The Annunciation
See ch. 3, § 36.

The birth of Jesus
See ch. 4, § 8.

**The boy Jesus
in the temple**
See ch. 4, §§ 38–40.

The Baptism of Jesus
See ch. 6, § 1.

A woman anoints Jesus' feet
See ch. 12, § 9.

**Jesus calms the
Sea of Galilee**
See ch. 13, §§ 5–6.

Jesus raises Jairus's daughter
See ch. 13, § 16.

**Jesus'
Transfiguration**
See ch. 18, § 8.

**Jesus'
triumphal entry**
See ch. 27, §§ 1–3.

KUEKER

Jesus' arrest
See ch. 33, §§ 4–8.

"Behold the Man!"
See ch. 34, § 22.

Jesus' crucifixion
See ch. 35, § 7.

Jesus' burial
See ch. 36, § 11.

The empty tomb
See ch. 37, § 3.

The risen Christ
See ch. 37, § 5.

The Ascension
See ch. 37, § 31.

KUEKER

THE LIFE OF CHRIST

THIRD EDITION

ADAM FAHLING

CONCORDIA PUBLISHING HOUSE · SAINT LOUIS

This edition © 2017 Concordia Publishing House
3558 S. Jefferson Ave., St. Louis, MO 63118–3968
1-800-325-3040 • cph.org

Manufactured in the United States of America

Library of Congress Cataloging-in-Publication Data

Names: Fahling, Adam, 1892-1945, author.
Title: The life of Christ / Adam Fahling.
Description: Third edition. | St. Louis, MO : Concordia Publishing House,
   2017. | Includes bibliographical references and index.
Identifiers: LCCN 2017000010 (print) | LCCN 2017000411 (ebook) | ISBN
   9780758644497 | ISBN 9780758644503
Subjects: LCSH: Jesus Christ--Biography.
Classification: LCC BT301.3 .F34 2017 (print) | LCC BT301.3 (ebook) | DDC
   232.9/01 [B] --dc23
LC record available at https://lccn.loc.gov/2017000010

1   2   3   4   5   6   7   8   9   10   26   25   24   23   22   21   20   19   18   17

Dedicated to the Christian pastor,

teacher, and student who seeks but

cannot always quickly find detailed,

authentic, satisfactory, scriptural, and

collateral information on the life of Christ.

CONTENTS

Appendixes

Abbreviations

AD	*anno Domini* (in the year of [our] Lord)	Ru	Ruth
		1Sm	1 Samuel
AUC	*ab urbe condita* (from the founding of the city [of Rome])	2Sm	2 Samuel
		1Ki	1 Kings
		2Ki	2 Kings
BC	before Christ	1Ch	1 Chronicles
c.	circa	2Ch	2 Chronicles
cf.	confer	Ezr	Ezra
ch.	chapter	Ne	Nehemiah
chs.	chapters	Est	Esther
e.g.	for example	Jb	Job
ESV	English Standard Version	Ps	Psalms
Gk	Greek	Pr	Proverbs
Grm	German	Ec	Ecclesiastes
Hbr	Hebrew	Sg	Song of Solomon
KJV	King James Version	Is	Isaiah
Lat	Latin	Jer	Jeremiah
		Lm	Lamentations
		Ezk	Ezekiel

Canonical Scripture

Gn	Genesis	Dn	Daniel
Ex	Exodus	Hos	Hosea
Lv	Leviticus	Jl	Joel
Nu	Numbers	Am	Amos
Dt	Deuteronomy	Ob	Obadiah
Jsh	Joshua	Jnh	Jonah
Jgs	Judges		

Mi . . . . Micah

Na . . . . Nahum

Hab . . . . Habakkuk

Zep . . . . Zephaniah

Hg . . . . Haggai

Zec . . . . Zechariah

Mal . . . . Malachi

Mt . . . . Matthew

Mk . . . . Mark

Lk . . . . Luke

Jn . . . . John

Ac . . . . Acts

Rm . . . . Romans

1Co . . . . 1 Corinthians

2Co . . . . 2 Corinthians

Gal . . . . Galatians

Eph . . . . Ephesians

Php . . . . Philippians

Col . . . . Colossians

1Th . . . . 1 Thessalonians

2Th . . . . 2 Thessalonians

1Tm . . . . 1 Timothy

2Tm . . . . 2 Timothy

Ti . . . . Titus

Phm . . . . Philemon

Heb . . . . Hebrews

Jas . . . . James

1Pt . . . . 1 Peter

2Pt . . . . 2 Peter

1Jn . . . . 1 John

2Jn . . . . 2 John

3Jn . . . . 3 John

Jude . . . . Jude

Rv . . . . Revelation

The Apocrypha

Jth . . . . Judith

Wis of Sol . . . . . The Wisdom of Solomon

Tob . . . . Tobit

Ecclus . . . . Ecclesiasticus (Sirach)

Bar . . . . Baruch

Lt Jer . . . . The Letter of Jeremiah

1Macc . . . . 1 Maccabees

2Macc . . . . 2 Maccabees

Old Grk Est . . . Old Greek Esther

Sus . . . . Susanna

Bel . . . . Bel and the Dragon

Pr Az . . . . The Prayer of Azariah

Sg Three . . . . . . The Song of the Three Holy Children

Pr Man . . . . Prayer of Manasseh

Commonly Cited Works and Authors

ABD Freedman, David Noel, ed. *The Anchor Bible Dictionary.* New York: Doubleday, 1992.

AE Luther, Martin. *Luther's Works.* American Edition. General editors Jaroslav Pelikan, Helmut T. Lehmann, Christopher Boyd Brown, and Benjamin T. G. Mayes. 82 vols. St. Louis: Concordia, and Philadelphia: Muhlenberg and Fortress, 1955–.

Against Apion Josephus, Flavius. *Flavius Josephus Against Apion.* In *The Works of Josephus.* Translated by William Whiston. Peabody, MA: Hendrickson Publishers, 1987.

ALEN Engelbrecht, Edward A., gen. ed. *The Apocrypha: The Lutheran Edition with Notes.* St. Louis, Concordia, 2012.

ANF Roberts, Alexander, and James Donaldson, eds. *The Ante-Nicene Fathers: The Writings of the Fathers Down to AD 325.* 10 vols. Buffalo: The Christian Literature Publishing Company, 1885–96. Reprint, Grand Rapids, MI: Eerdmans, 2001.

Ant Josephus, Flavius. *Jewish Antiquities.* In *The Works of Josephus.* Translated by William Whiston. Peabody, MA: Hendrickson Publishers, 1987.

Concordia McCain, Paul Timothy, ed. *Concordia: The Lutheran Confessions.* 2nd ed. St. Louis: Concordia, 2006.

ISBE *International Standard Encyclopedia of the Bible.* Chicago: Howard-Severance Co., 1939.

Life Josephus, Flavius. *The Life of Flavius Josephus.* In *The Works of Josephus.* Translated by William Whiston. Peabody, MA: Hendrickson Publishers, 1987.

LSB Commission on Worship of The Lutheran Church—Missouri Synod. *Lutheran Service Book.* St. Louis: Concordia, 2006.

LXX Septuagint. Koine Greek Old Testament.

NPNF2 Schaff, Philip, and Henry Wace, eds. *A Select Library of Nicene and Post-Nicene Fathers of the Christian Church*, Series 2. 14 vols. New York: The Christian Literature Series, 1890–99. Reprint, Grand Rapids, MI: Eerdmans, 1952, 1961.

SC   Luther, Martin. *Luther's Small Catechism with Explanation*. St. Louis: Concordia, 1986.

TLSB   Engelbrecht, Edward A., gen. ed. *The Lutheran Study Bible*. St. Louis: Concordia, 2009.

War   Josephus, Flavius. *The Jewish War*. In *The Works of Josephus*. Translated by William Whiston. Peabody, MA: Hendrickson Publishers, 1987.

ZPBD   *Zondervan Pictorial Bible Dictionary*. Grand Rapids: Zondervan, 1963.

ZPEB   *Zondervan Pictorial Encyclopedia of the Bible*. Grand Rapids: Zondervan, 1975.

FOREWORD TO THE THIRD EDITION

In 1936, Concordia Publishing House published Adam Fahling's *The Life of Christ*. An updated second edition was published in 1946. It included improvements and revisions that Fahling had suggested before his death in November 1945.

From the time it was first printed, this book has been a great resource for pastors, Sunday School and Bible class teachers, and lay students of the Bible. It gives the reader an inside look into the life of Jesus and the era in which He graced the world by His life, death, and resurrection.

This new edition has updated Fahling's language and included insights from more recent scholarship. We pray this third edition of Adam Fahling's great work will exalt Jesus Christ, our Savior, in your heart and life.

Concordia Publishing House

PREFACE

The subject needs no introduction. It concerns the earthly life of our Lord Jesus Christ, after the date of whose birth practically the whole civilized world numbers its years. He Himself is the Son of God, the Light, the Life, and the Truth; the First and the Last; the One and All; and the Way to life everlasting. "And there is salvation in no one else, for there is no other name under heaven given among men by which we must be saved" (Ac 4:12).

This book is written from the standpoint of a believer. It takes for granted the existence of miracles, the verbal inspiration, and the interpretation of Holy Scriptures according to the intended sense of the holy writers. This is not done in ignorance of the many charges of inaccuracy raised against the statements of the Bible, but rather with the knowledge that these charges cannot be successfully maintained.

The author is indebted to the best biblical scholarship of ancient and modern times. While the general structure and scope of the work is his own, he was guided by the books listed in the bibliography and among these is especially indebted to Farrar, Edersheim, Andrews, Schuerer, Bruce, Dods, Meyer, and others, not only for the subject matter, but also for literary expression.

The encouragement to begin this work grew out of a succession of manuscripts on related subjects, which led to the appointment to write this book. The consideration with which the present manuscript was received in its original, revised, and rewritten form is herewith gratefully acknowledged. Particular thanks for their kindness, advice, and assistance are extended to the Rev. L. Buchheimer of the Synodical Literature Board, Dr. W. Arndt of Concordia Seminary, the Rev. E. Eckhardt, Dr. F. Rupprecht, Dr. Edmund Seuel, and his able assistants at Concordia Publishing House.

The reader is naturally interested in the result of an author's investigation, not the process of that investigation. A tremendous amount of work and study awaits anyone who attempts to write a book on the life and time of Christ. An immense amount of material must be examined. The wide fields of ancient history, archaeology, geography, chronology, the Greek New Testament, the ancient manuscripts, the transmission of the sacred text, the harmony of the Gospels, the synoptic problem, and the like, must be investigated. All this the reader is spared. The author prays that God's blessings will accompany this volume, written to glorify our divine Savior.

A. F.

THE FOURFOLD GOSPEL

The outline harmony of the Gospels, upon which this work is based.
The marks of parentheses indicate that the passage has been taken out of its order.

	MATTHEW	MARK	LUKE	JOHN	CHAPTER/ SECTION
I. GENERAL SCOPE AND PURPOSE OF THE GOSPEL					
1. The Prologue of Luke			1:1–4		See pp. 6–7
2. The Prologue of John				1:1–14	See pp. 7–8
II. THE TWO GENEALOGIES					
3. Apparently Joseph's in Matthew and Mary's in Luke	1:1–17		(3:23–38)		See pp. 475–76
III. EVENTS PRECEDING THE BIRTH OF JESUS					**CH. 3**
4. The Annunciation of the Birth of John to Zechariah			1:5–25		§§ 1–29
5. The Annunciation of the Birth of Jesus to Mary			1:26–38		§§ 35–38
6. Mary's Visit to Elizabeth			1:39–45		§ 39
7. Mary's Song of Praise			1:46–56		§ 40
8. The Birth of John the Baptist			1:57–80		§§ 42–45
9. The Annunciation of the Birth of Jesus to Joseph	1:18–25				§§ 46–49
IV. THE BIRTH AND CHILDHOOD OF JESUS					**CH. 4**
10. The Birth of Jesus	2:1		2:1–7		§§ 1–8
11. The Angels and Shepherds			2:8–20		§§ 9–11
12. The Circumcision			2:21		§ 12
13. The Presentation in the Temple			2:22–38		§§ 13–16
14. The Visit of the Wise Men	2:1–12				§§ 17–27
15. The Flight to Egypt	2:13–18				§§ 28–29
16. The Death of Herod and Return to Nazareth	2:19–23		2:39		§§ 30–33
17. Childhood at Nazareth			2:40		§ 34
18. Visit to Jerusalem			2:41–49		§§ 37–40
19. Eighteen Years at Nazareth			2:50–52		§§ 41–42
V. THE PERIOD OF JOHN					**CH. 5**
20. The Beginning of the Gospel		1:1			
21. The Exact Time	3:1		3:1–2		§ 1

	MATTHEW	MARK	LUKE	JOHN	CHAPTER/ SECTION
22. The Character and Mission of John	3:2–6	1:2–6	3:3–6		§§ 2–4
23. John Warns the Pharisees and Sadducees	3:7–10		3:7–9		§ 5
24. Individual Directions to Inquirers			3:10–14		§ 5
25. Announcement of the Coming Christ	3:11–12	1:7–8	3:15–18	1:15–18	§ 6
(Announcement of the Imprisonment of John, see no. 50 below)			(3:19–20)		
VI. THE BEGINNING OF CHRIST'S PUBLIC MINISTRY AND CONTEMPORANEOUS MINISTRIES OF JESUS AND JOHN					CH. 6
26. The Baptism of Jesus	3:13–17	1:9–11	3:21–22	(1:32–34)	§ 1
(Luke's Genealogy, see no. 3 above)			(3:23–38)		
27. The Three Temptations of Jesus	4:1–11	1:12–13	4:1–13		§§ 2–7
28. John's Testimony to the Delegation from Jerusalem				1:19–28	§§ 8–13
29. "Behold, the Lamb of God!"				1:29–34	§ 14
30. The First Three Disciples—John, Andrew, and Peter				1:35–42	§§ 15–17
31. Philip and Nathanael				1:43–51	§§ 19–20
32. The First Miracle, at Cana				2:1–11	§§ 21–24
33. A Brief Visit to Capernaum				2:12	§ 25
VII. THE EARLY JUDEAN MINISTRY					CH. 7
34. The First Cleansing of the Temple				2:13–17	§§ 1–3
35. Jesus' First Prediction of His Death and Resurrection (see nos. 116, 123, 205, 245 below)				2:18–22	§ 3
36. Miracles in Jerusalem				2:23–25	§ 4
37. Interview with Nicodemus				3:1–21	§§ 5–10
38. Parallel Ministry of Jesus and John				3:22–24	§ 11
39. John's Loyalty to Jesus				3:25–36	§ 12
40. Jesus' Departure for Galilee				4:1–3	§ 13
41. The Gospel in Samaria				4:4–26	§§ 14–17
42. The Report of the Samaritan Woman to the People of Her Town				4:27–30	§ 18
43. The Discourse of Christ on the Fields White for Harvest				4:31–38	§ 19
44. Reception of Christ by the Samaritans				4:39–42	§ 20

	MATTHEW	MARK	LUKE	JOHN	CHAPTER/ SECTION
45. Return to Galilee				4:43–45	§ 21
46. The Official's Son Lying Sick at Capernaum, Healed at Cana				4:46–54	§§ 22–24
VIII. THE UNNAMED FEAST					**CH. 8**
47. A Feast of the Jews				5:1	§§ 1–2
48. The Healing at the Pool of Bethesda				5:2–13	§§ 3–6
49. Christ Defends His Action				5:14–47	§§ 7–10
50. Imprisonment of John and Christ's Return to Nazareth	4:12	1:14a	(3:19–20) 4:14a		§ 11
IX. THE BEGINNING OF THE GREAT GALILEAN MINISTRY, OPENING EVENTS					**CH. 9**
51. The Time is Fulfilled and the Kingdom of God is at Hand	(4:17)	1:14b–15	4:14b–15		§§ 1–2
52. The First Rejection of Jesus at Nazareth (see no. 90 below)			4:16–30		§§ 3–9
53. A New Home at Capernaum	4:13–16		4:31–32		§ 10
54. Jesus Calls Four Fishermen, Miraculous Catch of Fish	4:18–22	1:16–20	(5:1–11)		§ 11–12
55. Christ Teaches in a Synagogue and Heals a Man with an Unclean Spirit		1:21–28	4:33–37		§ 13–19
56. The Healing of Peter's Mother-in-Law	(8:14–15)	1:29–31	4:38–39		§ 20
57. In the Evening Many Others are Healed	(8:16–17)	1:32–34	4:40–41		§ 21
X. FROM THE FIRST GALILEAN CIRCUIT TO THE CHOICE OF THE TWELVE					**CH. 10**
58. Christ Retires to a Solitary Place and Is Found by the Disciples and the People		1:35–38	4:42–43		§ 2
59. Jesus Went throughout All Galilee	4:23–25	1:39	4:44		§ 3
(The Miraculous Catch of Fish, see no. 54 above)			(5:1–11)		
60. A Leper Healed and Much Popular Excitement	(8:2–4)	1:40–45a	5:12–15		§§ 4–9
61. Christ Withdraws into the Wilderness		1:45b	5:16		§ 9
62. The Paralytic Healed Who Was Lowered through the Roof	(9:2–8)	2:1–12	5:17–26		§§ 10–14
63. The Call of Matthew	(9:9)	2:13–14	5:27–28		§§ 15–18
64. Matthew's Feast	(9:10–13)	2:15–17	5:29–32		§§ 19–21
65. A Question about Fasting	(9:14–15)	2:18–20	5:33–35		§§ 22–23

	MATTHEW	MARK	LUKE	JOHN	CHAPTER/ SECTION
66. Two Parables: New Cloth and New Wine	(9:16–17)	2:21–22	5:36–39		§§ 24–25
67. The Disciples Plucking Grain on the Sabbath	(12:1–8)	2:23–28	6:1–5		§§ 26–28
68. The Man with a Withered Hand	(12:9–14)	3:1–6	6:6–11		§§ 29–31
69. Jesus Teaches and Heals by the Sea of Galilee	(12:15–21)	3:7–12			§§ 32–33
XI. THE CHOOSING OF THE TWELVE AND THE SERMON ON THE MOUNT					**CH. 11**
70. A Night of Prayer		3:13a	6:12		§§ 1–2
71. The Choice of the Twelve	(10:2–4)	3:13–19	6:13–16		§§ 3–17
72. The Sermon on the Mount	5:1–48 6:1–34 7:1–29 8:1		6:17–49		§§ 18–26 §§ 27–34 §§ 35–41 § 42
(Here follows in the order of Matthew: A Leper Healed, see no. 60)	(8:2–4)				
73. The Centurion's Servant	8:5–13	3:20a	7:1–10		§ 43
(Here follows in the order of Matthew: The Healing of Peter's Mother-in-Law, see no. 56)	(8:14–15)				
In the Evening Many Others are Healed, see no. 57)	(8:16–17)				
XII. A SECOND PREACHING TOUR, INCLUDING THE PARABLES BY THE SEA					**CH. 12**
74. The Raising of the Widow's Son at Nain			7:11–17		§ 1
75. John the Baptist Sends Two Disciples to Jesus	(11:2–19)		7:18–35		§§ 2–4
76. Woe to Unrepentant Cities (see no. 146)	(11:20–30)				§§ 5–7
77. Jesus Anointed by a Sinful Woman			7:36–50		§§ 8–10
78. With the Twelve and a Few Women Followers on a Tour through Galilee			8:1–3		§ 11
79. Christ Defends Himself against the Blasphemous Accusation of His Being in League with the Devil (see no. 152)	(12:22–37)	3:20–30			§§ 12–15
80. Scribes and Pharisees Demand a Sign; The Sign of Jonah (see nos. 111, 153)	(12:38–45)				§ 16
81. Jesus Is Called by Mother and Brothers	(12:46–50)	3:31–35	(8:19–21)		§ 17
82. The Parables by the Sea	(13:1–53)	4:1–34	8:4–18		§§ 18–32

	MATTHEW	MARK	LUKE	JOHN	CHAPTER/ SECTION
(Here follows in the order of Luke: Jesus Called by Mother and Brothers)			8:19–21		
XIII. THE GADARENE JOURNEY					**CH. 13**
83. Christ Commands His Disciples to Cross over to the Other Side of the Sea of Galilee	8:18	4:35	8:22		§ 1
84. Christ Replies to Applicants for Discipleship (see no. 144)	8:19–22		(9:57–62)		§§ 2–4
85. The Stilling of the Storm	8:23–27	4:36–41	8:23–25		§§ 5–6
86. In the Country of the Gadarenes	8:28–9:1	5:1–21	8:26–40		§§ 7–12
(Here follow in the order of Matthew: The Paralytic Healed, see no. 62)	(9:2–8)				
Matthew (Levi) Called (see no. 63)	(9:9–13)				
A Question about Fasting (see no. 65)	(9:14–15)				
Two Parables: New Cloth and New Wine (see no. 66, all in order, but transposed.)	(9:16–17)				
87. Jairus's Daughter and the Woman with the Discharge of Blood	9:18–26	5:22–43	8:41–56		§§ 13–16
88. Two Blind Men Healed	9:27–31				§ 17
89. A Demon Driven Out and a Blasphemous Accusation	9:32–34				§ 18
XIV. A THIRD PREACHING TOUR, INCLUDING THE MISSION OF THE TWELVE					**CH. 14**
90. The Last Visit to Nazareth. The Second Rejection (see no. 52)	(13:54–58)	6:1–6a			§§ 1–2
91. Jesus Preaches in the Villages of Galilee	9:35	6:6b			§ 3
92. "Pray Earnestly to the Lord of the Harvest" for Laborers	9:36–38				§ 4
93. The Mission of the Twelve	10:1–42	6:7–12	9:1–5		§§ 5–10
94. Jesus and the Disciples Preaching and Healing	11:1	6:12–13	9:6		§ 11
(Here follow in the order of Matthew: The Message from John the Baptist, see no. 75)	(11:2–19)				
Woes upon Cities of Opportunity (see no. 76)	(11:20–30)				
The Disciples Plucking Grain on the Sabbath (see no. 67)	(12:1–8)				
The Man with a Withered Hand (see no. 68)	(12:9–14)				
Jesus Teaches and Heals by the Sea (see no. 69)	(12:15–21)				

	MATTHEW	MARK	LUKE	JOHN	CHAPTER/SECTION
Jesus Defends Himself against an Accusation (see no. 79)	(12:22–37)				
Scribes and Pharisees Demand a Sign (see no. 80)	(12:38–45)				
Jesus Called by Mother and Brothers (see no. 81)	(12:46–50)				
The Parables by the Sea (see no. 82)	(13:1–53)				
The Last Visit to Nazareth (see no. 90) This is the end of the transpositions, with the exception of a few details.	(13:54–58)				
XV. THE DEATH OF JOHN THE BAPTIST					**CH. 15**
95. The Guilty Fears of Herod	14:1–2	6:14–16	9:7–9		§ 1
96. The Story of John the Baptist's Death	14:3–12	6:17–29	(3:19–20)		§§ 2–10
XVI. PERIODS OF RETIREMENT AND SPECIAL TRAINING OF THE TWELVE, THE FIRST RETIREMENT					**CH. 16**
97. The Return of the Disciples; Report to Jesus	14:13	6:30–33	9:10	6:1–2	§ 1
98. The Feeding of the Five Thousand	14:14–21	6:34–44	9:11–17	6:3–13	§§ 2–3
99. Prevention of the Revolutionary Purpose to Make Jesus King	14:22–23	6:45–46		6:14–15	§ 4
100. Jesus Walking on the Water	14:24–33	6:47–52		6:16–21	§§ 5–6
101. The Reception at Gennesaret	14:34–36	6:53–56			§ 7
102. The Sermon on the Bread of Life				6:22–59	§§ 8–10
103. The Collapse of the Scheme to Make Jesus King				6:60–71	§§ 11–12
104. Jesus Reproached by Pharisees from Jerusalem for Permitting His Disciples to Disregard Ceremonial Traditions	15:1–20	7:1–23	The Great Gap in Luke		§§ 13–17
XVII. THE SECOND AND THIRD RETIREMENTS					**CH. 17**
105. Jesus Avoiding the Hostility of the Jews				7:1	§ 1
106. Retirement into the Region of Tyre and Sidon	15:21–28	7:24–30			§§ 2–4
107. Retirement into the Decapolis	15:29	7:31			§ 5
108. The Healing of the Deaf Man with a Speech Impediment	15:30–31	7:32–37			§ 6
109. The Feeding of the Four Thousand	15:32–38	8:1–9			§ 7
110. A Short Visit to Magadan	15:39	8:10			§ 8

	MATTHEW	MARK	LUKE	JOHN	CHAPTER/ SECTION
111. A Sharp Attack of the Pharisees and Sadducees; The Sign of Jonah (see nos. 80, 153)	16:1–4a	8:11–12			§ 8
112. Jesus Returns to the Eastern Side of the Sea of Galilee	16:4b	8:13			§ 8
XVIII. THE FOURTH RETIREMENT, INCLUDING THE TRANSFIGURATION					**CH. 18**
113. The Disciples Who Had Forgotten to Take Bread	16:5–12	8:14–21			§ 1
114. The Blind Man near Bethsaida		8:22–26			§ 2
115. Peter's Wonderful Confession	16:13–20	8:27–30	9:18–21		§§ 3–5
116. Christ Distinctly Foretells His Death and Resurrection (see nos. 35, 123, 205, 245)	16:21–23	8:31–33	9:22		§ 6
117. Taking Up the Cross with Jesus	16:24–28	8:34–9:1	9:23–27		§ 7
118. The Transfiguration	17:1–8	9:2–8	9:28–36a		§§ 8–9
119. The Question of the Three Disciples	17:9–13	9:9–13	9:36b		§ 10
120. The Demon-Oppressed Boy Whom the Disciples Could Not Heal	17:14–18	9:14–27	9:37–43a		§ 11
121. "Faith Like a Grain of Mustard Seed"	17:19–21	9:28–29			§ 12
XIX. THE CLOSE OF THE GALILEAN MINISTRY					**CH. 19**
122. Jesus Returns to Galilee	17:22a	9:30			§ 1
123. Third Announcement of His Death and Resurrection (see nos. 35, 116, 123, 205, 245)	17:22b–23	9:31–32	9:43b–45		§ 2
124. Jesus Pays the Temple Tax	17:24–27	9:33a			§§ 3–4
125. "Who is the Greatest in the Kingdom of Heaven?"	18:1–5	9:33b–37	9:46–48		§ 5
126. John's Mistaken Zeal Rebuked by Jesus		9:38–41	9:49–50		§ 6
127. Warning against Causing Others to Sin	18:6–14	9:42–50			§§ 7–9
128. Right Treatment of a Brother Who Has Trespassed against Us	18:15–22				§§ 10–12
129. Parable of the Unforgiving Servant	18:23–35				§ 13
XX. AT THE FEAST OF TABERNACLES IN JERUSALEM					**CH. 20**
130. The Unbelieving Brothers of Jesus Counsel Him to Show Himself in Jerusalem as a Political Messiah				7:2–9	§§ 1–2

	MATTHEW	MARK	LUKE	JOHN	CHAPTER/ SECTION
131. Jesus Goes Privately to Jerusalem				7:10–13	§ 3
132. Intense Excitement concerning the Messiahship of Jesus				7:14–53	§ 4–12
133. An Overnight Visit at Bethany				8:1	§ 13
134. The Woman Caught Up in Adultery				8:2–11	§§ 13–14
135. Jesus the Light of the World				8:12–20	§§ 15–16
136. The Sinfulness of the Jews Exposed				8:21–30	§ 17
137. Who Are True Disciples of Christ?				8:31–32	§ 17
138. Spiritual Liberty, Abraham's Children				8:33–58	§§ 18–20
139. Attempt to Stone Jesus				8:59	§ 20
140. A Man Blind from His Birth Given His Sight				9:1–41	§§ 21–26
141. Christ the Good Shepherd and the Door to the Sheepfold				10:1–21	§§ 27–30
XXI. THE FINAL WITHDRAWAL OF JESUS FROM GALILEE AND THE LATER JUDEAN MINISTRY					**CH. 21**
142. Leaving Galilee as a Field of Operations			9:51		§ 1
143. Rejected by the Samaritans			9:52–56		§ 2
144. Application for Discipleship (repetition of no. 84)			9:57–62		§ 3
145. The Mission of the Seventy-Two			10:1–12		§ 4
146. Woe to Unrepentant Cities (repetition of no. 76)			10:13–16		§ 5
147. The Return of the Seventy–Two			10:17–24		§§ 6–7
148. The Parable of the Good Samaritan			10:25–37		§ 8–9
149. Jesus the Guest of Mary and Martha			10:38–42		§ 10
150. The Lord's Prayer Again Given to the Disciples (compare Mt 6:9–13, no. 72)			11:1–4		§ 11
151. The Parable of the Impudent Friend			11:5–13		§ 12
152. Healing of the Mute Demon-Possessed Man (see no. 79)			11:14–28		§ 13

	MATTHEW	MARK	LUKE	JOHN	CHAPTER/SECTION
153. The Sign of Jonah (sayings repeated; see no. 80)			11:29–36		§ 14
154. Woes against Pharisees (see no. 230)			11:37–54		§§ 15–17
155. Warnings against the Leaven of the Pharisees			12:1–12		§ 18
156. Christ Refuses to Divide an Inheritance			12:13–15		§ 19
157. Parable of the Rich Fool			12:16–21		§ 20
158. Worldly Anxieties			12:22–34		§ 21
159. Parable of the Waiting Servants			12:35–40		§ 22
160. Parable of the Wise Steward			12:41–48		§ 23
161. The Discourse Continued			12:49–59		§§ 24–26
162. The Galileans Slain by Pilate			13:1–5		§ 27
163. The Parable of the Fig Tree			13:6–9		§ 28
164. The Crippled Woman Healed on a Sabbath			13:10–17		§ 29–30
165. The Parable of the Mustard Seed (repeated; see no. 82; Mt 13:31–32; Mk 4:30–32)			13:18–19		§ 31
166. The Parable of the Leaven (repeated; see no. 82; Mt 13:33)			13:20–21		§ 31
XXII. AT THE FEAST OF DEDICATION IN JERUSALEM					**CH. 22**
167. Christ in Jerusalem at Feast of Dedication				10:22–23	§§ 1–2
168. "If You Are the Christ, Tell Us Plainly"; Plainly Told; Attempt to Stone Jesus				10:24–38	§§ 3–6
169. Jesus' Withdrawal into Perea				10:39–42	§ 7
XXIII. THE LATER PEREAN MINISTRY					**CH. 23**
170. Journeying toward Jerusalem			13:22		§ 1
171. The Question whether Few Are Saved			13:23–30		§§ 2–3
172. A Warning against Herod			13:31–33		§ 4
173. "O Jerusalem, Jerusalem!" (see no. 231)			13:34–35		§ 5
174. A Man Healed Who Had Dropsy			14:1–6		§§ 6–7
175. A Parable on Humility			14:7–11		§ 8
176. The Parable of the Great Banquet			14:12–24		§§ 9–12

	MATTHEW	MARK	LUKE	JOHN	CHAPTER/SECTION
203. Peter's Question: "What Then Will We Have?"	19:27–30	10:28–31	18:28–30		§ 17
204. The Parable of the Laborers in the Vineyard	20:1–16				§§ 18–19
205. Jesus Again Foretells His Death and Resurrection (see nos. 35, 116, 123, 245)	20:17–19	10:32–34	18:31–34		§ 20
206. The Ambition of James and John	20:20–28	10:35–45			§§ 21–22
207. Blind Bartimaeus and His Companion at Jericho	20:29–34	10:46–52	18:35–43		§ 23
208. Jesus Goes to the House of Zacchaeus			19:1–10		§§ 24–25
209. The Parable of the Ten Minas			19:11–28		§§ 26–29
XXVI. ARRIVAL AT BETHANY					**CH. 26**
210. The Passover of the Jews Was at Hand				11:55	§ 1
211. The Order is Given to Arrest Jesus				11:56–57	§ 1
212. Mary Anoints Jesus in the House of Simon the Leper	(26:6–13)	(14:3–9)		12:1–11	§§ 2–7
XXVII. PASSION WEEK—PALM SUNDAY					**CH. 27**
213. "Behold, Your King is Coming!"	21:1–9	11:1–10	19:29–40	12:12–19	§§ 1–4
214. But Jerusalem Is Blind to Jesus' Gracious Visitation			19:41–44		§ 5
215. Jesus Briefly Visits the Temple and in the Evening Returns to Bethany	21:10–11	11:11			§ 6
XXVIII. PASSION WEEK—MONDAY					**CH. 28**
216. The Cursing of the Fig Tree	(21:18–19a)	11:12–14			§ 1
217. The Cleansing of the Temple	21:12–16	11:15–18	19:45–48		§ 2
218. Jesus Returns to Bethany	21:17	11:19			§ 3
XXIX. PASSION WEEK—TUESDAY MORNING					**CH. 29**
219. The Fig Tree Withered Away	21:19b–20	11:20–21			§ 1
220. The Great Power of Faith	21:21–22	11:22–26			§ 2
221. The Authority of Jesus Challenged	21:23–27	11:27–33	20:1–8		§§ 3–4
222. The Parable of the Two Sons	21:28–32				§ 5
223. The Parable of the Wicked Tenants	21:33–44	12:1–11	20:9–18		§§ 6–8
224. Effect of These Parables	21:45–46	12:12	20:19		§ 9

	MATTHEW	MARK	LUKE	JOHN	CHAPTER/SECTION
225. The Parable of the Wedding Feast	22:1–14				§§ 10–12
226. A Question of the Pharisees and the Herodians	22:15–22	12:13–17	20:20–26		§§ 13–14
227. A Question of the Sadducees	22:23–33	12:18–27	20:27–40		§§ 15–16
228. Another Question by the Pharisees	22:34–40	12:28–34			§§ 17–19
229. "What Do You Think About the Christ?"	22:41–46	12:35–37	20:41–44		§ 20
230. The Scribes and Pharisees Denounced (see no. 154)	23:1–36	12:38–40	20:45–47		§§ 21–23
231. Jesus Weeps over Jerusalem (see no. 173)	23:37–39				§ 24
232. The Widow's Offering		12:41–44	21:1–4		§ 25
233. The Greeks Who Wished to See Jesus				12:20–36	§§ 26–28
234. Reflections on the Unbelief of the Jews				12:37–50	§ 29
XXX. PASSION WEEK—TUESDAY AFTERNOON					**CH. 30**
235. Prophetic Discourses: The Destruction of the Temple	24:1–2	13:1–2	21:5–6		§ 1
236. Prophetic Discourses: The Second Coming	24:3–14	13:3–13	21:7–19		§ 2
237. Prophetic Discourses: Signs of the Destruction of Jerusalem	24:15–22	13:14–20	21:20–24		§ 3
238. Prophetic Discourses: False Christs	24:23–31	13:21–27	21:25–28		§§ 4–5
239. The Parable of the Fig Tree	24:32–35	13:28–31	21:29–33		§ 6
240. Watchfulness Urged; Parables	24:36–51	13:32–37	21:34–36		§§ 7–10
241. The Parable of the Ten Virgins	25:1–13				§§ 11–12
242. The Parable of the Talents	25:14–30				§§ 13–15
243. Picture of the Day of Judgment	25:31–46				§§ 16–18
244. Jesus Returns to Bethany at Night			21:37–38		§ 19
245. Jesus Again Predicts His Death (see nos. 35, 123, 116, 205)	26:1–5	14:1–2	22:1–2		§§ 20–21
(Here follows in the order of Matthew and Mark: The Anointing of Jesus in the House of Simon, see no. 212)	(26:6–13)	(14:3–9)			
246. Judas Bargains for the Betrayal of Jesus	26:14–16	14:10–11	22:3–6		§ 22

	MATTHEW	MARK	LUKE	JOHN	CHAPTER/ SECTION
XXXI. PASSION WEEK—THURSDAY AFTERNOON TO THURSDAY NIGHT					**CH. 31**
247. The Preparation of the Paschal Meal	26:17–19	14:12–16	22:7–13		§§ 1–5
248. The Beginning of the Paschal Meal	26:20	14:17	22:14–18		§§ 6–8
249. The Contention among the Disciples			(22:24–30)		§§ 9–10
250. Jesus Washes the Disciples' Feet				13:1–20	§§ 11–13
251. The Traitor Is Revealed	26:21–25	14:18–21	(22:21–23)	13:21–30	§ 14
252. Upon the Departure of Judas, Jesus Indicates His Glorification				13:31–35	§ 15
253. Institution of the Lord's Supper (1Co 11:23–26)	26:26–29	14:22–25	22:19–20		§§ 16–19
(Here follow in the order of Luke: The Traitor is Revealed, see no. 251)			(22:21–23)		
The Contention of the Disciples (see no. 249)			(22:24–30)		
XXXII. PASSION WEEK—THURSDAY NIGHT—FAREWELL DISCOURSES					**CH. 32**
254. Peter's Denials are Foretold	26:30–35	14:26–31	22:31–39	13:36–38	§§ 1–3
255. Jesus Comforts His Disciples and Promises the Comforter				14:1–31	§§ 4–7
256. Christ the True Vine				15:1–27	§§ 8–9
257. The Disciples Warned of Persecutions; The Holy Spirit Promised				16:1–33	§§ 10–11
258. The Great Intercessory Prayer				17:1–26	§§ 12–15
XXXIII. PASSION WEEK—THURSDAY NIGHT TO FRIDAY MORNING					**CH. 33**
259. The Agony in Gethsemane	26:36–46	14:32–42	22:39–46	18:1	§§ 1–3
260. The Arrival and Betrayal of Judas	26:47–50	14:43–46	22:47–48	18:2–9	§§ 4–6
261. Peter's Untimely Zeal	26:51–54	14:47	22:49–51	18:10–11	§ 7
262. The Arrest of Jesus	26:55–56a	14:48–49	22:52–53	18:12	§ 8
263. The Disciples Flee	26:56b	14:50–52			§ 9
264. Jesus is First Brought before Annas				18:13–14 (18:19–23)	§§ 10–12
265. Jesus is Next Led to Caiaphas	26:57, 59–66	14:53, 55–64	22:54a	(18:24)	§§ 13–15
266. The Denials of Peter	26:58, 69–75	14:54, 66–72	22:54c–62	18:15–18, 25–27	§§ 16–20
267. Jesus Mistreated during the Night	(26:67–68)	(14:65)	22:63–65		§ 21

	MATTHEW	MARK	LUKE	JOHN	CHAPTER/ SECTION
268. Formally Condemned by the Council	27:1	15:1a	22:66–71		§ 22
XXXIV. PASSION WEEK—FRIDAY MORNING. "SUFFERED UNDER PONTIUS PILATE"					**CH. 34**
269. Jesus Brought before Pilate	27:2	15:1b	23:1	18:28a	§ 1
270. Remorse and Suicide of Judas (Ac 1:18–19)	27:3–10				§§ 2–3
271. Jesus before Pilate, the First Time	27:11–14	15:2–5	23:2–5	18:28b–38	§§ 4–9
272. Jesus before Herod			23:6–12		§§ 10–13
273. Jesus before Pilate, the Second Time	27:15–31a	15:6–20a	23:13–25	18:39–19:15	§§ 14–24
XXXV. PASSION WEEK—FRIDAY. "CRUCIFIED"					**CH. 35**
274. Jesus on the Way to Golgotha	27:31b	15:20b	23:26a	19:16–17a	§ 1
275. Simon of Cyrene Compelled to Bear the Cross	27:32	15:21	23:26b		§§ 2–3
276. Lamentation of the Daughters of Jerusalem			23:27–31		§ 4
277. "Crucified"	27:33–38	15:22–28	23:32–34 23:38	19:17b–24	§§ 5–9
278. Mocked and Reviled by Passersby	27:39–44	15:29–32	23:35–37		§ 10
279. The Penitent Thief			23:39–43		§ 11
280. Jesus Commends His Mother to John				19:25–27	§ 12
281. The Three Hours of Darkness	27:45–50a	15:33–37a	23:44–45a, 46a	19:28–30a	§§ 13–18
XXXVI. PASSION WEEK—FRIDAY. "DEAD AND BURIED"					**CH. 36**
282. "Dead"	27:50b	15:37b	23:46b	19:30b	§ 1
283. The Phenomena Accompanying the Death of Christ	27:51–56	15:38–41	23:45b, 47–49		§ 2
284. The Bones of the Criminals Are Broken				19:31–37	§§ 6–7
285. "And Buried"	27:57–60	15:42–46	23:50–54	19:38–42	§§ 8–11
286. Women Followers Witness Jesus' Burial	27:61	15:47	23:55–56a		§ 12
287. The Guard at the Tomb of Jesus	27:62–66				§ 13
288. The Rest on the Sabbath			23:56b		§ 14
289. The Visit of the Women to the Tomb—Saturday Afternoon	28:1				§ 14

	MATTHEW	MARK	LUKE	JOHN	CHAPTER/ SECTION
290. The Purchase of Spices—Late Saturday Night		16:1			§ 142
XXXVII. THE RISEN AND EXALTED SAVIOR					**CH. 37**
291. The Earthquake and the Rolling Away of the Stone	28:2–4	16:2–4	24:1–2	20:1	§§ 2–3
292. "He is Risen!"	28:5–7	16:5–7	24:1–8		§ 4
293. Jesus Appears to the Returning Women	28:8–10	16:8	24:9–11		§ 5
294. The Race to the Grave—Peter and John			24:12	20:2–10	§§ 6–7
295. Jesus' Appearance to Mary		16:9		20:11–17	§ 8
296. Mary's Message Is Not Believed		16:10–11		20:18	§ 8
297. The Report of the Guard	28:11–15				§ 9
298. Jesus Appears to Two Disciples Going to Emmaus		16:12	24:13–32		§§ 10–11
299. The Two Disciples Tell the Glad Tidings to the Eleven and Learn of the Risen Savior's Appearance to Peter (1Co 15:5a)		16:13	24:33–35		§§ 12–13
300. Jesus Appears to the Disciples and Others with Them; Thomas Absent. (1Co 15:5b)		16:14	24:36–43	20:19–25	§§ 14–16
301. His Appearance a Week Later; Thomas Present				20:26–29	§§ 17–18
302. Unrecorded Miracles; The Truth of the Gospel				20:30–31	§ 19
303. Jesus Appears to Seven Disciples by the Sea of Galilee				21:1–14	§ 20
304. Peter Reinstated in His Apostleship				21:15–23	§§ 21–22
305. The Close of John's Gospel				21:24–25	§ 23
306. The Appearance of Christ on a Mountain in Galilee (1Co 15:6); The Great Mission Command	28:16–20	16:15–18			§§ 24–27
307. Jesus' Appearances to James and Paul (1Co 15:7–9)					§ 28
308. Jesus' Last Appearance in Jerusalem (Ac 1:3–8)			24:44–49		§§ 29–30
309. The Ascension of Our Lord (Ac 1:9–12)		16:19–20	24:50–53		§§ 31–32

Why a Harmony?

Followers of Jesus Christ believe and confess that the four Gospels of Jesus Christ—Matthew, Mark, Luke, and John—were inspired by the Holy Spirit. This means each Gospel is reliable and accurate, even if details differ from one to the next. On this firm basis we are able to combine the events given in the four Gospels to gain a fuller, more complete picture of Jesus and His life among us.

This is especially important since many critics attempt to discredit the accuracy of these accounts by pointing to seeming contradictions between the Gospels. A harmony allows us to explore these difficult questions and provide feasible resolutions.

The first harmony of the Gospels was called the *Diatessaron* (*ANF* 9:43–129). It was prepared by a pupil of Justin Martyr named Tatian about AD 160–75 at Rome. Many harmonies have been written in the years since then.

But with any harmony there is a caution. None of the Gospel writers intended to give a complete picture of Jesus or flesh out every detail of His life. Each Gospel was inspired by the Holy Spirit for its own audience with a specific purpose in mind. Blending these Gospels into one account requires the harmonist to honor the specific purposes for which each of the Gospels was originally inspired.

This is something Fahling has done masterfully. His harmony provides us a new view of Jesus Christ, filled with grace, depth, and truth.

INTRODUCTION

Nearly 280,000 books have the word *Christ* in their title, according to WorldCat, the international library catalog. And that result is just for English titles! That number is easily several miles of books on library shelves—all dedicated to one person, one life.

This book is one of that number, and a very special one that takes into account the four great Gospels, the earliest records of Jesus of Nazareth, whose life forever changed the world. Fahling's *The Life of Christ* is a companion to those earliest accounts from eyewitnesses and disciples of Jesus. It is written with respect for those great Gospels, and unlike most books about Christ, it helps the reader easily understand those early accounts together. As you read this life of Christ as a companion to the canonical Gospels, you will grow in your understanding of the history of Jesus. But most important, you will grow in your love for Jesus, who taught:

> He who loves Me will be loved by My Father, and I will love him and manifest Myself to him. (Jn 14:21)

THE RECORDS

Before exploring the life of Christ, we need to familiarize ourselves with the records of His life and teaching. The principal, and practically the only, reliable sources of our knowledge of the life of Christ are the four canonical Gospels, the first three of which are called the Synoptic Gospels because they present a very similar view and outline of Jesus' life. The few notices of Christ in the writings of non-Christian authors, the references made to Christ in the other books of the New Testament, and those made in later Christian literature all add to the information that the four Gospels already supply. The supposed additional sayings of Jesus and incidents of His life found in the so-called apocryphal gospels are of questionable character. They were written late, and the early Christians regarded them as altogether worthless in authority. Before considering these other later documents, we do well to learn about the Gospels universally received by the early followers of Christ.

THE WRITERS OF THE FOUR CANONICAL GOSPELS

Matthew   We do not know too much about the writer of the Gospel according to St. Matthew. From the beginning of the postapostolic age, Church Fathers universally identified him with the apostle Matthew, and his Gospel was placed first in order among the books of the New Testament. Matthew, also called Levi (Mt 10:3; Lk 5:27), was a disciple and apostle of the Lord. When Jesus left Capernaum, "He saw a man called Matthew sitting at the tax booth, and He said to him, 'Follow Me.' And he rose and followed Him" (Mt 9:9). Matthew was a tax collector and, as such, belonged to that class of people whom the Jews mentioned in one breath with sinners. Tradition relates that he preached in Israel for fifteen years and then went to the Ethiopians, Syrians, Persians, Parthians, and Medes. There is also a tradition that says he died a natural death.

The Early Church accepted the apostolic origin and canonicity of the Gospel that bears Matthew's name. The late-first-century *Letter of Barnabas*, chapter 4, written by an apostolic father, quotes Matthew 22:14 distinctly with the formula "It is written" as though he was quoting the authority of Holy Scripture. Origen (c. 185–c. 254) refers to the Book of Matthew as the first of the four Gospels that the Church of God received without doubt (Eusebius, *NPNF2* 1:273). Its identity with our Matthew is confirmed by the presence of the Gospel in the first Gospel harmony, the *Diatessaron* (*ANF* 9:43–129) of Tatian (Justin Martyr's pupil), who prepared his work at Rome about AD 160–75.

The purpose of Matthew's Gospel is indicated in almost every section of the book. His object was to prove to his fellow countrymen that the entire life as well as the passion, death, and resurrection of Jesus Christ is the fulfillment of the Old Testament prophecies concerning the Messiah. The fifteen references to fulfillment are abundant evidence of this.

The date of composition is probably AD 50,[1] but it is unknown where this Gospel was written. Ancient tradition states that Matthew wrote it originally in Hebrew, which may mean the Aramaic spoken by Jewish people in the first century. Papias, bishop of Hierapolis in Phrygia, wrote about AD 140: "Matthew composed the Logia in the Hebrew dialect, and each one interpreted them as he was able" (Eusebius, *NPNF2* 1:173). But this is debatable. It may be fairly inferred that Papias himself had this Gospel in Greek. And there is no evidence that he had ever seen a copy of Matthew in Aramaic. Barnabas, who wrote before Papias, quotes the Gospel of Matthew in Greek. If Matthew originally wrote in Aramaic, we might assume that he also composed his Gospel in Greek, for it strikes one as altogether an independent composition and not as a mere translation.

From a closer examination of the Gospel itself, as compared with Mark and Luke, it is clear that the material is arranged not strictly chronologically, but by similarity of material. Matthew tends to gather the sayings of Jesus into five great discourses, or sermons (chs. 5–7; 10; 13; 18; 24–25). This is a problem that has always troubled the harmonists, especially in the arrangement of the material contained in Matthew 8:14–13:58. Some harmonists even suppose a shifting of pages in some ancient manuscripts. However, understanding this portion of the Gospel as a topical arrangement best explains the matter.

Mark

The writer of our second and shortest Gospel has from the earliest times till now been identified with John Mark of Jerusalem, the son of a well-to-do woman by the name of Mary, in whose house the disciples used to gather (Ac 12:12–17). He was a companion of Paul and Barnabas on their first mission journey (Ac 13:5). His intimacy with Barnabas is explained by the fact that he was his cousin (Col 4:10). Through Barnabas, he came in contact with the apostle Paul. But at that time, he still lacked fortitude and constancy; at Perga, in Pamphylia, he left the two apostolic missionaries and returned to Jerusalem (Ac 13:5, 13), much to the displeasure of Paul (Ac 15:38). On the next journey, Paul refused to take Mark along, while Barnabas was willing to overlook the temporary weakness. There was a sharp contention over the matter between the two leaders, resulting in Paul and Barnabas parting company. Barnabas took Mark to Cyprus, and Paul chose Silas as his fellow missionary (Ac 15:36–40). But later, we find Mark again as one of the fellow workers of Paul, who said Mark was of great assistance to him (Col 4:10–11; Phm 24; 2Tm 4:11).

However, we also find Mark connected especially with Peter, whom he assisted in his work and whom he accompanied to "Babylon" (1Pt 5:13). The Early Christian Church particularly remembered Mark as Peter's attendant and assistant. According to the earliest statement in the Church Fathers, "Mark, having become the interpreter of Peter, wrote accurately what he remembered of the things said or done by Christ" (Papias, in Eusebius, *NPNF2* 1:172). Mark is said to have lost one finger, and the nickname "stump-fingered" was given him on that account (Zahn, *Introduction to N. T.*, 3:428). He is represented as having been present at the death of Barnabas on Cyprus, after which he went to Alexandria, where he founded the first Church of St. Mark, of which he became the first bishop.

The Gospel that bears his name was most likely written in Rome before the destruction of Jerusalem (cf. Eusebius, *NPNF2* 1:115–16). An outstanding characteristic of Mark is his realism, and his pithy style and vivid flashes of portrayal confirm the historicity of his Gospel. All this is a guarantee of a firsthand historical record, a record such as might be expected from so lively a character as Peter, since, as Papias would have it, Mark neither saw the Lord nor followed Him (Eusebius, *NPNF2* 1:116). Commentators speak of the "Petrine character" of his Gospel.

As to the canonicity and the authenticity of this Gospel, there can be no doubt, for it is supported by the unanimous testimony of the Ancient Church, represented by writers from practically every quarter of the Roman world (cf. Eusebius, quoting Origen, *NPNF2* 1:273). There is a theory that would make Mark the first writer of the Synoptic Gospels—the other writers following his lead. We are not concerned with that issue here. However, the more we study the Gospels in Greek, especially when we compare again and again every word of each account, the more we are convinced that the three Synoptists wrote independently of one another.[2]

Luke   According to the testimony of early writers, Luke was the associate of Paul as Mark was of Peter. Luke does not mention his own name in the Gospel. Yet there is no reason to doubt the tradition transmitted by Eusebius that "the beloved physician" and companion of Paul is the author of the Acts of the Apostles and also of the Gospel that bears his name (Eusebius, *NPNF2* 1:136–37; 1:222; 1:273; cf. Col 4:14).

Little is known of Luke's personal history. He had not known Jesus personally, but determines to set forth faithfully "a narrative of the things that have been accomplished among us, just as those who from the beginning were eyewitnesses and ministers of the Word have delivered them to us" (Lk 1:1–2).

By birth, he seems to have been a Greek, possibly from Antioch, and by profession a physician. The apostle Paul may have converted him in Antioch, where the disciples were first called Christians. We find him connected with the great apostle in a lifelong, intimate friendship (2Tm 4:11). When Paul set out on his second missionary journey, Luke joined him at Troas and accompanied him to Philippi (Ac 16:10–17; the "we" passages, in which the author of Acts writes as though he was a traveling companion of Paul). On the third missionary journey, he was again with Paul (Ac 20:5–21:17). Afterward, he went with the now captive Paul to Rome (Ac 27:1–28:16); during the apostle's second captivity he was again with him (2Tm 4:11), for which the apostle was duly thankful.

Beyond these facts, nothing definite is known as to circumstances either of his life or of his death. But from his own writings we may gather that Luke had received a good education since he writes in an easy, flowing, and elegant style, which may be colored at points by the language of his profession (Lk 8:43; Ac 28:8; etc.); he was a historian of the highest order.[3]

That the Early Church regarded the Book of Acts and the Gospel of Luke as authentic is established by the fact that the Muratorian Canon, a Latin list of New Testament books, c. AD 170, both names Luke the physician as the author and lists his Gospel and Acts as Scripture. His Gospel was also used as one of the four recognized Gospels in the earliest account of the life of Christ, Tatian's *Diatessaron*.

The date of writing of this Gospel cannot be definitely fixed. But it might be said that Luke surely wrote his Gospel before the year AD 70, since there is no reference to the destruction of Jerusalem, concerning which a complete prophecy is given in Luke 21. From the last verses in Acts, it is probable that this book was written before the death of St. Paul (AD 68). And Luke's Gospel preceded the Book of Acts (cf. Ac 1:1). Perhaps c. AD 55–60 would fit the circumstances.[4]

In spite of the difficulties that for a long time puzzled historians, we now find that Luke is not only a reliable historian, but that he is *the* historian among the New Testament writers. Not only can Luke be checked against other historical accounts of that era, but in fact other historians ought to be compared with Luke.

The level of detail in the four Gospels presents a dilemma not commonly experienced by historians, who typically have only one or two accounts of an event or of a person's life rather than four detailed accounts. We have no basis to declare that one biblical account is apparently out of harmony with another or to credit one writer at the expense of the other. Nevertheless, qualities in John's Gospel, written by "the beloved apostle," have won first place in the hearts of many Christian readers. Looking at the matter from the point of view of the historian, we have to say that as an eyewitness from the beginning to the end, John was singularly able to tell the truth. In addition, we must consider his remarkably long life and the fact that he who heard the Lord formed the connecting link between the apostolic generation and other remarkable men living well along into the second century. All this confirms the reliability and trustworthiness of his account. For example, there is Irenaeus (bishop of Lyons c. AD 177) who had spent his early childhood in Asia Minor, where he heard the preaching of the aged bishop Polycarp of Smyrna (died c. AD 155). And Polycarp reported that he had heard John, who had heard the Lord (Eusebius, *NPNF*2 1:238–39; 161).

John

Although the writer of our fourth Gospel does not expressly mention his own name, he describes himself with sufficient clearness, so we know that he is one of the sons of the Galilean fisherman Zebedee (cf. Mt 4:21; Lk 5:10; Jn 21:2) and his wife Salome (cf. Mt 27:56; Mk 15:40–41). He is "the disciple whom Jesus loved" (Jn 13:23; 19:26; 20:2; 21:7, 20). A close comparison of a few passages has suggested the inference—although some do not accept it—that Mary, the mother of Jesus, and Salome, the wife of Zebedee, were sisters (cf. Mt 27:56; Mk 15:40; Jn 19:25). This would make John a cousin of Jesus, placing him all the nearer to the Lord and commending him to us all the more as a reliable and trustworthy biographer of Christ.

In his earlier days, John had been a disciple of John the Baptist, by whom he was directed to Christ. This was an experience that he never forgot, for he records for us even the hour of the day when he first followed Jesus (Jn 1:39). Together with Peter and his own brother James, he later became one of the most confidential disciples of Christ, and he was with the Lord as an eye- and ear-witness of the Master's labors, journeys, discourses, miracles, crucifixion, resurrection, and ascension.

Unlike the fiery character of Peter—although in John's earlier days he evinced a fiery temper himself (Mk 3:17; Lk 9:49, 54)—he was one of those quiet, modest, unassuming personalities who avoids even the mention of his own name. He had a receptive nature, following every move and listening most intently to every word of the Lord.

It seems that John, writing later than the other three evangelists, was acquainted with the Synoptic Gospels. In fact, it seems that it was his purpose to supply things the other evangelists had omitted in their accounts. Thus we have in John the particulars of the early Judean ministry of Jesus and His various journeys to Jerusalem.

Of John's later life, history reports that he went to Asia Minor, probably after the death of the apostle Paul. Emperor Domitian, in AD 95, banished John to the island of Patmos, where he wrote the Book of Revelation (cf. Rv 1:9). After regaining his liberty, John returned to Ephesus, where he died about AD 100.

His Gospel was evidently written shortly before the end of the century. It is undeniably present as one of the four interwoven Gospels in Tatian's *Diatessaron*. This first harmony of the Gospels begins with John's prologue and ends with the last verse in the appendix of St. John. The Gospel according to St. John is listed in the Muratorian Canon, and Eusebius wrote that all the Christian churches under the sun knew and accepted the Gospel of John (Eusebius, *NPNF*2 1:154).

Our introduction to the life of Christ would be incomplete without pointing to the introductions prepared by the evangelists themselves. There are two, prepared by Luke and John.

THE PROLOGUE OF LUKE

Luke 1:1–4

An Authentic Account of the Historic Christ

Following the literary style of Luke's day, he composes a classical prologue to his Gospel, in which he declares the motive, plan, and purpose of his work. As a late contemporary, he sets himself upon the task of writing a history of the recent past. Others had been doing this—gathering testimony, taking notes, and writing accounts in their attempt to preserve in writing the evangelical memorabilia—which moved Luke to do the same. "Many have undertaken to compile" an account of those things that now lie before us as a complete whole (Lk 1:1). The facts were gathered from those who had been eyewitnesses of Jesus and ministers of the Word. But Luke does not tell us who these writers were, nor does he say anything about the nature of their writings. He merely asserts the existence of certain written accounts, records, narratives, or sayings, which moved him, after due investigation, to write an independent and full account of his own. Luke made no explicit reference to the other Gospels. Matthew's and Mark's Gospels were probably written about the same time and, like Luke's Gospel, were independent productions.[5] Luke was well qualified to do this writing because, in his inquiries, he had followed all things from the beginning. (The fact that he made these investigations does not at all conflict with the doctrine of inspiration.) And in carrying out this difficult task, he plans to write "in order." This refers not to a detailed, mechanical sequence, but rather to a well-planned and well-arranged, reliable history. "That you may have certainty concerning the things you have been taught" (Lk 1:4). Of the "most excellent Theophilus," to whom Luke dedicated the Gospel, we know nothing. It has been suggested that he was a moneyed layman of Antioch who paid for the research and production expense. At any rate, he had already received "catechetical" instruction (Gr *katecheo*; Lk 1:4), and Luke was now supplying him with a reliable textbook for continued study.

THE PROLOGUE OF JOHN

In a beautiful prologue, the evangelist John identifies the person of Jesus Christ, who is to be the subject of his narrative. Jesus is the Logos, or the eternal and pre-existing Word, the Son of God—God Himself. John uses a term already familiar in Greek philosophy to denote the principle that maintains order in the world[6] but is here given a meaning all its own. "In the beginning was the Word, and the Word was with God, and the Word was God" (Jn 1:1). In tracing the antecedents of Jesus, John steps into prehistory (but not unhistory) and proclaims Jesus as the fountain of life and light, adding the sad note, however, that "the light shines in the darkness, and the darkness has not overcome it" (v. 5).

Not that the appearance of this Light came unheralded into a blinded world. For there was John the Baptist, the apostle John's former teacher. Although John the Baptist was not that Light, God sent him "to bear witness about the light, that all might believe through him" (v. 7). But the personified Light and Word, the way for whose coming John the Baptist prepared, "came to His own, and His own people did not receive Him" (v. 11). Still, the gracious operation of the Spirit through the Gospel overcame some who naturally opposed what was first preached to them, and they received "the right to become children of God." They "believed in His name" (v. 12). And thus they "were born"—reborn—"not of blood nor of the will of the flesh nor of the will of man" (v. 13). They were born not through anything that man can do, not in a natural way, "but of God," by the power of the almighty and gracious One.

The Son of God is eternal. But like the Father and the Holy Spirit, He was invisible to sinful man (1 Tm 6:16) until "the Word became flesh and dwelt among us" (Jn 1:14). Then all among whom He sojourned could see Him in the flesh. "We have seen His glory, glory as of the only Son from the Father" (v. 14). John the Baptist bore witness to the Lord's preexistence when he said: "He who comes after me ranks before me, because He was before me" (v. 15). And from John the evangelist's own

John 1:1–18

Exhibiting the Historic Christ as the Eternal Son of God Incarnate for Our Redemption experience, he joyfully states: "From His fullness we have all received, grace upon grace" (v. 16). This statement can be made because "the law was given through Moses; grace and truth came through Jesus Christ" (v. 17). Thus, John the evangelist formally identified "the Word" with Jesus Christ. The Law alone did not convey this fullness of God's grace. God revealed it in this wonderful incarnation. "No one has ever seen God; the only God, who is at the Father's side, He has made Him known" (v. 18).

NON-CHRISTIAN WITNESSES TO THE LIFE OF CHRIST

Lest anyone conclude that Christians were the only ones writing about Jesus in those early years, we include comments from authors who were not Christians but who referred to Christ. They include the following:

Josephus (AD 37–c. 100). In *Ant* 18:63–64, he wrote:

> Now there was about this time Jesus, a wise man, if it be lawful to call him a man; for he was a doer of wonderful works, a teacher of such men as receive the truth with pleasure. He drew over to him both many of the Jews and many of the Gentiles. He was [the] Christ. And when Pilate, at the suggestion of the principal men amongst us, had condemned him to the cross, those that loved him at the first did not forsake him; for he appeared to them alive again the third day; as the divine prophets had foretold these and ten thousand other wonderful things concerning him. And the tribe of Christians, so named from him, are not extinct at this day.

It is very likely that Josephus made some reference to Jesus, but most scholars agree that Christians revised this passage, if it is not entirely spurious. (The present writer is inclined to accept its authenticity; but this is not the place to enter into the argument.)

Pliny the Younger (AD 61–c. 113). Pliny, writing from Bithynia to Trajan, referred to Christians meeting on certain days and singing hymns "to Christ as to a god" (*Letters* 10.96).

Tacitus (c. AD 56–c. 117). The well-known Roman historian, in a passage relating to the persecution of Nero, wrote how the Christians, already a great multitude, derived their name "from one Christus, who was executed in the reign of Tiberius by the procurator of Judea, Pontius Pilate" (*Annals* 15.44).

Suetonius (c. AD 69–after 122). In his *Lives of the Caesars* (*Claudius* 25.4), Suetonius spoke of the Jews as expelled from Rome for the raising of tumults at the instigation of one "Chrestus," a mistaken name for "Christus." Suetonius was also mistaken about the cause of the disturbance, but the incident is likely that referred to in Acts 18:2.

APOLOGISTS FOR CHRISTIANITY

Of the ancient Christian apologists, mention may be made of the following:

Quadratus (died AD 129). This missionary of apostolic times wrote an apology for the Christian faith and presented it to Emperor Hadrian. The work has been lost; only a fragment has been preserved. Here is an interesting passage, which is found in the *Church History* of Eusebius:

> But the works of our Savior were always present, for they were genuine. Those that were healed and those that were raised from the dead, who were seen not only when they were healed and when they were raised, but were also always present—and not merely while the Savior was on earth, but also after His death—they were alive for quite a while, so that some of them lived even to our day. (Eusebius, *NPNF*2 1:175)

Aristides (writing c. AD 125). In his *Apology*, likewise addressed to Emperor Hadrian, Aristides included the following beautiful reference to Jesus:

> Now, the Christians trace their origin from the Lord Jesus Christ. And He is acknowledged by the Holy Spirit to be the Son of the Most High, who came down from heaven for the salvation of men. And being born of a pure virgin, unbegotten and immaculate, He assumed flesh and revealed Himself among men that He might recall them Himself from their wandering after many gods. And having accomplished this wonderful dispensation, by a voluntary choice He tasted death on the cross, fulfilling an august dispensation. And after three days He came to life again and ascended into heaven. (*ANF* 9:276)

Justin Martyr (c. AD 100–65). His *Apology*, addressed to Emperor Antoninus Pius, contains the following references to the time, birth, and life of Christ:

> Christ was born one hundred and fifty years ago under Cyrenius and subsequently, in the time of Pontius Pilate, taught what He said He taught. (*First Apology* 46)

> Our teacher of these things is Jesus Christ, who also was born for this purpose and was crucified under Pontius Pilate, proconsul of Judea, in the time of Tiberius Caesar. (*First Apology* 13)

> Now, there is a village in the land of the Jews [Bethlehem, mentioned before], thirty-five stadia from Jerusalem, in which Jesus was born, as you can ascertain also from the register of the taxing made under Cyrenius, your first procurator in Judea. (*First Apology* 34)

> And after He was crucified, they cast lots upon His vesture, and they that crucified Him parted it among them. And that these things did happen you can ascertain from the *Acts of Pontius Pilate*. (*First Apology* 35)

> In these books, then, of the prophets we found Jesus, our Christ, foretold as coming, born of a virgin, growing up to man's estate, and healing every disease and every sickness, and raising the dead, and being hated, and unrecognized,

and crucified, and dying, and rising again, and ascending into heaven, and being called the Son of God. (*First Apology* 31)

The Falsely Signed and Gnostic Gospels

Lastly, one cannot write about the Gospels today without also mentioning the falsely signed gospels (the Pseudepigrapha, or apocryphal gospels) and the Gnostic gospels. This is because manuscript discoveries in the twentieth century brought many of these works back to light. We write "back to light" because the early Christians knew and commented on these writings, rejecting them as unfaithful accounts. Although it remains possible that here and there these accounts preserve some credible sayings or stories from Jesus (cf. the independent saying from Jesus in Ac 20:35), there is no reliable way to confirm which sayings or stories these might be. Unlike the canonical Gospels that Christians universally received and regarded as faithful testimony, none of the falsely signed gospels or Gnostic gospels attained such status. Gnostics, for example, valued some of them and so preserved them, but Christians generally saw no reason to preserve them and in many cases warned against them. Most of these documents exist in one or a limited number of copies, in contrast with the canonical Gospels, which were preserved in many thousands of copies.

The earliest among these falsely signed or Gnostic gospels may be the *Gospel of Thomas*, which is a collection of sayings attributed to Jesus. Many of the sayings are like those in the canonical Gospels and may have been drawn from them or from the sayings passed down orally. The *Gospel of Thomas* likely dates to the early years of Gnosticism, sometime in the second century, though obviously much later than the time of the apostles and the canonical Gospels.

The value of these gospels today is that they tell us much about some fairly early and diverse beliefs and practices that sprang up among or alongside early and medieval Christian communities. They also illustrate the mixing of religions (syncretism) that can take place in a diverse culture.

1

The State of the World

The time was ripe for the coming of Christ. In all the world's history there never was such a combination of favorable circumstances for the birth of Christ and the introduction of Christianity—political, social, economic, intellectual, linguistic, religious, and moral. Divine providence itself had foreseen and provided for "the fullness of time" (Gal 4:4). Daniel's prophetic vision of a mighty kingdom of iron (Dn 2:40) was now reaching the height of its power. In ever-widening circles, the legions of Rome were extending her boundaries. From Rome to all of Italy, to the neighboring isles, to Carthage, to the right, to the left, they marched until finally they crushed all the countries of the Mediterranean basin under their iron heels, or the nations had voluntarily accepted the Roman peace (*pax Romana*). The whole world was at rest. From the wooded swamps of Britain to the sands of Egypt, from the Pillars of Hercules to far-off Mesopotamia, the famous *pax Romana* prevailed. And it was to prevail for centuries to come when the message of Jesus Christ would travel.

There had been mighty empires in the ancient world. History relates, and archeology reveals, the glories of the early Babylonian, the Egyptian, the Assyrian, the Chaldean, the Persian, and the Macedonian past. And even Israel had its brief spell of political glory. But in general, these older empires owed their rise to the success and ability of some adventurous conqueror. When the master-hand was withdrawn, they fell asunder or were swept away to make room for some new kingdom or dynasty that sprang up with the same rapidity and in its turn experienced the same fate.[1] This refers in particular to a number of ancient Asiatic kingdoms. But it is also true of Alexander's Greek monarchy that issued from Europe, was broken up at his death into several conflicting kingdoms, and yet survived in its influence and passed on to its heirs an heirloom of far-reaching importance.

With the coming of the Romans, a new era began. The Romans founded their monarchy on principles yet unknown. After ruthlessly conquering a nation, the Romans did not continue to oppress them but governed them so that conscious

1
The Roman Empire

2
Asiatic Monarchies

3
Roman Principle of Moderation

strength was tempered with consideration for local customs and ensured military protection, public safety, and domestic peace.[2] This refers, of course, to the general policy, not to local tyranny that an individual provincial governor might practice. By this general policy, the edifice of Roman power was gradually built up, and the wisdom of the ages preserved it. Here was the first Western empire that endured for a long period of time and whose yoke was rather endurable. In view of its size, its character, its composition, its lasting structure, and its success, one can justly call the *pax Romana* the grandest political achievement ever accomplished by Western culture.[3] With it, the monarchies of Alexander, of Charlemagne, and of Napoleon cannot be compared. Greeks, Romans, Gauls, Britons, Jews, Syrians, Egyptians were all peacefully and seemingly permanently united in one common fatherland (*communis omnium patria*). The general principle of government was wise and yet simple as well as beneficent. The various nationalities, though differing among themselves, felt as one. Their obedience to the central government, upon the whole, was voluntary, uniform, and permanent. The vanquished nations, blended into one great people, resigned the hope, nay, even the wish of resuming their independence and scarcely considered their own existence as distinct from the existence of Rome.[4]

4
Voluntary Submission

Never before had so many nations been so bloodily conquered and so peacefully ruled. The established authority of the Caesars was exercised with the same facility on the Thames, the Orontes, and the Nile as on the banks of the Tiber.[5] The Thracians were kept in subjection by two thousand Roman guards; the Dalmatians lived in peace under a single Roman legion. The tribes of Gaul had fought for independence for nearly eighty years, and when defeated, they submitted to the orders of twelve hundred men. A single legion sufficed to govern Spain. But one legion was quartered in Northern Africa, and a few legions curbed far-reaching Egypt and the proud nobility of Greece. Although it was still necessary to keep the German peace with eight Roman legions and to pacify the Britons with four, generally speaking, the conquered nations bowed respectfully to the proud Roman mistress and believed their own best interests to coincide with the common interests of Rome.

5
The Stewardship of Empire

Thus, Rome blended the nations and prepared them for the preaching of the Gospel among them. With the exception of a few inconsequential barbarian tribes beyond well-patrolled frontiers and outside the interest of the Roman horizon, now for the first time we may speak of "the world" (Lk 2:1) as embracing broad humanity or the *genus humanum*. For practical purposes, it was the whole Western world, united and largely at rest. Rome's enemies were conquered, peace was everywhere established, and her program of expansion concluded with Europe, Asia, and Africa firmly united. When her own civil wars ended, Rome finally settled down on January 16, 27 BC, to put the principle of the empire formally into operation. This was the day when Gaius Octavius became *Imperator* Caesar Augustus and was invested with absolute power under republican titles. For after the Battle of Actium, Augustus found himself at the head of nearly forty veteran Roman legions and the Roman world at his feet.

Happily for the tranquility of mankind and for the coming of the Prince of Peace, whose advent Caesar Augustus was unwittingly to usher in, Augustus was himself a prince of peace. His imperial policy was not aggression, but firm, yet peaceful, administration.[6] He was satisfied to relinquish the ambitious design of subduing the whole earth and to preserve those dominions that Rome won in the first seven centuries of its history. He concluded his last will and testament, written in his own hand, with the counsel to his successors never to aim at an extension of the empire.[7] And on the whole, the Julian-Claudian line adhered to this policy in the period with which we are now concerned, that is, during the life of Christ and in the first days of the Christian Church. The doors of the temple of Janus Quirinus, which were kept open only in time of war, were closed three times during the reign of Augustus.[8]

6
Caesar Augustus

Ever since the dawn of history, there had been a gradual intermingling of peoples around the shores of the Mediterranean Sea. Early Phoenician settlers formed colonies in Northern Africa and Spain, but in the course of time, many of them were made citizens of Rome. The Romans conferred the same honors upon Greek settlers of Italy, Sicily, Sardinia, Corsica, and Southern Gaul. As a result of the many wars, deportations, captivities, and colonizations, the Middle Eastern peoples had already become thoroughly acquainted with one another. After the Macedonian conquests, the whole East was covered with Greek colonies and cities. Greeks settled everywhere as professors, merchants, physicians, artists, actors, and acrobats. And now, with the coming of Rome, the East was to become thoroughly and permanently acquainted with the West. The members of each nationality discovered how much they really had in common with one another. Although the Greeks brought civilization and culture, the Romans brought law, order, and peace; and the entire nation was to enjoy the blessings of both groups of gifts. This peaceful and ordered state of affairs in the empire contributed largely to the spread of the cosmopolitanism already in progress. In an empire that was international in character, it was natural that national barriers were largely removed. The great cities of the empire—Rome, Alexandria, Jerusalem, Antioch, and others— became meeting places of all races and languages. The polyglot character of the legions recruited from every quarter of the empire was in itself a contributing factor in the breaking up of national barriers. On the front, soldiers of various nationalities fought their battles, became companions in arms, and then returned to their distant homes as brothers. Previously, it had been no strange experience for Jews and Egyptians, Germans and Gauls, to meet one another in Rome. Now, one could frequently see blond hair and blue eyes in the marts and camps even of the East. After the death of Cleopatra, the services of her splendid bodyguard of

7
Cosmopolitanism

four hundred Gauls were no longer needed in Alexandria, so Augustus generously sent them over to Herod.[9] There were Germans in Jerusalem at the time of the birth of Christ. When Herod the Great died, a Thracian-German-Gallic guard escorted his body to its resting place.[10] During Christ's sojourn on earth and until the last Jewish war, the stalwart and burly figures of soldiers from northwest Europe were familiar sights in the streets of Jerusalem.[11]

8
Domination of Greek Culture

Originally, the Romans were little more than conquering barbarians who had small regard for civilization and culture. Already, they had wiped out two ancient and, in some respects, superior civilizations—those of Etruria and Carthage—so that hardly a trace of them remained. The ancient languages and dialects of Italy, for instance, the Sabine, the Etruscan, and the Venetian, sank into oblivion. The language of the conqueror, though with some inevitable mixture, was adopted in Italy, Africa, Spain, and Gaul. Only in the mountains or among the peasants were preserved faint traces of the Punic, Celtic, or other idioms. However, the children of Mars left a cold civilization to the conquered nations. And it is hard to conceive what a scourge Rome would have proved to the world had she merely continued in her victorious course without the tempering influence of civilization and culture. The shades of night would have descended upon the Roman world. But with the conquest of Greece, untutored Mars came under the spell of cultured Pallas Athene.[12] The arts of Greece intellectually subdued victorious Rome. The immortal writers of classical Greece—Homer, Sophocles, Herodotus, Aristotle, and others—were soon made the favorite objects of Roman study and imitation. Of course, these elegant pastimes were not suffered to interfere with the more serious business of the Roman peace (*pax Romana*) and the policies of imperial rule. Nevertheless, the contact was of the greatest importance. It marked the end of a pure, independent Latin civilization—if there ever had been any—and the beginning of a culture known as the Greco-Roman civilization. Latin poets and historians might complain that captured Hellas (Greece) led captive her captor,[13] but it was a good thing that it happened. For thus Christ was ushered into a civilized and Greek-speaking world.[14]

9
A Limited Preparation for the Gospel (*Praeparatio Evangelica*)

Although it must be admitted that Roman protection and the adoption of Greek culture were important, it must be pointed out that this factor has been wrongly represented as a *praeparatio evangelica*. Socrates, Plato, Aristotle, the eclecticism of Greek thought, and Stoic philosophy cannot be called schoolmasters leading men to Christ. For, after all, Greek civilization, in spite of some beautiful aspects, was pagan, degenerate, and corrupt. Its true character was quickly recognized, even in Rome. Oriental extravagance, luxury, and vice tended to replace the simplicity, frugality, and morality of an earlier day. Along with the many helpful elements of culture that the Romans had received from the East, they also received the germs of moral and social disease. "To learn Greek is to learn knavery" became a proverb in Rome.[15]

In its far-reaching consequences, however, one of the results of the Greco-Roman civilization was to be of the greatest importance. For example, the worldwide spread and dominating influence of the Greek language was a most valuable aid to the cause of Christ's kingdom. As a result of the Macedonian conquests, Greek thought and culture not only pervaded the entire East, but the people from Asia Minor to India also generally spoke the Greek language. Many Greek colonies of the Mediterranean basin had previously known and spoken the Greek language, along with Latin, except where forcibly and successfully suppressed. But now Greek had entered and permanently established itself in even the strangest surroundings. Who would have dreamed of finding flourishing Greek cities in the land of Israel[16] and among the extraordinarily home-loving Palestinian Jews? Thus, our Savior was intimately brought into contact with Greek and occasionally may have spoken it. Some Jews even officially recognized Greek as a proper language for religious services. They translated their sacred writings, the Old Testament, into Greek.[17] Some of their books, not part of the canon, did not have to be translated because they were originally written in Greek.[18] The inscription on the wall of the outer temple court in Jerusalem forbidding Gentiles to enter under pain of death was posted in Greek.[19]

10
The Greek Language Aids the Spread of the Gospel

And when the Romans came upon the scene, they found the Greek language so widely known and so deeply rooted that they could not hope to suppress it. Indeed, they did not even try to do so. Merely asserting the dignity of the Latin tongue and employing it in the administration of civil and military affairs in their Eastern dominions, the Romans gladly accepted the Greek language as a common means of communication. And so it came about, at first in the East, but gradually throughout the whole empire, that the language of Alexander became both the language of the Gospels and the *lingua franca* of the Greco-Roman world. People in the Roman Empire used it to a much greater extent than Latin.[20] It was almost impossible in any province to find a Roman subject of liberal education ignorant of Greek.[21] No businessman of consequence could afford to be a stranger to Greek. Due to an overestimate of Greek literature, the only books read, studied, and imitated as to style—except Law, and that for good reasons—were Greek. So it was in Alexandria, in Jerusalem, in Antioch, in Rome, yes, even in Cadiz and Lyons. Alexander's ambitions of a world conquest had, in a way, been fulfilled. His language was spoken from the many Alexandrias that had been founded—in Babylonia, in Africa, etc.—to the statue of Alexander before which Julius Caesar sighed in Spain.[22] It is true, Alexander's kingdom was shattered since Rome largely swallowed it up, but his language remained. His successors, the masters of Rome, themselves studied Greek and were able to use it. Julius Caesar did not say, "*Et tu, Brute?*" as usually reported, but his dying words were Greek.[23] Some of the famous sayings of Augustus were originally uttered in Greek.[24] Tiberius understood Greek.[25] Caligula

11
The Romans Adopted Greek as a World Language

could quote Homeric verses.[26] Nero, it seems, could compose imitations of them on the spot.[27] And Marcus Aurelius, though born in Rome in AD 121, nevertheless wrote his philosophy in Greek.

12
The Early Christian
Church Was Greek

It was but natural that the Early Christian Church was Greek. With its universal appeal, it could hardly be anything else. The Gospels were written in Greek. The apostle Paul writes an epistle to the capital city of a Latin empire—and is understood—in Greek. In fact, all the early Christian writings that appeared in what would seem the Latin half of the empire—the epistles of Clement, the *Shepherd of Hermas*, the *Apology* of Tatian, and others—were Greek. The Christian churches of the first three hundred years, East and West, their language, their confessions, their hymns, their liturgy,[28] and many vestiges and traditions were Greek. And Latin Christianity, when it did come, did not originate in Rome, but in Africa.[29] We find the very same thing in Gaul (now France). Irenaeus, bishop of Lyons, wrote in Greek. And the first Christians in Gaul settled in Greek cities, which owned Marseilles[30] as their parent.

13
Separation of East
and West

The Greek language as an aid to the cause of Christ can hardly be overestimated. Without it, the spread of Christianity would hardly have been possible. Latin never was popular in the East. As late as the third century AD, Cornelius of Rome wrote to Fabius of Antioch in Greek. When Cyprian (bishop of Carthage, Northern Africa) also wrote to Fabius—but in Latin—Eusebius reported it[31] almost as though it was an innovation. As the West, centering around the bishop of Rome, gradually became Latin, a separation took place. It was a separation of Latin and Greek, of East and West, in Church and empire. And it really was a loss to the world in more than one respect. How noteworthy that after a thousand years, just before the Protestant Reformation, it was again the Greek language that ushered in a revival of Renaissance learning. Incidentally, this served the cause of the Reformation, the dispelling of spiritual darkness, and the dispensing of the saving light of "the everlasting Gospel" through Luther, who proclaimed the Christ.

14
Koine (Common)
Greek

Biblical scholars were long at a loss and at loggerheads with one another about how to classify New Testament Greek. Although the language of the Gospels is not on a par with literary Attic Greek, it is now clear that the Gospels were not written in a corrupt Jewish-Greek,[32] nor was their language a distinctive creation of the Holy Spirit.[33] It was simply the Greek language of the first century AD. It was the *lingua franca* of the Greco-Roman Empire. This legacy of Alexander the Great was a world-speech—with Attic Greek as the base—but affected and influenced by dialectal and provincial idioms. Just as the language used in these pages is not the English of Shakespeare or of Addison, but the language commonly used in the present-day English-speaking world, so the Greek of Paul and John compares favorably with the style of Greek authors of those days. For had they used a Greek of special creation or one that Jewish dialects corrupted, how could readers of Greek descent understand them? But as it was, the Lord in His wisdom used the existing world-language as a means of preparing the world for the reception of the message of Christ. The *koine* was the language that Christ heard and probably also used at times, although Aramaic was His native tongue. There really exists an intimate linguistic bond, therefore, between all students of the Greek New Testament and their Master in the very words presented in the Greek of the Gospels according to Matthew, Mark, Luke, and John.

A cruel hand of destiny seems to have shook "the house of Israel among all nations as one shakes with a sieve, but no pebble shall fall to the earth" (Am 9:9). Yet this sifting of Israel among all nations is one of the marvels of divine purpose in preparing the advent of Christ. In addition to the above preparations, we may mention this circumstance that aided the spreading of Christianity. We read in the Old Testament that Shalmaneser, the king of Assyria, "captured Samaria, and he carried the Israelites [the northern tribes] away to Assyria and placed them in Halah, and on the Habor, the river of Gozan, and in the cities of the Medes" (2Ki 17:6). Judah, about 125 years later, met with a similar judgment when Nebuchadnezzar, the king of Babylon, swooped down upon the Southern Kingdom and "carried away all Jerusalem and all the officials and all the mighty men of valor, 10,000 captives, and all the craftsmen and the smiths," so that only the poorest in the land remained (2Ki 24:14). Besides these, there were other captivities. For example, Ptolemy I of Egypt captured Jerusalem in 320 BC and took many Jews with him to Egypt,[34] adding largely to the Jewish population of Alexandria. Antiochus the Great of Syria (r. 223–187 BC) removed two thousand Jewish families from Babylon and settled them in Phrygia and Lydia.[35] (Their ancestors had elected to remain in Babylon when Cyrus [538 BC] earlier permitted the Jews to return to the land of their fathers.) And after Pompey captured Jerusalem (63 BC), he carried off hundreds of Jews to be sold as slaves in Rome.[36]

There was, however, also a voluntary emigration of Jews, for the purpose of trade and commerce, into all the chief cities of the ancient world.[37] Nearly a million Jews are said to have settled in Egypt alone.[38] For the sake of consolidating their possessions, the Diadochi, the successors of Alexander, attracted masses of Jewish settlers into their newly founded towns. Attractive offers were made; rights of citizenship and other privileges were granted.[39] As a consequence, the seed of Abraham was found in large numbers in every section of the Roman world; at the mouths of all principal rivers, the Nile, the Euphrates, the Tigris, and the Danube; in all the principal cities of the empire, Alexandria, Antioch, Damascus, Athens, Corinth, Thessalonica, and Rome; on the islands of the Mediterranean; from Babylonia to the south of France and Spain; and myriads in Parthia beyond the Roman Empire.[40]

15
The Jewish
Dispersion

16
Voluntary Jewish
Emigration

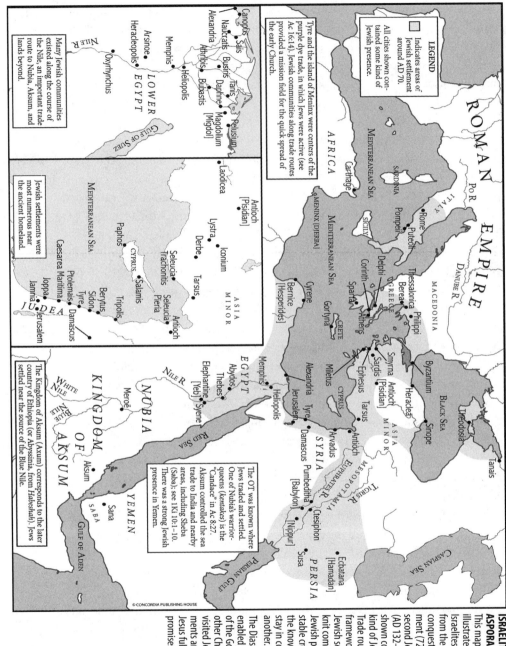

LEGEND

☐ Indicates areas of Jewish settlement around AD 70.

All cities shown contained some kind of Jewish presence.

Tyre and the island of Meninx were centers of the purple dye trade, in which Jews were active (see Ac 16:14). Jewish communities along trade routes provided a mission field for the quick spread of the early Church.

Many Jewish communities existed along the course of the Nile, an important trade route to Nubia, Aksum, and lands beyond.

Jewish settlements were most numerous near the ancient homeland.

The Kingdom of Aksum (Axum) corresponds to the later country of Ethiopia (or Abyssinia, from *Habeshah*). Jews settled near the source of the Blue Nile.

The OT was known where Jews traded and settled. One of Nubia's warrior-queens (*kentakes*) is the "Candace" in Ac 8:27. Aksum controlled the sea trade to India and nearby areas, including Sheba (Saba); see 1Ki 10:1–10. There was a strong Jewish presence in Yemen.

© CONCORDIA PUBLISHING HOUSE

ISRAELITE/JEWISH DI-ASPORA SETTLEMENTS.

This map illustrates the spread of Israelites and Judeans from the Assyrian conquest and resettlement (722 BC) to the second Jewish revolt (AD 132–135). All cities shown contained some kind of Jewish presence. Trade routes provided the framework for expanding Jewish settlement. Close-knit Jewish communities allowed Jewish people to trade on stable credit throughout the known world and to stay in contact with one another.

The Diaspora also enabled the early spread of the Gospel as Paul and other Christian leaders visited Jewish settlements and preached that Jesus fulfilled the OT promises of the Messiah.

Thus even in ancient times, the total numbers of the Jews in the Diaspora were not to be counted by the thousands, but by the millions.[41]

When the Roman conquerors came upon the scene, they witnessed the strange spectacle of a scattered race and millions of potential disturbers of the peace within their borders. In the interest of the peace (*pax Romana*), they bestowed upon a despised population particular favors and protection. This was a wise move. At home, the Jews were the greatest revolutionists, but abroad, they were typically the staunchest loyalists and supporters of Rome.[42] The Roman senate at one time had a special circular letter written in their favor and sent it to all the kings of the East and to all the cities, islands, and provinces of the Mediterranean (1 Macc 15:15–24), where presumably a larger or smaller number of Jews was to be found. Because the Jews established religious colonies wherever they went and at the same time kept in touch with Jerusalem and the temple, it is not surprising that on Pentecost Day, Jews from every quarter of the Roman Empire could be addressed (Ac 2:1–12). They established contacts for the message of the Gospel in the uttermost parts of the earth.

17
Roman Protection of Jewish Settlers

In an economic and material respect also, the world was ripe for the coming of Christ. It was natural for commerce to follow order and peace. Travel was safe by land and sea. Gnaeus Pompeius had destroyed the pirates, and after the death of Sextus Pompeius, no hostile maritime forces remained. As to intercommunication by land, it was one of Rome's first concerns in her policy of expansion to secure her conquests by means of splendid military roads. Rome began a road-building campaign in 312 BC with the construction of the Via Appia, which continued until all parts of the empire were connected with one another by well-kept highways issuing from the capital, passing through the provinces, and terminating only at the frontiers.[43] They erected roadhouses everywhere at a distance of only a few miles from one another. They constantly provided each of them with horses, and by the help of relays, it was possible to cover a hundred miles in a single day.[44] In the first century of the Christian era, it was possible to travel by land or sea through the length and breadth of the empire, from Alexandria to Cadiz or from Jerusalem to York, with safety and comfort. All this served the Gospel. Five centuries later, such travel would have been well-nigh impossible.[45] To this day, the great system of well-constructed Roman highways and bridges in some places has not entirely yielded to the devastating efforts of nearly two thousand years.[46] It served not only the legions and imperial escorts and made possible the carrying out of the decree of Emperor Caesar Augustus that "all the world should be registered" (Lk 2:1), but it was also of equal service in conveying the message of the ambassadors of Christ to all parts of the Western world.

18
Roman Roads as a Preparation for the Gospel

But there was something that Rome could not offer its subjects. It could give them a wonderful government, peace, protection, culture, commerce, a universal

19
Negative "Preparation"

language, prosperity, good roads, and material blessings. But it was not able to supply them with a religion that satisfied human need. The original Romans practiced extremely simple religion. Even the usual idols of paganism were missing. The mysterious influences or forces of nature that were supposed to direct the visible phenomena of the physical world were considered the "powers"[47] whose favor was necessary to the material prosperity of man. The objects around which this worship centered—not so much as objects of worship, but rather as symbols of the forces for which they stood—were the fireplace, the pantry,[48] the door,[49] the spear,[50] and others. Especially the spear, because, betraying their warlike impulses, the Romans delighted to call themselves the children of Mars. And since their gods were not originally conceived as having human form, it was not necessary to carve out their likenesses or to cast them into a certain form; besides, they did not know how. A spear stuck into the ground represented Mars. But later, when they came into contact with the Etruscans and Greeks, they discovered that their gods were all given a human form. Thus the Romans called upon Etruscan artists to aid them in giving a respectable appearance to their local gods.

20
Polytheism

In her march of conquest, however, Rome was confronted with a serious religious problem. Although it was a rather simple matter to impose the terms of Roman peace upon those who fell before her arms, she was at a loss as to what should be done with the gods of the newly conquered nations. Of course, Rome's gods must have been stronger; otherwise, how could one explain the victories? In some cases, the defeated nations could be induced to forsake their inefficient protectors. But even though the deities of the conquered nations could not withstand the mightier gods of the invading Romans, yet the Romans did not deny the existence of the defeated divinities.[51] But suppose the foreign divinities should unite and fight against the Roman gods. That would not be according to the policy of "divide and conquer" (*divide et impera*), and it would not be conducive to the expansion of Rome. Therefore, to solve a problem that might conceivably prove rather vexatious, both the conquered nations and their gods were admitted as members into the empire. The Romans treated the foreign gods with marked respect and invited them to transfer their abode to hospitable Rome and to bestow their favors upon it. Their devoted followers were granted a license or privilege, and their worship was recognized as a fully accredited Roman religion.[52] This was done according to the principle of Roman religious liberty and toleration. The persecution of Christians of a later date was a different matter and need not concern us here. People in the empire considered all religions equally true, the philosophers considered them equally false, and the rulers considered them all equally useful.[53]

21
Bankruptcy of
Paganism

However, not only gods, but also superstition, magic, sorcery, immorality, vice, and every form of corruption flourished under the Roman sun. Rome was a cesspool of everything infamous and abominable.[54] The religious life and morals of imperial Rome were hopelessly steeped in paganism and polytheism and were utterly corrupt. Every throne was occupied: the thrones of power, art, law, and culture; also the thrones of vice and sin; but one throne was vacant, the throne that Christ was to fill.

And was He expected? A few ancient writers mentioned a prevalent belief that a deliverer was to come from the East. These ancient writers asserted that Rome was awaiting the coming of a Savior—the references appear in Suetonius,[55] Tacitus,[56] and Josephus.[57] As a result, modern interpreters have often claimed that messianic expectations were universal in the Roman Empire. These interpreters connect the references with the destruction of Jerusalem, which took place after the appearing of Jesus. However, ancient Romans interpreted them as referring to Titus or Vespasian, so they are not helpful examples of a widespread expectation of a Messiah who was to come (cf. Jn 1:10). Two other references—the *Sibylline Oracles*[58] and the "Messianic" *Eclogue* of Virgil[59]—are too vague to merit any serious consideration. But for the sake of argument, supposing that they actually referred to Christ, they would not have proved the existence of a universal expectation in the Roman world. In contrast, the hope of a coming Redeemer was never absent in the heart of believing Israelites. Many who lived in heathen countries came into contact with Israelites and may have received some glimmering of Israel's hope. Yet the world at large was in ignorance of, and not consciously prepared for, the coming of Christ. Indeed, to a large extent, the Jews themselves were ignorant (Rm 9:30–33; 11:25) of the true nature of the promised Kingdom and its King. The time, however, as we have seen—God's time—was ripe for the coming of Christ.

22
Messianic
Expectations

2

THE STATE OF THE JEWS

The scepter had departed from Judah, but not yet completely. This did not happen definitely until the removal of Archelaus in AD 6,[1] when Judea was turned into a Roman province. The Romans broke even the last slender thread of Maccabean connection and the Jews willingly admitted: "We have no king but Caesar" (Jn 19:15). But until the coming of Christ, according to divine promise (Gn 49:10), the scepter continued with the descendants of Judah, at least in name and in prophecy, or rather, in the hands of the Levite high priests, who adhered to Judah. Let us briefly review the circumstances that brought about this state of affairs.

1
The Scepter of Judah

The key to Israel's involved history lies in the geographic position of the country, in its relation to the surrounding nations. It is frequently called the Holy Land because the footsteps of our Savior hallowed it. It is also still lovingly called the Land of Israel[2] in the Hebrew readers of Jewish schools and by those nations that recognize the modern state of Israel, but in our geography textbooks, it is often given the name *Palestine*. This is, however, really a misnomer, since Palestine denotes the territory of the Philistines. David and later kings claimed and ruled over the Philistine territory. However, the proverbial expression "from Dan to Beersheba" (Jgs 20:1) preserved an indication of the normal north-to-south limits of the Land of Israel. Compared with many modern states, this is a small land, only one-hundred-fifty miles in length and twenty-five to eighty miles in breadth. The total area is about seven thousand square miles—not as large as Massachusetts or New Jersey—and yet in certain respects, it was the very heart of the ancient world. The attention of the student of history is at once attracted by the immensely favorable strategic position of this little bit of soil. By depicting the world as a circle, with Jerusalem as its center, medieval cartographers displayed their theological motives; and history has confirmed their good judgment.[3] We can only marvel at divine providence for choosing this particular tract of largely sandy and rocky soil as the abode of a people that was to receive the divine message throughout the Old Testament and as the

2
The Land of Israel
(*Erets Israel*)

actual scene of the revelation and physical manifestation of God's grace in the person and work of Christ.

Between the twenty-fifth and thirty-fifth parallels northern latitude, there lies a strip of territory in the Old World of fairly uniform type beginning at the Straits of Gibraltar, embracing both shores of the Mediterranean, and extending to the border of the great Asiatic mountain systems of the distant East. Today, most of this is barren, except on the north Mediterranean coastline and in the tillable, great river valleys. But in earlier times, it likely consisted of grassy steppes until a northward shift of moist, westerly winds.[4] Now, it happens that in this general belt of land and sea occurred nearly all of what we know and what was recorded from earliest human history and western civilization.

In Western Asia, this territory may be roughly divided into three great belts.[5]

First, a northern belt of mountains and high tablelands extends from the eastern shores of the Persian Gulf through Persia and Kurdistan into Asia Minor.[6] This formidable barrier prevented the cradle civilization from coming into contact with its unknown northern neighbors and, at the same time, served as a protection against the Scythians, Gog and Magog, and such barbarian dangers as might be lurking beyond. Only once in Old Testament times, during the reign of Josiah, was this barrier crossed,[7] and ancient Middle Eastern civilization—Assyria, Babylon, Media, Israel, Egypt, and even Asia Minor and Greece—stood aghast at the spectacle of northern barbarians rushing down on the seats of luxury and power.[8]

Second, a vast belt of forbidding deserts extended in ancient times along the twenty-fifth parallel. It still extends from the Persian Gulf through Arabia and across the whole of Northern Africa to the Atlantic Coast.[9]

And third, between these two regions, another belt is placed, a large semicircle, with its open side to the south, on which was staged most of the world's ancient history. Because land suited for agriculture is found nearly all along this belt—at least grass and pasture during the rainy season—geographers and historians suggested the title *Fertile Crescent*, which is still widely used.[10] In the shape of a crescent or an inverted U, it can easily be traced from the valley of the Nile northward, then along the Mediterranean to Israel, east of the Lebanon Mountains to the Euphrates, eastward to the Tigris, and then southward to the Persian Gulf. Babylon and Assyria occupy its eastern arm, Syria the crest, and Israel and Egypt its western wing. Or, starting from Ur in Chaldea, one may trace it by following the travels of Abraham to Haran, northern Canaan (perhaps "Dan" or Laish), Shechem, Bethel, Jebus (Jerusalem), Kiriath-arba (Hebron), Beersheba, and Egypt.

On this general belt, the Land of Israel occupied the key position and lay like a bridge or corridor for the trader as well as for the conqueror between Asia and Africa, with solid barriers on both sides. To the west and north was the Mediterranean, an open route to Europe. But the Phoenicians jealously guarded passage to sea trade, securely barricaded with the Lebanon Mountains at their back,[11] and until the coming of the Romans, the Mediterranean Sea was also the realm of pirates. On the south side of the Fertile Crescent were the shores of a vast desert bay some five hundred miles across, not of water, but of the sweeping sands of the Arabian Desert. The strategic position of the Land of Israel was apparent to all; it was the only open and firm ancient highway between Asia and Africa. After the time of Alexander, its importance only increased; for then it became a turntable for Western civilization on the three continents: Europe, Asia, and Africa.[12] And finally, after Rome completed its own crescent all the way around the Mediterranean Sea, is it just mere coincidence that these two crescents, the eastern and the western, should form a conjunction and meet in a letter X on Jewish soil? In a wonderful way, at the right moment and at the most suitable spot, divine providence directed all circumstances to the coming of Christ. Rome itself would not have provided a better place for the appearance of Christ. (It was not even the best location for Rome, since three hundred years later, when it was too late, Constantine moved the capital of the Roman Empire to the East.) It is, therefore, no overstatement to call the Land of Israel the very center of the ancient world.

But Israel's eminently favored geographic position also had grave disadvantages. The Land of Israel lacked size, agricultural wealth, natural resources, harbors, and other regular empire builders' assets. It was fated to be the coveted prize of succeeding kingdoms rising on both arms of the Fertile Crescent. Egypt, 120 miles away, greatly yearned to dominate an area that might serve both as a buffer and a jumping-off place against Mesopotamia. Besides, there was also the highly desirable Phoenician timber of the Lebanon, and to the imperial aspirations of Babylonia and Assyria, it was almost mandatory to be provided with an outpost against Egypt. They wanted to control a district that commanded the last section of the great trade routes between the Euphrates and the Nile and to have access to the commerce deflected from the Orient by means of the Phoenician cities on the Mediterranean coast. Therefore, on both extremities of the Crescent, the possession of Israel was of vital importance for both commercial and military reasons. The march of empire in the end all hinged on business, and the only question was whether the military flag should precede and secure or follow and protect the caravan. Thus Israel's favored position—a highroad of commerce or a vantage ground of empire, the one contingent upon the other—meant that it was never left unmolested. In the gradual progress of human civilization, it was—humanly speaking—impossible for the indwellers of the Land of Promise to live at peace. Israel enjoyed peace only when it was united and strong—and that was not often and never long—but at the first sign of weakening, it had no more chance of avoiding being crushed than a tiny grain between

6
Coveted Prize of
Empire Builders

two millstones, no matter which way it turned.[13] This brings us back to our opening remark: The scepter had departed from Judah.

Of course, Israel enjoyed a brief spell of political glory. During the times of David and Solomon, it had won and held a considerable portion of the Fertile Crescent: from the River of Egypt to the crossing of the Euphrates known as Tiphsah.[14] Moreover, during the whole course of its checkered history, true to divine promise, the scepter did not depart from Judah altogether. Israel departed from the Lord, fell into discord, became subject, paid tribute, returned to the Lord, united, revolted, collected tribute, and in turn became subject again. But Israel somehow always succeeded, at least nominally, to manage its own affairs. In all the pages of world history, there are not to be found chapters of greater patriotism, bravery, loyalty, suffering, sacrifices, and more soul-stirring and heart-touching accounts of political martyrdom than are to be found in the pages of Judah's own historical tragedy.[15]

But that is not the important consideration. It seems that Israel on the whole constantly misconstrued and deliberately misunderstood the true nature and character of the divinely promised messianic kingdom. Thus, it sadly overlooked its real, divinely appointed place and purpose in history. This purpose was not imperial glamour or political glory, a Jewish world empire. It was an infinitely greater honor and privilege to be the people from which the Savior was to come, to provide His earthly abode, to prepare His way, to set the stage, and to usher His coming into this world. An Israelite world empire, continued Jewish national and political glory, would not have helped the cause of Christ. Had Christ appeared in the flesh in a firmly established, powerful Jewish state, then, from a human perspective, Christianity might have been essentially Jewish. Had He been born in Rome, Christianity might have been essentially Roman. But because He was born in a country such as Israel was then and among a people such as the Jews were politically at that time, Christianity, again humanly speaking, could more easily become universal. This agrees with God's promise to Abraham: "In you all the families of the earth shall be blessed" (Gn 12:3). The Lord was not referring to a political empire, but to the universal spiritual kingdom of grace when He promised that a descendant of David "shall build a house for My name, and I will establish the throne of his kingdom forever" (2Sm 7:13). This thought ought to reconcile us to the tragic course of Israel's history, though it is a puzzling problem to such students of history and a source of sorrow for such Jews as do not accept the Savior-King of promise. This fact relieves us of the need to explain in detail just what happened to the Jewish state, and how and why. Nevertheless, a brief outline of Israel's history is a fitting introduction to the state of the Jews with reference to the life of Christ.

Almost immediately after the death of Solomon, in 931 BC, the empire that David had won and Solomon had elevated fell into disruption, never to be reunited. For the next two hundred years, the fragments into which it had broken were to be found either fighting for their place or for supremacy on the Israelite land bridge.[16] Only once in the history of the divided kingdoms did it seem as though the political glory of David and Solomon would return. But that was due to the collapse of Syria and while Assyria was still asleep. Profiting by these circumstances, Jeroboam II of Israel, a grand, but very wicked king, regained nearly all of Syria. He made Judah tributary, restored the "border of Israel from Lebo-hamath as far as the Sea of the Arabah" (from Orontes to the Dead Sea), and gave Uzziah, the king of Judah, a chance to take Elath (on the Red Sea) after which "[Uzziah's] fame spread even to the border of Egypt" (2Ki 14:23–29; 2Ch 26:1–8). It was the Indian summer of Israel's history. Commerce increased, cities grew, and the people felt safe and secure, but this glory did not last. Spiritual decay accompanied outward splendor. It was the lull before the storm. The prophets Hosea and Amos preached repentance and threatened punishment and captivity in vain (Hos 14:1–3; 9:3; Am 7:8–11). But on the other hand, Jonah, who had promised this last flare of prosperity, was sent down to Nineveh to preach repentance, against his will; and his word took effect in Nineveh rather than Israel (2Ki 14:25; Jnh 1:2; 3:5).

9
The Divided Kingdom

The wild roar of strange beasts was soon to be heard in the Land of Israel; that is, the symbolic roaring of the winged, human-headed, and bearded bulls and lions of ancient Assyria. "They growl and seize their prey; they carry it off, and none can rescue" (Is 5:29). In 744 BC, a new king ascended the throne of Assyria, Tiglath-pileser III, who opened his reign with a whirlwind conquest of his neighbors. In three years, he overawed his opponents, and then he began to rule the Crescent. In c. 742 BC, both Syria and Israel "gave" their annual "presents."

10
The Fall of Israel

> Pul [Tiglath-pileser] the king of Assyria came against the land, and Menahem [king of Israel] gave Pul a thousand talents of silver, that he might help him to confirm his hold on the royal power. (2Ki 15:19)

But in four years, Tiglath-pileser had to return, because Israel had joined a coalition to throw off the Assyrian yoke. In a short time, Assyria crushed the revolt, and in order for them to secure their conquest and to prevent future occurrences of this nature, they employed an imperial invention on a larger scale; namely, the policy of deporting rebellious conquered people.[17] They carried into captivity thousands of the inhabitants of the territory that was afterward commonly called Galilee (2Ki 15:29). This territory, first to be depopulated, was later first to see the Light (Is 9:1–2 [the promise]; Mt 4:15–16 [the fulfillment]).

The cruel breakup of local ties was effective, making the new settlers in their alien surroundings completely dependent upon the central government. Yet it was also politically unwise, because it crippled tribute-bearing areas. Thus, Israel was punished; but it did not humble itself nor hearken to the Lord (2Ki 17:13–17). After Tiglath-pileser died, Hoshea, king of Israel, decided to rebel. Foolishly depending upon the support of King So of Egypt, Hoshea failed to send the annual tribute to Assyria (2Ki 17:4). Egypt—the "Rahab who sits still" (Is 30:7), the "broken reed of a staff, which will pierce the hand of any man who leans on it" (Is 36:6)—was anxious to have a buffer state between itself and Assyria. It was, therefore, ever ready to incite Israel to hopeless rebellion and to promise help, but never to supply it. Thus, after Hoshea's foolish act, the new king of Assyria, Shalmaneser V, struck at once and hard. Israel resisted for three years, and Shalmaneser was killed before Israel fell—an amazing testimony to the desperate resistance Israel offered. But Sargon, Shalmaneser's successor, defeated the army of Israel, and Hoshea was taken prisoner. In 722 BC, the kingdom of Israel came to an end.

> In the ninth year of Hoshea, the king of Assyria captured Samaria, and he carried the Israelites away to Assyria and placed them in Halah, and on the Habor, the river of Gozan, and in the cities of the Medes. (2Ki 17:6)

The Assyrians imported foreign colonists and "placed them in the cities of Samaria instead of the people of Israel. And they took possession of Samaria and lived in its cities" (2Ki 17:24). These heathen colonists intermarried with the remnants of the ten tribes that the Assyrians did not carry away into captivity. Probably, as in the case of Judah later, they were the poor of the land, which resulted in the planting of a mixed religion in the confines of the former kingdom of Israel (see 2Ki 17:24–34, 41). Ten tribes of Jacob thus faded out of history's picture. Judah was spared—for the present—and at a price.

11
The Fall of Nineveh

After the ten tribes had passed out of history, the kingdom of Judah continued for more than a century. But most of that time, Judah was a nation subject to the "great king" of Assyria, to whom Ahaz and his successors annually sent their "presents," that is, until Nineveh itself was doomed. The Assyrian war lords were great conquerors, but they did not know how to rule. The Scythian invasion definitely put an end to Assyria's control.[18] And south of Assyria, there was the more ancient Babylon, whose pride had never readily accepted the Assyrian rule. In July, 612 BC, Cyaxares destroyed Nineveh with the help of the Medes, Babylonians, and Scythians. They warred so effectually that two hundred years later, Xenophon, passing near its former site, did not even know that the ruins of that great city lay before him.[19] And in the book of the prophet Nahum, we hear the exulting shout that the terrible, bloody city of the East shall be laid low (2:10–13; 3:7–19). A new power, the later Babylonian Empire, was in the ascendant, in the lower arm of the ancient Crescent.

12
The Egyptians

But for the present, this was Egypt's chance. And again, Judah, alone on the land bridge between Africa and Asia, was like a tiny grain between two millstones, doomed to be crushed, no matter which way it turned. First, it fell into the hands of Egypt. It was during the reign of Josiah, the best king that Judah ever had, including even David and Solomon:

> Before [Josiah] there was no king like him, who turned to the LORD with all his heart and with all his soul and with all his might. . . . Still the LORD did not turn from the burning of His great wrath. (2Ki 23:25–26)

Bravely, Josiah went out to meet Pharaoh Neco, but in the first skirmish, he was killed, and his army was destroyed. The Egyptians swept northward as far as the Euphrates, exacted silver and gold as tribute, deposed a Judean king, and put another in his stead. However, the triumph of Egypt did not last.

Nebuchadnezzar is now introduced into history as the rod of God's anger to bring about that awful day of judgment that the prophets had foretold (Jer 34:2–3; Is 10:5–11). The Egyptians were soon driven back to the Nile, and the land of Judah had to recognize its new overlord. But after three years, the foolhardy Jehoiakim (2Ki 24:1) "forgot" the annual tribute, and then the trouble began. The Babylonians took Jerusalem, robbed the temple of its treasure, and in order to make submission permanent, they likewise deported citizens from the land. They carried off Jehoiachin,[20] the nobles, and thousands of captives so that only the poorest of the land remained (2Ki 24:15). The year 605 BC marks the beginning of the seventy years of the Babylonian captivity (Jer 29:10). But the Babylonian king had underestimated the inflexible patriotism of the Judeans, a patriotism that inflamed them to desperate resistance. The foolish remnants listened to Egyptian and Syrian intriguers. The die, however, was cast, and Jerusalem's last hour had struck. Nebuchadnezzar returned and directed his battering-rams against the walls of Jerusalem, but after a year and a half—this shows the desperate resistance—only a breach was made. The Babylonians then utterly destroyed the city. They captured and blinded Zedekiah, the last appointed king. They killed his sons and sixty leading citizens. They led about 25,000 of the inhabitants into exile and only the dregs of the land remained (2Ki 25; Jer 39; 52). Thus, the curtain descended upon the first act of Judah's historical tragedy. A man of fine character, named Gedaliah, whom Nebuchadnezzar appointed governor of Judah, tried his best to give the remaining poor wretches a sort of government; but they rebelled against him and slew him. Dreading the certain consequences of this final revolt, a large portion of the remaining terrified element fled to Egypt (2Ki 25:25–26; Jer 43:7), forcibly taking the old and protesting prophet Jeremiah with them.[21]

13
The Fall of Judah

Babylonia, however, was not long permitted to retain her ascendency on the Fertile Crescent. The center of gravity was gradually shifting to the Medes and Persians. A new sun had risen in the distant East, the hereditary king of Persia, Cyrus the Great. After heading a revolt against the Medes, he conquered Lydia,

14
Fall of Babylon

entered Babylon in 538 BC, killed Belshazzar (Dn 5:28–31), and soon established himself from the Indus to the Hellespont and from Armenia to the Nile as the new great monarch.

15
The Return of the Exiles

In accordance with prophecy and in obedience to divine command (Is 44:28; Jer 25:12; 29:10; Ezr 1:1–2), Cyrus gave the Babylonian exiles from Judah permission to return to the country of their fathers. In a short time, thousands of returning Judeans, or Jews, as they were ultimately called, were again settled on their ancestral soil. This was a wise political move on the part of the Persian king. Not only did it restore a tribute-paying area, but with the settlement of a friendly colony of home-loving inhabitants on that most important sector, it also decreased the danger of an Egyptian approach.

16
Temple Rebuilt

The two centuries of Persian government (538–332 BC) were a period of comparative rest for the returned Judean exiles. Although many did not return,[22] still about 50,000 (Ezr 2:64–65), mostly from Judah and Benjamin, gathered again on Judean soil. To these were added those who had fled to Egypt immediately before the final doom. They at once began to rebuild the temple, and in 516 BC, it was dedicated to the Lord. Although the restored temple could not compare with the temple of Solomon, God's prophet held out the comforting promise that "the latter glory of this house shall be greater than the former." Christ was to preach in its courts. "In this place I will give peace, declares the LORD of hosts" (Hg 2:9). When Ezra returned to Jerusalem with an additional group of exiles and Nehemiah returned to rebuild the walls of the holy city[23] (445 BC), Judeans again made a firmer hold on the famous Israelite land bridge. The government itself lay virtually in the hands of the Levite priests, among whom the high priest, chosen from the descendants of Zadok (1Ch 29:22), was practically king. From now on, the language spoken in Israel was Aramaic, a Semitic language, which largely displaced Hebrew and became the language of commerce and diplomacy of the entire Fertile Crescent, from the Nile to the Persian Gulf. Until Greek displaced Aramaic, it was the *lingua franca* of the Oriental world.[24] In the synagogue, likewise originating with the captivity, the Law was read in Hebrew and interpreted in Aramaic—the Targum. The Persian period finally marks the close of the long line of holy prophets from Moses to Malachi, who concluded the writings of the Old Testament with the promise of the forerunner of Christ (Mal 3:1).

17
The Fall of Persia

On the whole, the Persian government was an excellent one. For proof of this, we may point to the fact that it held together as long as it did. It was a precursor, as it were, of the Roman Empire, the first government to establish a sort of imperial organization. The 120 satrapies into which the Persians divided it were generally peaceful and prosperous. There was little oppression, and religious toleration was the universal rule. But in the end, it wore out. It was an unnatural empire in that it was sprawled all across Asia, its tentacles thrusting way into, but weakly connecting it with, Africa and Europe.[25] The Persian Empire was a premature attempt at something that was not successful until Rome gained world dominion. Until then, it lasted principally because there was no power at hand to end it.[26] The Eastern world had worn out. The world was waiting for a new master; and when he came, the Persian Empire collapsed like a house of cards.

His name was Alexander. The center of gravity had suddenly shifted from Asia and Africa to Europe. In the fateful year 333 BC, Alexander of Macedon defeated the Persian army in the Battle of Issus, and a year later, he was already crossing the Israelite land bridge on his way to Egypt. After founding Alexandria there, he returned, descended the Fertile Crescent, and soon made himself sole master of Western Asia as far as India. But this Alexander was quite unlike the usual ancient empire builders. He aimed not so much to establish brutal power as to make the world safe for Greek civilization. And in this he succeeded, although he died at the age of thirty-three (323 BC). His Greek colonies dotted western Eurasia. His immense conquests resulted in greater consequences for the Jews, both at home and in the Diaspora, than those of any other non-Jew in history.[27] He was generous to them and gave them a fair measure of liberty.[28] But at the same time, he located peaceful Greek settlements throughout Israel.[29] The result was a growing familiarity in his Asiatic dominions with all things Greek. The Greek language, Greek thought, manners, culture, literature, and art, Greek civilization, and Greek games were largely introduced; but also Greek vice and corruption infiltrated into the body politic. The career of Alexander himself was brilliant, but brief. Yet his victorious Asiatic campaigns, coupled with the founding of his marvelous world monarchy, were vastly more important than he could foresee. It is almost impossible to overestimate the magnitude of his bequest to succeeding generations and peoples on account of the universal use of the Greek language,[30] for Greek made possible the promulgation of the Gospel throughout "the ends of the world" (Rm 10:18).[31]

18
Alexander the Great

The death of Alexander was followed by bitter strife among his ablest officers, the *Diadochi* or "successors."[32] Each leader aimed at a dominant position in the empire that their great leader had left masterless. In the end, the confusion of competing claimants—omitting minor contenders—was reduced to the Ptolemies in Egypt and the Seleucids of Syria.[33] Between these two powers, the Eastern world was again divided, and Israel was once more the battleground of both. But let us note that both powers were and continued to be Greek kingdoms—true, Greek with a difference, as it was now called Hellenistic[34] and thus distinguished from the pure Hellenic culture of Greece. Both the Ptolemaic and the Seleucid courts were predominantly Hellenistic, and the monarchs of both lines aspired to be the champions of the new Hellenistic craze. And still, all this had to serve the cause of Christ.

19
The *Diadochi*

The two dynasties stood in the breach. They protected Hellenism from succumbing to an Asian culture or empire, until Rome, already in the rising, was ready to take their place.

For the first one hundred and twenty-three years of this period (321–198 BC), the high priests ruled the land of Judea, but under the suzerainty of Ptolemaic Egypt and with much confusion and bloodshed back and forth across the Israelite land bridge. The most important religious event in this epoch was the translation of the Old Testament into the Greek language. This version was commonly called the Septuagint (LXX). It owes its name to the story, now discredited, that it was the work of seventy-two translators who were sent to Egypt to prepare a version of the Jewish Law for the royal library at Alexandria.[35] This story is a legend; but the translation itself is a fact and was of the greatest importance for the New Testament Church. Greek-speaking Jews adopted this translation, Paul and the apostles used it for missionary work, and some of the early Christian Fathers even regarded it as inspired. As a true preparation for the Gospel, the Septuagint was of the greatest service. Without it, Hellenistic Judaism would have been as inconceivable as the Church of the Reformation without Luther's translation of the Bible.[36]

At the beginning of the second century before Christ, the kingdom of Syria grew more powerful and prepared to wrest the land of the Jews from Egypt. In a bloody battle in 198 BC, Antiochus III of Syria drove back the Egyptians and formally annexed Israel.[37] Hellenism, which had been steadily seeping into Israel, was now threatening to extinguish the Jewish religion altogether. The priesthood was corrupt, circumcision was neglected, and heathenish playhouses were erected in Jerusalem. It seemed as if even reactionary Judea had been made safe for Greek civilization.[38]

But one day, there arose a king in Syria named Antiochus Epiphanes, who spoiled everything.[39] On the way home from a successful campaign against Egypt (167 BC), he stopped in Jerusalem to accelerate the already quickly advancing process of Hellenization by force. He looted the temple, carried off the sacred vessels, killed many Jews, and ordered Judaism to cease (1 Macc 1:20–28). Just like that! No more Sabbath, no more circumcision, no more clean and unclean food, and no more Holy Scripture. Henceforth, swine's flesh was to be laid on the altar of sacrifice (1 Macc 1:47), and all their sacrifices were to be made either to Antiochus or to Zeus. Disobedience was to be punished with death. According to the blind Latin Tacitus,[40] he meant well with the Jews; he wanted to improve the condition of this "detestable nation." Many of the Jews obeyed man rather than God; yet not a few refused to forsake the Law and statutes of the Lord.[41] Stark horror swept the land as the army of Antiochus began to put his orders into effect. There was looting and murder, wailing and shame, and greater trials than in any previous period of Jewish history. But then, like the breaking out of mad fire, the nation blazed into rebellion.[42]

A pious priest named Mattathias ran his sword through one of the Syrian officers and started what is possibly the first war for religious liberty in history.[43] This introduces us to the brief spell of glorious Jewish history, the Maccabean[44] period (164–134 BC), with its chief figures, the brave members of the Hasmonean house. Fleeing into the wilderness with his five sons, Mattathias gathered around himself a band of desperate zealots. Fierce warfare ensued, in which repeated losses were inflicted on the Syrian forces. Four great armies were sent against Jewish rebels, but Judas, who succeeded his father, Mattathias, defeated them all. Then came a lull in fighting. The temple was cleansed of its swinish filth and rededicated to God (1Macc 4:42–59).[45] Then war commenced again. The Syrian king sent army after army into Judea, but the revolt could not be stamped out. Fighting for a most glorious principle, religious liberty, Judas and his followers withstood the onslaught of the best-equipped armies of the time, infantry, cavalry, and elephants. Although the Maccabees were defeated at times,[46] and Judas and three of his four brothers were killed, they still won in the end. After repeated reverses, the Syrians gave up the attempt as hopeless and withdrew from Israel forever in 142 BC (1Macc 13:31–41). At last, but also for the last time, Judea was again gloriously independent and free.

23
The Maccabees

But the triumph of the Maccabees was too complete. The war that at first had been waged only for religious freedom ended, as we just said, with complete political independence. For centuries, the Jews had little occasion to indulge in political aspirations. However, now drunk with recent success, they again became king-minded; but there was a little difficulty. Their present Hasmonean leaders were of priestly rather than of royal stock, from the tribe of Levi rather than the tribe of Judah. Moreover, as descendants of Jehoiarib (1Ch 24:7) rather than of Zadok (1Ki 2:35), Hasmoneans were not even entitled to the high-priestly office,[47] which had become vacant by the recent murder of Onias (2Macc 4:30–38). However, the national crisis overrode ceremonial scruples, and the high priesthood passed over to Jehoiarib's Maccabean descendants when Jonathan was made high priest, about 152 BC (1Macc 10:18–21).

24
Monarchic
Aspirations

But there was another, and it seemed a greater, difficulty. What about the royal dignity? What about the King who, according to the divine promise, had to be a son and heir of David (2Sm 7:12–16)? They made a provisional solution for this difficulty. They combined the royal and priestly office by making Simon, the last surviving son of Mattathias, both high priest *and* king (140 BC). There was, however, a significant reservation. This arrangement was to continue in full force "forever"; that is, his royal office was to be hereditary "until a trustworthy prophet should arise" (1Macc 14:41; see Dt 18:15).[48] In other words, Jewish royalty was to be held in trust for Christ. But the Hasmonean rulers did not succeed in holding the kingly office—they did not even succeed in holding onto the priestly office—nor did they

25
Jewish Royalty Held
in Trust for the
Coming Christ

likely even intend to hold it in trust for the coming Christ. However, one valuable service they did perform was that they kept Judaism intact and preserved it against the threats of Hellenism.[49] For the present, it seemed that bright Old Testament sunshine flooded the land of Judah. The force of victorious arms won independence. They set up a throne, and popular acclaim crowned and hailed a king. Moreover, Egypt, Syria, Cyprus, yes, even Sparta and Rome officially recognized Jewish rule as an independent state (cf. the official correspondence in 1 Macc 12:2–23; 14:20–23; 15:1–9, 16–21). But, alas, this light was but the last bright, flickering rays of a foreboding sunset, for Rome introduced into Jewish history a ruler (Herod) who would ever after be associated with the political doom of the Jews.

26
Pharisees and Sadducees

It was during the reign of Simon's successor, John Hyrcanus I (135–104 BC), that a beginning of the end was made. First of all came the conflict between the Sadducees and the Pharisees, whose names here for the first time enter into the arena of history.[50] As a power, these two influential Jewish religious parties had their rise at the same time with the Maccabees, but properly the Maccabees belonged to neither of them. Zeal for the Law and for religious liberty at first gave the Maccabees the support of the Pharisees.[51] But the Pharisees would not have a son of Levi ascend the throne of David, and they could not forgive Judas Maccabaeus for making an alliance with idolatrous Rome (1 Macc 8:17–29). And, on the other hand, the Sadducees saw the descendants of Jehoiarib as upstarts who took away the high priesthood from the time-honored sons of Zadok, to whose party they adhered or to whose supposed descendants they belonged. That is why they called themselves Zadokites, which is likely the origin of the name *Sadducees*.[52] As Hellenized aristocrats, they were willing, however, to set aside religious scruples as long as they could meddle with power. Their strong point was politics.[53] While the Pharisees enjoyed a popular following and represented the religious world, the Sadducees represented money and class, and it was only natural that the ruling powers, from the Hasmonean to the Herodian-Roman period, should cater to them. Of course, at the same time, they were careful not to ignore the power of the Pharisees as the leaders of the common people. But the dissension of these two religious parties resulted in severe internecine struggle and shedding of blood.[54] It was not good for the newly founded Jewish state.

27
Enforced Idumean Conversion

John Hyrcanus not only broke with the Pharisees, but he also became guilty of an offense that in its baneful consequences brought about the fall of his own house and added to the misery of the impending Jewish doom. This otherwise very able prince forgot that he owed his throne to the Maccabean struggle for religious liberty. In a quick campaign, he built up a sizable kingdom, conquered the trans-Jordan territory, added Samaria to his rule, and defeated the unruly sons of Esau, the Idumeans. Yet here is where he made his mistake: he compelled the Idumeans to accept circumcision and the same sort of corrupted Jewish religion to which he adhered.[55] That was religious persecution, enforced conversion. Little did Hyrcanus dream that he had fostered the political power of the Herodians in Israel, which helped to end the Jewish rule.

What remains now of the Maccabean period is but the story of the death throes of their dynasty—internecine strife, war, bloodshed, the Herods, and Rome. The seventh empire, and the most terrible of all, was to enter into the tragic history of the Jews; after Egypt, Syria, Assyria, Babylonia, Persia, and Greece, Rome now appeared on the scene. It was in the year 63 BC, the same year in which Caesar Augustus was born. Pompey had just cleared the Mediterranean of the pirates and was bringing the *pax Romana* to Asia. Rome defeated Mithridates, the marvelous king of Pontus, it dissolved the last remnant of the Syrian monarchy at Antioch, and then the Roman general Pompey advanced to Damascus. It was only natural for him to turn to the bridge that connects Asia with Africa. Like every world-conqueror before him, he wanted that little bit of vital territory, the key to the Orient and now the very center of the ancient world. It was not difficult to satisfy his desire. At Damascus, a Jewish delegation met him, extending an invitation to come to Israel.

28
The Coming of Rome

After the death of Queen Alexandra (76–67 BC), her two sons quarreled over the tottering Maccabean throne. Hyrcanus II was the elder of the two and, as such, had the better claim. But he was weaker than his brother. Although Hyrcanus II enjoyed the support of the rich and powerful Idumean governor Antipater,[56] whose father had been appointed as the first native governor of Idumea, his younger and abler brother Aristobulus had the support of the priestly Sadducees. Both parties sent delegations to Pompey with presents and the request to intervene in their favor.[57] But there was also a third party, the Jewish people, led by the Pharisees. They were sick of the unending evils that the priest-kings had brought and were begging for a chance to get rid of royalty altogether. These three requests for intervention gave Pompey a perfect excuse to invade Israel.

29
Pompey

Originally, the Romans intervened for Aristobulus; but through the machinations of scheming Antipater, Rome turned its favor toward Hyrcanus, so Aristobulus prepared for war. After a stubborn siege of three months, the Romans took Jerusalem, but even then only because Pompey took advantage of a religious scruple and built his siege works up to the walls on fast-days,[58] when the Jews would not take offensive action. With Jerusalem in his hands, Pompey proceeded at once to put fear into the hearts of the Jews. He ordered twelve thousand rebels put to the sword, and then he investigated the temple. He was curious to see the deity that this strange and stubborn people so zealously worshiped. He entered the Most Holy Place—a mortal sin for all except the high priest—drew the curtain aside, and received perhaps the greatest surprise of his life.[59] He found nothing. This may have been the first

30
Jerusalem Taken in 63 BC

time that he had ever entered a temple where there was no image of a god. Pompey tried to settle Jewish affairs for the present by imprisoning Aristobulus and giving the conquered territory over to Hyrcanus, who was recognized as high priest and nominal ruler, but without the title of king, and then he returned to Rome for one of the grandest triumphs that Rome had ever seen.[60]

31
Antipater

It was some time, however,[61] before the Jews submitted to their new Roman overlord. The Maccabean sons of Aristobulus,[62] who had graced Pompey's Roman triumphal procession, escaped and started trouble. Civil war ensued, in which the Idumean Antipater shrewdly kept himself in the background, making himself useful to the Romans in various ways,[63] while the talons of Rome crushed and tore the wretched little land of Judea. Finally, events took a new turn. The Roman generals Pompey and Caesar began fighting for political supremacy. It was now that the scheming Antipater and his old friend, the high priest Hyrcanus, came forward. They immediately attached themselves to Caesar's party, for Antipater was an astute man. He had a keen perception, especially for shifting political winds. He clearly beheld two things: the unconquerable power of Rome and the pitiful weakness of the decadent Hasmonean house. Out of these two factors, he hoped to build a house of his own. As a result, when Caesar emerged as victor in the Roman civil war,[64] Antipater came in for a rich reward. He was appointed to no less a position than that of procurator of Judea, while Hyrcanus, the innocent dupe, received merely the high-priestly title.[65]

32
The Last Maccabean
King

The government of Judea now passed over to the Herodians under Roman control. Antipater immediately proceeded to secure his power by appointing his sons Phasael and Herod governors of Jerusalem and Galilee, respectively. The latter, the young governor of Galilee, we now meet for the first time. Already at an early age, he gave proof of the abilities that later placed him on the throne. Meanwhile, with the murder of Julius Caesar (44 BC), there occurred another change in the Roman world. At first, Cassius became powerful in the East. Immediately, Antipater and Herod made themselves useful to him, but soon Antipater was killed (43 BC). Young Herod, however, avenging his father's death, was able to play the political game alone. When Brutus and Cassius were defeated (42 BC), Mark Antony and Octavian divided the Roman dominions between them. With one stroke, the East fell into the hands of Antony, thus cueing Herod to fawn on him. He sent Antony nice presents and flattered him with pretty speeches, and in return was confirmed governor of Judea and Galilee, yet still under the nominal rule of doting Hyrcanus. But when the Parthians invaded from eastern Asia, Herod was soon left high and dry. The Parthians took Herod's possessions, carried off Hyrcanus, and then slashed off the latter's ears in order to make him unfit for the high priesthood.[66] Then they set up Antigonus as the last of the Maccabean kings (40–37 BC).[67]

But Herod was not discouraged. It was not in the interest of the Romans to permit the Parthians to control the Israelite bridge. They soon appointed Herod king of Judea;[68] but he had to go and win his own recognition, his crown, and his kingdom. And this is exactly what he set himself to do. In less than three years, with the help of Roman soldiers—Samaritans, Idumeans, and hired troops—he literally carved his way to the Jewish throne. The country was taken, Jerusalem was stormed, and the mercy-imploring Antigonus was led to the blocks.[69] However, in the hope of healing the breach that his success would only widen, but also for love, Herod married the granddaughter of Hyrcanus, Mariamne, to whom he was previously engaged. Thus, the Maccabean kingdom came to an end, and a despised and much-hated half Jew inherited the kingdom.[70]

33
Herod, 40 BC

Herod was a born ruler. He was endowed with a powerful body, with great mental gifts, was highly ambitious, and was untiring in his efforts to reach his goal.[71] His insatiable ambition was kindled already in tender youth, when an Essene seer saluted him as king of the Jews,[72] and this soon became his one aim in life. With an equally cunning and scheming father preparing the way, Herod directed all his plans and plots, intrigues and crimes, to this one end—to make himself king of the Jews. This ambition is the key to his whole career. Difficulties that beset his path were but inducements to put forth added strength. This unwearied striving continued to characterize him until his miserable death. Only by a combination of cunning native shrewdness, unpitying cruelty for those who crossed his path and fell into his hands, and cringing servility before those whose favor it was necessary to obtain, was it possible for him to exist in the first few years of life-and-death struggle. Still, he reached unenviable greatness.[73]

34
Herod's Ambition

In the first period of his reign, Herod had to contend with many powerful adversaries: the Jewish people under the leadership of the Pharisees, the wealthy nobility as represented by the Sadducees, the surviving members of the displaced Hasmonean family, and—Cleopatra.[74]

Herod was well aware of the unconquerable strength of Rome. His view was wide enough and his judgment sufficiently keen to perceive that in order to maintain his position, he could gain nothing except through the favor of the Romans—at all costs. And on the other hand, the Romans knew the value to them of Herod. He was the one strong man in the East to hold the Israelite bridge, and the whole security of Rome in the East depended upon his loyalty. So there was mutual, albeit selfish, love between Herod and Rome. But the Jewish people, wholly in the hands of the Pharisees, spat at the very mention of his name and submitted only with the deepest aversion to the rule of the Idumean half Jew and friend of the Romans.[75] No application of torments could force the Jews to call him king. Only by the utmost rigors was Herod able to secure from them an obedience that at its best was

35
Herod's Reign, Part I

hypocritical submission. He won over the more pliable members of the population by the bestowal of honor and favors.

36
Forty-Five Nobles Slain; Aristobulus Drowned

Among the Sadducean nobles in Jerusalem, there remained numerous adherents of Antigonus. Herod got rid of them at the outset by executing forty-five of the most wealthy and prominent members. And by confiscating their property, he gained great wealth, which he employed to secure the friendship of Antony.[76] But members of the Hasmonean family also still stood in his way. First of all, there was his mother-in-law Alexandra, Mariamne's mother, who pursued him with unremitting enmity. By appealing to, and even instigating, Antony and Cleopatra, Alexandra forced Herod to appoint her son Aristobulus, a stripling youth of seventeen years, to the office of high priest. However, shortly after his appointment, Aristobulus was mysteriously drowned.[77]

37
Cleopatra

The fourth hostile power at the beginning of Herod's reign was the scheming queen of Egypt, Cleopatra. On account of the influence she had on Antony, Herod was forced to give up valuable territory to her.[78] Cleopatra even tried to draw him into her net, but Herod was cunning enough not to surrender himself completely to her power.[79]

38
Battle of Actium, 31 BC; Murder of Hyrcanus II

Then there came another change in the Roman political world. Antony (Herod's patron; Cleopatra's lover) and Octavian were engaged in a death struggle for Roman supremacy. Herod at first supported the cause of Antony; but just at the right time, he turned over to the camp of the conquering Augustus and by a clever act gave him proof of his change of heart.[80] Before presenting himself, however, to his new master Augustus for confirmation of his possessions, Herod secured himself against a possible "miscarriage of justice" by putting out of the way a rival to the throne who had better claims to it than he had. This rival was none other than Hyrcanus II, the former high priest, a feeble and babbling memorial to a grand Hasmonean past. The mere existence of an altogether harmless eighty-year-old man who was entitled to the throne more than Herod was to him sufficient reason for the bloody deed. Herod invited Hyrcanus II to return from his exile in Parthia in order to assert power over him.[81] And Hyrcanus, who had already lost his ears, then also lost his life.[82]

39
Again Confirmed by Augustus as King of the Jews

When Herod presented himself to Augustus at Rhodes in 30 BC, he played his part skillfully. He boasted of his friendship with Antony and of the services that Herod had rendered him in an effort to prove how useful he might be to anyone whose party he might join. In whatever else he may have been deficient, Herod certainly did not lack ability, and Augustus found it to his advantage to favor this crafty Idumean. Augustus confirmed Herod in his royal rank and gave him not only Cleopatra's domains in Israel, but other valuable possessions as well—practically all of ancient Israel.[83] To show his gratitude, Herod accompanied Augustus on his way home from Egypt as far as Antioch,[84] and again Herod was fully confirmed as the king of the Jews.

But now, Herod had trouble with his queen. According to all reports, Mariamne was the noblest of women. Unlike her mother, she never shared in any mean plots in the interest of the Hasmonean house. When she charged Herod with the death of her kindred, she spoke to him courageously and honestly as to a husband, on whose affections, if he was left to himself, she knew she could rely.[85] However, she failed to reckon with a real serpent, Herod's sister Salome, who managed to fabricate a plot according to which the queen was charged with, and convicted of, conspiring against Herod. Now, Herod was passionately in love with Mariamne, and undoubtedly she was innocent; but it was extremely dangerous even to be accused, let alone convicted, of such a crime. He was, after all, the king of the Jews. Thus, Mariamne was led to execution. With her, Herod threw away a pearl of greater value than all that he had gained, a deed for which he was afterward sorry almost to despair.[86] Mariamne's mother, Alexandra, was the next to fall. This scheming woman had long deserved her fate far more than others when she paid the price of Maccabean striving against the Herodian rule.[87] Finally, in order to rid himself of the hateful Hasmoneans altogether, Herod also had some distant relatives tracked down and killed who, it seems, had been preserved by his own Idumean brother-in-law Costobar for possible future use. It is questionable whether they were guilty or not; at any rate, Costobar and his protégés paid the penalty that Herod had provided for conspiring against the king of the Jews. At last, Herod's mind was at rest. For the present, none survived who could set up a claim to the Jewish throne.

40 Mariamne, Alexandra, and Others Executed

With the consolidation of Herod's kingdom and with his subjects so thoroughly in his power that they could not revolt against him, he began a period of glamour in his reign the like of which had not been seen since the days of Solomon. His dominion was almost as large as Solomon's. In order that it might pay tribute to his genius and gain glory for its builder, he began to embellish it with magnificent structures and strong fortifications, for which he made his subjects pay.[88]

41 Glamour; Herod's Reign, Part II

For the advancement of his people, Herod reared a theater, an amphitheater, and a hippodrome in Jerusalem, besides hippodromes and playhouses in other cities. For himself, Herod built a royal palace, upon which he lavished marble and gold in profusion. Already during the time of Antony, he rebuilt the citadel north of the temple and named it Antonia in honor of his patron. In this fort were kept the paraphernalia of the high priest, without which he could not perform his duties and the retention of which controlled the office.[89] He also built many cities throughout the land, including a new city with powerful breakwaters on the site of ancient Strata's Tower, which he named Caesarea.[90] At Jericho, he erected a fort and named it Cypros after his mother, and he founded other places that he named after his brother and father. Old Samaria was reconstructed and renamed Sebaste[91] in honor of Caesar Augustus, and two forts were honored with his own name—Herodium. Two ancient

42 The Builder

strongholds were restored and fortified, Machaerus and Masada, the former the probable scene of John the Baptist's death, the latter one of the last strongholds in the last Jewish war. Herod erected these fortresses not only to protect himself from foreign foes, but also to keep his own subjects in check.[92]

43
The Temple Rebuilt

Herod was a master builder in an age of builders. He even reached beyond his own boundaries to bring honor to his name, at Jewish expense.[93] But his most magnificent building operation was the restoration of the temple at Jerusalem, which has been called "a monument of penitence."[94] The old temple of Zerubbabel was no longer in harmony with its more beautiful surroundings; the neighborhood palaces quite eclipsed it in grandeur. Thus, Herod decided to completely restore the temple, and the rebuilding[95] began in 20 BC.[96] After eighteen months of building, during which it is said to have rained only at night, so that construction would not be interrupted, the temple proper was dedicated.[97] Its beauty was widely known and heralded: "He who has not seen Herod's building has never seen anything beautiful."[98] But Herod combined beauty with usefulness:

> There was also an occult passage built for the king; it led from Antonia to the inner temple, at its eastern gate; over which he also erected for himself a tower, that he might have the opportunity of a subterraneous ascent to the temple, in order to guard against any sedition which might be made by the people against their kings.[99]

44
The Much-Hated Jewish Humanist

Yet in spite of Herod's restoration of the temple, the Jews never ceased to hate him; for they knew that vanity had prompted him to rebuild the temple, not love for God. In addition, they knew that with the same money he used to restore the temple he also sponsored pagan exhibitions in which the life of men and animals were but little valued, and he erected temples to pagan gods as well. To all appearances, Herod took little interest in the Jewish religion. Although as king of the Jews, he at times insisted upon the observance of ritualistic forms of Judaism, as a Jewish humanist, he was ambitious to foster liberal arts and culture. His architectural proclivities served him an ill turn with the common people, who hated him for imposing heavy taxes upon them in order to carry out his extravagant building program. Foreign glory and Roman friendship were distasteful to them, because it was secured by oppression and accompanied by departure from the laws of the fathers. The Jewish Council, the highest court of the nation, was stripped of all its powers, causing doubts as to its very existence under Herod.[100] High priests were appointed and removed at will. The Sadducean nobles were tossed aside with ruthless violence because of their Maccabean sympathies. The legalistic Pharisees with their popular following never could regard the government of a Roman vassal king seated on David's throne as existing by right. Thus, in all quarters, the "Edomite slave" was equally hated and despised.

And still, in some respects, Herod's government benefited the people. He was the second man in the Roman Empire.[101] Many of the buildings he erected served useful purposes.[102] By his strong hand, he created conditions that encouraged trade and protected travelers, and he at times made attempts to win the hearts of his subjects by remitting taxes.[103] Herod sought by all means to lend assistance in a famine that spread over the land, even by converting his furniture into money.[104] Of course, he was careful to let the people know that the help came from him.[105] And by keeping on the friendliest of terms with Rome at all times, he secured the Jews of the dispersion against all oppression and infringements on their rights. For all this, however, he received but little thanks.

45
Herod's Good
Qualities

Now, we come to the third period of Herod's reign, which was as bloody as the beginning.[106] This period constitutes the period of domestic misery. Again, we notice that the unforgivable sin of the Jews against Herod was their failure to recognize him as king of the Jews. Herod thought he had fully suppressed the Hasmonean royal aspirations, never thinking of the fact that on the maternal side, his own sons were of half Hasmonean blood. Herod had a large family; he had at least ten wives, which, Josephus wrote, was in line with ancient custom.[107] This is a striking proof of his sensuality and political ambition. His first wife was Doris, by whom he had one son, Antipater. Mariamne bore him five children, of whom only two, Aristobulus and Alexander, interest us here. Of the other eight wives, only the Samaritan Malthace (mother of Archelaus and Antipas) and Cleopatra of Jerusalem (the mother of Philip) need now be mentioned.

46
Domestic Misery;
Herod's Reign,
Part III

Around 23 BC, Herod sent Aristobulus and Alexander to Rome to be educated.[108] After their return some years later, they married at an early age, according to custom, and were thereby brought into closer relation with the Idumean house. But still their pride would not let them forget their supposedly superior Maccabean blood. As a result, there was continual quarreling between the Hasmonean and Idumean half brothers and sisters. This is where Antipater, the son of Doris, comes in. Herod himself preferred the sons of Mariamne and would not let the wrangling amongst his children interfere with his love for these sons. But Antipater (not in his father's good graces for a time, but later restored to favor) labored incessantly in true Herodian fashion to carve his way to the Jewish throne.[109] By slandering his—probably guilty—half brothers, Antipater finally enticed his father into siding with him.[110] Plotting against his throne was the one sin that Herod could not forgive, and so he decided to accuse his sons before Augustus. The earnest, yet mild Augustus temporarily restored peace, but scarcely had the contending parties returned from Rome when the old feud was renewed. Antipater was aided by the old serpent Salome, Herod's sister. They revived old slanders, possibly to some extent founded on facts, and then Augustus finally authorized Herod to proceed against his sons as

47
Aristobulus,
Alexander, and
Three Hundred
Adherents Put
to Death

he thought best.[111] The sons were tried, convicted, and, together with three hundred adherents, put to death.[112]

48
Antipater Put to Death

Antipater was now all-powerful in court, but he overshot his mark. He could not await his father's death and therefore conspired against him. This was reported to the king. Antipater, the heir to the throne, had made himself guilty of the unpardonable sin: plotting against Herod.[113] Thus, he also was brought to trial, convicted, and put in fetters. A report was made to the emperor;[114] and when the permission came from Augustus, Antipater, too, was put to death, just a few days before Herod's own death.

49
Key to Herod's Character

This, then, is the key to Herod's whole career—he wanted to be king, so he put to death whoever else aspired to the Jewish throne. His insane ambition reached its most ghastly height in "the slaughter of the innocents" at Bethlehem (Mt 2:16). When this life of seemingly unceasing crime finally came to an end at Jericho in the first quarter of 1 BC, it was amid the rejoicing of his subjects. Unmourned and unwept he was carried to his grave.[115] The Jews afterward regarded the day of Herod's death as a day when they would not allow fasting and public mourning.[116]

50
Herod's Place in History

Thus ends the story of Herod the Great, of whom it is said that he stole his way to the throne like a fox, ruled like a tiger, and died like a dog.[117] He was a successful, but an extremely wicked despot. Nevertheless, God made even so wicked a king as Herod serve His wonderful purpose. After Herod's death and the misrule of Archelaus, the Jews had enough of kings, even expressing the desire to be ruled by Roman governors.[118]

And now, we are ready to take up the story of the King of kings, the Christ.

3
—

The Threshold of the New Testament

c. November 15, 4 BC

The story of Christ begins with the story of His forerunner.[1] In the days of King Herod, there lived in the hill country of Judah (Lk 1:39) a priest by the name of Zechariah and his wife Elizabeth, who was of the daughters of Aaron.[2] On account of his rural residence, he was most likely treated with benevolent contempt by the highbrow, city-dwelling Zadokites,[3] but he was to be honored beyond all his fellows.

After Joshua led the invasion of Canaan, he divided the land among the descendants of Jacob's twelve sons (Jsh 14–19), except the tribe of Levi, which formed a priestly caste. The Levites did not have a separate possession, but were allotted certain cities throughout the tribes (Jsh 21). These so-called Levitical cities were of two classes: those for the priests proper, or descendants of Aaron (thirteen cities in the territory afterward called Judah), and those for the Levites or subordinate priests (thirty-five cities distributed among the other tribes). On account of the great number of priests, already in the time of David,[4] it was simply impossible for all to officiate at the same time. In order to work out a plan according to which all could serve in regular rotation, David organized the whole body of priests and Levites into twenty-four families, or divisions of service (1Ch 24). Each division served one week at a time, the change being made on the Sabbath, between the morning and the evening sacrifice.[5] Likewise, all the people were distributed into twenty-four divisions of service. That way there was always, besides the other worshipers, a representation of Israel at hand, which "stood by" while the sacrifices were offered.

This priestly institution of David and Solomon continued until the captivity. But after the captivity, only four[6] of the original families returned. The remaining divisions were artificially supplied from the returning number. Naturally, the priesthood could now claim only continuity with, not identity with, those divisions

1
Zechariah, the Priest
Lk 1:5

2
The Twenty-Four
Priestly Divisions

3
The Division of
Abijah
Lk 1:5

whose names they actually bore. Still, strange to say, it was afterward considered a mark of great advantage to belong to the first of the twenty-four divisions, the class of Jehoiarib. This class had the honor of being the ancestors of the Maccabean family and the Hasmonean princes.[7] Now, Zechariah belonged to the eighth of the priestly divisions, the division of Abijah (1Ch 24:10). But we do not know from which priestly branch he was actually descended, whether from Zadok (which is unlikely), from Eleazar, or from Ithamar (1Ch 24:2–3). Nor does it matter. At any rate, being a descendant of one of these branches, he was a true priest of the sons of Aaron, and his wife Elizabeth, too, was of true priestly descent.

4
"Righteous before God"
Lk 1:6–7

When this honorable priestly couple was introduced into history, they were both well advanced in years. Zechariah was probably about as old as Caesar Augustus. He was an upright and righteous man before the Lord and enjoyed the honor and respect of his community. Being a priest, he was entitled to his share of the many sources of income, so we can therefore suppose that he was living in comfortable circumstances.[8] Although well advanced in years, he was still sound in body and able to meet the physical requirements that were necessary for the performance of his sacred office, for an officiating priest had to be totally free from every sort of physical defect (Lv 21:16–23).[9] Yet, though blameless, honorable, healthy, and in comfortable circumstances, there was still a shadow that like a dark cloud bore down on Zechariah's declining years: "They had no child." This was a calamity from the Jewish point of view and for many a year must have been the burden of thoughts and prayers as well as a burden of reproach that Elizabeth always seemed to carry about with her. But a wonderful thing was to happen.

5
The Time

It was about November 15, 4 BC. At this point, let us say something about the division of time. Our present era, called the Christian or the Dionysian Era, is computed from the supposed year of the birth of our Lord (that is, *anno Domini* [AD] or *annus ab incarnatione Domini*). The Roman abbot Dionysius Exiguus introduced this practice in AD 525 while preparing the Easter tables for that year.[10] According to his calculations, which slowly won acceptance throughout the Christian world, Jesus was born in the year AD 1. However, historians today conclude that Dionysius's calculations were off by a few years and that Jesus was most likely born in 2 BC.[11] But let us accompany Zechariah to the temple in Jerusalem, where reconstruction was still carried on.

6
The Temple

The temple itself with its surrounding courts was reared on the heights of Mount Moriah (2Ch 3:1). It was separated from the upper city by a deep valley, the Valley of Tyropoeon, and connected with it by a wonderful bridge on arches, or a set of steps from the height of the temple to the floor of the valley, its usual approach.[12] From the height of the temple courts, the city spread out to the observer like a map. Immediately in front (that is, to the east) were seen the rows of Corinthian monoliths surrounding the outer courts of the temple area. Towering beyond them could be seen the Mount of Olives with its orchards and trees. The mount was separated from the temple area itself by the Kidron Valley, four hundred feet below. To the left (north) lay the lower city and the Hill of Akra, and in particular that mighty fortress, guarding and controlling the temple, called the Tower of Antonia. To the rear (west), Herod's beautiful palace and the upper city fell into view. To the right (south) appeared the hill Ophel with its crowded and narrow streets and the priests' quarters. A well-paved valley street was immediately below.[13] Striking indeed must have been the appearance of this sacred place—the lower courts, standing on its magnificent terraces; the inner courts on a higher level and surrounded by massive towers and gates; and within this, the temple itself with its white walls and golden roof crowning the view. The whole scene soared out of the depths of the dark glen that lay below. It must have been one of the most splendid architectural combinations in the ancient world.[14]

Herod's workmen had artificially leveled and enlarged the temple plateau at immense labor and cost. In order to gain room for all the temple courts, they increased the small surface of the hill by building out from its sides successive platforms, supported by immense substructures of brick and stone, so that the whole hill is now honeycombed with artificial caves. The four principal entrances to the temple area, all of them from the west,[15] led the visitor through the outer row of pillars into the large Court of the Gentiles, which surrounded the temple proper on all sides. It was so named because it was the only part of the building in which foreigners were allowed. On two sides, there was a covered corridor: the colonnade of Solomon on the east, where the Savior walked at the Feast of Dedication (Jn 10:22–23), and Herod's Royal Portico on the south. Seats were placed in these halls or porches around the Court of the Gentiles, which must have been convenient places for friendly meetings or religious discussions.[16] Here, Jesus, while still a child, was found disputing with the doctors. Here, He afterward so often taught the people. And here, the first assemblies of Christians were held.[17] On the floor of this court, there was a market for sacrificial meats with the tables of the money-changers, twice broken up by our Lord.[18]

The Court of the Gentiles, the largest of the courts, was three-fourths of a mile in circuit. The court surrounded the so-called Sacred Enclosure, or *Chel*, on all sides. This enclosure included the Court of the Women, the Court of Israel, and the Court of Priests. It measured about 650 feet on the north and south and three hundred feet on the east and west. No Gentile was allowed to enter the Sacred Enclosure; there were signs erected at different places forbidding their entrance under penalty of death.[19]

7
The Court of the Gentiles

8
The Sacred Enclosure

Passing through one of the doors of the thick walls in the eastern half of the enclosure, the Jewish visitor—for none other was allowed to enter—now found himself in a 240 square-foot open court called the Court of the Women. It was called the Court of the Women not on account of its exclusive use by the women, but because this was as far as the women were allowed to go.[20] It was also called the Treasury on account of the thirteen chests, or trumpets, into which the worshipers deposited their temple dues or freewill offerings. There were four gates leading into this court. The eastern gate was called the Beautiful Gate, where beggars customarily sat (Ac 3:2). The western gate led into the Court of Israel. It was called the Gate of Nicanor, because, as some hold, the head and hand of Nicanor (a Syrian enemy in the time of the Maccabees) had once been placed upon it (1Macc 7:47; 2Macc 15:35). Here in the Gate of Nicanor, all that was ordered to be done "before the Lord" took place. For example, purified women, cleansed lepers, and others seeking confirmation of ritual purity would be examined by the priests. Under the floor of this court, and with an opening and a guardroom near the Beautiful Gate, there was a subterranean passage, by which Paul was at one time rescued from a Jewish mob (Ac 21:31–32). It led from the Tower of Antonia, by which Herod and afterward the Romans assured themselves of military control.

Passing through the Gate of Nicanor and up fifteen steps, another court was entered, which was called the Court of Israel, or the Court of the Men. It occupied the western end of the Sacred Enclosure and was really a narrow corridor that completely surrounded the next court, the Court of the Priests. In the Court of Israel, the men of Israel stood to view the sacrifices, which could also be viewed from the Court of the Women, only at a greater distance. Three gates led up to the Court of Israel from both the north and the south and the Gate of Nicanor from the east. This was as far as the Lord Jesus was allowed to go, because He was not of priestly descent. In the southeastern corner of this court, there was a room called the Hall Gazith. Members of the Council, seated in a semicircle on stone seats, usually assembled there to render judgments on behalf of Israel. Chambers were built into the temple walls and furnished for storehouses and living rooms for the officiating priests and the temple attendants.

11
The Court of the
Priests and the
Great Altar

On a raised platform, a few steps higher and surrounding the temple proper on three sides—east, north, and south—was the Court of the Priests. This court, about 275 feet long by 200 feet wide, was mainly occupied by the house of God, the sanctuary, which stood in the western half of the Court of Israel. The temple was itself divided into the Holy Place and the Most Holy Place (Holy of Holies). In front of the temple proper and in the eastern section of the Court of the Priests stood the great altar, or altar of burnt offerings, built upon the site that today lies under the Dome of the Rock, a Muslim mosque. In its construction, only unhewn stones were used, which no tool had ever touched (Ex 20:25; 1Macc 4:47). Upon it, the priests performed every act of sacrifice, with the exception of the burning of incense.[21] It was fully forty-eight feet square and fifteen feet high, diminishing in size toward the top, around which ran a circuit for the administering priests. They kept fire burning continually upon this altar by night as well as by day. Between the altar and the porch of the temple proper, toward the left (that is, to the south), there was at one time a large laver of brass, supported by twelve colossal lions. The priests used mechanisms to drain the laver every evening and fill it every morning so they could perform the washing required prior to their duties in the sanctuary. Indeed, the water supply as well as a perfect sewer system into the Brook of Kedron was one of the sanctuary's most wonderful arrangements. An aqueduct over forty miles long supplied the temple with water from the hills about Hebron, from Bethlehem, from Etham, and from the pools of Solomon.[22]

The temple proper, or house of God, was not a large and somewhat dark building but a handsome edifice. It included the projections of the porch, about 150 by 150 feet, and occupied about one half of the space in the Court of Priests. Its floor was eight feet above the level of the Court of Priests. In the front part, toward the east, was a porch, or vestibule, which extended across the temple. It was built of richly ornamented marble, was about 120 feet high, and consisted of several stories. Its roof was steep and covered with golden spikes to keep birds from settling upon it and defiling it.[23]

12
The Temple Proper

Two-leaved doors with gold plating formed the entrance from the porch into the Holy Place, which was about thirty by sixty feet. Above the entrance hung the symbol of Israel, a gigantic vine of pure gold, each cluster the height of a man. In the Holy Place itself, to the right, stood the table of the bread of the Presence. The priests placed twelve loaves on the table every Sabbath day (cf. Lv 24:5–9).[24] To the left (that is, to the south) stood the golden lampstand.[25] The priests had to keep its seven lamps burning constantly (cf. Lv 24:1–4).[26] And at the farther end of the Holy Place, toward the west and near the entrance to the Most Holy Place, was the golden altar of incense. Upon this altar, also called the inner altar, the appointed priest burned incense every morning and evening (cf. Ex 30:1, 7–8).

13
The Holy Place

Beyond the Holy Place, separated from it by a heavy curtain, or veil, which was rent from the top to the bottom at our Savior's death (Mk 15:38), was the room called the Most Holy Place. This room, the most sacred place, was a cube, each dimension being thirty feet. It was empty, containing only a large stone, upon which the high priest sprinkled the blood of the sacrifices on the Day of Atonement. The stone occupied the place where once the ark of the covenant, surmounted by the Mercy Seat, had stood in Solomon's temple. No one was allowed to enter the Most Holy Place except the high priest, and he but once a year, on the Day of Atonement.

14
Most Holy Place

This is the sanctuary of sanctuaries that Pompey insisted upon entering, expecting to find some idol—and "found nothing."[27]

15
The Beauty of the Temple

Such was the beautiful temple on which Herod, as a monument of penitence for the murder of Mariamne,[28] had lavished marble, gold, and brass and for which he received no thanks from the Jews. Although they passed over the name of the builder with absolute silence,[29] the rabbis were never weary of praising its beauties. Unfortunately, of the great building not one stone has remained.

16
c. November 15, 4 BC
Lk 1:8–9

One November morning in 4 BC, Zechariah stood among the priests who had assembled for the distribution of lots in the Hall of Hewn Stones, the Hall Gazith. He was a priest upon whom the snows of at least sixty winters had fallen.[30] His division, the division of Abijah, was on duty for the week and the house of his fathers for that particular day. During his week of duty, he slept in a room in the inner court. Already before dawn, he had submersed himself in a well-appointed subterranean bath in order to be Levitically clean.[31] Then he put on his official dress, which the priests wore only while on actual duty: short white linen breeches, a long white linen, close-fitting coat, a girdle of white linen (byssus), with embroidery work on it in scarlet, purple, and blue. He also wore a kind of turban on his head, because priests were not permitted to present themselves before the Lord with uncovered head (Ex 28:40–43; 39:27–29; Ezk 44:17–19). As shoes are nowhere mentioned, we can safely suppose that he had nothing on his feet.[32]

17
The First Lot

In all, four lots were taken for the purpose of deciding how the various functions of the day were to be apportioned. The first lot decided who was to prepare the great altar, carry away the ashes, and carry the wood and lay it on the altar. This lot was drawn while it was still dark, with no light except a flickering blaze from the fire on the great altar. Immediately, the designated priests washed their hands and feet in the great laver and set themselves to perform their appointed tasks. After they had performed their duties and once more washed their hands and feet, they again presented themselves in the Hall of Hewn Stones for a further drawing of lots.

18
The Second Lot

The second lot, taken while it was still dark, determined which priest would kill the morning sacrifice, prepare its body, and sprinkle the blood upon the altar. It also determined who was to prepare the altar of incense, trim and replenish the lamps, and attend to various other duties. The next step was to go out and see whether there was as yet any sign of day. As soon as the gray dawn was breaking, the lamb was led forth from the lamb house. Ninety-three[33] sacred utensils were brought from the utensil house. The lamb was watered out of a golden bowl, suspended from a ring on the north side of the altar, and its fore and hind feet were tied together.

19
The Slaying of the Lamb

Immediately upon this, there was heard the blast of a silver trumpet, which signaled several events. The great gates leading into the Holy Place would be opened; the Levites would make ready the music and prepare to perform their duties; and the representatives of the people, the so-called stationary men, would present themselves to witness the morning sacrifice. The opening of the gates was also the signal for the slaying of the sacrificial lamb.[34] While the lamb was slain and its blood sprinkled on the altar, the priests who had been chosen for that purpose entered the now open doors of the Holy Place to dress the golden lampstand and to prepare the altar of incense. Then the priests prepared the body of the victim for the burnt offering and went again to the Hall Gazith for the third drawing of lots.

The most solemn part of the service was now to begin, the determining by lot who was to offer the incense. The president of the division called upon all the assembled priests to join in the prescribed prayer and the repeating of the Shema,[35] which might be called a sort of creed, or confession of faith: "Hear, O Israel: The LORD our God, the LORD is one." After the Shema, the lot was cast for the burning of incense, which was regarded as the most solemn stage of the whole sacrificial act. No one might take part in this drawing of lots who already previously had been called upon to offer incense. In other words, only once in a lifetime would a priest receive this honor, after which he would be called rich and holy.[36] Now Zechariah, the aged priest from the hill country of Judea, was accorded this honor. But before taking up the story of Zechariah, let us finish the account of the service.

20
The Lot for the Burning of Incense
Lk 1:8–9

The fourth (and last) lot immediately followed the lot for the burning of incense. This lot ascertained whose duty it was to put the various parts of the slaughtered lamb on the fire of the altar of burnt sacrifice. Those upon whom no lot had fallen took off their official attire, hung it in the proper place, and were then at liberty to leave the sanctuary.

21
The Fourth Lot

The incense-offering priest with two assistants now entered the Holy Place, the temple proper. One of the assistants carried live coals from the fire of the great altar and the other the incense, which was composed of twelve kinds of sweet-smelling spices.[37] As they passed into the Holy Place, a signal was given at the sound of which all priests hastened from all parts to worship. The Levites occupied the places allotted to them for the playing of the stringed instruments and the singing of psalms. The chief of the stationary men arranged his course at the Gate of Nicanor while the incense-burning priest slowly approached the altar. One of the assistants reverently placed the coals on the altar and then withdrew. Another arranged the incense and then withdrew. The chief officiating priest was then left alone to await the signal for the burning of incense. It was always a solemn moment. Throughout the temple courts, silence reigned, while within the sanctuary itself the solitary priest laid the incense upon the fire and thick clouds of sweet-smelling odor rose up before the Lord.

22
The Burning of Incense

After the offering up of incense, the officiating priest and his assistants, as well as those of the second lot who had prepared the lamp and the altar of incense,

23
The Burnt Offering and the Benediction

proceeded to the steps in front of the sanctuary. The officiating priest solemnly recited the benediction (Nu 6:24–26), pronouncing the Lord's so-called ineffable name of "Yahweh" during the course of the blessing.[38] (Jews had the custom of replacing the name "Yahweh" with "Adonai," a euphemism meaning "the Lord.") They then began the sacrificing of the burnt offering, laying upon the altar those parts of the lamb that had been designated by the Lord to be burned.[39] Besides this regular daily burnt offering, the priests presented other offerings—meat offerings and drink offerings—of the people. While a priest bent forward to pour out the appropriate drink offering, a signal was given for the musical part of the service to begin. The twelve-voiced Levite choir sang the psalm appointed for the day, accompanied by the musical instruments. At the blast of the silver trumpets, the people bowed to the ground and worshiped. This ended the morning service. The evening service was similar to the morning service. The only difference was that lots were drawn only for the burning of incense, and the burnt sacrifice was offered before the burning of the incense. Thus the daily burnt offering was encircled by the offering of incense.[40]

24
A Celestial Visitor
Lk 1:10–12

Now, let us return to Zechariah. Deep silence had fallen upon the worshipers as prayerfully they waited for the ascending clouds of sweet odors to fill the house of God. Zechariah paused until he saw the incense burning. Then he, too, bowing, would have reverently withdrawn had not a startling sight arrested his attention.[41] Was he dreaming? There on the right side of the golden altar,[42] he clearly beheld an angelic form. One of those holy beings of God's invisible creation here assumed visible form, and it is evident why Zechariah was—and for that matter, why anyone in his place would have been—troubled with fear.

25
John the Baptist
Promised
Lk 1:13–17

But except for the fact of the sudden appearance of God's holy messenger to Zechariah, a sinful man, there was no reason for fear. "Do not be afraid, Zechariah," the angel said, "for your prayer has been heard, and your wife Elizabeth will bear you a son, and you shall call his name John." This does not mean that Zechariah had been praying at that moment for the birth of a son, for as the incensing priest, he was serving in an official capacity. His prayer likely concerned the deepest desire of all true Israel; namely, the messianic deliverance of the people:

> Be graciously pleased, Lord, our God, with Your people Israel and with their prayer. Appoint peace, goodness, and blessing, grace, mercy, and compassion, for us and for all Israel, Your people.[43]

"Oh, that salvation for Israel would come out of Zion! When the LORD restores the fortunes of His people, let Jacob rejoice, let Israel be glad" (Ps 14:7). This prayer had been heard. But the Lord had held in remembrance also the other prayer of Zechariah, that oft-repeated private prayer. And now as a sign of the advent of the Messiah in the near future, the son Zechariah prayed for would be born to serve as the Messiah's forerunner. What honor and glory for the humble priest from the hill country!

There was a peculiar significance in the name that God selected for the unborn child, John, which refers to the grace of God.[44] The time for the gracious coming of Christ, whose forerunner John was to be, had finally arrived. Therefore, many would rejoice at his birth. According to the word of the angel, this child was to be "great before the Lord," a truly great man. Moreover, like Samson (Jgs 13:7) and Samuel (1Sm 1:11) of old, he was to consecrate himself as a lifelong Nazirite unto the Lord.[45] The angel said he would be filled with the Holy Spirit already before his birth. In the strength of God, the forerunner would lay the ax to the root of the tree, bare the sin and corruption of the people, go to the root of evil—the sinful heart— by preaching the Law of God as it should be preached and showing the wrath of the holy God upon all sinners. Like Samuel, he would turn many of the children of Israel to the Lord, their God. And like Elijah (1Ki 18:37), he would "turn the hearts of the fathers to the children, and the disobedient to the wisdom of the just." He would point those who, after hearing the curse of the Law, truly repented of their sins to Him who alone can save them from their sins. So, by the grace of God, they would return to the faith of little children and thus become truly wise. His real mission was to "make ready for the Lord a people prepared"; that is, willing and eager to receive the Messiah (Mt 3:1–6; 11:10, 14; Mal 3:1).

These words of the angel filled the soul of Zechariah with bewilderment and his heart with doubt. But it was inexcusable doubt. He demanded some visible sign by which to know "this." His doubt was different from the reaction of Abraham and Manoah (Gn 17:17; Jgs 13:17) to somewhat similar announcements. (Even a cursory reading of the passages conveys the impression of a marked difference.) The doubt of Zechariah was, however, not to make the promises of God come to naught. Zechariah asked for a sign and he received it. Before giving the sign, the angel, by way of justifying the penalty that he had to announce, said, "I am Gabriel. I stand in the presence of God, and I was sent to speak to you and bring you this good news."[46] Gabriel means "the Strength of God" (*Vir Dei*);[47] he was a special messenger sent by God to Zechariah for this particular purpose.

And now the sign. "You will be silent and unable to speak until the day that these things take place, because you did not believe my words, which will be fulfilled in their time." Immediate muteness was to be the sign; however, it was not caused by a stroke of apoplexy or by terror, nor was it a state of prolonged surprise, as some surmise.[48] It was a *miraculous* penalty for the reason that the "good news" was not believed. In the course of a few minutes, three miracles took place: the appearance of an angel, a prediction of an extraordinary event, and miraculous muteness.

26
The Doubt of Zechariah
Lk 1:18–19

27
The Sign
Lk 1:20

28
The People Outside
Lk 1:21–23

Considerable time had passed since the signal for the burning of incense had been given. The people had said the prayers. They were now waiting for the return of the priest to lead in the priestly blessing that preceded the daily burnt offering and the psalm of praise. It was a rule with the priests to spend only a short time in the sanctuary, because otherwise the worshipers might fear that God had slain them for having become guilty of some wrong.[49] Thus, the unusually long delay of Zechariah in coming forth from the Holy Place caused the people to wonder (Lk 1:21). When he finally did emerge and tried to speak but could not, he helplessly endeavored by signs to indicate his inability to pronounce the Benediction. The awestruck assembly knew that something uncommon had happened and that he had received a revelation or seen a vision in the temple. After the first excitement had passed over, it is probable that by means of a written communication, Zechariah gave an explanation.[50] Wondering, all disperse—priests and worshipers.

29
Zechariah Returns
Home
Lk 1:23

The day's service over, another priestly family would take the place of Zechariah's priestly family. The ninth, the division of Jeshua (1Ch 24:11), was ready to relieve the division of Abijah. The priests returned to their homes, some to Ophel, some to Jericho. Zechariah, now "rich and noble"[51] on account of the lot that had made him an incense-offering priest, was mute, and yet happy to trace a silent homeward course to the hill country of Judea. God fulfilled the promise that He had given by His angel, and the more Zechariah meditated on all these things—the vision of the angel, the wonderful announcement, the punishment his doubting had brought upon him, and now the cheering pregnancy of his devoted wife—the more fully he must have realized that in truth the redemption of Israel was drawing nigh. As for Elizabeth, we can suppose that she marveled and devoutly meditated on those things like her husband.[52] Rejoicing in her heart, she was satisfied for the present that the Lord had looked upon her and taken away her reproach among men. And so the next five months passed by in deepest silence.

30
Galilee

From the hill country of Judea, we now proceed to Galilee, to a town called Nazareth. Galilee, meaning "circuit" or "border," included a territory originally claimed, but never completely possessed, by the tribes of Naphtali, Zebulun, Issachar, and Asher. Hence, it is called "Galilee of the Gentiles" (Jgs 4:2; Is 9:1; Mt 4:15; 1Macc 5:15), on account of its mixed population of Phoenicians and Arabs, and because in the time of our Lord, Greek was spoken there. In the time of David, this territory was united with his kingdom. For services rendered in the building of the temple, Solomon gave Hiram, the king of Tyre, twenty cities in the land of Galilee. But it seems that Hiram was not quite satisfied, for when he came out to look at the cities, "They did not please him. . . . So they are called the land of Cabul to this day" (1Ki 9:12–13).[53] From that time on, it seems always to have been the fate of Galilee to be despised. Following Jeroboam after the death of Solomon, Galilee helped to form the Kingdom of Israel; but in the time of Tiglath-pileser, it was the first to fall. Eleven years before the final doom of Israel, Assyria carried away thousands of the inhabitants of Galilee (c. 735 BC; 2Ki 15:29). But this territory, first to fall, was also first to see the Light (Is 9:1–2; Mt 4:13–16). After the Babylonian captivity, it was largely settled by returning Jewish colonists. They carefully avoided the schismatic Samaritans by faithfully maintaining religious fellowship with Jerusalem. Since they did not belong to Judea proper, Jews in Galilee were considered part of the Jewish Diaspora. During the Maccabean uprising, a closer contact was established with the mother country. One of the first acts of the Maccabee brothers, after the restoration of worship in Jerusalem, was to defend their northern brethren against heathen persecution; Simon went to Galilee and Judas to Gilead (1Macc 5:9–58). But beyond bringing help to their brethren and transporting them safely to Jewish soil, properly so called, no attempt was made to subjugate the territory itself. This was not done until the short reign of Aristobulus I, when a large portion of the northern territory, including Galilee, was conquered and made subject to the high priest at Jerusalem.[54] Thus, Galilee was again politically embodied with the ancient Land of Israel, but still within its own boundaries and under foreign rule. The Romans left the weak Hyrcanus II as high priest and nominally as "ethnarch" of the Jews, although Antipater was the real power behind the throne. Phasael was appointed governor of Jerusalem and young Herod governor of Galilee. So it happened that Herod began his political career as governor of Galilee and was later called "King of the Jews."

In the course of time, a nationalism and patriotism developed in Galilee as intense as that in Judea itself, notwithstanding the disdain with which the highbrow metropolitans of Jerusalem regarded the Galilean provincials. They had contempt for their very speech, their amusing Galilean dialect, which was probably a confusion in the pronunciation of gutturals (Mt 26:73). They hurled belittling proverbial sayings against them, such as, "See that no prophet arises from Galilee" (Jn 7:52). But what about Deborah, Jonah, Elisha, and probably Hosea? Of the Galileans' intense Jewish patriotism, of Galilean manhood and womanhood, there was no question, as witnessed by Josephus,[55] himself a Galilean governor at the outbreak of the last Jewish war. The soil of Galilee was richer than that of Judea, and its inhabitants were more prosperous, according to a common saying: "If a person wishes to be rich, let him go north; if he wants to be wise, let him come south."[56] And still, Galilee was to Judaism only the "Court of the Gentiles," while Judea was its "innermost sanctuary." Yet some of the best Jewish families had made Galilee, or specifically, Nazareth, their home.

Scholars offer many conjectures about the etymology of Nazareth. On account of the quotation of St. Matthew "He would be called a Nazarene" (2:23), it is

31
The Galileans

32
Despised Nazareth

probably best to connect Nazareth with *netzer*, a branch or twig, conforming to the prophecy: "There shall come forth a shoot from the stump of Jesse, and a branch from his roots shall bear fruit" (Is 11:1; cf. Zec 6:12).[57] The town is not mentioned in Josephus or in the Old Testament;[58] however, the New Testament Scriptures not only mention it, but give it due prominence. It was a small and secluded town of a few thousand inhabitants. "Can anything good come out of Nazareth?" (Jn 1:46)[59] was an insult that lent the town's inglorious name to the scornful title on the cross, "Jesus of Nazareth." Yet the Lord Himself did not despise to use that title when He appeared to persecuting Saul (Ac 22:8).

33
Nazareth's Beautiful Setting

Nazareth was beautifully situated. Travelers tell us that the beauty of its surroundings must be seen to be appreciated. It lies on the western and northwestern slopes of a hollow among the hills of Lower Galilee, away from the main caravan route[60] and just north of the great Plain of Esdraelon, from which it is reached by a steep and rocky path. Still, the quiet little town was no stagnant pool of rustic seclusion; for while its own immediate horizon was limited, there is a splendid view from the summit of a nearby hill. To the west are the low-lying hills stretching toward the Mediterranean Sea, whose blue waters turn to a silver sheen under the shining sun. Following the coastline to the left, the eye is arrested by the only promontory on the coast of Israel, the thickly wooded ridge of Carmel, where Elijah slew the prophets of Baal (1Ki 18:19). To the south, there extends the great Plain of Esdraelon, framed in by the bare mountains of Samaria, with its vegetation and trees looking like a sea of green, bordered by yellow shores.[61] The scene is crowned by the Hill of Moreh, or Little Hermon, with Nain clinging to its slopes. This is the battlefield of Gideon (Jgs 7:1) and Gilboa, where Saul was slain (1Sm 28:4). To the east, there first falls into view the rounded top of Mount Tabor. Behind it appears the deep valley of the Jordan. To the left, one sees the shining waters of the Sea of Galilee. Beyond the sea appears the yellow horizon of the heights of Gilead and Bashan, plowed, as it were, into sandy furrows by the desert winds. To the north, the eye rests on Cana and many other little villages, glittering like white spots here and there in the bright sunlight. Passing over romantic hills and glens and pausing for a moment on Safed, the supposed "city set on a hill" (Mt 5:14), the view is bounded by far-off Mount Hermon with its crest of snow.[62]

34
Nazareth's Importance

However, in spite of the seclusion of Nazareth and the fact that the Old Testament writers down to Josephus fail to mention it, we should not suppose that it was a place of little importance and that its inhabitants were people of but little culture. On the contrary, there was a synagogue at Nazareth (Lk 4:16), and according to some writers, it was a priest center, a gathering place for priests, from which they "went up in company to Jerusalem" and the temple.[63] Indeed, if a rabbinic tradition is to be credited, it was the home of the eighteenth division of priests, the division of Happizzez (1Ch 24:15).[64] But, what is more, at the time that we are taking up our story, it was also the home of ex-royalty. Two members of the house of David, a son and a daughter, and probably also their families, had made it their home.[65]

Fully five months after the conception of Elizabeth—that is, in the sixth month, and, as we take it, between April 17 and May 16, 3 BC—God sent the angel Gabriel to a virgin in Nazareth who was betrothed to Joseph[66] of the house of David and a carpenter by trade. This time, however, the appearance was not in the solemn grandeur of God's sanctuary, but in a humble private home.[67] The name of the virgin was Mary. Whether the prevalence of this name in the New Testament was a tribute to the popularity of Mariamne, the murdered wife of Herod, we do not know. It does not seem likely in the case of Mary, because Marys, or Miriams, are mentioned already in the Old Testament, such as the sister of Moses (Ex 15:20). Besides, Mary was a descendant of the royal house of David.[68] Of her age we know nothing. We may suppose that she was still quite young when betrothed to Joseph,[69] whom tradition has described as rather advanced in age.[70] But we must not forget that Joseph was still alive twelve years later and paid his annual visit to the temple (Lk 2:41–42). When or why these two persons of royal descent left the ancestral home of Bethlehem in Judea with their families and made Nazareth in Galilee their permanent residence is impossible to state. At the time of their entry into the story, they had been recently engaged.[71] It was probably a simple betrothal, not because Joseph was a carpenter—since among the Jews it was regarded as almost a religious duty for every boy to learn a trade—but because they were poor (Lv 12:8; Lk 2:24). A promise was given in the presence of witnesses, a pledge was added with a small coin or coin's worth, a meal was enjoyed, the Benediction was spoken over the statutory cup of wine, and a son and a daughter of David became groom and bride.[72] From that moment, Mary was the betrothed wife of Joseph. Their relation was as sacred as if they had been already wedded. Any breach of this relation would be treated as adultery. But before the actual marriage of Joseph and Mary took place a few months later,[73] a remarkable thing happened. Both Mary and Joseph received revelations that proved most momentous for the history of mankind.

A greeting from heaven was brought to Mary. "Greetings, O favored one, the Lord is with you!" Naturally, the awe of the supernatural fell upon her.[74] But it was not so much the appearance of the mysterious stranger as the words of greeting, implying most distinctive blessings, that disturbed the humble maiden. After a friendly "Do not be afraid," the blessings are unfolded, which are not awarded on account of merit but are bestowed upon her as a special favor by the grace of God. She, a virgin, was to conceive and bear a son and call His name Jesus.[75] He would be great and would be called the Son of the Most High. Upon Him, God would confer the title to the throne of His father David[76] and give Him *eternal* dominion. It

35
Mary of the House of David
Lk 1:26–27

36
The Annunciation
Lk 1:28–34

is evident from this message of the angel that the long-awaited fullness of time had come and that the promised Messiah was now to appear on this sin-cursed earth, to be born of a virgin (Is 7:14; 9:6, 7; 2Sm 7:12). It is clear that Mary of the house of David was directly conscious as to *who* was meant. Not for a moment did she entertain any doubt as to the possibility and truth of the promise.[77] She simply expressed perplexity as to certain details: "How will this be, since I am a virgin?" For, she was betrothed to Joseph of the royal line, but she was not yet married to him. Besides, the promise of the angel was given to her without reference to her impending marriage to Joseph.[78] The angel had not spoken of a child of which Joseph was to be the father. Still, the fulfillment of the promise of the incomprehensibly wonderful event is taken confidently for granted. And her humble inquiry for additional enlightenment is not at all a word of trembling doubt. She did not require a sign on which to lean, but rather requested guidance in obedient self-surrender.[79] To her who believed, the angel pointed out a glorious path. That did not seem strange. Only that *she* was favored to walk in it seemed so.[80]

37
"Conceived by the Holy Spirit"
Lk 1:35

And now the angel comes to her aid with an explanation in words tender and chaste about the miraculous conception. "The Holy Spirit will come upon you, and the power of the Most High will overshadow you; therefore the child to be born will be called holy—the Son of God." This is the answer to Mary's perplexity—how will I be a mother if I am still a virgin? Because she would conceive by the power of the Holy Spirit, her virginity would not be affected. And, moreover, the holy child would not only be called, but would truly *be* the Son of God.[81] In this way, the divine mystery of the miraculous conception of the Son of God is most tenderly, suitably, and most clearly expressed.

38
The Sign
Lk 1:36–38

Mary did not ask for a sign. Yet unasked, the angel gave a sign to strengthen her faith and to confirm the words that he spoke. He showed her an example of God's omnipotence by telling her that her relative Elizabeth, notwithstanding her age and supposedly hopeless barrenness, has been with child for the past six months. Elizabeth's conception was not like Mary's conception, but on account of Elizabeth's age, it was nevertheless also beyond the ordinary course of nature and therefore likewise a miracle wrought by the hand of God. Just how Mary (of the tribe of Judah and of the house of David) and Elizabeth (of the tribe of Levi and a daughter of Aaron) were related, the Bible does not state.[82] Most likely, however, they were related on the maternal side, since the priests were not compelled to marry within their own tribe. With the devotion of a childlike and firm faith, Mary replied, "Behold, I am the servant of the Lord; let it be to me according to your word." Then the angel departed from her.

39
Visit of Mary to Elizabeth
Lk 1:39–45

The information concerning Elizabeth provided Mary with some direction. She may not have communicated with Joseph[83] or with anyone else, which in her circumstances seems natural. Instead, trusting in the Lord for guidance in the whole matter, Mary immediately[84] arose and hastened to the hill country of Judea[85] to communicate and confide her deepest feelings to that kinswoman and friend who also was highly favored. The whole narrative implies that both Mary and Elizabeth, full of faith, quietly waited for God to reveal what He had done. Elizabeth must have learned from her husband the destiny of her unborn child and the near advent of the Messiah. But she could not know either when or of whom the Messiah was to be born.[86] Upon the arrival of Mary in the house of Zechariah, full confirmation was made of what the angel said concerning Elizabeth. And now the mother of her Lord was standing before her! Immediately, Elizabeth's own child leaped in her womb and gave signs of life and faith. Elizabeth was filled with the Holy Spirit[87] and replied to Mary's greeting:

> Blessed are you among women, and blessed is the fruit of your womb! And why is this granted to me that the mother of my Lord should come to me? . . . Blessed is she who believed that there would be a fulfillment of what was spoken to her from the Lord.

Two mothers meet: the mother of the way-preparer and the mother of Him whose way he would prepare. Elizabeth, filled with the Holy Spirit, expresses the homage that her unborn child offered to his Lord. Then Mary replies, offering her own homage to God. The words of her hymn are taken from the Old Testament (1Sm 1:11; 2:1–10; Ps 103:17; 107:9; Is 41:8–9; etc.), but the music is of the New.[88] The keynote of all is the grace and favor of God—shown to Abraham, to Israel, to Elizabeth, and to her, the handmaid. God shows grace and favor to the humble and poor, to all believers who rejoice in their Savior and their God. Elizabeth praises Mary and her faith, but Mary gives all glory to God:[89]

40
The Magnificat of Mary
Lk 1:46–55

> My soul magnifies the Lord, and my spirit rejoices in God my Savior, for He has looked on the humble estate of His servant. . . . For He who is mighty has done great things for me, and holy is His name. And His mercy is for those who fear Him from generation to generation. He has shown strength with His arm; He has scattered the proud in the thoughts of their hearts; He has brought down the mighty from their thrones and exalted those of humble estate. . . . He has helped His servant Israel, in remembrance of His mercy, as He spoke to our fathers, to Abraham and to His offspring forever.

Thus Mary, in a hymn that the Church has called the Magnificat, gives expression to her exceeding gladness and to the cause of her joy. Then she describes the new order in Christ's kingdom and sets it all down as a deed of divine mercy and grace.[90]

After a stay of some months, for which no details are given, and before the birth of John the Baptist, Mary again returned home. Some think that Mary stayed with Elizabeth and helped her until after the birth and circumcision of John.[91] But it

41
The Return of Mary
Lk 1:56

seems more likely that she would return now in an arrangement that is permissible and by which she is screened from public view.

Elizabeth's conception took place contrary to the common laws of nature. But now, after it had taken place, the time for her delivery arrived in the ordinary course of time.[92] In the whole community, it was an unexpected event. When the neighbors and more distant relatives heard that the Lord had magnified[93] His grace upon her—for by this birth, so long deferred and so contrary to all expectation, they clearly saw a proof of special divine compassion—they came and cordially congratulated her. On the eighth day, the divinely prescribed day for circumcision (Gn 17:12), a special gathering was arranged. "They came to circumcise the child"; namely, the relatives and friends and those who were invited for that purpose. Since Zechariah and Elizabeth were most likely living in comfortable circumstances, they were able to prepare a little celebration for this highly exceptional event. As it was, a day of circumcision in a Jewish family was always a day of domestic solemnity and joy, in which a son of Abraham was put under the yoke of God's holy law, with all the duties and privileges that this implied.[94] With the circumcision itself there was also associated, according to ancient custom, the giving of the name (Gn 21:3–4).[95] Ordinarily, the head of the family made all arrangements, but in the house of Zechariah, it seems, the relatives and friends had matters pretty well in hand, including even such important details as selecting the name. Without consulting Elizabeth in the matter or endeavoring to communicate with the mute-stricken Zechariah, they attempted to call[96] the infant "Zechariah" after his father. It obviously was, they thought, the proper thing to do. What greater honor could be accorded Zechariah than to have his name so unexpectedly perpetuated by the birth of a son? But Elizabeth objected. "No; he shall be called John." This was not merely the expression of a personal desire; it was a mother's decision, and it was final. Very likely, Zechariah had in some way communicated to her what the angel had told him regarding the name his child should receive.[97] The visitors said to her: "None of your relatives is called by this name," not as if the name of John had been unknown. There were certain well-known Johns of priestly lineage; Herod murdered the last one[98] about twenty-seven years before. However, even that event would have been considered too remote to suggest the selection of that name. To overcome the difficulty, and to confirm the name, those present decided to communicate with Zechariah, who but for this incident would probably have been well-nigh forgotten by the happy gathering. All this happened while Zechariah sat there as a deaf[99] and mute witness, until Elizabeth interrupted the solemn proceeding when it came time to name the child in the Benediction.[100] Then the appeal was made to Zechariah to name his son. Zechariah asked[101] for a writing tablet, most likely a small tablet covered with wax. Upon this he inscribed the words,[102] "His name is John." Thus, firmly and finally, he expressed himself in agreement with Elizabeth for a name foreign to the family. He did this not, however, merely to assert his parental authority, but to indicate that he was obeying a divine command. The assembled guests marveled at this strange way of giving assent to his wife, no doubt feeling that there must be something behind it all. But this was not the sole cause for their astonishment. For, immediately Zechariah's mouth was opened and his tongue loosed, and he burst forth into rapturous praise of God. A mute Zechariah, an unusual birth, a singular name, and the sudden recovery of speech—surely sufficient cause for a religious awe!

The last words Zechariah had spoken in the temple were words of unbelief and doubt, but now his first words after his son's birth are an expression of faith. He could not even utter the name of his child, but now he bursts into a lengthy praise of the name of God. The first evidence of his muteness had been when his tongue refused to pronounce the Benediction upon the assembled worshipers, but now, filled with the Holy Spirit, he speaks a message embodying sublime praise of God. Just as Mary's song is called the Magnificat from its opening word in the Latin version, so Zechariah's song is similarly named the Benedictus. It begins in the Old Testament and ends in the New.[103] The hymn itself sees the fulfillment of the messianic prayers that the priests said in the temple before the lot was cast for the incense offering, as well as the prayers by the people during the offering.[104] Then it speaks of the ministry and mission of John. "Blessed be the Lord God of Israel, for He has visited and redeemed His people and has raised up a horn of salvation for us in the house of His servant David." Thus it was promised in Paradise, then to Abraham, to David, through Moses and the prophets,[105] "that we, being delivered from the hand of our enemies, might serve Him without fear, in holiness and righteousness before Him all our days." It is the fulfillment of the promise of salvation from sin by the coming Savior, for whom his child was to prepare the way.

44
The Benedictus
Lk 1:67–79

> And you, child, will be called the prophet of the Most High; for you will go before the Lord to prepare His ways, to give knowledge of salvation to His people in the forgiveness of their sins, because of the tender mercy of our God.

By the virtue of this mercy, "the sunrise[106] shall visit us from on high to give light to those who sit in darkness and in the shadow of death." Thus, the Benedictus of Zechariah, steeped in Old Testament language, is at the same time a commentary for the correct understanding of the Old Testament messianic promises. At that time, thousands of Abraham's descendants were groaning under Herod's yoke. They may have been tempted to entertain the false hope of being delivered from the yoke of a pagan ruler by the yearned-for Messiah. But Zechariah here plainly told them what kind of Messiah to expect—namely, one who would gain for them and grant them remission of sins. That was the kind of salvation that the Messiah was to bring and the kind of Messiah whose way John was to prepare.

Far and wide, these marvelous tidings spread through the hill country of Judea. Awe fell upon the people. The long and dreary night had at last given place to day, and the light of hope had begun to fill their hearts. Reflecting upon the utterances of Zechariah, an uncommon future was rightly expected for the child. The question was asked, "What then will this child be?" (v. 66). There was good reason to expect great things of this child, because "the hand of the Lord was with him." Zechariah and Elizabeth pass out of the picture; instead we learn that "the child grew and became strong in spirit, and he was in the wilderness until the day of his public appearance to Israel." The desert that he loved was the foster mother of him who was to be the stern preacher of repentance in the wilderness: "Repent, for the kingdom of heaven is at hand" (Mt 3:2). The Qumran community that preserved the Dead Sea Scrolls was not far off. But there is no clear indication of contact with them.[107]

Now, let us return to Nazareth.[108] After her stay of about three months with Elizabeth, Mary returned to her home in Nazareth (Lk 1:56). A number of months had passed since the Annunciation, and although Mary was fully aware that the Holy Spirit caused her condition, others did not know. Therefore, it must have felt as if a sword pierced her heart when her secret became known and she was found to be with child. Naturally, one of the first to find out was Joseph, to whom she was betrothed.[109] There was a discovery and a surprise. In order to forestall any unholy thoughts, the evangelist quickly inserts: "She was found to be with child *from the Holy Spirit.*" Of course, Joseph was ignorant of this. This belongs to the realm of revelation and faith. Therefore, as the betrothed husband of Mary, with a husband's rights and responsibilities, and acting in a strictly legal manner, he could not over-look what appeared as adultery. On the other hand, however, still loving Mary and unwilling to expose her to public shame, he resolved to divorce her quietly. Of course, even this action—a quiet canceling of the betrothal bond—opposed the strict application of the Mosaic Law. The least that the Law required in such a case[110] was a bill of divorcement,[111] and that, as a public document, would have been opposed to the gentle course of action Joseph resolved to take.[112]

While Joseph, at first wavering between two plans, finally resolved[113] on the course of abandoning[114] Mary privately and probably was painfully deliberating on even so harsh a measure, an angel appeared to him in a dream and delivered him from his perplexity. We need not enter into the question of dreams and visions, except to state that we are here dealing with a divine revelation. "Joseph, son of David,[115] do not fear to take Mary . . . your wife."[116] Before God, she is already his lawfully wedded wife. He should not leave her. An explanation is offered concerning her present condition: "For that which is conceived in her is from the Holy Spirit." Thus at once, briefly and definitely, the suspicion that had tormented Joseph was shown to be without foundation. The angel continues, "She will bear a son." But he is careful not to add "to you," as was done in the case of Zechariah (Lk 1:13), as if Joseph were the physical father. Still, Joseph is to take a real father's place—namely, in the naming of the child. "And you shall call His name Jesus." This is a command and a prediction. There is a singular significance connected with this name. "For He," emphatically,[117] He and none other, "will save His people from their sins." What a glorious prediction about a child whose approaching birth had filled Joseph with such keen sorrow and toward whom he was privileged to occupy the relation of father! The still unborn child was to be the Messiah, the Christ, the Savior, who was to "save His people from their sins."[118]

In all this, the evangelist sees a fulfillment of prophecy—not merely in the singular name nor in the mere fact of a miraculous virgin birth; but these matters were as links welded into a golden chain. "All this took place to fulfill what the Lord had spoken by the prophet: 'Behold, the virgin shall conceive and bear a son.' " This is the fulfillment of the sign Isaiah gave Ahaz to confirm the promise he had made to him that Syria and Israel (Ephraim) should not prevail against Judah and "set up [a] king in the midst of it" (Is 7:6). In other words, "Behold, the virgin shall conceive" (Is 7:14) meant that God would secure the royal line of Judah. This promise was not forgotten, for here is that virgin[119] of whom Isaiah spoke. In passing, it may be noted that the Hebrew word for virgin,[120] as translated by the Septuagint into Greek and used by Matthew, is sufficient evidence for understanding the term used by Isaiah as a virgin in the strictest sense. " 'And they shall call His name Immanuel' (which means, God with us)." In this child, God is to be with us in His loving kindness and grace.

Joseph hesitated no more. He understood and believed. He rose from his sleep and did as the angel had commanded him. This is indeed a characteristic of the silent saint, of whom in all the Scriptures not a word or phrase is recorded. Silently he performed his duty. And the highest duty toward Mary and the unborn Jesus demanded immediate marriage,[121] which would afford not only outward, but also moral protection to both.[122] So he "took his wife, but knew her not until[123] she had given birth to a son. And he called His name Jesus." Thus, Joseph showed his faith. He married her to legitimize the child, the Messiah, whose advent was now at hand.

48
The Virgin Birth
Mt 1:22–23

49
"He Called His Name Jesus"
Mt 1:24–25

4

The Birth and Childhood of Jesus

Between late 3 BC/early 2 BC and
Nisan (March/April), AD 10

From Jerusalem to the Judean hill country, to Nazareth, to Rome! It is remarkable how the course of ancient history is wrapped up in the destiny of Rome. Rome rises as Israel and other nations fall. The rising of the mighty power on the banks of the Tiber was sensed in the Eastern world, as evidenced by an ancient legend[1] that makes the founding of Rome an instrument of divine wrath. After the marriage of Solomon to the daughter of Pharaoh (1 Ki 3:1), the angel Gabriel—according to the legend—descended into the sea and fixed a reed in it, around which a mud bank gathered and on which a forest sprang up. On this site imperial Rome was built. The meaning of this legend is that, when Israel began to fall away from God, the punishment was prepared that culminated in the dominion of Rome. This agrees with history. But Rome was not only the instrument of wrath with respect to Israel; it was also in a way an ally to the coming Christ.[2] The periodic and universal enrollments inaugurated by Caesar Augustus, by the governance of God, ushered in the birth of Christ.

Julius Caesar had put an end to the Roman republic and made himself master of Rome. But it was Augustus who became the real founder of the empire. His dominion embraced the *orbis terrarum*, practically the whole of the Western world. It was in his interest to know both the strength and the weakness of the vast empire that he had consolidated. Likewise, he wanted to know the strength of potential rebels and the dangers to the *pax Romana* that might be lurking in certain quarters. Thus, he inaugurated the system of periodic universal enrollments by issuing the decree that "all the world should be registered"; that is, enrolled.[3] The ancient historical writers do not directly mention a general imperial census.[4] However, it has

1
Rome

2
The Decree of Caesar Augustus
Lk 2:1–2

/ 63

now been established that Caesar Augustus laid down the principle of systematic, periodic enrollments, to take place every fourteen years. These enrollments lasted for over two hundred and fifty years. This first general enrollment likely took place in late 3 BC or early 2 BC.[5]

3
Herod

The will of Augustus was supreme in Judea when he willed it. Yet the dominion of Herod enjoyed official Roman recognition, and it was in the interest of Rome to retain the good will and services of Herod to preserve order on the land bridge between Africa, Asia, and Europe. It was also Herod's policy to retain the good will of the Romans at all costs. It would certainly not be in keeping with his character to accept what would seem to him a degrading Roman imperial measure without some form of protest. For was he not a "fellow king" (*rex socius*)[6] and Augustus his friend? The prime requirement of his government was to maintain order and peace. If he had endeavored to force upon his people anything Roman, insurrection would have been almost certain to follow, as it did come in AD 6, in "the days of the census" (Ac 5:37). Ever since the days of David's folly, when he said to Joab, "Go, number Israel and Judah" (2Sm 24:1), his people were opposed to the numbering of persons.[7] Therefore, if a census was to be taken, it would have to be given a different name. Jewish concerns had to be taken into account. And besides, there were internal difficulties in the last years of Herod's reign. Ordinarily, a census would presuppose a period of domestic peace. However, Herod was involved in a war with his Arabian neighbor. Sylleus, the Arabian minister, who was in Rome, obtained the ear and confidence of Augustus and made him believe that Herod had made war upon his people on his own account, without Roman permission. This roused the ire of Augustus, and he wrote to Herod that, whereas he had treated him until now as a friend, he would henceforth treat him as a subject.[8] Therefore, when the decree of Augustus reached Jerusalem via Antioch,[9] we can well imagine Herod to have been in a plight. He had to deal with a census, the war with the Arabians, disgrace before Augustus, and the prejudices of his Jewish subjects. He could say with perfect truth that the census would endanger the peace. Furthermore, according to Josephus, his case was a good and strong one, and Sylleus was a slanderer.[10] An embassy was sent to Rome, but it was not even given an audience and returned without having accomplished anything. After some time, a second embassy was sent, headed by Nicolaus of Damascus, which in all probability was commissioned not to suggest exemption from enrollment, but to promise unconditional obedience in the matter. This embassy was successful. Sylleus was condemned, and Augustus was reconciled to Herod. Augustus had even resolved to bestow the government of Arabia upon his reconciled friend. But upon second thought, this resolution was not carried out, the determining factor being Herod's age and his abominable relation to his sons.[11] In respect to the census, however, Herod had to obey.

As a concession to Herod's pride and to soothe the ever wakeful jealousy and prejudices of his Jewish subjects, the enrollment was given a tribal character. His subjects were called upon to return to their own ancestral cities for enrollment, as if they were still living in the days of David and Solomon. The marvelous success of Rome in the administration of its provinces was due to its tolerant attitude toward the prejudices of its subject population. Rome humored the Jewish religious prejudices (Jn 18:28–29) with rare exceptions. Augustus did not care what form the enrollment took as long as his orders were obeyed. It may even be said that this form of Roman census in Israel was an advantage to Augustus. Judea had always been a troublesome province to rule. Now, this enrollment by tribes would mark off by a clear line the true Jews—potential rebels—from the loyal mongrel population of Israel. All who claimed to be true Jews were to report at the respective city of their tribe and family. The census of the rest could be taken at their ordinary places of residence. There was thus an obvious advantage in knowing the exact strength of potential rebels.[12]

During the last year of Herod's life, all arrangements were made in Judea for the carrying out of the decree of Augustus that together with the other parts of the world it should be registered. The census decreed that everyone be personally presented to the officer for enumeration. It is likely that the last few weeks[13] of the year were most generally used.[14] "And all went to be registered, each to his own town." Already in Egypt[15] and in other parts of the Roman Empire people had gone by households. In Herod's kingdom, the same thing was to be done, only by tribes, according to the Jewish method. What power in the word of an emperor! What a stir in Israel! What thought must not the term "own town" have aroused in those who were patriotically inclined! And which Jew was not a patriot at heart?

It almost seemed as if Old Testament times had come back. Of course, the proud and high-brow Zadokites (1Ch 29:22) would very likely stay right in Jerusalem.[16] The members of the once proud and now dispossessed Hasmonean house; that is, if there were any left, could safely have a Maccabean family reunion at Modein (1Macc 2:1, 17, 70). And David's descendants would report at Bethlehem, the city of David. Although they constituted some of the renowned people in the land, most of them were now living in humble circumstances. For example, the famous Hillel—the supposed grandfather of Gamaliel (Ac 5:34)[17] and reputed president of the Sanhedrin (30 BC–AD 10)—is said to have claimed descent from the house of David.[18] If this was true, and if this fact was not kept in the background on account of Herodian rule, then it is likely that very distinguished company from Jerusalem made its appearance in Bethlehem. But most of the descendants of David very likely were of modest estate. Years later, in the time of Domitian, the combined wealth of David's heirs as represented by the members of the Lord's family amounted to no

4
The Enrollment
Lk 2:3

5
By Tribes
Lk 2:3

6
David's Descendants
Lk 2:4

more than about eighteen hundred dollars[19] (this not in silver, but as represented by thirty-nine acres of no doubt sandy Israelite soil).[20] They belonged to the poor of the land. There were some obscure members of the family coming from Kochaba,[21] in Iturea, near Damascus.[22] There were others. And there was a carpenter from Nazareth in Galilee, with Mary, his betrothed, who was with child.

7
Bethlehem
Lk 2:4

Bethlehem! Not the Bethlehem of Zebulun (Jsh 19:10, 15), seven miles north-west of Nazareth, but the Bethlehem of Judea (Bethlehem Ephrathah) about six miles south of Jerusalem.[23] Rachel died there (Gn 35:19–20), and a tomb has been erected in her memory just where the road to Bethlehem leaves the main highway to Hebron. Bethlehem is also where the rich farmer Boaz lived (Ru 2:4), who was one of the owners of the cornfields that gave the city its name—the House of Bread. That is where he married Ruth, the lovely Moabite widow who became the ances-tress of David (Ru 4:13–17). From the heights of her new home, 2,350 feet above the sea, through a break in the Eastern hills and across the heavy surface of the Sea of Judgment, she could even then view the mountains of her native land. Southward, the horizon was bounded by the highland wilderness and hill country of Judea, the home of John the Baptist. The main highway passed Bethlehem and wound its way to Hebron. To the north lay the valleys and hills that separated Bethlehem from Jerusalem, just concealing the Holy City. From that direction, leaving the high-way at Rachel's tomb, came the white-bearded priest Samuel with his cruse of oil to anoint David, at that time still a brown-eyed shepherd lad (1Sm 16:11–13). Thus, Bethlehem became the home of kings. But still greater fame was promised it. For in the time of Hezekiah, the prophet Micah pointed out that Bethlehem should become the birthplace of the Christ (Jn 7:42).[24] "But you, O Bethlehem Ephrathah, who are too little to be among the clans of Judah, from you shall come forth for Me one who is to be ruler in Israel" (Mi 5:2). And this promise was not discarded, for after the captivity, one hundred and twenty-three Bethlehemites returned to reoc-cupy the ancestral site (Ezr 2:21).

8
The Birth of Christ
Lk 2:4–7

It was very likely on a wintry day, not improbably December 25,[25] that Joseph and Mary[26] arrived in Bethlehem as a result of the decree of Caesar Augustus. And it happened that with their arrival the days were accomplished for Mary to be deliv-ered. Now, the first concern for Joseph was to find shelter and rest. But the little town of Bethlehem was crowded with many other sons and daughters of David who had come from different quarters of Herod's kingdom to register their names. Joseph and Mary were poor[27] and otherwise unable, by virtue of mere prominence, to secure desirable accommodation. The inn was filled, and the only available space was a sheltered place, where the cattle were stabled.[28] "And she gave birth to her firstborn[29] son and wrapped Him in swaddling cloths and laid Him in a manger, because there was no place for them in the inn." Simple language records the most important birth in human history. For the moment, the birth is unnoticed and unheralded, like other momentous occasions in history. Yet all the previous history of Rome and Israel gathers about this manger. Caesar Augustus, though ruler of the whole civilized world, unconsciously brought this about: the Messiah, the Son of God, but also the son of David, born of the Virgin Mary, was born in a "stable" at Bethlehem, though His mother's home was Nazareth.

The world was still unaware of the birth of the Messiah, but the Lord was not. There were shepherds near Bethlehem, watching their flock that night. This does not disagree with the tradition that Christ was born in December, because due to frequent dry spells between December and February in Judea, it was possible to keep sheep in the open.[30] It is also possible that the flocks were temple herds, destined for temple sacrifices, which, according to rabbinical references, lay out all the year round.[31] While the shepherds were thus camping in the open, watching their herd, "Heaven and earth seemed to mingle, as suddenly an Angel stood before their dazzled eyes."[32] Awe came upon them as supernatural light flooded the darkness, and they were filled with fear. But their fears were soon "hushed" when the angel began the first Christmas sermon with the words: "Fear not, for behold, I bring you good news of great joy that will be for all the people." The words that he then spoke were nothing less than the message that the long-promised Messiah and Savior of all nations had just been born in the city of David and that they might go and see Him and recognize Him by the humble circumstances attending His birth that the messenger of God had mentioned (Lk 2:12).

9
The Shepherds
Lk 2:8–12

It seems as if the celestial choir could hardly await the last words of this message; for suddenly there was with the announcing angel a multitude of the heavenly host, praising God and saying: "Glory to God in the highest, and on earth peace among those with whom He is pleased!"[33] In Isaiah's "rapt vision, heaven's high temple had opened,"[34] seraphim appeared and were heard crying one to another: "Holy, holy, holy is the LORD of hosts; the whole earth is full of His glory" (Is 6:3). Never before had, and never afterward did, the entire multitude of heavenly hosts become audible and visible to man.

10
The Gloria in
Excelsis
Lk 2:13–14

When the hymn was ended and the strains of the heavenly music had faded away, darkness returned, and the shepherds were left alone. But they remembered the message and welcomed the sign by which they could find the newborn Savior— the babe was wrapped in swaddling cloths and lying in a manger. Overcome with emotion, they said one to another: "Let us[35] go over to Bethlehem and see this thing that has happened, which the Lord has made known to us." Quickly climbing the terraced heights, they soon found the holy group: the virgin mother, Joseph, and the child lying in a manger. It all corresponded to the angelic announcement. What else happened we do not know. At least, they told what brought them there and

11
Adoration of the
Shepherds
Lk 2:15–20

what they had seen and heard. And they published it all around—in Bethlehem, in the field, probably also in nearby Jerusalem and in the temple, to which they might bring their flocks. All who heard wondered at the things that the shepherds told them. It seemed so sudden, so strange. But what these humble men told was the glad tidings that every Jewish ear tingled to hear and every tongue was eager to repeat. If only no deception was practiced upon them! But Joseph knew. And Mary knew. And she "treasured up all these things, pondering them in her heart."

12
The Circumcision and the Name Jesus
Lk 2:21

Eight days pass, and the day of circumcision has arrived. Nothing is said about a celebration, nor does this surprise us, in spite of the fact that a lowly born, yet royal son of David is "born under the law" (Gal 4:4). He received a share in the ancient covenant that God made with Abraham (Gn 17:4–14; Lv 12:3). Considering the divine origin and mission of this child, it may be mentioned that the rite in this case also implied voluntary submission to the will of the Father and the first shedding of blood "to redeem those who were under the law" (Gal 4:5). In connection with His circumcision, as was the custom, the child for the first time publicly received the name that Gabriel by divine command had revealed to both Joseph and Mary.[36] Ordinarily, there would have been nothing significant in giving a child this name. Jesus, meaning "Yahweh is Salvation," was a name quite common among the Jews. It had been the name of Joshua,[37] who led the children of Israel into the Promised Land. Another great leader by this name was the high priest Joshua, or Jeshua (Ezr 2:2; 3:2; Zec 3:1), who with Zerubbabel brought a band of former captives from Babylon to Jerusalem. In the intertestamental period, Jesus son of Sirach was a famous teacher. And in the New Testament we find one "Jesus who is called Justus" (Col 4:11). In Josephus, no fewer than twelve persons of the same name are mentioned besides those mentioned in Scripture. But here the name acquired a significance infinitely more sacred as the human name of the Son of God.[38] The Hebrew *Messiah* and the Greek *Christ* were titles that represented His office as anointed Prophet, Priest, and King. But *Jesus of Nazareth* was the personal name, which He bore when He "emptied Himself" of His glory (Php 2:7) and became the world-redeeming Son of Man. "There is salvation in no one else, for there is no other name under heaven given among men by which we must be saved" (Ac 4:12).

13
The Presentation in the Temple
Lk 2:22–24

Two other legal ordinances still remained to be observed, one affecting the child and the other the mother. The first was to "present" the infant Jesus to the Lord. Originally all the healthy, firstborn sons of Israel were the special property of the Lord (Ex 13:2) and destined to do sacred service at the tabernacle. But after the separation of the Levites (Nu 3:45; 8:14) for this particular duty, the firstborn among the other tribes were exempted. However, it was still necessary to present them to the Lord and to redeem them from this obligation with five shekels of silver (Nu 3:47; 18:16).[39] This ransom could be paid to any priest; personal appearance in the

temple was therefore not necessary. But it was otherwise with another legal ordinance, the purification of the mother (Lv 12:4, 6–7). After a number of weeks of
seclusion,[40] she was to offer a gift of thanksgiving. In the case of a male child, forty
days had to elapse. The payment was prescribed: a lamb of the first year for a burnt
offering and a young pigeon or turtledove for a sin offering. But if the parents were
poor, a pair of young pigeons or turtledoves would suffice, one for the burnt offering and the other for the sin offering (Lv 12:6, 8). Therefore, in obedience to divine
command and, as we take it, in the beginning of February, 2 BC,[41] we find Joseph
and Mary with the holy child on their way to Jerusalem for a twofold purpose. The
Lord of the temple went up to the temple of the Lord.[42] But of this there was no
external or material evidence. Although there was no discount in the redemption
money, Joseph and Mary made the offering of the poor. We have no further details
of the presentation and purification, except that this visit to the temple resulted in
a double recognition of the infant Savior.

There was living in Jerusalem at that time Simeon, an aged and devout Israelite,
of whom we have little—except legendary—knowledge. The little that Scripture
does say of him combines all the chief characteristics of Old Testament piety. He
was just in his relation to man, pious in his devotion to God, and, above all, "waiting for the consolation of Israel."[43] The Holy Spirit was upon him, and an answer to
his greatest longing had been communicated to him; namely, "It had been revealed
to him by the Holy Spirit that he would not see death before he had seen the Lord's
Christ."[44] We do not know the details. But tradition, interestingly enough, tells
us that while Simeon read the Scripture, he stumbled at the words: "Behold, the
virgin shall conceive and bear a son" (Is 7:14). There was doubt in his heart. And
then the revelation was made that he would not die before taking that virgin's son
into his arms.[45] Whatever historical basis there may be for this tale, the fact is that
God fulfilled His Word. By some inspired impulse, Simeon entered the temple just
when the "parents"[46] of Jesus brought in the child to do for Him what the Law commanded. Simeon immediately recognized the child, took Him into his arms, and
burst into that glorious and inspired swan's song, "Lord, now You are letting Your
servant depart in peace" (the Nunc Dimittis), which for twenty centuries has been
so dear to Christian hearts.

14
Simeon
Lk 2:25–32

After Simeon had seen the infant Messiah, he was content to be released from
service and to depart in peace. His eyes had actually seen the Salvation, so long prepared for a weary world. He was the first prophet who could say that Christ *had*
come.[47] It was an old man's happy Christmas. His eyes had seen the true Christmas
light in its manifestation to all. Not only a beam to shed the light of salvation upon
God's chosen people and to reflect glory upon the Jewish nation (Jn 4:22), but a
"light for the nations" (Is 42:6; 49:6). Except in its direct application, like in the

15
The Nunc Dimittis
Lk 2:29–35

Magnificat and the Benedictus, there was really nothing new in the Nunc Dimittis. It rested altogether on the Old Testament messianic promises, correctly understood. Moreover, it was in accordance with the angelic revelations made to Zechariah and the Virgin Mary. But its unexpected pronouncement in the sacred place, not by a priest, but by a devout Israelite, filled the hearts of Joseph and Mary with wonderment and silent awe. After blessing them and probably returning the child to His mother's waiting arms, Simeon addressed himself in particular to the Virgin. The Holy Spirit illumined him to recognize her marvelous relation to the child. The blessing of privileged parenthood to this child was undoubtedly great, but not unmixed with pain and sorrow. For this child was to be a "rock of stumbling" (Is 8:14) to all who would crash against Him. But He was also a solid rock of salvation (Ps 89:26) to all who would cling to Him in faith. "This child is appointed for the fall and rising of many in Israel, and for a sign that is opposed." The sword of deep personal sorrow would pierce the mother's heart. She would see the true inner nature of those who opposed the promised bringer of salvation. The hatred of His enemies would culminate in His crucifixion. Such, as regards Israel, was the history of Jesus, from His flight into Egypt until His death on the cross. And such, as regards natural man, has always been the history of the Gospel, which to them that perish is foolishness and a stumbling block, but to those who believe in Him, a power of God for salvation (Rm 1:16; 1Co 1:18, 23, 24).

16
The Prophetess Anna
Lk 2:36–38

And now another charming bit of the Old Testament projected into the New. There lived at this time in Jerusalem a pious and aged widow of whom just enough is known to make us anxious for more. She was a descendant of the "happy" tribe of Asher (Gn 30:13), which occupied a region toward the Phoenician seacoast and dipped its foot into the rich Galilean oil (Dt 33:24). Curiously enough, the tribe of Asher, "the favorite of his brothers" (Dt 33:24), "alone is celebrated in tradition for the beauty of its women, and their fitness to be wedded to High-Priest or King."[48] Much of the tribe vanished because it belonged to the ten tribes that did not return from captivity. However, we know from 2 Chronicles 30:1–12 that some members of the tribe celebrated the Passover with Hezekiah at Jerusalem. This took place in 715 BC after the Assyrians conquered the northern kingdom of Israel. So some remnant of the tribe of Asher bound its future with the Judeans. And the fact that Anna, the daughter of Phanuel, could still trace her ancestry back to this tribe is valuable proof for the carefully preserved genealogical traditions in the time of Christ[49] and seems to imply that hers was a family of distinction.[50] Ancient Asher sat still at the haven of the sea and "stay[ed] by his landings" (Jgs 5:17). The tribe produced no prophet, raised no hero, and gave no deliverer to the nation. Still, as a belated contribution in the time of Christ, it produced a prophetess to proclaim the advent of the Messiah to all those "who were waiting for the redemption of Jerusalem." Anna had a brief wedded life of seven years. From that time until she was eighty-four years old,[51] "she did not depart from the temple"[52] and devoted herself to praying and fasting night and day. The near extinction of her own tribe, the political state of the land of Israel, Herod, the conditions of the Holy City, the Hellenizing Sadducees, the externalizing Pharisees—these all kindled in her widowed heart, as well as in those who were like-minded, an earnest longing for the promised redemption. And now, the Messiah *was* come. Being a prophetess, Anna recognized Him. She joined Simeon in giving thanks to the Lord and in proclaiming to Jerusalem the advent of her Messiah and her King.

Shortly after the events just related, Jerusalem was to experience a remarkable confirmation of the shepherds' startling tale. Star-guided Magi came with the question: "Where is He who has been born king of the Jews?" We might as well admit at the outset that we do not know just who the Magi were and where they came from. Even their designation is obscured with ambiguity. Originally, the Magi seem to have been members of a priestly order, the Levites, as it were, of the Median tribes in Chaldea.[53] If the Magi and Chaldeans are practically the same, then Daniel was one of their presidents in the time of Nebuchadnezzar.[54] They were the learned men and scientists of their day, who devoted themselves to the study of nature, medicine, mathematics, physics, astronomy, and the like. These studies, however, were not always untinged with superstition. The name Magi, at first a title of honor, gradually lost its better meaning. Among the Greeks and Romans, it practically became the general designation of all who made pretensions to supernatural knowledge: magicians, interpreters of dreams, astrologers, necromancers, soothsayers, sorcerers, conjurers, false prophets, and all dealers in the black arts. In this lower sense, we find the term applied to the Magus or Magian (the sorcerer) who opposed Paul on the island of Cyprus (Ac 13:6, 8). However, as to the Wise Men who sought Christ, we do not consider them astrologers, soothsayers, skillful dissemblers, medicine men, or the like, nor do we hold that a delusion was used by providence to guide them to the Light. That would be ascribing to a pseudo-science a reality that it does not possess. At any rate, they were upright men, honorable in their vocation, and showed their wisdom in seeking Christ.

We know neither their number nor the country whence they came: Arabia, Persia, Parthia, Babylonia, or even Egypt, all of which countries have been suggested.[55] The expression "from the east,"[56] as viewed from Israel, is indefinite. They might have come from any of these countries and still have been Eastern Magi. But from the form of their question: "Where is He who has been born king of the *Jews*?" we can safely suppose that they were not Jewish. They were the firstfruits among the Gentiles rather than Jews living in the Diaspora. It is quite baseless to regard them as kings,[57] although this view was held already in ancient times.[58] As regards

17
The Magi
Mt 2:1–2

18
Legendary
Embellishments
Mt 2:1–2

their number, there is a double tradition. Some of the Fathers[59] held that there were twelve. But the common belief, arising probably from their three gifts, is that there were three.[60] The Venerable Bede has even supplied them with names, family, and nationality, as it were, and given us a description of their personal appearance. There was old Melchior of Asia, a descendant of Shem, a patriarch with a long white beard. Caspar was a dark-skinned youth of Africa, a strong and passionate son of Ham. The European son of Japheth, Balthasar, was swarthy and in the prime of life. The skulls of these three worthy representatives of the three sons of Noah and of the three periods of life, each encircled with a crown of jeweled gold (kings, if you will), are exhibited among the relics in the Cologne Cathedral.[61] Although the fictions regarding these men are valueless for historical purposes, they are nevertheless interesting due to their influence on splendid productions of religious art.

19
Messianic Expectations
Mt 2:1–2

And now, let us return to the story. What brought these Magi to Jerusalem? "Where is He who has been born king of the Jews? For we saw His star when it rose." It is commonly supposed that general messianic expectations pervaded the entire East at this time to the effect that a king should arise in Judea and gain dominion over the world.[62] But there is no historic evidence of such widespread messianic hope. There are references in the Roman writers, most likely derived from Josephus and referred by him to the Flavian dynasty seventy years *after* the advent of Christ, which might be indirect proof that there were messianic expectations. But they are not evidence of the Gentile's hopes. The Fourth Eclogue of Virgil, regarded as the "unconscious prophecies of heathendom,"[63] may be based on the Sibylline Oracles that were of Jewish authorship, dating probably from 160 BC.[64] If a diffuse knowledge of the messianic hope existed,[65] Jewish sources likely provided it, and Jewish misinterpretation probably also corrupted it. Others commonly assume that people in the Eastern world expected a Messiah. According to this view, the Magi, as learned men and zealous partisans of the East against the West, *knew* of this expectation. And in particular, as astrologers, when they saw a rare planetary conjunction in the supposed Jewish sign of the fish, they immediately interpreted it as indicating the advent of the promised Jewish deliverer and king. But even outside of the political considerations and misinterpreted messianic expectations, there is no satisfactory proof that at the time of the Lord's birth Judea was astrologically designated by the sign of the fish.[66] The whole theory rests upon an altogether arbitrary and untenable supposition.

20
Balaam's Prediction
Mt 2:1–2

However, admitting for the present that the Jews connected the advent of Christ with the appearance of a star—for which we have no historical proof till *after* the birth of Christ[67]—there still remain some difficulties in connecting the narrative of the Magi with Balaam's prediction: "A star shall come out of Jacob, and a scepter shall rise out of Israel" (Nu 24:17).[68] This is not a prediction of a literal star, but a promise of the King.[69] The Star, the Scepter, and the King are one.[70] Magi could hardly understand the predicted star in this peculiar sense, except through a "decided astrological tendency."[71] If Matthew regarded Balaam's prophecy as actually referring to a star, and the star of the Magi was a fulfillment of Old Testament prophecy, Matthew certainly would not, according to his well-known custom,[72] fail to express it. At any rate, even if this promise of Balaam was remembered and understood as actually indicating a star, this prophecy alone, without other revelation, would hardly have been sufficient to set the Wise Men on their way.

Astronomically, a most remarkable conjunction of planets *did* take place in the constellation of Pisces, which occurs only once in about eight hundred years.[73] Jupiter and Saturn first appeared together, with Mars added later, in c. 7 BC. But a conjunction of planets does not fit the case. At the outset, there is no scriptural evidence that a planetary configuration can be drawn upon to indicate or foretell *anything*, much less the birth of Christ. To accept it would be to encourage astrological superstition. And it does not help us to suppose that in this instance delusion providentially ended in truth.[74] According to Jewish tradition, knowledge is not found with astrologers, and he that learned even one thing from a Magus deserved death.[75] The Scriptures are plain in their denouncement of astrologers, star gazers, and of those who use divination (Dt 18:9–12; Is 47:12–14). Moreover, there were other conjunctions before and after, and even a closer conjunction fifty-nine years before the birth of Christ, which did *not* lead an investigating committee to Jerusalem. And finally, the planets never approached closer to each other than twice the apparent diameter of the moon, so that they could not have appeared as one star. It has been suggested[76] that the observing Magi had weak eyes! But even if the planets stood as one bright light in the southern sky over Bethlehem as the Wise Men left Jerusalem, they would not a few hours later, when the Magi arrived in the city of David, be resting "over the place where the child was" (Mt 2:9).

Neither can it have been a fixed star, because the degree of light of these heavenly bodies is constant, and their apparent movement with respect to one another is regular.[77] Nor can it have been a new star.[78] For no previous knowledge of it existed, so it could not have any astrological value. The same applies to comets.[79] Though popularly considered portents, they cannot astrologically indicate events.[80] We cannot make satisfactory explanation based on the supposition that the Magi were astrologers.

These theories may be fascinating. Yet it seems necessary to admit the occurrence of a miracle.[81] Nothing is gained by way of a natural explanation in the attempt to defend the evangelist or to fix the date of the Savior's birth. It is evident, however, that the whole story of the visit of the Magi places the nativity not long before the slaughter of the infants and before the death of Herod.

21 Planetary Conjunctions

22 New Stars and Comets

23 A Miracle

24
"Where Is He Who
Has Been Born King
of the Jews?"
Mt 2:2

Whatever the physical nature of the star of the Magi—whether it was one of the known or unknown heavenly bodies, whether previously existing, still existing, or not, or whether it was only a star-like supernatural light[82] that moved in the earthly atmosphere[83]—its purpose was evidently to serve as a sign and as a guide. One verse more, and the evangelist could have explained all. But he does not provide that verse. And therefore, accepting the miraculous and without attempting further explanation, we hold that the Magi saw a star in their Eastern native land. For some undisclosed reason of divine providence, they had both a revelation[84] and an astral phenomenon, a sign, which betokened the birth of the Jewish Messiah King.[85] It led them to make the inquiry: "Where is He who has been born king of the Jews?"

25
The Effect of the
Inquiry upon
Jerusalem
Mt 2:2–3

The Magi are called "Wise Men," and they showed their wisdom by seeking Christ.[86] Concerning the *fact* and the *time*[87] of the Savior's birth, there is no question; "for we saw His star when it rose and have come to worship Him." They only asked about the *place* of His birth.[88] They inquired in Jerusalem, not because they imagined that He must be born in the Jewish capital, but because they naturally expected to find there additional necessary and authentic information. But to ask this question in Herodian Jerusalem was like setting fire to dry thorns. For were not Herod's lifelong plans, intrigues, efforts, yes, many murders, wound up in the one aim to make himself and no one else king of the Jews?[89] And had he not practically succeeded? Of course, there was Rome, his late disfavor with Augustus, the enrollment, and the ideal of complete independence. Still, he was quite satisfied with existing arrangements. And there was another matter. There was the question of *birth*, a very difficult matter for a born Edomite to improve. Eusebius wrote that Herod ordered all family records to be committed to the flames, since the foolish Israelite scruple about accurate genealogical records contributed nothing to his advantage.[90] He also encouraged the circulation of a flattering legend that credited him with descent from a noble Babylonian *Jew*.[91] But the consciousness of his ignoble origin must have secretly goaded him. He must have felt guilty as a pretender to the Jewish throne. Therefore, when he heard of these tidings, the dread of possibilities must have crept over his frame.[92] "He was troubled, and all Jerusalem with him." He had reigned long and with a heavy hand for thirty-seven years, and he liked it. He did not want himself nor his family to lose this power. The inhabitants of Jerusalem, on the other hand, had other reasons to be seized with fear. Those secretly opposed to the Idumean rule knew only too well the character of Herod and the consequences to anyone who might, justly or unjustly, be suspected of sympathy with, and support of, any claimant to the royal throne. Still, the Sadducean nobles favored Herod because they had similar interests; therefore, they were satisfied to have things remain as they were.[93]

Herod was resourceful and took measures he considered necessary to protect his throne. Whatever posterity may say of him, it cannot deny his uncanny ability and craftiness. He called together the high priests, past and present, the chairmen of the various priestly orders, and the scribes—that is, the learned rabbis.[94] Without committing himself, he put before them a theological problem: *Where* is Christ to be born? The answer was easy: According to prophecy (Mi 5:2),[95] He was to be born in the Judean Bethlehem (not the Bethlehem of Zebulun). Then Herod called the Wise Men privately, and without revealing his real intentions to them, he questioned them about the precise time when the astral phenomenon had first attracted their attention. From his subsequent course of action, it seems that their answer was: more than one year before their arrival at Jerusalem.[96] Then he directed them to Bethlehem, at the same time giving them instructions to report to him again, so that he also might "come and worship" the newborn King. Here we have a picture of Herod as he was during his entire reign.

As the Wise Men left Jerusalem,[97] they looked up to the heavens.[98] To their surprise and joy, the star that had attracted their attention in the East and which, it seems, had disappeared for a while, appeared again. It moved from north to south, a most unusual course for a star,[99] and led them directly to the house[100] where the young child was. No details of the first meeting and greeting are given, except that they fell down and worshiped Him. At last, they had found the object of their quest. And then, they opened their treasures and presented their gifts: gold, frankincense, and myrrh. These gifts, except probably the gold as a tender aid to a poverty-stricken King,[101] seem strangely inappropriate. They were evidently intended as specimens of the product of their country. But the Christian Church has from ancient times seen in these gifts a special significance: "gold as to a king, incense as to God, myrrh as to one destined to die";[102] or gold for Shem, myrrh for Ham, and incense for Japheth;[103] or gold for faith, myrrh for repentance, and incense for prayer.

Danger threatened the child. The Magi, however, were not to be the innocent instruments of Herod's murderous designs.[104] Warned by God in a dream, they did not return for their report to Herod, but departed into their own country another way. And Joseph also had a dream. God directed him to flee from Herod's dominion into nearby Egypt, the home of many Jews since the days of Alexander the Great. Although at one time Egypt had been the house of bondage, still in Israel's history it had at many times served as a place of sheltering refuge. The reason given by the angel why Joseph should take the Christ Child to Egypt was: "For Herod is about to search for the child, to destroy Him." Thus, early on, the cross was placed beside the cradle of David's royal Son.[105] Scripture gives us few particulars about the flight into Egypt and its duration, which cannot have been long. It was a hasty departure by night. According to instruction, this exile was to last until after the death of

26
"Bethlehem, in the Land of Judah"
Mt 2:4–8

27
The Adoration of the Magi
Mt 2:9–11

28
Flight into Egypt
Mt 2:12–15

Herod. We are not concerned with the apocryphal legends,[106] immortalized by the genius of Italian art. The evangelist,[107] alluding only to the causes of the flight and the return, sees in it all a deeper significance, calling it the fulfillment of the words of Hosea: "Out of Egypt I called My Son" (11:1).[108]

29
The Massacre of the
Innocents
Mt 2:16–18

When Herod saw that he was duped,[109] from his point of view, his jealous fury against a possible future rival knew no bounds. For once, his cunning had failed. Maddened with anger, he resolved upon even more cruel and fierce measures than he had at first intended—to kill all male inhabitants of Bethlehem of a certain age in order to exterminate the supposed claimant to his throne. Incredible? Anything is credible of the man who murdered his own wife and killed his sons. He sent forth and slew all the male children of Bethlehem and its environs, "two years old or under, according to the time that he had ascertained from the wise men." He may have made his net wide. He may have kept the time learned from the Magi and added a liberal margin. This dreadful butchery of helpless innocent little children was wholesale murder, almost unparalleled in the annals of history.[110] Of their number we know nothing. Very likely, there were only twenty or twenty-four, considering the probable population of Bethlehem.[111] But the deed was still more than savagely atrocious. We do not know how the decree was carried out. The most terrible deeds of tyrants such as Herod are sometimes hushed into oblivion.[112] According to a vision of the prophet Jeremiah, the sympathizing tears of a typical mother of all Israel were shed for these infants. Rachel, Jacob's beloved wife, had died in the pains of childbirth and was buried on the way to Bethlehem (Gn 35:19). Her tears had already flowed at Ramah when the exiles were led into captivity in Babylon (Jer 40:1). They again flowed: "Rachel is weeping for her children; she refuses to be comforted for her children, because they are no more" (Jer 31:15). A sad tragedy, this merciless massacre of the innocents, but also an honor, since the Church has rightly regarded them as the protomartyrs,[113] or the first witnesses of Christ.[114]

30
The Plotting
of Antipater

The exile of the Holy Family in Egypt was probably of brief duration because the cup of Herod's misdeeds was full. After gaining the Jewish throne, one thought still haunted the whole later part of his life: the dread of a possible rival. This fear had the habit of making its appearance in the midst of his most intimate surroundings. He nominated his eldest son, Antipater, as the successor to the throne, and he became all-powerful at court. But it seems that Antipater overshot his mark.[115] Not satisfied with clearing his own way to the throne by instigating the murder of his half brothers Alexander and Aristobulus, he grew impatient because of the long reign of his father. He complained that he was growing old himself, and when the kingdom would come to him, it would afford him no pleasure.[116] Indeed, it seems that he contrived to hasten Herod's end in connection with the mysterious poisoning of Pheroras, Herod's brother. Herod heard about it. He was told that the potion supplied by Antipater—now in Rome—and administered to his brother was actually intended for Herod himself. Under all sorts of pretenses, Antipater was recalled for the purpose of being put on trial at home. Immediately upon his return, unsuspecting Antipater was arrested and tried before Varus, the governor of Syria. He was convicted, and a report of the matter was made to Emperor Augustus.[117]

But there was something else that made the future look very gloomy for Herod. A most loathsome and dreadful disease, phthiriasis,[118] had fastened itself on his body. In plain words, it was an excessive multiplication of lice and worms in his body. Josephus speaks of a slow-burning fire and a worm-producing putrefaction in the bowels and private parts.[119] As soon as the news spread that his disease was incurable, two rabbis stirred up the people to tear down the golden eagles from the temple gates. But they rejoiced too soon. Herod was still strong enough to pass sentences of death and to carry them out. The ringleaders were burned alive. That very night, there was an eclipse of the moon.[120] By the advice of physicians, Herod was carried to the soothing waters of Callirhoe, east of the Jordan; but death was rapidly approaching. The baths were in vain, and the old king was carried to Jericho. He was fully cognizant of the fact that death would soon claim him. But there were still a few things that increased the torments of his putrefying body. When a king dies, there ought to be public mourning. But Herod had reason to believe that only tears of rejoicing would be shed at his grave, and so he decided to provide such mourning as would befit his death. He ordered all the noblest of the land of Israel to assemble in the hippodrome at Jericho. When they were all seated there, he shut them up and gave orders to his sister Salome to kill them all at the first news of his death. Thus, he thought he would provide for himself the honor of a memorable mourning.[121] Another worry on Herod's mind was Antipater, who had made himself guilty of an unpardonable sin. But five days before Herod's death, some joyful news momentarily lightened his terrible pains: the permission from Rome to act as father or king—to banish his son or to put him to death, as he pleased.[122] When he heard this, he felt somewhat better. But when the pains suddenly returned, he forgot his thoughts of revenge and wanted to turn a knife against himself. Woeful lamentation echoed through the palace and reached the ears of fettered Antipater, who thought that his father was already dead. Antipater already pictured himself as ascending the throne. But he rejoiced too soon, of which Herod was informed. In a fresh outburst of rage, he ordered that his son be killed without delay and ignobly buried.[123]

Five days later, the terror of Judea himself expired.[124] According to Josephus, it was thirty-seven years after his appointment as king of Judea and thirty-four years after his conquest of Jerusalem and the execution of Antigonus, the last of the Maccabean rulers.[125] Salome did not carry out Herod's instructions with regard to

31
Herod's Disease

32
The Death of Herod

his provision for a memorable national mourning.[126] The date of Herod's death and the release of the imprisoned Jewish nobles from the hippodrome was remembered by the Jews as a day of national rejoicing. Henceforth, it was a day on which fasting and mourning were not allowed.[127] The royal corpse, with a crown on his head and a scepter in his hand, was placed on a splendid bier, covered with purple. Thracian, German, and Galatian guards carried it to its resting place in the Herodium,[128] a fortress that Herod had built not far from the place where Christ was born. This concludes the story of a highly successful villain, a private man who became a king, and, though encompassed by ten thousand dangers, escaped them all and continued in power to a ripe old age. According to the provisions of Herod's thrice-altered will, Archelaus was to receive Judea, Idumea, Samaria, and the crown; Antipas, the Herod of the Gospels, was appointed tetrarch of Galilee and Philip tetrarch of the territories east of the Jordan.[129] Even in death, the sly old fox showed his cunning, as seen from another provision of his will. For he bequeathed ten million silver coins[130] to his friend Caesar Augustus and exceedingly fine and costly garments to Her Imperial Highness Julia, the empress (better known as Livia). It need therefore scarcely be said that the will was confirmed and that, for the present at least, his rule passed on to his descendants.[131] However, less than a century later, the whole race of Herod was swept away.

33
Return to Nazareth
Mt 2:19–23; Lk 2:39

It must have been after the death and burial of Herod and before the tidings of the actual accession of the cruel and suspicious Archelaus reached Joseph in Egypt that the Holy Family returned[132] to the beloved "land of Israel" (*Erets Israel*). An angel of the Lord appeared to Joseph in a dream, saying: "Rise, take the child and His mother and go to the land of Israel,[133] for those who sought the child's life are dead." But to whom does "those" refer? Certainly, Herod and perhaps others of his household or court (e.g., the lately executed Antipater). We do not know. Perhaps the plural form[134] is used in studious avoidance of Herod's dreaded name.[135] Or it could express a general idea, although only a single person is meant.[136] It seems that Joseph at first intended to return to Bethlehem, the home of his fathers and now made memorable by the birth of Jesus. As a carpenter, his trade would have easily supplied the modest needs of his household there. But when, on reaching Israel, he heard that the mean and contemptible[137] Archelaus reigned,[138] he did not know what to do. However, divine counsel, given in a dream, directed him to turn toward Galilee,[139] and he again made Nazareth in Galilee his home. It is true, another son of Herod ruled in Galilee, the equally unscrupulous and immoral Antipas. But since he was at the same time more good-natured and indifferent, the life of the Holy Family under his dominion was secure, especially in consideration of the storms that were soon to break out in the South. In all this, however, the inspired evangelist sees a prophetic significance. He states that the return of the Christ Child to

Galilee and His living in the lowly and despised Nazareth is a fulfillment of divine prophecy: "He would be called a Nazarene."[140]

Of the childhood of Jesus, we have only the notice from St. Luke that He grew and developed like any other normal child, mentally and physically.[141] Dear to God, He was the unique subject of His paternal care. "The child grew and became strong, filled with wisdom. And the favor of God was upon Him." We can safely ignore the legendary embellishments.[142] The simple statement of St. Luke tells us more than all the pretended omniscience of the apocryphal gospels with their silly legends about the omnipotence and miraculous prowess shown by the infant Jesus. Eleven years pass by in sacred silence; that is, as we reckon it, from 1 BC to the spring of AD 10. However, politically a great change had taken place in the land of Israel. Beyond all doubt, and undisguised, yes, even by request, the scepter had actually departed from Judah. The weak and wicked rule of Archelaus lasted only nine years. Already at the beginning of his reign, shortly after the death of Herod, a Jewish delegation appeared before Augustus protesting against the imperial confirmation of Herod's will and petitioning him to deliver them altogether from a royal form of government and to add Judea to the province of Syria.[143] This was a most remarkable request and a significant commentary on that much earlier request, made to Samuel in Old Testament times: "Now appoint for us a king to judge us like all the nations" (1Sm 8:5). But at the time, and for reasons of his own,[144] Augustus saw fit to deny the request and to confirm the will of Herod. A few days afterward, he appointed Archelaus, not indeed king of the whole country, but ethnarch of one half of it, with the promise of the royal title if he would deserve it.[145] The delegation returned, and Archelaus—minus the coveted royal title and with a reduced income[146]—entered his ethnarchy. Nine years later, a delegation[147] returned to Augustus on account of Archelaus's rough, tyrannical rule and the scandal caused by his unlawful marriage. This time, the emperor was in a receptive mood. The charges were serious, and Caesar was angered. Thinking it beyond his imperial dignity to write to Archelaus, he sent the Jewish ambassador to Jerusalem to tell his master, Come. Archelaus came. And when he had come, Augustus made short work of him. He took away his government and banished him to Vienne, a city in Gaul. He also took away his money.[148] The portion over which Archelaus had ruled was united to the Roman province of Syria, as had already been desired by a large Jewish party at the time of Herod's death. Caesar appointed P. S. Quirinius, who once before the birth of Christ had been governor of Syria, to a second term of office.[149] The new arrangement of things, although brought about by Jewish request and no doubt entered into with good intentions on both sides, was nevertheless not completed without violent convulsions.

34
Childhood in Nazareth. The Removal of Archelaus
Lk 2:40

35
Reported Census
and Revolt of Judas

As noted earlier, many scholars date the census under Quirinius to 6 or 7 AD.[150] We mention it here because many resources do as well. However, Steinmann argues convincingly that the census happened when Christ was born, when also "Judas the Galilean[151] rose up and drew away some of the people after him" (Ac 5:37). Judas's insurrection was effectually crushed by Coponius, whom Augustus appointed procurator of Judea, endowed with supreme power (the power of life and death), and sent out to accompany Quirinius, the governor of Syria.

36
Silence in Galilee

Although there were often troublous times in Israel, these storms likely did not affect the home of Jesus. The childhood of Jesus probably passed in calm and peace, under the reign of an easy-going, pleasure-seeking, and characterless prince. Antipas entirely lacked his father's ability and strength of will. He seems at least to have inherited the art of winning, and for many years holding, the favors of powerful Rome.[152]

37
Passover

It was in the spring of AD 10, after order had again been restored in Judea, that the silence of the Gospels with regard to the life of Jesus was broken with the account of His visit to the Passover Feast in Jerusalem. According to the strict application of Mosaic Law, God required all the male Israelites to present themselves in the sanctuary for the three chief Jewish feasts: Passover, Pentecost, and Booths (Ex 23:17; Dt 16:16). But it seems that because of the national dispersion this rule could not be strictly observed, especially not by those living at a great distance from Jerusalem. However, if at all possible, every law-abiding Jew would try to make a journey to Jerusalem at least once a year, preferably at Passover, for the purpose of appearing before the Lord. This accounts for the almost incredible number of annual Passover pilgrims.[153] Of the obligation of women to make this journey, there is no mention; but it seems that Mary, being a very pious woman, made this journey annually.[154] Up to a certain age, a Jewish boy was called *katon*, "little." From his thirteenth year,[155] or up to a year earlier, he would be called *gadol*, "big." Henceforth, he would begin to wear the *tefillin*, or phylacteries (Mt 23:5).[156] At this age, his father presented him at the local synagogue and called him a "son of the Law" (*Ben ha Torah*). Now, he was bound to a full observance of the Law, and rabbinical injunction and national custom obliged him to learn a trade.

38
The Journey
to Jerusalem
Lk 2:41–42

It was in accordance with these customs that the parents[157] of our Lord made their annual Passover journey. Joining their friends and neighbors in a company, they took the twelve-year-old Jesus with them. Nazareth is over sixty miles from Jerusalem. We do not know by which road they traveled, but in spite of the evident hostility of the Samaritans, the traditional and more direct (and also safer) route through Shechem might be taken.[158] The profane plumage of the Roman eagles overshadowed the Holy City, but it was still the Jerusalem of which David sang (Ps 48; 122) and for which the exiles yearned (Ps 137). Towering above its walls still glittered the great temple with its gilded roofs and marble colonnades. Who shall fathom the unspeakable emotion with which the boy Jesus, nearing the city, gazed on that memorable and never-to-be-forgotten scene? It may have been His first visit to the Holy City and His first appearance in the halls of the temple. At the time of the Passover Feast,[159] Annas, that wily diplomat, whom the then youthful Jesus would later meet under other circumstances (Jn 18:13), was ruling the temple.[160] Living in Jerusalem at the time was probably also the great Hillel, the eminent jurist—mild, and now white with the snows of nearly one hundred years—whom the Jews reverenced almost as a second Moses. Hillel's rival, the stern Shammai, was also likely there. They were the two founders of opposing Jewish schools.[161]

There is no record of the Passover Feast itself as observed by the Holy Family and a group of Galilean friends. But it would include the selection and slaying of the paschal lamb, the sprinkling of the blood upon the altar, the meal itself, and the Days of Unleavened Bread.[162] We are only told that, when the days were fulfilled and all the legal ordinances had been observed and the vast multitudes were returning to their homes, the child Jesus tarried behind, and His parents[163] did not know it. This was, however, not a case of careless negligence. On account of some circumstance unknown to us, they were confident that the missing boy could be found in the caravan made up of Galilean relatives and friends. A day elapsed before the parents discovered the loss. This probably happened as they arrived at the place that had been designated by the caravan as the evening rendezvous.[164] On the next day— we can well imagine their anguish and concern—they returned to Jerusalem. Yet there was still no trace of Him at the temporary dwelling place or camp where they had made their stay during the days of the feast. Not until the third day did they find Him, strangely enough, in the place where they had least thought of searching for Him: "in the temple, sitting among the teachers, listening to them and asking them questions." This was not in a synagogue that some suppose to have been located in the temple area, but most likely in one of the halls where such popular discourses were held.[165]

We do not know the particular subject of the discourse. On this occasion,[166] Jesus was not taking the part of a teacher. Like a truly developing child, He was humbly seeking to learn. At the same time, His fitting replies gave evidence of His deep interest and His remarkable intelligence. There was no forwardness in His behavior, which would have been entirely foreign to Him "who knew no sin" (2Co 5:21) and contrary to His upbringing.[167] And still, all who heard Him were astonished at His marvelous understanding and wisdom and at His discerning answers. When His parents saw Him in this austere presence and so occupied, they were amazed. The daily contact with this obedient child may have blunted the memory of His wonderful origin.[168] Mary spoke, venturing to address Him in language of tender reproach: "Son, why have You treated us so? Behold, Your father and I have

39
Jesus Missing on the Return Journey
Lk 2:43–46

40
Found in His Father's House
Lk 2:47–49

been searching for You in great distress." To this mild chiding, Jesus replied—His first recorded utterance: "Why were you looking for Me? Did you not know that I must be in My Father's house?" Jesus' noble reply and His earthly parents' confused response revealed how little they had understood Him up to that point. Yet these events all agree with His mission, person, and work. Mary referred Him to His "father"; but in His reply, Jesus reminded them that He was sent to this earth to do the business of His Father in heaven.[169] In the "Did you not?," He delicately recalled to them the fading memory of all they *did* know. And in the "I must," He laid down the law by which He had to walk to the day of His death upon the cross.

41
Return to Nazareth
Lk 2:50–52

"And they did not understand the saying that He spoke to them." Their lack of understanding was mournfully prophetic of what became so manifest throughout His ministry: "He came to His own, and His own people did not receive Him" (Jn 1:11).[170] And yet, though conscious of His divine origin, and though one ray of hidden glory had flashed forth, in dutiful and willing obedience "He went down with them and came to Nazareth and was submissive to them." But Mary remembered. She kept all these sayings in her heart (Lk 2:19, 51).[171] And again the Gospel lets fall the veil upon this youthful life. The child became a youth, and the youth a man. This life, truly human and yet without sin, the evangelist sums up in the words: "And Jesus increased in wisdom and in stature and in favor with God and man."

42
Education

Eighteen years of deep silence followed in Nazareth and also general silence in Galilee, Judea, and Rome. For this obscure period in the life of Jesus, we have no direct knowledge and must satisfy ourselves with what can be inferred with more or less certainty from a few incidental references in the scriptural account. Because of His humble circumstances, it is not likely that this royal Son of the house of David enjoyed any special education and training. He likely learned from His mother and father and in the local synagogue.[172] He may have naturally acquired further knowledge through His cosmopolitan Galilean surroundings and in the process of normal development (Lk 2:40–52). His language was undoubtedly common Aramaic;[173] but He also knew Hebrew, for some of His scriptural quotations refer directly to the Hebrew original (Mk 12:29, 30; Lk 22:37; Mt 27:46). He was able to read (Lk 4:16–21);[174] for in His disputes with the Pharisees and Sadducees He could, by appealing directly to Scripture, meet them on their own ground with the challenge, so often repeated: "Have you not read?" (Mt 22:31; etc.). And it seems that He could write.[175] He also likely understood conversational Greek; for whenever He spoke to those who used that language—the Roman centurion (Mt 8:5), the Canaanite woman (Mt 15:22), the Greeks who wished to see Jesus (Jn 12:20–21), and Pilate—no mention is made of an interpreter.[176] Whether He showed extensive familiarity with Latin we cannot say. A number of Latin words occur in His teaching.[177] And on one occasion, He referred to an inscription on a Roman coin (Mt 22:19). The use of these languages, however, does not at all presuppose a special training, but is easily accounted for in the life of a Galilean Jewish boy in a surrounding Greco-Roman world. If this boy received any special school education, which is doubtful, at any rate we assume that it must have ceased soon after His first paschal visit to Jerusalem. For now He was humbly engaged in learning His father's trade. For almost twenty years there was nothing that distinguished Him from any other youth of Nazareth, as far as the eye of man could see. He was a plain carpenter (Mk 6:3) and a carpenter's son (Mt 13:55). A hundred years later, according to Justin Martyr, people in Galilee could still show some plows and yokes that they said were made by Joseph and Jesus.[178]

We have no record of the members constituting the intimate household of the Holy Family in Nazareth. But it seems that besides Joseph and Mary and the boy Jesus there were other children, boys and girls, in Joseph's house. They appear afterward as the Lord's brothers, but we do not know for certain who they were. The Gospels give us the names of James, Joses, Judas, and Simon,[179] while the *History of Joseph the Carpenter*[180] supplies the names of Anna and Lydia.[181] But we do not know whether they were children of Joseph by a former marriage,[182] whether they were cousins, the children of a deceased brother—Alphaeus or Clopas[183]—and now legally adopted by Joseph,[184] or whether they were actually the children of Joseph and Mary.[185] And it does not matter greatly. We are not compelled to accept the literal sense of the term *brother* because the same evangelist also refers to Jesus as the carpenter's *son* (Mt 13:55), while expressly stating in another passage that He was not his son (Mt 1:20). Much can be said for and against each view. For instance, if Joseph had any children before he legally adopted Jesus, what about the status of Jesus as the rightful heir to the throne of David in the eyes of His followers? If they were cousins of Jesus, how is it that they are always called brothers and sisters and not cousins or kinsmen?[186] If they were the nephews of Joseph, how is it that they are invariably found in the company of Mary (Jn 2:12; Mt 12:46; Mk 3:31; Lk 8:19)? Or were their mothers likewise sisters?[187] And if they were so devoted to Mary, or if they were actually her own children,[188] how is it that their opposition to Jesus (Jn 7:5)[189] was apparently also extended to Mary, since the Lord entrusted the care of His mother to John (Jn 19:27)? And if they were not actually the children of Joseph and Mary, what about the statement that Joseph "knew her not *until* she had given birth to a son" (Mt 1:25)?[190] And finally, if they were actually the sons of Joseph and Mary, what about the doctrine of the perpetual virginity? Without going farther into this vexed question[191] and with the admission of our own inability to determine the precise relation between Jesus and these "brothers and sisters," we can at least safely assume, whatever theory we may be inclined to accept, that the relation must have been a most close and intimate one, exercising a certain influence

43
The Lord's Family

upon the human development of the youthful Jesus. We are inclined to accept the view of Hegesippus[192] that they were the children of Joseph's brother Alphaeus and another Mary. This is not on account of any dogmatic interest in the perpetual virginity of Mary, but only our preference in a matter about which the Scriptures have not definitely spoken and tradition disagrees.[193] To the members of that family in Nazareth—now numbering six or seven children, boys and girls—we might also add two more cousins in Capernaum as belonging to the family circle—namely, James and John, the sons of Zebedee and Salome, the sister of Mary.[194] Jesus grew up in this circle. We lose sight of Joseph and suppose that he must have died some time during these silent years.

44
Conditions in the
Roman World

What happened in Rome while Israel was waiting? In AD 9, sad news reached Rome from Germany. Quinctilius Varus, the same Varus who was governor of Syria at the time of Herod's death, had been disgracefully defeated by Arminius in the Battle of the Teutoburg Forest. This was the second of the only two severe defeats, both in Germany, that Augustus suffered in the forty-one years of his reign. For months, he expressed his grief by letting his beard and hair grow and repeating, "Quinctilius Varus, give me back my legions."[195] In AD 13, Tiberius Claudius Nero, a son of the Empress Livia Drusilla by a former marriage and now Augustus's own adopted son and heir, was made "colleague in empire."[196] On August 19, AD 14, Augustus died and was promptly deified, and the reins of government passed on to Tiberius. Meanwhile, as well as later, there was little change in Judea outside the succession of procurators and high priests. Of the latter, a few names are of interest: (1) Annas, the son of Seth, who was himself high priest from AD 6–15 and after a short interval was followed by (2) his son Eleazar, AD 16–17, and by (3) his son-in-law Joseph, called Caiaphas, from AD 18–37.[197] Annas and Caiaphas are the two ecclesiastical rulers who appear as the "high priests" in the New Testament. There was only one high priest, Caiaphas, actually holding office. However, Annas was the real power behind the throne (Lk 3:2; Jn 18:13–24; Ac 4:6). There were also a number of procurators following Coponius, of whom, however, with the exception of the last, little is known: Marcus Ambivius, probably AD 9–12; Annius Rufus, probably AD 12–15; Valerius Gratus, AD 15–26, and Pontius Pilate, AD 26–36.[198] Gratus and Pilate held office for a longer period due to the consideration of Tiberius for the provinces. He held that governors acted like flies upon the body of a wounded animal. However, if the governors were gorged once, they would become more modest in their demands.[199] And in Galilee, which witnessed the luxurious, dissipated life and the Herodian building operations of the tetrarch Antipas, there was hardly any change at all.

5

THE PERIOD OF JOHN

SPRING AD 29 TO THE BEGINNING OF AD 30

AUC	782	783	784	785	786
AD	29	30	31	32	33
Approx. age of Jesus	30	31	32	33	34
Passovers		I	II	III	IV

In the fifteenth year of the reign of Emperor Tiberius, the entire nation of Israel was aroused by a powerful movement such as it had not experienced since the great days of the Maccabees. In the spring of AD 29, the call came to John, the son of Zechariah, in the wilderness, to be followed shortly afterward by the beginning of Christ's public ministry, when both Christ and His forerunner were about thirty years of age. Nothing is known of John's earlier life since his circumcision, when he received the name John, except that he "was in the wilderness until the day of his public appearance to Israel" (Lk 1:80). The Essenes, being desert-dwellers, were nearby. But there is no scriptural evidence that John, like Josephus (who speaks of his three-year discipleship with Banus in the desert[1]), had any inward or outward contact with them.[2] Nor is there any significance in the fact that he began his public career at the age of thirty because the Levites began their service at that time.[3] Although he was by birth entitled to the priesthood, it is mere conjecture, in the absence of scriptural proof, to assume that the priests entered upon their duties at the same age as the Levites. The rabbinical tradition states that a priest was duly qualified as soon as the first signs of manhood appeared, although there was no installation until the candidate had reached the age of twenty.[4] And besides, there is no evidence that John assumed the priesthood at all. Rather, it is as a prophet that he is introduced in the Gospel account, and the divine call to this office was not bound

1
The Exact Time
Mt 3:1; Lk 3:1–2

by age, rule, custom, or tradition. It is, therefore, all the more interesting to notice that in Luke's account of John's ministry, this prophet is introduced with the same historical accuracy as, for instance, the prophet Jeremiah (Jer 1:1–3), or Ezekiel (Ezk 1:1–3). There are exactly six historical references to define the date of John's ministry with respect to the reigning Roman emperor and the civil and ecclesiastical rulers within the confines of ancient Palestine. The first, which has already been considered, refers to the fifteenth year of Emperor Tiberius (AD 29). Pontius Pilate was ruler of Judea. This well-known Roman governor was appointed around AD 26 and held office until he was recalled in AD 36 (c. 779–789 AUC).[5] Herod Antipas was still in possession of the governorship of Galilee, which he held until he was finally deposed in the autumn of AD 38 (791 AUC). His own half brother Philip, son of Herod the Great and Mariamne II, daughter of Simon the high priest, was tetrarch of Iturea and the territories east of the Sea of Galilee, Batanea, Trachonitis, Auranitis, Gaulanitis, and Panias.[6] He seems to have been the best of the Herodian princes, enjoying Roman favor from the time of his appointment to the time of his death in AD 34 (787 AUC).[7] A certain non-Jewish prince, Lysanias of Abilene, occupied the outlying territory between the Lebanon ranges near Damascus. This notice is relevant because this territory belonged to the Land of Israel in ancient times and because subsequently, nearer to the day of the evangelist, it formed a part of the territory assigned by Caligula to his favorite Herod Agrippa I (AD 37).[8] Although long doubted, this notice of Luke is now acknowledged as historically correct by competent scholars. It has been shown that Lysanias ruled over this region as a contemporary of Antipas and Philip (not to be confounded with the Lysanias who had ruled over it sixty years before).[9] The ecclesiastical rulers Annas and Caiaphas, that notorious pair, divided the honors, if not the functions, of a sacred office that they disgraced.[10] Of course, there could only be one actual high priest, and that position was held by Caiaphas (c. AD 18–37). But Annas,[11] as the influential former high priest, father-in-law of Caiaphas, and the real power behind the throne, was also given this title.[12]

2
The Appearance of John
Mt 3:2–4; Mk 1:2–6;
Lk 3:2–6

This, then, was the political and ecclesiastical situation when the word of God came to John in that wild range of uncultivated wilderness, stretching forth from Jericho to the fords of the Jordan and southward to the shores of the Dead Sea. He would prepare the way for Christ by "proclaiming a baptism of repentance for the forgiveness of sins." Thus, his aged father, in agreement with what the angel Gabriel had told him, proclaimed on the day of John's circumcision: "You will go before the Lord to prepare His ways" (Lk 1:76). And thus it was written in the combined promise of Isaiah and Malachi: "Behold, I send My messenger before your face, who will prepare Your way, the voice of one crying in the wilderness: 'Prepare the way of the Lord' " (cf. Mal 3:1; Is 40:3).[13] This is an announcement of the coming Lord and the identification of John as the herald to prepare His way. Repentance was preparation for the reception of the coming King and admission into His kingdom. "Every valley shall be filled, and every mountain and hill shall be made low." This is figurative language for the direct admonition: "Repent, for the kingdom of heaven is at hand." Although the nature of this kingdom was probably entirely different from that expected by his hearers, John makes it quite clear that he was not preaching the hoped-for deliverance from foreign oppressors. He was preaching the kingdom of heaven, the redemption of all mankind from sin, and life everlasting through the Messiah. This kingdom was now approaching. Although spiritual (yet quite real), it would not bring about glorious material changes. Admission into it required sincere repentance, a complete change of heart. Believing Israel was aware of this. So close was repentance connected in their thoughts with the advent of the Messiah that it was said in one of the rabbinical traditions: "If Israel repented but one day, the Son of David would immediately come."[14] John's own personal habits—his dress and food—were in striking harmony with his call to repentance as the proper preparation for the reception of the Messiah. Like Elijah, the prophet of judgment to the Northern Kingdom (2Ki 1:8), he was dressed in hairy garments. He was clothed with camel's hair and wore a leather belt around his waist. This coarse, Bedouin-like tunic emphasized the profound earnestness of his call to repentance. Everything in the man was real and true. He preached with his voice, with his dress, and with his food. His food was such as the desert supplied: roasted locusts (Lv 11:22)[15] and wild honey (either such as he found in the clefts of the rocks or as flowed from a hole in lightning-riven trees).[16]

In addition to his call to repentance, a new rite, Baptism, accompanied his word. It was this rite which gave him the name "the Baptist" (Mt 3:1).[17] The baptisms that he performed are not to be confused with the Levitical purifications.[18] John's Baptism was a divine institution, as he said himself: "He who sent me to baptize with water" (Jn 1:33; cf. Lk 3:2–3). It was not merely an initiatory ceremony but an actual and effectual Means of Grace, bestowing forgiveness of sins upon those who received it in sincere repentance (Mk 1:4; Lk 3:3).[19] Christ Himself acknowledged its effectiveness and referred to it as a means by which the Holy Spirit wrought regeneration: "Unless one is born of water and the Spirit, he cannot enter the kingdom of God" (Jn 3:5).

3
John's Baptism
Mt 3:5–6; Mk 1:4–5;
Lk 3:3

In a short time, John became a powerful influence in the midst of his people. It soon became widely rumored that a prophet had arisen whose burning words it was worthwhile to hear. This was a man, talking about judgment and the Kingdom, who by his expressions recalled Isaiah and by his life Elijah. It may have been in a Sabbath year,[20] when the people could rest from agriculture, business, and other labor. The news spread from the wilderness to the surrounding country, and the

4
The Aroused Jewish
Population
Mt 3:5; Mk 1:5;
Lk 3:3

movement soon reached colossal dimensions. In widening circles it embraced Judea and even affected disdainful Jerusalem (Mt 3:5). Twenty years later, disciples of John were found as far abroad as Ephesus in Asia Minor (Ac 19:1–3).

Among those coming to John's Baptism were also the self-glorifying professors of Jewish orthodoxy, the Pharisees, the strict exponents of piety and external righteousness, according to law and statute. But also the liberal element made its appearance; that is, the exclusive and wealthy Sadducees, mostly men of affairs and largely belonging to the priestly class. They came "to"[21] John's Baptism, not because they were truly repentant (Lk 7:30), nor because they were exactly opposed to his Baptism and resolved to put down the movement. They came either as curious and interested witnesses of a strange phenomenon or perhaps with the intention of submitting themselves, at least externally, to John's Baptism as preparation for reception of the Messiah. After all, they shared with the common people a messianic hope. But John had no words of welcome for them. "You brood of vipers! Who warned you to flee from the wrath to come?" They owed this harsh greeting to their well-known insincerity and deception (Mt 16:1). In their minds, they had connected judgment with a messianic advent that would drive out the Roman oppressors. But now a warning of general wrath is sounded, and individual and universal repentance is demanded. Independently of their own personal faith and obedience to God's commandments, they thought their mere physical descent from Abraham entitled them to seats of honor in the kingdom of heaven. But John told them: "God is able from these stones to raise up children for Abraham. . . . Every tree therefore that does not bear good fruit is cut down and thrown into the fire." This stinging rebuke, directed against the leaders of the Jewish people, instilled fear in others. The multitudes asked, "What then shall we do?" A simple answer was given them. Although John ate locusts and clothed himself in hairy garments, he did not require others to do the same. He did not tell his hearers to quit their honest calling, but only to change their way of living. Simple justice, mercy, and charity were imposed upon all. "Whoever has two tunics is to share with him who has none." To the inquiring, deeply hated tax collectors, he replied: "Collect no more than you are authorized to do." Soldiers also came to him; but John did not ask them to give up their calling. We do not know who they were, whether they were Jews, Romans, Thracians, or Germans. Neither is there any evidence that there was any war in progress in that region at the time.[22] Most likely they were soldiers in some way connected with the Roman provincial government. John told them not to extort money by threats or false accusations and to be content with their wages.

In addition to these simple precepts, John had another and a stranger message to deliver. While the people mused in their hearts whether John was Christ, he made the statement that he would claim no authority for himself except as the divinely commissioned forerunner of another.

I baptize you with water, but He who is mightier than I is coming, the strap of whose sandals I am not worthy to untie. He will baptize you with the Holy Spirit and fire. His winnowing fork is in His hand, to clear His threshing floor and to gather the wheat into His barn, but the chaff He will burn with unquenchable fire.

It was a useful evangelic ministry, but it was cut short, as St. Luke notes, when John was cast into prison (Lk 3:19–20).[23]

6

THE BEGINNING OF CHRIST'S PUBLIC MINISTRY

SUMMER OF AD 29, OR 782 AUC

Contemporaneous Ministry of Jesus and John

A few months have passed. It is perhaps the summer of AD 29 (782 AUC).[1]
John, whose ministry began in the wilderness of Judea (Mt 3:1; Mk 1:4; Lk 3:2), in
the neighborhood of the Dead Sea, may have gradually ascended the El Ghor (the
Jordan Valley). He may now have reached the most northern point of his activity.
Tradition commonly placed "Bethany across the Jordan" (Jn 1:28), or rather the
"Bethany beyond the Jordan" (to distinguish it from the Bethany near the Mount
of Olives[2]), east of Jericho.[3] But it may have been located at Arbarah, a ford of the
Jordan above Beth-shean, and near the Sea of Galilee. This was about twenty miles
from Nazareth. But long before John reached Bethany, tidings of his words and
deeds must have penetrated the silent carpenter shop in the Galilean hills.[4] Jesus
knew John and his mission, and He also knew that the time for the beginning of His
own public ministry had come. However, although Jesus and John were distantly
related on their maternal side, we have no evidence that the cousins were otherwise
acquainted with each other and that John knew Jesus. Twice, John emphatically
declares: "I myself did not know Him" (Jn 1:31, 33). Although John knew that the
Messiah had appeared in the flesh, he had not met Him face-to-face. When he saw
Jesus for the first time, there was something in His look, something in His bearing, something in the sinless beauty of His ways, or some revelation, which at once
overawed and captivated him. Therefore, when Jesus came to be baptized by him,
he tried to hinder Him, saying: "I need to be baptized by You, and do You come
to me?" It was his mission to baptize sinners with the Baptism of repentance. John
knew that Jesus was the Holy One of God. But Jesus answered—the second recorded

1
The Baptism
of Jesus
Mt 3:13–17; Mk 1:9–
11; Lk 3:21–22;
Jn 1:32–34

utterance since His boyhood visit to the temple and the first word recorded since His entrance into His public ministry: "Let it be so now, for thus it is fitting for us to fulfill all righteousness." In saying this, Jesus admitted that, as far as obtaining remission of sins was concerned, He did not need to be baptized. However, because, as Luther aptly says, he had taken the place of all sinners and must fulfill the entire Law for them, John should "let it be so *now.*" With His Baptism, Jesus began His messianic work. Thus He became Jesus, the Savior of mankind. Upon hearing Jesus' answer, John "consented," baptizing Him in the Jordan. No details are given about how He was baptized.[5] Immediately after the Baptism of Jesus, and while He stood praying, John beheld that wonderful sign that God promised to him to make him absolutely sure that this was indeed He who was to come: "He on whom you see the Spirit descend and remain, this is He who baptizes with the Holy Spirit." There occurred a most exceptional manifestation of the triune God. The incarnate Son of God was standing on the banks of the Jordan. The heavens were opened, actually rent asunder,[6] and the Holy Spirit descended in the form of a dove. And a voice from heaven was heard and understood by those who stood by, especially by Jesus and by John, as saying: "This is My beloved Son, with whom I am well pleased."[7] Now John was divinely certain that here was God's own Anointed, the Messiah, the Christ, anointed with the Holy Spirit and with power (Ps 45:7; Ac 10:38). The Father Himself duly invested Him with His messianic office. Luke adds the chronological note that we have already previously observed: when Jesus began to teach, He was about thirty years of age.

2
The Temptation
Mt 4:1–11; Mk 1:12–13; Lk 4:1–13

From the banks of the Jordan to the wilds of the desert. From the smiling sunshine of opened heavens to the assaults of the evil one.[8] Immediately after Jesus' Baptism, the Spirit led Him into the wilderness to be tempted by the devil. Thus the fact, the impulse, and the purpose of this withdrawal are at once briefly and simply stated. In the solitude of the desert He sought communion with His Father. In fervent prayer, He sought strength for the superhuman task that was awaiting Him (cf. Mk 1:13a), a task necessary for the deliverance of mankind from the power of the devil (Heb 2:14–15; 1Jn 3:8). The struggle was real, the account of it no allegory, its outcome the ignominious defeat of the hellish foe.

3
The Sinlessness of Jesus
Mt 4:1–11; Mk 1:12–13; Lk 4:1–13

There is a question whether Jesus, because of His absolute sinlessness, *could* be tempted to sin; that is, whether He was actually *capable* of committing a sin.[9] Despite this question, the sinlessness of Jesus must be maintained according to Scripture (2Co 5:21).[10] Since the human nature of Christ had personal existence only in the Son of God, it was as little possible for Him really to sin as it is possible for God to sin.[11] Jesus, being "*full* of the Holy Spirit" (Lk 4:1), was led by the Spirit into the wilderness. There Satan futilely assaulted Him with temptations. But was His great conflict, then, merely a deception?[12] Was not His temptation the semblance of a battle against an apparent foe? By no means. A battle can be a real battle even if there is no doubt as to the outcome. It was in the interest of Satan to strain every effort to frustrate his own predicted ultimate defeat (Gn 3:15). The same Satan whom Holy Scripture pictures as exceedingly cunning is also shown to be at the same time stupid and blind so that he defeats his own ends. It may properly be stated that Satan hoped he might gain the mastery over this Jesus whom he saw in the likeness of sinful flesh. But Jesus overcame him to the glory of God.

No definite place is given where the temptation took place. It was in the wilderness, most likely not so very far from the place of John's Baptism, and among the wild animals (Mk 1:13). The latter are not mentioned to hint at the danger in which our Savior was, but rather to indicate the uninhabited nature of that region. Food and supplies were not considered, and hunger was necessarily a part of His experience. A tradition, but no older than the Crusades, fixes the scene at a mountain to the south of Jericho, which from this circumstance has received the name of Quarantana.[13] But the scene may also be laid beyond the Jordan, in the hills of Moab, where the Lord promised Moses a view of the Promised Land.[14] Forty days of fasting,[15] of solitude, and of various temptations (Lk 4:2), probably in summer or early autumn, filled the period. Three particular temptations are mentioned.

4
The Time and Place
Mt 4:1–2; Mk 1:12–13; Lk 4:1–2

The whole time had been one of moral and spiritual tension. Soldiers on battlefields fight through battles unconscious of wounds and exhaustion; but when the enthusiasm is spent, nature asserts itself. Jesus was weary with the contest, alone in the desert, and faint with hunger. The moment was favorable for the satanic temptations recorded by the evangelists. Let us suppose that in the dim light of the dawn, the stones of the desert assumed the form of little loaves of bread.[16] Satan, the tempter, appeared to Jesus, in which disguise we do not know. He said: "If You are the Son of God, command these stones to become loaves of bread." Now, Satan is not omniscient (cf. 1Co 2:7–9). But he had been a witness of the incident of the opened heaven on the banks of the Jordan and had heard the voice calling Jesus the Son of God. This was, of course, interesting to one who since the fall of Adam, as a strong man armed, had kept his palace and enjoyed the fruits of his original victory (Lk 11:21). As an attack, his assault upon Jesus was in true satanic form. Simulating compassion with the hungry Jesus, he repeated his tactics of pretended friendship successfully employed in the case of Eve (Gn 3:1). Likewise, he injected the element of doubt: "*If* You are the Son of God." However, granting this divine Sonship for the present, he asks Jesus to "command these stones to become loaves of bread." Since the heavenly Father evidently failed to provide for His beloved Son, Satan incited Jesus to rebellious thoughts and invited Him to help Himself by virtue of the miraculous powers bestowed upon Him. Jesus does not deny His hunger nor His ability to carry out the suggestion. In fact, it would not have been impossible or wrong for

5
The First Temptation
Mt 4:3–4; Lk 4:3–4

Jesus to relieve His need in the manner Satan suggested. But under these circumstances—"led up by the Spirit into the wilderness to be tempted by the devil"—and at the direction of Satan, Jesus' action would have indicated despair of God, disobedience to His Father's will, and failure to trust in His divine providence. He would have done the will of God's inveterate enemy. This He could not and would not do, neither as the Holy One of God nor as man's substitute in this combat with the Prince of Darkness. On the contrary, He pointed the tempter to Scripture: "It is written," and repelled the temptation by quoting a passage of Deuteronomy (from the Septuagint): "Man shall not live by bread alone, but by every word that comes from the mouth of God" (cf. Dt 8:3). God, He said, can preserve man's life without bread. His Father had sustained Him without food of any kind for forty days, and therefore He would commend also the future to Him.[17]

6
The Second Temptation
Mt 4:5–7; Lk 4:9–12

Satan tried again. Jesus next[18] permitted Himself to be bodily transported to Jerusalem, the Holy City,[19] and to be let down on the pinnacle of the temple. This was probably at the southeastern angle of the temple cloisters, "whence the view into the Kidron Valley beneath was to the stupendous depth of 450 feet."[20] If we may venture a guess as to the time, we should say that it was probably at the hour of the morning sacrifice.[21] The vanishing dawn broke into the morning light and the temple gates were slowly opened. The blast of the silver trumpets summoned Israel to begin a new day by appearing before the Lord. Jesus had just proved His trust in God. And now Satan tried to tempt Him to an apparently greater trust. However, had Jesus yielded, it would have been sheerest fanaticism and wicked presumption. "If You are the Son of God"—Satan very shrewdly observed that Jesus had not replied to these words, already used in the first temptation. So he attacked Him again, "Throw Yourself down." Surely no harm can come from that! Not if He is God's beloved Son and if He confidently trusts in God! As Jesus surveys the scene, the dizzy heights of the columns, the wall of the temple, and then the dark depths of Kidron, Satan quotes a passage of Scripture to encourage Him to attempt the leap. Yes, Satan plays Rabbi and quotes (rather misapplies) the words of a psalm: "He will command His angels concerning you . . . On their hands they will bear you up, lest you strike your foot against a stone" (Ps 91:11–12). But what about the omission of the words "to guard you *in all your ways*"? This was not a lapse of memory but was intentional. Surely God protects His children—in the lions' den, in the fiery furnace—by a miracle if need be. But in this case, it would have been a most wicked presumption and desperate recklessness to test divine providence. However, as some think, there may also have been another consideration that prompted Satan to venture this temptation. The sudden appearance of Jesus among a gaping multitude below might easily have gained for Him popular recognition as the Messiah. For, according to popular belief, the Messiah would appear suddenly and in a marvelous manner.[22] However, repelling the temptation to gain for Himself easy recognition by way of spectacular demonstration and also disregarding the suggestion to thrust Himself needlessly into reckless perils, Jesus replies by quoting another Scripture passage: "Again it is written, 'You shall not put the Lord your God to the test" (Dt 6:16). True, God will protect His children; but they have no right to claim His miraculous intervention to keep them from harm if they actually court danger. They have no right to challenge His power to the proof.[23]

The scene changes. By a supernatural mode of transportation, the Lord is placed on the top of a high mountain. We do not know its exact geographical location. In the bright morning light, let us suppose, the devil dazzles the carpenter's son from Nazareth, just now entering into His messianic office, with something of the worldly glory. Satan brazenly attempts to fill Jesus with unhallowed personal ambition. He points out the enticing prospects of a universal messianic kingdom and claims the power and authority of disposing of it at will. The world in all its beauty and glory, with all its treasures and the immense power their bestowal includes, is unveiled to Him. On one side lies Africa and Egypt. In the sandy regions are the kingdoms of the Arabian Desert. On another side, the snowy crest of distant Hermon points the way to Damascus and to the mighty empires that once flourished between the Tigris and Euphrates. He also views His beloved Land of Israel, Judea, Samaria, and Galilee, once the kingdom of David and Solomon, but now in the grasp of a foreign oppressor. Beyond it stretches forth the shiny waters of the Mediterranean Sea, on the northern shores of which the glory of Greece and the power of Rome beckon Him. Dazzling prospects! "All these I will give You, if You will fall down and worship me." Not only is Satan very liberal with another's possession—"The silver is Mine, and the gold is Mine, declares the LORD of hosts" (Hg 2:8)—but he also blasphemously makes a bid for divine honor. There is only one answer therefore to this preposterous request: "Be gone, Satan! For it is written, 'You shall worship the Lord your God and Him only shall you serve.' " Be gone! the Savior shouts, manifesting at this point a ray of the divine glory that was His even in the state of humiliation. Yet He condescends to support this peremptory dismissal of Satan with an appeal to Scripture: "For it is written." For the third time, He refers the infernal spirit to the Book of Deuteronomy (6:13), which seems to have been one of His favorite books. The Tempter is foiled. He departs from Him, yet only for a while. He postpones his return to a more convenient season, probably presenting his temptations in a different manner, hoping in his blindness to have better success at some other time (Lk 4:13).[24] Now the angels of heaven came and ministered to Jesus (Mk 1:13)[25] in reply to the insinuation of Satan that God the Father did not treat Him as though He were His beloved Son. Since there were no human witnesses to the temptation,

7
The Third
Temptation
Mt 4:8–11; Lk 4:5–8

the story must have been related by Jesus Himself. By inspiration of the Holy Spirit, it was afterward included in the Gospel account.

8
A Delegation to John
Jn 1:19–28

Now let us return to the banks of the Jordan. At the end of this forty-day period of Christ's temptation in the wilderness, in fact, a day before His return (see Jn 1:29), John the Baptist received an official visit. A number of Pharisees and Sadducees had already made their appearance among the multitudes coming to be baptized. In promptly calling them to repentance, John employed no ambiguous language (Mt 3:7–10). Of course, they returned to Jerusalem with their report. But the scattering multitudes had also published their version. They mused in their hearts whether John was the Christ (Lk 3:15). Thus an investigation was needed. According to a rabbinic tradition, the Council was under a special obligation to prevent the appearing of false prophets.[26] Hence, a special deputation of priests and attending Levites, but with strong pharisaic tendencies (Jn 1:24–25), was dispatched with the commission to find out what it was all about. We remember that John's father was a priest, but since he lived in the country, he did not belong to the ruling priestly class. What little the aristocratic Sadducees had seen of John's work and heard of his preaching must have convinced them that "his views and aims," his calling the people to repentance as a proper preparing of the way for the Messiah, "lay entirely beyond their horizon."[27]

9
Time and Place
Jn 1:19–28

The scene is placed at "Bethany across the Jordan," not the Bethany near Jerusalem, but near the Sea of Galilee and north of Jericho. As we shall see, there was a wedding at Cana in the following week. And now, assuming that the bride of this wedding was a maiden and that in accordance with "uniform custom"[28] her wedding took place on a Wednesday, by counting back, we arrive at a Thursday for the day on which the committee of the Council (Jn 1:19) called on John.[29] The interview was rather laconic: formal in inquiry with little time wasted for polite sentiment, as we would naturally expect from a somewhat suspicious investigating committee. John replied straightforwardly, in harmony with his character.

10
"Who Are You?"
Jn 1:19–21

The interview began with the question, "Who are you?" Not, What is your name or the date of your birth?—for John's questioners were evidently supplied with this data. Instead, they asked, Who are you? What personage do you claim to be? "He confessed, and did not deny, but confessed, 'I am not the Christ.' " The answer of John seems to indicate that his questioners had hinted at the possibility of his being the Messiah. This, in view of his popularity, was no small temptation. But the manner in which he replied to the question brought out the earnestness, almost horror, with which he disclaimed the ascription to himself of messianic honors.[30] If not Christ Himself, the next possibility was that he was His forerunner. "What then? Are you Elijah?" This was in reference to the prophecy of Malachi: "Behold, I will send you Elijah the prophet before the great and awesome day of the LORD comes" (4:5). Now, John actually was the forerunner of the Messiah. He was that promised Elijah. Christ Himself paid him that tribute: "Elijah has already come" (Mt 17:12). But John was not Elijah in the sense in which they had put the question; for they expected a physical return of that prophet before the coming of the Lord. Therefore, he could not admit the suggested identity without misleading them. "He said, 'I am not.' "

Another possibility presented itself: "Are you the Prophet?" "And he answered, 'No.' " This question was also based upon a misunderstanding. Many Jews were expecting a special prophet to terminate the prophetic era and to usher in the messianic reign.[31] There was also the particular prophet promised by Moses: "The LORD your God will raise up for you a prophet like me from among you" (Dt 18:15). This referred to Christ Himself, and so it was also generally understood (1Macc 14:41; Ac 3:22). Therefore, since John was neither that anticipated special prophet, according to the understanding of some, nor the prophet[32] in the promise of Moses, he could only answer, "No."

11
The Witness of John
Jn 1:21–28

But now their stock of leading questions was exhausted. John the Baptist was not Christ, not Elijah, not the anticipated intermediary prophet. In fact, he was no prophet at all in their sense and according to their expectations. Thoroughly disappointed and baffled by the plain and austere wilderness preacher, they requested that he give an account of himself. "Who are you? We need to give an answer to those who sent us." In his reply, John cited the prophecy of Isaiah: "I am the voice of one crying out in the wilderness, 'Make straight the way of the Lord' " (cf. Is 40:3). By applying this prophecy, John identified himself as the immediate precursor of the Lord.

12
"I Am the Voice of
One Crying Out in
the Wilderness"
Jn 1:22–23

But this answer did not satisfy his questioners. If he was not the Christ, nor Elijah, nor "the prophet," nor any kind of prophet—since he claimed to be only a voice, a mere noise, in a pathless, barren waste—"Then why are you baptizing?" If he disclaimed for himself the office and honor of a prophet, why assume its rights and privileges? If he was no prophet, why did he act like one? In attacking John's Baptism, they probably referred to certain peculiar symbolic actions and habits. At one time, Jeremiah walked about with a wooden yoke dangling from his shoulders as a sign that Judah would have its neck put under the yoke of the king of Babylon (Jer 27:2, 8). For three years, Isaiah went naked and barefoot to symbolize that the king of Assyria would lead the Egyptians prisoners, old and young, naked and barefoot (Is 20:2–4). Other examples might be mentioned. These and other prophetic peculiarities the people in Old Testament times were accustomed to as attending the sacred office. But if John was no real prophet, what, then, was the idea of his wilderness life, his hairy garments, the leather belt, his peculiar food, wild honey and roasted grasshoppers? In particular, what about this novel rite, the Baptism of

13
"Then Why Are You
Baptizing?"
Jn 1:24–28

repentance for remission of sins? But now, John delivered a blow, claiming no particular honor and distinction for himself on account of his Baptism with water as a divinely appointed preparation for the immediate advent of the Messiah: "I baptize with water, but among you stands One you *do not know*." There is the trouble. Not only did they not know that He had come, which would excuse them, but they did not even care to know whether He had made His appearance. They, the investigating committee, were on the lookout for false prophets, but missing the Prophet of all prophets, the Messiah! What they ought to have done was to form a messianic reception committee. But they were evidently not interested in preparing for the advent of the Messiah such as the Baptist demanded—repentance and humble craving for the forgiveness of sins. Finally, in true humility and abasing himself in all sincerity, John made a beautiful confession of Christ: "He who comes after me, the strap of whose sandal I am not worthy to untie."

Thus the interview ended. We are not told what effect the testimony of John had upon the investigating committee. Most likely, they were not very much pleased with it. However, what he had replied to their questions gave them no sufficient grounds for citing him before the Council. When John later lost his life because of his courageous testimony, it was not the Council that caused his death, but someone else. Although the Council in a certain sense exercised jurisdiction over every Jewish community in the world, it was only within the limits of Judea proper that it exercised any *direct* authority.[33] Even if they had cause for action, John, across the Jordan, had no reason to fear anything.

14
"Behold, the Lamb of God"
Jn 1:29–34

On the following day, Jesus again made His appearance on the banks of the Jordan. The motives that brought Him back to the scene of His Baptism are not explained in Scripture.[34] So far as we know, there was no interview then or afterward between Jesus and John; just a meeting in the distance, as it were. Jesus approached John, came toward him,[35] but not directly *to* him. Yet He was close enough to him to be pointed out by him. Although it seems that Jesus had nothing to say to John, John had something wonderful to say about Jesus. Pointing out the approaching Jesus to those who were around him, John uttered these remarkable words: "Behold, the Lamb of God, who takes away the sin of the world!" This was a reference to Isaiah's picture of the suffering Messiah (Is 53:7) and an unmistakable testimony of Jesus as the Savior of the world. In the Old Testament, lambs were sacrificed daily and on all festival days for the atonement of the sins of the people. They were types of the supreme and perfect sacrifice to be brought by Him on whom the Lord would lay "the iniquity of us all." Therefore, in John's designation of Jesus as the Lamb of God who takes away the sin of the world, there was already a forecast of Good Friday, of His suffering and death on the cross. We do not know whether God revealed to John the details of Christ's suffering and death apart from the fact of the slaughter of the innocent Lamb as depicted by Isaiah. But he was fully assured that Jesus was the Savior of the world. For he continued: "This is He of whom I said," (namely, to the delegates from Jerusalem) "After me comes a man who ranks before me, because He was before me." And he explained *how* he knew that Jesus was the Redeemer promised since the fall. Without any personal knowledge of Jesus, whom he was to introduce to Israel as the Messiah, John had gone about his mission of preparing the way for Him, preaching repentance and baptizing with water. But then he had received a divine revelation, a sign, now fulfilled: "'He on whom you see the Spirit descend and remain, this is He who baptizes with the Holy Spirit.' And I have seen and have borne witness that this is the Son of God." To whom these words were spoken we do not know, but most likely they were uttered in the hearing of John the evangelist, in whose Gospel this account is given. For the evangelist had himself been a disciple of the Baptist but, on hearing this beautiful testimony, became a disciple of Jesus.

Again on the next day, John the Baptist was standing with two of his disciples as Jesus walked by. He fixed upon Him an earnest and intense gaze[36] and said, "Behold, the Lamb of God!" John's two disciples had already been impressed with this statement and its explanation as made by their master on the previous day. But now that they heard it again, they immediately left John and followed Jesus. A loss for John, it is true; but it was in accordance with his mission—to prepare the way for Christ. As they followed Jesus in modest silence, He turned and asked, "What are you seeking?"[37] This was a master question, penetrating their inmost souls. It is evident that they were seeking Him, but the form of the question compelled them to consider carefully the object of their search and to examine the motive that prompted them to forsake John and follow Him. Their reply was simple and plainly showed their sincerity of purpose. "Rabbi," (that is, Master or Teacher) they said, addressing Jesus with a title of honor and respect, suggesting that they desired to become His pupils, "where are You staying?" This, in effect, meant, We are seeking You. This frank and sincere expression of their desire was met with a kind and generous response, "Come and you will see." We do not know where Jesus was at that moment. Most likely, He was at a modest and temporary dwelling place in the neighborhood where John was preaching and baptizing, probably some sort of tent or booth,[38] which served as the only shelter to the hundreds who had come to the Baptism of John. They came and saw where Jesus dwelt, stayed with Him that day, and probably slept there that night. Before their first visit was over, they were fully satisfied that they had been in the presence of the promised Messiah. It was an unforgettable experience, this first hour of their personal communion with Jesus. John the evangelist remembered this even in his old age, when he wrote his Gospel, as having been the tenth hour of the day. "It was about the tenth hour." But what is meant by the tenth hour? The most

15
The First Disciples
Jn 1:35–39

learned commentators struggle in the attempt to answer the question of how the evangelist calculated his hours.[39] We suppose that John employed the Jewish mode of reckoning time, from sunrise to sunset (Jn 11:9), as marked off on the sun dial,[40] except in the one instance at the trial of Jesus before Pilate (Jn 19:14). There, following strict Roman computation, he employed the language of the court. Therefore, according to our view, this memorable first meeting with Jesus took place at the tenth hour of the civil day; that is, at four o'clock in the afternoon.[41]

16
Andrew and John
Jn 1:40–42

One of the two who heard John the Baptist speak and followed Jesus was Andrew.[42] The name of the other is not mentioned in the Gospel; but we are left to infer that it was the evangelist John himself. Since tradition states that he died at the end of the century, he must have been a youth of seventeen or eighteen years when he first met Jesus.[43] His consistent refusal to mention himself by name is one of the characteristics of his Gospel.[44] While he has praise for others, he only faintly alludes to himself. Andrew is the one to receive the honor of becoming the first disciple of Christ. We don't know much about him. He was a fisherman from Bethsaida, near the Sea of Galilee, which was the original home also of Peter (Jn 1:44). His father's name was John, or Jonah (Jn 1:42; Mt 16:17). Presumably, he was no longer living at the time of this story. He had an elder brother by the name of Simon, who was to play an important part in the Gospel history and whom Andrew, as we shall presently learn, was instrumental in leading to Christ.

17
Peter
Jn 1:41–42

"He [Andrew] first found his own brother Simon"—the word "found" shows that he had been looking for him—and led him to Christ. " 'We [Andrew and John] have found the Messiah'[45] (which means Christ)." That was his great moment. "He brought him to Jesus." That is the greatest service that one brother can render another. Thus, Andrew is praised for his missionary zeal, and Peter is introduced. In company with his younger brother Andrew, and with James and John and their father Zebedee, Simon Peter was engaged in the fisherman's trade, with headquarters at Capernaum, where he owned a home (Lk 5:10; Mk 1:29). Originally, he hailed from Bethsaida. If, as tradition states, he was about seventy-five years old at the time of his martyrdom in AD 68, he must have been already thirty-five years old at this important period of his life.[46] Andrew presented him to Jesus, who fixed His royal gaze upon him and read his inmost thoughts. At a glance, He saw in that simple fisherman a fiery nature, impulsive enthusiasm, potential service of a high character to be rendered His kingdom, but also a great weakness—inconsistency.[47] At once, He accepted him as His disciple with the greeting: " 'You are Simon the son of John. You shall be called Cephas' (which means Peter)." And history shows that Christ was not mistaken. By divine grace, weak Peter became a rock. Upon the solid rock of his confession, the Church of Christ is built. "And the gates of hell shall not prevail against it" (Mt 16:18).

Andrew was *first* to bring *his* brother. But unassuming, contemplating John was not altogether to be outdone. He likewise had a brother, who, too, was probably near at hand. Andrew "first[48] found his own brother." Now, John, in his usual delicate reserve, does not say it directly, but something is clearly implied by the word "first." For he also went out and found *his* brother and led him to Christ. Thus, at the very beginning of His ministry, two pairs of brothers—Andrew and Peter, James and John—were brought into contact with Christ. And it seems that this latter pair, James and John, were Jesus' own cousins. Their father, Zebedee, the husband of Salome, was a prosperous fisherman, with hired servants (Mk 1:19–20) and connections as far as Jerusalem. For only so can we explain that afterward John had connections with the high priest's house (Jn 18:15).[49] According to tradition, their mother, Salome, was a sister of Mary, the mother of Jesus (Mt 27:56; Jn 19:25).[50]

18
James
Jn 1:35–42

Another disciple was added, the fifth, to the list of future apostles,[51] who at first were occasional companions of Jesus and then became His constant attendants, until He solemnly chose them as His apostles and expressly designated them as such. The Sabbath was over. On the next day, Sunday, Jesus intended to go forth again into Galilee. Then He found Philip, who was of Bethsaida, Peter's native town. Like Andrew and Simon, Philip also very likely had come to John's Baptism and was now on his way back home. Among the apostles, he is one who had a typical Greek name,[52] being named perhaps after the tetrarch Philip.[53] (The custom of naming children after celebrities was as common then as it is now.) If so, he must at this time have been younger than thirty years old. Possibly, his Greek name suggests familiarity with the surrounding Greek-speaking population. At any rate, he was singled out by the Greeks who in the last week of Christ's life wished to see the Lord (Jn 12:21). At his first meeting with Jesus, a simple "Follow Me" made him a disciple. We are not told what Philip answered, but his hearty assent is fully implied by all that follows.

19
Philip
Jn 1:43–44

Jesus found Philip, and Philip found Nathanael. Eager to communicate his rich discovery, Philip sought out his friend and jubilantly said to him, "We have found Him of whom Moses in the Law and also the prophets wrote, Jesus of Nazareth, the son of Joseph"; that is, the promised Messiah. The last-named details Philip must have learned in his conversation with Jesus or from the newly accepted disciples. Nathanael, however, was not so easily convinced. He was from Cana (Jn 21:2), only a few miles from Nazareth, but he had not heard about Jesus, the son of the carpenter Joseph of Nazareth, before. At least he had not been told that He was the Messiah. And now Nathanael found it hard to believe that despised Nazareth[54] could produce the Messiah. He therefore said to Philip, "Can anything good come out of Nazareth?" Philip, however, did not try to argue with him. He made a very wise reply, one that recalls the words of Jesus to Andrew and John, "Come and see." Now,

20
Nathanael
Jn 1:45–51

who was this Nathanael? His name, Nathanael (like Gr Theodore, "gift of God"), gives us no clue. His name does not appear at all in the list of apostles, but he is usually identified with Bartholomew, the sixth in the list.[55] This name, however, means merely Bar-Tolmai; that is, "the son of Tolmai" (a family name).[56] According to a legend of his later martyrdom, Bartholomew was sewed in a sack and cast into the sea.[57] That is about all we know of him. Jesus' words tell us that he was a man without duplicity, thoroughly sincere, and probably well versed in Scripture. His initial prejudice was soon removed. When Jesus first saw him, He remarked, "Behold, an Israelite indeed, in whom there is no deceit!" This was praise indeed, and more. It was a revelation, a hint, and the suggestion of some secret knowledge of something that Nathanael thought nobody else possessed. Of course, like every true Israelite, he shared the waiting for Israel's salvation (Gn 49:18). And if at first, by asking questions and making objections—probably secretly hoping that the news *was* true—he did not immediately recognize and acknowledge Jesus as the promised Messiah, what wrong was there in that? However, it seems that already by His opening words, "Behold, an Israelite indeed, in whom there is no deceit!" Jesus wrought in Nathanael the conviction that He was truly what Philip had called Him. Nathanael already half submitted when he asked, "How do You know me?" Not only did Nathanael seem to have had no previous knowledge of Jesus, but he also thought that Jesus had no knowledge of him. By asking now, "How do You know me?" he virtually admitted that Jesus *did* know him, indeed, had a very intimate knowledge of him. And Jesus now gave him a manifest proof of this by the following answer, which was a testimony of His divine omniscience: "Before Philip called you, when you were under the fig tree, I saw you." Nathanael must have been doing something noteworthy under the fig tree. Some think that Nathanael had been praying for the coming of the Messiah.[58] At any rate, Jesus' words thoroughly convinced him. He confessed: "Rabbi, You are the Son of God! You are the King of Israel!" to which Jesus replied:

> Because I said to you, "I saw you under the fig tree," do you believe? You will see greater things than these. . . . Truly, truly,[59] I say to you, you will see heaven opened, and the angels of God ascending and descending on the Son of Man.

What Jacob beheld in his dream was realized in Christ (Gn 28:10–15). Not only once, but on many future occasions did he and his companions see this promise fulfilled. With the eyes of faith, they saw the heavens open and the angels of God ascending and descending upon the Son of Man. By calling Himself the "Son of Man," Jesus wished to indicate that He is the Messiah, true God and true man. This is the first time that He used this title in speaking of Himself.[60]

21
The Wedding at Cana
Jn 2:1–2

Three days afterward,[61] there was a wedding in Cana of Galilee, to which Jesus and His newly won disciples were invited. If we assume that the bride was a maiden, we arrive at a Wednesday.[62] It was probably in the autumn of AD 29. After an absence of about two months, Jesus had returned from the banks of the Jordan. He probably stopped first at Nazareth, where He heard about the wedding at Cana and received the invitation, and then proceeded to join His mother and the members of His family who were already there. While Cana was the home of Nathanael-Bartholomew (Jn 21:2), there is no evidence that he had anything to do with the marriage.[63] Other details are equally uncertain. However, it is probable, because of the prominent position accorded Mary there, that it was the wedding of one of her or Joseph's nephews or nieces. Joseph is no longer mentioned, probably because he was already dead. We need not go into details about the ceremonies or proceedings connected with a Jewish marriage in New Testament times, except to point out that the marriage customs prevailing in Galilee are said to have been pure and simple.[64] There was probably a procession to the house of the bridegroom on the eve of the wedding, the prescribed washing of hands, the signing of a formal legal instrument, and a simple benediction, followed by a liberal wedding feast. It was for this joyous occasion that preparations were made in Cana of Galilee; but, strangely, we are not able to fix definitely the location of this little town, though a number of different sites have been proposed.[65]

As we pass through the court of a festively adorned house in Cana, we notice six large stone water pots, arranged after the manner of the Jews for purification, for the washing of the feet and hands, before and after eating, and also of the vessels used.[66] As we enter the lofty dining room, brilliantly lighted with lamps and candles, the guests are seen disposed around tables or seated on chairs. The feast proceeds. Oriental hospitality demands a sufficient supply of food and drink for the requirements of the invited guests. But at some point, the wine suddenly ran out. This unexpected failure may have happened because Jesus and His disciples were added to the number of expected guests. Or was it the poverty of the bridal pair? At any rate, the watchful eye of Mary quickly observed the imminent embarrassment and communicated the fact to Jesus: "They have no wine." This remark was evidently a pointed one. Mary did not want the bridegroom's family to be disgraced. Now, if anyone ought to have known who Jesus really was, it was Mary. She was probably not aware of it at the moment, but consciously or unconsciously she was calling upon Jesus to exercise His messianic power or influence. He could supply a need that His and His disciples' presence at the wedding had possibly occasioned. At any rate, her words contained an indirect appeal for help. And from Jesus' reply, it would indeed seem that Mary had suggested that Jesus intervene for the benefit of the wedding guests. But He would do so in His own manner and at His own appointed time. Jesus said to her, "Woman, what does this have to do with Me? My hour has not yet come." In Greek, the term *woman* is not one of disrespect.[67] Jesus does not call Mary "mother," for in this matter of performing miracles and

22
"They Have No Wine"
Jn 2:3–4

manifesting His power, the two—mother and Son—stand on different grounds. "What does this have to do with Me?" The performance of miracles belongs to His office. In this matter, He allows no interference, neither from His disciples nor from His brother or mother (Mt 12:46–50). He, too, had seen the lack of wine. He was probably even now waiting for an opportunity to grant aid in His own way and His own time. But "My hour has not yet come."

23
Water Changed
into Wine
Jn 2:5–10

Mary was gently checked. She did not understand—and still she understood. Jesus' reply was not altogether a refusal. In the little words "not yet" she beheld a distinct ray of hope. For she said to the servants: "Do whatever He tells you." We have already noticed the jars near the entrance of the house. Probably, the water supply was nearly exhausted when Christ gave the strange command "Fill the jars with water." Water was specified in view of what was to follow. In their great zeal, the servants filled the vessels to the brim. This is probably stated for the purpose of pointing out the large quantity as well as to exclude the possibility of someone adding anything to the water. But why go into apologetic details? The miracle that follows is either a miracle, or it is not. And we are either going to accept or reject the simple account. No argument is likely to convince the skeptic, and no amount of rationalizing is going to make a miracle more comprehensible.[68] Thus, we shall attempt neither, but rather make it our purpose to tell the story. "And He said to them, 'Now draw some out and take it to the master of the feast.' " The servants were ordered to draw out the contents of the large jars, to put them into smaller vessels, and to carry these to the guest who, according to the custom of the time, had been elected "master of the feast."[69] We might call him a butler or head waiter, whose duty it was to arrange the table and to taste the food and wine.[70] "So they took it." But meanwhile, a most remarkable thing had happened. A situation that had threatened to become very embarrassing had been quickly relieved. What the servants poured in as water flowed out as wine. The master of the feast did not know what had taken place. When he tasted the water that had become wine and did not know from where it had been procured, impartially judging it as wine among wines, he mirthfully remarked to the bridegroom that in offering the good wine last, he had deviated from the rule observed at banquets. Commonly, the best wine was offered first, and when the sense of taste had been somewhat dulled and the wedding guests could no longer appreciate a choice product, an inferior vintage was offered. But we need not suppose that the remark was intended to imply that the guests were well-nigh intoxicated. It merely establishes the superb quality of Christ's wedding gift. Here was a miracle and not a mesmeric trick. The wine was real and it was of the very best.

24
The Manifestation
of His Glory
Jn 2:11

Abruptly the story closes. This is divine reticence in contrast to our shallow talkativeness.[71] We can only surmise what the bridegroom said, the company thought, and Mary felt. But the narrator, St. John, tells us what the Synoptics have not recorded.[72] "This, the first of His signs, Jesus did at Cana in Galilee, and manifested His glory." These words are not to be construed as if the evangelist did not consider certain previous incidents as miraculous, for instance, the remarkable insight Jesus showed in the choice of His disciples. What Jesus wished to state was that here we have the beginning of those marvelous works, viewed as signs[73] or object lessons of Him whose very existence was the greatest miracle of all ("He was manifested in the flesh" [1 Tm 3:16]). "And His disciples believed in Him." By this miracle, He strengthened His disciples' faith in Him as the Messiah, which had been kindled a few days previously (Jn 1:37–49). He manifested His glory, in particular proving Himself as the Lord of nature, God Omnipotent, and the benevolent friend of man. By His presence at a humble wedding, the incarnate Son of God sanctified the holy estate of matrimony. In the beginning of His public ministry, with much work awaiting Him, He still found time to attend the marriage of a country couple and to exercise His sovereign transforming power to relieve their perplexity.

Shortly after this, Jesus went to Capernaum with His mother, brothers, and disciples.[74] Whether He first returned to Nazareth after the wedding and then proceeded to Capernaum the evangelist does not state. From Cana, the distance would have been about seventeen miles. His sisters are not mentioned, probably for the reason that they were already married and returned to Nazareth or else remained behind. Later we find them living at Nazareth (Mk 6:1, 3). The reason Jesus' family departed from Nazareth is not mentioned. It seems, however, that Jesus visited Capernaum to see the closely related family of Zebedee, whose sons, James and John, had now joined Him as disciples with Andrew and Simon, in order to draw tighter their mutual bond.[75] It was only a brief visit, but later Capernaum was to be His permanent home. The evangelist remembered this visit as the first of God's Chosen One in his fisherman's home. At that time, Capernaum was a city of considerable importance.[76] There was the residence of a royal officer and a custom station (Mt 9:9; Jn 4:46; etc.), and a detachment of Roman soldiers occupied the town. It was located on or near a great trade route from Damascus to the Mediterranean Sea and Egypt, with a flourishing fish trade, its own synagogue, and so forth. There also stood Peter's home, which may likewise have been the home of Christ (cf. Mt 8:14; Mk 1:29, 35; 2:1) before the town became desolate and lost.[77] "And you, Capernaum, will you be exalted to heaven? You will be brought down to Hades. For if the mighty works done in you had been done in Sodom, it would have remained until this day" (Mt 11:23; Lk 10:15). This was Capernaum, the home base of Jesus' ministry and the scene of many of His mighty works, where even now a few unrecorded mighty deeds may have been performed.[78] No long stay was made at this time, probably a few days at the end of February and beginning of AD 30, because the Jewish Passover was at hand.

25
Brief Visit
to Capernaum
Jn 2:12

7

THE EARLY JUDEAN MINISTRY

PASSOVER, AD 30, TO WINTER, AD 31

AUC	782	783	784	785	786
AD	29	30	31	32	33
Approx. age of Jesus	30	31	32	33	34
Passovers		I	II	III	IV

Absolute certainty about dating of biblical events is hard to achieve. But if our computations are tenable, and if John began his ministry in the spring of AD 29,[1] and if Jesus was baptized in the summer following,[2] then the first Passover of Christ's public ministry must have taken place in the spring of AD 30. Preparations for the festival had indeed been in process for a number of weeks before. There was the necessary domestic preparation for those making the pilgrimage. Bridges and roads were put in repair. The sepulchers were whitewashed to prevent an accidental pollution of the pilgrims.[3] The whole land was in a state of preparation. The roads were filled with pilgrims. As many as two and a half million worshipers gathered at Jerusalem from all parts of the Jewish world,[4] and among the Galilean pilgrims from Capernaum was Jesus of Nazareth with His little band of disciples (Jn 2:17; 3:22). The time had come for Him to present Himself to the nation as the promised Messiah. Of the journey itself and the particular route—probably along the Jordan valley to Jericho and then to Jerusalem—no details are given, except the notice that He "went up"[5] to Jerusalem, an expression literally accurate. For coming from Galilee one ascends from 680 feet below sea level near the Lake of Gennesaret to 2,500 feet above the Mediterranean Sea, the altitude of Jerusalem.

1
The Jews' Passover
Jn 2:13

On reaching Jerusalem, the Lord of the temple presented Himself at the temple of the Lord.[6] Yet, what He saw in the Court of the Gentiles did not at all please Him. He again noticed the disorder that may have vexed Him on earlier occasions. It is true, the Gospels mention only one previous visit, but we may well take it for granted that there had been others. The majestic temple, rising above the surrounding courts, included in its area an extensive southern space, into which the magnificent outer gates opened directly, the Court of the Gentiles. Gentiles might walk there, but not beyond a stone railing, the Soreg, which surrounded the Sacred Enclosure and menaced with death any Gentile who would enter.[7] In this space, a temple market had long ago been established. This was contrary to the Lord's purposes for His temple: (1) a "house of prayer" (Is 56:7), (2) the habitation where all His wondrous deeds should be proclaimed (Ps 26:7–8), and (3) the site for the Messiah-typifying sacrifices. Now, one of the courts had become a mart of trade where all that was needed for the sacrifices was offered for sale. The idea of making sacrificial animals readily available for people travelling from distant lands was a good one (cf. Dt 14:24–26), but the temple court was the wrong place for it. Even more troublesome, the money changers exchanged—at a premium of not less than five percent[8]—the image-bearing foreign currency for the lawful temple coin. Usually, the foreign coins were also defiled with heathen symbols and inscriptions. When it is remembered that, in addition to Israelite silver and copper coin, Persian, Tyrian, Syrian, Egyptian, Grecian, and Roman money circulated in the country—besides the foreign coin brought directly by the pilgrims from the Diaspora—it will be understood that both the work and the profit must have been enormous. All Jews and proselytes—with the exception of women, slaves, and minors—had to pay the annual temple-tribute of half a shekel in statutory coin (Ex 30:11–16).[9] In addition, there was a great deal to be bought at the temple bazaars for the feast, for the sacrifices, and for purification. There stood the cattle dealers with their animals for sacrifice: oxen, heifers, and lambs. Beside their cages sat the sellers of doves, offering to the poor worshipers what they needed for sacrifice. Oil, wine, and incense—the accessories of sacrifice—were also kept ready within the booths. This was all quite convenient for the sacrificers, but the booths and stalls should have been outside of the temple area. For all of these purchases, the right money was needed, and the prices charged were often exorbitant. The revenue realized by the regular temple tribute was immense, and the vast accumulation of illegally acquired wealth as realized by the temple bankers and traders must have been simply enormous. No wonder that, despite many previous spoliations, Crassus could carry away from the temple treasury ten thousand talents in gold (54–53 BC).[10] What became of the profit of the money changers? And who were the real owners of the temple market? Most likely Annas and the members of his high-priestly family.[11]—But to return. There was the disputing at the tables and the chattering beside the livestock. Loud noises disturbed the worship, while usury and deceit desecrated the sanctuary. Every finer religious feeling must have revolted against this state of things.

To Jesus, the temple market constituted an intolerable abuse. Stooping down, He made a whip of ropes made of rushes,[12] probably designed as an emblem of His power. Then, in order to cleanse the sacred court of its worst pollutions, He drove out the oxen, sheep, and cattle, along with the people who sold them. Then, going to the tables of the money changers, He overthrew them with their carefully arranged piles of various coins. To the sellers of doves, He issued the command: "Take these things away; do not make My Father's house a house of trade." In His word and action, His Messiahship was clearly implied. He does not merely say "your Father" or "our Father," but "My Father's house."[13] This, then, was Christ's first public act in Jerusalem: the first cleansing of the temple. (There was another at the close of His ministry.) Of course, ordinarily a Jewish religious enthusiast would have had no actual right to interfere. That was the duty of the temple police, assigned to it by the supreme ecclesiastical court. But this body had failed in its duty, and in a most particular sense Jesus was now about His Father's business (Lk 2:49, KJV). In spite of the fact that the messianic import of the cleansing was not recognized, all true friends of the Law saw the righteousness of the action. The disciples of Jesus saw the fulfillment of a messianic psalm: "Zeal for Your house has consumed Me" (Ps 69:9). The Jewish authorities, however, saw in the act and word of Jesus only unauthorized interference and unwarranted assumption of authority. It was quite characteristic of them to ask for a sign. "What sign do You show us for doing these things?" This was not the last time that such questions would be asked. Jesus gave the enigmatic answer: "Destroy this temple, and in three days I will raise it up." In reply to their challenge He referred them to the greatest messianic sign. This was Jesus' first prediction of His death and resurrection, as remembered by His disciples after He was risen from the dead. The Jews misunderstood, but they did not forget the words. Later on, during His final trial, they used His words for their false charge (Mt 26:61). Christ spoke of the temple of His body, as the evangelist observes. But the Jews thought that He was thinking of the still unfinished Herodian temple. "The Jews then said, 'It has taken forty-six years to build this temple, and will You raise it up in three days?" These words serve as a chronological tag. The rebuilding of the temple was begun in Chislev (November–December) in the eighteenth year of the reign of Herod, corresponding to 20–19 BC. The temple itself was finished in mid to late 18 BC. The temple precinct was completed in 12 BC. However, work on the edifice continued until the time of Herod Agrippa II (AD 64).[14] If the Jews spoke to Jesus about the completion of the temple in c. 18 BC, then the forty-sixth

3
Cleansing the
Temple
Jn 2:15–22

anniversary of the temple would have occurred in mid to late AD 29, meaning the Passover of John 2 took place in AD 30.[15]

During Jesus' stay in Jerusalem for the Passover, He performed a number of miracles of which we have no particular account. "Many believed in His name when they saw the signs that He was doing." But this faith was only a milk faith, as Luther calls it,[16] which fed on signs and required miracles for its sustenance. It was a faith that was not genuine and did not reach down to the heart. And Jesus, who is a discerner of men and looks into the heart, would not commit Himself to such followers or enter into any intimate relation with them such as He did, for instance, with His newly won Galilean friends.

The reformatory act of Jesus in the temple naturally aroused the enmity of the ecclesiastical powers. There was as yet no hostile step, but a bitter feud had begun, of which the sequel could not be doubtful. Nevertheless, even among the Jewish authorities an early follower was found, a Pharisee, a rich man, a ruler—Nicodemus, a member of the Council (Jn 7:50; 19:39). A certain Bonai, surnamed Nakdimon, appears in the Talmud. He was one of the richest and most distinguished citizens of Jerusalem, whose daughter, after inheriting immense wealth, was reduced to abject poverty. But it seems that this legendary Nakdimon was not the Nicodemus of the Gospel.[17] According to a tradition in the Gospel of Nicodemus and in other apocryphal works, after Nicodemus testified in favor of Christ before Pilate, the hostile Jews divested Nicodemus of his office and banished him. It also states that Peter and John baptized him, and that his remains were found in a common grave beside those of Gamaliel and Stephen.[18] But our only authentic information of this interesting rabbi is derived from the few scattered notices in the Gospel of John (Jn 3:1–15; 7:50–52; 19:39). He came to Jesus by night. His secret visit was probably because he feared he would be exposed to the ridicule and hatred of his fellow Jewish leaders, or because he thought himself too eminent a person to compromise his dignity by making this visit in public.[19] Be that as it may, he came. There was something about this young Galilean prophet that attracted him. There was a desire in his soul, though he was "a teacher of Israel" (Jn 3:9), to become more closely acquainted with the doctrine of this Teacher come from God. Possibly he had previously heard, and seriously meditated on, the message of John the Baptist: "Repent, for the kingdom of heaven is at hand" (Mt 3:2). Nicodemus was now conceiving it to be possible that the recent deeds of Jesus were signs of the Kingdom.

We do not know where the meeting took place. But since John was the reporter and also perhaps a witness of the interview and seems to have had a house in Jerusalem (see Jn 19:27), it is probable that the conversation took place in his house and in his presence. It was on an evening in spring. A whispering breeze gently disturbs the evening air (Jn 3:8). The city rests. But Nicodemus, a noble member of the Council, has something on his mind. He comes to Jesus for direction on a most delicate point of Jewish or Christian theology—the King and admission into the Kingdom. Or we might state it in an unexpressed "What must I do in order to enter the Messiah's kingdom?"[20] Nicodemus was an unexpected and uncommon nightly visitor. But as Jesus was not intimidated by the questioning Jewish authorities (Jn 2:18) nor deceived by the "milk faith" of acclaiming multitudes (Jn 2:24), so He was not now flattered into eager politeness by the possibility of gaining a convert from the Great Council of the Jews. There is neither undue deference nor, on the other hand, an air of superiority. An atmosphere of calm and earnest dignity prevailed. Probably not every word of the interview has been recorded. What the Holy Spirit inspired the evangelist to write is an outline, the gist, of an extended conversation, which, however, gives us all that is necessary to know. We can almost imagine the scene beside a flickering lamp. Nicodemus began: "Rabbi, we[21] know that You are a teacher come from God, for no one can do these signs that You do unless God is with him." Thus by way of introduction he paid a fine tribute to Jesus. He thought well of Him, but not well enough. He regarded Him as a teacher, but not as the Savior. In speaking of Him as a miracle-working divine prophet, Nicodemus probably thought he had made a great confession. But he had not yet entered the porticoes of true knowledge.[22] He was still ignorant of the way to salvation.

Jesus did not respond to the words of esteem directed to Him. Jesus replies—if not to the *words*, then at least to the *question in the heart* of Nicodemus: "Truly, truly, I say to you, unless one is born again[23] he cannot see the kingdom of God." He tells him point-blank that the righteousness of works, upon which he, as a Pharisee, builds his hope of heaven, cannot avail before the just and holy God. No man is able to fulfill His Law. If he desires to enter the Kingdom, he must experience a radical change of heart and will; he must become an entirely new creature; a spiritual rebirth must take place. What Jesus says to Nicodemus corresponds to the message of the Baptist and to His own words: "The time is fulfilled, and the kingdom of God is at hand; repent and believe in the gospel" (Mk 1:15). Nicodemus could not understand. He thought Christ was referring to a physical rebirth. "How can a man be born when he is old? Can he enter a second time into his mother's womb and be born?" Jesus replied: "Unless one is born of water[24] and the Spirit, he cannot enter the kingdom of God. That which is born of the flesh is flesh, and that which is born of the Spirit is spirit." This rebirth is the spiritual regeneration most marvelously brought about by the Holy Spirit in Word and Sacrament. It is necessary for every man on account of his sinful nature, original sin, inherited from our first parents; for "that which is born of the flesh is flesh." A new God-pleasing life is possible only in those regenerated by the Spirit. An expression of confusion registers

7
"Unless One Is Born Again"
Jn 3:3–8

itself on the face of Nicodemus as he listens to these bewildering words. But did he hear the brief rushing of the night breeze as it rose and fell?[25]

> Do not marvel that I said to you, "You must be born again." The wind blows where it wishes, and you hear its sound, but you do not know where it comes from or where it goes. So it is with everyone who is born of the Spirit.

Even as—for example—the wind, the thunder, the human soul, are invisible, though their existence and operation are evident, so also the effects of regeneration are apparent. But the process of regeneration, the manner in which the spiritual rebirth is brought about, is incomprehensible to human reason.

8
"How Can These Things Be?"
Jn 3:9

Jesus' explanation does not make the matter clear to the bewildered mind of Nicodemus. He asks, "How can these things be?" Nicodemus held the opinion that the mere fact of his physical Jewish birth entitled him to admission into the kingdom of heaven, and now he hears: Not birth, but rebirth. As a teacher of Israel, he was supposed to lead others on the way to salvation, and now he learns that he must be shown that way himself. And then this reference to the mysterious working of the Spirit. Question after question arises in his heart, "How can these things be?" Jesus replies, "Are you the teacher of Israel and yet you do not understand these things?" These words are not to be taken as reproachful irony, but rather as an expression of sincere sadness over this sorrowful state of ignorance. If the teacher is so obtuse, how great must be the dullness of those whom he teaches![26]

9
"Whoever Believes in Him"
Jn 3:10–21

The dialogue ceases. But Jesus does not leave Nicodemus in a state of bewilderment. His nightly visitor's searching questions stirred Him into offering him a fuller explanation of heavenly things. Coordinating His teaching with that of the prophets, John the Baptist, and all divinely appointed messengers of the truth, Jesus continues: "Truly, truly, I say to you, we speak of what we know, and bear witness to what we have seen, but you do not receive our testimony." This is a sad complaint. The spiritual regeneration, though a wonderful work of God, is yet an earthly thing in the respect that it takes place on earth, in the hearts of men. But "if I have told you earthly things and you do not believe, how can you believe if I tell you heavenly things?" That is, if you have questions about matters open to human observation (at least in their effect), what if Christ teaches about things unseen (Wis of Sol 9:13–19)?[27] And this He now does. As the apostle later wrote, the Gospel is "a stumbling block to Jews and folly to Gentiles, but to those who are called, both Jews and Greeks, Christ the power of God and the wisdom of God" (1Co 1:23–24). He speaks of the mysteries concerning His own person and of the gracious counsel and purposes of God. He shows that to this category belongs especially the messianic mysteries, the divine decrees for the redemption and salvation of man. Only the Lord can reveal these things. For "no one has ascended into heaven except He who descended from heaven, the Son of Man." He came down from heaven being true God from eternity together with the Father and the Holy Spirit, and still is in heaven, also according to His human nature and in His present state of humiliation.[28] Without controversy, great is this mystery: God was manifest in the flesh. The purpose of His incarnation is stated in the following: "And as Moses lifted up the serpent in the wilderness, so must the Son of Man be lifted up." Already Christ makes an allusion to His redeeming death by crucifixion.[29] "Whoever believes in Him may have eternal life." And, continuing, Christ utters those wonderful words, the kernel of the Gospel:[30] "For God so loved the world, that He gave His only Son, that whoever believes in Him should not perish but have eternal life." Jesus is the universal, the only, Savior of all mankind. Whoever believes in Him will not be condemned. But whoever does not believe is condemned already; he already has hell on his neck.[31] But, alas! men prefer sin and destruction to the Savior, the Light of life, of their salvation. They love darkness rather than light. This they show in their everyday life.

> For everyone who does wicked things hates the light and does not come to the light, lest his works should be exposed. But whoever does what is true [i.e., receives Christ] comes to the light, so that it may be clearly seen that his works have been carried out in God.

But did not Christ contradict Himself? First He said: "Unless one is born again he cannot see the kingdom of God," and then He says: "Whoever believes in Him is not condemned." How do these statements agree? There is no contradiction in these two statements. He that is born of the Spirit believes in Christ. And he that believes is reborn and shows his faith in a new, a Christian, life. Thus the interview with Nicodemus came to an end. He came seeking and left believing. At least, when he appears again, there is evidence that the Spirit of God had moved his heart (Jn 7:50–52). Born again? How can these things be? But why ask? Even in his own heart, these things had actually taken place.

10
A Question
Jn 3:1–21

After the interview with Nicodemus, Jesus and His disciples left the capital city for the rural section of the Judean country. The location is not given, but most likely He traveled in a northeasterly direction, toward the banks of the Jordan. We now hear that Jesus baptized. However, whereas John baptized with his own hand, Jesus Himself did not baptize (Jn 4:2), but delegated the Baptism with water to His disciples. Thus Jesus rendered the act of Baptism independent of His own personal presence and so provided that it would continue in His Church after His departure. We do not know how long Jesus continued His ministry here, but His stay must have been prolonged,[32] covering, as we suppose, the summer of AD 30.[33] In this same period, John, after transferring the scene of his ministry from Bethany to the west side of the Jordan, was similarly engaged. But why did John continue to baptize? Was it because Jesus had not yet come forth, as John mistakenly thought He

11
The Parallel Ministry
of Jesus and John
Jn 3:22–24

should? Or was it because John was not convinced of the messiahship of Jesus? Or must the parallel ministry be looked upon as a splitting asunder of the messianic movement?[34] Certainly not. John's work and mission, to which his administration of Baptism belonged, was from God (Lk 20:4), and God had not yet ended it. Although we do not know the exact location of our Lord's baptismal activity, the scene of John's ministry at that time is given as "Aenon near Salim, because water was plentiful there." We have not yet definitely identified this site, though a number of localities have been proposed.[35] The tradition that places it a few miles south of Beth-shean, Scythopolis, has this in its favor, that it was on the west side of the Jordan[36] and that it locates the scene of John's last public labors close to the seat of Herod Antipas, into whose power he was soon to be delivered.[37]

During this period, there arose a discussion between John's disciples and the Jews[38] about purification. Most likely, the argument was about the relative importance of the two baptisms, the relation of one to the other, and the like. The disciples of John, it seems, began the questioning.[39] They possibly challenged some Jew for desiring to be baptized by Jesus. In zeal, John's disciples brought tidings to John of which he seems not to have been aware. They complained indirectly about what to them seemed interference with his work and something approaching presumption on the part of Jesus.[40] "Rabbi, He who was with you across the Jordan, to whom you bore witness—look, He is baptizing, and all are going to Him." The significant suppression of the name of Jesus reveals a jealous irritation.[41] John's disciples complained because they thought that Jesus, who had gone forth from the fellowship of the Baptist, owed His standing to John's favorable testimony; yet He now arose in competition with John and put him in the shade. John, however, made a noble reply to this complaint, in which his inherent greatness shone forth. "A person cannot receive even one thing unless it is given him from above." That is, all success, including that of the preacher of God's Word, comes from above. And in John's case, had he not testified: "I am not the Christ, but I have been sent before Him"? Jesus' success should not be an occasion for complaint to them, but rather a source of joy. It is to the bridegroom, and to him alone, to whom the bride belongs. He was not the Bridegroom, but the Bridegroom's friend,[42] and even now he was greatly gladdened by the Bridegroom's voice—unmistakable evidence that the moment for the marriage had arrived. "He must increase, but I must decrease." The setting of his sun was the signal of the rising of One infinitely brighter. The end of his mission marked the beginning of another's. Although John was indeed a prophet, his words were only "of the earth," while Jesus, "who comes from heaven is above all." John's disciples complainingly said of Jesus: "All are going to Him." If only it were true! John's complaint was that the number was much too small. "No one receives His testimony." And still, there were some that believed. "The Father loves the Son and has given all things into His hand. Whoever believes in the Son has eternal life; whoever does not obey the Son shall not see life, but the wrath of God remains on him." A wonderful tribute to Christ. "He must increase, but I must decrease." What a depth of unselfish, humble loyalty! John spoke from the bottom of his heart, because it was for the very thing of which his disciples complained that he had waited and worked. Now that Jesus had come, he was content. It was all in order. Moses disrobed Aaron (Nu 20:28), but this Aaron of the New Testament (John) unrobed himself before he lay down to die.[43] "Truly, . . . among those born of women there has arisen no one greater than John the Baptist" (Mt 11:11).

"Now when Jesus[44] learned that the Pharisees had heard that Jesus was making and baptizing more disciples than John,[45] . . . He left Judea and departed again for Galilee." Here we have the facts: first, that Jesus made more disciples than John, which led the forerunner's disciples to complain; second, that the Pharisees, who evidently watched both Jesus and John, knew this; and third, that Jesus, well aware that the Pharisees were watching,[46] left Judea. But are these all the facts, or were there other reasons why Jesus ceased to baptize and why He left Judea? The question is of some importance for chronological considerations. Readers often attempt to make this passage agree with the notice about John's arrest and imprisonment (Mt 4:12; Mk 1:14; Lk 4:14; 3:19–20).[47] They say that the Pharisees were instrumental in arresting John at this time and that Jesus, fearing a similar fate, retired through Samaria to Galilee, beyond the jurisdiction of the Council, and there began His great Galilean ministry. But this solution does not agree with our present text, which leaves us under the impression that John's work was still in progress. It is true that Jesus did not begin His own great Galilean ministry until John had run his course; but it seems improbable that the arrest of John took place at this time. Although Jesus' greater success was offensive to the Pharisees, there is no evidence that the Pharisees were instrumental in delivering John over to Herod. Jesus did not leave Judea because He was concerned about His own personal safety, but rather because He did not want to place Himself in competition with John, His friend and divinely commissioned forerunner. Jesus withdrew to avoid any hindrance that His own baptismal activity might make for John. There are also other considerations that cause us to believe that John's imprisonment and the beginning of Jesus' Galilean ministry did not take place at this time. According to John 1:35–51, Jesus met some of the disciples right after His Baptism, before later calling them as described in Mt 4:18–22; Mk 1:16–20; Lk 5:1–11. The calling, or rather the recalling, of the disciples at Capernaum, as related by the Synoptists, presupposes a period of retirement.[48] During Jesus' baptismal activity in Judea, His disciples were His helpers; but after the return of their Master to Galilee, they seem to have returned to their old calling. He did not recall them until He began His labors at Capernaum. That, by the way,

13
Departure for Galilee
Jn 4:1–3

is probably the reason why this period of the life of Christ is passed over in silence by the Synoptists, while it was the purpose of John to fill this gap. Therefore, if it is now late in AD 30 or early in 31, we place the imprisonment of John and the beginning of Christ's great Galilean ministry after the unnamed feast.[49]—We now proceed with our story.

14
Samaria
Jn 4:4

"And He had to pass through Samaria." If we place the scene of Jesus' ministry in Northern Judea, He would pass through Samaria on the way to Galilee. And if we may credit the report of Josephus, the road through Samaria was generally taken by the Galilean pilgrims on their way to the capital,[50] especially if they were in a hurry.[51] On the other hand, the traveling Judeans[52] seem chiefly to have made a detour through Perea in order to avoid the hostile and Levitically impure Samaritans. We need not enter into all the details of Samaritan history. We remember that after the fall of the Northern Kingdom[53] and the carrying away of the ten tribes, the Babylonians repeopled the wasted and depopulated districts of this territory with heathen colonists. There was thus formed a mixed people with a mixed religion. Although the name Samaria and Samaritans still clung to the territory,[54] the principal settlers, "men of Cuth" (2Ki 17:30), contributed the name Cutheans, by which the Jews afterward persistently designated the Samaritans.[55] This was intended as a term of reproach to mark them as a foreign race and to repudiate all connections between them and the Jews. The colonists brought by the Babylonians naturally introduced a number of idols (2Ki 17:29–31); but as these heathen people gradually intermingled with the remnants of the Israelitish population, they generally accepted the worship of Yahweh—with exceptions. They strongly believed in the unity of God. They most strictly and zealously observed what they still retained of biblical Law.[56] They observed the Sabbath and practiced circumcision. They held to the doctrine of angels and devils, and it is doubtful whether they shared the Sadducean denial of the resurrection.[57] Of the Old Testament writings, only the five Books of Moses, the Pentateuch, were accepted as canonical.[58] They, too, hoped for the Messiah, expecting Him, however, to be a religious reformer, a prophet,[59] not a king in the nationalistic, Jewish sense. After the return of the Jews from the Babylonian captivity, Ezra and Nehemiah insisted upon a strict separation between the Samaritans and the faithful Jews. So the Samaritans erected a rival temple on Mount Gerizim, above Shechem. A violent and constant hostility resulted, which was modified only on occasions. When the Jews were in the ascendency and it suited their purposes, the Samaritans would call themselves Jews, at least descendants of Jacob and Joseph through Manasseh and Ephraim. But when the Jews were in adversity, then the Samaritans would claim to be of the stock of the Medes and Persians.[60] In the troublesome times of enforced Hellenization under Antiochus Epiphanes, when the temple in Jerusalem was desecrated, sacrifices of swine were commanded, and Judaism was ordered to cease,[61] the Samaritans escaped a similar fate by repudiating all connection with Israel and dedicating their temple to Jupiter. In the last Jewish struggle with Rome, the Samaritans remained neutral. Since the time of Herod, Samaria had been a province of the Jewish kingdom, passing on to Archelaus and, after his deposition, to the Roman procurator. Pontius Pilate ruled both Judea and Samaria in the days of our Lord. But despite unified administration, there was no love lost between the Jews and the Samaritans. When Jewish pilgrims passed through Samaria, scoffing was not lacking, nor were malicious deeds of violence wanting. The Jews, on the other hand, treated the Samaritans with every mark of supreme contempt. They excluded them entirely from their fellowship. They accused them of falsehood, folly, and irreligion, and this in the most offensive terms of assumed superiority and self-righteous, pharisaic bigotry.[62] The expression "You are a Samaritan and have a demon" (Jn 8:48), which they hurled at Jesus, shows in what egregiously low esteem the Jews held the Samaritans.

It was without this racial prejudice that Jesus entered Samaria in late AD 30. He came to rest at Jacob's well, just outside Sychar, near the estate that Jacob had bequeathed to his favorite son and where Joseph himself had commanded his bones to be buried (Gn 33:19; 50:24–26; Jsh 24:32).[63] This well is located at the fork of an old Roman road, with Joseph's tomb and Sychar (Al Askar) to the right (northeast) and Shechem (Nablus) to the left (northwest). Just off the road to the south, the giant bulk of "this mountain" (Jn 4:20), Gerizim, overshadows the rear.[64] It was, as we take it, between 11 a.m. and noon, "about the sixth hour," that Jesus, "wearied as He was from His journey, was sitting beside the well."[65] The disciples had gone away into nearby Sychar to purchase food, Samaritan food, which curiously enough was declared lawful in the time of Christ.[66] Jesus rested at the well alone—unless John, the recorder of this event, was with Him. As He waited for His disciples to return, "A woman from Samaria[67] came to draw water." Jesus said to her, "Give Me a drink." Everyone who has traveled in the hospitable East knows with what ready response a request of this nature is usually met.[68] But here was a delicate situation. Jesus' clothing or appearance would tell the woman He was a Jew. And His speech, His pronunciation and enunciation, would beyond doubt have revealed His nationality.[69] She well knew how haughtily the Jews generally looked down upon her despised race. With a certain satisfaction, she noticed that thirst had forced a member of that proud race to make a request that, as she thought, would ordinarily not have been made. "How is it that You, a Jew, ask for a drink from me, a woman of Samaria? (For Jews [adds the evangelist] have no dealings with Samaritans.)"

The woman did not seek this meeting; it was providential in the truest sense of the word. Our omniscient Savior knew that He would meet her, and He was seeking to save her soul. Gently, He turned the request and the reply to the Samaritan

15
At Jacob's Well
Jn 4:5–9

16
Living Water
Jn 4:10–15

woman's spiritual welfare. The woman was utterly unconscious of standing on the threshold of the greatest possibilities. Jesus told her that if she had known the gift of God and Him who was making the request, she would have asked Him to give her living water. This gift of God is the Messiah and the living water His salvation. But the woman did not understand. She pointed to the well, a hundred feet deep.[70] And still, she must have been impressed, for she now addressed her Jewish stranger with a title of respect: "Sir,[71] You have nothing to draw water with, and the well[72] is deep. Where do You get that living water?" Or was He probably thinking of other and better water; that is, living and running spring water, which He could procure independently of the well? But then, even so, why should that water be better than that which she could draw for herself, consecrated by the memories of the patriarchs, and which had sufficed for the ancient fathers, for their household and cattle? "Are You greater than our father Jacob? He gave us the well and drank from it himself, as did his sons and his livestock." Jesus did not expect the woman to understand. His purpose was to attract and then to fix her attention. The hard literalism of her reply did not deter Him. On the contrary, He seized upon it to bring home to her that He was speaking of living water in a figurative sense.[73] Certainly, His water was better in quality than that of the patriarch's well, better than all earthly things.

> Everyone who drinks of this [well] water will be thirsty again, but whoever drinks of the water that I will give him will never be thirsty again. The water that I will give him will become in him a spring of water welling up to eternal life.

But even this explanation suggested nothing to the woman. While a desire had been awakened in her, she was still thinking of the laborious drudgery and tiresome daily journey to the well. If she could only do away with that! "Sir, give me this water, so that I will not be thirsty or have to come here to draw water."

17
God Is a Spirit
Jn 4:16–26

Jesus changes the subject. He strikes out on a different avenue in His approach to the woman's heart. The woman's material interests, as revealed in her reply, indicate that as yet she feels no spiritual need. There was only one way to open that understanding, and that was to awaken in her a sense of guilt. "Go, call your husband, and come here." The woman answers, "I have no husband." Jesus replies, "You are right in saying, 'I have no husband'; for you have had five husbands,[74] and the one you now have is not your husband." Here we have the same proof of divine omniscience that He revealed in His talk with Nathanael (Jn 1:48). He knew that she had been married five times, but that the man with whom she was now living was not her husband, but only her paramour. He certainly knew about her past (Jn 4:29) and now reminded her of her sin and shame. The woman did not dare to deny her sin, but was forced to acknowledge that Jesus was right. "Sir, I perceive that You are a prophet." But she did not yet recognize in Jesus *that* prophet. Neither was she ready to ask, What must I do to be saved? In true artfulness, she clouded the issue.

Partly exposing her views, yet not completely confiding in the newly discovered prophet, she challenged Jesus with a standing problem of the Samaritan religion.[75] It was a question that divided the Jews and the Samaritans and struck at the heart of their respective national and religious interests. If this question was answered to her satisfaction, then she could also tell whether He was truly a prophet or whether His detailed knowledge was only a trick. "Our fathers worshiped on this mountain, but You say that in Jerusalem is the place where people ought to worship." In His reply, the Lord showed marvelous wisdom and both tender human insight and consideration. As to the proper place for worship, the Jews were undoubtedly right. Jerusalem was the place that the Lord had chosen. As compared with the hybrid and defective Samaritan worship, the worship of the Jews was pure and true.[76] Even if inwardly they had betrayed their solemn trust, outwardly they still *had* Moses and the prophets. The Messiah was of the seed of David, and salvation was of the Jews, from which race it was to pass on to all. But before and after entering into the merely formal and physical phase of the controversy, Jesus pours out to the woman a taste of the living water. The hour shall come, indeed, has already come, "when neither on this mountain nor in Jerusalem will you worship the Father." "The hour is coming, and is now here, when the true worshipers will worship the Father in spirit and truth." It is not a question of *where* you worship, but *whom* you worship and *how*. "God is spirit, and those who worship Him must worship in spirit and truth." His presence is not confined to a temple built by the hand of man, nor are those who worship Him bound to mere forms, ceremonies, rituals, symbols, and sacrifices. Jesus gives a picture in miniature of the New Testament Christian Church, which is not bound to a certain place of worship and its prescribed ceremonies. The true children of God, the believers in Christ, need not observe such and such outward forms; it is all a matter of a truly believing heart.

The woman was deeply touched and moved. Her heart was directed to messianic thoughts. In her heart a longing was awakened for the Messiah. She shared with her people the Samaritan conception of the promised Messiah. "I know that Messiah is coming (He who is called Christ). When He comes, He will tell us all things." As opposed to the Jewish imperial messianic expectations, the Samaritans saw in the expected Christ chiefly a teacher and a guide. With a sigh, she would refer the final solution of this and other difficult problems to that expected teacher. And now Jesus opens wide the floodgates of living water: "I who speak to you am He."

In the meantime, the disciples returned. They were astonished at finding their Master in conversation with a Samaritan woman. To talk with a strange, particularly a Samaritan, woman was supposed to be against the dignity of a Jewish rabbi.[77] But they were gradually learning that Jesus would at times do strange things for reasons that were not always clearly evident. Awe of Him, however, prevented them

18
The Woman Speaks to Her Samaritan Friends
Jn 4:27–30

from making any inquiries as to the motive or as to the subject matter of the exceptional conversation that they had just interrupted. At the arrival of the disciples, the woman withdrew. Only conscious of the new well-spring that had risen in her heart, she forgot all about her water-bearing errand. She left her water jar at the well, hastened to the city, announced her great discovery, and called upon her townspeople to seek with her the prophet whom she ventured to describe as the Messiah: "Come, see a man who told me all that I ever did. Can this be the Christ?" This statement, on the part of the woman, was skillful leading without seeming to lead. She aroused the curiosity of the townsfolk, and a number of them immediately set out on a mission to seek Christ.

19
Discourse on the Fields White for Harvest
Jn 4:31–38

The disciples now urged Jesus to eat of the food that they had brought from the city. But the soul of Jesus was otherwise engaged. At the moment, He felt no need for bodily food. "I have food to eat that you do not know about." There was food and satisfaction for Him in things of which the disciples were not aware. The disciples did not understand. No one could be seen who had given Him food. But Jesus explained: "My food is to do the will of Him who sent Me." And, looking up, He saw the Samaritan townsfolk approaching through the fresh green of the springing grain. This, in line with His thoughts about the newly won Samaritan woman, probably suggested a notable discourse on the harvest fields. The seed had been recently sown that autumn. Now, a little later, the fields were already fresh and green.[78] "Do you not say, 'There are yet four months, then comes harvest'?" That is, the sixteenth day of Nisan, on which day harvesting legally commenced by the offering of the first sheaf (Lv 23:10–15; Dt 16:9). "Look, I tell you, lift up your eyes, and see that the fields are white for harvest." The disciples saw only the green fields of springing corn. But in the approaching Samaritans, the prophetic eye of Jesus saw a harvest field (Ac 8:5). There were the real firstfruits of a promising mission-harvest. In this field, there was a sowing and a reaping unto life everlasting. "One sows and another reaps"; but both he that sows and he that reaps should rejoice together. Jesus, the Sower, had just sown the seed. But already there was a harvest, not only in the Samaritan woman, but in the friends whom the woman was bringing to Christ. There would also be a harvest for the disciples, even in Samaria, and to the ends of the earth. "I sent[79] you to reap that for which you did not labor. Others have labored, and you have entered into their labor."

20
Reception by the Samaritans
Jn 4:39–42

It was as Jesus had said, "The fields are white for harvest." The newly won Samaritan woman missionary had done good work. "Many Samaritans from that town believed in Him because of the woman's testimony." And the conversation with Jesus convinced others. "And many more believed because of His Word." As a result of the first interview with the stranger at Jacob's well, the Samaritans invited Jesus to stay with them. He accepted the invitation, stayed with them two days, and

His Word established faith in Him as the Messiah. Apparently, they did not need the aid of signs and wonders to believe. The final result of this visit is summed up in an expression by the believing Sycharites to the first Samaritan missionary for Christ: "It is no longer because of what you said that we believe, for we have heard for ourselves, and we know that this is indeed the Savior of the world."

After a stay of two days with the friendly Samaritans, Jesus returned to Galilee. His absence had extended over eight months, since the Passover in spring, shortly after His first miracle in Cana. We remember the reason for His departure from Judea at this time;[80] namely, the fact that more people were flocking to Him than to John (Jn 4:1–3), while in the counsel of God, John was to continue for a while yet to prepare the way for Him. Jesus withdrew to Galilee to seek retirement for Himself and to await such a time as He would see fit to begin His own great ministry in earnest. In Galilee, He would not likely receive high honor on account of His humble origin and the familiarity created by the knowledge of His home surroundings. "For Jesus Himself had testified," either now or previously,[81] "that a prophet has no honor in his own hometown." Nor was He mistaken. In the beginning of His great Galilean ministry, His first public appearance in Nazareth was promptly followed by His first rejection (Lk 4:22–30). This first gleam of transient reception did not deceive Him (compare Jn 2:23–25). "So when He came to Galilee, the Galileans welcomed Him, having seen all that He had done in Jerusalem at the feast. For they too had gone to the feast." They "welcomed" Him. The evangelist is very careful in His statement. The reception of the Galileans, based only upon signs and wonders, was not true, genuine faith such as was that of the Samaritans, which was grounded upon His saving Word.[82]

Jesus returned to Galilee, but we don't know whether He made a short stopover at Nazareth, which was just off the main caravan road. He had lived in Nazareth for many years and probably even now it was the home of His sisters (Mk 6:3).[83] Such a visit is not stated or even intimated in any of the four Gospels. Most likely, He continued His journey, at least as far as Cana, with Capernaum as a possible objective. Capernaum was the home of Simon and John and, it seems, the present home of Jesus' mother and His brothers (Jn 2:12).[84] Cana was the home of Nathanael, and it was there, we remember, that Jesus performed His first miracle, about a year or so previously. On His way to Capernaum, He met an officer of King Herod's court. We do not know the name of the royal officer nor the nature of his office. However, it is reasonable to conjecture that it was Chuza, Herod's household manager, for afterward, Chuza's wife Joanna appears as a follower of Jesus (Lk 8:3). In consequence of the miracle Jesus performed here, this courtier believed, as did all his house.[85] An urgent need prompted the court official to leave the bedside of his dying son at Capernaum and to walk the sixteen miles of hard travel up the steep

21
Return to Galilee
Jn 4:43–45

22
The Official's Son
Jn 4:46–47

Way of the Sea across the hills to Cana where he could make an earnest appeal to Jesus, whose fame had preceded Him to Galilee and of whose arrival there he had heard. "When this man heard that Jesus had come from Judea to Galilee, he went to Him and asked Him to come down and heal his son, for he was at the point of death." Outside of the general designation "fever" (v. 52), the nature of the sickness is not described. We need not assume that this officer appealed to Jesus for help because he believed in Him as the Messiah.[86] Most likely, he despaired of a cure through other means already employed. So he resolved to appeal to the new Galilean prophet. He believed that Jesus was able to heal his son, but he considered the personal presence of Jesus necessary to effect the cure. Thus, he "asked Him to come down," sixteen miles, "and heal his son." Being a person of high standing, he did not hesitate to make the request.

23
"Unless You See Signs and Wonders"
Jn 4:48–49

Jesus replied: "Unless you see signs and wonders you will not believe." It was not the purpose of Jesus to set Himself up as a miracle-monger, to gain fame for His healing powers, but through the miracles that He performed He desired to attest His doctrine and the truth that He was indeed that Prophet who was to come. Even without miracles, people should have believed His divine Word. But the official was in no mood for spiritual discussion. As a parent, he thought only of his sick child. It was already between noon and one o'clock,[87] and Capernaum was sixteen miles away. "Sir, come down before my child dies." His confidence in the Lord's ability to help was still unshaken; that is, under the condition that He would personally appear at the bedside, and as long as there was still life in his son. Notice the little word "before" in verse 49. Would it be too late after his son had passed away? Would the faith of the tormented father then have faced too great a test?

24
"Your Son Will Live"
Jn 4:50–54

But Jesus knew what He was doing. After checking the request, which appears to have had little root in spiritual conviction, and rebuking the spirit that demanded signs as the ground of faith, He still showed that the official's confidence was not misplaced. He was actually the benevolent physician the man expected—and more. "Go; your son will live." It is not necessary for Me to go along with you. "Your son will live"; that is, he is cured and no longer at the point of death. "The man believed the word that Jesus spoke to him and went on his way." That was faith based upon the Word, as it should be, and not merely upon a miracle. And it was faith unmixed with doubt; he "went on his way," believing, rejoicing, although he could not yet see that Jesus had kept His word. Believing and trusting, he did not even hurry. "Whoever believes will not be in haste" (Is 28:16). He could have reached Capernaum that night, but, calmed by faith in the promise, he slept at some point along the way. The next morning, his servants met him with the joyful news. When he inquired about the time when his son improved, they replied, "Yesterday at the seventh hour," (that is, at 1 p.m.) "the fever left him." "The father knew that was the hour when Jesus had said to him, 'Your son will live.' And he himself believed, and all his household." Notice the remarkable progress his faith had made. From a mere belief in the healing power of Jesus to faith in His Word, and then to absolute faith in Him as the Messiah, with a blessed effect upon the members of his house. Thus for a second time, Jesus performed a miracle immediately upon His return from Judea to Galilee (Jn 2:11).[88]

8

THE UNNAMED FEAST

THE IMPRISONMENT OF JOHN, AD 30

AUC	782	783	784	785	786
AD	29	30	31	32	33
Approx. age of Jesus	30	31	32	33	34
Passovers		I	II	III	IV

Following the return of Jesus from His early Judean ministry in late AD 30, our Lord seems to have lived in retirement until He again went up to Jerusalem to attend an unspecified feast of the Jews. Neither do we hear of the disciples until the Synoptics take up the account. In the Gospel of John, they do not appear again until at the feeding of the five thousand (6:3). It seems that after the return of their Master through Samaria to Galilee they were permitted to return to their families and their accustomed labors, not to be recalled[1] until the beginning of the great Galilean ministry. Possibly, there was one exception: John, the beloved disciple, who, as a probable witness, brings the account of the story we are about to relate.

"After this there was a feast of the Jews, and Jesus went up to Jerusalem."[2] We would indeed welcome a definite proof that this festival was the Passover; for then we would have a chronological tag for determining the length of Christ's ministry. But it seems that the evangelist's inclusion of this notice was not prompted by chronological considerations. From a reference to a Jewish festival, which explains the presence of Jesus in Jerusalem, the evangelist proceeds to the account of a miracle, which, in turn, is introduced by the information that "there is in Jerusalem"[3] a well-known pool, called Bethesda in Aramaic, and enclosed within five arches, or colonnades, presumably near the Sheep Gate, at the northeastern corner of the city.

1
The Connection
Jn 5:1

2
"A Feast of the Jews"
Jn 5:1–2

Various interpretations are offered for the term, which, contrary to his usual practice (compare 19:13, 17), John himself has left indefinite. No doubt the name Bethesda had meaning, and we are quite willing to accept the common explanation that it is from Beth Chisda—that is, "House of Mercy"; for this it was about to become. According to the King James Version, its location is "by the sheep *market*." The English Standard Version and other translations have "by the Sheep Gate" (cf. Ne 3:1, 32; 12:39). The translators have supplied the term that describes its more precise location. All that we know from the Greek is that it was a pool provided with a pentagon of covered porticoes, or colonnades, at a site in or near Jerusalem that had something to do with sheep. The Sheep Gate (St. Stephen's Gate?) has been suggested as the location. Through this gate, the sheep destined for sacrifices were led into the city. There was likewise a market in which sacrificial sheep were sold and a pool in which the sheep used for sacrifice were washed.[4] Of the several sites proposed—all in the same general vicinity—the traditional pool rediscovered a little northwest of the Church of St. Anne seems to have the greatest probabilities in its favor, although it is impossible to speak on this matter with authority.[5] All of this, however, is of subordinate importance compared with the marvelous facts of the event itself.[6]

In the five colonnades surrounding the pool, a great multitude of invalids—blind, lame, and paralyzed—lay in anxious hope of a miraculous cure. They were waiting for the moving of the water (5:7). Bethesda was most likely an intermittent pool, with periodic bubbling and gushing of waters, which is still the character of a number of springs in Israel.[7] Many later manuscripts of the Gospel include these words or something similar:

> For an angel of the Lord went down at certain seasons into the pool, and stirred the water: whoever stepped in first after the stirring of the water was healed of whatever disease he had.

In the King James Version, the explanation is John 5:4; but modern translations put this text in a footnote since it does not appear in the earliest manuscripts or is marked as an addition to the Gospel. However, the passage does appear as early as the fifth century and may be based on common belief about the pool in ancient times. In this view, at the first moment of bubbling, the water possessed the highest degree of healing quality for the first person who could scramble into it. We know that the Lord can and does employ angels as His ministering spirits in the service of mankind sent forth to carry out His commands (Heb 1:14; it is not stated that the angel was visible). The account is wholly unlike anything related in any other part of Scripture. However, we do know that the evil angels afflict man with all kinds of sicknesses and maladies while the holy angels give suffering mankind various remedies that tend to restore their health.[8]

We are introduced to a man who had been helplessly invalid for thirty-eight years, possibly due to youthful excesses (v. 14). For many years, he had haunted the porticoes of this health-giving pool. Friends had carried him there; but when the favorable moments of periodic troubling of the waters occurred, others more fortunate and less feeble had always managed to struggle in before him. The result was a life of hopeless despair. Thus, Jesus looked on him with heartfelt pity. According to His omniscience, He knew how long the poor man had suffered (v. 6). He resolved to help him whom no one had helped before. "Do you want to be healed?" But why ask that question? Certainly, he wanted to be delivered. But it was not a question of will and desire, but of opportunity.[9] Hopelessly, he describes his discouraging condition: "Sir, I have no one to put me into the pool when the water is stirred up, and while I am going another steps down before me." He did not yet realize how this unknown stranger could help him, and he was still futilely trusting that someone would put him in the pool. If only I had a *man* to help me! But Jesus had resolved upon a speedier and more effectual aid. "Get up, take up your bed, and walk." With the Lord it was not a question of opportunity or of human aid. He *gave* what He commanded, and He commanded what He would. "And at once the man was healed, and he took up his bed and walked." For a moment, the sick man hardly realized what had happened to him. He did not even know who had spoken the words. In glad amazement, he looked around to thank his unknown benefactor. But the crowd was large, and Jesus, anxious to escape noisy excitement, quietly turned from observation.

5
"Do You Want to Be Healed?"
Jn 5:5–9a

But it was on a Sabbath! In spite of the marvelous cure, many scrupulous and jealous eyes were upon this happy bed-bearing and freshly discharged member of the House of Mercy. Immediately he was rebuked by the Jews:[10] "It is the Sabbath, and it is not lawful for you to take up your bed." They did not see the cure, but only, as they thought, a flagrant violation of the Law. Had not a man during the wandering in the wilderness been stoned to death for gathering sticks on a Sabbath (Nu 15:32–36)? Did not the prophet Jeremiah say: "Take care for the sake of your lives, and do not bear a burden on the Sabbath day" (Jer 17:21)?[11] It is true. But this was not rebellion (cf. Nu 15:30–36). Nor was it marketing or trading or carrying burdens for personal interests and gain (compare Ne 13:15–18). This was not a case of desecrating the Sabbath, but of honoring God for the cure that had been marvelously wrought and a sign or a witness to that effect, even if the impotent man was as yet ignorant of the fact that he had been cured by Christ. The man had not violated the Law of God, the basic principle of which is love (Rm 13:10); he had merely acted contrary to rabbinic traditions. According to the rabbis, a nailed shoe might not be worn on a Sabbath because it was a burden, and one man might carry a loaf of bread, but two men must not carry it between them, and so forth, to the utmost

6
"It Is the Sabbath"
Jn 5:9b–13

limit of tyrannous absurdity.[12] Sensing a higher Law than that of the Sabbath, the healed man replied: "The man who healed me, that man said to me, 'Take up your bed, and walk.' " This simple statement was followed by an angry reply, "Who is the man?" They did not ask "Who made you whole?" but "Who said to you" (i.e., who gave the wicked command), "Take up you bed and walk"? However, Jesus was generally unknown in the suburbs of Jerusalem so neither the healed man nor any of the witnesses of the miracle could identify him.

7
The Council
Informed
Jn 5:14–15

The scene changes. Not long afterwards, Jesus found the formerly invalid man in the temple, where he had evidently gone to thank God for his recovery. Jesus admonished him not to bring upon himself a return of the infirmity by a relapse into former sinful excesses: "Sin no more, that nothing worse may happen to you." Jesus was interested not only in the welfare of his body, but also, and particularly, in the welfare of his immortal soul. He endeavored through His miracle to bring the man to repentance, in which, we assume, He was successful. No other conversation is recorded. But on this occasion, the healed man learned, either directly or indirectly, that he owed his bodily health, gratitude, and obedience to Jesus. The man now left his benefactor and told "the Jews" that it was Jesus who had made him whole. But why must a special report be made to the religious authorities? Was it gratitude, the desire to gain recognition for Jesus among the members of the ruling class? Or was it a defiance against constituted authorities? Or was it even, as has been suggested,[13] base ingratitude in seeking self-protection at the expense of another? Hardly. It was but natural for him to go to the Jews. He had been accused of Sabbath-breaking. And now he was in a position to supply the name of Him who had made him whole. He could furnish a sufficiently complete vindication of the authority in obedience to which he had been charged with breaking the Law. He answered the question the Jews had put to him, likely suggesting at the same time that He who had the power to perform so great a miracle had a right to give him the command that He did. Since the man obeyed such an authority, the Jews ought to acquit him of the charge of having broken the Sabbath.

8
Beginning of
Conflict with Jewish
Authorities
Jn 5:16–18

But the consequences of this report were immediate and momentous. For the first time, Jesus was brought into direct conflict with the Jewish authorities, and this changed the entire tenor of His remaining life. Untouched by the evidence of tender compassion, unmoved by the display of truly miraculous powers, the Jewish inquisitors were at once up in arms against Him with their favorite piece of legalism.[14] "And this was why the Jews were persecuting Jesus, because He was doing these things on the Sabbath." A bitter conflict began, which did not end until the death of Jesus on the cross. And not even then. In defending His action, Jesus made the statement: "My Father is working until now, and I am working." As a result, the Jews sought all the more to kill Him, "because not only was He breaking the Sabbath, but He was even calling God His own Father, making Himself equal with God." Their inference was very correct. But to their horrified ears, the words sounded like blasphemy.

Now follows an extensive and powerful discourse of Christ concerning Himself. Whether the words were spoken publicly in the temple or more privately before some committee of the Council, we do not know. At any rate, the great rabbis who had brought Jesus into their presence in order to warn Him were infuriated because Jesus was warning *them*. They thought they could overawe Him; but they trembled and gnashed their teeth, though they dared not act, as Jesus overawed *them* by assuming the awe-inspiring dignity of the Son of God. In reply to the charge of Sabbath-breaking, Jesus had pointed them to the example of His heavenly Father. The work of the Father did not end on the seventh day of creation, but continued to the present hour. "My Father is working until now, and I am working." Jesus asserted that He was the Son of God, not in the sense in which other men may be called the sons of God, but in the sense that He was equal with God. The accusers of Jesus understood this implication. But far from denying or hiding this equality with the Father in order to placate the Jewish authorities, Jesus insisted upon it in a powerful discourse, which explained His relationship to the heavenly Father. There is perfect equality and agreement between the Son and the Father. "The Son can do nothing of His own accord, but only what He sees the Father doing." And the Father takes a loving interest in the Son (Mt 3:17). The same divine works and honor are equally shared between them. For instance, as the Father gives life, even so does the Son. It does not matter much what kind of life-giving is meant. "The Son gives life to whom He will," even though a person has lain as long and has been as incapable of helping himself as the invalid man, indeed, even though he be dead, spiritually or physically. In addition, the Father has committed all judgment to the Son because He is the only mediator between God and men. It might seem incredible to them that the apportioning to men their eternal destiny should be assigned to the Son. But so it is. This supreme authority is given with the purpose "that all may honor the Son, just as they honor the Father." In denouncing Him for breaking the Sabbath, the Jews were really committing the great sin of dishonoring the Father. And by rejecting His Word, which has the power to give them eternal life, they were shutting the gates of heaven against themselves. "Truly, truly, I say to you, whoever hears My Word and believes Him who sent Me has eternal life. He does not come into judgment." Even now, He had given evidence of the power of His Word by granting health to the invalid man and reviving him to a new spiritual life through it. Neither is this power confined to the care of this invalid man or merely to the spiritual sphere. "An hour is coming, and is now here, when the dead will hear the voice of the Son of God, and those who hear will live." Yes, "an hour is coming when all who are in the tombs will hear His voice and come out." On the

9
Testimony of Jesus
Concerning Himself
Jn 5:19–29

Last Day, the Lord will raise the believers to the resurrection of life and unbelievers to the resurrection of judgment. Spiritual enlivening, raising the dead, and final judgment are the works committed by the Father to the Son.

Affidavits and certificates are not necessary for these truths, because these are statements made by One who is Himself Life and Truth. But according to human standards, the Speaker is making statements concerning Himself which, considering their nature, require verification. So Christ appeals to a number of witnesses. The Jewish authorities are reminded of the delegation they sent to John. "You sent to John, and he has borne witness to the truth." Whatever report this committee had made of the interview with John, it is a fact that John had given this testimony of Jesus: "But among you stands one you do not know" (Jn 1:26). "He must increase, but I must decrease" (Jn 3:30). These words had been fulfilled, for it seems that John had now been imprisoned. "He was[15] a burning and shining lamp, and you were willing to rejoice for a while in his light." But the Jews here were not willing to heed John's call to repentance. Another witness appears in the Father, rather in "the works that the Father has given Me to accomplish, the very works that I am doing, bear witness about Me that the Father has sent Me. And the Father who sent Me has Himself borne witness about Me." The Father already bore witness in the sacred writings of the Old Testament. But unbelief is perverse.[16] It searches the Christ-containing Scriptures and still does not find Christ. And that is exactly what happened to this group at Jerusalem in spite of the fact that they occupied themselves so much with the Scriptures. They searched them, even counting the very letters; for in them they imagined they had eternal life. Theoretically, this was true, but practically it was not the case, because they did not find Christ. You "search the Scriptures because you think that in them you have eternal life; and it is they that bear witness about Me." A close study of them reveals to us many testimonies to Christ as the Messiah—even the Books of Moses, another witness of whom they boasted, but whom they did not understand. "There is one who accuses you: Moses, on whom you have set your hope. For if you believed Moses, you would believe Me; for he wrote of Me" (see Gn 3:15; 12:3; 18:18; 22:18; 49:10; Dt 18:15, 18). But since they evidently had already rejected the true meaning of the messianic promises in the written words, how would they now believe the spoken word to which they were listening with rage? This dispute caused a breech between Jesus and the Jewish authorities. They were horrified at what seemed to them the pinnacle of blasphemy. They would struggle unto death with their Messiah, who had come to give them life. The hour of conflict, however, had not yet arrived. At this point, the evangelist John interrupts his account of the life of Jesus, not to take it up again until the feeding of the five thousand.

It was probably in autumn of AD 30 that John the Baptist was cast into prison. When we last met him, he was still engaged at Aenon, near Salim, in his work of preparing the way of the Lord (Jn 3:23–24).[17] At that time, a question arose between his disciples and the Jews about purifying, which caused the former to complain to their master that Jesus was making more disciples than John. At the news of this, and out of consideration for His friend and forerunner, Jesus withdrew until such time as the work of the forerunner would be finished, when His own public ministry would begin in earnest. This time had now arrived. The public testimony of the forerunner was forcefully and suddenly checked. It seems that John had brought the message of repentance from Aenon northward into Galilee or across the Jordan into Perea. The last scene of his public ministry was in the neighborhood of both. At any rate, he brought his message of repentance and preparation for the coming Kingdom too close to the ears of Herod Antipas, to whom Galilee and Perea belonged. John was very outspoken in his language. Not only did he preach repentance in general, but he mentioned particular sins. And especially did he incur the hatred of Herodias, the former wife of Philip, now illegally married to her brother-in-law and uncle Herod Antipas. But in the eyes of the Galilean rulers, the pet sins of the Herodian family—adultery, marriage irregularities, and other dark deeds—were not a matter for a coarse wilderness preacher to criticize or discuss. And what about this talk of the Kingdom? Had Herodias not severed her marriage bond with Philip[18] in her ambition[19] to make Antipas king of the Jews? Whereupon "Herod the tetrarch, who had been reproved by him for Herodias, his brother's [Philip's] wife, and for all the evil things that Herod had done, added this to them all, that he locked up John in prison." In addition, Josephus suggests that Herod "feared lest the great influence John had over the people might put it into his power and inclination to raise a rebellion."[20] But if fear of a rebellion was an additional motive with Herod to imprison John the Baptist, he altogether misunderstood the work and mission of this great preacher. The place of imprisonment is given[21] as Machaerus, a castle east of the Dead Sea. With this removal of John from the scene of activity, the heavenly Father moved Jesus to enter fully upon His messianic career.[22]

11
The Imprisonment of John
Mt 4:12; Mk 1:14a;
Lk 3:19–20; 4:14a

9

THE BEGINNING OF THE GREAT GALILEAN MINISTRY

OPENING EVENTS

Perhaps January, AD 31

The imprisonment of John marked a great turning point in the life of Jesus.[1] With the removal of the forerunner, the time had arrived for Jesus to identify Himself as that Prophet who was to come. This He had already done when He proclaimed Himself in Jerusalem as the Son of the Father. But the leaders of the Jews had not received Him. They accused Him of breaking the Sabbath, charged Him with blasphemy, and contemplated taking His life. The introductory labors of the Baptist and His own work had been unavailing toward gaining their hearts, so that they would have accepted and proclaimed Him as the Messiah. David's city was no safe place for David's Son. The temple of His heavenly Father contained no auditorium for the saving message of His Son. And since in Judea the influence of a now hostile Council was supreme, there was little likelihood of His winning recognition among the Judeans at the present time. But the rejection in Jerusalem was not regarded as final. If they, the leaders, would not recognize Him as what He truly was, He would present Himself to the nation at large. Thus a great ministry was begun in and around the still predominantly Jewish[2] Galilee, where the Council had no civil jurisdiction[3] and Herod Antipas was not likely to interfere.[4] Thus the early Judean ministry had come to a close.

The general character of the message of Jesus was the same as that of John: "Repent, for the kingdom of heaven is at hand." But there is an additional note sounded in the word *believe*, which settles the nature of the Kingdom: "Repent and believe in the Gospel." John, in keeping with his character, sought his listeners in the wilderness. Jesus, besides carrying on an open-air ministry, sought His hearers

1
A Great Turning Point
Mt 4:17; Mk 1:14b–15; Lk 4:14b–15

2
The Galilean Ministry Begun
Mt 4:17; Mk 1:14b–15; Lk 4:14b–15

also "in their synagogues, being glorified by all." And as to His success: "A report about Him went out through all the surrounding country." But at first, at the very outset, a very bitter rejection awaited Him.

3
At Nazareth
Lk 4:16

According to the sequence of events that seems correct to us,[5] the Sabbath controversy in Jerusalem was followed by the Sabbath rejection at Nazareth, possibly even on the following Sabbath. It must have been with mingled feelings that Jesus "came to Nazareth, where He had been brought up." Great changes had occurred since He had left Nazareth.[6] This is the town where He had lived with His mother and His foster-father since the days of His early childhood.[7] Here, He likely helped bury His foster-father Joseph, the husband of Mary and faithful guardian of His tender youth. Here, He had received His training, learned His trade, formed His associations, and "increased in wisdom and in stature and in favor with God and man" (Lk 2:52). Here, He had waited in silence to take up the work upon which He had now fully entered. He honored this town in His first visit within its walls as the great Galilean Prophet. It was on a Sabbath day. He entered the synagogue, as was His custom since His childhood days. Sabbath after Sabbath He had occupied His usual place and listened to the Word of God read and expounded there. But now—since the opening of His public ministry—He Himself preached the Gospel of God.

4
Synagogues

Although rabbis traced the synagogues back to patriarchal times, it is quite generally supposed that these institutions of Jewish worship and instruction originated during, or in consequence of, the Babylonian captivity.[8] We can easily understand how the exiles keenly felt the need of places and opportunities for common worship on Sabbath and feast days in those trying times.[9] After they returned to Jerusalem, they transplanted the institution to Israel and at the same time regarded it as all the more necessary for the perpetuation of Judaism on foreign soil. In the scattered Jewish communities, those ignorant of Hebrew would not only gather for prayer, but also have the assigned Scripture lessons read and paraphrased to them.[10] In the course of time, a confession of faith, prayers, and sermons or addresses were added. Thus the regular synagogue services were gradually introduced, first on Sabbaths and holidays and then on ordinary days, at the same time as, and in a sort of internal correspondence with, the worship at the temple. The services on the market days, Mondays and Thursdays, were special, these being the days when the country people usually came to town. As a rule, every community would build its own synagogue. These houses of worship, erected by popular subscription or private generosity, were often built of local stone. In wealthier communities, they used white marble. Their simple porticoed rectangular halls usually pointed toward Jerusalem.[11] The furnishing was simple. Seats were arranged for the men and likewise for the women, who, however, shrouded in their long veils, were seated behind a lattice or in a gallery. At one end, there was a painted ark, or chest, which contained the rolls of Sacred

Scripture. In front of this, facing the congregation, the chief seats were placed for the ten or more men of leisure, the leaders of the synagogue. Preeminent among them was the seat of the presiding elder, or chief of the synagogue. On one side, there was an elevation, or platform, on which there was a lectern, or desk, from which the Law was read. Properly speaking, there were no clergy, since the offices of priests and Levites for the temple worship in Jerusalem were altogether different. There were, however, a number of officials. Besides the elders, who constituted the local tribunal, there was the presiding elder, or ruler, whose duty it was to keep order and to appoint at each meeting the reader or expounder of the Law and the Prophets. The servant, or Chazzan, was the custodian of the Sacred Rolls and a sort of elementary school teacher. He would also act as janitor and wielded the scourge when punishment was inflicted.[12] The reader, or delegate of the congregation, was appointed at each meeting by the ruler, whose duty it was to read and explain the Scriptures and to lead in prayer. Usually a scribe was appointed to this office. He had to be a man of good character. There was also the interpreter, or Targumist, the Methurge man, whose duty it was to render the Hebrew reading of the Scriptures immediately into the vernacular. And since this had to be done without written sketch[13] and on the spot, even without previous preparation, the person serving in this capacity would have to be a man of some learning. And finally, there were the alms gatherers (almoners), who collected for the poor.[14] A public worship presupposes a congregation. They would only erect a synagogue at a place where there were ten men of leisure (Batlanim), who could devote their time and services to the worship and the local administration. Tradition had it that the number ten was chosen because God said to Abraham that if ten righteous had been found in Sodom and Gomorrah, these doomed cities would not have been destroyed (Gn 18:32).[15]

The services in the synagogues were in some respect somewhat like our own. The service began with the recitation of "Hear, O Israel" (the *Shema*; Dt 6:4–9; 11:13–21; Nu 15:37–41). This confession of faith in the unity of God was followed by the prayers, in which *Adonai* was substituted for the unspeakable name *Jehovah*.[16] The liturgical part was concluded with a benediction.[17] If a priestly descendant of Aaron was present, he pronounced the blessing; if not, the leader of the devotion pronounced it. After this the servant (Chazzan) stepped to the painted ark, or chest, and brought out the Sacred Roll (Megillah) for the assigned readings from the Law (Parashah) and the Prophets (Haftarah).[18] Since the original Hebrew was no longer generally understood, an interpreter (Targumist) stood by the side of the reader (Maphtir) and translated the reading into the vernacular verse by verse, except in the section of the Prophets, which was rendered into Aramaic after three verses of reading. Since the Targum was not considered inspired, the interpreter might paraphrase freely for the better popular understanding. Only the substance of the text

5
The Service

had to be correctly given. This may help us in a measure to understand the popular mode of the Old Testament quotations in the Septuagint and in the New Testament writings. This reading was immediately followed by an address or sermon, delivered by the appointed reader; that is, where a scribe or rabbi capable of giving such instruction, or a distinguished stranger, was present.[19]

6
"The Year of the Lord's Favor"
Lk 4:17–20

On this particular Sabbath there was a distinguished rabbi in the synagogue of Nazareth. In recognition of His reputation, Jesus was requested to perform the honorable function of reader (Maphtir).[20] When He ascended the platform (Bima) and stood up at the lectern (Luach) "to read," the servant (Chazzan) drew aside the silk curtain and brought forth the scroll (Megillah), which contained the reading from the prophets (Haphtarah) of the day. Our Lord unrolled the volume and found the well-known passage in Isaiah 61.[21] The congregation stood as He read:

> The Spirit of the Lord is upon Me, because He has anointed Me to proclaim good news to the poor. He has sent Me to proclaim liberty to the captives and recovering of sight to the blind, to set at liberty those who are oppressed, to proclaim the year of the Lord's favor.

This is a free reproduction of the Septuagint, which freely reproduces the original Hebrew. It was probably first read in Hebrew, thereupon translated (targumed) into Aramaic, and then preached on by Jesus.[22] Stopping short before the stern phrase "and the day of vengeance of our God" (Is 61:2), the last words He read to His listeners were the gracious words "the year of the Lord's favor."[23] Curiously enough, this phrase has led a number of the Fathers to argue that our Lord's ministry lasted but a single year.[24] After the reading, the Lord rolled up the Megillah, handed it back to the Chazzan, and, as was customary among the Jews, sat down on the chair (Kisse) to deliver His sermon.[25]

7
"Today This Scripture Has Been Fulfilled in Your Hearing"
Lk 4:21–22

Whether the selection of this text was by choice or, as some think, part of the ordinary lesson of the day, the Spirit of the Lord was indeed upon Jesus in prompting Him to make it the basis of His first recorded messianic sermon. It struck the keynote of His whole prophetic ministry. In breathless silence, all people focused on Him as He made the astounding disclosure: "Today this Scripture has been fulfilled in your hearing." There was no doubt as to the messianic character of the text. But the people of Nazareth were taken by surprise at the announcement that the very voice of Him of whom the prophet prophesied had entered into their ears. From the very beginning of His ministry, Jesus had the clear and certain consciousness that He was the Messiah. How clearly this passage gives the lie to the supposed gradual development of messianic consciousness on the part of Jesus! We can imagine the awesome thrill that passed through the hearts of His hearers as Jesus identified Himself with the subject of the prophecy: "He has anointed *Me* to proclaim good news to the poor." At any rate, before the reaction set in, there was one point in which they were all agreed: marvelous words of grace proceeded out of His mouth.[26] At first held spellbound, they gradually began to realize the full meaning of the words. Breathless silence and devout attention gave way to the after-sermon buzz. Since it was customary among the Jews to remain absolutely silent during the synagogue discourse and then to give vent to their feelings in full, it was not long before Jesus became sensible of rebellious murmurs.[27] What is that? The Messiah? "Is not this Joseph's son?" Did we not know Him all this time as the carpenter's son? What business has He to teach? They wondered how He could know letters,[28] having never learned (Jn 7:15). Small-town jealousy raised voices of disparagement against the success of a distinguished native son.

Jesus was aware of the change of feelings, but He did not deny the fact of His Messiahship in order to placate His listeners.[29] He passed by the slur on His humble origin. Other men of yet humbler origin had become distinguished. Amos, "no prophet, nor a prophet's son," was taken from his flocks with the summons: "Go, prophesy to My people Israel" (Am 7:14–15).[30] Likely the Nazarenes would next demand visible proof of His being the Anointed of God. They had *heard* the claim. But now He should let them *see*. Let Him *do* here in His own country—indeed, here all the more because it was His own country—"what we have heard You did at Capernaum."[31] Should not charity begin at home? And what about the proverb "Physician, heal yourself"? If You desire to be a helper of others, the poor, blind, brokenhearted, and bruised, then why not begin at home, or first help Yourself from the lack of consideration and esteem that attaches itself to You?[32] In reply to these objections in their hearts, and all but on their lips, Jesus points to the truth of another proverb as applied to His own sad experience: "No prophet is acceptable in his hometown." And then He shows them that, unless they accept Him in faith, the mere fact of compatriotism establishes no particular claim. "Miracles are not limited to geographical relation."[33] This is clearly seen from two well-known instances in which not Jews, but Gentiles were most particularly favored in the ministry of Elijah and Elisha.

> There were many widows in Israel in the days of Elijah, when the heavens were shut up three years and six months,[34] and a great famine came over all the land, and Elijah was sent to none of them but only to Zarephath, in the land of Sidon, to a woman who was a widow. And there were many lepers in Israel in the time of the prophet Elisha, and none of them was cleansed, but only Naaman the Syrian.

The Nazarenes were not slow in grasping the reference. A ministry that smacks of universalism! What is that? Pagans, Gentiles, not to mention the inhabitants of Capernaum, are better than we? There was but one answer, Away with Him!

8
"No Prophet Is Acceptable in His Hometown"
Lk 4:23–28

9
Rejected by the
Nazarenes
Lk 4:29–30

Nathanael was almost right: "Can anything good come out of Nazareth?" (Jn 1:46). The Nazarenes were filled with fury. They rose and thrust Him out of the synagogue, out of the city, and led Him to the "brow" of the hill on which the city was originally built, in order to throw Him over the cliff.[35] And all this on the Sabbath! But His hour was not yet come. His majesty overawed His infuriated townsmen; He passed through the midst of them and went away, which was certainly a sad parting from the town of His youth. Did He cast a longing glance at the humble home in which He had played and toiled and waited? Such questions are natural, but they are left unanswered.[36] Resting probably in the neighborhood until the Sabbath was spent, He pursued His downward[37] journey to Capernaum, which was henceforth to be His Galilean home.

10
A New Home
at Capernaum
Mt 4:13–16;
Lk 4:31–32

Friendly Capernaum on the sunlit shores of the Galilean Sea. Our Lord was there before. For a brief spell after the marriage of Cana, He made it His residence with His mother and brothers (Jn 2:12).[38] His own town had cast Him out, but here devoted friends and believing disciples would welcome Him. Either here or in the immediate vicinity were the homes of Simon and Andrew, and James and John. They, it seems, had returned to their accustomed labors after their Master returned through Samaria to Galilee.[39] Soon, they were to become His constant attendants and chosen apostles. Capernaum was probably already the home of Mary and His brothers,[40] while it seems that His sisters were married at Nazareth.[41] In this city, He would preach on the Sabbaths in the synagogue that the good centurion had built (Lk 7:1–5) and of which Jairus was one of the rulers (Mk 5:22). Here was also the home of the now believing official, whose son Jesus restored to life at a distance through His word (Jn 4:46–53). And thus in Capernaum, as far as the Son of Man had a place to lay His head, He was among friends. Added to this, Capernaum and its vicinity were situated on the Sea of Galilee, with the great trade routes to Egypt and Syria, to Jerusalem and Damascus, passing through or by it. This gave Jesus opportunities to speak with people as He could not have in the more secluded Nazareth.[42] Finally, the removal of Jesus to Capernaum fulfilled a prophecy. "The land of Zebulun and the land of Naphtali, the way of the sea, beyond the Jordan, Galilee of the Gentiles—the people dwelling in darkness have seen a great light, and for those dwelling in the region and shadow of death, on them a light has dawned."[43] These regions, first to be depopulated at the time of the fall of Israel (2Ki 15:29),[44] were the first to see the Light. The bright sunshine of messianic summer now flooded Galilee of the Gentiles. This must have been of peculiar interest to St. Matthew, the writer of the first Gospel. Seated at the tax booth (Mt 9:9), he had perhaps often seen Jesus pass by and heard His words, until he himself heard and gladly obeyed the gracious summons, "Follow Me!"[45]

The first notice we have of our Lord after His rejection at Nazareth brings Him before us as standing on the shores of the Galilean Sea, surrounded by people who were eager to hear the Word of God. His growing reputation as a prophet, joined to what happened in Nazareth, would have provided Him with an audience in whatever village He entered, especially in the populated regions of the Sea of Galilee. How long an interval had elapsed since He left Nazareth, we do not know. Most likely, it was on the Friday in the week following His rejection at Nazareth, before the Sabbath of His first synagogue appearance in Capernaum (Mk 1:21).[47] Approaching the lake, He again met His former disciples, Simon, Andrew, James,[48] and John, who, it seems, had left their Master after His journey through Samaria and returned to their fishing trade. The sea swarms with fish, and in the Lord's day its waters were covered with boats. A flourishing fish trade was carried on with Jerusalem, where one of the gates was called the Fish Gate (Ne 3:3). The rabbis were veritable connoisseurs of fish,[49] and it seems that Zebedee, the father of James and John, was a prosperous fisherman with connections in Jerusalem. Later, we learn, if our interpretation of the respective passage is correct, that John was known in the high priest's palace (Jn 18:15).[50] Very likely, Andrew and Simon had formed a partnership with them in a prosperous fish business and had their own boats and nets as well as hired servants. But this time, they had not been successful. It had probably been a stormy night.[51] At least their toil had brought them no fish. Two of them, Simon and Andrew, were now washing and mending their nets. At a short distance, James and John, seated in their boat with their hired servants and Zebedee, their father, were similarly engaged. Thus Jesus found them. Very likely, they were unconscious of His presence and surely unaware of the fact that the time had come for them to be recalled—and this time permanently—into His service. As He addressed Himself to them, the multitude that had followed Him gathered around. Beckoning Peter, Jesus stepped into his boat and requested him to pull out a little from the land. "Seated in this pleasant pulpit, safe from the inconvenient contact with the multitude, He taught them from the little boat as it rocked on the blue ripples, sparkling in the morning sun."[52] We need not ask what He spoke. It would be words of Life, of their need, and of the beauty and glory of the Kingdom that was "at hand." When the sermon was over, Jesus made preparation to carry out what He had in mind.

11
The Recall of the Four Fishermen
Mt 4:18–22;
Mk 1:16–20;
(Lk 5:1–11)[46]

"When He had finished speaking, He said to Simon, 'Put out into the deep and let down your nets for a catch.'" In the ears of an experienced fisherman, this was certainly a strange command. Success was doubly improbable both as to time and place, for fish were caught at night and near the shore.[53] But when the Lord bids us to let down our nets, there *must* be fish. Peter, however, was filled with gloom. "Master,[54] we toiled all night and took nothing!" Still, discarding his initial objection and speaking as the captain, he replies: "But at Your word I will let down the nets."

12
The Miraculous Catch of Fish
(Lk 5:1–11)

This obedience was rewarded. Instantly, a vast number of fish crowded into the net. A busy scene followed as the instinct of work first prevailed.[55] "They signaled to their partners in the other boat to come and help them. And they came and filled both the boats, so that they began to sink." When Simon Peter[56] now realized the greatness of the miracle, he thought only of his own unworthiness and of the presence of Jesus with him in the boat. "He fell down at Jesus' knees, saying, 'Depart from me, for I am a sinful man, O Lord.'" Not that he really wanted the Lord to depart or to dismiss him from His presence; but he was overcome by the sense of his own unworthiness and sin. These passionate words are really a humble prayer, requesting the Lord to receive him and to stay. Peter's companions were also overcome. It was a miracle that only experienced and hardened fishermen could fully appreciate. It was a real miracle. Yet it was also a symbolic miracle and performed by Jesus for a definite purpose. "Do not be afraid!" "Follow Me, and I will make you fishers of men." It was not at all a strange command. Neither Peter and Andrew nor the sons of Zebedee could have misunderstood the call or even regarded it as strange. They had heard it before. But now, the call for *permanent* discipleship had come. And there was only one answer: they forsook all, the boats, nets, hired servants, the fish,[57] Zebedee, and the members of their families, and followed Him.

13
**In the Synagogue
at Capernaum
Mk 1:21–22;
Lk 4:31–32**

Followed by His first four permanent disciples, Jesus proceeded to nearby Capernaum, which was henceforth to provide Him with an earthly home.[58] This must have been a memorable occasion for the four Galilean friends and a day of which especially Peter loved to speak frequently and fully to Mark, the disciple and "interpreter of Peter, [who] wrote down accurately, though not in order, whatsoever he remembered of the things said or done by Christ."[59] Though originally from Bethsaida (Jn 1:44), it seems that Andrew and Peter now owned a house and lived with their households (Mk 1:29) at Capernaum. Although Jesus had been in Capernaum before (Jn 2:12),[60] this is the first time after the beginning of His great Galilean ministry that He publicly appeared in Simon's town. He was probably even now honoring Peter's house with His personal presence. On the next morning, He presented Himself at the local synagogue, again to serve as the reader (Maphtir), as He had previously done at Nazareth. The Sabbath services in the synagogue usually began at nine in the morning and lasted until noon,[61] after which the worshipers would gather in the house of some friend for a festive meal (Lk 14:1–3). We do not know the subject of this particular Sabbath discourse. But we are told that the Lord astonished His listeners; for He taught them as having authority and not as the scribes, who as the men of letters of the day, teachers and lawyers, were usually appointed to serve as the lecturers in the synagogue.[62] There was no appeal to human authority, neither did He resort to subtle logical distinctions, legal niceties, witticisms, or clever sayings.[63] Clear words flowed from the spring, which was itself life and truth.

But suddenly, the service was interrupted by the obscene cries and blasphemous ravings of an unhappy wretch who had a spirit of an unclean demon. "Ha![64] What have You to do with us,[65] Jesus of Nazareth? Have You come to destroy us? I know[66] who You are—the Holy One of God." A testimony for Jesus by a demoniac.

14
A Demoniac
Mk 1:23–24;
Lk 4:31–34

But what is a demoniac? Whatever difficulty the term may offer, every reader of the New Testament cannot but form a definite idea of what a demoniac is. Scripture itself throws enough light upon the subject. In diverging for a brief discussion of demoniacal possession, we may state at the outset that all kinds of ancient superstitions, beliefs, and irrational fears were prevalent in the days of Christ. Educated men of the time, Jews and Gentiles, were not free from it, neither the postapostolic Christians nor the Fathers of the Church, and we may add, neither are the people of our own day and age. Mysterious occurrences were promptly ascribed to supernatural forces. And strange maladies, psychical and physical disorders, were attributed to the invasion of spirits, or demons. By means of magic, incantation, and exorcism, people frequently attempted to free those possessed. In order to gain reputation among the superstitious for their pretended arts, the professional Jewish exorcists credited the invention of their spells to Solomon. In apostolic times (Ac 19:13) and in the Middle Ages, the name of Jesus was used in the adjuration of wicked practitioners who pretended to effect a cure of a particular spell, and it is so used today. Widespread belief in the power of omens, signs, charms, and the like, based on fear gullibility, including the possession and dispossession of demons, had taken root in the popular mind. Some information on those views and practices has reached us. Jesus, at one time, pointed to exorcism engaged in by some Jews when, in defense of His own real power over actual demons, He conceded: "If I cast out demons by Beelzebul, by whom do your sons cast them out?" (Mt 12:27). They used the name of God, and with their activities the Pharisees found no fault. An example of superstitious exorcism is given by Josephus:

15
Ancient
Superstitions

> I have seen a certain man of my own country whose name was Eleazar, releasing people that were demoniacal in the presence of Vespasian, and his sons, and his captains, and the whole multitude of his soldiers. The manner of the cure was this: He put a ring that had a root of one of those sorts mentioned by Solomon to the nostrils of the demoniac, after which he drew out the demon through his nostrils; and when the man fell down immediately, he abjured him to return into him no more, making still mention of Solomon, and reciting the incantations which he composed. And when Eleazar would persuade and demonstrate to the spectators that he had such a power, he set a little way off a cup or basin full of water, and commanded the demon, as he went out of the man, to overturn it, and thereby to let the spectators know that he had left the man.[67]

Now, the evangelists were simple men, yet would not people scorn them and ridicule their gullibility if they had related the story of an exorcism such as this? However, they did not. Their account, told in simple language, deals not with superstitions but with facts. And we can rest assured that they did not share the erroneous opinions of their age.

16
Demoniacal
Possession as
Viewed by Jesus

But did Jesus perhaps *accommodate* Himself to the popular conceptions of the day? It has been said that like a good physician He *seemed to agree* with the popular notion and to enter into the fancy of the afflicted patient in order the more easily to effect a cure.[68] But outside of the fact that this view would transform all cases of possession into hallucinations, this method of treatment would not have been honest. If this "canon of accommodation" were true, then Jesus—by the same argument—might have possessed advance information in other matters, and all His miracles might have been performed by applying until then or even to this day undiscovered natural forces.[69] Then the inspired Gospel narratives might be treated as a series of historically untrustworthy legends. No! Far from accommodating Himself to a supposed popular prejudice, Jesus regarded His own cures of demon possession as direct conquests of Satan and his powers. In sending out His disciples, He did not equip them with supposed might against nonexistent, fictitious devils, but He gave them real power against unclean spirits, power to cast them out, and power to heal all manner of sickness and disease. He said: "Cast out demons. You received without paying; give without pay" (Mt 10:1, 8). When the Seventy-Two returned and reported of their success, He acknowledged that He gave them such authority (Lk 10:17–20).

17
The Demonized
State

The inhabitation of an unclean spirit in some cases affected the possessed person physically, producing ordinary diseases. Some commentators think the Jews believed that service to sin and enslavement to Satan accounted for the mental and physical diseases and for the visible effects on both body and mind. However, as we have pointed out, this view would deny the fact of diabolical possession in an attempt to explain the phenomenon as due to the popular ignorance of natural causes. And what was the character of this remarkable phenomenon? The answer is as simple as the statement of the Gospels. Without apparent reason or cause, the victims appear as "demonized," as "having a demon, or spirit," who is called "evil" or "unclean." This, of course, correctly presupposes the existence of a personal demon together with a host of evil spirits. Although one may admit that a mass of superstition is popularly associated with the notion "devil," one cannot deny that Scripture plainly teaches the existence and manifestation of Satan and innumerable evil spirits.[70] From the Gospels, we see that demons were at times divinely permitted to take bodily possession of people, so that for a longer or shorter period of time the demonized person was no longer himself. In this demonized state, sometimes accompanied with physical suffering, the afflicted person was in the power of the evil spirit. The spirit tormented him, robbed him of his senses, turned him into a raving maniac, and made him utter indecencies and even blasphemies. The irresponsible sufferer may or may not have previously led an exceptionally sinful life. Really, we know very little about the character of the maladies that were conjoined with demoniacal possession. In the Gerasene demoniac, we have a case of violent madness (Mk 5:1–5). Another one of the sufferers was only mute (Mt 9:32–33). The mute boy in the region of Caesarea Philippi had a demon that made him an epileptic and raving maniac (Mt 17:14–21; Mk 9:17–29; Lk 9:37–43a). The sick daughter of the Syrophoenician woman was "severely oppressed by a demon" (Mt 15:21–28; Mk 7:24–30).

Whether there are still cases of demoniacal possession is hard to decide. However, as we can little deny the possible occurrence of present-day miracles, we can little deny the possibility of demon possession, though it can be difficult to establish particular cases.[71] And still, physicians admit and family members sometimes sadly experience cases where sickness (in particular, mental diseases and nervous disorders) produces almost unbelievable phenomena in a patient: gigantic strength in an emaciated body; the senses, eyesight and hearing, so sharpened as to be most uncanny; the mental faculties so keen as to be almost supernatural; and ravings so fierce as to be almost diabolical. There are still many phenomena "in heaven and earth" of which even our enlightened philosophy has no adequate conception.[72] However, in the time and land of Jesus the appearance of demoniacs must have been quite prevalent. And for this, there was a very good reason. Because the Son of God came into the world for the purpose of destroying the works of the devil, we can well understand a corresponding period of developed enmity in the satanic kingdom of darkness. Jesus Christ assumed human nature for the purpose of taking our infirmities (Mt 8:17). Above all, He came to bear our sins and save our souls (Is 53:5; 1Pt 2:24). We can well understand why the prince of darkness in the days of Christ sought to injure and destroy more people by sending out his evil spirits to possess them bodily and to rob them of their salvation. Add to this the *time* of the coming of Christ.[73] It was a time when the ancient world to a peculiarly large extent seemed to have been abandoned by all the forces of health and vitality and therefore to have fallen more deeply into sin and under the powers of darkness.[74] We are now ready to proceed with our story.

In one respect, all demoniacs in the Gospels were alike: they all owned the power of Jesus. The Jewish nation, upon the whole, still remained in ignorance as to the identity of Jesus. But ever since the opening of the heavens at the banks of the Jordan and the temptation in the wilderness, the devils knew—and shudder (Jas 2:19). But if Jesus checked the nation's revolutionary hopes by discouraging

18
Present-Day
Occurrences?

19
"Be Silent, and Come
Out of Him!"
Mk 1:25–28;
Lk 4:35–37

direct testimony as to His Messiahship (Mk 1:44), He least of all desired a satanic testimony as to His origin and office (Lk 4:41). No matter what the motive of the prince of darkness was, it was bound to be satanic. "But Jesus rebuked him, saying, 'Be silent [literally, "Be muzzled"] and come out of him!'" The ring and magical root of certain Jewish exorcists was not required. Jesus' word sufficed. One wild outburst, and the poor sufferer was free from demoniacal possession; one final fit, and he was perfectly healed.[75] Stupor and astonishment fell upon the assembly in the synagogue. Questioning remarks passed from one to another. What is this? What new, powerful teaching is this? "He commands even the unclean spirits, and they obey Him!" There was no question as to the miraculous powers displayed. Neither was there any questioning this time as to Christ's doing this on the Sabbath day. As a result, the fame of Jesus spread along the lake north and south, back into the hill country, and into all the nearby regions of Galilee.

20
**The Healing
of Peter's
Mother-in-Law
(Mt 8:14–15);[76]
Mk 1:29–31;
Lk 4:38–39**

From the synagogue, we follow the Savior and His four called disciples into Peter's wedded home (cf. 1Co 9:5). But no festive Sabbath meal, as was the Jewish custom,[77] awaited Him there. A sudden and severe fever had stricken down Simon's mother-in-law, who lived with him. Again, the Lord was in the presence of suffering and pain. And He "rebuked the fever." Standing over her, "He touched her hand, and the fever left her." "Immediately she rose and began to serve them."[78] She was now able and willing to serve.

21
**In the Evening Many
Others Are Healed
(Mt 8:16–17);[79]
Mk 1:32–34;
Lk 4:40–41**

While they were still sitting at the meal, the daylight faded. The Sabbath had come to an end. The report of the wonderful occurrence in the synagogue had been whispered from door to door. The people, no longer restrained by the rule of rest, brought all manner of sick and possessed people and began to flock to Simon's house. At last, the whole town was gathered at his door. What a strange scene! The clear waters of the Galilean Sea. The last flush of sunset gilding the ascending western hills.[80] A motley crowd casting curious glances at Simon's door. But for many, it was a door of longing hope. Parents, children, husbands, and wives brought, led, and carried their beloved sick. A peaceful scene of faith and hope. But also a scene of suffering humanity. Suddenly, the wild shrieks of demoniacs disturbed the evening stillness. Satanic testimonies to the presence of the Son of God were heard: "You are the Son of God!" But the Lord would have none of that. Rebuking the evil spirits, He did not allow them to speak and commanded them to leave their afflicted victims. And He "healed all who were sick. This was to fulfill what was spoken by the prophet Isaiah: 'He took our illnesses and bore our diseases'" (see Is 53:4). How well the ideas are associated: sin and sickness, healing and the Savior! Thus, the healing ministry of Jesus is placed into the proper light. And thus on the Sabbath eve, we see the God-given hope of the prophet initially fulfilled.[81]

10

FROM THE FIRST GALILEAN CIRCUIT TO THE CHOICE OF THE TWELVE

PERHAPS SPRING, AD 31

A modern book must have divisions and parts. Thus we begin a new chapter, although there are no mechanical divisions in the life of Christ. An examination of our Lord's ministry, however, seems to point to a number of stages distinctly marked. The first is the period immediately following His Baptism and extending from the first Passover (Jn 2:13) to the unnamed feast, when the invalid man was healed, and embracing a little over one year. It extended from the first calling of His disciples, the first miracle, and the first cleansing of the temple to the attempt of the Jews to kill Him a year later because He declared Himself equal with God (Jn 5:15, 18). During this time, His labors were chiefly confined to Judea. Near the close of this period, we have placed the imprisonment of John. The second stage is the period following His return to Galilee immediately after the Feast of the Passover. It embraces the whole duration of His great Galilean ministry, about a year and six months, and may be divided into the period preceding and following the death of John. The third stage begins with His final departure from Galilee and ends with the death on the cross. This period embraces about five or six months. The first part of the second stage of our Lord's ministry, the great Galilean ministry before the death of John, is before us now. For the sake of giving the crowded events a place in our minds, we have grouped them under the heads of Galilean circuits, with intervening chapters for the Sermon on the Mount and the parables by the sea.

> **1**
> Divisions in the Lord's Ministry

The closing events of the last chapter present Jesus as a much-sought healing guest in Peter's home. Jesus devoted the evening hours to the healing of the sick, and the night was spent in Peter's house. Day had not yet dawned, however, when Jesus quit the dwelling and withdrew to a nearby desolate place to be alone with His

> **2**
> Retirement to a Solitary Place
> Mk 1:35–38;
> Lk 4:42–43

/ 145

Father in heaven. Again and again during His public ministry, we shall find the Lord seeking retirement for the purpose of prayer (Lk 6:12; Mt 14:23; Lk 5:16; 9:28; Mk 14:32). There was probably an additional reason for this particular retirement. He had healed many the evening before. He knew that, as the news was carried from door to door, many others who had not been healed would scarcely await the dawn in their search of aid. However, it was not His purpose to establish a clinic at Capernaum, although this seems to have been what the people at Capernaum expected. While He was engaged in prayer, throngs of petitioners were storming Peter's door. They impelled him to seek after Jesus and to return with Him at once. Peter and his companions set out to search for their Master. When they found Him, they tried to convince Him to return with them and to keep Him from doing what He seemed inclined to do, to leave Capernaum for the present with some of the sick still unhealed. "Everyone is looking for You," they said. But to escape the multitudes was one reason why He had left Capernaum. It was not His object to become the center of a miracle-admiring population. The purpose of His miracles was to gain the hearts for the good tidings of the Kingdom. And besides, His blessings were not to be confined to Capernaum. There were Dalmanutha, Magdala, Chorazin, Bethsaida, and other towns and villages near at hand. "Let us go," He said, "on to the next towns, that I may preach there also, for that is why I came out"; that is, out from Capernaum. "I must preach the good news of the kingdom of God to the other towns as well; for I was sent for this purpose." Whether Jesus yielded to the anxiety of the waiting multitude or instantly carried out[1] His intention, Mark and Luke do not expressly state. At any rate, a Galilean preaching and healing circuit was now begun.

3
"And He Went Throughout All Galilee"
Mt 4:23–25; Mk 1:39; Lk 4:44

The general character of the Galilean preaching tour in which Jesus now engaged is given as preaching, teaching, and healing. Galilee at this time was extremely populous.[2] Jesus was assured of an audience wherever He went. The joy that He brought to some afflicted sufferer would give Him a chance to announce the good tidings of the kingdom of heaven to the gathering attracted by His miracles. This was an open-air ministry. But especially did He desire to bring His message to the congregations assembled in the synagogue. His activities were not those of a political agitator; His purpose was to announce the coming of the heavenly kingdom. And subordinate to this ministry of preaching and teaching was His ministry of healing. Those afflicted with fever, the blind, paralytics, demoniacs, and epileptics[3]—whose seizures followed upon the phases of the moon—were brought to Him. He healed them all. Naturally, the report spread. His fame spread through Galilee and then through Syria, the Roman province to which Galilee and the whole of Israel belonged. Multitudes were attracted from all quarters: Galilee, Decapolis, Jerusalem, Judea, and Perea beyond the Jordan.[4]

During this journey, one smitten with a loathsome and terrible disease—leprosy[6]—approached Jesus. Even today, the name of this dreadful scourge of the Eastern world strikes terror into our hearts. Egypt is called its cradle, but it also appeared in Assyria, Babylonia, India, and China two to three thousand years ago. The father of medicine, Hippocrates (c. 460–c. 375 BC), called it the Phoenician disease, and Galen (AD 130–200) named it elephantiasis. In the Old Testament, it first appears as a sign given by God to Moses (Ex 4:6),[7] but shortly afterward Miriam, the sister of Moses, was stricken with it (Nu 12:10). In the Mosaic Law, definite rules for its recognition, the preliminary quarantine period, and ceremonial methods of cleansing are given (Lv 13–14). The Alexandrian conquerors returned to Eastern Europe with the disease. The Romans contracted it from the Greeks. Pompey carried it into Italy. The Muslims brought it into new areas. Pilgrims from the Holy Land introduced it into England. And the returning crusaders brought it into other parts of Europe. Thus in the course of time, this dreadful disease made itself felt all over Eurasia. According to Herodotus, the ancient Persians exiled the lepers. The Chinese burned them alive. But segregation was practiced at an early date. This was the custom of the Egyptians, the Jews, and the afflicted European nations. In the beginning of the thirteenth century, there were two thousand leper houses in France and nineteen thousand in Europe, excluding those of Russia and Sweden.[8]

The invasion of leprosy is usually slow and intermittent. White shining spots are seen, appearing to be deeper than the skin. Red or coppery patches appear on face, hands, feet, or other parts of the body. Lumpy excrescences arise, at first pink, but changing to brown. The skin of the face and the mucous membranes[9] of the nose and throat are thickened, producing a distorted appearance, impeding breathing, and impairing the voice. The eyebrows drop off, and the eye tissues undergo degenerative changes. The ears and the nose become thickened and enlarged. As the disease progresses, the knotty surface breaks down in ulcerating sores. The nails of the fingers may become hard and clawed. Portions of the extremities, including whole fingers and toes, die and drop off. The gums are absorbed, and the teeth disappear. The nose, eyes, tongue, and palate are gradually consumed. Slowly and surely, the malady progresses. Living death seizes upon one organ after another, until, perhaps after the lapse of years, the patient is carried off, death often hastened by some intervening disease.

Among the Jews, those afflicted with leprosy were shunned by their fellow men not only because of the loathsomeness of their disease, but also because they were in a special manner regarded as ceremonially unclean. There was more than concern about contagion; mere contact with a leper defiled whoever touched him. While the cure of other diseases was called healing, the cure (if there was any) of leprosy was usually called cleansing. A leper was considered an outcast, socially and morally,

4
Leprosy
(Mt 8:2–4);[5]
Mk 1:40–45;
Lk 5:12–15

5
The Character
of Leprosy

6
"Unclean, Unclean"

although it is not possible to determine precisely to what extent the unfortunate sufferers were excluded from interaction with other people. A place was set aside for them in the synagogues, and the strictest precautionary measures were taken.[10] The leper was obliged to avoid the towns and to go about with torn garments, bared head, and covered chin. The only care he received was from such as were similarly afflicted. As he passed by, wrapped in a mourner's garb, as it were, he was required to cry, "Unclean, unclean" (Lv 13:45), thus proclaiming that his was both a living and a moral death.[11] There was no special treatment. If he recovered from the disease, he was obliged to submit to an extended priestly inspection and to prolonged ceremonial purifications. And not until after the presentation of the legal offering was he pronounced clean.

7
"Be Clean!"
(Mt 8:2–3); Mk 1:40–42; Lk 5:12–13

While Jesus was in a certain city,[12] a man "full of leprosy" came to Him, threw himself down before Him, and pleaded with Him in the manner of all true Christian prayer: "Lord, if You will, You can make me clean." That was faith in the power of Jesus and absolute committal to Him in the man's helpless and, generally speaking, hopeless state. The Lord was moved with compassion. There was not a moment's hesitation on the part of Jesus. "Prompt as an echo"[13] came the reply: "I will; be clean."[14] Almighty power spoke. Stretching forth His hand, the Lord touched the leper—there was no shrinking from the loathsome disease—and as soon as Jesus had uttered those words, the leper was cleansed. "The touching hand of Jesus was not defiled by the leper's body, but the leper's body was cleansed by Jesus' touch. Thus Jesus touched our sinful nature and yet Himself remained without the touch of sin."[15]

8
"Show Yourself to the Priest"
(Mt 8:4); Mk 1:44; Lk 5:14

"And Jesus sternly charged him and sent him away at once." Almost vehemently, the Lord dismissed him from His presence with a twofold charge: keep silent and obtain the legal priestly certificate of his cleansing. The latter command was most likely given for the purpose of establishing the proof of the miracle, out of consideration for the sufferer, whose social rehabilitation might otherwise be frustrated. Jesus would also obey the Levitical law (Lv 14:2–32). According to the Law of Moses, anyone who claimed to be cured of the plague had to submit to a rigid priestly inspection for the purpose of obtaining the legal certificate that he was actually clean. In many cases, the person suspected of having contracted the malady was not afflicted with true leprosy, in which case the priest could announce a cleansing after fourteen days. But a true leper usually remained a leper.[16] However, if the priestly inspection proved favorable, an offering was both permitted[17] and required, after which the former leper was again admitted to the society of his family and friends. Jesus' command clearly shows that it was His desire to fulfill all righteousness (Mt 3:15; 5:17), even to submit to the ordinances of the ceremonial law. There was to be no just cause of complaint against Him nor against the person whom He had helped. "Go, show yourself to the priest[18] and offer the gift that Moses commanded, for a proof to them"; namely, as evidence and testimony to the people that you have been healed.[19]

"And He charged him to tell no one." But why this command of silence? We can only guess at the answer. Was it that the healed man should "silently reflect upon the wonderful work of God"?[20] Was it to "avoid the excitement and tumult of the already overexcited multitudes of Galilee"?[21] Or was it, as seems most likely, the desire to discourage any publicity that might lead to a false conception of His messianic work, of the purpose for which He had come into the world?[22] It seems that the leper complied with the Lord's direction concerning his purification and social rehabilitation. "But he went out and began to talk freely about [his cleansing], and to spread the news."[23] The result was that the Lord's work was hindered on account of the man's well-meant disobedience. It is true, great multitudes flocked to Jesus. However, their purpose was not so much to hear the Word of God (Lk 5:1) as "to hear" about the great miracle-worker and to secure healing for themselves. But this was not the popularity that the Lord desired. In order to counteract this unwanted publicity, He made Himself inaccessible for the time being by avoiding the open cities and retiring to desolate places for the purpose of solitude and prayer.[24] And still they came to Him from every quarter.

We know neither the extent nor the route of our Lord's first Galilean circuit. Returning quietly to Capernaum "after some days,"[27] it was reported abroad that He was at home, presumably in Peter's house.[28] Soon a crowd gathered in ever-growing numbers, filling the house and the surrounding courtyard and occupying every foot of available space without and within. Peter's house was packed to the door.[29] Among those gathered were believing disciples, friendly neighbors, and curious strangers, generally sympathetic. But there were also Pharisees and doctors of the Law from Galilee, Judea, and Jerusalem, who, it seems, had come for a purpose. Following the encounter in Jerusalem at the unknown feast, it appears that representatives had been sent for the purpose of watching, opposing, and, if possible, entrapping Jesus. And so we might say there was a gathering in Peter's home "like the gathering of Israel on Mount Carmel to witness the issue as between Elijah and the priests of Baal."[30] Jesus had the power to heal. But the first thing He did was preach.

While Jesus was busily engaged in preaching "the Word,"[31] a remarkable thing happened. Four men approached, bearing a paralytic on his pallet. Of course, this was not strange. Of late it had become too common a scene to see sick people carried to Jesus to attract special attention. But with the house packed to the doors and no one apparently willing to leave his place, access to Jesus was simply impossible. What was to be done? The four men were absolutely determined and probably solemnly pledged to bring their patient to Jesus. We do not know who the sufferer

9
"See that You Say Nothing to Anyone"
Mk 1:45; Lk 5:15–16

10
Returning to Capernaum
(Mt 9:1–8);[25] Mk 2:1–12;[26] Lk 5:17–26

11
The Paralytic
(Mt 9:2); Mk 2:1–4; Lk 5:17–19

was. He was "a paralytic."[32] The disease or injury causes extreme loss of the power of motion by affecting either the motor centers of the brain or the spinal cord. It is always serious, usually intractable, and generally sudden in its onset (1 Macc 9:55–56). Though the Lord addressed him affectionately as "son," this was not necessarily a proof that he was young.[33] And though He prefaced the cure by declaring to him the forgiveness of sins, we need not infer from this that the disease was the result of a wicked life, although it may have been. It seemed impossible to bring the sufferer into the presence of Jesus. But necessity is the mother of invention. When the four men saw that they could not approach Jesus by clearing a path for themselves through the crowd, they made their way to the roof of the house, perhaps by an outer staircase.[34] There, they removed the tiles and, through an opening, let down their burden exactly in front of the place where Jesus was. We can imagine the surprise of the assembly within as a disturbance overhead interrupted Jesus' discourse and a pallet slowly lowered, on which a paralytic lay, silent.[35]

12
"Your Sins Are Forgiven"
(Mt 9:2); Mk 2:5; Lk 5:20

Many sick had been brought to Jesus. But such a display of purposeful energy, unhesitating boldness, and unyielding determination of a heroic faith had never been witnessed before. And it was faith, at least a firm belief in the almighty healing power of Jesus, both on the part of the sufferer and of his friends, but probably also a faith in Jesus as the promised Messiah of God. Jesus saw, and Jesus spoke. "And when Jesus saw their faith,[36] He said to the paralytic, 'Take heart, My son; your sins are forgiven.'" Certainly, a strange greeting to one whose strange coming had a different purpose. But whether the man had brought on his suffering by a previously licentious life, it was the purpose of Jesus to set the temporal and the spiritual into proper relation. The first and greatest need of every person, whether sick or healthy, is the gracious forgiveness of sins. And regardless of the degree of his knowledge and faith in Jesus as the Messiah, the sufferer was apparently a repentant Israelite, who acknowledged himself a sinner, felt the need of forgiveness, and as such was beyond "the coarse Judaic standpoint, which viewed suffering itself as an expiation of sin."[37] As the kind Physician, Jesus inspires confidence at the outset with a tender, cheering word: "Take heart, My son." And then, He deals first with the disease of the soul: "Your sins are forgiven."

13
"Who Can Forgive Sins but God Alone?"
(Mt 9:3–5); Mk 2:6–9; Lk 5:21–23

And now, the scribes[38] played their part. The sufferer appeared before Jesus only by the most unusual means; but it seems that the scribes and the Pharisees were early on the spot and in a position to hear and see Jesus distinctly. Although many others were standing, they had even found comfortable seats[39] and were now in sullen silence carrying on a dialogue[40] in their hearts: "Who is this who speaks blasphemies? Who can forgive sins but God alone?" From their point of view, they were right. But Jesus was God, which truth, however, they were not ready to accept. Immediately, Jesus gave a proof of His divinity. The reasoning of their hearts was known to Him.

It is true, He was a man like all other men in every respect except sin, but also the "Son of Man" in the emphatic and well-understood sense,[41] the promised Messiah and Mediator between God and men. When He perceived in His spirit that they so reasoned within themselves, He said to them: "Why do you think evil in your hearts? For which is easier, to say, 'Your sins are forgiven,' or to say, 'Rise and walk'?" As regards the mere words, both were just as easy to say. If merely saying them constituted blasphemy and pretense, accomplishing them would demonstrate divine authority and power. Also, the healing would prove the forgiving.[42]

"Which is easier?" If Jesus could by one word of His divine power heal this man, who was hopelessly paralyzed, would the crowd not have to admit that He had power on earth to forgive sins? "The unanswerable question was received with the silence of an invincible obstinacy."[43] But in order to prove that the declaration of forgiveness was no pretense and "that the Son of Man has authority on earth to forgive sins," He turned once more to the paralytic and said to him: "Rise, pick up your bed, and go home." "At once power was restored to the palsied limbs and peace to the troubled soul."[44] The man was healed, spiritually and physically. He arose, took up his pallet, opened a passage through the crowd, and went to his house, glorifying God. Said, done. Who could now, in the face of this visible proof, persist in the charge of blasphemy against Jesus? The effect the miracle had upon the scribes and the Pharisees is not recorded. Very likely, their "evil" thoughts remained unchanged (cf. Mt 9:11; Mk 3:6). The multitude dispersed, glorifying God. Exclamations of astonishment were heard, intermingled with expressions of amazement and fear. "We never saw anything like this!" "We have seen extraordinary things[45] today."

And now, comes a memorable day for the evangelist St. Matthew. Shortly after the healing of the paralytic, Jesus seems to have departed to His nearby favorite shore. As usual, an ever-increasing multitude surrounded Him. At or near Capernaum, there was a tax booth. Passing by the place, after having taught the people, He beheld a tax collector, or customs official, sitting at the place of toll, to whom He extended the call, "Follow Me." We are quite safe in supposing a previous acquaintance and friendship. But the time had now come for Jesus to include him among the number of constant companions. However, before directing our attention to this new disciple of Jesus, this is probably the place to say something about the office of a tax collector and the reputation of that class of officials to which Matthew had belonged.

The scepter had indeed departed from Judah, and the Jews were made to feel the weight of the tribute-taking hand of a foreign ruler, although the Roman government as such could not be called particularly rapacious in this respect. Indeed, the Romans had changed the financial administration of the provinces since the days of the republic. In the imperial era, the direct taxes, ground, income, and poll taxes, were no longer sold or farmed out to the highest bidders; that is, the revenues

14
"Rise, Pick Up Your Bed, and Go Home" (Mt 9:6–8); Mk 2:10–12; Lk 5:24–26

15
At the Tax Booth Near Capernaum (Mt 9:9);[46] Mk 2:13–14; Lk 5:27–28

16
Taxes

of a particular district or province were not leased to the so-called *publicani* for a fixed period or sum. The procurators, or ruling princes, now collected them in their regular routine of official duty.[47] Indeed, it seems that in order to check the rapacity of the provincial rulers, the Romans provided the territorial princes with a fixed annual salary in the days of Caesar Augustus.[48] And lest they be still tempted to take advantage of their position, Tiberius, the emperor at the time, introduced the policy of leaving them at their posts as long as possible. The hope was that, after having gorged themselves at the beginning, they would become more moderate in their exactions.[49] But while the Roman government in general adopted a milder policy with respect to provincial administration, the actual governing hand was often cruel and harsh. The taxes were heavy. And what has just been said applies only to the direct taxes. In spite of all leniency and consideration in many matters—no tribute in sabbatical years[50]—the fact could not be disguised that a proud nation, which felt itself called upon to govern the world, found itself paying tribute to Caesar.[51]

17
Customs

It seems that the aversion to paying taxes is ingrained in human nature. But the Jewish hatred of Roman taxes was directed especially against one source of revenue, the customs, and the officials who collected them. This tax, which was still farmed out, was collected at various places and levied not only upon exports and imports but also upon all goods in the hands of merchants passing through the country. Its collectors were the familiar tax collectors of the New Testament. The name[52] was extended from the Roman farmer-general of an entire province to his subordinate local officials. Sufficient cause for their unpopularity in New Testament times is not far to seek. Customs officials are always unpopular. The man who opens boxes and bundles for the purpose of appraising their value and is on the lookout for mostly nonexistent hidden pearls is at best a tolerated evil. Among the Jews, all circumstances combined to send the tax collector beyond the social pale. He was the very embodiment of antinationalism. He represented, and at a very sore spot brought the individual into contact with, the hated power of Rome. The tax was looked upon not only as a civil imposition but also as a religious wrong. Many even considered its payment a sin, an act of disloyalty to God. If the tax collector was a Jew, as many of them were, he was a renegade in the eyes of his fellows. Since he had to pay for his concession, he had to be a man of some wealth. It was in his interest to make a sound financial investment. If the sum of the fixed revenue exceeded the expected amount, it was his gain. If, however, he failed to collect the specified amount, he had to bear the loss. The tariff rates were vague and indefinite, which permitted him to protect his investment with a liberal margin. In collecting the dues, he was always under the suspicion of extortion, and in many instances he actually *was* an extortionist. Where tax collectors are mentioned in the New Testament, they are usually associated with "sinners." Edersheim tells the story of the death of a tax collector and of a very pious man. The tax collector, at his burial, received all honor from his townsmen, while the pious man was carried to his grave unmourned. This anomaly was explained in this way, that the pious man had committed one sin, while the tax collector had done one good deed. Later, however, the fate of the two men was satisfactorily adjusted. The pious man was seen walking beside the heavenly waterbrooks, while the tax collector was burning in hell.[53] This illustrates the low esteem in which the tax collectors were popularly held. On the other hand, examples could also be given of contrivances and ways for defrauding the revenue.[54] There were three principal stations in Israel for the collecting of customs: Caesarea, Jericho, and Capernaum.

We are now ready to make the acquaintance of one of the tax collectors at Capernaum. Whether he was the principal customs collector of the Capernaum district or one of his subordinates, we do not know. From the fact that he was seated at the place of toll, it has been argued[55] that he was a subordinate official and tax collector of the worst kind,[56] who had secured a concession for himself in the hope of making profit on his own account. Capernaum itself was ideally located, and for that reason probably chosen, for a customs station. Touching the lake in the neighborhood was the great road of Eastern commerce, which led from Damascus and beyond to the harbors of the west. The lake itself and the caravan route around the shores would serve in transferring goods to and from the Arabian interior. Diverging from the Way of the Sea, there was a choice of roads southward to Jerusalem and Egypt.[57] At the juncture of these roads, customs stations would be located, with the tax collectors sitting at the place of toll. Levi was the name of one of them, the son of an otherwise unknown Alphaeus, not to be identified with the father of James the younger and of Jude (Mt 10:3; Mk 3:18).[58] But it seems that, in conformity with Jewish custom on the occasion of a decisive change of life, he received or adopted a name indicative of his entry into the discipleship of Jesus. Very fittingly, Levi the tax collector called himself Matthew—that is, Theodore, or "gift of God."[59] Or the name may have been changed by Jesus (cf. Jn 1:42), perhaps partly to "obliterate the painful reminiscences of his late discreditable calling."[60] In this case, we note the touching humility with which in the list of the apostles he alone among the evangelists gives to himself the dishonorable title of "Matthew the tax collector" (Mt 10:3).[61] That the former tax collector Levi is to be identified with the apostle Matthew and that he wrote the first of the four Gospels was universally accepted in the Christian Church.[62] He must have heard and seen Jesus frequently as He taught by the seaside. He may have witnessed the call of the first disciples. His calling would make him acquainted with the fishermen and ship owners of Capernaum. He had probably become a disciple of Jesus in his heart long before the eventful day that forever decided his future life. But on account of his social standing as a despised

18
Levi-Matthew
(Mt 9:9); Mk 2:13–
14; Lk 5:27–28

tax collector, he did not dare to hope for personal recognition, much less a call to discipleship. He was mistaken. When Jesus fixed His look of love upon him, which pierced the inmost depths of his soul, and said to him, "Follow Me," the summons needed not a moment's consideration. "His past was swallowed up in a heaven of bliss."[63] He said not a word, but rose, left everything, and followed Him.

19
Matthew's Feast
(Mt 9:10); Mk 2:15;
Lk 5:29

The progress of the story infers a return to nearby[64] Capernaum. Matthew's first act as a disciple of Jesus was to prepare a great feast in honor of His new Master. The invited guests, besides Jesus and His disciples, included a multitude of those who in the pharisaic vocabulary were classified as "tax collectors and sinners." But disregarding this for the present, we take it that Matthew was a man of some wealth. He also had some social standing, at least in the circle in which he moved, and was the owner of a large house or roomy court, spacious enough to accommodate a large number of guests. As tax collector, he would be acquainted with the representatives of the Roman government, with whom he very likely was able to converse in Greek. His acquaintance may have included some of the officers of Herod's court. And he would be known to the traders and businessmen of Capernaum. His feast was a farewell feast, as some take it. It would afford Matthew's associates, who were contemptuously designated sinners and excluded from the synagogue because of some offense against the traditions, an opportunity to hear the Gospel of the Kingdom and to meet Jesus. To sit at a meal with such guests was in full accord with the mission of Jesus, but in the eyes of the "orthodox" it was a scandalous affair.

20
"Tax Collectors and
Sinners"
(Mt 9:11); Mk 2:16;
Lk 5:30

When some members of the pharisaic party "saw it,"—namely, when they beheld Jesus at Matthew's festive gathering—they became indignant that one who passed for a rabbi should have so little consideration for the honor of the learned profession. He who "pretended to be a preacher of virtue did not hesitate to contaminate Himself by the society of such disreputable characters."[65] But how could they see Him? Were they present themselves? Most likely not, at least not as invited guests. At such occasions, however, there is no privacy in the East.[66] In exercising their functions as guardians of the Law, they may, in passing by, have looked in; for otherwise "their presence as invited guests would have involved them in the same blame which they were now casting upon the Lord."[67] Under the circumstances, none of them dared to reproach Jesus directly; they contented themselves for the time being with making spiteful observations to His disciples: "Why does your teacher eat with tax collectors and sinners?" In putting this question to the disciples rather than to Jesus, the critics showed a certain amount of cowardly cunning. The disciples were but "initial learners." The question was one that concerned Jewish social norms. "Had they been able to shake the confidence of the disciples in their new Master, they would at the same time have seriously injured the cause of Christ."[68]

As soon as Jesus heard of it, He took the faultfinding and "murmuring respect-ability" to task.[69] In defending His own conduct, He quotes a proverb, implying at the same time a criticism of their own self-righteous attitude. "Those who are well have no need of a physician, but those who are sick." This is true in the spiritual as well as in the physical sense. "I came not to call the righteous, but sinners." Not as if there were actually any "righteous," but the trouble with the Pharisees was that they considered themselves whole and righteous. They felt no need of a Savior from sin—a miserable delusion. They were sinners as well as others, howbeit self-righteous sinners, blind to their real condition, while those whom they called "tax collectors and sinners" were conscious of their sin. In their self-righteousness, they would now combine against Jesus, not on account of any sinful act of His, but on account of His association with sinners. Applying "a rabbinic formula,"[70] Jesus bade them, "Go and learn what this means, 'I desire mercy, and not sacrifice'" (Hos 6:6; LXX). Mercy goes before sacrifice. Love is the fulfilling of the Law. Outward formalism, mere Levitical piety, and dead orthodoxy are an abomination to the Lord. In the number of sin-sick and salvation-needing souls, they had forgotten to include themselves. Had it never occurred to their scandalized minds, "overlaid with a crust of mere Levitism, that the love which condescends to mingle with sinners in the effort to win their hearts is more pleasing to God than a century of accumulated fasting, a hecatomb of rams, or a river of oil"?[71]

Not only was the association of Jesus with tax collectors and sinners offensive to the pharisaic mind, but the feast itself seems to have been in conflict with current opinion and practice: instead of a fast, a feast. The feast of the converted Levi-Matthew in honor of Jesus probably took place on one of the two days appointed for weekly fasts.[72] There was another reason for complaint. By this time, John the Baptist "lay in the dreary misery of a Machaerus dungeon,"[73] east of the Dead Sea. Misunderstanding the austere manner of their master and imitating it in a false manner, a number of John's disciples had not followed his suggestion to leave him and follow Jesus, but had associated themselves with the Pharisees, who above all wanted to regulate the piety of Jesus by their own practices. A number of men of both parties approached Jesus with a question concerning the strict observance of prayers and fasting (Lk 5:33), regarding which they and the party of Jesus were apparently at variance. "Why do we and the Pharisees fast, but Your disciples do not fast?" The attack was cunning. If the exact relation of Jesus and John was not known and accepted, it was at least a matter of common knowledge that Jesus highly respected John. The question drew from Jesus three of His first "parabolic impromptus."[74] In replying, He both shielded His forerunner and gently answered His critics.

The last recorded public testimony of John had pointed to Jesus as the Bridegroom (Jn 3:29). His presence marks the marriage week. Even according to

21
Jesus' Self-Defense
(Mt 9:12–13);
Mk 2:17; Lk 5:31–32

22
Fasting
(Mt 9:14); Mk 2:18;
Lk 5:33

23
The Wedding Guests
(Mt 9:15); Mk 2:19–
20; Lk 5:34–35

rabbinic law, this was to be a time of unmixed festivity.[75] During the marriage week, all mourning was to be suspended, and even the daily prescribed prayers were not obligatory. Was it not, then, inconsistent to "make wedding guests fast while the bridegroom is with them"? Jesus is the Bridegroom. His disciples are the sons of the bridal feast, the best men at the wedding. The title "sons of the bridechamber"[76] explains all companions of the bridegroom, who act for him and in his interest and bring the bride to him. How can they be sad? When the bridegroom is conducted by his friends into the bridal chamber, that is the time for perfect enjoyment. If it should happen, however, that sudden death seizes the bridegroom in the midst of the marriage rejoicing, then indeed there would be a time for them to fast. And calmly looking toward "the deep abyss which yawned before Him,"[77] Jesus again[78] alluded to the violent end that awaited Him: "The days will come when the bridegroom is taken away from them, and then they will fast in those days." The disciples did not yet know what this would mean.

24
New Cloth
(Mt 9:16); Mk 2:21;
Lk 5:36

In Jesus' defense of His disciples, He emphasizes fasting in ways that are fitting. So He also insists upon proper "congruity in religion."[79] "No one puts a piece of unshrunk cloth on an old garment, for the patch tears away from the garment, and a worse tear is made." This happens when a piece of unshrunk cloth[80] or a piece cut from a new garment[81] is taken to repair an old.[82] The process would only make matters worse. When the new cloth shrinks, it would draw apart the threads from the weak part of the old garment. At best, it would make the patch all the more conspicuous. It is useless "to mix heterogeneous things,"[83] indeed, worse than useless. The observance of fasting, prayers, and days in a self-righteous spirit does not agree with the doctrine of grace and therefore shuts one out from the Kingdom.

25
New Wine
(Mt 9:17); Mk 2:22;
Lk 5:37–39

The illustrations are beautiful. The introductory figure of a wedding feast suggests images of the bridegroom, fasting, clothing, and wine. "Neither is new wine put into old wineskins;" (that is, skins used as bottles) "if it is, the skins burst and the wine is spilled and the skins are destroyed. But new wine is put into fresh wineskins, and so both are preserved." Until it is thoroughly aged, new wine, still in its expansive strength, must be kept in fresh and elastic containers. Thus, in a gentle manner Jesus gives His questioners more than they had asked for. All that He has said answers the question raised at Matthew's feast: "Why does your teacher eat with tax collectors and sinners?" (Mt 9:11). Mercy goes before sacrifice. All service of the lips and sacrifice of the hands—all mere outward worship, self-righteous fasting, prayers, and observance of days—are an abomination to the Lord. The piety of the Pharisees (based on ultra-legalism) and the doctrine of Jesus will not agree. The old garments, the filthy rags, must not bind the heart in its own righteousness. Neither can the new and sweet wine of the Gospel be contained in carnal hearts. The Gospel does not require the Old Testament form, but faith. "No one after drinking old wine desires new, for he says, 'The old is good.'" The haggling Pharisees and the misunderstanding disciples of John still loved the "old wine of legal piety and did not care for the new"[84]—the fulfillment of prophecies that the Lord proclaimed in the Gospel. They found the old wine so good that they did not wish to taste any other and therefore disdained the doctrine of salvation full and free in Christ Jesus.[85]

According to the chronology that we have adopted, it was now late spring or early summer of AD 31 (784 AUC). We suppose that what is related here happened near Capernaum.[87] Those following Jesus passed through a field of wheat[88] on a Sabbath day,[89] the exact time of which cannot be determined. The disciples of Jesus, being hungry, began to pluck ears of the ripe wheat and to eat the kernels, after rubbing off the chaff with their hands. To spying Pharisees, who were ever on the lookout for offenses committed by someone, this action was a fortunate discovery. According to their statutes, the disciples of Jesus entangled themselves in at least two sins. With a "contemptuous gesture towards them"[90] (the disciples), the Pharisees approach our Lord with an angry question: "Look, why are they doing what is not lawful on the Sabbath?" It seems that Jesus Himself was not directly implicated. It also seems that the rabbinic rule of the Sabbath day's journey, which was not to exceed two thousand cubits, was not transgressed.[91] Neither was their action looked upon as stealing, for the plucking of ears from the neighbor's grain was not only sanctioned by custom, but permitted by law (Dt 23:25). But a far more heinous crime was discovered, which, technically speaking, might render the offenders liable to death by stoning: the plucking and rubbing was done on a Sabbath. According to rabbinic interpretation, these acts constituted reaping and threshing.[92] Of course, there was no wrong done, even from the standpoint of the strictest interpretation of the Jewish Law. But the Pharisees—always unable to penetrate to the principle of a thing and engrossing themselves in a maze of rules—so construed it and incidentally accused Jesus as an accomplice for permitting the assumed sacrilege.

Jesus defends the action of His disciples with unassailable arguments and then declares Himself to be the Lord of the Sabbath. The first argument was taken from a well-known incident of biblical history. When David fled before the wrath of Saul, he was in need and hungry. David came to the sanctuary of God at Nob. There Abiathar, most likely the assistant at the sanctuary, with the distinct sanction of his father Ahimelech (1Sm 22:20),[93] supplied David with bread of the Presence, "which it was not lawful for him to eat nor for those who were with him, but only for the priests" (cf. Lv 22:10; 1Sm 21:6; Lv 24:8–9). David's fleeing men needed food. It was an emergency. What constituted the particular emergency in the case of the disciples that forced them to appease their hunger in the fields of grain, we do not know. Now, if David, their national hero and saint, had thus violated the letter of the Law

26
Plucking Heads of Grain on a Sabbath
(Mt 12:1–2);[86]
Mk 2:23–24;
Lk 6:1–2

27
Jesus Defends His Disciples
(Mt 12:3–7);
Mk 2:25–27;
Lk 6:3–4

(Lv 24:5–9) and had yet been held blameless because his men needed the grain,[94] why should the disciples be blamed for the harmless act of appeasing their hunger?

The second argument is taken from the discharge of priestly duties on the Sabbath days.

> For certainly to hew the wood for the burnt offering, to light the fires, to place hot, fresh-baked show-bread on the table, to slay the victims, and to circumcise children on the eighth day, involved work for the servants of the temple of the Lord. And if they were held blameless, should not the servants of the Lord of the temple be excused?[95]

"I tell you, something greater than[96] the temple is here." Jesus returns to the charge made at the feast given by Matthew of eating with tax collectors and sinners (Mt 9:11, 13). He strikes at the principle: "If you had known what this means, 'I desire mercy, and not sacrifice,' you would not have condemned the guiltless." Here, Jesus defends His conduct of shielding the disciples by an appeal to the voice of prophecy (Hos 6:6). The Pharisees were men of a thousand "rules, not accustomed to go back on principles";[97] but love clearly is the fulfilling of the Law (Rm 13:10). "Ceremonial rules may be overruled by higher considerations."[98] With the sacrificing priests, it was the temple. Here was One greater than the temple (compare Mt 12:6). In the case of Abiathar or Ahimelech, it was the love of a needy neighbor. In the case of the disciples, it was hunger that must be appeased. Why did it not occur to them to offer food instead of spying? And as to the Sabbath rest, this applied only to the regular work of weekly labor. Deeds of love and mercy were at all times permitted.

28
The Lord of the Sabbath
(Mt 12:8); Mk 2:27–28; Lk 6:5

That this is the correct interpretation of the Sabbath law and that the great underlying principle of the Sabbath is only a means to an end, man's highest good, Jesus now states in a great word, preserved only in Mark: "The Sabbath was made for man, not man for the Sabbath."[99] The Sabbath, as God intended it for the Jews, was to serve them as a day of rest, but His intention never had been to make them slaves of its observance and to bind them with fetters. The Sabbath was given for their highest good. And as far as the whole question is concerned, Jesus points to Himself as being greater than the temple and greater than the Sabbath. The old injunctions concerning sacrifices, new moons, and Sabbaths were in force until He came. They were "a shadow of the things to come, but the substance belongs to Christ" (Col 2:17). This truth stands for all times. Upon the believers in the New Testament, the Third Commandment of the Decalogue enjoins only this, that they gladly hear and learn the Word of God. Whether the Pharisees understood it, we do not know, but the fact is that "the Son of Man is Lord of the Sabbath."[100] One fifth-century manuscript concludes this story with a remarkable addition.[101] It reads as follows: "On the same day, seeing one working on the Sabbath, He said to him, O man, if indeed you know what you do, you are blessed; but if you know not, you are accursed and a transgressor of the Law." The incident is curious. But no doubt the paragraph is a late addition. At most, it contains one of those so-called "unrecorded sayings" of our Lord.[102] However, it illustrates the spirit of our Lord's teaching as understood by St. Paul: "Whatever does not proceed from faith is sin" (Rm 14:23).[103]

The Pharisees were corrected, but not convinced. At the first opportunity, they renewed their attack upon the Lord because of His alleged breaking of the Sabbath. This took place, as it would seem, the following Sabbath[104] in Capernaum.[105] According to the custom of His earlier life as a worshiper and since the beginning of His public ministry as a teacher, Jesus entered the synagogue. Among those present in that Sabbath gathering was a man whose right hand was dry, or withered,[106] as a result of an accident or a disease. According to legend, he was a stone mason, maimed by an accident, who implored Jesus to restore the use of his working hand, that he might not be forced to beg.[107] The evangelists do not state whether the Pharisees were responsible for his presence. At any rate, his presence and his condition were known, and it was their purpose to watch Jesus, "whether He would heal him on the Sabbath, so that they might accuse Him." By this time, Jesus had gravely offended them on a number of different points: (1) He had assumed the right to forgive sins; (2) He associated with tax collectors and sinners; (3) He disregarded their traditions of fasting; (4) He was guilty of Sabbath infractions. And although He had fully justified His actions and ably defended His position, their hatred was intensified with each new defeat. If by reasoning with Him they did not succeed in gaining their end, they hoped to do so by prosecuting Him according to the Mosaic Law. In the end, they could resort to violence. If it must be admitted according to their own statutes that emergencies and danger to life warranted a breach of the Sabbath observance,[108] surely here was a case of healing that one could easily postpone until the next day. In their eagerness to provoke the Lord, they asked the question: "Is it lawful to heal on the Sabbath?"

Jesus did not leave His questioners long in doubt. First, He requested that the man with the withered hand stand forth in their midst. Then He asked a counter-question: "Is it lawful on the Sabbath to do good or to do harm, to save life or to kill?" In agreement with the principle stated the week before, Christ taught that "the ethically good coincides with the humane."[109] Deeds of love and mercy are never limited to days. Then there is also the possibility of doing evil by failing to do good (Jas 4:17). To neglect to do good that it is in one's power to do is sinful. And not to save life when an opportunity to do so presents itself is to kill. Would it be a proper observance of God's holy day to do evil, to kill? "But they were silent." They could not answer such an argument, for here was an altogether different point of view. Neither were they anxious to "go and learn" (Mt 9:13). Their whole purpose was to find a transgression upon which they could successfully base a charge before

29
The Man with a Withered Hand (Mt 12:9–10); Mk 3:1–2; Lk 6:6–7

30
Jesus Defends His Healing on a Sabbath (Mt 12:11–14); Mk 3:3–6; Lk 6:8–11

the Council or, if not, to turn the admiration of the people for Jesus into suspicion and to mark Him with the stigma of a Sabbath breaker. In an appeal to their well-nigh dead feelings of humanity, Jesus justified His action by citing a practice that they themselves followed: "Which one[110] of you who has a sheep, if it falls into a pit on the Sabbath, will not take hold of it and lift it out?" Their own rabbis made provisions for such cases.[111] "Of how much more value is a man than a sheep!" The argument is unanswerable. "So it is lawful to do good on the Sabbath." Kindness is never unseasonable. And looking upon His silent and sullen accusers in just anger, He "grieved at their hardness of heart, and said to the man, 'Stretch out your hand.' He stretched it out, and his hand was restored." Thus, Jesus had not broken the Sabbath law, not even according to their strictest interpretation of it. Surely, it was not wrong to speak a word! For neither by touch nor by remedy nor by outward application, merely by His word of power, had He healed the man. But the Pharisees, now filled with an insane rage, went out and took counsel with the Herodians how they might destroy Him.

31
The Herodians
(Mt 12:14); Mk 3:6;
Lk 6:11

This was the second direct plot against the life of Jesus—first in Jerusalem at the unnamed feast (Jn 5:18) and now in the Prophet's own home province, Galilee. This is the first time that the Herodians are mentioned. The Herodians were people who favored rule by the Herodian family. Although both the Herodians and the Pharisees hated the Roman rule (and each other), just why the Herodians, a political party with Sadducean tendencies, should now combine with the Pharisees against Jesus is not clear. However, in a false understanding of the King and the Kingdom, they would naturally be jealous and watchful of anyone whom they supposed to put forth any messianic claims. And because the Pharisees were angry with Jesus on religious grounds, yet unable to take any measures against Him without the assent of Herod, the two parties easily united for the destruction of Jesus.[112]

32
Jesus Sought
by Multitudes
(Mt 12:15–16);
Mk 3:7–12

The hatred of the religious and the political leaders did not cause Jesus to lose popular favor. However, their constant attacks upon Him did make it desirable for Him to remove to some other place. Jointly with His disciples, who by this time were His constant companions and were soon to be appointed to permanent apostleship, He sought a retreat on the shores of the Galilean Sea. If the need should arise for another withdrawal, He could follow the shore or retire to a secluded place across the sea. But the opposition that rose against Him was accompanied by a popular prestige in a manner no one had anticipated. His visit to the unnamed feast in early spring, followed by the opening of His great Galilean ministry, had caused His fame to spread in every part of the land. It has always been a Near Eastern characteristic to flock to a prophet or popular leader (Mk 1:5).[113] Multitudes flocked to Him from every part of the region of Israel. There were the people of nearby Galilee. Others came from the North and South, from the busy ports of Tyre and

Sidon to the hills of sandy Idumea (Mk 3:8).[114] Even exclusive Judea and haughty Jerusalem were represented, the land of Israel from Dan to Beersheba, from Perea to the Mediterranean Sea. There was hardly a person of average intelligence who had not heard of the preaching and healing of this great Galilean Prophet. From all directions, they came. The onrush was so great that Jesus had to take precautionary measures. His disciples were instructed to have a small boat in readiness at all times, so that He could at once withdraw from the press should necessity so demand. "For He had healed many, so that all who had diseases pressed around Him to touch Him." It seems that it was mainly the desire for miracles that attracted the crowds. While Jesus' sympathy went out to all those afflicted with plagues and scourges,[115] while He healed "them all" (Mt 12:15), even permitting some to be healed by the mere touch of His garments, yet that was not the chief purpose of His miracles. It was not His aim to set Himself up as a miracle-monger, but for believing hearts to receive Him as the Messiah and Son of God. That is why He "ordered them," almost vehemently, "not to make Him known."[116] Neither did He want a confession as to His divine Sonship at the urge of demons. "And whenever the unclean spirits saw Him, they fell down before Him and cried out, 'You are the Son of God.' And He strictly ordered them not to make Him known."[117]

But there was an acknowledgment that befitted His ministry: the sincere faith of those who accepted Him as the Savior and depended upon Him for help not only for the body, but also for the soul. Thus, the prophecy of Isaiah was fulfilled (Is 42:1–4).[118] The Messiah, the beloved Servant of God, had at His Baptism received the Spirit of God without measure. His gentle Gospel shall be a light to lighten the Gentiles to the end of the earth. His spirit would not be the sensation-seeking self-advertisement of a demagogue, but the gentle and sympathetic ministry of One who supplies strength to the "bruised reed" and fresh oil to the "smoldering wick." By this ministry, He will bring final victory over Satan's forces and human pride. "And in His name the Gentiles will hope."

33
"In His Name the Gentiles Will Hope"
(Mt 12:17–21)

11

CHOOSING OF THE TWELVE AND THE SERMON ON THE MOUNT

PROBABLY SPRING OR EARLY SUMMER, AD 31

Events of far-reaching importance were soon to happen. The King rapidly shaped His work. Friends and enemies either flocked to His banner or banded themselves together to plan His ruin. The time had come for Jesus to select, and attach to His person, a definite number of accredited ambassadors—not simply friendly disciples—who might take an actual and authorized part in His work. He would deliver to them, as well as to the acclaiming multitudes, a manifesto of His kingdom. With these things in mind, probably after a brief return to Capernaum, Jesus went out[1] one evening in the spring of AD 31 to some nearby height to spend a night in prayer.[2] How often did our Lord in the days of His flesh offer up prayers and supplications (Heb 5:7) to His Father to gather strength for the superhuman task He had undertaken to perform—the redemption of mankind! How eagerly He set aside long hours for communion with Him in conjunction with whom He had formed the loving decree to gain fallen man back for the abodes of bliss! And in the morning, as we shall soon hear, He wanted to choose those men who were to be His messengers unto the ends of the earth. For this most important work, He asked for wisdom and guidance.

The scene of this elevated and lonely vigil is not known, although there is evidence that it was near Capernaum.[3] The hill that tradition has chosen, known as the Kurn (Horns of) Hattin, from its peculiar shape, has impressed scholars who believe it fits the circumstances described in the Gospels.[4] It lies about eight miles from Capernaum, off the road from Tiberias to Nazareth, at an elevation of 1,720 feet above the waters of the nearby Galilean Sea.[5] Its peculiar shape attracts the attention of travelers—a ridge about a quarter of a mile in length, running east and west,

1
A Night in Prayer
Mk 3:13a; Lk 6:12

2
The Mount

with a small cone, or horn, on each end. Thus with its two horns, the hill closely resembles the form of a camel saddle.[6]

Whether the disciples were with Jesus during His night of prayer we do not know. At any rate, they knew where He was to be found, and it was probably through them that the multitudes who were soon to assemble knew as well. It was at dawn of day and before the crowd arrived that our Lord summoned into His immediate presence the disciples, who had gradually made their appearance, very likely by special appointment.[7] The time had come when out of the number of general followers He wished to make a final choice of those whom He designated apostles. They were to be His present helpers in proclaiming the kingdom of God and in calling their countrymen's attention to the fact that Jesus was the promised Messiah. They were commissioned to preach, and in confirmation of their testimony and their appointment they were empowered to heal and authorized to cast out devils. But, as the result showed, their work had its chief significance, not in their present witness and work, but in their future labors when they were instrumental in establishing the Church, "built on the foundation of the apostles and prophets, Christ Jesus Himself being the cornerstone" (Eph 2:20). It is doubtful, however, whether at this time they realized the significance. They themselves above all needed to be thoroughly instructed as to the Lord's person and work. We are later told that their qualification for the office consisted in having been in the company of Jesus as witnesses from the time of the baptizing activities of John to the Lord's ascension (Ac 1:21–22). The selection of twelve men was likely based on the number of tribes of Israel (Mt 10:6; 19:28; Rv 21:12–14). By what formal act or process, if any, He ordained or "made"[8] them apostles we do not know. And now, without entering deeply into the many disputed points of names and relationship, let us take a look at the list.

It is interesting to compare the lists of the apostles as given by Matthew, Mark, Luke, and the Book of Acts. (See chart at right.)

First of all, leading the lists, is *Peter*, the eager, impulsive, faithful, and loving disciple who suddenly became weak, unsteady, and staggering. His name is perhaps mentioned first, not as if the lists were arranged according to rank—for Jesus reproved the apostles for disputing about that privilege (Mk 9:33–35)—but according to the common rule of priority or seniority. In the apostolic circle, the group of four fishermen who were first called naturally took precedence. And in that particular group it was Peter who took the lead. Most likely, he was a little older than the rest, probably about forty by this time. By occupation, he was a fisherman (Mk 1:16), originally an inhabitant of Bethsaida, on the Sea of Galilee, but subsequently living with his family at Capernaum (Jn 1:40–41; Mt 8:14; Mk 1:30). We shall meet him again and again in the Gospel history. His Lord and Master predicted a violent death for him (Jn 21:18–19), and there is a tradition that he died a martyr at Rome around AD 68, when he was about seventy-five years old. He is believed to have been crucified under Nero. It is said that at his own desire he was crucified head downward, feeling unworthy to die exactly like his Master.[9] The feast day for St. Peter is June 29.

	MATTHEW	MARK	LUKE	ACTS
1	Simon Peter	Simon Peter	Simon Peter	Peter
2	Andrew, his brother	James, son of Zebedee	Andrew, his brother	John
3	James, son of Zebedee	John, his brother	James	James
4	John, his brother	Andrew	John	Andrew
5	Philip	Philip	Philip	Philip
6	Bartholomew	Bartholomew	Bartholomew	Thomas
7	Thomas	Matthew	Matthew	Bartholomew
8	Matthew, the tax collector	Thomas	Thomas	Matthew
9	James, son of Alphaeus	James, son of Alphaeus	James, son of Alphaeus	James, son of Alphaeus
10	Thaddaeus	Thaddaeus	Simon the Zealot	Simon the Zealot
11	Simon the Zealot	Simon the Zealot	Judas, son of James	Judas, son of James
12	Judas Iscariot	Judas Iscariot	Judas Iscariot	

Strictly speaking, it was really the mission-minded *Andrew*, the brother of Peter, to whom the honor goes of being the first to be called into the intimate fellowship of Jesus. On learning of John the Baptist's powerful preaching of repentance, he left Bethsaida for the banks of the Jordan, there to become a disciple of the forerunner of Jesus. Upon the announcement that Jesus was "the Lamb of God" prophesied by Isaiah, he left John and followed Jesus (Jn 1:36–42). This great moment moved him to look for his brother Simon and to say to him: "We have found the Messiah." Outside of the few references in the Gospel narrative, nothing trustworthy is recorded of his subsequent life. According to a tradition, he suffered martyrdom in Greece by crucifixion on a cross shaped like the letter X, which therefore is called

6
Andrew
(Mt 10:2); Mk 3:18;
Lk 6:14; (Ac 1:13)

St. Andrew's cross. It is also said that a ship bearing two supposed relics of him was wrecked in what is now called St. Andrew's Bay in Scotland. The mariners who reached the shore introduced the Gospel in that region. Thus Andrew became the patron saint of Scotland. His festival is kept by the Greek and Latin churches on November 30. In the Church of England it has become customary on that day to preach on the subject of missions.[10]

7
James
(Mt 10:2); Mk 3:17; Lk 6:14; (Ac 1:13)

Next in the list, we have *James* and John, the sons of Zebedee and Salome, who, it seems, was the sister of Mary, the mother of Jesus.[11] Together with his sons, Zebedee carried on a flourishing fishing trade. He had boats and hired servants (Mk 1:20), and his connections may have extended to Jerusalem; this explains how it was that John was known in the house of the high priest (Jn 18:15–16).[12] That Zebedee was a man of some wealth is also usually inferred from the fact that his wife was one of those women who supported Jesus' ministry (Mt 27:55–56; Lk 8:2–3).[13] As the Synoptists usually place the name of James before that of John, it is supposed that he was the elder of this pair of brothers. That James was also among the first of the disciples of Jesus is inferred from the words of the evangelist John: "He *first* found his own brother Simon" (Jn 1:41), the inference being that, after Andrew had found his brother Simon, John, who does not name himself, found his brother James. He and John received from Christ the surname Boanerges, Sons of Thunder, probably on account of their desire to punish the Samaritans by fire from heaven (Lk 9:54). The few notices of James contained in the New Testament close with the account of his death at the hands of Herod Agrippa I, who had him beheaded probably in AD 41 (Ac 12:2). Thus he was the first of the apostles to seal his testimony with his blood and to drink of the cup of his Lord and Master (Mk 10:39). The feast day for St. James is July 25.

8
John
(Mt 10:2); Mk 3:17; Lk 6:14; (Ac 1:13)

We now come to *John*, the disciple "whom Jesus loved" (Jn 13:23). At least, we are convinced that it was this disciple who appears in the synoptic account as John, the son of Zebedee and (as is supposed) Salome,[14] was the brother of James, and is the author of the Gospel that bears the name of John. From the Synoptic Gospels, we gain the information that he became a disciple of Jesus, that together with Peter, James, and probably Andrew he belonged to the "inner circle" (Mk 5:37; Lk 9:28; Mk 9:2; 14:33; Mt 26:37; Mk 13:3), and that he was continually with our Lord to the end. From the fourth Gospel, we gain additional intimate glimpses, confirming our belief that this Gospel was written by him. This Gospel supplies us with many incidents of our Lord's ministry in Judea and sayings that have been entirely omitted by the other evangelists. It was evidently written by an eyewitness for the purpose of supplementing the synoptic account. And incidentally, also we learn certain facts about the writer—that he leaned upon the Savior when He celebrated the last Passover with His disciples and instituted His Holy Supper (Jn 13:25), that the grief-stricken mother of the Savior was conducted to his house (Jn 19:27), and that he outstripped Peter in running to the Savior's grave on that memorable Easter morning (Jn 20:4). John's was a meditative and contemplative disposition, and he deeply absorbed the doctrine and spirit of his Master. On account of his shrinking disposition (he does not directly mention himself, his mother, or even his brother) and the tenderness and depth that his writings reveal, his character has often been misjudged. He was far from being a mystic and pietist, as he has been represented.[15] The theological heights to which he soared in his Gospel, the intensity of his devotion and zeal, and the wonderful revelations recorded in the Apocalypse show that in him was "the spirit of the soaring eagle, which, rather than the dove, has been his immemorial symbol."[16] If, according to a thoroughly credible tradition, John lived in Ephesus until toward the end of the century,[17] he must have been very youthful at the time of his call to the apostleship in AD 31. Unlike most of his associates, he is said to have died a natural death. He reached an age of about a hundred years. The feast day for St. John is December 27.

Matthew and Luke group the apostles in pairs, but it seems that they can be arranged also in groups of four, the second group beginning with *Philip*.[18] Along with his fellow townsmen Andrew and Simon, he also had journeyed from Bethsaida to Bethany to hear the teaching of John the Baptist and there had received the first call of Jesus (Jn 1:43–44). Like Andrew, he, too, immediately won a fresh follower, Nathanael, for Christ (Jn 1:45). His was a Greek name, Philip, lover of horses, and it seems that he also possessed a knowledge of Greek; for a few days before the final Passover we find him acting as spokesman for certain Greeks who sought an interview with Jesus (Jn 12:20–22). The tradition identifying him with the disciple who asked permission to go and bury his father (Mt 8:21; Lk 9:59) is not likely based on fact.[19] With the notice of his presence in the upper chamber at Jerusalem (Ac 1:13), his name passes into confused ecclesiastical tradition. According to one account, he is said to have proclaimed the Gospel in Asia Minor, where he suffered death by crucifixion.[20] The feast day for St. Philip is May 1.

9
Philip
(Mt 10:3); Mk 3:18;
Lk 6:14; (Ac 1:13)

Because the name of *Bartholomew* is closely associated with Philip in three of the lists of the apostles, this disciple is usually identified with Nathanael of Cana, whom we remember as the disciple under the fig tree, to whom our Lord paid the tribute: "Behold, an Israelite indeed, in whom there is no deceit!" (Jn 1:47).[21] If so, then Bartholomew is probably a family name, the apostle's full name being Nathanael Bartolmai, i.e., the son of Tolmai. After the ascension of the Lord, he is said to have gone on a missionary tour to India (which at that time was a very wide geographical designation), where he left behind a copy of the Gospel of St. Matthew.[22] According to a legend, he suffered martyrdom, being sewed in a sack and cast into the sea. Another account relates how he was flayed alive and then crucified with his

10
Bartholomew
(Mt 10:3); Mk 3:18;
Lk 6:14; (Ac 1:13)

head downward. In works of art, he is generally represented with a large knife, the instrument of his martyrdom, or, as in Michelangelo's "Last Judgment," with his own skin hanging over his arm. The festival of St. Bartholomew is celebrated on the 24th of August. This completes the group of earlier disciples gained from the circle of John the Baptist. They were present with Jesus at the marriage of Cana and subsequently followed Him to Capernaum (Jn 2:12).

11
Matthew
(Mt 10:3); Mk 3:18;
Lk 6:15; (Ac 1:13)

We have already made the acquaintance of *Matthew*, the next member of the apostolic band. Modest Matthew, we are inclined to say. The commonly accepted author of the Gospel according to St. Matthew calls himself "the tax collector," referring to his former occupation. He also mentions his name second after that of Thomas, whereas Mark and Luke mention him first. It is practically beyond all doubt that he is that Levi, the son of an unknown Alphaeus, who sat at the tax booth near Capernaum and to whom the call of the Lord came "Follow Me." "And he rose and followed Him" (Mk 2:14; Mt 9:9; Lk 5:27–28).[23] No other information is furnished of this very important apostle and evangelist until the notice of his appearance with the other apostles at Jerusalem (Ac 1:13). According to an old tradition, he is said to have written his Gospel in Aramaic or Hebrew.[24] But both his own original Greek style and his evident purpose in writing his Gospel for Greek-speaking Jews,[25] as well as other considerations,[26] speak against this view.[27] He is said to have been the first apostle from Ethiopia, where according to some he died a natural death, while according to others he suffered martyrdom, nails being driven through his body.[28] The feast day for St. Matthew is September 21.

12
Thomas
(Mt 10:3); Mk 3:18;
Lk 6:15; (Ac 1:13)

Associated with Matthew is Didymus (Jn 11:16 [KJV]), the Greek name for the Hebrew *Thomas*, or Twin.[29] On account of his doubt or disbelief regarding the resurrection of Jesus, the term *doubting Thomas* has become proverbial. He is generally described as a fearless, upright man, but slow of apprehension. Still, he was the first to clearly apprehend that the Master was going forward to certain death (Jn 11:16). From the point of view of his own dark outlook, the Lord's comforting farewell addresses missed their mark. Puzzled, Thomas interrupted the Master with the question: "Lord, we do not know where You are going. How can we know the way?" (Jn 14:5). Not that he was frightened, but he was frankly in the dark. Thomas was no coward. When the other disciples were in hiding, although he ought to have been with them, he was out. When the joyful news of the resurrection reached his ears, he would not believe except on the evidence of his senses. Yet in the end, he made a glorious confession: "My Lord and my God!" (Jn 20:28). He was sincere to the core, but very human. Tradition has it that he labored in Parthia and Persia. At a later period, India is named as the place where he preached and suffered martyrdom. An elevation near Madras is called St. Thomas Mount.[30] The feast day for St. Thomas is December 21.

The third group of four apostles each is headed in all the lists by *James, the son of Alphaeus.* He is also called James the younger (Mk 15:40), in order to distinguish him from James, the brother of John. His father Alphaeus is not to be identified with the father of Matthew; for otherwise Matthew and this James would have been brothers—a view, it is true, which has also been held.[31] So many considerations enter into the discussion that we cannot hope to solve the problem. According to our view, this Alphaeus, the father of James, was the brother of Joseph. He was also called Clopas[32] and was married to a certain Mary (Jn 19:25; Mk 15:40).[33] Alphaeus and Clopas are probably both Greek variations of the same Hebrew name. And Mary, the wife of Clopas, is mentioned among the women standing below the cross of Jesus and also appears as the mother of James the younger and Joses (Mk 15:40). Therefore, it seems that the apostle James the younger was the son of Mary and Alphaeus.[34] Thus, he was a close relative of the Lord. We identify him as the head of the church in Jerusalem in the apostolic age (Ac 12:17; 15:13; 21:18),[35] as the James who is referred to by St. Paul as the "Lord's brother" (Gal 1:19), and as the "James, a servant of God and of the Lord Jesus Christ," in the General Epistle of James (1:1).[36] It seems that it was this James, "the Lord's brother," who was hurled from the pinnacle of the temple and stoned in AD 62.[37] The feast day for St. James the younger is May 1. There is a separate day for St. James of Jerusalem, Brother of Jesus and Martyr on October 23. This is due to uncertainties about which James is meant in some texts.

13
James the Younger
(Mt 10:3); Mk 3:18;
Lk 6:15; (Ac 1:13)

As with James, the son of Alphaeus, so we meet with a problem of relationship also respecting *Judas,* "not Iscariot" (Jn 14:22), the son of James, also called *Thaddaeus* or *Lebbaeus* (KJV). In his case, we have a multiplicity of names and a paucity of knowledge. Thaddaeus and Lebbaeus, both terms of endearment, are believed to mean the same thing, the hearty or beloved one.[38] Since the names of Thaddaeus and Judas occupy corresponding places in the apostolic roster, it is believed that they signify the same person. There is some dispute as to whether "Jude of James"[39] is to be rendered son or brother of James.[40] For example, the King James Version and some others have "brother of James." I believe that Jude was the brother of James and the author of the Epistle of Jude. The traditions concerning this apostle are contradictory and confusing. The general consensus, however, seems to be that he labored in Edessa. His burial is placed in Beirut and in Egypt. Of more interest is the story that concerns his grandchildren, who were brought before the suspicious Emperor Domitian, who, like Herod, it seems, feared the descendants of David. The emperor assured himself of their royal descent and heard of the spiritual character of the Kingdom. After he inquired about their thirty-nine acres of sandy soil in Israel and noticed their calloused hands, he felt relieved.[41] The feast day for St. Jude is October 28.

14
Judas the Son of
James/Thaddaeus
(Mt 10:3); Mk 3:18;
Lk 6:16; (Ac 1:13)

15
Simon the Zealot
(Mt 10:4); Mk 3:18;
Lk 6:15; (Ac 1:13)

Of *Simon the Zealot*, still less is known. By some, he is connected with Cana and identified with Nathanael of Cana.[42] By others, he is considered a former member of the Rome-hating Zealots, headed by Judas of Galilee.[43] This Judas "in the days of the census" (Ac 5:37) bitterly opposed the threatening increase of taxation and would have hastened by the sword the fulfilment of the messianic prophecies. And there is still another view, according to which he, as a third brother, joins James and Judas as sons of Alphaeus (Mt 13:55; Mk 6:3). Eusebius refers to a Simon who succeeded James as bishop of Jerusalem and suffered martyrdom under Trajan (AD 98–117) at the age of one hundred and twenty.[44] And Hegesippus, whom Eusebius professes to quote, calls this son Simon a son of Clopas and Clopas a brother of Joseph. The feast day for St. Simon is October 28.

16
Judas Iscariot
(Mt 10:4); Mk 3:19;
Lk 6:16; (Ac 1:13)

It seems that all these apostles were Galileans. Only one, *Judas Iscariot*,[45]—that is, the man from Kerioth, located "in the extreme south, toward the boundary of Edom" (Jsh 15:21, 25)[46]—seems to have been a native Judean.[47] His name invariably appears last, and always the fatal epithet clings to him "who betrayed Him." He presents the dark problem in the apostolate. We have the express testimony that Jesus knew from the beginning that he would betray Him (Jn 6:64). And yet He chose him. He did not take Judas for the purpose of proving him a traitor. That he afterward became a traitor can no more be charged to Jesus than the denial of Peter, which Jesus also foreknew. Judas may have been sincere when he entered the ranks of the apostles, and he may have possessed special qualities that made him desirable as a disciple. In choosing His apostles, Jesus considered the special gifts and qualities of the men whom He desired to associate with Him. As everything else that Jesus did, so this was also done in full agreement with the Father (Jn 5:19) and in order that the Scriptures might be fulfilled (Jn 13:18). That is about all we can say in the matter.

17
"The Glorious
Company"
(Mt 10:2–4);
Mk 3:13b–19a;
Lk 6:13–16;
(Ac 1:13)

This, then, is "the glorious company of apostles"[48] whom the Lord united into one band. They were men of different ages, tribes, abilities, occupations, training, relationship, connections, character, and disposition. All were chosen for a purpose. "They had now definitely attached themselves to the leadership of a Master whose fortunes they were willing to share. If need be, they would be weary with Him under the burning sun or sleep, as He did, under the starry sky."[49] And now, let us return to the story.

18
The Gathering
Multitudes
Mt 5:1–2;[50]
Lk 6:17–20a

While the Lord was choosing His apostles, a vast multitude began to gather. From the densely populated shores of the Sea of Galilee, from Judea and Jerusalem, even from the coasts, or borders, of Tyre and Sidon, people came to Him in vast numbers, hoping to be healed by Him (compare Mk 3:10) and eager to hear His words. From the peak of the mount, He descended to a flat space lower down the hill.[51] We thus combine the account of Luke and Matthew, assuming the identity of both accounts.[52] There is "no objection at all to the supposition that our Lord may have repeated parts of His teaching at different times and places and to different audiences and that the discourse may have summarized the contents of other sermons delivered on the Galilean hills."[53] But before the Savior began His great discourse, His heart went out in divine pity to those of His anxious hearers who approached Him with their physical ailments. He healed all who were afflicted with diseases or were vexed with unclean spirits. And when the whole audience was seated—the newly appointed group of twelve apostles, the larger circle of disciples, and the great multitude of people[54]—He lifted up His eyes (v. 20), opened His mouth, and delivered that memorable discourse ever since known as "the Sermon on the Mount." The words may have been chiefly directed to the disciples, but they were intended also for the multitudes within reach of His voice and, since the sermon has been recorded, for all who hear or read these words.

The Sermon on the Mount is a long sermon with many parts, the longest uninterrupted discourse recorded by any of the Gospel writers.[55] As recorded by Matthew, it may be the condensation of a still longer address or the inclusion of parts of other addresses delivered also on other occasions. It is not within the sphere of this work to present a detailed analysis, and therefore we shall merely attempt a brief review of what already is a masterpiece of brevity. The Sermon on the Mount is essentially a proclamation of the Law, but not in the fiery manner of Sinai, where thunder, lightning, and the voice of the trumpet shook the hearts with terror and agitation (Ex 19:16). Nor is it a new law and the abrogation of the old (Mt 5:17), but the words that the Lord spoke at this time were addressed principally to such as were children of God through faith in Him, His disciples (Mt 5:2). Some have contended that the Sermon on the Mount was not original to Jesus.[56] It is claimed that every item of our Lord's teaching can be paralleled in either the Old Testament, the Apocrypha, or in the Talmudic and Midrashic literature of the period near to the time of Jesus.[57] We need not be disturbed by the criticisms leveled against Him who taught with authority and not as the scribes (Mt 7:29). He began His sermon with the word *blessed* and with eight[58] Beatitudes. Just what the thought connection was for the introduction, we do not know. An expectant multitude of people was gathered around Jesus as around its Messiah and King. According to the hope and wish of many, if not of most of them, the Messiah should break the heavy Roman yoke resting on their necks and establish an earthly kingdom with the pomp of victory and vengeance. Probably in order to dispel this incorrect view of His person and His kingdom, the Lord immediately set forth in unmistakable terms to explain the principles of His kingdom, to expound its laws, and to exhibit its righteousness. While it is true that He is a blessing-bestowing King, the subjects of His kingdom should not hope to be covered with jewels and showered with manna. "Blessed,"

19
Beatitudes and Woes
Mt 5:3–12;
Lk 6:20b–26

yes, blessed and happy, "are the *poor in spirit*, for theirs is the kingdom of heaven." His royal blessings reverse the world's standard of blessings in similar matters. He calls His subjects blessed, happy—why? (1) True, most of them have not much of this world's goods, nor do they set their affections on them. In addition, they do not boast of good works and saintly virtues, but rather deplore their spiritual poverty in the sight of God. However, since they seek and partake of the imperishable riches of the kingdom of God through faith in Christ, they are truly to be accounted happy. (2) In this life, they mourn and weep while the world rejoices. As a rule, they bear a heavier load of ills and afflictions than "the wicked; always at ease" (Ps 73:12). They particularly lament their sins. However, they shall be comforted, already in this life; above all, however, in the life to come. (3) With regard to earthly possessions as well as to honor before men, they do not insist on what is due them. Men of the world consider such possessions and honor the only proper course. However, the blessed are not proud and arrogant, but meek and submissive. They nevertheless "inherit the earth," receiving many temporal blessings from God and enjoying them in peace and contentment. (4) They lead a life of external, or civic, righteousness on earth, endeavoring to shine as lights in this godless world. They crucify their flesh with the affections and lusts, which seems foolish to those who are not of Christ. However, in the life to come they will, by the grace of God, eat the fruit of their works and thus be filled. (5) They are merciful; that is, they have compassion with their needy and suffering fellow men and therefore are rich in deeds of mercy, which are an outflow of a heart filled with love. Blessed are they; for their works of charity please the Lord. On that Great Day, He will graciously reward them for all the love and mercy shown by them in this life. (6) Although *in* this world, they are not *of* the world. The Lord cleanses them from all filthiness of the flesh and spirit, perfecting holiness in the fear of God. As a result, they enjoy a good conscience during their sojourn here, and when they awaken in the likeness of God, they will behold His face in righteousness. (7) Being justified by faith, they have peace with God, and they therefore desire to have peace with all men, as far as this is possible, and also use their best efforts in promoting peace. That proves them to be true children of the God of peace. On Judgment Day, He will acknowledge them to be such before all people. What great honor! (8) Because they confess Christ and follow after holiness and are not conformed to this world, the world hates them as it did their Savior. It persecutes or at least ridicules their faith, reviles and abuses them, and tries to harm them. But what a glorious prospect opens up before them! "Theirs is the kingdom of heaven" with its unspeakable bliss—a glorious compensation for all that they suffered for Christ's sake.—"But woe to you who are rich" (that is, "rich" in the same sense as above,[59] rich, filled up, satisfied in laughing self-righteousness) for then you have your consolation, the only consolation, in advance! Jesus adds another woe, of particular interest to His newly appointed apostles: "Woe to you, when all people speak well of you." Chances are that undue popular praises would indicate that the apostles omitted the fearless denunciation of sin.

Possessing true godliness of character, His followers act as the salt of the earth and shine as the light of the world.[60] The purpose of salt is to give flavor to food and to preserve it against corruption. Now, if salt loses its virtue, "it is no longer good for anything except to be thrown out and trampled under people's feet."[61] Notice our Lord's apt illustrations and concrete, forceful language. "You are the light of the world." The disciples illumine. The very nature of light is to shine. Otherwise, it is no light. And "a city set on a hill cannot be hidden." No particular city is named, but lofty Safed, located on a prominent elevation and visible about twelve miles to the north, has been proposed.[62] "Nor do people light a lamp and put it under a basket."[63] The meaning is obvious. And as applied to the high calling of His followers: "In the same way, let your light shine before others, so that they may see your good[64] works and give glory to your Father[65] who is in heaven." Of course, Jesus is the only true Light of the world (Jn 8:12). But the disciples, who receive their illumination through Him and power to give light to others from Him, are cautioned against hiding their beliefs and convictions. The world observes keenly how they live, and they are to show that, as God has called them to holiness, so they are truly "holy in all [their] conduct" (1Pt 1:15).

Good works had been urged. Jesus now explains to His listeners what really makes a work good before the Law. But, first of all, He defines His own position with respect to the Mosaic Law. Although the teaching of His kingdom, the Gospel, is a doctrine radically different from the Law of Moses, it does not abrogate that Law. On the contrary, One that is greater than the temple and the Law (Mt 12:6–8) solemnly[66] affirms that He did not come to destroy, but to fulfill, and that "until heaven and earth pass away, not an iota, not a dot,[67] will pass from the Law until all is accomplished."[68] This being His own attitude toward the Law, Jesus takes a firm stand against those who transgress it. He who sets aside the least of its injunctions "will be called least"; that is, shall not be received into His kingdom, shall be excluded from its glories.[69] And he who teaches the Law in its great purpose of preparing the heart for the Gospel shall receive the reward of faithfulness. This is a strong statement from One whom the scribes and Pharisees[70] accused of breaking the Law. The trouble with these people was, as Jesus shows, that they were setting aside the "moral for the ritual, the divine for the traditional."[71] They were making a show of their pretended piety before the multitude, but in their hearts they departed from the Lord. They altogether missed the righteousness that they so ardently sought. Lacking true righteousness, they would receive no reward for righteousness. Better righteousness was necessary. For "unless your righteousness exceeds

20
The Salt of the Earth and the Light of the World
Mt 5:13–16

21
"I Have Not Come to Abolish Them but to Fulfill Them"
Mt 5:17–20

that of the scribes and Pharisees, you will never enter the kingdom of heaven." That there is a higher righteousness in the fulfilling of the Law, Christ shows in a number of striking illustrations.

22
"You Shall Not Murder"
Mt 5:21–26

Referring to the customary reading of the Law in the synagogues, Christ takes His first argument from the commandment "You shall not murder" (Ex 20:13). But He notes the addition of a penalty (Gn 9:5–6; Lv 24:17; Nu 35:16–21) for this breech of the Law: "whoever murders will be liable to judgment." The rabbis restricted this penalty to actual murder, whereby the commandment of God was made a mere external legal enactment. Striking at the root of the matter, Jesus explains that unrighteous anger[72] was in God's sight an offense equal to murder and punishable by the fires of hell.[73] This anger directed not against the sin (holy wrath), but against one's neighbor, used insulting language[74] that disregarded one's standing in the sight of God.[75] The obligation of this commandment does not merely include the avoidance of actual killing, but reconciliation and a forgiving heart. If in the very act of sacrifice the worshiper suddenly remembers an offense against his brother, let him interrupt his worship, and first seek forgiveness. Mercy before sacrifice. There will be plenty of time for sacrifice later, "lest your accuser hand you over to the judge, and the judge to the guard, and you be put in prison. Truly, I say to you, you will never get out until you have paid the last penny."[76] Jesus depicts walking to court to face the one who loaned him the money. Jesus has in view anyone who has insulted or provoked his brother by demeanor or language and does not seek reconciliation. The Judge, on the Last Day, will condemn him to that prison from which there is no escape in all eternity.

23
"You Shall Not Commit Adultery"
Mt 5:27–32

In like manner, Jesus opened to His hearers the proper understanding of the commandment "You shall not commit adultery." According to rabbinical interpretation, adultery meant only deliberate unfaithfulness of those joined together in wedlock. But Jesus explains that already a lustful look is a transgression of the Sixth Commandment in the sight of God. The eye must therefore be closely guarded. And not only the eye, but also the hand and foot. Figuratively speaking, these members and all other members of the body must be controlled, if necessary, by an absolute and painful severance, or amputation, as it were, lest the whole body be condemned (Mk 9:43–47; repeated Mt 18:8–9). Spiritual plucking out and cutting off is meant here, as Luther remarks; or as St. Paul puts it, we mortify the members of our body by battling against "impurity, passion, evil desire" (Col 3:5) in our hearts.—Continuing His explanation of the commandment, Jesus adds a word about divorce. Because of the hardness of hearts, Moses had, as a civil measure, permitted a husband to divorce his wife if she "finds no favor in his eyes" (Dt 24:1; Mt 19:7–8). In the eyes of God, however, there is only one true cause for divorce,[77] and that is adultery. "Whoever divorces his wife, except for sexual immorality, and marries another, commits adultery" (Mt 19:9; Mk 10:11–12; Lk 16:18).

Better righteousness than that of the Pharisees is necessary also with regard to the commandment "You shall not swear falsely, but shall perform to the Lord what you have sworn." The words as heard in the synagogues are correctly given (Lv 19:12; Nu 30:2; Dt 23:21). But it seems that the interpretation left much to be desired. Among the Jewish doctors, there was much sophistical and also superstitious quibbling as to the degree of the oath, whether "the ineffable name" of Jehovah was used (Dt 6:13) or whether the oath taken was "by heaven," "by the earth," "by Jerusalem," or "by your head" in an attempt to evade or diminish the obligatory powers of the pledge. As Christ points out, it all amounts to the same. In the end, all such oaths involve reference to God. The Lord's command is "Do not take an oath at all." Develop such a love of, and reputation for, truthfulness that there will be no need for oaths. Of course, in this world full of falsehood, an affirmation must sometimes be fortified with a solemn oath, for instance, in court, "because of the untruth and consequent distrust prevailing in the world."[78] For all general purposes, a simple " 'Yes' or 'No' " should suffice among God's children.

24
"You Shall Not Swear Falsely"
Mt 5:33–37

The next reference of Jesus is to the common law of retaliation as contained in the Old Testament ordinance: "An eye for an eye and a tooth for a tooth" (see Ex 21:24). This was a good rule for the judge, but should not be privately applied. A disciple of Jesus should be willing to suffer patiently, even wrongfully, and not seek revenge by returning evil for evil. "If anyone slaps you on the right cheek, turn to him the other also. And if anyone would sue you and take your tunic, let him have your cloak as well [see also Lk 6:29]. And if anyone forces you to go one mile," probably a soldier forcing you to carry his baggage,[79] "go with him two miles." A strange doctrine! Does this mean that all outrages should henceforth go unchallenged? The meaning is that the followers of Jesus, "so far as their own person is concerned, will wisely submit to abuses and cheerfully render exacted service and even do more than is asked rather than stubbornly resist the inevitable."[80] There is a time to submit, but there is also a time to fight. Passive behavior ceases when it comes into conflict with the law of love. Naturally, a Christian's duties to his family, community, or country may compel him to resist rather than to submit to injustice and insult. But that is not the point in the present consideration. Rather than harbor evil and vengeful thoughts in the prosecution of his individual interests, a Christian should be ready to render assistance: "Give to the one who begs from you, and do not refuse the one who would borrow from you" (see also Lk 6:30).

25
Retaliation
Mt 5:38–42

A final illustration of the righteousness of the Kingdom as compared with the righteousness of the synagogue is taken from the general law of love: "You shall love your neighbor." But it seems that the rabbis had added: "and hate your enemy." In

26
Love of Enemies
Mt 5:43–48;
Lk 6:27–30, 32–36

the Old Testament, the whole verse reads: "You shall not take vengeance or bear a grudge against the sons of your own people, but you shall love your neighbor as yourself: I am the LORD" (Lv 19:18). In understanding "neighbor" to refer to an Israelite, it seems the inference was made that it was permissible to hate a Gentile. For did not God in many passages command Israel to destroy the heathen nations? It was, however, forgotten that in these instances Israel was merely the instrument of God's penal justice.[81] The argument could therefore not stand, especially not in view of the precept not to wrong or oppress sojourners (Ex 22:21). For this reason, the spirit that at the time fostered an ever-increasing hostility toward the Gentiles, or Goyim,[82] was altogether wrong. Whether it was a personal or a national enemy, or an enemy or the true religion, Jesus insists that all hatred is contrary to the Law of love and the spirit that He was striving to foster. "But I say to you, Love your enemies and pray for those who persecute you." Certainly a strange doctrine, contrary to natural, carnal urge and instinct. And it is to be applied at all times and in all places. Whatever means the enemy may devise, "love's ingenuity must find a way to overwhelm him with goodness."[83] This is sound practice, for which we have the example of our Father in heaven, who "makes His sun to rise on the evil and on the good, and sends rain on the just and on the unjust." And in following this practice, a Christian will not seek his own advantage or gain. "For if you love those who love you, what reward do you have?" "And if you do good to those who do good to you, what benefit is that to you? For even sinners do the same." Nay, since love is the fulfilling of the Law, it must also, and especially, be directed toward someone who will test it and so establish whether it is love. For this, a Christian has the example of his Master (Lk 23:34): the command, the example, and the promised reward of the merciful Father in heaven.

27
Giving to the Needy
Mt 6:1–4

A right interpretation of the Mosaic Law makes it clear that the law of the scribes fell far short of the standards of true righteousness. And now, Jesus directs His attention to hypocritical pharisaic practice. Certainly, real righteousness is not ostentatious hypocrisy, which the Pharisees affected in their trumpet-sounding[84] almsgiving in the streets and synagogues. "Truly, I say to you, they have their reward. But when you give to the needy, do not let your left hand know what your right hand is doing." But this is not opposed to the command that the disciples should let their light shine before men (Mt 5:16). The difference is in the motive: the glory of God or the self-glorification of man.

28
Prayer
Mt 6:5–8

The same applies to the theatrical and public-attracting synagogue or street-corner prayers. The practice of reducing prayers to a system is contrary to the very nature of prayers.[85] With the exception of the public invocation of a worshiping group, or congregation, this act of individual worship is a matter of strictest privacy between the person praying and his Maker. Therefore, "when you pray, go into your room and shut the door and pray to your Father who is in secret. And your Father who sees in secret will reward you." Neither is there any merit in vain repetitions. As if much speaking or iteration were needed to reach the divine ear! This was the Gentile practice and belief; with them a very flood of words or a repetition of phrases should suggest sincerity and practically weary the gods into complying with their request (1Ki 18:26; Ac 19:34). Babbling prayers are utterly absurd. We need not teach God what to give, but in the habit of prayer we should learn what we need.

The Lord next instructs His disciples as to their various needs and God's manifold gifts. He also gives them a brief formula of a proper prayer—not to be abused. He teaches them a prayer that, because it comes from Him, has always been called *the Lord's Prayer.*[86] As to its form, it matters little or nothing whether some of the phrases have their parallels in rabbinic expressions. Its beauty lies in this, that the Lord has gathered matchless pearls and arranged them into a priceless chain. It is usually divided into the introduction, the seven petitions, and the conclusion, or doxology. It begins with the words *"Our Father in heaven."* The disciples are invited to approach God "with all boldness and confidence [and] ask Him as dear children ask their dear father."[87] *"Hallowed be Your name."* The Father receives this prayer on behalf of the Holy Trinity, the only true God, who is the universal and the only object of worship. We duly honor Him in faith and life, by what we teach and believe and by all our deeds and actions. *"Your kingdom come."* That was the prayer of all Jews. But it all depends upon what kingdom is understood. The kingdom of the Lord comes to those who truly hallow the Lord and receive Jesus as their King. We pray that His Kingdom may come also to those who do not as yet know, and believe in, the Savior King. *"Your will be done, on earth as it is in heaven."* Since God is our Lord and Sovereign and the Kingdom that Christ preached is a kingdom of grace, it follows that both His holy and His good and gracious will is to be done. It is done perfectly by the angels in heaven, whose example we, God's children, should follow. We obey God in all things and under all circumstances, and that willingly and cheerfully. *"Give us this day our daily bread."* This includes temporal gifts, daily bread—to be asked for humbly and confidently. Our wise and gracious Father in heaven gives them, and with a grateful and contented heart we receive them.[88] *"And forgive us our debts, as we also have forgiven our debtors."*[89] This petition refers to man's greatest spiritual need, the forgiveness of sins. Forgiveness is needed daily, yes, every minute, and it is graciously granted for the sake of Christ. The more conscious people are of their own sins and anxious for forgiveness, the more forgiving they should become of the shortcomings of others (vv. 14–15).[90] *"And lead us not into temptation."* This does not mean God tempted anyone to sin. The Christian beseeches God that, if he faces tests according to God's wisdom and will, he may "finally overcome them and win the victory." *"But deliver us from evil."*[91] All contingencies are provided for.

29
The Lord's Prayer
Mt 6:9–15

As the sum of all, Christians ask to be delivered "from every evil of body and soul, possessions and reputation, and finally, when [their] last hour comes, . . . graciously [to be taken] from this valley of sorrow to [their Father] in heaven."[92] Some manuscripts include, "*For Yours is the kingdom and the power and the glory, forever. Amen.*"[93] This glorious doxology and fervent amen closes this epitome of the Gospel (*breviarium Evangelii*).[94]

30
Fasting
Mt 6:16–18

What has been said of show-making almsgiving and prayers also applies to the deception of gloomy-faced fasting. Without condemning fasting itself,[95] Jesus next attacks the pharisaic practice that reduced an otherwise laudable custom to a show-making system. It is the heart that should show sorrow and humility, not the body or face. We should not parade an act of self-glorification to make an outward sign of repentance. "Truly, I say to you, they have received their reward." Rather than present a haggard appearance, the fasting penitent should not neglect his usual daily washing and anointing in order that people may not even know that he is fasting. "And your Father who sees in secret will reward you."

31
Treasure-Hoarding
Mt 6:19–21

Passing on, the Lord admonishes His disciples to have single-hearted devotion toward God as opposed to worldly aims and anxieties. In spite of their pretended piety, the Pharisees were, after all, a greedy and covetous lot. The disciples are therefore warned not to hoard up "treasures on earth, where moth and rust destroy and where thieves break in and steal" (compare Lk 12:33). The heavenly treasures are the lasting spiritual gifts offered to them in the Word of God's grace. And in seeking them, their hearts become heavenly-minded. "For where your treasure is, there your heart will be also" (compare Lk 12:34).

32
The Parable
of the Eye
Mt 6:22–23

On the other hand, if one seeks the treasures of this world, there also his heart will be. And what covetousness leads to, Jesus explains in the parable of the eye (compare Lk 11:34–35). The eye is the lamp of the body. If the eye is healthy,[96] it gives light for all bodily functions so that you can see what you are doing. But if it is diseased,[97] it cannot serve as a guide. So it is with the eye of the soul. If the light of the love of God is shed abroad in it, love of the neighbor will follow and manifest itself in deeds of love and mercy, and the whole body will be full of light. But a soul in which this light is not found begrudges the needy its temporal and spiritual welfare, and then the whole body is in darkness. And therefore, if the light-giving eye itself is dark, how great is the darkness![98]

33
God and Money
Mt 6:24

Covetousness perverts the heart. In fact, it is idolatry. "No one can serve two masters, for either he will hate the one and love the other, or he will be devoted to the one and despise the other." A new master is chosen, to whom attachment is made. A new god is set up, whose name is Mammon.[99] "You cannot serve God and money" (see also Lk 16:13). It is impossible for a Christian to be faithful to God and make an idol out of wealth.

However, a person need not necessarily be rich to be a servant of money. So Jesus follows up with a warning against worries and cares. "Therefore I tell you, do not be anxious about your life, what you will eat or what you will drink, nor about your body, what you will put on" (see also Lk 12:22–31). Trust in the Lord. "Look at the birds of the air: they neither sow nor reap nor gather into barns, and yet your heavenly Father feeds them. Are you not of more value than they?" Cares are needless and unprofitable. "Which of you by being anxious can add a single hour to his span of life?"[100] Or take the example of flowers. "Consider the lilies of the field,[101] how they grow: they neither toil nor spin." How affectionately the Lord speaks of flowers! "The lilies are viewed individually as living beings, almost as friends."[102] "Solomon in all his glory was not arrayed like one of these." Jesus speaks of creation like an adoring poet. So the lesson follows, "If God so clothes the grass of the field, which today is alive and tomorrow is thrown into the oven,[103] will He not much more clothe you, O you of little faith?" The disciples of Jesus should therefore guard against the Gentile practice of distrust and sinful cares. "Your heavenly Father knows that you need them all." There is only one permissible care: "Seek first the kingdom of God and His righteousness." Then the little things of this earthly body and life will come as a matter of course. "Therefore do not be anxious about tomorrow, for tomorrow will be anxious for itself. Sufficient for the day is its own trouble."

34
"Do Not Be Anxious"
Mt 6:25–34

Not only a pharisaic vice, but a common sin found in everyday life, is the sin of fault-finding, of criticizing or condemning others. To this subject, Jesus turns without apparent connection. A very cheap way of claiming moral superiority over others is to exalt oneself by disparaging others. But Jesus says: "Judge not, that you be not judged." This command does not including the sober, moral judgment enjoined in Scripture, such as admonishing an erring brother (Mt 18:15), or of people in public office. He rejects the sin of freehandedly condemning others. Besides its general injustice and its being committed in a spirit of self-satisfaction, such condemnation does nobody any good. Before anyone attempts to censure others, he ought, first of all, to have a proper self-knowledge. "Can a blind man lead a blind man?" Very often, he that sees the faults of others is blind to his own. "Why do you see the speck[104] that is in your brother's eye, but do not notice the log[105] that is in your own eye? . . . First take the log out of your own eye, and then you will see clearly to take the speck out of your brother's eye."

35
"Judge Not;
Condemn Not"
Mt 7:1–5;
Lk 6:37–42

A sort of corresponding reverse to uncharitable judging is to give holy things to the dogs and to cast pearls before the pigs. A Christian's most holy things are the pearls of God's Word and the Sacraments. To cast these before dogs and pigs—that is, before people who abuse what is sacred—is to cause desecration. In the blasphemous attacks "some of the mud will spatter on him who lacked judgment,

36
Casting Pearls
before Pigs
Mt 7:6

and the offender will be responsible for the desecration and therefore also guilty before God."[106]

The subject of prayer is taken up again. In the struggle for true righteousness, prayer is necessary if any progress is to be made. "Ask" in all humility, "seek" with untiring application, and "knock" with earnestness and perseverance (see Lk 11:9–13).[107] Everyone will receive if he approaches God in prayer as a child comes to his father. A parable explains this truth. "Which one of you, if his son asks him for bread, will give him a stone? Or if he asks for a fish, will give him a serpent?"[108] A loving father may be unable to comply with the request made to him, but he would not add mockery to inability. And the application: "If you then, who are evil,[109] know how to give good gifts to your children, how much more will your Father who is in heaven give good things to those who ask Him!"

And now, a rule for all men and all times. It is generally known as *the Golden Rule*. Since it agrees with the fundamental requirements of the law of neighborly love, it sums up the Law and the Prophets. Jewish, Greek, Roman, and Eastern teachers held a similar view,[111] but not quite like it—Jesus gives a revolutionary commandment in the ethical experience of mankind.[112] "So whatever you wish that others would do to you, do also to them, for this is the Law and the Prophets." Probably, this precept is more frequently quoted than any other divine rule of Christian conduct. However, we may hope that people would practice the good toward others that Jesus teaches rather than make the usual appeals for others to start showing goodness to them. Then peace, love, and harmony would soon generally prevail in the world.

In conclusion, a few lessons of personal righteousness are driven home by powerful parables. Two ways are briefly sketched, leading from the present life to that beyond the grave. "Enter by the narrow gate. For the gate is wide and the way is easy that leads to destruction, and those who enter by it are many" (compare Lk 13:23). This is the way of the Kingdom as outlined by Christ, the way of righteousness, strait, narrow, contracted; but it "leads to life, and those who find it are few." The broad way is the way of sinful indulgence and unrestricted liberty; but it "leads to destruction."

The way to life is easily missed. In fact, a warning must be posted against such as would deliberately misdirect travelers on their way to heaven. "Beware of false prophets, who come to you in sheep's clothing but inwardly are ravening wolves." Certainly, a striking description of those soul murderers who falsify God's Word and substitute for it their own "tongues and declare, 'declares the LORD' " (Jer 23:31). Even as in the Old Testament they caused God's people to fall into error and in the time of Christ raised their voice of deception, so they are still doing their nefarious work today. Many of them are greedy for money and eager for power. Therefore, "test the spirits to see whether they are from God" (1Jn 4:1). The principle of testing them is to look at "their fruits." "Are grapes gathered from thornbushes, or figs from thistles?" "Thus you will recognize them by their fruits." And what are these fruits? Their professed loyalty, their apparent sincerity, and evident zeal? No. "Not everyone who says to Me, 'Lord, Lord,' will enter the kingdom of heaven." They and their followers may display the greatest piety and religious fervor. But are deeds of charity, even prophecy, the casting out of devils, healing, or some other wonderful works the fruits by which they are to be known? All these are no safe criteria. Fruits of this kind may be the deceptive sheep's clothing that the Lord mentions. Looking forward to a later day, when false prophets and "Gospel merchants" and their followers would deceive people in the name of Christ and to the day when they will be finally judged, Jesus says: "On that day many will say to Me, 'Lord, Lord, did we not prophesy in Your name, and cast out demons in Your name, and do many mighty works in Your name?' And then will I declare to them, 'I never knew you; depart from Me, you workers of lawlessness.' " The fruits by which we are to recognize them as false prophets are their pernicious doctrines, which destroy the souls of men. Their false teachings make them not murderers or thieves or tyrants, but *false prophets*.[113]

And now, in the form of a majestic parable, a grand finale. A proper hearing of Christ's words implies appropriate obedience to them (Jas 1:22). He who heard and did these sayings is compared to a wise man who built the house of his life upon the solid foundation of a living rock. "And the rain fell, and the floods came, and the winds blew and beat on that house, but it did not fall, because it had been founded on the rock." To "evangelic ears this eloquent description may, in the first instant, have a legal sound, but the doing which Christ had in mind is the opposite of pharisaic legalism."[114] Not the builder's doing or obedience makes him firm, but the foundation upon which his house is erected. "On Christ, the solid rock, I stand; All other ground is sinking sand."[115] Storms and tempests will not blow down this house, and trials and temptations will find the builder prepared. But the playhouse of life easily and quickly erected upon smooth sands of good-weather Christianity, of hearing and not doing, is inevitably destined to collapse before the onrushing surge. "And everyone who hears these words of Mine and does not do them will be like a foolish man who built his house on the sand. And the rain fell, and the floods came, and the winds blew and beat against that house, and it fell, and great was the fall of it."

41
The Two Builders
Mt 7:24–27;
Lk 6:46–49

The Sermon on the Mount left a profound impression upon the multitudes. "They were astonished at His teaching, for He taught them as one who had authority, and not as the scribes" (Mk 1:22).[116] Here was a teacher with a message of eternal truth. The professional teachers "droned out their traditions and the injunctions

42
Teaching as One
Having Authority
Mt 7:28–8:1

of a Law which was in effect dead in their own lives."[117] They never passed a hair's breadth beyond the carefully watched boundary lines of commentary and precedent. Jesus preached with authority; it was the voice of Him who was both God and man in one person. At the conclusion of the sermon, the immense throng dispersed. But there were still many, most likely those whose homes lay in the Plain of Gennesaret, who followed their Teacher, once more on His way to nearby Capernaum.

In the order of Matthew, the cleansing of the leper (Mt 8:2–4; see ch. 10 § 4) would come next.

43
The Centurion's
Servant
Mt 8:5–13;
Mk 3:20a; Lk 7:1–10

Our Lord had scarcely arrived at His "home," in Peter's house, when He was approached by a delegation of Jewish elders. They were probably the leaders of the local synagogue,[118] who were acting in the interest of a centurion whose faithful and beloved servant lay in the agony and peril of paralytic attack.[119] Most likely, this captain of a hundred soldiers—whether Roman or not, we do not know, but certainly of heathen descent—was a military officer of Herod Antipas[120] and probably stationed just out of Capernaum, on the Way to the Sea. From the glimpse that we get of his person and character, we are not surprised that he appealed to Jesus for help. He was a worthy man, who loved Israel, a thing most rare in any Gentile, and reverenced Israel's God. This affection for God's people took visible form when he built a beautiful synagogue at his own expense, the ruins of which, it is believed, can still be seen today.[121] Nor was the name of Jesus unknown to him. Capernaum was the headquarters of this new Galilean Prophet and the scene of many of His recent miracles as well as the home of a fellow official of the court of Herod, the *basilikos*, whose son Jesus had healed from a distance at Cana, about seven months before (Jn 4:46–54).[122] He made a direct and personal appeal to Jesus. The more highly he esteemed Jesus, the more he felt his own unworthiness, probably on account of his Gentile birth. Therefore, Jewish friends interceded on his behalf. Their willingness to plead the cause of a Gentile speaks well for them as well as for the centurion. Incidentally, it also shows that not all the Jewish leaders had turned against Jesus, especially not in Galilee. Not only did these elders plead the cause of the centurion, but they pleaded it well. Immediately, Jesus promised to grant the request. "I will come and heal him." We are led to infer that the house of the centurion was not in Capernaum itself, but rather in the neighborhood, probably on the road southward to the nearby Galilean capital Tiberias, recently rebuilt by Herod. But on the way, other messengers stopped the approaching Lord with the request not to enter under the roof of an unworthy Gentile,[123] but to heal the suffering servant by a mere word of power. An argument is advanced from the centurion's own military experience. Though a subordinate officer himself, "under authority," yet he had well-disciplined servants, ever ready to do his bidding. "And I say to one, 'Go,' and he goes, and to another, 'Come,' and he comes, and to my servant, 'Do this,' and he does it."

How much more, then, could not Jesus, with the hosts of heaven at His command, send His "viewless messengers to do His will without undergoing all this personal labor"![124] The Lord was struck by this remarkable faith. What He expected in Israel, He received from the Gentiles. Turning to the multitude following Him, He stated the solemn truth that many of those called by the rabbis "children of darkness"[125] would come from the East and West and recline with Abraham, Isaac, and Jacob at the tables of the messianic banquet hall. But the "children of the Kingdom," or "the children of the banquet hall," would be cast into outer darkness, where there is weeping and gnashing of teeth. "The imagery is Jewish, but the truth is universal and lasting."[126] To stress the greatness of the miracle, the remark is added that the suffering servant—of whom no details are given—was "healed at that very moment," as was ascertained by the messengers at their return.

In the order of Matthew, the healing of Peter's mother-in-law and in the evening the healing of many others (Mt 8:14–17; see ch. 9, §§ 20–21) would come next.

12

A SECOND PREACHING TOUR, INCLUDING THE PARABLES BY THE SEA

PROBABLY SUMMER AND AUTUMN, AD 31

After a brief stay in Capernaum, in fact, the very next day,[1] we find Jesus on a twenty-five-mile journey to a city in Southern Galilee on the slopes of Jebel el Duhy, or Little Hermon. The name *Nain*—or Nein, which the city still retains— means "green pastures" or "vale of beauty." Its location, commanding an extensive view of the Plain of Esdraelon and the northern hills, justifies its flattering title.[2] It is a long journey, but if the Israelites walked rapidly and started early in the morning, the town may have been reached sometime in the afternoon.[3] Traveling with Jesus were His disciples and an adoring and rejoicing crowd. As the glad procession was climbing to the gates of the city, it was met by another—and sad—procession issuing forth to bury a dead youth outside of the walls. It was an exceptionally sad funeral, since the young man was an only son and his mother was a widow. We can picture the mournful scene: the flute players and the mourning women; the simple bier—that is, an ordinary open wooden frame—on which the body was carried to the grave; the lonely widow accompanied by her relatives, neighbors, and a host of sympathizing friends. "And when the Lord saw her,"—this is the first time that the evangelist Luke uses this title[4]—"He had compassion on her and said to her, 'Do not weep.' " This was not only a pious phrase, but what Jesus thought, Jesus wrought. The grief-stricken widow could not yet fully comprehend what Jesus meant, especially when He "came up and touched the bier." It was a moment of breathless expectation. "And the bearers stood still." Here was one who unconcernedly disregarded the greatest of all defilements, that of contact with the dead.[5] But His touch rendered clean (Mt 8:3) and removed that which made the ceremonial ordinances (Nu 19:11–20) necessary.[6] Immediately, the heart-thrilling and life-giving utterance

1
The Raising of the Widow's Son at Nain
Lk 7:11–17

was heard: "Young man, I say to you, arise." But would this word pierce "the more than midnight darkness of the world beyond the grave"?[7] It did. It was a word of sovereign command. The supposedly impossible happened. Life itself again pulsated through the lifeless body. "And the dead man sat up and began to speak." Truly, the days of Elijah and Elisha had returned (1Ki 17:21; 2Ki 4:35). Yes, far greater days had come. The miracle was not the result of earnest supplication and much wrestling in prayer, but here was the Source of Life, personally restoring a dead person to life. "And Jesus gave him to his mother." The miracle could have but one effect: "Fear seized them all." The manifestation of the almighty power that had just been witnessed moved many to glorify God—at least for the moment—and to admit that a great prophet had risen up and that God had visited His people. There was no doubt about the miracle because its reality was undeniably evident. Here was a living and walking witness who could testify to the truth that Jesus was the Lord. Many years later, an apologist of the Early Christian Church, Quadratus, whom Eusebius called a pupil of the apostles (*auditor apostolorum*), could point out to the Roman Emperor Hadrian:

> The works of our Savior were always present, for they were genuine:—those that were healed, and those that were raised from the dead, who were seen not only when they were healed and when they were raised, but were also always present; and not merely while the Savior was on earth, but also after His death, they were alive for quite a while, so that some of them lived even to our day.[8]

The rumor of the astounding miracle performed by the Lord spread to Judea and to all the region around, to the north, south, east, and west. The news also penetrated the prison walls at Machaerus, where John the Baptist lay imprisoned.

2
The Message from John the Baptist
(Mt 11:2–6);
Lk 7:18–23

By this time, John the Baptist had spent a number of months in prison.[9] When the report of our Lord's wonderful ministry reached him, he sent two of his disciples who still clung to him to Jesus with the question, "Are You the one who is to come, or shall we look for another?" Not that there was any doubt in the mind of him who had said, "Behold, the Lamb of God, who takes away the sin of the world!" (Jn 1:29). John had already released some of his best disciples to Jesus. But some of his disciples refused to give up their allegiance to him. They could not distinguish between essentials and nonessentials and felt that the austere habits of John belonged to the substance of a truly moral life. A number of them were even now allying themselves with the Pharisees (Mt 9:14),[10] and others, still adhering to him, would probably be tempted to perpetuate their allegiance to him by organizing a sect of Johannites instead of following Christ and becoming Christians.[11] True to his God-given mission, which was to direct the people to Christ as the Redeemer, John improved this favorable opportunity by sending two of his disciples to Jesus with a definitely worded question. What John failed to do by testimony and direction, he hoped Jesus would accomplish by drawing these followers and identifying Himself as the Messiah. The moment was auspicious; for just then Jesus was performing miracles. The proof of His Messiahship was before their very eyes. In His answer, Jesus definitely identified Himself as the Messiah by an appeal to prophecy: The blind see, the lame walk, the lepers are cleansed, the deaf hear (Is 35:5–6), and—for no doubt they had heard of the miracles at Nain—the dead are raised up; and the poor have the Gospel preached to them (Is 61:1). Let them draw their own conclusions from this prophetic summary of what the Messiah would do. The reply was directed to John, "Go and tell John," but it appealed to John's disciples, especially the final remark: "Blessed is the one who is not offended by Me."[12] This is a word of warning directed especially to the two messengers. Some of the disciples of John were not satisfied with the manner in which Jesus and His disciples were conducting themselves as to fasting, washing of hands, and other Levitical regulations (Lk 5:33). "If anyone is so carried away with a false asceticism as to want to curtail the liberty of the New Testament and for that reason is offended at Jesus, he has only himself to blame for the consequences."[13]

No sooner had John's messengers departed than Jesus delivered that memorable eulogy over His friend and forerunner, not in the spirit of idle flattery nor for the purpose of restoring John's supposedly endangered authority.[14] Instead, Jesus wanted to convince the people, especially their leaders, of their inconsistency in accepting John as a divinely appointed prophet, but rejecting Him to whom he had always pointed. "What did you go out into the wilderness to see? A reed shaken by the wind?" A public-pleasing demagogue? A well-fed and -clothed, man-serving court preacher? A prophet? "Yes, I tell you, and more than a prophet. This is he of whom it is written, 'Behold, I send My messenger before Your face, who will prepare Your way before You' " (Mal 3:1). Not only of all Old Testament prophets but also of all Old Testament people, indeed, of all "those born of women," John was the greatest. There was no one in Old Testament times that approached him in the capacity of rendering such direct, such way-preparing service to the kingdom of God. Other prophets had pointed from the dim distance, but John stood on the threshold. And yet, as compared with the children of the Kingdom, even John remained a child of the Old Testament. He introduced, but did not fully see and enjoy, the day of Jesus Christ. His career closed before Jesus entered into His glory. In this respect, therefore, it is true: "Yet the one who is least in the kingdom of God is greater than he." Until the day of John, the children of God were kept under the Law, the guardian (Gal 3:23–24); but since John, the Gospel ruled. As a result, many who by Pharisaic legislation had previously been ruled out of the Kingdom—the tax collectors, the sinners, and heathen coming to sincere repentance—were now storming the kingdom of heaven, taking it by force (Mt 11:12). In one prophecy, the herald of the

3
Encomium of the Baptist
(Mt 11:7–15);
Lk 7:24–28

Messiah is also called Elijah (Mal 4:5–6).[15] This prophecy does not refer to a return of Elijah in person. Correctly understood, John was this Elijah, sent to make ready people's hearts to receive the Messiah. In fact, the correct understanding of the whole matter is this: The purpose and the person of the herald, the nature of the preparation, the nature of the King and the Kingdom, required intelligent attention and believing hearts. "He who has ears to hear, let him hear."[16]

4
"Wisdom Is Justified by All Her Children"
(Mt 11:16–19);
Lk 7:29–35

In spite of his greatness, John did not receive the general recognition that he deserved. Many among the common herd, the tax collectors and sinners, acknowledged the prophetic legitimacy and power of John's office. They "justified," or endorsed, God in sending him as a herald of the Messiah-King. However, the accredited leaders and teachers "rejected the purpose of God for themselves." Not only did they take offense at John's message of repentance, but they were also greatly displeased with his austere ways and manner of living. This so biased them against him that they declared him to be possessed by a demon.[17] But their attitude toward Jesus was no better, even though, in contrast to John the Baptist, His demeanor and address drew the masses to Him and His mode of living did not differ from that of other people. These leaders were men of peculiar whims and fancies, whom no one could please. They were like capricious children, who aren't happy no matter what game their playmates propose. "We played the flute for you, and you did not dance; we sang a dirge, and you did not weep." When some want to play at a marriage, others want to play at a funeral. John was a madman because of his rigorous life; Jesus, because He ate and drank as did other men. So they called Him "a glutton and a drunkard, a friend of tax collectors and sinners!" "Yet," said Jesus, "wisdom is justified by all her children." John and Jesus taught the true heavenly wisdom. There were, by the grace of God, always some who were thankful for this wisdom unto salvation. For instance, the disciples of Jesus believed, and "the tax collectors and the prostitutes" (Mt 21:32) realized that they were sick and therefore needed a physician: Jesus, a physician for their souls (Mt 9:12–13).

5
"Woe to You, Chorazin!"
(Mt 11:20–24)[18]

The Lord is kind and gracious; but woe to those who reject His grace! It was during the time of this portion of His Galilean ministry, it seems,[19] that Jesus delivered His famous woes over the cities that had been so highly favored. The land of Zebulun and Naphtali had seen a glorious light (Mt 4:15–16); its inhabitants had been filled with astonishment. They had praised the manifest glory of God and they had flocked to the Great Prophet arisen in their midst. They had eagerly sought and received His help for their bodily needs, *but* they did not repent. There was Chorazin, otherwise unmentioned, a town near the northwestern shore of the Sea of Galilee, where Jesus performed mighty unrecorded works. If these same works had been performed in the heathen cities of Tyre and Sidon, rarely visited by the prophets of old, these cities would have repented in sackcloth and ashes. And there was Bethsaida, on the northern shore of the lake, in whose streets Andrew, Philip, and Peter had played in their boyhood days. Christ's works here are likewise unrecorded. "It will be more bearable on the day of judgment for Tyre and Sidon than for you." And especially there was Capernaum, which Jesus had honored more than any other city on Jewish soil. Bethlehem was justly honored as the town of the Savior's birth. Nazareth received the privilege of sheltering Him in the days of His childhood and youth. But Capernaum, the scene of His greatest activity and His headquarters and home during the greater part of His public ministry, had been "exalted to heaven." However, had it repented? The greater the opportunity, the greater the responsibility. "If the mighty works done in you had been done in Sodom, it would have remained until this day. But I tell you that it will be more tolerable on the day of judgment for the land of Sodom than for you." Such is the curse. And these words are no idle threat; for it is a terrible thing to despise God's visitation of grace.

On the other hand, may the Lord be thanked that some *did* see the light. Probably, these were not always found among the wise and intelligent generally, the scribes and Pharisees, who deemed themselves the custodians and dispensers of true wisdom. Rather, God revealed His ways among the novices and babes, those unversed in scholastic wisdom, such as the fishermen disciples, tax collectors, prostitutes, and sinners. This came about by the gracious will of the Father, and in perfect accord with it Jesus was at particular pains to reveal the way of salvation to this despised class of people. So He thanked the Father for having given success to His preaching.[21]

6
"Revealed to Little Children"
(Mt 11:25–27)[20]

Now He extends a gracious invitation to all who feel the burden of their sin and yearn to be relieved of it to seek refuge with Him. "Come to Me, all who labor and are heavy laden, and I will give you rest." These wonderful words of universal grace should receive individual application. If offered to all, then they are also offered to you personally. Receive Christ in childlike faith as your Lord and Savior. In rabbinical imagery[22] and Old Testament words (Jer 6:16), New Testament Gospel truths are expressed. "For My yoke is easy, and My burden is light." Notwithstanding the strait gate, the narrow way, and the cross that is to be imposed, all believers in Christ will find true rest for their souls in Him who has taken the burden of their sins from their shoulders and put them upon His own.

7
"Come to Me, All Who Labor"
(Mt 11:28–30)

"Come to Me, all who labor and are heavy laden, and I will give you rest." Jesus' infinitely tender and inviting words could be put to a practical test. While the Lord was in an unknown city in this period of His Galilean ministry, He received and accepted an invitation into a Pharisee's house. Some think that it was at Nain, but it seems that some time must be allowed for the report to John the Baptist and the embassy of His disciples. And on account of the progress of the story, others think that it was at Magdala, on the western shore of the Sea of Galilee. This is on account

8
An Invitation to the House of Simon the Pharisee
Lk 7:36

of the popular identification of the unknown sinner with Mary Magdalene. But we are not so sure of that. Neither do we know the particular cause or object of the invitation. There was not yet an open rupture with the Pharisaic party. Jesus did not avoid the Pharisees and gave them no excuse for saying that He ate only with tax collectors and sinners. He still had no reason to refuse the invitation. Of one thing, however, there is no doubt: the inviting host, whose name was the common Simon, but who otherwise is unknown,[23] was a Pharisee both by party affiliation and character. In a few lines, the term *Pharisee* is repeated four times by the evangelist, almost, as it were, by intention. Although Jesus outwardly enjoyed the hospitality of the Pharisee, it seems that Simon purposely omitted the ordinary attentions paid to an honored guest. "There was no water for the weary and dusty feet, no kiss of welcome upon the cheek, no perfume for the hair, nothing but a somewhat ungracious admission to a vacant seat, and the distant courtesies, so managed that the Guest might feel He was receiving, and not conferring, an honor."[24] In order that the mats, or carpets, which were hallowed by domestic prayer, might not be rendered unclean by the pollution of the street, the entering Guest took off His sandals and left them at the door. He then assumed a recumbent posture in the banquet room, with His left elbow resting on the table, His body reclined upon a couch, and His feet turned in the direction of the wall.[25]

9
The Anointing of Christ's Feet by a Sinful Woman
Lk 7:37–38

The story that follows is perhaps a "history more fit to be wept over than to be commented upon."[26] While Jesus was supping in the Pharisee's house, a woman—probably known to the host and to some of the guests—entered the banquet room. On account of her past unchaste life, she was called, and from the standpoint of public opinion still was, a sinner. According to popular opinion, it was Mary Magdalene. Her very name has in all civilized languages become a byword for "accepted penitence and pardoned sin."[27] But we are going to follow the lead of the apostle Luke. He, as we take it, introduces Mary Magdalene as a new historical figure in the next section and not as a woman of a previously unchaste life, but as one out of whom the Lord had cast out seven demons (Lk 8:2). And that is quite a different matter. By the way, this touching story in the record of St. Luke along with the annunciation of Mary, the stories of the infant Jesus, the women followers in the next section, the story of Mary and Martha of Bethany (Lk 10:38–42), and the like, has led some writers[28] to believe that Luke had women reporters from the intimate circle of Jesus among his sources. In the present instance and for reasons of his own, it seems that the evangelist concealed the identity of the fallen woman by covering her with a cloak of namelessness. She came to the house of the Pharisee with a purpose. Summoning up courage to intrude upon that respectable house and company, she made her way through the throng, carrying with her an alabaster flask of perfume. She found the object of her search. As she stood behind Him and thought of what He had said and of what she had been—of His sinlessness and of her life of vice and shame—she began to weep. As it happened, teardrops fell upon His unsandaled feet. There was no napkin at hand, and bending down to hide her confusion and shame, she quickly wiped the tears away with the long tresses of her disheveled hair. Overcome by emotion and seeing that no resistance was offered her, she kissed those holy feet again and again and anointed them with her costly and fragrant nard. At the proper moment, according to her purpose, she probably had hoped to anoint His head, but because of the unexpected turn of events she had instead anointed His feet!

Not a word had as yet been spoken in this silent drama. The woman was touching Jesus, who did not repel her. A tense situation. But the scene could not have been more natural and more human even if it had been prearranged. And also the Pharisee played his part true to form. First of all, in some way acquainted with the woman and her history, he had looked on with icy dislike and disapproval. A self-righteous and impenitent saint. The heartbreaking scene of sincere penitence left him unmoved. If this man, Simon thought, had been a prophet and not simply ignorant like any other man, and if He had known who and what sort of woman had imposed upon Him her defiling touch, He would immediately have repulsed her with contempt and indignation, as he himself would have done. But Jesus *was* a prophet, and in a fuller sense than Simon had imagined. Replying to the thought concealed in Simon's heart and to the contempt probably written on his face, Jesus addressed Himself to Simon with the words: "Simon, I have something to say to you." "Say it, Teacher" (politeness demanding the title) was his constrained reply. Then Jesus told the parable of the two debtors and one creditor. One of the two debtors owed five hundred denarii and the other fifty. Both were unable to pay. And the creditor forgave them both. "Now which of them will love him more?" Thrown off his guard, Simon may have had no suspicion that Jesus was applying the parable to him. Rather indifferent to the whole matter, he answered: "The one, I suppose, for whom he cancelled the larger debt." In agreement with Jewish theology, so much for so much, that would be the natural conclusion. Although Simon, like David in Nathan's parable (2Sm 12:1–8), was slow in making the application, perhaps the penitent woman had grasped the point. For the first time, Jesus turned to her directly and also asked Simon to notice her whom he had so despised. Probably at her entry, he had not even given her the attention of a condescending glance. But Jesus sharply contrasts her behavior with Simon's behavior. As regards Jesus, Simon had not even observed the courtesies commonly extended to invited guests.

> I entered your house; you gave Me no water for My feet, but she has wet My feet with her tears and wiped them with her hair. You gave Me no kiss, but from the time I came in she has not ceased to kiss My feet. You did not anoint My head with oil, but she has anointed My feet with ointment. Therefore I tell

10
"Your Faith Has Saved You; Go in Peace"
Lk 7:39–50

you, her sins, which are many, are forgiven—for she loved much. But he who is forgiven little, loves little.

Simon had no consciousness of sin. He believed he had no particular need of forgiveness, and therefore there was no expression of love. Although he knew of the woman's great sin, he did not believe her to be penitent. The woman did not receive forgiveness as a result of her love. Rather, coming to Jesus, as she did, with a truly contrite and believing heart, she sought and received forgiveness, and her love was the result of her forgiveness. And giving her the assurance that this was actually the case, Jesus said: "Your sins are forgiven." In surprised silence, the guests heard these words. But frowning faces clearly expressed the familiar "Who can forgive sins but God alone?" (Mk 2:7). Concerned, however, only with the penitent sinner, Jesus uttered the peace-bestowing and rest-giving words: "Your faith has saved you; go in peace."

11
With the Twelve and a Number of Women Followers on a Tour through Galilee
Lk 8:1–3

The evangelists do not present, nor do they intend to present, a complete life of Christ. In one place, they give a glimpse, probably an incident related with fullest details, and then a gap or a summary of unrecorded events. In another place, they give the exact time and strict chronological sequence, and then only a loose chronological connection. Thus, we continue our narrative with the notice of our Lord's itinerant preaching ministry through Galilee. He travels in the company of the Twelve, properly so called, and a number of loving, grateful women followers drawn to Him by His healing deeds of love. Among these women, three are especially named. The first is Mary Magdalene, of Magdala, a Sabbath's journey from Tiberias. She had received special benefits for body and soul from Jesus. From her, seven devils had been cast out. She is not, we believe, the unknown sinner whose history ends with the previous section but a new historical figure, whom we shall meet again during Passion Week at Jerusalem (Mt 27:56, 61). The second is Joanna, the wife or widow of Herod's steward Chuza, probably the court official whose son Jesus had healed by the word spoken at Cana (Jn 4:46–54).[29] Last is Susanna, otherwise unknown. The evangelist did not inscribe the names of the others in the sacred records, but their names are recorded in the Book of Life.[30] Being women of some means, they provided for Jesus and the disciples, thus returning love for love and illustrating the rule of Christ's kingdom: The one forgiven much loves much.

12
The Friends Concerned about Jesus
Mk 3:20–21

We are again in Capernaum.[31] It is remarkable how much of what is connected with our Lord's life and ministry centers about this thriving fishing town on the shores of the Galilean Sea. No sooner had the news spread than the multitudes were at hand, so that the party of Jesus "could not even eat." Cure-seeking crowds imposed upon the Savior to the extent that His family[32] feared for Him. They thought the constant strain and His own all-consuming zeal (Jn 2:17) would seriously injure His health. They considered it their duty to rush to His rescue and take Him into their hands, because in their opinion, He was in a state of excitement bordering on insanity; "for they were saying, 'He is out of His mind.' "

The opinion expressed by well-meaning but mistaken friends was certainly not flattering to Jesus. But it was a small insult compared with what the scribes and Pharisees said. When Jesus healed an unfortunate victim of demon possession, stricken dumb and blind, the amazed multitude was almost convinced that Jesus must be the Son of David in the sense of Old Testament Scripture. In reaction, certain scribes and Pharisees from Jerusalem declared that the devils who possessed that man had been cast out by Beelzebul, the prince of the devils. We remember that after the raising of the widow's son at Nain, reports concerning Jesus had gone out to Judea and the surrounding country (Lk 7:17). As the result, a delegation had come from John's prison at Machaerus (Mt 11:2–6). And now, the reaction from Jerusalem.[34] With regard to the cures of demoniacs, the theory was advanced that these deeds were performed with the help of Beelzebul, the prince of the devils. The name of this patron idol of Ekron, a city of the Philistines (2Ki 1:2–3, 16), was really Baal-zebub, "Lord Prince." But the Israelites may have perverted his name to Beelzebul, the Lord of dung, in order to show their contempt for this heathenish god.[35] It was a blasphemous accusation to assert that Christ cast out devils with Satan's help. But whether they were conscious of it or not, what they said was an involuntary admission that He *cast out demons.*

To this charge, Jesus replied that it would be utterly absurd to suppose that Satan would be so foolish as they made him out to be. That would be against his own best interests. "How can Satan cast out Satan? If a kingdom is divided against itself, that kingdom cannot stand." Satan casting out Satan would be self-defeating.[36] It is evident that Satan, as a strong man, would not yield unless overcome by someone endowed with superior strength. Jesus did not ally Himself with Satan. He overpowered Satan by the Spirit of God and took possession of "his goods"; that is, He released human souls previously held by Satan in bondage. Moreover, it was a well-known fact that the Jews practiced a certain kind of exorcism with Pharisaic sanction. In the name of the Lord, they and their disciples attempted to cast out devils. Without entering into the merit or the effectiveness of the practice itself, Jesus raises a personal argument (*ad hominem*):[37] "If I cast out demons by Beelzebul, by whom do your sons cast them out? Therefore they will be your judges." Jesus' accusers would thus be silenced, judged, and condemned by their own practice.

If the devil was not helping Jesus, and if He did not practice fraud and deception, then there could be only this alternative—He delivered people by the power and Spirit of God. And the accusation just made against Jesus was really a sin against the Spirit of God. By discrediting and rejecting Jesus in the face of all evidence and better conviction, they deliberately and blasphemously rejected the work of the

13
"He Is Possessed by Beelzebul" (Mt 12:22–34); Mk 3:22[33]

14
The Defense of Jesus (Mt 12:25–29); Mk 3:23–27

15
The Sin against the Holy Spirit (Mt 12:30–37); Mk 3:28–30

Spirit of God. If in their judgment the Pharisees would have been mistaken only in theory, they would have been guilty of an offense against the Son of Man, a less heinous sin by comparison. But they willfully hardened their hearts against the gracious operation of the Holy Spirit. " 'Truly, I say to you, all sins will be forgiven the children of man, and whatever blasphemies they utter, but whoever blasphemes against the Holy Spirit never has forgiveness, but is guilty of an eternal sin'—for they were saying, 'He has an unclean spirit.' "[38] For all sins, there is forgiveness; but the final rejection of the only saving grace of God in Christ, the "malicious and persistent resistance against the converting and sanctifying work of the Holy Ghost"[39] in and through the Gospel, is the rejection of the only possibility of forgiveness, the rejection of forgiveness itself. And that in the last analysis is the sin against the Holy Spirit. And in the Sermon on the Mount, Jesus points to the fruit of His critics and to the evidence of their own conduct, which all goes to show that they were dangerously near, if not already fatally affected with, this terrible hardening of their hearts.[40]

16
The Sign of the Prophet Jonah (Mt 12:38–45)[41]

These were strong words, especially since they were spoken in the hearing of the great teachers from Jerusalem, who in all probability had been sent by the Council to pay close attention to every word Christ would utter. They resented that He assumed such royal and judicial authority, and they immediately demanded of Him a sign from heaven with which to substantiate this claim. The implication, of course, was that the sign they had just seen was insufficient. But their request was declined. It came from such as were guilty of spiritual adultery, having by their rejection of Jesus as the true Messiah become unfaithful to God, their Husband (Is 23:17; Jer 31:32). The sign given to them would be the death and resurrection of Jesus as typified in the history of Jonah (Jnh 1:17).[42] "For just as Jonah was three days and three nights in the belly of the great fish, so will the Son of Man be three days and three nights in the heart of the earth." A veiled reference is made to Christ's death and resurrection. They would put Him to death, "but He would rise again to their confusion, if not to their conversion."[43] By the way, the Lord accepted the story of Jonah. And the reference to this prophet leads to another thought. The people of Nineveh repented—"and, behold, something greater than Jonah is here." After the queen of Sheba returned from her visit to Solomon, she brought true wisdom to her country (1Ki 10:1–10)—"and, behold, something greater than Solomon is here." But the wicked generation Jesus faced was like a demoniac from whom evil spirits had been cast out. They could have been rid of the evil one forever, but rather than enjoy being permanently released from evil, they actually prepare for the evil spirit's return to them. The homesick spirit, roaming in a far off desolate waste, is welcome to take possession again of those from whom he had been cast out, and he says, "I will return to my house from which I came." "And when it comes, it finds the house empty, swept, and put in order. Then it goes and brings with it seven other spirits more evil than itself, and they enter and dwell there; and the last state of that person is worse than the first." This is the sin of sins, the damnable, final, fatal self-surrender to Satan, resulting from the rejection of Christ. "The end is damnation, yes, twofold damnation, by nature and by choice."[44]

The discourse was broken at this point by a sudden interruption. News had reached the family of Jesus—His mother and His brothers[46]—of the dense throngs surrounding His person, of the strange and threatening words uttered by Him, and probably also of the presence of the spying delegation from Jerusalem. Alarm seized them, and they felt it their duty to save Jesus from Himself. But they had some difficulty in reaching Him on account of the crowds. They were standing outside the home where Jesus was teaching. And it was not for the purpose of attracting attention to themselves that they sent word to Jesus: "Your mother and Your brothers are outside, seeking You." But Jesus would not tolerate any interference. Without denying the rights of relationship "nor condemning them, but placing His Father first"[47] (Lk 2:49), Jesus looked around, His eyes sweeping the whole circle of His audience, and stretching forth His hand toward His disciples, He said: "Here are My mother and My brothers! For whosoever does the will of God, he is My brother and sister and mother."

> **17**
> Interfering Kinsmen
> (Mt 12:46–50);
> Mk 3:31–35;
> (Lk 8:19–21)[45]

On the same late summer or autumn day of AD 31, we find our Savior leaving the house where He was staying in Capernaum on His way to the nearby shores of the Sea of Galilee. This, by the way, was to be one of the busiest days of which we have any knowledge in the life of our Lord. The account extends from the time when He was besieged by the multitudes upon His return to Capernaum until late in the same day, when He rested His weary head in the rocking bed of a storm-tossed ship on the Sea of Galilee. As the multitudes gathered, He seated Himself in a boat in preparation for a lengthy discourse, while His hearers stood upon the beach. Thus, He began what is known as the great group of parables by the sea.[48] Without going into details about parables, an introductory word about them may prove helpful. They are a method of speech used by many other teachers, but especially developed by Jesus, in which moral or religious truths are illustrated from comparison with human experience. They were used by Jesus in every period of His public ministry. But there came a time, it seems, when a larger and a special place was given to parables in His ministry. In His public ministry, there seems to be a ratio of parabolic speech to the popular opposition against His work. When it became increasingly evident that the great bulk of the Jewish people, especially the leaders, would not accept Him as the promised Messiah and continued tenaciously to cling to their carnal messianic ideas and ideals, Christ ceased largely to direct Himself to them and confined His instructions chiefly to His disciples and special friends, to whom He addressed Himself in parables. By these means, spiritual truths, clothed in images,

> **18**
> Parables
> (Mt 13:1–3a);
> Mk 4:1–2; Lk 8:4

were shielded from public attack. The purpose of parables was both to reveal and to conceal. Two reasons for parabolic speech are given. One is that the Scriptures might be fulfilled (Mt 13:14, 34–35).[49] The other reason was the policy of our Lord not to cast pearls before the swine. The time had come to instruct His followers, who were to carry on His work after His departure. But, as Jesus Himself indicates,[50] the truth should be hidden from those who would only hear it without repenting of their sins. In the presence of hard-hearted enemies, who were only watching to employ His words against Him, the truth was to be cautiously uttered. The fickle multitudes, who would have refused to accept Jesus' words if they had perceived their full import, likewise needed instruction. Jesus carefully veiled the depth of His meaning from them. On the other hand, with but a very gentle hint at what He meant to teach, a simple-minded follower of Christ would nevertheless readily understand figurative illustrations of spiritual truths that would be absolute enigmas to the most educated doctors and scribes. They were trained in the Law,[51] the Word of God, but were impervious to its saving truths.

19
First Parable:
The Sower
(Mt 13:3b–9);
Mk 4:3–9; Lk 8:5–8

Like a number of other parables, the first one of the nine is taken from agricultural life. "Listen!" Jesus said. "A sower went out to sow." And as he sowed his seed, some fell on the footpaths in the field, where it was either trampled underfoot or the birds of the air came and devoured it. Other seed fell upon shallow ground, with rock near the surface. It made a lively start but was quickly killed because of the lack of deep soil and moisture and on account of the burning sun. Some fell among the thorn-infested soil, and when, in competition, the thorn seeds or roots grew up and choked it, it yielded no fruit. Other seed, however, fell into soft, clean, and good ground. There, it grew and yielded fruit, wholly satisfactorily. Some yielded thirtyfold, some sixtyfold, and some a hundredfold—thirtyfold, good; sixtyfold, better; a hundredfold, best. And giving His listeners an invitation to think of the hidden meaning or rather a hint that there was a hidden meaning, Jesus said: "He who has ears to hear, let him hear."

20
The Reason for the
Parables
(Mt 13:10–17);
Mk 4:10–12;
Lk 8:9–10

There must have been a short pause. During the brief interval when the boat was probably withdrawn a little from the shore so that they might be strictly alone (Mk 4:10), the Twelve and other disciples asked Jesus about His method of teaching in parables. They also requested an explanation of this particular parable. There was an answer for both questions. As to His method, Jesus said: "To you has been given the secret of the kingdom of God, but for those outside everything is in parables." These words are to be understood in the light of the terrible warning against the sin of blasphemy against the Holy Spirit (Mk 3:28–30; Mt 12:31–32), spoken by Christ on the same day (Mt 13:1). Since they who asked the question are believing disciples and as such are not offended at His doctrine, the "secrets" of the Kingdom are no longer mysteries to them because the doctrines have been revealed to them.[52]

Christianity has no secret doctrines; for what has been publicly proclaimed is no longer a secret. As believing disciples, this knowledge has been given *them*, but to others "everything is in parables, so that,[53] 'they may indeed see but not perceive, and may indeed hear but not understand, lest they should turn and be forgiven.' " This does not refer to a decree of God by which some people are predestined to eternal condemnation. There is no such terrible decree. Nor does it mean that Christ used parables to blind the people on account of the increased opposition. This is rather one of those notable passages in which it is pointed out, as a solemn warning, what deliberate rejection and self-hardening leads to. Thus, the same sweet Gospel that is to believers the aroma of life to life becomes to unbelievers the stench of death to death (2Co 2:15–16; 1Co 1:18). A terrible judgment of God will befall those who harden their hearts against the Gospel of mercy, whose purpose is to save souls. This judgment upon Israel, as Jesus points out,[54] began in the days of Isaiah and was now fulfilled. "But blessed are your eyes, for they see, and your ears, for they hear."[55] Judgment for rejecters, but blessings for believers.

And now, the explanation of the parable. "The seed is the word of God." Now, when one hears the Word of the Kingdom, preached either by Christ or by His ministers, and does not "take it in,"[56] "the evil one comes and snatches away what has been sown in his heart." This is the seed that was sown along the path. That which is sown on the rocky ground is that sown in shallow and emotional hearts. The ready acceptance of the Gospel by such hearers is sometimes almost embarrassing. But they have no root. And in times of tribulation, adversity, and persecution, they fall away. That which fell among the thorns are they who, having heard the Word, promise well indeed. But the cares of the world, the deceitfulness of riches, and the lusts of other things choke the Word so that it brings no fruit. Thus with some of the unfruitful hearers, it is a case of lack of interest at the outset. With others, it is a case of want of steadfastness. With still others, there is a deplorable absence of real sincerity. Only those of another class, by the grace of God, present soil ready for a crop of fruit that is well-pleasing to the Lord. They are those who receive the Word into fine, good hearts, "hearing the word, hold it fast in an honest and good heart, and bear fruit with patience." With them, the heart was properly plowed and prepared by the Law. After they have heard and received the Gospel, they bring forth God-pleasing fruit in accordance with the gifts received and opportunities offered them in their individual lives.

21
The Explanation
(Mt 13:18–23);
Mk 4:13–20;
Lk 8:11–15

Sometimes a speaker tells one story to illustrate another. Christ's purpose in telling the parable of the sower was to show His hearers that, after hearing the Word, they must yield God-pleasing fruit. It was the disciples' privilege to receive a special explanation of the parable. In giving them the requested explanation, Jesus admonished them to make the proper use of this special instruction. "No one after lighting

22
The Proper Use
of the Explanation
Mk 4:21–25;
Lk 8:16–18

a lamp covers it with a jar or puts it under a bed, but puts it on a stand."[57] The Lord often repeated His sayings. "Take care then how you hear, for to the one who has, more will be given, and from the one who has not, even what he thinks that he has will be taken away." To him who has Christian knowledge, the Lord gives an additional store of it. But if one is indifferent about growing in knowledge and manifesting his faith in life, then even what little he has will be taken from him. Privileged possession entails increased responsibility. And even as in other matters, the rule applies, "With the measure you use, it will be measured to you," so also in this case the reward of prayerful attention to the Word is an increase of saving knowledge.

23
Second Parable:
The Seed Growing
Mk 4:26–29

Even in the case of the fourth class of hearers, the yielding of fruit is a gradual process, demanding time. This the Lord sets forth in a beautiful parable, peculiar to the Gospel according to St. Mark: The kingdom of God is as if a man should scatter seed into the ground and then sleep night and day, with nothing in particular to do beyond patiently waiting for the result of what he has already done. For what else is there for him to do? Should he worry about the outcome? Should he go out into the wheat fields and disturb the roots or forcibly stretch the plants in a harmful attempt to hasten the crop? "The earth produces by itself, first the blade, then the ear, then the full grain in the ear." It is not until the fruit is ripe that he "puts in the sickle, because the harvest has come." Thus it is also in spiritual matters. Worrying about results is foolish and useless. The power of God is in the Word, and He has promised that it shall not return to Him empty (Is 55:10–11).

24
Third Parable:
The Weeds
(Mt 13:24–30)

By this time, it seems, Jesus again directed His attention to the assembled multitudes.[58] The present parable is also taken from agricultural life. But while the parable of the sower describes disappointing past experiences, the parable of the weeds is prophetic of a future state of things. The kingdom of heaven is compared to a man who sowed good seed in his field. But, as afterward became evident, while the man slept, his enemy came with a certain malignant seed, a degenerate form of wheat, whose stalks and spikes closely resemble the true grain,[59] and maliciously sowed it into the ground. Not until the crop began to mature was the spiteful trick discovered. The surprised farm laborers suggested to the householder to have them go and pull it out. But the householder, who knew the reason for the presence of the weeds and also knew that an uprooting at this time would be harmful to the wheat, arranged for a different course of action: "Let both grow together until the harvest, and at harvest time I will tell the reapers, Gather the weeds first and bind them in bundles to be burned, but gather the wheat into my barn." This parable, which Jesus Himself explains (vv. 36–43), illustrates the truth that in the visible Kingdom, or Church, the bad, or hypocrites, are mingled with the good, the true believers. Forceful means for an attempted elimination of the wicked, heretics, and false Christians are not to be employed. This, of course, does not deny to the visible

Church the right of discipline by way of individual excommunication or restoration. But even so, a visible Church consisting only of saints cannot be established. And if we attempt to separate believers and unbelievers absolutely, we will find that we are not competent for the task. It must be left in the hands of the Judge. "They who today are tares may tomorrow be grain."[60]

Sore disappointments, extended waiting, fiendish opposition to the Kingdom— and still marvelous growth. This the Lord sets forth in the parable of the mustard seed. "With what can we compare the kingdom of God, or what parable shall we use for it?" "The kingdom of heaven is like a grain of mustard seed." Among the rabbis, the phrase "like a grain of mustard seed" was a common expression for anything very minute.[62] A number of varieties of the mustard plant, all having very small seed and in a short time reaching a striking growth of treelike proportions, meet the requirements of the parable. "That a man took and sowed in his field." This tiny seed is "the smallest of all seeds on the earth, yet when it is sown it grows up and becomes larger than all the garden plants and puts out large branches, so that the birds of the air can make nests in its shade." Thus, the preaching of the Gospel may be considered insignificant before men, but from it the Christian Church was born, a power that has changed the course of the world's history and is a source of true rest and peace for all nations under the sun.

25
Fourth Parable:
The Mustard
Seed
(Mt 13:31–32);
Mk 4:30–32[61]

A mere handful of disciples were gathered in the Upper Room at Jerusalem, and in a short time they and their followers went out and conquered the world. And what brought about this remarkable change? Clearly, it was the hidden, silent, mysterious, and still all-pervading and transforming power of the Word. That seems to be the point in the next parable, in which the Lord speaks of the leaven "that a woman took and hid in three measures of flour, till it was all leavened."

26
Fifth Parable:
The Leaven
(Mt 13:33)[63]

Thus Jesus, for reasons indicated above,[64] addressed the multitudes in parables. And without parables, He would not speak to the people. Privately, He expounded the parables to His disciples that they "might understand the better."[65] A few of His interpretations have been recorded. As regards the various details of the parables, we must remember that all comparisons are limited. To attempt to interpret all the details, for instance, in the parable of the leaven, that the woman took *three* measures of meal, and so forth, is both needless and fruitless. We get the main point, and we must guard against going beyond the point of comparison. And as regards the whole matter of parabolic teaching, the evangelist Matthew points to a fulfillment of prophecy (Ps 78:2).[66]

27
The Parabolic
Method
(Mt 13:34–35);
Mk 4:33–34

After Jesus had spoken His fifth parable, He dismissed the multitude and "went into the house."[67] Most likely, it was His home in Capernaum. The parable of the weeds must have made a deep impression upon His disciples for they came to Him, saying: "Explain," interpret,[68] "to us the parable of the weeds of the field." Point for

28
Explanation of the
Weeds
(Mt 13:36–43)

point, the parable was thereupon explained by the Lord. The wide world is the harvest field of the Son of Man, who here represents Himself as the Lord of the Church. The good seed represents—not the Word this time (Lk 8:12), but—the children of the Kingdom, while the weeds are the seed and children of the devil. In the time of harvest, at the end of the world, the unbelief of the latter will become apparent, though during their lifetime they skillfully hid it behind a semblance of piety and hindered the development of the good grain. At the command of the Son of Man, the reaping angels will then issue forth and gather out of His kingdom the offenders and "throw them into the fiery furnace. In that place there will be weeping and gnashing of teeth." But the righteous shall "shine like the sun in the kingdom of the Father." At this final harvest, and not before, a forceful sifting of believers and unbelievers is to take place. On the one hand, there is the outlook of everlasting bliss and a glorious reward; on the other, a terrible and eternal punishment. "He who has ears, let him hear."

29
Sixth Parable:
The Hidden Treasure
(Mt 13:44)

As Christ next points out in two brief parables, the supreme value of the bliss of heaven and the promised gracious reward outweighs everything else. The man who understands this will happily part with all. "The kingdom of heaven is like treasure hidden in a field, which a man found and covered up. Then in his joy, he goes and sells all that he has and buys that field." Jesus is here not concerned with the moral aspect of the act, if indeed this comes into consideration here at all. It is a story that has found its parallel often enough. A certain treasure that had been hidden in the ground was found by a man, who then, eager to secure the treasure, carefully covered it up again. He sold his property and bought this extremely valuable piece of ground. The salvation offered in the Gospel is such a find. Although it cannot be earned or purchased, no sacrifice is too great to obtain possession of it and to retain it by the grace of God (Lk 10:42; Php 3:8, 13).

30
Seventh Parable:
The Pearl of Great
Value
(Mt 13:45–46)

"Again, the kingdom of heaven is like a merchant in search of fine pearls, who, on finding one pearl of great value, went and sold all that he had and bought it." A "*connoisseur*" of valuables is completely taken by surprise."[69] A pearl merchant, an expert in his line, finds a pearl of rare beauty and worth. Recognizing its value, he sells all that he has and buys this pearl of great price. He strips himself of all his possessions and risks all in the one great venture of his life. So also, the earnest seeker of the saving truth is completely taken by surprise when he finds the pearl and realizes the value of the treasure contained in the Gospel of Christ. Although he is a seeker, still the true treasure comes to him as a find. Nor is he able actually by purchase to gain its possession, but after "he has learned to know this priceless gift, he will gladly renounce all goods, joys, and delights of this world and consider all human wisdom and righteousness but loss in order to gain Christ."[70]

Christ's parables are taken from everyday life. The parable of the net especially offered a picture with which the disciples were very familiar. The kingdom of heaven is like a large net that is cast into the sea. In the great number of fish enclosed, good and bad, the value of the catch among fishermen is in the edible fish, the rest being carefully separated and thrown away. They are not really counted as belonging to the catch. Thus also, the kingdom of heaven as it appears here upon earth is such a net. The preaching of the Gospel results in an outward collection of such as are really members of the Kingdom as well as of such as merely have a semblance of membership. Upon earth, the entire netful is drawn toward the shores of eternal life. But on the Last Day, "the angels will come out and separate the evil from the righteous and throw them into the fiery furnace. In that place there will be weeping and gnashing of teeth." As distinguished from the true believers in the kingdom of heaven, similar to the parable of the weeds, nominal Christians and hypocrites are depicted here.

31
Eighth Parable:
The Parable of
the Net
(Mt 13:47–50)

In concluding this great series of parables, Jesus asked His disciples the question: "Have you understood all these things?" As far as their understanding went, they unhesitatingly said they did. Pleased with this profession of understanding, which reflected favorably both upon the ability of the Teacher and the aptitude of the learners, the Lord gave them some additional instruction pertaining especially to their future work as teachers. "Therefore every scribe," in this case, every Christian teacher, "who has been trained for the kingdom of heaven is like a master of a house, who brings out of his treasure what is new and what is old." Unlike the scribe, rabbinical in spirit, who produces only the old and stale, the disciple of the Kingdom, like the Master, is always fresh-minded and able to present the old Gospel in a new dress.[71] And as he himself grows in knowledge, so he is able to aid also his hearers to increase therein.[72]

32
Ninth Parable:
The Master of the
House
(Mt 13:51–53)

13

THE GADARENE JOURNEY

PROBABLY AUTUMN, AD 31

A busy day in the life of Christ was coming to a close—the same day on which He returned to Capernaum after His second tour of Galilee (Mk 3:20).[2] It was probably in the morning that Jesus taught a dense throng of people, some of whom insulted and blasphemed Him, while others demanded a sign. Jesus' friends considered Him beside Himself, so that at length His mother and His brothers felt it their duty to interfere and to save Him from Himself.[3] In the afternoon, He chose as His method of instruction a group of most remarkable parables, several of which He explained. And now, toward evening, tired and worn out, He entered a boat "just as He was" (Mk 4:36)[4] in order to escape the great multitudes about Him. He then gave His disciples the command to depart with Him to the other side.

But before Jesus could sail out into the lake, a remarkable interruption occurred. Three of His listeners, struck perhaps by "the power of His teaching or dazzled by the zenith of His popularity, desired, or thought that they desired, to attach themselves to His person as permanent disciples."[6] The first applicant was a scribe. If he already belonged to the outer circle of disciples,[7] the designation *scribe* seems to indicate that he was still attached to a party utterly opposed to the ways of Jesus. "Teacher, I will follow You wherever You go." Have we here a "Saul among the prophets"?[8] Did the good man really think that he was able to follow Jesus in any way he should choose or be obliged to go? In his enthusiasm, he was evidently ignorant of the real cost of being a disciple of Jesus. Jesus did not turn him away, but very likely He chilled his enthusiasm by telling him: "Foxes have holes, and birds of the air have nests,[9] but the Son of Man[10] has nowhere to lay His head." Now, Jesus was no pauper. The picture of His poverty must not be overdrawn. His wants and needs were always provided for. But according to His will and purpose, He had no house or piece of

1
The Command to Cross Over to the Other Side
Mt 8:18;[1] Mk 4:35; Lk 8:22

2
Three Applicants for Discipleship
(A) Inconsiderate Impulse
Mt 8:19–22;
(Lk 9:57–62)[5]

land that He could call His own. In pointing to His personal poverty, He shows the manner in which His disciples are to follow Him. That indeed, as far as the enthusiastic scribe is concerned, was the decisive and necessary thing.

3
(B) Conflicting
Duties
Mt 8:19–22;
(Lk 9:57–62)

The second applicant already was a partial disciple, but before complying with Jesus' request to follow Him, he wished first to bury his father. We do not know whether he wished to live at home until his aged father died or whether the father had just died, in which case the permission would have involved very little delay. We cannot say whether the burial included also the arranging of the family affairs and the distribution of the inheritance.[11] Neither have we any information as to the identity of this or the other applicants.[12] The answer of Jesus is, "Follow Me, and leave the dead to bury their own dead." It seems that the word *dead* must be taken in a twofold sense: Let the spiritually dead bury the physically dead. According to another explanation, the meaning is, "Let the dead be taken care of by those whose occupation it is to inter the earthly remains."[13] At any rate, it is a hard answer, although Jesus knew to whom He spoke. If there is a conflict of interests, even duties, in the service of Christ, there can be but one choice—to follow Christ (Mt 10:35–39). "And the saying can also be misunderstood and abused; but woe unto him who does so!"[14]

4
(C) A Divided Heart
Mt 8:19–22;
(Lk 9:57–62)

A third would-be disciple[15] likewise pleaded for delay. He first wanted to bid farewell to those at home in his house. Seemingly a small request,[16] but at the same time a dangerous thing. Many times, the influence of family, relatives, and friends has prevented new converts from coming under the full power and into the full service of Jesus. This man seems like those who always "want to do something else first in which they are personally interested before addressing themselves to the main duty to which they have been called."[17] Jesus answers him: "No one who puts his hand to the plow and looks back is fit for the kingdom of God." This saying has become proverbial for all time. In the service of the Kingdom, there can be no divided mind. There must be firm intention and a steady eye. The ambition of all plowmen is to make a straight trench. This skill, like the highest calling in the Kingdom, needs a forward-looking eye. "When the East calls, thoughts must be turned from the fading West."[18] In the Lord's kingdom, there must be no "inconsiderate impulse, no conflicting duties, and no divided mind."[19]

5
"Save Us, Lord; We
Are Perishing!"
Mt 8:23–27;
Mk 4:36–41;
Lk 8:23–25

After all these delays, the trip across the lake could finally begin. The departure was hasty, for the disciples had taken Jesus into the ship "just as He was." But even now, others followed Him for "other boats were with Him." However, these were probably soon scattered or frightened back on account of an approaching storm. At any rate, in His own boat[20] and among His trusted disciples He could soon rest His head on a cushion, or pillow, in the steersman's seat. Yet this rest, so sorely needed, was soon violently disturbed. One of those fierce storms of which travelers tell us, "peculiar to that strange hollow in the earth's surface, swept down with sudden fury upon that little inland sea."[21] To understand the causes of these sudden and violent tempests, we must remember that the lake lies over six hundred feet below the level of the Mediterranean Sea. One commentator writes:

> Naked plateaus rise upward and backward to the snowy heights of distant Hermon, that the watercourses have cut deep ravines converging at the head of the lake, and that these gorges act like gigantic funnels to conduct the descending cold winds down the valley of the Upper Jordan against the surface of the lake.[22]

At scarcely a moment's notice, the air was filled with a whirlwind, and the smiling evening waters were whipped into a boiling sea. The wild waves rose and fell and tossed, lashed, and broke over the ship, rapidly filling it with water, and threatened to hurl it into the deep. The danger was extreme. The violence of the tempest caused even the strong hearts of experienced and weather-beaten fishermen to quake with fear. But Jesus was asleep. With a cry of terror, the imperiled disciples aroused their sleeping Master. "Save us, Lord; we are perishing." Just what they expected Jesus to do, we do not know. They hardly wanted what actually happened, since "great fear came over them as they had witnessed it."[23] At any rate, with cries of terror and excitement, they implored Jesus' help.

Calmly, Jesus awoke from His slumbers and addressed His disciples from the dripping stern: "Why are you afraid, O you of little faith?" And then, rising to His feet and standing in the dashing spray, the hurricane raging, and His garments and hair fluttering in the wind, He rebuked[24] the wind and the wild waters of the raging sea: "Peace! Be still!" The double imperative "Silence! Be muzzled!"[25] reveals an energy almost untranslatable.[26] And the wind ceased, and there was a great calm—instantaneously. In the calm starlight, a moment later, the trembling and dripping disciples could gaze into the quiet waters. Awesome fear overcame them, causing them to whisper to one another, "What manner of man is this?" It was a stupendous miracle. Three evangelists relate the event in almost the same words. "It was one of those miracles of power which cannot be explained away by existing laws."[27] Yes, "what sort of man is this, that even winds and sea obey Him?"

6
"Peace! Be Still!"
Mt 8:23–27;
Mk 4:36–41;
Lk 8:23–25

The next morning,[28] we find Jesus and His companions on the other side of the lake. But He could not find seclusion and rest even on the farther shore. He reached that part of ancient Manasseh directly East of Galilee, now included in the tetrarchy of Philip and the confederacy of the Decapolis. It was properly called either the land of the Gerasenes or Gergesenes (Gerasa or Gergesa), with reference to the local center, or the land of the Gadarenes (Gadara), with reference to the superior city.[29] He was "met with such an exhibition of human fury and degradation as was even more startling than the rage of the troubled sea."[30]

7
In the Country of
the Gadarenes
Mt 8:28; Mk 5:1;
Lk 8:26

Matthew writes, "Two demon-possessed men met Him, coming out of the tombs, so fierce that no one could pass that way." But Mark and Luke single out

8
The Two Demoniacs
Mt 8:28–29;
Mk 5:1–8;
Lk 8:26–29

and describe one man, probably as the more grievously afflicted and the spokesman of the two. The evangelists describe the men's fierceness, the unclean nature of their dwelling places in the tombs, or limestone caves. Others cannot control them. Their supernatural strength breaks chains and shackles, their suicidal frenzy gashes and cuts them with stones. Their yells and cries night and day disturb the solitude, they bare themselves of every rag of clothing. As Jesus touched the shore, He drew them to Himself with irresistible force. However, their first contact with Jesus was not the occasion of a fresh outbreak of fury. As at other times, the demons knew Jesus. His presence forced them to identify themselves and incidentally also to acknowledge His superior power. They sensed from Christ's manner and look that He would soon deliver the men from them, so they begged the Lord not to torment them before the time of final judgment. In Jesus, they recognized their Judge, who would certainly consign them to everlasting punishment. They addressed Him in the well-known Jewish formula: "What have You to do with us," or rather, "What is there between us and You,"[31] "O Son of God? Have You come here to torment us before the time?" They apprehended their defeat and ultimate punishment based upon the fact that Jesus had said, or rather, was about to say, "Come out of the man, you unclean spirit!"

9
"My Name Is Legion"
Mk 5:9; Lk 8:30

Instead of insisting upon immediate release, Jesus adopts a roundabout way of dealing with the case.[32] He addresses one of the victims with the question, "What is your name?" Still absorbed "in the hideous tyranny of a multitude of demons, under whose influence his own true personality was destroyed,"[33] the unfortunate sufferer replies: "My name is Legion, for we are many." This designation, by this time naturalized into Greek and Aramaic,[34] does not mean exactly six thousand soldiers, but conveys the idea of a multitude of armed and strong warriors of evil. Incidentally, it is also a tribute to the universal and well-organized power of imperial Rome. Like the well-organized legions everywhere seen and felt in the Roman world, so also the demons were well-organized; and there were many of them.

10
The Demons
Enter Pigs
Mt 8:30–32;
Mk 5:10–13;
Lk 8:31–33

And now we come to a difficult part of the story. The devils felt that their time for torturing these victims would soon be over. But if Jesus would send them away, they begged Him not to banish them from the area that was so favorable to their infernal purposes nor to cast them into the abyss "before the time." And if they had to leave mankind, they begged to enter pigs. This is certainly a strange suggestion, but also truly devilish and cruel. Satan's one desire is to destroy the life that God has created. As a roaring lion, he walks about, seeking whom he may devour (1Pt 5:8), if not the soul, then the body of man; and if not the human body, then the mute beast.[35] Now, at a distance, yet within view, there was a herd of about two thousand pigs feeding on the hillside. They probably belonged to some Gentile inhabitants, but they may have belonged to some apostatizing Jews in violation of the Law. With a laconic "Go," Jesus allowed them to enter into the pigs. Thus in a self-staged infernal finale, the devils wreaked their fiendishness, their mania for destroying God's creatures, on beasts. "So they came out and went into the pigs, and behold, the whole herd rushed down the steep bank into the sea and drowned in the waters." But was not the demons' request to enter the pigs and then immediately to destroy their new hosts extremely stupid? As we shall see, this act of the demons allowed them to stay in that country and effected the removal of Jesus from that region. The incident has exhausted the wit of the critic and apologist in every age. Truly, the sufferers were free from their hellish tormentors, but what about the property rights of others and the loss of the pigs? We answer: Is He not the Lord? And are not two souls worth more than two thousand pigs?[36] Besides, the loss of the pigs punished the indifferent Jews of the Decapolis, who tolerated the pigs more than they did the Lord.[37]

In wild terror, the pig-herders brought the news of the terrible catastrophe to Gerasa and the surrounding region. They knew or felt that there must be some connection between the coming of Jesus, the release of the demoniacs, and the headlong rush of their herds into the sea. A multitude soon gathered, probably with thoughts of revenge on whoever destroyed their pigs. But the truth was soon learned. There sat the man who had been a terror to the country, clothed and in his right mind. A charitable hand flung a robe over his naked figure. There was the proof of the power of the mighty Stranger who had thus visited their country. "And they were afraid." Jesus' presence awed them. He demonstrated His power over the demons beyond a doubt. Truly, it was a remarkable cure. But there was also the matter of the pigs! Although they could not deny the cure, it was also a calamity to them. Here was both a benefactor and a dangerous man! "With disgraceful and urgent unanimity they request Jesus to leave the coasts."[38] His presence might cause another cure—and catastrophe.

Jesus did not need much urging. Since the people of that region were evidently little interested in the person of the Miracle-worker and the purpose of His miracles, He left them. But while the multitudes requested His departure, one of the healed demoniacs asked to remain in Jesus' presence. He requested this just as Jesus entered the boat, but He "did not permit him." Nevertheless, while Jesus refused his request, He did not dispense with his services. He commissioned him as the first missionary to the heathen of those parts. He commanded him to go to his home and friends and give them a full account of the great blessings of God he had experienced and especially also of the mercy the Lord had bestowed upon him. This he did. He "began to proclaim in the Decapolis how much Jesus had done for him, and everyone marveled." The evangelists have not stated what events followed his testimony. At any rate, the population had the opportunity to hear about the great

11
The Sequel
Mt 8:33–34;
Mk 5:14–17;
Lk 8:34–37a

12
"Tell How Much the Lord Has Done for You"
Mt 9:1; Mk 5:18–21;
Lk 8:37b–40

Prophet in whom the Gentiles would hope (Mt 12:21). In the meantime, Jesus returned to Capernaum.[39]

The friends of Jesus in Capernaum who had witnessed His sudden departure the evening before, as well as the furious tempest while He was crossing the lake, were by this time concerned about His safety and that of His companions. Therefore, when He returned safe and sound, the people gladly received Him. As the tidings of His return rapidly spread, the usual multitude gathered. One of them was Jairus, an elder in the local synagogue. It is possible that on a previous occasion Jairus belonged to a delegation sent to Jesus on behalf of the centurion's servant who was at the point of death, although the words used are not quite the same (Lk 7:3).[40] At any rate, as one of the synagogue rulers of Capernaum, he had witnessed Jesus' words and deeds. He had seen and heard others appeal to Jesus, and this time he was in need himself. Casting himself at Jesus' feet, he told Him that his twelve-year-old daughter, his "little daughter," his "only daughter," was dying. Moments later, after hearing the last report, he had to say that she had "just died" (Mt 9:18).[41] Still, even now, if Jesus would but come and lay His hand on her, she would live. But if Jairus's daughter was seriously ill, why did he not apply for help earlier? Why wait? Only in the hour of supreme need did he resort to Jesus. There was faith, but there was also need to perfect such faith. The merciful Savior was not deaf to the heartbroken father's cry. He at once set out to go to Capernaum, followed not only by His disciples but by a dense and thronging crowd, anxious to witness a scene.

At this point, an interlude occurred. While Jesus was on the way to the ruler's house, an afflicted woman prayerfully touched Him. She secretly hoped "to steal from Jesus a blessing for which she longed."[42] For twelve years, she had suffered from a distressing malady, an issue of blood, peculiar to her sex. This was not only extremely afflicting, but it also rendered her Levitically unclean (Lv 15:25), making her unfit for all the usual relationships of life. She had spent all her money on physicians in search of a cure and found none; if anything, her condition had grown worse. As a last desperate recourse, she determined to gain relief "from the Great Physician without money and without price."[43] Having heard the things concerning Jesus, she came into the crowd behind Him and quietly and quickly touched the fringe of His garment.—The evangelists do not mean the inner garment, "seamless, woven in one piece from top to bottom" (Jn 19:23).[44] They mean the outer garment, the mantle,[45] upon which were fastened fringes, or tassels, in accordance with the Law (Nu 15:38–41; Dt 22:12).[46]—"For she said, 'If I touch even His garments, I will be made well.' " According to her secret hope, the least possible degree of contact was enough to cure her. This was faith. "But it was also mingled with superstition and cunning"[47] because she hoped to gain a cure by touch, even though the Law would prevent her from touching Him (cf. Lv 15:19–27). Immediately, there was a turn for the better. "And immediately the flow of blood dried up, and she felt in her body that she was healed of her disease."

Others did not notice the incident, but Jesus did. He knew and felt, and He instantly complied with the woman's unspoken request. Many in the crowd had touched Jesus, but only one had touched Him in faith. Perceiving that healing power had gone forth from Him, He turned about and asked "Who touched My garments?" It is not as if He did not know or as if He were giving vent to rabbinical anger because the touch of an unclean woman had polluted Him. His touch cleansed her, her touch did not pollute Him.[48] The purpose of the question was to reveal the faith of the woman. Of course, the disciples could not know. They had not noticed anything, and in view of the crowd the question seemed strange. Peter was almost impatient with his Master, which is evident from his reply: "You see the crowd pressing around You, and yet You say, 'Who touched Me?'" But Jesus, His eyes still sweeping over the many faces, insisted that there was a difference between the accidental touching of curiosity and the intentional touching of faith. Naturally, the woman was an interested witness of the dialogue. Seeing that neither she nor her action could any longer be hidden, she came forward with fear and trembling, "fell down before Him and told Him the whole truth." This included the cause of it all, her purpose, and the cure. She probably feared Jesus would be angry because she had exposed Him to her defiling touch (Lv 15:19). Still, her faith was now fully revealed and Christ's purpose in asking the question was achieved. In all kindness, Jesus dismissed her with the assurance: "Daughter, your faith hath made you well; go in peace."

In consequence of this delay, the urgent need of Jairus was almost forgotten. But this was wholly in line with Jesus' plans. At this point, messengers reported to Jairus that his daughter had really died, and the suggestion was added: "Why trouble the Teacher any further?" All help was now too late. However, Jesus, overhearing but not heeding the message, calmly continued on His way to Jairus's house, addressing him with the memorable words: "Do not fear, only believe." Upon His arrival at the house, He found it already occupied by the customary company of wailing women and flute players. The women wept, howled, beat their breasts, and tore their hair, according to contract. The players struck up mournful dirges. It was a veritable mockery of true sorrow and in weird contrast with the awful silence of death. "Mourning like everything else had been reduced to a system. At least two flute-players and one mourning woman at the burial of a wife, for instance, was incumbent on the poorest man."[49] The whole procedure repulsed Jesus. "Why are you making a commotion and weeping?" Moreover, "the child is not dead but sleeping." They "laughed at Him," and Jesus ejected them all from the house, the crowd as well as the paid mourners. Only the father and the mother of the departed maiden and

15
"Who Touched Me?"
Mt 9:22;
Mk 5:30–34;
Lk 8:45–48

16
"Talitha, Cumi"
Mt 9:23–26;
Mk 5:35–43;
Lk 8:49–56

three disciples—Peter, James, and John—stayed with Him. (We here read for the first time that Jesus specially favored these three.[50]) He grasped the cold little hand and uttered the life-giving words: " 'Talitha, cumi,' which means, 'Little girl, I say to you, arise.' "

> Jesus may have been bilingual and expressed Himself in Greek or in Syriac [Aramaic], as the occasion demanded. On a pathetic occasion like this He would naturally express Himself in the mother tongue of the sorrowing mother and father.[51]

"And immediately the girl got up and began walking." Amazement seized the parents, but Jesus calmly directed them to give her something to eat. And again, Jesus added His customary warning that they should not speak of what had just happened. He evidently intended that they should not so much peddle His miracle as rather reflect upon it in silent faith and spread His doctrine. He would have nothing of that fanatical and extravagant enthusiasm that made Him a miracle-monger and often disturbed the progress of faith. Although Jesus often forbade miracle-spreading reports, He never forbade the spreading of His doctrine, which had the power to kindle faith. In this case as well as in others, His charge did not prevent people from talking.

17
Two Blind Men
Mt 9:27–31

On His return from Jairus's home, two men addressed Jesus with a familiar messianic title publicly for the first time. They uttered the cry: "Have mercy on us, Son of David." Now, Jesus *was* the Son of David. In certain quarters, He was intimately known and believingly acknowledged. But it seems that at this time He did not welcome this title,[52] which may have nourished false messianic expectations. An incorrect understanding of the title might have led to a popular uprising in His favor against the Roman government. The title must therefore be correctly understood and a test made of the faith of those who applied it to Him for help. He permitted the blind men to follow Him to His house. Then He turned to them with the question, "Do you believe that I am able to do this?" A prompt "Yes, Lord" was the reply. The confession revealed both their confidence in the mighty power of Jesus as well as their faith in Him as their Messiah and merciful Lord. Without further hesitation, Jesus touched their eyes and gave them their sight. The purpose of the touching probably was to impress upon them that the healing came from Him. Again, there was a command of silence, most sternly given this time.[53] Jesus probably did not want people to rouse one another for a rebellion against Rome. But the men disregarded the command. Their publicity was an act of disobedience, and we should not excuse it by assuming that these men believed it was only Jesus' modesty that had prompted the command.

18
A Mute Demoniac
Mt 9:32–34

Jesus had hardly healed the two blind men when others brought a mute person into His presence. In this case, the muteness was not due to a physical cause, but an evil spirit had blunted the faculty of speech. No sooner was the devil cast out than the mute man was able to speak. This again filled the crowd with wonder, and they said, "Never was anything like this seen in Israel." Such miracles, signs, and wonders! It had gradually entered into the consciousness of the people that it was the promised Messiah who was blessing them with His presence among them. "The crowds marveled. . . . But the Pharisees said, 'He casts out demons by the prince of the demons.' "

14

A Third Preaching Tour, Including the Mission of the Twelve

Probably early in AD 32, January to March

After the crowded events related in the last chapter, we picture solitude and rest for our Savior—probably at Capernaum. Henceforth, His beloved city ceases to be the center of His activities; He will visit it only occasionally. According to our chronology, we have reached the winter months of AD 31 to 32 (the time is fixed by the death of John the Baptist). Already, the public ministry of Jesus was drawing to its close, at least as far as some sections of the land of Israel were concerned. Jesus of Nazareth was to visit the city of Nazareth, again to be rejected as at the beginning of His great Galilean ministry (Lk 4:16–30). There is no sufficient reason to equate this visit with that described by Luke. The time and the details are quite different. It is perfectly natural that Jesus should give the Nazarenes another opportunity to hear His teaching.[2] But what surprises us is what Jesus marveled at: the unbelief of His townsmen, which lay at the bottom of their estimate and treatment of a "native son."

When Jesus arrived at Nazareth in the company of His disciples, it was natural for Him to make His Sabbath appearance in the local synagogue. And on account of His fame, it was also quite natural that synagogue leaders would invite Him to teach as a visiting rabbi. Even if His address on that morning provoked astonishment, we are surprised at the reaction to His teaching. Regardless of the fact that He happened to be a townsman, if He was a prophet, people might expect the extraordinary. The comments were many and varied. "Where did this man get this wisdom and these mighty works?" The answer is, of course, from God. And both the particular words and deeds argue for His Messiahship. But the Nazarenes were unwilling to concede this distinction to a "native son." "Is not this the carpenter's son?[3] Is not His mother called Mary? And are not His brothers James and Joseph and Simon

1
The Last Visit to Nazareth (Mt 13:54–58);[1] Mk 6:1–6a

2
"Is Not This the Carpenter's Son?" (Mt 13:54–58); Mk 6:1–6a

/ 213

and Judas?[4] And are not all His sisters[5] with us?"[6] "And they took offense at Him." Jesus could only refer to the proverb "A prophet is not without honor except in his hometown and in his own household."[7] Therefore, outside of a few minor works of healing performed upon those who *did* accept Him in faith, Jesus "could do no mighty work there" on account of the general unbelief. For unbelief shuts people out of the blessings God intended for them. Neither was it fitting that Jesus should benefit these people against their will. But the attitude of His townsmen caused Him to wonder. Their reasoning against His Messiahship based upon residence and previous acquaintance was most unreasonable.

3
A Brief Itinerancy
Mt 9:35; Mk 6:6b

After His rejection at Nazareth, Jesus again assumed the role of an itinerant preacher, visiting Galilean cities and villages, teaching in the synagogue on the Sabbath, "proclaiming the gospel of the kingdom and healing every disease and every affliction."

4
"Pray Earnestly to the Lord of the Harvest"
Mt 9:36–38

This itinerant preaching brought our Lord into the most intimate touch with the people, giving Him an insight into their moral and religious condition. Two pictures came to His mind: a neglected flock of sheep and a harvest going to waste for lack of reapers. Both imply not only the plight of the people but a blameworthy neglect of duty on the part of their religious guides.[8] As usual, where Jesus was, the crowds gathered. And when He saw the multitudes, He was moved with compassion because they were "like sheep without a shepherd."[9] A shepherdless flock, what a pitiful sight!—unprotected, distressed, and scattered, "footsore and fleece-torn."[10] Then a new figure flashes into the Lord's mind, not only reflecting His divine sympathy but showing His ardent desire to help these poor people spiritually. "The harvest is plentiful, but the laborers are few; therefore pray earnestly to the Lord of the harvest to send out laborers into His harvest."[11]

5
The Mission of the Twelve
Mt 10:1–4; Mk 6:7; Lk 9:1

Immediately, the Savior decided upon a special mission for His twelve apostles. Of course, "they will be but poor substitutes for Him, but they had already received some training and had imbibed somewhat of His spirit of love."[12] He called them to Himself for the purpose of sending them forth to preach the kingdom of God and to perform works of mercy in His name. Out of consideration for their initial timidity and for the purpose of giving them moral backing, He sent them out two by two. In order that they might prove their divine calling, He equipped them with power—probably only for this mission—"over unclean spirits, to cast them out, and to heal every disease and every affliction."[13] We have already become acquainted with the individual members of the apostolic band,[14] but the evangelist Matthew finds here a convenient place in his account for giving the names of the Twelve, to whom a number of special instructions are given.

6
Their Instructions
Mt 10:5–15; Mk 6:8–11; Lk 9:2–5

Someday, the Gospel would be brought to all, but during the period of this mission the apostles should not go "among the Gentiles" nor enter any "town of the

Samaritans."[15] But they should "go rather to the lost sheep of the house of Israel." And wherever they would go, they should above all preach that "the kingdom of heaven is at hand." And that their message might bear weight, they should back up their preaching with such signs as would be accepted as proofs of their divine mission. "Heal the sick, raise the dead,[16] cleanse lepers, cast out demons." However, this power was not to be for hire nor to be sold for money. "You have received without paying; give without pay." Regarding provisions for the journey, they should take nothing along, no bread, no wallet, no money, neither two coats, nor shoes; and if they had no staff, they should not procure one.[17] "For the laborer deserves his food." Upon entering a village, they should establish a center of activity and carefully inquire into the moral worthiness of a probable host. Having found a favorable prospect, they should enter his house with the time-honored and much-valued blessing, "Peace be with you." If the house sheltered children of peace, then this blessing would be effective. If not, then "let your peace return to you." Then they were to shake the dust off their feet in witness of the fact that they had spoken faithfully. They symbolically cleared themselves of all responsibility for the wrath of God that would come upon the haters of the Word of God. "Truly, I say to you, it will be more bearable on the day of judgment for the land of Sodom and Gomorrah[18] than for that town."

It seems that the evangelist Matthew, "guided, as usual, by the unity of subject, has collected into one focus the scattered rays of instruction,"[19] delivered perhaps on several occasions.[20] Some of the expressions, while applying to the present apostolic mission, refer to experiences that lie in the future. But that need not disturb us. What applies to the apostles in particular might apply also to disciples of Christ in general. It is a great honor to be a follower of Jesus. But there are also perils of discipleship; Jesus predicted persecution. Although Jesus sent forth the disciples on an errand of peace, people would not always peacefully receive them and their followers. "Behold, I am sending you out as sheep in the midst of wolves." The situation calls for diplomacy both blameless and prudent. "So be wise as serpents and innocent as doves." It is not as though "serpents and doves are in themselves exceptionally cunning or particularly harmless,"[21] but what matters is what serpents and doves represent in Scripture and in the popular mind (Gn 3:1; Hos 7:11). Neither have we here a license for Christians to practice the duplicity of serpents; for that would be out of harmony with the proverbial sincerity of the dove. It may be difficult in practical life to combine the sagacity of a serpent with the simplicity of a dove; but these are traits that every believer must cultivate. We will find enemies on every hand. Generally speaking, the natural mind is unfriendly toward the Gospel. Therefore, "beware of men, for they will deliver you over to courts[22] and flog you in their synagogues" (cf. Ac 22:19; 26:11). Even the civil courts, provincial rulers, and

7
Persecutions
Predicted
Mt 10:16–23

Herodian princes would pronounce judgment upon the followers of Christ. The outlook is not pleasant, but believers have many opportunities to witness for the cause of Christ. However, in the critical hour they need not trouble themselves as to manner or matter of word or thought. "For what you are to say will be given to you in that hour."[23] They were to boldly confess; God would defend them. "The grandest utterances in defense of Christianity have sometimes been made by the simplest minds."[24] Gold is tested in the trial of fire. And some of the trials are fiery indeed, especially when the enmity against the Gospel makes itself felt among those who are otherwise bound together by the strongest ties of love. "Brother will deliver brother over to death, and the father his child." But even in spite of this most painful opposition, a disciple of Christ must persevere. "But the one who endures to the end will be saved." Discipleship might end in martyrdom. But this does not mean that the disciples should rush headlong to such a death. "When they persecute you in one town, flee to the next." Thus persecution might serve the spreading of the Gospel. And as to persecution and opposition, there is also judgment in the end. Now Jesus makes a solemn declaration: "You will not have gone through all the towns of Israel before the Son of Man comes." We must feel our way as to the thought connection and meaning of some of the sayings of Jesus. Evidently Jesus does not mean the second coming directly. It seems to us that we have here a veiled reference to the destruction of Jerusalem; namely, a "coming of the Son of Man." This is not in the understanding of the Jews and according to their wish, but in judgment upon their city and state in vindication of the Kingship that Israel had disowned.[25]

8
Encouragement
Offered
Mt 10:24–31[26]

But Jesus also offers encouragement. There is a source of consolation in the companionship of suffering with the Master. "A disciple is not above his teacher, nor a servant above his master." And if the enemies have gone so far as to call "the Master of the house Beelzebul" (cf. Mk 3:22), how can they of the household expect less? Reference might here be made to the time when pagans heaped the vilest epithets upon the Christians, such as "atheists" and "worshipers of the ass's head." They accused Christians of the most scandalous crimes, Thyestean banquets, Oedipean incest, nightly orgies, child murder, and the like.[27] Tacitus said they were given to "abominable and atrocious superstition" and were guilty of "hatred of the human race."[28] But "have no fear of them," the Lord encouraged them; "for nothing is covered that will not be revealed, or hidden that will not be known." If the apostles and missionaries were to be useful, they would naturally achieve publicity, some of which would bring upon them the hatred and hostility of men. Nevertheless, "what I tell you in the dark, say in the light, and what you hear whispered, proclaim on the housetops." Fearless testimony should not be silenced on account of threatened persecution. And the proper antidote for the fear of man is the fear of God. "A mighty fortress is our God." "Do not fear those who kill the body but cannot kill the soul.

Rather fear Him who can destroy both soul and body in hell." And as to earthly persecutors, why fear at all? Are you not in the hands of the heavenly Father? "Are not two sparrows sold for a penny?"[29] We are surprised that they had any value at all. "And not one of them will fall to the ground"—a beautiful expression—"apart from your Father. But even the hairs of your head are all numbered." Not as if they had been counted once for all, but that "one hair cannot go a-missing unobserved."[30]

This, then, is encouraging. However, not only does Jesus offer encouragement, but He also demands a steadfast defense of the truth. "Everyone who acknowledges Me before men, I also will acknowledge before My Father who is in heaven, but whoever denies Me before men, I also will deny before My Father who is in heaven." And what will be the result of such brave and uncompromising Christian confession? Cannot the Gospel of forgiveness and the new religion of peace propagate itself quietly and peacefully? The question is answered decidedly in the negative. "Do not think that I have come to bring peace to the earth. I have not come to bring peace, but a sword." A surprising statement. Of course, the purpose of Christ's coming was to bring peace. "Peace on earth" the angels proclaimed. But to a great extent, the opposite was the result. Not as though Christ or His Gospel were to blame, but it was due to fleshly strife, which found its expression in the hatred against Christ and the persecutions that followed the introduction of the Gospel. And "there is no more bitter hatred and strife than that due to religious difference. It estranges relatives, disrupts families, and causes lasting enmities between the closest of friends."[32] "A person's enemies will be those of his own household. Whoever loves father or mother more than Me is not worthy of Me, and whoever loves son or daughter more than Me is not worthy of Me." Christ does not prohibit family love, but Christ must be loved more than father and mother or son and daughter. And in the event of a family disruption for the sake of Christ, the Christian must endure the ensuing hatred willingly. Thus a Christian must take up his cross.[33] But there *is* also a reward for loyalty unto death. "Whoever loses his life for My sake will find it."

9
Loyalty Demanded
Mt 10:32–39[31]

In a concluding reminder, Jesus points out to His apostles that in this mission they are His duly accredited and commissioned representatives and messengers. Whatever happens to them happens to Him. The treatment accorded the messenger reverts to his master. "Whoever receives you receives me, and whoever receives me receives him who sent me." The Savior will remember any kindness or courtesy extended to a true prophet (in this case, to a minister or disciple of Jesus because he *is* His disciple) as having been done unto Him. It is in His disciples that Jesus, as well as the Father who sent Him, would be loved and honored. And he that thus esteems and treats them, "truly, I say to you, he will by no means lose his reward."

10
The Proper Attitude to the Ministers of Christ
Mt 10:40–42

After Jesus had finished this discourse, He continued His labors in the usual manner, while the disciples set out two by two on their preliminary missionary

11
The Departure of Jesus and the Disciples
Mt 11:1; Mk 6:12–13; Lk 9:6

tour. The burden of their message was to preach repentance in order that the call of the Gospel might find ready acceptance. They cast out demons and healed the sick "everywhere," thus establishing their authority by miracles and signs. That they used oil, which Israelites regarded as a healing ointment, in some instances (Mk 6:13)[34] does not detract from the supernatural character of these works of healing.[35]

15

THE DEATH OF JOHN THE BAPTIST

MACHAERUS, EAST OF THE DEAD SEA. PROBABLY LATTER PART OF MARCH OR THE BEGINNING OF APRIL, AD 32

The scene changes. It is now about the latter part of March or the beginning of April, shortly before the Passover of AD 32 (Jn 6:4).[1] The spreading fame of Jesus had reached the ears of the tetrarch Antipas. In the north, his dominions embraced Galilee, west of the Jordan, and the Lake of Galilee; in the south, Perea, east of the Jordan. Like his father, Antipas was a builder and had a number of strongholds and royal palaces: Sepphoris, which he made his metropolis, and Tiberias in Galilee;[2] Julias, or Livias, opposite Jericho;[3] and Machaerus, east of the Dead Sea, in Perea. But because it was not until "at that time" that "Herod the tetrarch heard about the fame of Jesus," we suppose that during the nine or ten months of Christ's great Galilean ministry Herod Antipas must have resided in Perea. Most likely, he lived in Machaerus, that fortress on the Arabian frontier that must have required his particular attention. Josephus mentioned it as the place of the Baptist's imprisonment and death.[4] It is quite possible that Antipas fled from the scene of his crime soon after John's death and returned to his own Tiberias on the Galilean Sea. At any rate, when King Herod[5]—the title was freely applied to all Eastern rulers—heard of the ministry of Jesus, he was immediately reminded of his infamous act. Was it possible? Could there be two such remarkable men in the same land and period? Because of a wrong understanding of the prophecy of Malachi (chs. 3–4), some believed Jesus was Elijah come back to life with extraordinary power and mission. According to others, He was one of the prophets of old who had risen from the dead, or at least He was like one of them. But according to Herod himself, with a murder on his conscience and "the Baptist on his brain,"[6] "this is John the Baptist. He has been raised from the dead; that is why these miraculous powers are at work in Him." But

1
Herod's
Superstitious Fears
Mt 14:1–2; Mk 6:14–16; Lk 9:7–9

it was Herod's superstitious fear about the fame of Jesus that caused the first three Gospel writers to record how the "Heaven-enkindled and shining lamp of John the Baptist was suddenly quenched in blood."[7]

2
"It Is Not Lawful for You to Have Her"
Mt 14:3–12;
Mk 6:17–29;
(Lk 3:19–20)

When we last heard of John the Baptist, he was already in prison. There, John received a report of our Lord's wonderful ministry when he sent two of his disciples to Jesus with the question, "Are You the one who is to come, or shall we look for another?" (Mt 11:3).[8] This question led Jesus to that memorable praise of His friend and forerunner (Mt 11:2–15; Lk 7:18–28). Although imprisoned, John had some freedom to communicate with his friends and disciples. He was direct in his testimony. Because he had reproved Herod for his illicit marriage to his brother's wife, "Herod had seized John and bound him and put him in prison for the sake of Herodias, his brother Philip's wife, because John had been saying to him, 'It is not lawful for you to have her' " (cf. Lv 18:16; 20:21). For a subject to openly declare the unlawfulness of a Herodian ruler's marriage as both incestuous and adulterous was certainly dangerous—especially in this case, when the king was called to account because of pet Herodian family sins. John incurred the hatred of Herod's new wife, his former sister-in-law Herodias, the wife and niece of Philip. She was now illegally married to Herod Antipas, who was both her brother-in-law and her half-uncle.

3
The Political Aspect
Mt 14:3–12;
Mk 6:17–29;
(Lk 3:19–20)

Josephus mentioned that politics may also have led to the imprisonment of John. The interesting passage does not give us the real motive, supplied by the evangelists, who let us look behind the scene.[9] Yet Josephus's account at least demonstrates that we are dealing with history in presenting the external and public aspects of the imprisonment and death of the forerunner of Christ.

> John was a good man, who bade the Jews first cultivate virtue by justice towards each other and piety towards God and so to come to baptism; for immersion,[10] he said, would only appear acceptable to God if practiced, not as an expiation for specific offenses, but for the purification of the body, when the soul had already been thoroughly cleansed by righteousness. Now, when all men listened to his words with the greatest delight and flocked to him, Herod feared that the powerful influence which he exercised over men's minds—for they seemed ready for any action which he advised—might lead to some form of revolt. He therefore decided to put him to death before any revolution arose through him. To forestall events appeared far better policy than a belated repentance when plunged in the turmoil of an insurrection. And so, because of Herod's suspicions, John was sent as a prisoner to Machaerus, the fortress already mentioned, and there put to death. The Jews supposed that the destruction of Herod's army was the penalty expressly inflicted upon him of God to avenge John.[11]

Josephus does not mention Herodias. The last sentence refers to the war that followed with Aretas. On the one hand, we agree with the interpretation of Josephus as an outsider and with his ascription of fear to Herod as an additional motive for imprisoning John. But John was not a revolutionary. Herod feared the multitude "because they held [John] to be a prophet" (Mt 14:5). According to the evangelists' statements, Herod had John imprisoned because John declared his marriage unlawful. (Josephus not only calls that marriage unlawful, but he tells us how it came about).[12] On the other hand, John's influence with the multitude might eventually have led to a rebellion, which a suspicious and power-loving member of the Herodian family would not fail to consider.

We remember Herod Antipas as the son of Herod the Great by Malthace, the Samaritan. He had received the tetrarchy of Galilee after the death of his father. The title "king" is applied to him by courtesy only. For by the grace of the Romans, his domain extended merely over Galilee and Perea, east and west of the Jordan. Samaria separated his region from the now Roman province of Syria, to which Judea belonged, with Pontius Pilate as governor. Antipas was married to the daughter of King Aretas of Arabia, but while on a visit in Rome, he lodged with his half brother Herod Philip, the son of Mariamne II, the daughter of Simon the high priest. Antipas enjoyed his brother's hospitality, conspired with Herodias, and made the agreement with her that on his return he would repudiate the daughter of Aretas and wed Herodias. But Antipas's wife heard of the plot and fled to her father. The adulterous marriage with Herodias followed.

4
Herod Antipas
Mt 14:3–12;
Mk 6:17–29;
(Lk 3:19–20)

To keep matters clear, we must disentangle some of the already much-entangled Herodian family relation. There are two Philips. Josephus tells us that this Herod Philip was the son of Herod the Great by his wife Mariamne II, the daughter of Simon the high priest.[13] He is not to be confused with Philip the son of Cleopatra of Jerusalem, who appears as the tetrarch of East Jordan (Iturea). At one time, it seemed that the first Herod Philip, son of Mariamne II, would succeed his father as the sole heir to the kingdom. But because Mariamne II plotted against her husband, the old tyrant altered his will (he had done so before).[14] He left Herod Philip with great wealth but reduced him to a private person, apparently living at Rome. Herod Philip married Herodias, his (half) niece. She was the granddaughter of the ill-fated Maccabean princess Mariamne I (a wife whom Herod the Great had earlier put to death) and the daughter of Aristobulus, one of the sons whom Herod had also put to death. Together, Herod Philip and Herodias (uncle and niece) had a daughter, Salome,[15] now fully grown. She married the second Philip, tetrarch of Iturea, mentioned by Luke (3:1). Philip of Iturea seems to have been the best of the Herods, though by marrying Salome, his (half) niece, he was running true to Herodian form. If keeping track of these two Philips is not confusing enough, here is a puzzle for the curious: Salome married Philip of Iturea; her mother, Herodias, was at first the *niece* of Philip of Iturea. Through Herodias's second marriage to Antipas,

5
Herod Philip
Mt 14:3–12;
Mk 6:17–29;
(Lk 3:19–20)

she became *sister-in-law* to Philip of Iturea. Finally, through the marriage of Salome and Philip of Iturea, Herodias became *a mother-in-law* to Philip!

6
Herodias
Mt 14:3–12;
Mk 6:17–29;
(Lk 3:19–20)

Now, this much-related Herodias of the much-entangled Herodian family had a special grudge against John the Baptist. She "had a grudge against him and wanted to put him to death"; literally, according to the Greek, she had it "in for him."[16] "But she could not [kill him], for Herod feared John" (Mk 6:19–20a). But why this murderous hatred? Because John had condemned her adulterous marriage, which developed as follows. Herodias had first married a private person of great wealth: Herod Philip. But being married to a private person little suited this highly ambitious woman. Her intrigue with Antipas was in harmony with her character, as depicted to us by history. Antipas was her uncle. When Herodias married (Herod) Philip, Antipas also became her brother-in-law. Finally, Antipas became her husband. This intrigue was trouble enough. But there may have been other reasons for Herodias to hate John. Antipas did not have a drop of Jewish blood in his veins.[17] Herodias, through her grandmother Mariamne I, was a Maccabean princess, albeit from the priestly tribe of Levi rather than the Judean house of David.[18] And as a Maccabee—like her grandfather—she certainly had no use for John, who as the forerunner preached the advent of *the King of the Jews.* She also could not control the deep-rooted Herodian suspicions. It was and remained her ambition that her new husband should be the king of the Jews rather than the one John proclaimed.

> She proved to be the curse and ruin of Antipas. First came the murder of John the Baptist. Then came a war with Aretas on account of the daughter whom Herod Antipas had discarded, in which Herod was worsted.[19]

Josephus brings this defeat directly into connection with the death of John the Baptist. And finally, the wild ambitions of Herodias directed Antipas to Rome to solicit the title of king conferred upon her own brother Agrippa I. She failed in her schemes for Antipas, who lost even his own possessions to Agrippa (AD 39) and was banished to Lyons and died in Spain, "where his wife had followed him."[20] But we are a little ahead of our story.

7
Herod's Attitude
Mt 14:3–12;
Mk 6:17–29;
(Lk 3:19–20)

And Herodias had a grudge against him and wanted to put him to death. But she could not, for Herod feared John, knowing that he was a righteous and holy man, and he kept him safe. When he heard him, he was greatly perplexed, and yet he heard him gladly. There was "*one* thing that Herod would not do, and that was to give up his guilty love and to dismiss the imperious woman who ruled his life after she had mined his peace."[21] The feeble, vacillating Herod was between two fires. The people, on the one hand, esteemed John as a prophet who might start a revolution. Herodias, on the other hand, grimly demanded John's death. To these, we may add the little fire that was still burning in Herod's heart. After Herod had put John safely behind strong walls at Machaerus, he no longer had any reason to fear John for political reasons. He heard John often, even gladly. Yet this fearless preacher had many unpleasant things to say, which caused Herod to think twice or thrice, and even kept him from committing further deeds of violence. But oh! the "concentrated venom," the smoldering fire, in that revengeful woman's breast![22]

"But an opportunity came"—not for Herod nor for John, but for Herodias. It was most likely early spring again, just before the Passover. The "opportunity" was either the tetrarch's birthday, as seems most likely, or his accession anniversary, which the Herods kept as a festival according to an old custom.[23] In any event, it was a fit time for a "Herodian Belshazzar feast."[24] It is evening, and the castle is lit up. Lords, courtiers, generals, and Galilean nobles are the invited guests. The merriment is at its height. "The king has nothing new to offer his excited guests, no food, no drink, no fresh excitement, and so let other pleasures begin!"[25] In comes Salome! Josephus supplies her name. She is a princess herself, a daughter of that once noble Hasmonean or Maccabean house,[26] soon to become the wife of Tetrarch Philip of Iturea. After his death and a childless marriage, she would become the wife of Aristobulus, king of Chalcis, and, as it seems, the mother of a king.[27]

Salome enters the banquet of sensual and half-intoxicated guests. She "danced, she pleased Herod and his guests." In the delirium of his drunken approval, like the well-known Xerxes, or Ahasuerus (Est 5:3),[28] the king said to the damsel, "Ask me for whatever you wish, and I will give it to you." The girl, being trained and educated to seek the Herodian interests at all costs, hastened to her mother. "For what should I ask?" This was the moment Herodias had been waiting for; to her, revenge was sweeter than wealth or pride. She did not suggest robes, or jewels, or palaces, or whatever might please a maiden's heart. Quick as a flash, the answer "hisses out":[29] "The head of John the Baptist." And in order to make sure: "Give me at once the head of John the Baptist *on a platter*." Silence chilled the assembly, and our story draws to a close. In the dance, we have an example of the shameless Herodian ways. In the oath, we have an example of "maudlin amorous generosity."[30] In Herodias, we have the vengefulness and determination of a Jezebel to rid herself of a hated person. And even Salome is no better. Her impudent and pert manner in saying the gruesome words almost outdoes her mother. "And she came in immediately with haste to the king and asked, saying, 'I want you to give me at once the head of John the Baptist on a platter.'" The tetrarch was plunged into grief by this request. "Fear, policy, remorse, superstition, and whatever spark of better feeling still remained unquenched under the dense white ashes of a heart consumed by evil passions, made him shrink in disgust from this sudden execution."[31] He was sorry. "But because of his oaths and his guests he did not want to break his word to her." It was an oath that should not have been made and, after it had been made, should not have been kept. Herod wavers. But a despicable pride and fear of man prevails

8
The "Convenient Day"
Mt 14:3–12;
Mk 6:17–29;
(Lk 3:19–20)

9
"The Head of John the Baptist"
Mt 14:3–12;
Mk 6:17–29;
(Lk 3:19–20)

over his better impulses. Only for a moment, he battles with indecision, and then the order is given. The guardsman leaves the hall and enters the dungeon. "No time is given for preparation nor needed."[32] In a few minutes, it is all over. The ax falls. "The head of the noblest of prophets was shorn away,"[33] and Herodias received her "ghastly dish."[34] But even this feature is not overdrawn. In the same chapter where Josephus describes the marriage of Herodias to Herod, he also describes the war with Aretas. In this war, the emperor Tiberius ordered Vitellius, the president of Syria, "either to take [Aretas] alive and bring him in bonds or to kill him and send him [Tiberius] his head."[35]

10
"They Went and
Told Jesus"
Mt 14:3–12;
Mk 6:17–29;
(Lk 3:19–20)

Thus a "ruler's adulterous union was cemented with a prophet's blood."[36] When the disciples of John heard of it, they "came and took the body and buried it, and they went and told Jesus." What a depth of pathos and a wealth of suggestion in the three words "and told Jesus"! The dark deed was done. John's shining light was snuffed out.[37] This spreading news may have reached the Twelve while they were still happily engaged in their primary missionary endeavor. "The apostles returned to Jesus and told Him all that they had done and taught" (Mk 6:30).

16

THE PERIODS OF RETIREMENT AND SPECIAL TRAINING OF THE TWELVE

THE FIRST RETIREMENT

In Districts around Galilee. Probably early spring AD 32

AUC	782	783	784	785	786
AD	29	30	31	32	33
Age of Jesus	30	31	32	33	34
Passovers		I	II	III	IV

Both the imprisonment and the death of John the Baptist form important turning points in the life of Jesus. John's imprisonment is followed by Jesus' great Galilean ministry.[2] And John's death introduces a period of retirement and gradual withdrawal of Jesus from public labors. He devotes His time to the instruction of the Twelve, which finally terminates in His last journey to Jerusalem and His death on the cross.—The last year of the life of Jesus had come. Outwardly, it would seem, Jesus was at the height of His popularity. But His popularity did not rest upon the recognition of His true mission. He must either accept the false popular messianic expectations and begin the struggle for political freedom or refuse the popular view and meet the reaction that this refusal must inevitably bring. Therefore, Jesus begins to act in view of His approaching death. The "dread intelligence of His forerunner's sad death reached Him,"[3] presumably at Capernaum. The returning Twelve reported on their first missionary endeavors, after which He suggested a brief period of repose such as was not possible for them to enjoy at Capernaum. "'Come away by yourselves to a desolate place and rest a while.' For many were coming and going, and

1
Retirement to a Desolate Place
Mt 14:13–14;
Mk 6:30–34;
Lk 9:10–11;
Jn 6:1–3[1]

they had no leisure even to eat." In the words of the inspired preacher, "For every-thing there is a season, and a time for every matter under heaven" (Ec 3:1), even for a brief and well-earned pastoral vacation. The news of the death of Jesus' fore-runner deeply moved Him, and He felt the need for solitude and rest. Although we notice (here and later) that He withdrew from the territory of Herod, He did not fear personal violence, for on the very next day He returned to Capernaum (Jn 6:22, 24). Instead, Jesus was attempting to escape the crowds, which in their excite-ment might look to Him as the avenger of John. They would create a disturbance for Herod and cause a disastrous crisis in the ministry of Jesus.[4] As St. John notes, it was near the Passover season, when pilgrims filled all the roads and villages. If He stayed in the public eye and joined the pilgrims on their journey to Jerusalem,[5] His presence would almost certainly have led to a false messianic demonstration. Instead, Jesus took the Twelve down to the beach[6] for the purpose of quietly setting out on an excursion to a place of seclusion and rest.[7] Matthew and Mark tell us that Jesus and the disciples withdrew to a "desolate place" without naming it. Luke says it was Bethsaida, which means "fish house." However, Luke goes on to note that the feeding of the five thousand took place "in a desolate place" that lacked lodg-ing and food. So the "desolate place" was somehow associated with Bethsaida but was also out in the countryside. Jesus and the disciples visited a secluded and unin-habited little plain of rich silt soil, now covered with the green grass of early spring. This fact is especially noted because this is about the only time of the year when grass covered this region. Around the northeastern edge of the delta, the land rises to the hills.[8] To this uncultivated, "desolate"[9] place, the little vessel steered its course with its "freight of weary and saddened hearts."[10] Although they departed secretly, they did not pass unobserved, nor did they remain unknown. As the vessel slowly glided over the waters toward its goal, the people "ran there on foot from all the towns and got there ahead of them." As a result, there was already a throng at the landing place when the prow of the vessel touched the sandy shore. The quiet rest that Jesus had planned was spoiled. Sadly, this was a miracle-seeking crowd, not a Savior-seeking one. But even so, when Jesus saw so many people, the vision of Ezekiel flashed into His mind (Ezk 34:1–15; also Nu 27:17). He "had compassion on them, because they were like sheep without a shepherd." And though they were "following Him, because they saw the signs that He was doing on the sick," Jesus lost no time in preaching to them "many things," especially about the true nature of the kingdom of God. In addition, He "cured those who had need of healing."

2
"Where Are We to Buy Bread, So That These People May Eat?"
Mt 14:15–18;
Mk 6:35–38;
Lk 9:12–13; Jn 6:3–9

We picture the scene as follows. After ministering to the multitudes at the shore of the lake immediately upon His landing, Jesus "went up on the mountain, and there He sat down with His disciples." Thus, He tried to accomplish the purpose for which He had come. A few hours passed.[11] Already, the vast Safed heights to the northwest threw their gigantic shades across the landscape. The day began to wear away. Looking up, Jesus saw that the people to whom He had ministered after His landing had not dispersed. A still greater multitude was ascending the hill. We remember that "the Passover, the feast of the Jews, was at hand," and that travelers filled the roads. Approaching pilgrims most likely asked why there was an unexpected gathering in a "desolate place." They soon learned that Jesus was on the nearby hill. And once more, a multitude besieged the Savior. He lifted up His eyes and said to Philip, "Where[12] are we to buy bread, so that these people may eat?" The question had a purpose. "He said this to test him; for He Himself knew what He would do." Undoubtedly, Jesus intended to arouse loving concern for the people in the hearts of the disciples. After a brief twilight, the wandering crowds would suddenly find themselves hungry and in the dark. Jesus probably addressed Philip because of the character of this disciple. It seems that Philip was a matter-of-fact person (Jn 14:8) and more inclined to demand visible evidence than to rely on unseen resources.[13] While this conversation was going on, the disciples began to grow uneasy and to whisper to one another. Moving up from where they sat, they said to Jesus, "This is a desolate place, and the hour is now late. Send them away to go into the surrounding countryside and villages and buy themselves something to eat." But to this suggestion, Jesus replied, "They need not go away; you give them something to eat." The disciples then asked, "Shall we go and buy two hundred denarii worth of bread and give it to them to eat?" But quick-figuring Philip swiftly pointed out the impossibility of supplying the need. "Two hundred denarii[14] worth of bread," he said, "would not be enough for each of them to get a little."[15] This figure was probably what their common treasury contained at the time. Philip settled the matter of financial resources. But were there any provisions on hand? "How many loaves do you have? Go and see." Jesus thus prevented anyone from charging that the subsequent miracle was a fraud. Andrew volunteered the information about a little boy[16] with five barley loaves and two fish. "But this he said in a despairing way and, as it were, to show the utter helplessness of the suggestion which occurred to him."[17]

Yet the reply of Andrew suggested what Jesus might do. "Jesus said, 'Have the people sit down.'" Swiftly, the disciples, puzzled but obedient, arranged the multitudes in groups by hundreds and by fifties on the thick green grass. And then, standing in the midst of those who would forever after remember Him as Teacher, Healer, and Host, Jesus took the loaves and fish. He raised His eyes to heaven, gave thanks, and blessed the loaves. Then He broke them into pieces and began to distribute them as well as the fish to the disciples, and they in turn to the multitudes, as much as everyone desired.[18] "It was a humble, but a complete and sufficient and to hungry wayfarers a most delicious meal."[19] Out of His abundance, the Lord supplied the bread of life in unlimited measure. And when all were amply satisfied, He

3
The Feeding of the
Five Thousand
Mt 14:19–21;
Mk 6:39–44;
Lk 9:14–17;
Jn 6:10–13

proved to His disciples the extent and reality of the miracle. He also taught them a lesson about wastefulness, even after His miraculous power had supplied such wonderful plenty, saying "gather up the leftover fragments, that nothing may be lost." For "infinite resources" do "not justify waste."[20] The arrangement by fifties and hundreds easily showed that Jesus fed about five thousand men, besides women and children.[21] And yet, the disciples gathered twelve large baskets[22] of fragments.[23]

4
The Attempt to
Make Jesus King
Mt 14:22–23;
Mk 6:45–46;
Lk;[24] Jn 6:14–15

This miracle overwhelmed the minds of those present. Surely, here was a Messiah after their own heart! They began to whisper to one another that this must undoubtedly be "the Prophet who is to come into the world" (cf. Dt 18:15). This was "the beginning of that reign of earthly abundance which in their carnal desires and in a false interpretation of messianic promises they thought the prophets had foretold."[25] So great was their enthusiasm that they proposed among themselves to take Him by force, if necessary, and make Him a king. They could not imagine a better king than one who could effect cures, supply food, and provide prosperity for all! With Him at their head, endowed with the power of the eternal God, which He had just displayed, He could lead them on. He would rid them of the detestable Herods and conquer Rome. They dreamed sweetly of the Golden Age and the reign of God. Here was the time for instant action. The miracle confirmed them in their false messianic hope. Yet this "brief blaze of a falsely founded popularity"[26] did not deceive Jesus. He was aware of the danger of mob passion and instantly made His decision. First of all, He had to remove the disciples, who were only too prone to share the popular conception, for their own good. He ordered them, well-nigh compelled them, to go down to the beach and sail in the direction of Bethsaida,[27] or ultimately to Capernaum. The disciples left their Master in the midst of this outburst of unprecedented popularity. They may also have feared crossing the lake alone in the night on account of a former experience (Mt 8:24), especially, as again seemed likely, in view of an approaching storm. But "immediately He made His disciples get into the boat," with the promise, it seems, to meet them on some point along the shore later on.[28] The disciples departed. And now, gradually and gently, Jesus proceeded to dismiss the crowd. In the gathering dusk, all but the most persistent had streamed away. Based on the incidents of the following day (Jn 6:22, 24), we conclude that some lingered.[29] But leaving them, Jesus "went up on the mountain by Himself to pray. When evening came,[30] He was there alone." Again, a decisive hour had come. Once before, He had spent the solitudes of a night in lonely prayer. That was the night before He chose His associates or apostles for the proclamation of the Kingdom He was about to establish (Lk 6:12–13). Far different were His feelings on this night when He ascended the rocky heights. The Passover was near. The events of the next Passover unfolded themselves before His eyes. John the Baptist had been foully killed. The public was enraged. Now the attempt to make

Him king. Of a truth, He *was* a King! In due time, He would present Himself to the nation as Israel's promised King. But He had to refuse the crowd's attempt to crown Him this day.

Hours pass, and a storm begins to sweep down the barren hills. It is in the fourth watch of the night—that is, between three and six in the morning.[31] The disciples, hugging the shore, rowed furiously in the teeth of a gale. After eight hours of hard labor, they had not rowed more than three or four miles,[32] "and Jesus had not yet[33] come to them." While they were distressed with toiling at the oars and were tossed up and down on the perilous sea, there was not, as they probably had hoped,[34] any sign or signal of Jesus. With the surface of the sea like a boiling caldron and in the face of winds that were against them, the disciples could not possibly make a landing. They were experienced fishermen, well acquainted with the dangerous moods of this hill-bound, yet deep-lying[35] inland sea. We can imagine their alarm over the plight in which they suddenly found themselves.[36] But "man's extremity is God's opportunity."[37] Jesus was neither ignorant of, nor indifferent to, the plight of His disciples. It was He who had directed them into the boat. From the mountain, He perceived their distress. Even now, He was probably on the road running along the shore. But leaving the road, He turned down to the surf, walked out to the sea, and, contrary to the laws of nature, was *"walking on the sea."*[38] The disciples saw a gleam in the darkness and a figure of one who to them looked like Jesus. However, they could not believe that it was He—treading upon the waves of the sea (cf. Jb 9:8), calmly walking as if He meant to pass them by. They cried out in terror and rushed to the conclusion: an illusion, a ghost! If they would have recalled the crossing to Decapolis (Mt 8:26), they would, it seems, immediately have connected the Stiller of the storm with this Traveler on the sea. But here, we learn that, even in its repetition and familiarity, a miracle strikes renewed terror in the sinful heart. Only when Jesus spoke to them did their fear subside. Above the roar of the raging sea and through the darkness of a storm-tossed night came the well-known, the calming and cheering voice: "It is I. Do not be afraid."

With their terrors stilled and Jesus' identity established, the disciples were ready to take Jesus into the boat. But Peter's impetuous joy could not wait for his Master's approach. "Lord, if it is You, command me to come to You on the water."[39] The request was foolhardy and presumptuous but true to the character of Peter. The Lord bade him, "Come." And Peter actually left the boat and walked on the water.[40] "But when he saw the wind," (that is, the effect of the wind in a boisterous wave[41]) "he was afraid." It is one thing to view the storm from the deck of a ship and another to see it when one is in the midst of the waves. Then he began to sink and cried out, "Lord, save me." When his faith failed for walking, he forgot how to swim.[42] Immediately, Jesus stretched forth His hand and caught the struggling disciple with

5
Jesus Walking
on the Sea
Mt 14:24–27;
Mk 6:47–50;
Jn 6:16–20

6
Peter Walking
on the Water
Mt 14:28–33;
Mk 6:51–52; Jn 6:21

the gentle rebuke: "O you of little faith, why did you doubt?" Jesus satisfied Peter's yearning love and rebuked his overconfidence. At that moment, too, the storm was instantly stilled. And so, the One dry and the other dripping, they climbed into the boat.[43] After a night of distressing toil, the alarmed disciples were somewhat composed. But the effect of the miracle that they just witnessed still left them amazed. The significance of the miracle of the loaves had not yet entered their hearts. And now a few hours later, in rapid succession, three other miracles were added to their experience: Jesus and Peter walking on the water and the stilling of the storm. No wonder "they were utterly astounded." Despite doubting and a faltering faith, they saw that they were face-to-face with divine omnipotence. This caused them to fall at Jesus' feet with Nathanael's former confession on their lips: "You are the Son of God!" (Jn 1:49). Amid the rippling waves of a calmed sea and in the gentle light of an increasing Passover moon, Jesus was the captain of the elements and the possessor of all power in heaven and earth (Mt 28:18). His puzzled but joyful crew quickly reached land and moored the boat on their familiar shores.

7
Reception at Gennesaret
Mt 14:34–36;
Mk 6:53–56

It seems that the landing was not made at Capernaum, but just a little to the south, toward Magdala, in a district called the Plain of Gennesaret.[44] No sooner, however, was Jesus on the beach than He was recognized. Rapidly, the report spread that He was back. Soon, the usual crowds came to be healed, streaming down the rocky paths and along the shores from Magdala, Capernaum, Chorazin, and all the villages and towns. There were patients everywhere—some walking, others carried by sympathizing friends and deposited at His feet in streets and marketplaces.[45] So great was the patients' faith in Him and so great also His power that, if they only touched the fringe of His robe, they were healed (cf. Mk 3:10).

8
Revolutionists Seeking Jesus
Jn 6:22–24

What happened in the meantime to those "hot-headed nationalists" who wanted to make Jesus their king?[46] We remember[47] they remained all night in the desolate place in the hope of linking up with Jesus when He descended from His retreat in the hills. When dawn came, they were bewildered at His nonappearance. They had seen Him dismiss His disciples at dusk. They had perhaps seen glimpses of Him as He climbed the hill. They had also noticed that the wind was against them and that no boat had left the shore except the one that the apostles had entered. Still, when morning dawned, there was no trace of Jesus, neither on the hill nor on the plain. Meanwhile, a number of boats from Tiberias[48] had arrived "near the place where they had eaten the bread." They were perhaps driven to the shore by the same gale that had hindered the opposite course of the disciples on the night before.[49] They hired these boats. Going in search of Jesus, they at last found Him teaching on a Sabbath Day,[50] it seems, in the synagogue at Capernaum.

9
"You Are Seeking Me . . . Because You Ate Your Fill of the Loaves"
Jn 6:25–31

Here, they met Jesus with "Rabbi, when did You come here?" This was an expression of natural surprise. "At the same time the *when* includes the *how*."[51] To them, the whole matter was a mystery. In His answer, Jesus did not mention walking on water, which in no way concerned them. He directed His reply to the attitude of those who sought Him with a carnal heart. The fact of the matter was that the miraculous feeding had missed its purpose. They sought Him not for what He was, their Savior, but for what they wanted Him to be, a bread king, now that they had eaten the loaves and enjoyed a good meal. He did not want them to follow Him, since they merely sought physical satisfaction. Their efforts should be directed to a higher cause. "Do not work for the food that perishes, but for the food that endures to eternal life, which the Son of Man will give to you. For on Him God the Father has set His seal"—that is, confirmed and authenticated Him by great miracles as the Messiah (Jn 10:38). He was the giver of nourishment for life everlasting. These words of the Lord impressed at least some of the crowd. They were anxious to labor for this food and asked, "What must we do, to be doing the works of God?" Jesus answered, "This is the work of God, that you believe in Him whom He has sent." But since He was referring to Himself, they demanded that He produce His credentials. It seems that to them the miracles of the loaves[52] did not prove His Messiahship. What miracle would convince them and enable them to become believers in Him? Now, for instance, there was Moses. For forty years, he fed a whole nation in the desert. "Our fathers ate the manna in the wilderness" (cf. Ex 16:4), which the psalmist called bread from heaven (Ps 78:24). Again, they betrayed their desire to have a leader who would above all feed their bodies.

But at once, Jesus "leads His listeners to loftier regions than those of historical connection."[53] Jesus solemnly points out to them[54] that it was not Moses who gave the bread in the wilderness, but God. The heavenly Father is even now offering them the Bread of God "who comes down from heaven and gives life to the world." However, with their minds still attached to earthly things, they say, "Give us this bread always."[55] Jesus explains, "I am the bread of life; whoever comes to Me shall not hunger, and whoever believes in Me shall never thirst . . . whoever comes to Me I will never cast out." Then He gives an outline of His Savior-mission: He does the Father's will by coming into the world, He will rise again, and He will come again for judgment on the Last Day. But the people looked on with bewildered faces and objecting hearts. Quickly abandoning the objective argument, they became personal. How could He say that He had come down from heaven? "Is not this Jesus,[56] the son of Joseph, whose father and mother we know?"[57] Ignoring the personal reference, Jesus tells them to stop muttering and complaining. Nevertheless, it is true that He is the heaven-sent Way and Life. No man comes to the Father except by the Son.[58] And "no one can come to Me unless the Father who sent Me draws him." Coming to Christ is being drawn to Him by the Father. Certainly, "your fathers ate the manna in the wilderness." But what happened? They died. But here is the Bread

10
The Sermon on the Bread of Life
Jn 6:32–59

that comes down from heaven, which one receives by faith. "Truly, truly, I say to you, whoever believes has eternal life. I am the bread of life"; or "If anyone eats of this bread, he will live forever. And the bread that I will give for the life of the world is My flesh." He will give His body as a sacrifice for the salvation of the world.— At this point, the Jews[59] broke out in angry debate. What does He mean? "How can this man give us His flesh to eat?" Jesus refers to receiving Him and partaking of Him and of His work in faith. Thus, He is the bread of life. And "unless you eat the flesh of the Son of Man and drink His blood, you have no life in you." Not as the fathers ate manna and died, but "Whoever feeds on this bread will live forever."

11
"This Is a Hard Saying"
Jn 6:60–65

This, then, is a very brief outline of Jesus' discourse on the bread of life, the famous and probably final sermon Christ delivered in the synagogue of Capernaum. But its effect was very disappointing. It puzzled even His larger circle of friends and followers.[60] "When many of His disciples heard it, they said, 'This is a hard saying; who can listen to it?'" The expression "eating His flesh and drinking His blood" was on their minds. They did not understand, nor would they believe. That is why the saying was hard for them. Were the disciples of Jesus offended? Was the language of their Master too mysterious? Let them be patient. They will find it easier to believe that He came down from heaven when they see Him return to heaven. What then? Will they be more scandalized? Then they will be convinced that He is God. Of course, these are matters of faith. Sadly, Jesus knew that some in the larger group of disciples would not believe, yes, and there was one among the Twelve who would even betray Him.

12
"Do You Want to Go Away as Well?"
Jn 6:66–71

In sheer disgust, large numbers turned away. They had so ardently followed Jesus. They waited for Him through the hours of the night and then had sailed back to find Him at Capernaum. They now left Him forever. It was not that they could not understand. Now, they understood very well that Jesus was not what they wanted Him to be or at least did not declare Himself to that effect. It was the loaves of a political king that they wanted rather than the bread of everlasting life. The Galilean campaign to make Jesus king collapsed because He would not meet the people's messianic expectations. Turning to the Twelve, Jesus asked them, "Do you want to go away as well?" It was a test. Ever ready and on the alert, Simon Peter acts as spokesman for the Twelve: "Lord, to whom shall we go?" There is none other, none to whom we might apply. "You have the words of eternal life, and we have believed, and have come to know,[61] that You are the Holy One of God." It was a wonderful confession. And it was the confession not only of Peter, but also of every believer in Christ. At that moment, however, Jesus' heart was saddened. At the very moment when Peter wonderfully confesses that Jesus is from God, we also have a truly human touch of the Son of God. So many of His disciples had turned away. And there was disloyalty even among the chosen Twelve. "Did I not choose you, the Twelve? And yet one of you is a devil." Strong words and true, yet tender. For though Jesus uttered the warning, He did not reveal the identity of the betrayer. But based on subsequent events, the evangelist explains that Jesus spoke of Judas, the son of Simon Iscariot,[62] being "one of the Twelve."

A delegation of lakeside Pharisees arrives in Jerusalem. They make a report to the Jewish Council. It concerns the widely known and, in their minds, overly popular Galilean Prophet. They must investigate. Although the Jerusalem authorities could not make any arrests in Galilee, and although Jesus was safe as long as He stayed out of Judea, yet their power and influence was great throughout the Jewish land.[63] It would be their special duty to safeguard Jewish religion and morals, to be on the lookout for the Messiah, and to pass on any prophetic and messianic claims.[64] At any rate, "wise-looking and bearded scribes and Pharisees from Jerusalem"[65] make another appearance on the Galilean shore (cf. Mk 3:22).[66] It was probably shortly after the Passover of AD 32,[67] while Jesus was still at Capernaum before His journey to the north and west. They came here once before, after the raising of the widow's son at Nain (Lk 7:11–17). At that time, they regarded Jesus' miracles, in particular the casting out of demons, as the work of Satan. They said Jesus was his special representative—almost his incarnation (Mk 3:22). This time, they needed to carefully investigate the great miracle of the feeding and its effect on the popular mind as well as an act of unheard-of impiety. It concerned Jesus' indifference toward the sacred traditions of the elders, particularly eating with unwashed hands. They soon caught some of the disciples defiling themselves by eating bread with unclean hands.[68] This was probably the real offense[69] to them—not the miraculous feeding and the outburst of natural enthusiasm but the failure of the host to supply water or to insist upon the prescribed ceremonial washings. At any rate, this prophet must be watched. They would warn the public of His growing influence and, if possible, counteract it. With a "swelling sense of self-importance at the justice of their reproach,"[70] they came to Jesus with the question, "Why do Your disciples break the tradition[71] of the elders? For they do not wash their hands when they eat."

At some time after the days of Ezra, Jewish leaders added customs to the Old Testament canonical writings. These were called the traditions of the elders. Later Jews regarded them as having equal authority with the Old Testament. These traditions included (1) the oral laws of Moses, supposed to have been given by the great lawgiver in addition to the written laws; (2) the decisions of various judges, which had become precedents in judicial cases; and (3) the interpretations of great teachers.[72] In the time of Jesus, these traditions had grown into a maze of laws and ordinances touching every phase of Jewish life and conduct. Not only did the Pharisees prescribe washings, especially before partaking of food, but "all the Jews do not eat unless they wash[73] their hands" (Mk 7:3). Now, they based these rules

13
Scribes and Pharisees from Jerusalem
Mt 15:1–2; Mk 7:1–2

14
Eating with Unwashed Hands
Mk 7:3–4

about washing the hands, as well as the food that came from the market and their cups and containers, on ordinary cleanliness and sound ideas of good health. But the tradition of the elders had exaggerated this practice to such an extent that to eat without washing was likened to the lowest kind of vice.[74] Although the law of Levitical purification was in the background (Lv 15:11), the fear of defilement had even extended to precise washings[75] of cups, pots,[76] vessels of wood,[77] utensils of brass, and tables.[78] And in the face of these ordinances, the disciples dared to eat with unwashed hands!

15
Jesus' Reply
Mt 15:3–9;
Mk 7:5–13

The attack was clever. Either Jesus must defend what they asserted to be a sin, or the disciples must change their ways. Although they accused the disciples, Jesus Himself was their target. If He would defend the disciples, as He naturally would, they could accuse Him of contempt for sacred institutions. And if He would correct them, His standing as a prophet would be discredited, and their own battle would be won. But Jesus was not "overawed by the attacks of His sanctimonious critics."[79] In effect, He replies, Let your charge stand for the present. But here is a more serious matter: Suppose that, in some instances, time-honored traditions are disregarded for the sake of the commands of God. What about *you* who deliberately set aside the commandments of God for the sake of your miserable traditions?[80] For God[81] said, "Honor your father and your mother" (see Ex 20:12; Dt 5:16), and "Whoever reviles father or mother must surely die" (see Ex 21:17; Lv 21:9). But you gloss over the command. Instead of giving to father or mother, a man could simply give or designate the sum needed or intended for their support to the sacred treasury or for religious purposes. Then one pronounces the magic word: it is " 'Corban'[82] (that is, given to God)." The vow exempts one from further obligation and the burden of support. By this and other evasions of duty (Mk 7:13), their human traditions voided the divine Word. One might well apply the prophecy of Isaiah (Is 29:13) to such hypocrites,[83] obliterations of divine injunctions: "This people honors Me with their lips, but their heart is far from Me; in vain do they worship Me, teaching as doctrines the commandments of men."

16
A Puzzling Parable
Mt 15:10–11;
Mk 7:14–15

By this time, a multitude had gathered in the background. They were very much interested in the discussion because the people had been "trained to look up to the Pharisees as little gods."[84] Inviting them to step closer, Jesus said, "Hear Me, all of you, and understand: There is nothing outside a person that by going into him can defile him, but the things that come out of a person are what defile him."[85] At first glance, there seems to be no connection, but the point is that in their external ceremonialism the Pharisees had altogether overlooked the real issue. As long as they considered true morality a symposium of outward acts, they had not touched the spirit of the Law.

Jesus dismissed the people and returned to His home at Capernaum. Here, the disciples quickly informed Him of the indignation that His words caused. At the same time, Peter confessed the ignorance of the Twelve, including his own, as to the meaning of the concluding parable. Jesus expressed His indifference about the indignation of His enemies. Don't worry about the Pharisees! "Every plant that My heavenly Father has not planted will be rooted up. Let them alone." They are hopeless. "They are blind guides. And if the blind lead the blind, both will fall into a pit" (cf. Lk 6:39). As to His parable, however, Jesus expressed His surprise at their ignorance. "Are you also still without understanding?" Do you not grasp that what is swallowed into the stomach is afterward cast out from the body? But the things that proceed out of the mouth come from the heart. It is they that defile man. "For out of the heart come evil thoughts, murders, adultery, sexual immorality, theft, false witness, slander," and other sins. "These are what defile a person. But to eat with unwashed hands does not defile anyone."

17
The Parable Explained
Mt 15:12–20;
Mk 7:16–23

17

THE SECOND AND THIRD RETIREMENTS

IN THE REGION OF TYRE AND SIDON AND IN THE DECAPOLIS

Probably spring and early summer AD 32

Jesus counter-charged that the traditions of the scribes and Pharisees transgressed the holy Law of God. So there was no doubt as to the report that their incensed delegation would render in Jerusalem. It was only too clear that Jesus had become indifferent to the Pharisaic institutions. From their own observation and according to reliable testimony, charges would include disregard of fasting (Mk 2:18), Sabbath infringements (Mk 2:24), disreputable association (Lk 7:39; 15:2), affiliation with the devil (Mk 3:22), insurrectionary tendencies (Jn 6:15), and the "monstrous impiety"[1] of eating with unwashed hands (Mk 7:2). But as long as Jesus stayed in Galilee, He was safe from actual arrest. For although the influence of the Council was great, its judicial power did not extend to the tetrarchy of Herod Antipas.[2] Therefore, "after this Jesus went about in Galilee. He would not go about in Judea, because the Jews were seeking to kill Him." Not that He feared for His life, but it was not yet time to present Himself in the national capital as the promised Messiah and to expose Himself to the hostility of the judicial authorities. Yet occasion arose for Him to depart even from Galilee. This was not, however, because He feared Herod after the death of John the Baptist or because the people would make Him king. If Herod really wished to arrest Him, he could easily have done so. For on the very next day, Jesus returned, landing in Gennesaret, and then went to Capernaum attended by crowds, where He taught publicly in the synagogue. And even later, during the Perean ministry, He was in Herod's jurisdiction and was not molested.[3] Nor, as some suppose, did He now leave Galilee because He feared the local Pharisees, for they had no power to harm Him. They could do nothing beyond

1
Reason of
Retirements
Jn 7:1

annoy Him and discourage those who followed Him by threats of excommunication. The reason of His withdrawal from Galilee was threefold: to find seclusion and rest, to escape for a time the popular attention paid Him, and to devote Himself to the instruction of His disciples.

2
Phoenicia
Mt 15:21; Mk 7:24

According to our chronology, it was the spring of AD 32[4] when Jesus and His disciples turned their backs on the lake in a journey toward[5] Tyre and Sidon.[6] From more than six hundred feet below sea level, the travelers mounted the winding and rocky paths of the western hills until nearly two thousand feet above the Mediterranean Sea they felt the spring breezes whipping their tunics about their knees. Before them in the distance, they beheld the wide expanse of the great Western Sea. And below them, from Mount Carmel on the left, for about one hundred and fifty miles to the north, stretched out the long, tawny coast of ancient Phoenicia. Here dwelt the proud descendants of that portion of the original population of the land of Canaan (Gn 10:15), which Israel never fully subdued. In their long history, these pirating seafarers and outstanding traders of the ancient world, securely barricaded behind the sheltering ranges of the Lebanon Mountains (cf. Jgs 18:7),[7] were for the most part proudly independent. At different times, however, the ancient Assyrian, Babylonian, and Persian powers made them their subjects. But after their stubborn resistance to Alexander and the period of the Seleucids of Syria, they eventually passed—like the Punic kingdom of Africa, which they had founded—into the all-embracing power of Rome. Although originally Semitic, their language became largely Greek in the time of Christ,[8] as inscriptions and coins testify. We remember that it was a Phoenician king, Hiram of Tyre, who contributed to Solomon skilled labor and provided cedar and fir trees for the building of the house of God (1Ki 5:18).[9] Likewise, a Phoenician widow at Zarephath (Sarepta) fed Elijah the Tishbite (1Ki 17:9). Also, the wicked Jezebel was a Phoenician princess, who introduced the worship of Baal and Astarte into Hebrew life and contributed to the downfall of Ahab (1Ki 16:31). The Phoenicians were daring seamen. They ventured to push out of sight of land in their voyages and sailed through the Pillars of Hercules into the unknown sea. They were the founders of a number of colonies, the most famous of which was Carthage on the northern coast of Africa, which was for a long time the persistent rival of Rome, which finally crushed them. Popular history books credit them with a number of great inventions and discoveries: glass; the famous and precious Tyrian purple dye, obtained from a shellfish, that became a symbol of royalty; the practical application of astronomy in navigation; and the introduction of the alphabet to the Western world, if not even the invention of it.

3
The Syrophoenician
Woman
Mt 15:22–24;
Mk 7:25–26

Jesus went to Phoenicia for seclusion and rest. But even in this Gentile country, His presence became known, although the little company of wayfarers concealed themselves in a house. A woman whose daughter was being tormented by an evil spirit came to Him, fell down at His feet, and said, "Have mercy on me, O Lord, Son of David;[10] my daughter is severely oppressed by a demon." By language, this woman was a Greek. By birth, she was a Canaanite, a heathen. By allegiance, she was a Roman subject, a Syrophoenician of Syria, as distinguished from a Phoenician of Carthage. By faith, she was a firstfruit of that harvest that was to spring up in Phoenicia, in Greece, in Carthage, and in Rome.[11] Jesus understood the woman, "but He did not answer her a word." Certainly, a most strange behavior. This role of "indifference must have cost Him an effort."[12] Even among the disciples, it created surprise. When at last her persistent pleading annoyed them, they asked Jesus to aid her and "send her away, for she is crying out after us." But even this intercession was of no avail. Addressing His disciples, but probably speaking loud enough for the woman to understand Him, He said, "I was sent only to the lost sheep of the house of Israel." Thus, the Lord had instructed His disciples on their first missionary venture: "Go nowhere among the Gentiles and enter no town of the Samaritans" (Mt 10:5–6). In His state of humiliation, His prophetic activity was limited to Israel, according to the flesh. After He would be exalted, He would draw *all* people to Himself (Jn 12:32). Of course, there were exceptions, for instance, the woman of Samaria (Jn 4:7–26) and the centurion of Capernaum (Mt 8:5–13). But how unkind, even unfeeling Jesus' words sounded in the woman's ears!

And what was the effect of this seemingly ungracious refusal? Did she who had so confidently sought Him out with a grief-torn heart now leave Him in a boiling rage? No. She thought about the agony of her tortured child. She now "came and knelt before Him, saying, 'Lord, help me.'" She was not interested in any herd-dividing classification of sheep as to which did and which did not belong to the house of Israel. She was only interested in one thing: "Lord, help me." And it was now the Lord's turn to decide the issue. Would He be coldly indifferent to that heart-touching appeal? He replied to her earnest entreaty, but it seemed that He added insult to disdain. "Let the children be fed first, for it is not right to take the children's bread and throw it to the dogs." So He called her a dog! But the word is not as harsh as it sounds, for the expression used by the Lord refers to canine household pets rather than to the dogs on the street.[13] Jesus may have borrowed this illustration from the room where the gathering assembled. Even then, a child may have surreptitiously tossed a morsel to the household pet. His answer might have chilled the mother's soul, but in the allusion she quickly finds an object to which her heart might cling. "Yes, Lord," she agrees. For[14] "even the dogs under the table eat the children's crumbs."[15] Yes, I am a Gentile dog. So be it. But in many households, dogs are part of the family. The children indeed come first, but immediately after the children is the dog. If at the Lord's table she could not enjoy the position of a child, she could at least share in the portion given to dogs. The Lord is conquered. The successful

4
"It Is Not Right to Take the Children's Bread" Mt 15:25–28; Mk 7:27–30

struggling of this unhoused Gentile sheep brings to mind the wrestling of Jacob with God: "I will not let You go unless You bless me" (Gn 32:26). Not one moment longer did the Lord now prolong the agony of her suspense.[16] "O woman," He exclaimed, "great is your faith! Be it done for you as you desire." What a contrast between the native "traditionalism" that He had just experienced in the house of Israel and this "simple faith on pagan soil"![17] "And her daughter was healed instantly."

5
Retirement to Decapolis
Mt 5:29; Mk 7:31

Again, Jesus moved out on the trail, and we regret that we have no fuller details of this northern trip. As we picture it, for twenty-five miles He followed the road along the sea-washed shore. He crossed the Leontes and passed through Sarepta (Zarephath), where Elijah was entertained by the widow (1Ki 17:9). The hills rise to ever greater heights until they reach the Lebanon on the right and the Mediterranean on the left. He reached the bustling port of Sidon, famous throughout the Roman Empire for its exquisite glass and its purple dye. And then, turning to the right,[18] He probably returned by passing over the Lebanon ranges. He crossed the upper waters of the Jordan and then went southward through the territory of Philip. Once more, He reached the Galilean Sea, but this time on its eastern or southeastern shore. This we infer from the notice of His crossing over to Dalmanutha (Mk 8:10) or Magdala[19] and from there back to Bethsaida to the other, or northeastern, side (Mk 8:13, 22). It was this country that He had previously visited during the Gadarene journey, after the parables by the sea.[20] This country was called the Decapolis, or the Ten Cities. But the name is a somewhat loose geographical term. It refers to a number of urban communities, all except one on the eastern side of the Jordan, which after the conquest of Alexander became predominantly Greek. Wedged in between the tetrarchies of Philip and Antipas, this league of cities formed an independent political combination under the governor of Syria.[21]

6
"Ephphatha!"
Mt 15:30–31;
Mk 7:32–37

So Jesus returned from what seems to be the longest single journey in His public ministry. This journey took Him out of the confines of the ancient *Erets Israel*,[22] which He apparently had not left since the flight into Egypt shortly after His birth. We know nothing of this journey except the story of the Syrophoenician woman, but we are undoubtedly not far from the truth when we say that He employed the time in instructing the apostles for their future work. We also know nothing of His whereabouts in the Decapolis after His return. We suppose that He sojourned offshore in the rolling uplands,[23] east or southeast of the Galilean Sea. But while the evangelists have left us in the dark as to these details, the multitudes knew where He was to be found. Where Jesus was, even in the out-of-the-way and semipagan Decapolis, His fame had already gone before. Crowds gathered and, showing their chief interest, brought their sick to Him, and He healed them. Among them was a deaf man with a speech impediment, whose healing is briefly described. "They begged Him to lay His hand on him"; that is, to heal him, as symbolized by that universal gesture that illustrates the transmission or conveyance of blessing. Immediately, Jesus took him aside from the multitude, perhaps to impress upon him the greatness of the blessing he was to receive. Then "He put His fingers into his ears," probably one finger in each of the afflicted organs. Then "after spitting" (that is, moistening His finger), He "touched his tongue," pointing out also the afflicted ears and indicating the source of the blessing. He might have healed the man with one word, without these strange actions. But He made it plain to the man that "all help must and will come from Him."[24] And prayerfully "looking up to heaven, He sighed" in deepest sympathy with the sufferer. At last, He called out in His native Aramaic, "Ephphatha!"—that is, "Be opened." Immediately, the gates of the man's hearing were opened, and the fettering strings of his tongue were loosed. And since the purpose of Christ's healing was not to gain publicity as a miracle-monger but to bring those healed and their companions to faith in Him as the Savior, He charged the man and his friends to "tell no one" (cf. Lk 5:14; Mt 12:16).[25] But, as usual, the man and his companions disregarded the command, and all hope for seclusion was now at an end. "The more He charged them, the more zealously they proclaimed it." The result was that a great multitude followed Him to the summit of a hill, brought to Him their lame, blind, mute, crippled, and many others, and laid them down at His feet. And He healed them all. Filled beyond measure with astonishment and admiration, the semipagan population of the Decapolis could not tear themselves away from the beloved Jesus. Glorifying the God of Israel, they said, "He has done all things well. He makes the deaf hear and the mute speak."

Three hot summer days had passed, and the multitude was still encamped around the sun-scorched hill.[26] Jesus had pity on them and told His disciples, "I have compassion on the crowd because they have been with Me now three days and have nothing to eat. And I am unwilling to send them away hungry, lest they faint on the way." Jesus manifestly has the intention to perform a miracle again. But the disciples may have thought it would be presumptuous to suggest that He repeat the miraculous feeding.[27] They asked, "Where are we to get enough bread in such a desolate place to feed so great a crowd?" And Jesus replied, "How many loaves do you have?" A hurried search brings the answer: "Seven, and a few small fish." Again, as at the feeding of the five thousand, the people are commanded to sit down, but this time on the bare ground.[28] Again, there was a supply, small, but at any rate a supply. Again, Jesus blessed and broke the loaves and presented them with the fish so that the disciples could distribute them. Again, the miraculous multiplication of a small supply for the satisfaction of many. Again, and this time unbidden, the disciples gather up the remaining fragments. They filled seven large baskets[29] after four thousand people, excluding women and children, had been filled. Quietly and

7
The Feeding of the Four Thousand
Mt 15:32–38; Mk 8:1–9

orderly, not with that noisy exhibition of carnal excitement that marked the former miracle, Jesus peacefully dismissed a grateful and rejoicing multitude.

Immediately afterward, Jesus boarded a boat with His disciples for a brief return to Galilee. They landed some place on the Plain of Gennesaret near Magadan (Magdala), the home of Mary Magdalene (Lk 8:2), and an otherwise unknown Dalmanutha.[30] But barely had Jesus set forth on the shore when the Jewish leaders began to attack Him. As if watching for His return, the local Pharisees came with a demand for a sign from heaven,[31] this time in conjunction with their traditional rivals and enemies, the Hellenistic Sadducees. We do not know just what kind of sign they wanted—a meteor, thunder, a lurid light, the Messiah dropping down from heaven,[32] or something of that sort. They probably did not know themselves, except that they were not yet satisfied with the credentials God the Father gave Him, which showed He was the Messiah. Until now, the unbelieving and worldly minded Sadducees paid little attention to Jesus. Their interest was not religion and orthodoxy but wealth and power. They were the liberals of the day, who had rather "advanced" views about angels, devils, and life after death. They contented themselves with material things, things pertaining to this life. And in dealing with these, they were successful. They represented the priestly and ruling classes and counted the high priests in Jerusalem as well as the Herodian rulers among their members.[33] As long as Jesus limited His teaching to strictly spiritual matters, they were not much interested. But the movement to make Jesus king and the report of His sermon on the bread of life seem to have made them suspicious of Jesus. They were probably also concerned about their high-priestly rule and their own Herodian hero. In their minds, Jesus threatened to disturb the Sadducean idea of the Messiah, who was already here.[34] He also did not conform with the Pharisaic ideal of a Messiah, who was still to come. Therefore, although the Sadducees were not usually on friendly terms with the Pharisees, they now made common cause against Jesus. While the Sadducees doubted Jesus' ability to produce the desired sign, the Pharisees, for reasons of their own and in an effort to discredit Him before the people, "shrewdly counted on His repeated refusal to their presumptuous and unspiritual demand" (Jn 2:18; 6:30; Mt 12:38; Lk 11:29).[35] Again the request for a sign! It caused Jesus to sigh "deeply in His spirit." As if His miracles were not signs! He denounced them for their hypocrisy: being able to discern the face of the heavens but being blind to the signs of the time. "When it is evening, you say, 'It will be fair weather, for the sky is red.' And in the morning, 'It will be stormy today, for the sky is red and threatening.'" But they were blind to the notable phenomena that characterized their day—John the Baptist, Jesus' appearance, and the many signs that indicated the fullness of time. If these signs did not suffice to prove that He was in truth the Prophet who was to come, the Messiah, then nothing else would. And Jesus did not mince words as He addressed the vile and wicked brood: "An evil and adulterous generation seeks for a sign, but no sign will be given to it except the sign of Jonah" (cf. Mt 12:38–39; Lk 11:29). He refused to give them any other sign than the one that would only increase their hatred against Him—His resurrection from the dead. This was the greatest of all signs after the type of the prophet Jonah. Jesus would set it before them; they would harden their hearts. Having sternly pronounced this judgment upon them, Jesus abruptly turned His back and departed. After a brief stay, the great Galilean Prophet again left Galilee. Boarding a ship, He departed in the direction of Bethsaida (Mk 8:22), to the "other" (Mk 8:13; Mt 16:5), the northeastern, side.

18

THE FOURTH RETIREMENT, INCLUDING THE TRANSFIGURATION

INTO THE TETRARCHY OF PHILIP

Probably summer AD 32

After Jesus' returned from the Decapolis, He had a short stay in Galilee. While He was sailing with a heavy heart and with His mind still filled with the rejection, which caused Him to seek another place of retirement, He warned His disciples: "Watch out; beware of the leaven of the Pharisees[1] and the leaven of Herod." For different reasons, the two chief exponents of Jewish thought—the Pharisees with their extreme legalism and the Sadducees with their worldly interests—had just combined against Him. He warned His disciples against the teachings of both. The Pharisees, in a hypocritical manner, pretended to be strict in their mode of worship. Yet they transgressed the commandments of God. The Sadducees rather boldly cast off the skin of Pharisaic hypocrisy and introduced the religion of the flesh. But the disciples were dense as usual. Due to their sudden departure from Galilee, they had altogether forgotten to take bread, "and they began discussing with one another the fact that they had no bread." In His reply, Jesus complained about their little faith.[2] The disciples were always thinking about bread and its provision instead of the Kingdom and its extension. And with such little excuse! Where were their eyes to see, their ears to hear, their minds to remember, and their hearts to understand? Even if His reference had been to physical bread, would there have been any cause for worry? " 'When I broke the five loaves for the five thousand, how many baskets full[3] of broken pieces did you take up?' They said to Him, 'Twelve.' 'And the seven for the four thousand, how many baskets full[4] of broken pieces did you take up?' And they said to Him, 'Seven.' " After this explanation, it finally dawned on

1
The Leaven
of the Pharisees and
of the Sadducean
Herodians
Mt 16:5–12;
Mk 8:14–21

their minds that the Master was warning them not against the leaven of bread, but against the doctrine of the Pharisees and Sadducees.

2
The Blind Man
at Bethsaida
Mk 8:22–26

As we picture it, the little vessel in which Jesus and His disciples had embarked passed northward by the synagogue of Capernaum and past Chorazin, the scene of many unrecorded miracles (Mt 11:21). Then, following the curving shores to the east and crossing the inrushing waters of the Upper Jordan, they landed at Bethsaida Julias, in the territory of Philip. This was near the place where the first feeding of the multitudes had taken place. On their arrival, a blind man was led to Jesus with the request that He would touch him and restore his sight. It seems that the man had not been born blind, because the shapes of persons and trees were still vaguely impressed upon his memory from the time when he still had the gift of sight. In His cure, the Lord proceeded in a manner similar to that employed in the healing of the man who was deaf in the Decapolis (Mk 7:32–37). In order to avoid a run made on Him for cures, He took the blind man by the hand and led him out of town. There He moistened his eyes with spittle, laid His hands upon him, and touched his eyes.[5] Then He asked him whether he could see anything. The Lord did not have to cure him by stages, but this process impressed upon him that his cure was absolutely dependent upon the Lord. The man, looking up, answered that he could "see people, but they look like trees, walking." In other words, he saw something distorted: people who looked like trees, except that they were walking. Jesus thereupon touched his eyes again, and at once his eyesight was completely restored. Thus, the Lord shows that divine omnipotence may manifest itself in various ways. But in any event, whether the cure was gradual or instant, whether effected mediately or immediately, it must not lend itself to the creation of cheap sensation.—The Lord was withdrawing for rest and did not wish to be disturbed. The cured man was therefore dismissed with the express command to proceed directly to his house, "Do not even enter the village."

3
Caesarea Philippi
Mt 16:13–20;
Mk 8:27–30;
Lk 9:18–21[6]

From the deep-lying level of the Sea of Galilee, Jesus proceeded north past the marshy shores of Lake Huleh, the ancient Waters of Merom, to the borders of Caesarea Philippi in Gaulanitis, the capital city of the tetrarch Philip. In thirty miles, an ascent is made from nearly seven hundred feet below sea level to three thousand feet above the Mediterranean Sea. It is in this region where one of the largest fountains in the world is found. It pours down the valley as the river Leddan,[7] forming one of the four sources of the Upper Jordan. In ancient times, the Sidonians colonized this matchless spot of natural beauty under the name of Laish and it served as a center of the worship of Baal, their Phoenician god. However, after the Danites conquered it (Jgs 18:7, 29), they changed its name to Dan, and it formed the northern limit of the Land of Israel as remembered in the familiar phrase "from Dan to Beersheba" (Jgs 20:1; 1Sm 3:20; etc.). Here Jeroboam set up an image and instituted the worship of the golden calf (1Ki 12:28–29). About three miles to the east, at the southeast base of Mount Hermon, there is another famous fountain. At the foot of a cliff, a stream over thirty feet wide gushes out to form another source of the Jordan. After the conquest of Alexander, the mystery of this wonder of nature called out the worship of the Greeks. They believed this was the abode of the god of nature and of his dancing and laughing nymphs. Thus a temple to the worship of Pan was erected. One can still see there a Greek inscription in one of the niches on the face of the cliff, "Pan and his nymphs inhabit this spot."[8] On account of the worship of Pan, in spite of the subsequent history, the name of Banias still clings to the place. When the Romans followed the Greeks, they gave this territory to Herod, who built a temple on the ancient site and named Caesarea in honor of his patron, Emperor Caesar Augustus. After Herod's death, the district passed over to his son, the tetrarch Philip of Iturea. He made Caesarea the capital of Gaulanitis. After rebuilding and beautifying the city, he added his own name and called it Caesarea Philippi to distinguish it from the Caesarea on the Mediterranean Sea.[9]

It was in this delightful district, however, as we suppose, without entering into the capital of Philip itself, that Jesus sought seclusion and repose.[10] Although He was not blind to the beauties of nature, He had other matters on His mind. These He had just laid before His heavenly Father in solitary prayer. Having concluded His prayer, He beckoned His disciples and asked them two questions. The outcome of all His work depended on their answers. "Who do people say that the Son of Man is?" It was not for His sake, but for the sake of the disciples that Jesus asked the question. The disciples reported the popular reaction frankly. In spite of the bitter attack of the popular teachers, the Pharisees, and the rising opposition of the priestly rulers, the Sadducees, public opinion was favorable toward Jesus. However, Jesus did not fulfill the political expectations of the general public. They considered Him only the precursor of the Messiah, not the Messiah Himself. Echoing the opinion of the superstitious Herod, some held that He was John the Baptist come back to life (Mt 14:2; Mk 6:14). Some heard in His "mighty utterances the thunder-tones of a new Elijah."[11] Others believed Him to be the prophet Jeremiah, whom God resuscitated to bring back to His people the lost Urim, the sacred fire, the vanished ark, or something of that sort (2Macc 2:1–8).[12] "Or one of the prophets." That was about as far as the public cared to go. A prophet, but not *the* Prophet. They thought well of Him, but not well enough.

"But who do you say that I am?" That was the real question that the Lord's first question introduced. Again (cf. Jn 6:69), and with the correct word at the proper time, Peter acts as spokesman of his associates: "You are the Christ, the Son of the living God." This was the only and the correct answer, a wonderful confession, freely and frankly made.[13] In His reply to Peter, Jesus expresses pleasure and joy. "He would

4
"Who Do People Say
That the Son of Man
Is?"
Mt 16:13–20;
Mk 8:27–30;
Lk 9:18–21

5
The Confession
of Peter
Mt 16:13–20;
Mk 8:27–30;
Lk 9:18–21

have no one call Him Christ under a misapprehension, but He congratulated Peter in His right conception of what the title meant."[14] "Blessed are you, Simon Bar-Jonah!" In solemn address, the use of Peter's full name comes spontaneously. But He places the credit for this blissful knowledge where it rightly belongs. "For flesh and blood has not revealed this to you, but My Father who is in heaven."[15] After this explanation, Jesus continues: "You are Peter,[16] and on this rock[17] I will build My church,[18] and the gates of hell shall not prevail against it." Jesus does not say that His Church is to be built on the person of Peter, but upon "this rock." "Peter-like faith admits into the kingdom of heaven."[19] Upon this confession the Church is built. And in recognition of this faith Christ confers upon Peter and upon *all* (cf. Mt 18:15–18) that share this faith a special distinction: "I will give you the keys of the kingdom of heaven, and whatever you bind on earth shall be bound in heaven, and whatever you loose on earth shall be loosed in heaven." The possession of keys is an evidence of power and authority both to admit and to exclude. Thus also in the public exercise of the Great Commission given the Church, in the preaching of the Gospel and in the administration of the Sacraments, there is an authorized and effective bestowal of divine favor upon all who gratefully accept the proffered grace of God. Yet, there is also a pronouncement of judgment upon all those who reject it. But these things are still in the future. The time had not yet come for Jesus to fulfill His purpose by fully advancing His messianic kingdom. Serious implications might arise if the disciples prematurely were to begin to call Him Christ and proclaim Him as the Messiah. And, therefore, for the present, Jesus imposed strict silence upon them.

6
Christ Foretells His Death and Resurrection
Mt 16:21–23;
Mk 8:31–33;
Lk 9:22

It was still news to the disciples, but it was not news to their Master, that Christ must first suffer before He could enter into His glory (Lk 24:26). Jesus, therefore, makes a second, and this time unmistakable, announcement to this effect, to be followed by others in the course of time.[20] In order to free the disciples from false ideas about the Messiah and equip them to guide others in a correct appraisal of His redemptive work, Jesus began to show them "that He must go to Jerusalem and suffer many things from the elders and chief priests and scribes,[21] and be killed, and on the third day be raised." There is no mistaking the Lord this time. An outline of the whole Passion story is given, including place, persons, suffering, and death. Although there is as yet no notice of the manner[22] of death, the resurrection on the third day is clearly foretold. The dark prophecy was understood, at least that part that spoke of Jerusalem, of suffering and death. But Peter deemed the tragic outcome decidedly improbable and unnecessary. He therefore presumed to take Jesus in hand: "Far be it from You,[23] Lord! This shall never happen to You." Thus, Peter has turned prophet. A minute ago he was speaking under inspiration from heaven, but now under inspiration from another direction. However, he did not get far; he would have upset God's whole plan for the redemption of the world, including his own. He would place a stumbling block[24] in the way of Christ. This was a temptation to Jesus. His own beloved disciple had become a tool of Satan to defeat the purpose of His coming into the world. With a flash of sudden indignation, the Lord administered to him a crushing rebuke: "Get behind Me, Satan! You are a hindrance to Me. For you are not setting your mind[25] on the things of God, but on the things of man" (Mk 8:33; cf. Mt 4:10). Peter's views about His Master's messianic office were still decidedly carnal.

Certainly Peter meant well. But in his vehement protest against what he thought was the wrong course of Jesus to attain the goal of Messiahship, he clearly revealed the faulty nature of his own messianic ideal. Jesus must correct this fault in His followers, in the Twelve, in Peter, in all. Even in His retirement there were always some people in the background (Mk 8:34). Jesus called these followers into His presence and told them and His disciples that the messianic kingdom He was establishing did not consist in glory to its heralds and distinction to its chieftains. Rather, "if anyone would come after Me, let him deny himself and take up his cross[26] and follow Me." He who aims only at the life in this world will lose the life in Christ. And he who will cheerfully give up everything in this life, if need be, for the sake of the Gospel and of Christ will find true and everlasting life in the Redeemer. For, in the end, "what will it profit a man if he gains the whole world and forfeits his own soul?" and thus forfeit eternal salvation? "Or what shall a man give in return for his soul?" What purchase price may he substitute for his soul that he may have eternal life? There is none. And this is not mere talk about the hope of eternal life as well as the terrible possibility of judgment, as Jesus shows in His concluding remarks. Even as the Son of Man "must suffer many things" so shall there also be a coming of the Son of Man in glory, accompanied by angels. What if this adulterous and sinful generation that hears the Gospel, but is ashamed to confess it, should see the Son of Man turn on His rejecters as avenging Judge? But why think of the distant judgment at the end of the world? A sign, a complete vindication, of His rejected claim is near at hand. "Truly, I say to you there are some standing here who will not taste death until they see the kingdom of God after it has come with power." Three would clearly see a manifestation of Christ's glory at the transfiguration and many would see after His resurrection. Many would clearly see a prelude to His final judgment, at the capture of Jerusalem and the destruction of the temple in AD 70.

After six[27] days, about the events of which the records are silent, Jesus took the three disciples who belonged to the inner circle[28] "and led them up a[29] high mountain" to pray. The three apostles chosen were Peter, James, and John—the "man of rock"[30] and the two "Sons of Thunder" (Mk 3:17). They were to witness the Lord's greatest glory on earth as well as His deepest degradation in the Garden of

7
Taking Up the Cross with Jesus
Mt 16:24–28;
Mk 8:34–38; (9:1);
Lk 9:23–27

8
The Transfiguration
Mt 17:1–8;
Mk 9:2–8;
Lk 9:28–36a

Gethsemane. The name of the mountain is not recorded, and the ancient tradition that caused the erection of three churches on Mount Tabor in Galilee in commemoration of the great epiphany is evidently wrong.[31] We are left under the impression that Jesus had not departed from the neighborhood of Caesarea Philippi,[32] and hence the mountain that He ascended with those three disciples must have been one of the slopes of the gigantic, snow-capped Mount Hermon,[33] whose "glittering mass, the only snow-clad mountain in the Holy Land, is visible as far south as the Dead Sea."[34] And if Mount Hermon furnished the scene, then it is one of the few summits directly to gain the scriptural epithet of "the holy mountain" (2Pt 1:18).[35] It was in an evening hour,[36] as we suppose, that the Lord singled out His companions for a vigil of meditation and prayer far above the misery and toil of the world and to prepare Himself for the approaching outcome in Jerusalem that He had just foretold. While their Master knelt and prayed, the disciples, it seems, slept. After a long ascent, during which they had inhaled the thin mountain air, sleep was natural for these men of simple habits.[37] Thus, the first part of the celestial visitation was probably missed. It was most likely towards dawn that their Master, still praying, was transfigured or transformed[38] before their half-dazed eyes. No, it was no dream or deception, but a glorious reality that, as Peter himself testified, caused them to become suddenly wide awake and eyewitnesses of the majesty of Jesus (2Pt 1:16–18). Through the form of a servant they beheld the glory of His divinity (Php 2:6). Their Master was still there, but "the appearance of His face was altered," yes, it "shone like the sun." His whole figure was bathed in light; His clothes were glistening white, "as no one[39] on earth could bleach them." Only the choicest words descriptive of dazzling brilliance and only the best possible comparisons can portray to us, though but imperfectly, the celestial luster. Nor was this all. "Behold, there appeared to them Moses and Elijah, talking with Him." Both of these former prophets and now residents of heaven, whom they probably recognized by the nature of their conversation,[40] stood before them with glorified bodies (cf. Jude 9; Dt 34:6; 2Ki 2:11).[41] They heard them talking with Jesus. As God had preserved the bodies of these prophets from decay, so the body of Jesus would not see corruption (Ps 16:10; Ac 2:27–31). They had been zealous for the Lord and His Law, one as the lawgiver, the other as a fiery reformer. But neither of them could stop Israel's transgression. Now they were talking to Jesus of His "exodus"[42] at Jerusalem and the redemption that He was to accomplish.

9
"This Is My Beloved Son"
Mt 17:1–8;
Mk 9:2–8;
Lk 9:28–36a

The disciples were seized with nameless terror (Mk 9:6). And still they were overjoyed with the vision that never before had fallen on the sight of mortal man. They had heard "heaven's converse and had tasted angels' food."[43] They gladly would have held what now seemed to escape their grasp. They did not know how to express their ecstatic longing for the continuance of what they had seen and heard as well as their willing readiness to do their part. Peter volunteered: "Master,[44] it is good that we are here.[45] Let us make[46] three tents,[47] one for You and one for Moses and one for Elijah." But why three tents? One tent would have been better for meeting and conversing with Jesus and the prophets. Evidently, "he did not know what to say." His suggestion was well meant, but the whole scheme showed that it was not for Peter to

> construct a universe for his personal satisfaction. He had to learn the meaning of Calvary no less than that of Mount Hermon. Not in a cloud of glory or in a chariot of fire was Jesus to accomplish His work, but with His arms outstretched on a cross; not between Moses and Elias, but between two thieves who were crucified with Him on either side.[48]

No answer was awarded to Peter's pleasant dream. But while he was still speaking, a luminous cloud overshadowed them as a token of God's presence. A voice from the cloud repeated the message spoken at the Baptism of Jesus: "This is My beloved Son, with whom I am well pleased."[49] Thus God confirmed the confession Peter made a few days before, that Jesus was indeed the Messiah, the Son of the living God. But the manner and the circumstance of the divine revelation caused the disciples to "hide their faces in the grass."[50] Meanwhile the shining faces, the celestial figures, the dazzling robes, the luminous cloud, and the heavenly voices passed away. Jesus, ever kind and gentle, stepped forward, touched His fear-struck disciples, and encouraged them with reassuring words: "Rise, and have no fear." And as, at first startled, they looked suddenly up and around, "they saw no one but Jesus only."

It was, as we suppose, "the early dawn of another summer's day"[51] when the Master and His intimate friends made a silent descent to join the disciples whom on the previous evening they had left in the valley below. The glory that the three disciples had witnessed filled their hearts and minds. At last, Jesus broke the silence with the command to "tell no one the vision,[52] until the Son of Man is raised from the dead." "Visions are for those who are prepared for them."[53] The other disciples were but partially fit for them. There is no benefit in relating visions to those who are not able to receive them. The three to whom the Lord entrusted this vision should ponder over it in the depth of their hearts. To announce it to their fellow disciples might only tend to awake "jealousy and their own self-satisfaction. And besides, until the Resurrection it would add nothing to the faith of others and might only confuse their conception of what was to be Christ's work on earth."[54] The disciples heeded the Master's command, although they could probably attach no meaning to His allusion. It was only among themselves that they could ask each other "what this rising from the dead might mean." So entire was their submission that they did not even dare to ask Jesus for enlightenment regarding this personal reference. And there was another thing on their minds. They had seen Elijah; Elijah had come. They knew that Jesus was indeed Christ, the Lord; but now Elijah was

10
"Tell No One"
Mt 17:9–13;
Mk 9:9–13;
Lk 9:36b

also gone! "Then why do the scribes say that first Elijah must come?" According to Jewish legends, Elijah was to bring back the pot of manna and the rod of Aaron that were placed before the ark of covenant, but that had disappeared in the destruction of the temple of Solomon. He would settle quarrels, restore all things, and the like, in preparation for the Messiah. And then the Messiah Himself "should suffer many things and be treated with contempt." How does that agree with what the Jews expected? Jesus replied that Elijah should indeed first come, and he truly had come, not, however, in harmony with their false views, but in accord with the word of the prophet Malachi (Mal 3:1; 4:5; Lk 1:17; Mt 11:10). "And they did to him whatever they pleased." Suffering is the appointed lot of the faithful servants of God: Elijah at the hands of Jezebel, John at the hands of Herod, and Jesus, too, must suffer. "So also the Son of Man will certainly suffer at their hands."[55] The latter reference was still a dark mystery to them, but now they understood that Jesus spoke to them of John the Baptist.

11
The Demoniac
Whom the Disciples
Could Not Heal
Mt 17:14–18;
Mk 9:14–27;
Lk 9:37–43a

When Jesus and His inner circle rejoined the other disciples, He saw, even from a distance, that there was an unusual commotion. An excited crowd, scribes among them, probably from a neighboring synagogue, gathered with a heartbroken and disappointed father and his unhealed son around the "diminished band."[56] They brought a boy for healing who was mute and suffered from attacks of epilepsy that were "supposed to become aggravated with the phases of the moon,"[57] and who also suffered severe attacks of intermittent diabolical possession. In Jesus' absence, the father appealed to the disciples for help; and they, it appears, willingly attempted, but failed to heal the boy. As a result, the scribes sharply questioned them. They were always on the trail of Jesus and now were at hand to taunt His disciples in their hour of weakness and at the same time to cast insinuating aspersions upon the power and authority of the absent Lord.[58] At that moment, Jesus appeared. When the people saw Him, they greeted Him with joyful surprise.[59] Most likely, as reflecting the popular mind, they sympathized with the harassed disciples. Now, sensing the dramatic, they confidently hoped that the Master Himself would accomplish what they had failed to do. "What are you arguing about with them?" Jesus sharply asked of the scribes. But before the question could be answered, the man who had given the occasion for all this came forward and implored Jesus on his knees: "Lord, have mercy on my son!" The description of the affliction of his son reveals a pitiful case. First of all, the lad was mute. Added to this there were the symptoms of epilepsy, spasms, foaming at the mouth, grinding of the teeth, suicidal mania, and a final stage of atrophy and motionless stupor. At times the attacks were worse than at other times, which was popularly ascribed to the influence of the moon. But on the whole—and here the father rightly diagnosed the affliction—it was a case of demon possession. And then he told how he had come in search of Jesus, but having found only the nine disciples, he spoke to them "to cast it out, but they could not." Now I have brought to You "my only child" (Lk 9:38). The whole scene grieved Jesus at heart. "O faithless and twisted generation," He exclaimed, "how long am I to be with you?" This complaint included all "the malicious scribes, the miracle-seeking multitude, and His own faltering disciples."[60] Not that He had grown weary of well-doing, but He was grieved because the leaders would not accept Him as the Prophet that He was; because the people regarded Him as a prophet such as they hoped He was; and because the disciples, although He had given them power over demons (Mt 10:8), had lacked the faith to exercise it. He then directed the father to bring his boy closer to Him. But no sooner had the lad's eyes fallen on Jesus than he was seized with another attack of violent convulsions. The devil tore him grievously, so that "he fell on the ground and rolled about, foaming at the mouth." Jesus asked the father: "How long has this been happening to him?" The father answered: "From childhood. And it has often cast him into fire and into water, to destroy him. But if You can do anything, have compassion on us and help us." *If* You can? An ugly word! The leper said: "Lord, if You will" (Mt 8:2). Jesus replied that it was not a question of His power, but of the father's faith. " 'If you can!'[61] All things are possible for one who believes." The unhappy father accepted the correction. Humbled, but not discouraged, he cried out with agony in his soul: "I believe; help my unbelief!" These memorable words have been uttered by millions of souls who are painfully conscious of the weakness of their faith and then beseech the Lord to strengthen it. That cry of the father could not remain unanswered. Meanwhile, the crowd had become greatly excited and came running, no doubt eager to learn whether Jesus would succeed where His disciples had failed. Turning to the poor sufferer, Jesus "rebuked the unclean spirit, saying to it, 'You mute and deaf spirit, I command you, come out of him and never enter him again.' "[62] A wild cry and a final convulsion followed these words. And then the boy lay on the ground "like a corpse," and many said, "He is dead." But Jesus took him by the hand and, amid the exclamations of amazement at the majesty of God on the part of the people, restored him completely cured to his father.

Then Jesus retired to a nearby house. The puzzled disciples asked: "Why could we not cast it out?" Frankly, Jesus told them: "Because of your little faith."[63] At their first missionary venture, they had gone forth joyfully, preaching the Gospel, casting out demons, and healing everywhere (Mk 6:13; Lk 9:6). But here they had lacked faith. And had Jesus not just told the father of the demoniac boy: "All things are possible for one who believes" (Mk 9:23; cf. Mt 17:20; Php 4:13)? With the most solemn assurance, "Truly, I say to you," Jesus points toward faith like a grain of mustard seed (Mt 13:31; Lk 17:6), that is, sincere faith unmixed with doubt (Mt 21:21). Such faith could even say "to this mountain," towering Mount Hermon: " 'Move

12
"Faith like a Grain of Mustard Seed"
Mt 17:19–21;
Mk 9:28–29

from here to there,' and it will move, and nothing will be impossible for you." Mighty words. Faith apprehends God and His immeasurable power. "All things are truly ours if Christ is ours."[64] And who is going to limit God's power with respect even to the greatest physical barriers? This does not mean that all believers should now proceed to try out their faith, as it were, in the performance of miracles. They have not that command. But the disciples did have the authority and power. Still they failed, and the Lord tells them the reason why. Referring to the case at hand, He says: "This kind," that is, the demon that possessed the youth, "cannot be driven out by anything but prayer."[65]

19

THE CLOSE OF THE GALILEAN MINISTRY

A FEW DAYS IN GALILEE

Avoiding, as far as possible, public attention.
Probably late summer AD 32

Returning from His retreat in the utmost borders of the Land of Israel at Caesarea Philippi, our Lord seems to have crossed westward through the hills and valleys of Upper Galilee, avoiding public attention and the main thoroughfares. This journey would take Him once more, and, as far as we know, for the last time, to Capernaum. The purpose of this trip was not public teaching, as is stated: "They went on from there and passed through Galilee. And he did not want anyone to know." The reason given is: "For He was teaching His disciples." His one purpose was to instruct the Twelve and especially to prepare them for the approaching crisis.

Here, Jesus gave another (and we may call it a third) clear and emphatic announcement of His death and resurrection.[1] This one truth should sink into the hearts and minds of His disciples, that the consummation of their Master's messianic career would not be that kind of glory for which they so ardently hoped, but death and resurrection. They had heard that saying before. But they could make nothing of those mysterious words of doom, to be followed by a resurrection on the third day. They did not understand, and yet they were afraid to ask. They were exceedingly sorry and yet preferred to live on in the hope that their Master was under a spell of hallucination.

Again, and for the last time, it seems, Jesus had returned to His familiar Capernaum. Upon arrival at His home, He was usually sought by sufferers in need of help. This time, He was sought, though indirectly, by tax collectors. "From the Mount of Transfiguration to money demands that one is too poor to meet, what a

1
Returning to Galilee
Mt 17:22a;
Mk 9:30–31a

2
Another
Announcement
of Death and
Resurrection
Mt 17:22b–23;
Mk 9:31b–32;
Lk 9:43b–45

3
The Temple Tax
Mt 17:24–27;
Mk 9:33a

descent!"[2] Ever since the giving of the Law, every male in Israel from twenty years upwards, whether rich or poor, was required to contribute to the temple treasury an annual sum of one half-shekel (Ex 30:11–15) or an Attic double drachma.[3] This tax yielded vast sums. The purpose of the contribution was the purchase of all public sacrifices, that is, of those that were offered in the name of the whole congregation of Israel, such as the regular morning and evening sacrifices.[4] Even after the destruction of the temple, Vespasian ordered that the Jews pay this tribute wherever they were, which he used for the temple of Jupiter Capitolinus in Rome.[5] The time for the payment was from the fifteenth to the twenty-fifth of Adar, before the Passover, about the month of March.[6] The usual mode of procedure was to have local collectors gather all the contributions of one community and then send them to Jerusalem, where at the time of the Passover the payment was legally made. Quite naturally, delinquency was followed by a visit from those whose duty it was to receive the shekels. Jesus and Peter had not yet paid the tax. Nothing is stated about the other disciples. There was no payment recorded in Capernaum. Neither had Jesus been in Jerusalem for the Passover in spring, having at the time probably been on the borders of Tyre and Sidon. There was only the one consideration: Did He, after the manner of some famous rabbis, claim exemption for Himself?[7] At any rate, the local officers considered it their duty to inquire. They approached Peter, in whose house Jesus presumably dwelt, and asked him, "Does your teacher not pay the tax?" Without hesitation, Peter replied, "Yes." To the best of his knowledge, such was the custom of Jesus. Not as if the Redeemer of all souls was to pay a ransom for His own soul (Ex 30:12); but "He paid for what He did not owe to save them which owed and could not pay,"[8] as well as for reasons that will shortly appear.

4
"From Whom Do Kings of the Earth Take Toll or Tax?"
Mt 17:24–27;
Mk 9:33a

When Peter came into the house, there was no chance for him to explain or to inform his Master of the question that the taxman had just asked. Jesus prevented him[9] by addressing him first with "What do you think, Simon? From whom do kings of the earth take toll[10] or tax?[11] From their sons or from others?" The purpose of the question might have baffled Peter, but on the face of it, there was but one answer: "From others." Certainly a king, if he is at all worthy of his name, would tax his subjects, and not the members of his household, for the maintenance of his palace. Jesus replied: "Then the sons are free." As to Christ's payment of the temple tax, had not Peter himself confessed: "You are the Christ, the Son of the living God" (Mt 16:16)? And the temple in Jerusalem, was it not the house of God? Why, then, should the Son be taxed for His Father's house? And in the New Testament, even Peter and all followers of Christ would be sons, though in a different sense, and as such they could not be legally required to pay the temple tax. And if payments were made, it should not be a matter of positive obligation, but of free and cheerful giving. But, it is doubtful whether the tax collectors and others would have understood this principle by which Christ could justly refuse to pay temple tax. And there was another consideration: the matter of giving offense. "However, not to give offense to them,[12] go to the sea and cast a hook[13] and take the first fish that comes up, and when you open its mouth, you will find a shekel. Take that and give it to them for Me and for yourself."[14] The miracle is taken so absolutely for granted that its fulfillment is not even recorded.[15] Peter went out with hook and line, drew up a fish, opened its mouth, and took out of it a coin, a stater,[16] exactly equivalent to two double drachmas, sufficient for himself and for his Master.

Already on the way from Caesarea Philippi to Capernaum, the disciples had been disputing with one another as to who was to occupy the highest place in the temporal kingdom that they believed their Master was about to establish. They finally believed that He would soon reveal Himself as the Messiah of their hopes. In anticipation of the approaching fulfilment of their carnal desire, the ambitions of human nature began to assert themselves. Jealousy rose against those who, they feared, would be unduly preferred. Perhaps it was the misunderstood address to Peter about the keys of the Kingdom or the fact that only three of the Twelve had been privileged to be with the Master on the Mount of Transfiguration, not to mention the most recent occurrence, the prominence given to Peter in the payment of the temple tax. It was not until His arrival in Capernaum that Jesus took His muttering disciples to task. " 'What were you discussing on the way?' But they kept silent." However, their deep silence was in itself an eloquent confession of their sinful ambition. They were ashamed to confess, and yet they were anxious to hear what Christ would say. "Who is the greatest," that is, among us,[17] "in the kingdom of heaven?" Jesus called a little child in order to teach them that only those who are like little children—trustful, humble, unambitious—could enter the heavenly kingdom. He set the child in the midst of them, folded him in His arms, and warned them: "Truly, I say to you, unless you turn and become like children, you will never enter the kingdom of heaven." The point of comparison is not sinless innocence, but ingenuousness and simple humility. And how highly the childlike spirit is valued in the judgment of God is revealed in the words: "Whoever humbles himself like this child is greatest in the kingdom of heaven." It is easy to humble oneself in "self-disparaging words or by symbolic acts, as when the Egyptian monks wore hoods like children's caps; but to be, in childlike manner, humble in spirit is as great in the moral world as it is rare."[18] The disciples of Christ are to be like children in this world. This does not mean children do not need regeneration. But every disciple, as the result of regeneration by the Spirit, becomes a child, whether or not he is a child in years. And then, as the Lord turned to the child, considering his age as well as his faith, He made this statement: "Whoever receives one such child in My

5
"Who Is the Greatest in the Kingdom?"
Mt 18:1–5;
Mk 9:33b–37;
Lk 9:46–48

name receives Me." What a glorious promise for kindness bestowed upon forsaken, fatherless, Christ-redeemed little children for the sake of the Redeemer! Bruce adds:

> The legendary spirit, which dearly loves certainty in detail, identified this particular child with St. Ignatius, who later became the second bishop of Antioch and died as a martyr. As if that would make the lesson more valuable![19]

6
The Mistaken Zeal of John
Mk 9:38–41;
Lk 9:49–50

At that moment, the apostle John interrupted the discourse of Jesus. When Jesus used the expression "in My name," it seems to have suggested an experience that John and certain other disciples had at a time when they were separated from Jesus. In their work they had run across a man who was casting out devils. Ordinarily, these exorcists conjured with the name of Abraham or Solomon in their attempt to expel demons. But this man was no ordinary sorcerer. Nor was he like a Simon Magus (Ac 8:18–24) or one of the seven sons of Sceva (Ac 19:13–16), who would use the name of Jesus and still remain unbelieving in their hearts. This man actually cast out demons in the name of Christ. However, since he did not outwardly join the company of followers, John and those with him had forbidden him. And now John wondered whether what they had done was right. Jesus replied: "Do not stop him, for no one who does a mighty work in My name will be able soon afterward[20] to speak evil of Me. For the one who is not against us is for us." This man was a believer and was acknowledged as such by Christ, even if he did not reach the point of considering it his duty to join the fellowship of His followers. He was by no means a neutral person, to whom the word would have applied: "Whoever is not with Me is against Me" (Mt 12:30). The important thing is not always to follow disciples, but to follow Christ. And the important thing among followers of Christ is not to strive for an honorable position, but to willingly render the humblest service, even though it is as insignificant a thing as the giving of a cup of water for the sake of Christ. "Whoever gives you a cup of water to drink because you belong to Christ will by no means lose his reward."[21]

7
Warning against Causing Others to Sin
Mt 18:6–7;
Mk 9:42

And then, gently resuming His discourse at the point where John interrupted it, Jesus warns His disciples against the awful guilt incurred by causing youthful believers to stumble from the path of faith. What a sin to separate children from the salvation that Christ has come to bring! It would be better for such a person to have one of those large millstones turned by a donkey[22] hung about his neck and to be cast into the sea. That would keep him down and prevent him from doing mischief to others. But, however glaring the sin of offense may be, in a world that lies in wickedness, offense cannot be avoided. "But woe to the one by whom the temptation comes!"

8
"If Your Eye Causes You to Sin"
Mt 18:8–9;
Mk 9:43–50

Then there is another thing: the temptation into which one is not led by others, but which comes from the members of one's own body. It is the duty of every Christian to keep the members of his own body under perfect control. For, the end of him who yields to temptation and places his members in the service of sin will be the everlasting fires of hell,[23] where their worm will not die nor their fire be quenched (Is 66:24). The matter is so serious that the Lord repeats some of the warnings of the Sermon on the Mount (Mt 5:29–30).

> If your hand or your foot causes you to sin, cut it off and throw it away. It is better for you to enter life crippled or lame than with two hands or two feet to be thrown into the eternal fire. And if your eye causes you to sin, tear it out and throw it away. It is better for you to enter life with one eye than with two eyes to be thrown into the hell of fire.

This does not mean that a person should mutilate himself, but that he should subdue his members in the service of Christ, so they do not perform those things that the sinful heart desires. This may involve a sacrifice, a crucifying of the flesh with passions and desires (Gal 5:24). But this crucifying of the flesh is necessary. For, just as salt is sprinkled over every sacrifice for its purification (Lv 2:13), so every soul must be salted with fire, if need be, of the most painful self-sacrifice. "Salt is good" (cf. Mt 5:13). But let not the salt lose its savor nor this fire its purifying powers. "Have salt in yourselves, and be at peace with one another." Instead of permitting themselves to be led into sin, Christians, who are purified by the Word and the Spirit, should act as a salt in the world amid the surrounding corruption.

Once more, probably with the child still nestling in His arms, Jesus reverts to the "little ones" and charges His disciples of all times: "See that you do not despise one of these little ones," whose guardian angels do always behold the face of the Father in heaven. The Son of Man, who came to save that which is lost, takes particular interest also in children. It is His will that not one of them should perish. He is just like the man who has a hundred sheep[24] pasturing on a mountain meadow. He notices that one has gone astray. Leaving the ninety-nine, he climbs up to the mountain in search of the one that has gone astray. "And if he finds it, truly, I say to you, he rejoices over it more than over the ninety-nine that never went astray." The Lord Himself became a child at Bethlehem. And as great as is the sin that causes the loss of a lamb of Christ, so great is the joy in heaven at the gain of a youthful soul. It is the will of the Father in heaven that not one "of these little ones should perish."

9
Parable of the Lost Sheep
Mt 18:10–14

The heavenly Father has but one will, the will to save. This includes all, young and old. It also includes those who have fallen into sin, but who by loving patience and hard work might be won back. "If your brother sins against you," does not necessarily mean a strictly personal offense, but an evident act against a certain word of God. Treat him as an erring brother and "go and tell[25] him his fault, between you and him alone. If he listens to you, you have gained your brother." This is the general rule, which may be repeated patiently, as Jesus would soon explain to Peter (Mt 18:21–22). Its purpose is to provide personal care and to avoid sins of gossip

10
"If Your Brother Sins against You"
Mt 18:15–17

and revenge, which are most destructive to churches. And only upon failure to gain him privately may a second step be taken, namely: "Take one or two others along with you, that every charge may be established by the evidence of two or three witnesses." This is common sense. And as to the number of witnesses, the procedure is the same as that prescribed in the Old Testament (Dt 19:15). This second step may also be repeated with patience. If the purpose of these admonitions is not finally achieved, the case will have to be continued. The purpose is to lead the brother—for he is still to be regarded as a brother—back to the right path. And only after the failure of the second measure might the offense be made known to a larger circle. "If he refuses to listen to them, tell it to the church," the congregation of which he is a member. But even here the purpose must be to gain the sinner.—As regards the word *church*,[26] the New Testament Christian Church had not yet been established; but, while using the term in the sense of a Jewish community, Jesus looks forward to the time of the establishment of local Christian congregations. By the members of a Christian congregation, its verdict in the matter will be regarded as the verdict of Christ Himself. If, therefore, the offender who is requested to appear before this body "refuses to listen even to the church," he has deprived himself of the rights and privileges granted a Christian congregation and must henceforth be adjudged "a Gentile and a tax collector."

11
The Office of the Keys
Mt 18:18–20

This act of solemn excommunication, administered in the spirit of love, has as its objective the sincerely hoped-for restoration of the fallen. The excommunication is binding, provided that all has been done in accordance with the Word of God. "Truly, I say to you, whatever you bind on earth shall be bound in heaven, and whatever you loose on earth shall be loosed in heaven." This applies, whether the local congregation of disciples is large or small. When such a community on the basis of Scripture has reached a full agreement in the matter referred to above, the sad duty of dealing with a fallen brother, or in any other matter pertaining to the preaching of the Word and the furtherance of the Kingdom, it has the sanction of the Lord of the Church. Indeed, Jesus said that an assembly of Christians may ask about anything and "it will be done for them by My Father in heaven." What tremendous power Jesus grants to His Church on earth, even to the smallest Christian congregation! "For where two or three are gathered in My name"[27] as witnesses, "there am I[28] among them."

12
"How Often [Shall] I Forgive My Brother?"
Mt 18:21–22

The subject of dealing with a fallen brother attracted the particular attention of Peter. For the second time in this discourse, a disciple interrupted Jesus.[29] The disciples were at least paying attention. It seemed to Peter that Jesus was stretching the matter of brotherly love a little too far. Suppose a brother had to be dealt with again and again? According to the rabbinical rule, forgiveness had to be extended three times.[30] But Peter was willing to raise it to seven times. "Lord, how often will my brother sin against me, and I forgive him? As many as seven times?" But Jesus answered: "I do not say to you seven times, but seventy times seven."[31] That is a figurative term for always. Forgiveness is not a matter of pharisaic exactness, but love and forgiveness should always dwell in the Christian heart.

This truth is illustrated in the parable of the unforgiving servant. After all, even if the disciples of Christ would comply with the apparently unreasonable requirement of forgiving a fallen brother exactly four hundred and ninety times, what is that compared with what God has already forgiven them?[32] Among the debtors of a certain indolent and trusting Middle Eastern king, there was one whom he had fully trusted, but who now owed him ten thousand talents,[33] an immense sum, let us say, millions of dollars. We don't know how much, since it is not stated whether the weight was of silver or of gold. Nor does it matter. The case was hopeless. In accordance with the power of a monarch over the life and property of his subjects, this ruler commanded the servant "to be sold, with his wife and children and all that he had, and payment to be made." So the servant fell down on his knees and asked for mercy with a promise beyond his ability to keep: "And I will pay you everything." This pitiful plea moved the king. He set the servant free, canceled the debt, and forgave him all. Now comes the other side of the picture. The servant, happily restored to his master's favor, immediately afterwards seized by the throat a fellow servant who was indebted to him and would not forgive him a miserable little debt.[34] This was an insignificant sum as compared with the immense debt that had just been canceled for him. His fellow servant now also fell down and besought him: "Have patience with me, and I will pay you." But "he refused." Turning from the debtor in heartless cruelty, he "put him in prison until he should pay the debt." This merciless deed was reported to the king. Once more the servant was summoned into the royal presence. With words of severest condemnation, he turned him over to the jailers. And the lesson? "So also My heavenly Father will do to every one of you, if you do not forgive your brother from your heart."

13
The Unforgiving Servant
Mt 18:23–35

20

AT THE FEAST OF TABERNACLES IN JERUSALEM

PROBABLY OCTOBER, AD 32

If the unnamed feast (Jn 5:1) was the Passover of the year AD 31, one and a half years had elapsed since the last visit of Jesus to Jerusalem. At that time, the Jews had already sought to kill Him (Jn 5:16, KJV), but the time had not yet come for Him to present Himself as the Lamb of God, who takes away the sins of the world. This visit was followed by the great Galilean ministry, the death of John the Baptist, the period of retirement, and the close of the Galilean and the northern ministries. "Now the Jews' Feast of Booths was at hand." This was the second of the great annual Jewish harvest festivals[1] and the third of the three great annual pilgrimage feasts: Passover, Pentecost, and Tabernacles, observed in memory of the dwelling of Israel in tents in the wilderness (Dt 16:16; Lv 23:34–42).[2] It was held from the fifteenth to the twenty-first day of the seventh month, Tishri, which corresponds to our month of October. It was also the last annual feast of thanksgiving, when the harvest was celebrated with universal joy. The eighth day of the feast was observed with particular solemnity as a holy day of convocation (Lv 23:36; Jn 7:37). In order to recall the days of the desert wanderings, the pilgrims lived in branch-constructed booths, or tents, during the whole time of the feast. During the week, each of the twenty-four courses of priests were employed in turn. A special sacrifice of seventy bullocks for the seventy nations of the world[3] was made in a decreased daily scale (Nu 29:13–32).[4] And on each day, the temple trumpets sounded an inspiring and rejoicing blast twenty-one times.[5] The joy of the occasion was doubtless heightened by the fact that the feast followed five days after the awe-filled and comforting ceremonies of the Day of Atonement, on which a solemn sacrifice was made for the sins of all the people.[6]

1
The Feast
of Tabernacles
Jn 7:2

All Galilee was active in the preparation that preceded the starting of the caravans to Jerusalem. Jesus' brothers wanted Him to reveal Himself publicly in the capital city as the King of Israel. We understand these brothers of Jesus to be those of the Lord's family, Joses and Simon, who had not become apostles of the Lord like James and Judas (Mk 6:3).[7] They had a certain faith in the miracle-working power of Jesus. The fact that all who supported Jesus would be at Jerusalem seemed like an ideal opportunity for their Relative to advance His messianic claims. Their advice was: "Show Yourself to the world." No one who seeks public recognition confines his activities to a hidden corner. These brothers failed to believe in Him, not through active opposition, but through a relative unbelief[8] shared also by others in Jesus' circle. These supporters looked forward to a political Messiahship, failing to see the purpose of Christ's coming into the world. But Jesus rejected their carnal proposal. The proper time for His full messianic revelation had not yet arrived. In revealing their carnal hopes, they indicated that they were worldly. If they hoped in a political Messiah, and if that was the character of their discipleship, then their journey to Jerusalem was perfectly in keeping with the views of most Jews in that day. To the extent of their spiritual ignorance, they were really unbelieving disciples of Jesus. However, the Lord tells them: "You go up to the feast" and do your duty. "I am not going up to this feast," at any rate, not for the purpose that they had in mind, to make the display they believed He should make. Not until the following spring would He make His triumphal entry into Jerusalem, to be followed not by the fulfillment of false messianic hopes but by the establishment of a spiritual kingdom through suffering and death. And so, leaving His puzzled brothers in ignorance as to His references and plans, He stayed behind in Galilee.

But when the brothers were gone, Jesus also started out on the journey to Jerusalem, "not publicly but in private," and not for the purpose that they had suggested. If asked about the coming of Jesus, as they surely would be, Jesus' brothers could say in all truthfulness that He did not come with them. They did not know if He was coming at all. However, many confidently expected Jesus' presence in Jerusalem. Hardly had the party from Capernaum made its arrival when there were inquiries from all sides, "Where is He?" Likewise, there was also much wrangling concerning Him. Some said He was a good man; others, that He was a deceiver. But neither side dared to declare itself openly until the authorities of the Church had spoken.

Suddenly, in the midst of the feast, Jesus appeared in the temple and began to teach. Although His presence in Jerusalem had been expected, this sudden appearance came as a surprise. "The Jews therefore marveled." Jesus did not want to create a sensation, for His purpose was simply to attend to the duties of His prophetic office. For a while, the people listened in silence; but soon the old scruples recurred to them. "How is it that this man has learning, when He has never studied?" They thought that the only one who could excel in learning had to receive the prescribed course of formal educational training![9] Without training, Jesus excelled in what the scribes considered their responsibility: the interpretation of Scripture. Jesus understood the questioning glances and told them that His learning came from the heavenly Father. He who would earnestly seek to do the will of God would readily see that what He taught, both Law and Gospel, was the truth and that, therefore, He was "of God," the Son of the Father. There are two kinds of religious teachers: those who seek their own glory and those who seek the glory of Him whose ambassadors they are. And since it was plain that Jesus revealed the truth and advanced the glory of Him who had sent Him, they had no right to appear as the champions of the Law against Him. Yet that is what they did. In opposing Him and His Gospel, they appealed to Moses and the Law; "yet none of you keeps the law." If they would seriously examine themselves according to the Law, they would soon realize that they transgressed it and therefore needed a Savior. Then they might believe in Jesus and not "seek to kill" Him.

Now, this reference to the determination to kill Jesus, primarily a secret of the leaders, but in the end a general resolve, aroused the people. Indignantly, they resented the insinuation: "You have a demon! Who is seeking to kill You?" In His reply to this blasphemy uttered against Him, Jesus refused to be turned aside from His argument. He had no demon. Neither was He a "monomaniac, laboring under the hallucination that people wished to kill Him."[10] He knew perfectly well that the opposition to Him had reached the murderous stage (Jn 5:16, KJV). In opposing Him, they appealed to the Law. Yet, they did not keep the Law. They even sinned against it at times through a wrong interpretation of it—for instance, by insisting on strict observance of certain portions of the Law contrary to the spirit of the Law. A year and a half ago, He had healed a man on a Sabbath Day (Jn 5:5–9). They still marveled at this, but at the same time were horrified because Jesus did this work on a Sabbath Day (Jn 5:16). But there was no reason for this. According to a rigorous conception of the Law, the Sabbath law was regularly transgressed whenever the act of circumcision was performed on the Sabbath. Yet, no one ever paused to give that a thought. Now, if without scruple they sacrificed one ordinance for the sake of another (if, for example, the law of circumcision superseded a certain restriction of the Sabbath commandment), why not admit exceptions based on the supreme law of love and mercy?[11] And if it was right, for the purpose of ceremonial purity, to inflict a wound upon one member of the body, why, then, should it be wrong by one word to effect a cure of the whole body? Therefore, "do not judge by appearances," but by a sane judgment reach a righteous decision.

5
"You Have a Demon!"
Jn 7:20–24

These words made an impression upon the hearers. "Is not this the man whom they seek to kill?" Can He possibly be the very Christ? The leaders may have changed their opinion. For, "here He is, speaking openly, and they say nothing to Him!" Still, they found it difficult to believe that the authorities would relent to accept the Speaker as the promised Messiah, because He did not satisfy their messianic requirements in the first place, as to origin. The leaders had taught them, "When the Christ appears, no one will know where He comes from." According to the apocalyptic literature, Christ was to appear suddenly "in the clouds or from the sun,"[12] yet there was nothing miraculous in the arrival of Jesus in their midst. "But we know where this man comes from," Jesus of Nazareth, the Son of Mary and of the carpenter Joseph.

As these opinions were loudly discussed in the temple, Jesus shouted into the babel of voices: "You know Me, and you know where I come from. But I have not come of My own accord. He who sent Me is true, and Him you do not know." Jesus granted them the knowledge of His earthly origin. That was no secret. But their knowledge was clearly still deficient even in these matters. They did not know that He was born at Bethlehem (v. 42). But that did not matter. Of far greater importance was the fact that they were not aware of His preexistence, that they did not truly know the Father, who had sent Him, that they were ignorant of the purpose of His coming into the world, and the like. This frank statement of His divine origin they did not fail to grasp, but it made them furious. "So they were seeking to arrest Him"; still, they did not dare to do so. They were held back by a power that lamed their hands, "because His hour had not yet come." And besides, even at that moment, faith was wrought by the words of Christ. "Many of the people believed in Him." And immediately, they were willing to defend their faith. They were quite satisfied to cast their lot with Jesus. Even if Christ should come later, they argued, He would not be able to perform greater miracles "than this man has done," which the rulers had tried to make the people believe. At least the reality of Christ's miracles was not denied.

As the Holy Spirit moved many people to receive the teaching of Jesus, the Pharisees were alarmed. They persuaded the Council to send out officers, most likely members of the temple guard, for His arrest. But Jesus was not afraid, and there was no arrest. He continued in His testimony to the people: "I will be with you a little longer," then His earthly work would be finished: "then I am going to Him who sent Me." Then, when it is too late, "You will seek Me"—probably just then the officers of the Council were slinking behind the pillars—"and you will not find Me. Where I am you cannot come." This was an urgent invitation to make use of the brief period of grace. At the final destruction of Jerusalem, the Jews vainly clung to the promise of their leaders that the Messiah would yet come to deliver them; but they did not see Him (Lk 19:42–44). "You will desire to see one of the days of the

Son of Man, and you will not see it" (Lk 17:22). However, not only was the Lord's warning unheeded, but it was deliberately misinterpreted. "Where does this man intend to go that we will not find Him?" What is He talking about?, they asked and sneeringly conjectured that He intended to teach the Jews in the Diaspora and the Gentiles among whom they lived. It was a contemptuous remark. But that is exactly the course that the Gospel took. The children of the Kingdom who proudly declined the proffered grace were cast out, and the despised Gentiles were made to sit in the Kingdom. Thus passed this memorable day.

On "the last day of the feast, the great day," Jesus was once more in the temple.[13] The feast itself lasted seven days (Lv 23:34; Ne 8:18), and on the eighth day there was a holy convocation (Nu 29:35), when the people celebrated their entrance into the Holy Land. As their fathers abandoned their wilderness tents as soon as they occupied the Promised Land, so the booths were torn down on the last day of the feast, the leaves were shaken off the willow-boughs, the palm branches were waved against the altar, and everyone returned to his dwelling.[14] Another custom was that daily during the festival,[15] at the time of the morning sacrifice, a priest would fill a golden vessel with water at the Pool of Siloam.[16] He would pour it, together with the wine used for the sacrifice, on the altar in commemoration of the water from the rock in the wilderness (Ex 17:6) and their entry into the land of springs and water (Jsh 12:8). At the signal, "Raise thy hand,"[17] the water was poured out,[18] and the Great Hallel (Ps 113–18) was sung in the manner prescribed: "O give thanks to the LORD, for He is good; for His steadfast love endures forever" (Ps 118:29). Besides the historical reference, this ceremony of the pouring of the water was believed to have some bearing on the dispensation of rain, the annual amount of which was thought to be determined by God at that feast. But its main and real application was the misunderstood future outpouring of the Holy Spirit in fulfillment of prophecy: "With joy you will draw water from the wells of salvation" (Is 12:3). In their daily circuit around the altar, the chanting priests thought of the ingathering of the heathen nations. But on the eighth day, this procession was made seven times. Remembering how the walls of Jericho crumpled and fell down at the seventh march of the people round about them (Jsh 6:15–20), they pictured to themselves how God would bring down the walls of heathenism before them. All nations would convert to Judaism, and the land would lie open for the people to enter and possess it.

Whatever the significance of the various ceremonies, Jesus applied the prophecy of Isaiah to Himself (Is 12:3). And as He had done to the woman at the well of Sychar (Jn 4:10–26), so here, too, He pointed to Himself as the Water of Life. "If anyone thirsts, let him come to Me and drink." He is the only true fountain of living water; for in Him there is true, everlasting life. Not only shall the spiritual thirst of the believer be quenched, but he shall be the source of good for others. "Whoever

8
The Last Day
of the Feast
Jn 7:37a

9
Christ the Water
of Life
Jn 7:37b–39

believes in Me, as the Scripture[19] has said, 'Out of his heart[20] will flow rivers of living water.'" The believer's life will manifest itself in deeds of the Spirit for the benefit of others. And while the work of the Holy Spirit was effective in all ages, yet there would be a special manifestation of it, as the evangelist remarks, after the glorification of Christ in the gift of the Spirit at Pentecost. "Now this He said about the Spirit, whom those who believed in Him were to receive, for as yet the Spirit had not been given, because Jesus was not yet glorified."

10
The Effect of the Sermon
Jn 7:40–44

The effect of these words was instantaneous; but it manifested itself in various ways. The vast assembly could not help being aroused to the truth that they were suddenly brought face-to-face with the fulfillment of prophecy. Some were ready to believe that Jesus was the great Prophet promised by Moses (Dt 18:15), whom, however, they did not identify with the Messiah.[21] Others gained the conviction that He was the Christ Himself. Still others, believing that Scripture was on their side, objected: "Is the Christ to come from Galilee?" And what about the promise that Christ was to be born of the seed of David and come out of "Bethlehem, the village where David was?" (Mi 5:2; Is 11:1; Jer 23:5). Although this appeal to Scripture was perfectly in order, it was founded on ignorance of the fact that these requirements had actually been met. "So there was a division among the people over Him." The words of Jesus even forestalled those who had been sent to take Him. They would have made the arrest, but an unseen force rendered their hands impotent and checked their desire.

11
The Report of the Officers
Jn 7:45–49

For four days, the officers of the Council kept a close watch on Jesus, but in the end they had to return empty-handed. Their commission had kept them in the neighborhood of Jesus and in the hearing of His teaching. His words had a powerful effect upon them. When they returned to make their report to the Council, the reason for their failure was at once demanded. "Why did you not bring Him?" All they could answer was: "No one ever spoke like this man!" The Pharisees immediately suspected that the officers had come under Jesus' influence. "Have you also been deceived?" They felt that their power was slipping from their hands when even trusted underlings could not be depended upon. This was altogether out of order. It was theirs to act mechanically, to carry out the order, and to leave the matter of responsibility to their superiors. What right did they have to form an opinion of their own, especially if the opinion did not coincide with that of their masters? "Have any of the authorities or of the Pharisees believed in Him?" That ought to settle the matter as far as the servants were concerned. As to the "miserable mob, whose favorite Jesus had become,"[22] "this crowd that does not know the law is accursed."[23] Pharisaic pride expressed unbounded scorn for the "unlettered mob."[24]

12
Nicodemus: "Does Our Law Judge a Man without First Giving Him a Hearing?"
Jn 7:50–53

This was too much for one member of the Council, Nicodemus, the same man who had come to Jesus by night (Jn 3:1–15). He demanded to know whether it was in accordance with the Law to condemn a man unheard and in ignorance as to the nature of his deeds. Truth hurts. Since there was no reply to the "justice of the principle, the fellow members of the Council fell back on taunts."[25] "Are you from Galilee too?" and inclined to become a follower of this Galilean? Galilee is not the soil to produce prophets! Don't expect a prophet, much less the Messiah, to come from there! "Search and see that no prophet arises from Galilee." But their perverseness was equaled only by their denseness. What about Jonah of Gath-hepher in Zebulun (2Ki 14:25; Jsh 19:13)? And there may have been others.[26] And what about Naphtali and Zebulun in Galilee of the Gentiles, which should see the "great light" (Is 9:1–2; Mt 4:15–16)? "But there is no ignorance so deep as the ignorance that will not know, nor a blindness so incurable as that which will not see."[27] The meeting broke up in a deadlock. "They went each to his own house," the members of the Council and the worshipers in the temple, while Jesus, having no home of His own, went out to stay with some friends on the Mount of Olives.

From the home of Lazarus, where we imagine Jesus spent the night,[29] He returned early to the temple on the following morning. But while the Savior was about His Father's business, His old enemies, the scribes and Pharisees,[30] were busy with the work of their father, the devil (Jn 8:44). They brought to Him a woman caught up in adultery. Instead of delivering her to the proper authorities, they made her the instrument of satisfying their hatred against Jesus, by "subject[ing] her to the horror of odious publicity, and drag[ging] her fresh from the agony of detection into the sacred precincts of the Temple."[31] There they placed "her in the midst" and said to Jesus: "Teacher, this woman has been caught in the act of adultery." A shameful charge, but what about the witnesses and the partner of the crime? Evidently, they were not so much under the strain of moral outrage and anxious to charge the woman as they were interested in offering charges against Jesus. "Now in the Law Moses commanded us to stone such women.[32] So what do You say?" From the Law they cited (Dt 22:24), it would appear that the woman who had committed this sin was a betrothed virgin. Death generally, whether by stoning or by strangulation, was the punishment for adulteresses as well as for adulterers (Lv 20:10; Dt 22:22). The particular relation of this accused woman cannot definitely be inferred from the use of the term. And besides, the actual carrying out of these laws had long fallen into disuse. Be that, however, as it may; that was not the real point at issue. Rather: "This they said to test Him, that they might have some charge to bring against Him." They knew that Jesus had been lenient, according to their judgment, with tax collectors and sinners. According to their idea, He had deviated from the Law of Moses before. And now, would He acquit this woman and make Himself liable to a charge of heresy? In the face of the woman's flagrant transgression, would He openly disregard the fiery Law? Or would He belie His customary compassion so as

13
The Woman Caught up in Adultery
Jn 8:1–6a[28]

ruthlessly to condemn? How could He get out of doing either one or the other? In any event, it would either cost Him His popularity, or He would be accused before the Council. And if He would order stoning, then they could accuse Him before the governor of advocating sedition and mob violence. "What a chance a weak and erring woman had given them!"[33]

14
"Let Him Be the First to Throw a Stone at Her."
Jn 8:6b–11

Satan is never lacking in willing and able servants. But in order to convey to His enemies that He wanted nothing to do with this affair, "Jesus bent down and wrote with His finger on the ground." Whether the Savior wrote words or only traced some figures on the ground[34] as a symbol of indifference or distraction, we do not know. The punishment of adultery is a matter of the court. He did not have to involve Himself. He focused on His writing "as though He heard them not."[35] But impudently, the accusers pressed for an answer. Straightening Himself up, Jesus gave them a reply that came to them like a fiery bolt from the very Law to which they had appealed. "Let him[36] who is without sin among you be the first[37] to throw a stone at her." This was a startling solution. It was not an abrogation of the divine Law. "You shall not commit adultery" was, and still remained, in the Decalogue. Neither was the Law in need of a new interpretation. In no way was the sin of the woman excused. But the matter of dealing with the sinner, as Jesus' enemies requested, belonged to the civil law, with which Jesus did not meddle. They, however, had illegally brought her to Him. They demanded that He act in an unofficial capacity, as a private person. Since He knew their self-righteousness and hypocrisy, "He transfers the whole case from the forum of law to that of conscience."[38] The scribes and Pharisees should grieve over their own iniquities rather than judge the sins of others. After telling them exactly what they were in need of hearing, Jesus again "bent down and wrote on the ground." With burning cheeks, "being convicted by their own conscience" (KJV), one by one, from the eldest to the youngest, the accusers slunk away. When Jesus once more raised His head, He saw that all the accusers had melted away. "And Jesus was left alone with the woman standing before Him." She, too, might have gone, but the same force that had repelled the accusers kept her in the presence of Jesus. Her stay was a sign of repentance and no doubt she craved forgiveness. Addressing her, Jesus asked: "Woman, where are they? Has no one condemned you?" "No one, Lord," was all that her trembling lips could answer. And with the words "Neither do I condemn you; go, and from now on sin no more," does "divine Mercy graciously dismiss Misery from His presence."[39]

15
Jesus the Light of the World
Jn 8:12

Just where in the temple the above incident occurred is not evident. Because of the reference to stoning, some have thought that the words were spoken in the colonnades of an unfinished part of the temple. But Jesus might have said the words without a single stone lying about.[40] Of the following discourse, however, really a series of noisy interruptions, we are told that it took place "in the treasury, as He taught in the temple" (v. 20). It was also called the Court of the Women because this was as far as the women were allowed to go.[41] It received the name "the treasury" on account of the thirteen trumpet-shaped receptacles, or chests, for contributions. Nightly during the Tabernacle week, four large golden candelabras were lighted[42] to add to the joy of the feast. This brilliant illumination was perhaps a memorial of the pillar of fire that led the children of Israel during their wilderness pilgrimage (Ex 13:21). But like the pouring out of water, this brilliant light was also brought into connection with the time of the Messiah, when, it was hoped, all the Gentile nations would be led to the Jewish light. Ordinarily, in common houses, windows were made narrow without and wide within, so that the rays of the sun could pour in. But in Solomon's temple, the windows were made narrow within and wide without, "because the light issuing from the Sanctuary was to lighten that which was without."[43] And indeed this was fitting symbolism; for a light was actually to shine forth from out of Israel. There were prophecies to this effect. "The people who walked in darkness have seen a great light" (Is 9:2). "And the nations shall come to Your light, and kings to the brightness of Your rising" (Is 60:3)—namely, to the Messiah. We are reminded of the language of Simeon, whose eyes actually beheld that Light, "a light for revelation to the Gentiles, and the glory of Your people Israel" (Lk 2:32). But the eyes of the people who had gathered at the Feast of Tabernacles were still unopened, as Jesus, evidently referring to the illumination ceremony, pointed out: "I am the light of the world. Whoever follows Me will not walk in darkness, but will have the light of life." Even as Israel of old followed the pillar of fire to the Promised Land, so he that follows this Light shall be safely guided to life everlasting.

The reference was only too clear. Immediately, the ever-present Pharisees challenged the great declaration. They charged Jesus with an idle assertion about Himself. They maintained that this great claim lacked proper attestation, to say the least. "You are bearing witness about Yourself; Your testimony is not true." But Jesus replied that the ordinary requirements of law—since they purposed to enter into the formal aspect of the matter—did not apply to His witness regarding Himself. For He knew His origin and His destiny—a Savior coming from God and going to God. "Even if I do bear witness about Myself, My testimony is true, for I know where I came from and where I am going." Because they were unacquainted with His true higher position and His form as a servant, they passed judgment and rejected His messianic claims. They should not have done this. There was too much judging on their part, as could be pointed out in the case that Jesus had just dismissed (vv. 3–11). Now, in His Savior capacity, He said of Himself: "I judge no one." He had come to save and to bless. However, this principle did not bar exceptions. "Yet even if I do judge, My judgment is true, for it is not I alone who judge, but I and the Father who sent Me." He wants to be the Savior of all men. But so many did

16
Challenged by the Pharisees
Jn 8:13–20

not believe in Him. The Son of the Father, and therefore true God, would have to be also a Judge. And reverting from the idea of judging to that of witnessing and to the testimony concerning Himself, His self-witness was entirely in order. It agreed with the Law to which they continually appealed and which they so frequently disregarded (Dt 17:6; 19:15). He is in truth the light of the world. There are two witnesses: His own testimony and that of the Father who had sent Him. The Pharisees knew perfectly well what and who was meant. Although they transgressed the rule of supported evidence for an accusation, they demanded witnesses on the spot in frivolous mockery. "Where is Your Father?" Calmly, Jesus unveiled to them why they had put forward so wicked a question. "You know neither Me nor My Father. If you knew Me, you would know My Father also." Since they would not know the Son, the Father, too, would remain unknown to them. As Jesus spoke these words in the treasury, within a few feet from where the august Council held its sessions,[44] He could have been apprehended. But "His hour had not yet come." That was the reason why "no one arrested Him."

17
**Jesus' Departure and
Its Result for Israel
Jn 8:21–32**

Presently, we find Jesus teaching a more general audience,[45] presumably in one of the temple porches (v. 59). His words have a sad note. He again takes up the subject of His departure (cf. Jn 7:33) and emphasizes that those rejecting Him will not only vainly seek Him but will die in their sins. His departure to the Father seals the fate of Israel. And is it not true? These many centuries, Israel has sought its Christ and perished in the great sin of rejecting Him. Yet, Jesus' words are met with satanic disdain. What is He talking about? "Will He kill Himself, since He says, 'Where I am going, you cannot come'?" Is it by way of suicide that He wants to put Himself out of their reach? Jesus disregards this sneering interruption and points out the real cause of the separation between them and Himself. They are from below, in the worst sense of the term, while He is from above. And the testimony that He has given them as the only means of salvation they will not accept. But the adversaries will not admit this, and they do not inquire who He may be, so that they will come to faith in Him and thus gain life and salvation. With quiet dignity, Jesus tells them that He is the same person as He had said He was from the beginning. He directs them to the divine message that He has received from the Father, through which they will have salvation if they receive it. But if they obstinately refuse to believe the message, it will condemn them. And what He has received from the Father is the truth; for "He who sent Me is true." But they would not or could not understand that the Father sent Jesus. Therefore, Jesus explains: "When you have lifted up the Son of Man, then you will know that I am He, and that I do nothing on My own authority, but speak just as the Father taught Me." After His crucifixion and the miracles that would follow—His resurrection, His ascension into heaven, the outpouring of the Holy Spirit on Pentecost, and the establishment of the Christian

Church—and after the destruction of their city as a preamble to the final judgment, they would either know and joyfully confess or admit in grim despair that the Father sent Jesus to carry out the Father's will, and that He invariably did what was pleasing in the Father's sight. This announcement made a powerful impression. As a result, many were, at least temporarily, brought to faith. Jesus addresses these beautiful words to them for the purpose of encouraging them to continue in faith: "If you abide in My Word, you are truly My disciples, and you will know the truth, and the truth will set you free."

But hardly had some come to faith in Christ when the words He had just spoken offended a number of His hearers. How could He talk of liberty to such as felt that they already were free? "We are offspring of Abraham," they claimed, and God called them to rule over other people, "and [we] have never been enslaved to anyone." They regarded as altogether incidental that the Egyptians, Assyrians, Babylonians, and Greeks had subjected them and they were now under the dominion of the Romans. At all times throughout their checkered history, they had claimed and practically enjoyed religious independence. But Jesus points out to them that there is a servitude that may, and in their case really did, apply in spite of their descent from Abraham and of the enjoyment of outward religious liberty. The servitude of sin, to which by nature every human being is subject, also applied to them.[46] "Everyone who practices sin is a slave to sin." How can a worker of iniquity talk about being free when he is a slave of sin? Of what value is physical descent in a theocracy if in the end one loses his true membership and is cast out? It is only the Son of God who can bring about spiritual liberty, emancipation from sin and its service. Instead of tracing their ancestry to Abraham, they should have considered Abraham's faith. It is not their physical descent, but their moral condition that is so important. "I know that you are offspring of Abraham; yet you seek to kill Me" (Jn 5:16, 18; 7:19, 30). Their conduct showed that the Gospel of freedom that Jesus had proclaimed had not become effective in them.[47] While Jesus was carrying out His Father's will and expressing His Father's thoughts, their reaction betrayed their true parentage.

As if to resent the insinuation that they had learned something evil from their high ancestor, the Jews answer: "Abraham is our father." But Jesus replies: "If you were Abraham's children, you would be doing the works Abraham did." "[Abraham] believed the LORD, and He counted it to him as righteousness" (Gn 15:6). "But now you seek to kill Me." There is a difference between physical and true spiritual descent. Even though their physical origin may indeed be traced to Abraham, they are intent on doing something that Abraham never would have done—kill "a man"[48] who has proclaimed to them God's own truth. This murderous bent of mind is based upon hostility to God and shows that they are born of someone other than Abraham. "This is not what Abraham did." Now the Jews began to notice that Jesus was speaking of

18
Spiritual Liberty and Being Abraham's Children
Jn 8:33–38

19
"You Are of Your Father the Devil"
Jn 8:39–47

spiritual extraction. And this allusion only increased their anger. Was He alluding to them as idolaters and hinting at idolatrous practices that often were connected with idolatry (Ex 34:15; Lv 17:7; Is 57:3)? The idea was resented with indignation. "We were not born of sexual immorality. We have one Father—even God." The idea was preposterous. They belonged to the children of Israel in truth. Whatever else might be said to their discredit, they believed in one God, Yahweh, and had nothing to do with adulterous practices and the worship of idols. But even the outward worship of one God and conformity to high moral standards was not proof, Christ rejoined, that they were truly spiritual children of God. "If God were your Father, you would love Me, for I came from God." "That is His constant argument, that as He came forth from God and was sent by Him, they must have welcomed Him had they been God's children."[49] And this they did not do. "They did not recognize His speech as divine."[50] They were unwilling to receive Him and the saving truth He proclaimed, which made them reject the truth He uttered. There was but one explanation for this. And, therefore, since plain language must be used, He told them, "You are of your father the devil." From the beginning of the human race, the devil was a liar and a murderer. Their own murderous intentions and their opposition to the truth only proved their descent from the one who is the origin of all wickedness. Theirs was a complete perversity as compared with the sinlessness of Jesus. Owing to their self-righteousness and according to their standards, it was easy for them to accuse not only tax collectors and sinners but also those who walked in the statutes of the Lord but failed to keep all the ordinances and traditions of the elders. "Which one of you convicts *Me* of sin?" (emphasis added). Their own depravity was so great that if Jesus had "led them into sin, they would have followed, or spoken lies, they would have believed."[51] But since He spoke the truth, they did not believe Him because of their corrupt nature. Manifestly, this sad condition was both the result and the evidence of their paternity. "Whoever is of God hears the words of God. The reason why you do not hear them is that you are not of God."

20
"Before Abraham Was, I Am"
Jn 8:48–59

To this stinging rebuke, the Jews replied with a coarse invective. "Are we not right in saying that You are a Samaritan and have a demon?" Since Jesus refused to admit their true Abrahamic ancestry, they retorted with the taunt that Jesus was no pure Jew, but a Samaritan heretic and, as such, was Himself a child of the devil. (By the way, this shows how intensely the Jews hated the schismatic Samaritans.) Gently, the Lord puts the taunt aside. "I do not have a demon." One commentator observed, "The dishonor does not stir His resentment" for He does not seek His own glory. "Nevertheless, on account of His nature [because He is true God], His glory is not to be turned into reproach";[52] for "there is One who seeks it, and He is the judge." Those who dishonor the Son of God will one day be judged; and this judgment will be according to His Word (Jn 5:23–24). But from this judgment, there is an escape in the time of grace: "Truly, truly,[53] I say to you, if anyone keeps[54] My word, He will never see death." But this death-abolishing claim confirmed the Jews in their opinion that Jesus was demented and demon-possessed. "Now we know that you have a demon! Abraham died, as did the prophets, yet You say, 'If anyone keeps My word, he will never taste death.' Are You greater than our father Abraham, who died? And the prophets died! Who do you make Yourself out to be?" Once more, Jesus tells them that He was not seeking His own glory. But this is a matter in which the Father is involved, "of whom you say, 'He is our God.'" Now, if Jesus will disavow His knowledge of God and say: "I do not know Him," He "would be a liar like you." And as far as Abraham is concerned: "Abraham rejoiced that he would see My day. He saw it and was glad." The very Abraham in whose parentage they gloried sought salvation through Christ and received it of Him. But these Jews completely misunderstood the statement about Abraham's seeing the day of Jesus. If Jesus claimed that Abraham had seen the days of Jesus, then Jesus must have seen the days of Abraham. A true deduction, but it appeared ridiculous to them in the highest degree. "So the Jews said to Him, 'You are not yet fifty years old,[55] and have You seen Abraham?'" But even in that sense, Jesus solemnly answers the question in the affirmative. "Truly, truly, I say to you, before Abraham was, *I am*" (emphasis added). No stronger affirmation of the eternal existence of Jesus occurs anywhere in Scripture.[56] But this blessed truth is as blasphemy in the ears of His adversaries—claiming equality with the eternal I AM (Ex 3:14). "So they picked up stones to throw at Him." The unfinished state of the temple could easily supply them with such stones close at hand.[57] But Jesus would not permit Himself to be harmed that way, so He "hid Himself and went out of the temple."

As Jesus "passed by," probably on the next day,[58] at any rate on a Sabbath, He saw a man who was "blind from birth." We are not told where He met him. We assume that it was in Jerusalem, in the neighborhood of the Pool of Siloam and the temple, if not at one of the gates of the temple itself. There the objects of pity and charity would gather (Ac 3:2).[59] At the sight of the blind man, Jesus' disciples— who were again in the company of their Master[60]—asked Him: "Rabbi, who sinned, this man or his parents, that he was born blind?" In spite of their long contact with Jesus, they still thought that each particular sickness or sorrow was directly traceable to some particular sin. But Jesus answered: "It was not that this man sinned, or his parents" to cause this lifelong affliction. Indirectly of course, it was the result of sin in general. Moreover, by means of this affliction, "the works of God might be displayed in him." And, therefore, the proper question was not where the suffering had come from, but what was to be done with it.[61] In the brief spell of fleeting time, works of mercy brook no delay. Jesus says about Himself as well as all His followers, "We[62] must work the works of Him who sent Me while it is day"—that is,

21
Healing of a Man
Born Blind
Jn 9:1–7

while there is still the day of life. For "night is coming, when no one can work." This is in accordance with the purpose of His coming, as explained in His discourse of the previous day (8:12). "As long as I am in the world, I am the light of the world." Jesus does not lose any time putting the proverbial expression of working while it is day into practice. He proves that He is indeed the light of the world. "Having said these things, He spit on the ground and made mud with the saliva. Then He anointed[63] the man's eyes with the mud." No virtue lay in this particular mode of healing.[64] He did this in order to impress upon the afflicted man that the healing came from Him. For the purpose of placing additional emphasis, the direction is given: "Go, wash in the Pool of Siloam." From this pool the water was taken for the ceremony of the pouring of water on the last day of the Feast of Tabernacles to symbolize the pouring out of the Holy Spirit.[65] The evangelist adds: "which means Sent."[66] Thus the living water of the pool is connected with the Water of Life, the Light of the World, and the Sent (Gal 4:4) of the Father. Not doubting, and without a moment of hesitation, the blind man "went and washed and came back seeing."

22
Questioned by His
Neighbors
Jn 9:8–14

But the miracle led to serious results. When the healed man returned to his home, the neighbors and those who had known him as a blind beggar could hardly believe their eyes. "Is this not the man who used to sit and beg?" Although some were certain of his identity, others doubted on account of his altered appearance. However, the former blind man's emphatic "I am the man" scattered their doubts. But how did it happen? The amazed neighbors made him repeat the story of his cure. A man whom he at the time could not see and who even now was unknown to him, called Jesus, made clay. He anointed his eyes, and told him to go to the Pool of Siloam and wash his eyes, which he did, with the result that he recovered his sight.[67] A most astounding cure, simplicity itself and yet a true miracle. Yet, on account of one particular detail, they felt that something was not quite in order. If the marvelous tale was confirmed, there was a possibility that the deed itself might lack proper authorization. They therefore asked: "Where is He?" And when the man answered, "I do not know," they took him to the Pharisees (Jn 8:13), by whom they had been taught that, except in mortal danger, the use of medicine, even the application of spittle on the eyes, was a breach of the Sabbath if such action was intended as a remedy.[68] "Now it was a Sabbath Day when Jesus made the mud and opened his eyes." The mixing of clay was labor, the work of a mason, not to mention the order to go and wash himself, which was an unnecessary piece of work on the Sabbath. Thus, for dogmatic reasons and out of horror at the neglect of a Sabbath superstition, they entirely overlooked the fact that this was a unique miracle of mercy.

23
Examined by the
Pharisees
Jn 9:15–17

Immediately, the Pharisees[69] arrange for a hearing. Again he describes the miracle and they disregard the deed of mercy. Rabbinic wisdom as represented by some of the assembly decides: "This man is not from God, for He does not keep the

Sabbath." The miracle is not denied for the present, but it cannot be a work of God, because it was done on a Sabbath. But others said, "How can a man who is a sinner do such signs?" Whether it was a Sabbath or not, how can such a work be done at all by a sinner? "And there was a division among them."[70] And being in a quandary, they asked the blind man for his opinion. To the best of his knowledge and to the extent of his faith, he promptly answered, "He is a prophet." Without presuming to enter into the controversy, he was at least convinced that his benefactor was of God.

More information was needed. Probably it was no miracle at all! A fraudulent agreement between Jesus and the man was now suspected, which was not dispelled until they called the man's parents. They were showered with questions: Is he your son? Was he really born blind? And if so, "how then does he now see?" The first two questions the parents promptly answered in the affirmative. But as to the next question, they shammed ignorance in their own interest and referred the question to their son. "Ask him; he is of age. He will speak for himself." Not as if the parents were ignorant of the miracle or ungrateful to Jesus; it was fear that prompted the answer, because already the Jews, as incorporated in the Council, had agreed that if any man confessed that Jesus was the Christ he should be excommunicated.[71] There were three degrees to this excommunication. The first rebuke, or admonition (*neziphah*), if formally pronounced, lasted thirty days. At the end of that term, there was a second admonition (*niddui*), which also lasted thirty days. If the person so visited occupied an honorable position, the sentence was expressed in a euphemistic manner: "I think your companions are separating from you." And if the culprit was still impenitent, he was solemnly laid under the ban, or final excommunication (*cherem*). Its duration was indefinite and, accompanied with curses, entirely cut him off from interaction with his fellows. Henceforth, he was like one dead.[72] No wonder the parents of the formerly blind son dreaded to commit themselves. "This punishment to persons so poor as the parents of a beggar would practically have meant ruin and death."[73] "Therefore his parents said, 'He is of age; ask him.'"

But "the son was made of sturdier stuff."[74] What did he care about such an excommunication! If he had to choose, he would rather be socially dead than physically blind, not to mention the debt of gratitude that he owed to his Benefactor. Again they called him and said to him: "Give glory to God" (see Jsh 7:19); that is, tell the truth. He was placed under oath, as it were. "We know that this man is a sinner," a desecrater of the Sabbath Day and as such an ungodly man. But the man was unable or unwilling to enter into these speculations. "Whether He is a sinner I do not know." He knew only one thing, "that though I was blind, now I see." Then they began to subject him to a tiresome cross-examination. "What did He do to you? How did He open your eyes?" But no more of that! Should he needlessly repeat his testimony just because they had not listened? Or was it that they were wishing

24
Consultation with the Parents
Jn 9:18–23

25
Faith in Christ Confessed; "Cast Out"
Jn 9:24–34

to become disciples of Christ? "But no more galling gibe could be flung into their teeth"[75] than this man's "Do you also want to become His disciples?" This was more than they could bear. Expressing their true sentiment in the matter, they began to revile him. "You are His disciple, but we are disciples of Moses." Again they championed Moses and the Law. "We know that God has spoken to Moses." But "as for this man,"[76] they claimed, "we do not know where He comes from." Even to the untrained mind of the former blind beggar, this willful ignorance in the face of the undeniable miracle was altogether inconceivable. What astounding ignorance! "Why, this is an amazing thing! You do not know where He comes from, and yet He opened my eyes." Should it really be said that a former blind beggar must give these Pharisaic doctors a lesson in logic? "We know that God does not listen to sinners," but only those who worship Him and do His will. From the miracle that had been performed, it was certain that God had heard Jesus. And it was an astounding miracle; for, "Never since the world began has it been heard that anyone opened the eyes of a man born blind." Therefore, this Man is not a Sabbath-defiling sinner, but is from God. For "if this man were not from God, He could do nothing." But should this miserable beggar, this cursed member of the ignorant mob (7:49), teach *them*? "*You*[77] were born in utter sin," reproaching him even for his calamity (9:3), "and would you teach *us*,"[78] the pure and godly (emphasis added)? Such audacity! And they kicked him out,[79] not only from the hall, but also from the synagogue.

26
Christ
Acknowledged
His Faith
Jn 9:35–41

But Jesus heard that the man whom He had given his sight had been excommunicated. As He had wished and sought to do, He found him and asked him: "Do you believe in the Son of Man?" The healed man was a believing Israelite and as such placed his faith in the Messiah, knowing that He was the Son of God. His answer was an admission of this faith, but also an expression of his ignorance about who the Messiah was. "Who is He, sir, that I may believe in Him?" He did not doubt that Jesus, whom he had already declared to be a prophet (v. 17), could tell him who the Messiah was. Jesus answered, "You have seen Him, and it is He who is speaking to you." This blessed revelation was immediately received in faith. Here the Light of the World did not shine in vain. Sinking to his knees and worshiping Jesus as God,[80] he exclaimed, "Lord, I believe." Summing up the significance of the miracle, Jesus said: "For judgment[81] I came into this world"—that is, to bring to light and to exhibit the actual inward state of men—"that those who do not see may see, and those who see may become blind." Those who are by penitent admission spiritually blind shall receive spiritual sight; those who presume to have spiritual light, while in reality they are stone-blind, shall be hopelessly darkened. But immediately, this oxymoron[82] was attacked. The Pharisees, who were again dogging the footsteps of Jesus, correctly feared that the saying reflected upon them. "Are we also blind?" they asked. Christ answered, "If you were blind, you would have no guilt;

but now that you say, 'We see,' your guilt remains." For penitent sinners there is the light of forgiveness. But to those who bask themselves in the deceptive light of self-righteousness, the darkness of nonforgiveness remains. By rejecting Jesus, the Pharisees had shown that they were truly blind. And if the leaders, the teachers, are blind, how can those whom they teach see?

Judging by the character that the leaders and teachers of Israel had again displayed in the last few days, it was extremely obvious they were utterly unfit for their professed work of feeding the flock of God.[83] It was only too apparent that they were certainly not God's shepherds, having cast out the blind man miraculously healed, judging Jesus as they did, and excommunicating everyone who confessed that Jesus was the Christ. They had climbed into God's sheepfold, but not by the door of the Word and promise by which the Owner, God, had brought His flock into the fold. They were shepherds who had "climb[ed] in by another way" and "attained rule and leadership over God's flock in the same manner and by the same right as a robber and a thief."[84] This is the truth that Jesus solemnly[85] explained in a beautiful parable or allegory. He probably delivered it in the temple, in continuation of the conversation that arose out of the healing of the blind man. In the East, the flocks are driven at night through a portal into an enclosure that is surrounded by a protecting wall. They are left in the care of a gatekeeper, or guard. In the morning, the shepherd comes to the corral, the gatekeeper opens the door, and the shepherd raises his voice. When a number of herds are sheltered in the same fold, the sheep that belong to the calling shepherd will follow him as he calls them by name, and he leads them out. As actual tests proved,[86] sheep will not follow the shepherd's clothes if worn by a stranger, but will flee from him, because they do not know the stranger's voice. Of course, we should not press each detail of the parable. The point is that unlike the Old Testament prophets, who pointed forward to Christ, the members of the present hierarchical party, like thieves and robbers, had broken into the herd. They assumed authority over the people of God, misleading all but the true children of God, who in spite of force or persuasion would not permit themselves to be lured from the voice and promises of God. The parable[87] itself is clear. What Jesus described happened every day in the Judean hills. But what He allegorically delivered, He was compelled to explain. And that does not surprise us; for most of those who heard Him were not of His flock and knew not His voice.

The Savior Himself adds the solemn application: "I am the door of the sheep." He does this for the sake of His hearers and probably also to assure the excommunicated outcasts[88] that the Pharisees could not admit or reject them from the fold of God. Before Jesus appeared, thieves and robbers assumed that their own misguided directions could lead people into communion with God. But the real sheep of God had not given heed to their word. Christ is the door; only through Him shall

27
The True Shepherd
of the Sheep
Jn 10:1–6

28
Jesus the Door
to the Sheepfold
Jn 10:7–10

someone be saved who enters in. And led by Him, he is privileged to enjoy the full pasture of the Gospel. The thief, especially the thief in spiritual matters, comes "to steal and kill and destroy." But Jesus has come for the purpose of giving full, true, and everlasting life.

29
Christ the Good
Shepherd
Jn 10:11–18

Continuing the same image, viewed from a different angle, Christ says: "I am the good shepherd."[89] He is the Good Shepherd in the absolute sense, because "the good shepherd gives His life for the sheep." In contrast with this one Good Shepherd, who lays down His life for the salvation of the flock, no other shepherd deserves the description as "good," especially not those hirelings who preach what is in their own interest. In the face of danger, seeing the wolf coming, they flee shamefully and desert the sheep. The result is the slaughter and dispersion of the sheep. But a good shepherd, even in the literal sense, will fight wolves or thieves at the risk of his life, just as a conscientious preacher of the Gospel will suffer all, even martyrdom, rather than become unfaithful to his trust and disloyal to his charge. Christ is the Good Shepherd in contrast with all other shepherds also in another respect—namely, regarding the intimate knowledge and acquaintance between Himself and His flock. That knowledge and communion is so close and all-embracing, it is like that between Himself and the Father in heaven. According to the will of His heavenly Father and for the salvation of His sheep, this Shepherd, freely and unforced, lays down His life.[90] And since this ransom is for the whole world, He wants to gather also other sheep besides those of the house of Israel into His fold. "And they will listen to My voice. So there will be one flock, one shepherd," one holy Christian Church, the communion of saints, scattered throughout the world, in whatever visible Church they may be. They are all His by the Father's gift and design. And the chief proof of the Good Shepherd's love is that He will lay down His life for His sheep. Because of this consummate act of love, His Father loves Him. In the laying down of His life is implied that He will take it again. "No man takes it from Me, but I lay it down of My own accord. I have authority to lay it down, and I have authority to take it up again." The sacrifice on the cross must be followed by the return to life; otherwise His entire ministry would have been rendered void. And in this act of disposing of His life and taking it again, according to the divine plan of salvation, He again is in full harmony with the Father, whose commandment[91] He has received for the salvation of the world.

30
The Effect of the
Discourse
Jn 10:19–21

The immediate effect of these blessed and comforting truths was another (see 9:16) division among the Jews. Some held that Jesus was mad and possessed by a demon. But others objected to this insinuation. His words were not the usual ravings of demonized persons. And as to His acts, they were not satanic; they were not acts performed by him who is "a murderer from the beginning" (8:44). And besides, "Can a demon open the eyes of the blind?"

21

JESUS' FINAL WITHDRAWAL FROM GALILEE
AND THE LATER JUDEAN MINISTRY

END OF OCTOBER TO MIDDLE OF DECEMBER, AD 32

After the Feast of Tabernacles, in the autumn of AD 32, Jesus seems to have returned once more to Galilee. However, He was soon to leave Galilee as a field of operations and not return. The days were at hand for His "taking up,"[2] as ordained by God.[3] In fact, the beginning of the end had come as Jesus "set His face to go to Jerusalem." But while the face of Jesus was set toward Jerusalem, His mind was still occupied with other things.

1
Leaving Galilee as a
Field of Operations
Lk 9:51[1]

After His departure from Galilee, Jesus intended to proceed southward through Samaritan territory. Although there was little love between the Jews and the Samaritans, Galileans commonly crossed Samaria in their journeys to and from Jerusalem.[4] Thus, for the purpose of securing lodging for Himself and His party, Jesus sent messengers to a Samaritan village. But these returned with the report that the villagers declined to receive Him. When Jesus made an earlier journey through Samaria, the Samaritans were not only glad to receive Him, but anxious to have Him stay with them (Jn 4:40). But now the circumstances were different. At that time, attended by a few followers, He stayed with them. But now, acclaimed by multitudes, His face "was set toward Jerusalem." That was different. They had heard something about His being the Jewish Messiah-King—misunderstood, of course. And they would not provide a Jewish Messiah with the ordinary necessities of life if He were to set up a kingdom in Jerusalem instead of, as they hoped, restoring and glorifying the worship on Mount Gerizim.[5] The Samaritans' refusal to receive their Master filled the disciples, especially James and John,[6] with the hottest indignation. Personally convinced, as they were, of the nearness of the messianic kingdom, they would now usher it in with a flare of Sinai fire. "Lord, do you want us to tell

2
The Inhospitable
Samaritans
Lk 9:52–56

fire to come down from heaven and consume them?" (cf. 2Ki 1:10–12). Thus they seem to justify their fiery proposal with the example of Elijah. Whether the brothers received the name of Boanerges, or Sons of Thunder (Mk 3:17), from this circumstance, we do not know.[7] But Jesus rebuked them. Some manuscripts include Him saying: "You do not know what manner of spirit you are of." Jesus does not disparage the action of Elijah, whom they had seen on the Mount of Transfiguration, but that was a different matter. As His followers, the disciples were not to reflect Sinai and Carmel, but Hermon, Calvary, and His spirit. For the Son of Man did not come to destroy people's lives but to save them. To the Samaritans, for the present, the rejection of grace and salvation was punishment enough. Therefore, "they went on to another village."

3
Application for Discipleship
Lk 9:57–62[8]

"Along the road,"[9] there occurred a repetition of application for discipleship, which Matthew related in connection with the Gadarene journey (Mt 8:19–22). As happens to others in public life, so also in the extended ministry of our Savior circumstances recurred that gave occasion to a similarity of actions or replies. Jesus was always on the lookout for competent assistants and eager to use such as were available. But in many instances, whether they were invited or whether they presented themselves, these prospects for discipleship were not "fit for the kingdom of God."

4
The Mission of the Seventy-Two
Lk 10:1–12

The fundamental rules for those who were privileged to labor side by side with Jesus were laid down in the mission of the Twelve in Galilee (Mt 10).[10] And as others were sent out, they received substantially the same instructions. So also in this time of our Lord's closing ministry, a group of seventy-two from the outer circle of disciples received their commission for an extensive "go your way." We are unable to determine from where Jesus sent out these disciples. We conclude that it was in Southern Galilee, before Christ's crossing of the Jordan into Perea. This is because of the sad words He uttered over the Galilean cities (Lk 10:13–15), to which Luke added the recent rejection of the Samaritans. The immediate purpose of this mission was to make preparation for Jesus' reception in those parts of the land of Israel, especially in Perea and Judea (10:38), where He was still comparatively unknown. Neither do we know the reason for the particular number seventy-two. It may subtly symbolize the number of Gentile nations around Israel. What surprises us is the comparatively large number of efficient workers for a temporary mission. They were sent out two by two for the purpose of publicity in the places that the Savior intended to visit. The instructions differed from those issued to the Twelve in that they were briefer and the restrictions about not visiting the Gentiles and the Samaritans were omitted. Also, less ample miraculous powers seem to have been bestowed upon them (Mt 10:8).

5
The Doom of the Impenitent Cities
Lk 10:13–16

Although Jesus left faithful hearts behind, it was with sorrow that He started from the scenes of His glorious, but rejected, ministry. The base ingratitude of the highly exalted Galilean towns moved Him to repeat the woes that He had uttered on a previous occasion (Mt 11:21–24).[11] But the disciples should not be discouraged on account of the rejection that attended the gracious ministry of Jesus. The Lord assures them as well as every true servant of His: "The one who hears you hears Me, and the one who rejects you rejects Me, and the one who rejects Me rejects Him who sent Me."

The ministry of the Seventy-Two seems to have been brief. Strange things were joyfully reported to Jesus on their return. They were especially elated over the fact, it seems, that they had been able to accomplish more than had been expected or promised. "Lord, even the demons are subject to us in Your name!" Although Jesus shared the joys of this outer circle of disciples, their report was no news to Him. While they were working, He saw Satan falling. "I saw Satan fall like lightning from heaven." He who had left his celestial habitation to become the god of this world (2Co 4:4) was falling from the pinnacle of his power. But as the lightning descends in a flash and is suddenly extinguished, so Jesus saw how the foul flash of Satan had reached the end of its course. "The reason the Son of God appeared was to destroy the works of the devil" (1Jn 3:8). And this power of successfully opposing the devil was also transmitted to Jesus' disciples. Thus, they were able to "tread on serpents and scorpions" (symbols of Satan) and given power "over all the power of the enemy, and nothing shall hurt you."[12] In the exercise of their duties, they could at all times be assured of the protecting hand of God. But lest they be tempted to self-reliance and become overjoyed at their personal success, a warning word is given. The most important point for the individual Christian is not that he has been successful in an engagement with Satan, but that his name is "written in heaven." That is the greatest glory that a Christian can obtain; not that he has accomplished a great deed, be it even the performance of a miracle in the name of Christ, but that his name is inscribed in the Book of Life.[13]

6
The Return of the Seventy-Two
Lk 10:17–20

Rejoicing with and over His disciples, Jesus repeated the great "devotional utterance" that He had previously expressed (Mt 11:25–27).[14] In the Lord's ministry, there were not only seasons of sadness, but also seasons of joy.

7
The Joy of Christ
Lk 10:21–24

> In that same hour He rejoiced in the Holy Spirit and said, "I thank You, Father, Lord of heaven and earth, that You have hidden these things from the wise and understanding and revealed them to little children; yes, Father, for such was Your gracious will."

Uneducated disciples, novices, and babes, according to the will and by the revelation of God, saw what the custodians of wisdom, the scribes and Pharisees, did not: the salvation of Christ. Turning to His disciples, Jesus addresses them with the same words He used previously to explain the parable of the sower (Mt 13:16–17).[15] He impresses upon them in particular the glory of their blessed privilege as followers and believers: "Blessed are the eyes that see what you see! For I tell you that many prophets and kings desired to see what you see, and did not see it, and to hear what you hear, and did not hear it."

The story moves from the glorious promise of the Gospel as simply accepted by those of childlike faith to a matter of subtle reasoning as presented by one who represented the prudent and the wise (v. 21)! Just where it was that a certain lawyer, "an expert in Jewish Canon Law,"[16] "stood up" for the purpose of involving Jesus in a legal difficulty, we do not know. It was probably in a synagogue, although no reference is given.[17] It was a momentous question that he put to Jesus, concerning life everlasting. About what could and should a man be more concerned? But the question was not asked in good faith; for he tested Him, saying, "Teacher, what shall I do to inherit eternal life?" His purpose was not to learn something, but to involve Jesus in an unholy debate and to find reason for complaint. At the bottom was the notion that eternal life is the reward of merit and works. The only question was what these works might be. "The idea of sin, guilt, and need of forgiveness had not entered his mind. It was that old Judaism speaking without disguise."[18] Knowing Jesus' principle of appealing to Scripture, he was prepared for a response. The only difference was that, instead of giving the expected scriptural answer, Jesus parried by asking him a question: "What is written in the Law? How do you read it?" The reply of the legal expert was natural enough. He pointed to the passages that, as a part of daily prayer, every devout Jew was supposed to quote in connection with the words "Hear, O Israel: the LORD our God, the LORD is one." He said: "You shall love the Lord your God with all your heart and with all your soul and with all your strength and with all your mind, and your neighbor as yourself" (cf. Dt 6:4–5; Lv 19:18). What other answer could be given? Every Jewish child knew the words.[19] They were to be written on the doorposts of Jewish homes and were enclosed in phylacteries, those little boxes that they bound to themselves.[20] From the standpoint of the Law, there was no other answer. Jesus Himself would have given this answer; in fact, on another occasion He did so (Mt 22:37–40). Thus, Jesus replied: "You have answered correctly." But since the Lord was aware that the question was not asked because the lawyer was interested in the true way to life, He added: "Do *this*, and you will live" (emphasis added). Yet the lawyer thwarted Christ's purpose, which was to lead him to examine himself. In his spiritual blindness, he considered this the opening he had been waiting for. The lawyer was sure that he loved God with all his heart, soul, strength, and mind, according to a "fourfold analysis of the inner man."[21] No failure on his part there! But the second part, about loving one's neighbor, was not as easily settled as Jesus' answer, "Do this," seemed to imply. True, the Law commanded love of one's neighbor, but a person must know who his neighbor is. That gave him the chance to discuss the problem under a tempting question: "And who is my neighbor?" In his opinion, "neighbor" was an elastic term. Had Jesus asked for a definition, He would no doubt have received a reply in which the term *neighbor* would have been narrowed down to a restricted class of fellow beings. So, Jesus told the striking parable of the Good Samaritan to show the lawyer how far orthodox Judaism was from a true understanding, not to mention perfect observance, of the Law. Jesus would bring him to a true knowledge of his sins, as well as teach all people of all times a lesson of neighborly love.

The parable introduces "a man," probably a Jew, for the purpose of teaching that the duty of love is independent of race, religion, and color. The man is intentionally presented as an unnamed human being who went down the rapidly descending[22] desert road from Jerusalem to Jericho. Somewhere along this notoriously insecure "Bloody Gorge,"[23] the solitary traveler fell into the hands of robbers. They stripped him of his clothing, covered him with wounds, and left him as he was, half dead. Soon he would have breathed his last had not someone come to his help.[24] Now, it happened, by a providential combination of circumstances that a certain priest came down that way, which made it seem probable that help would be at hand when most needed. He had very likely returned from his weekly course of service in the temple to his home at Jericho.[25] But in spite of the fact that the wounded man was in full view of the priest and presented a sight fit to arouse compassion, "when he saw him," he quickly "passed by on the other side." Likewise an attendant of the priesthood, a Levite, with still cooler indifference, "came to the place and saw him, [passing] by on the other side." And why did they pass by? It was due to their wrong answer to the question, "Who is my neighbor?" and the fear lest they make someone the object of their love whom God had probably made the object of His wrath[26]— or simply to lack of love. It probably was the same spirit of quibbling that would prefer to speculate on the problem "Who is my neighbor?" rather than be spurred on to action by asking, "Whose neighbor am I?"[27] But the unexpected happened. A semi-heathen Samaritan, of all men most despised and hated by the Jews, came upon the half-dead man. No Jew, probably not even the suffering man on the roadside, would have expected mercy from the Samaritan, nor would a Jew have made the Samaritan the object of his mercy. It seems that the traveler was on a longer journey[28] than merely from Jerusalem to Jericho. But he did not use haste or business as an excuse for passing by the unfortunate man. Neither did he ask who the man was in order to learn whether he was his neighbor. He did not determine the extent of the suffering man's actual need. Perhaps in less time than we have consumed in explaining this, the Samaritan saw him, had compassion on him, went to him, and made preparations to apply medical aid from his traveler's supply. "He bound up his wounds, pouring on oil and wine." On the bandages he poured a mixture of what was commonly regarded and used as a dressing for wounds. Then he lifted him up

9
The Good Samaritan
Lk 10:30–37

"on his own animal," which he would otherwise have mounted himself, and shuffled along beside them until he arrived at an inn, where he could give him additional care. He deferred business or whatever awaited him at the end of his journey. He spent the night with the wounded man, who perhaps had a high fever. Not until the next morning, when the patient had sufficiently improved, did he leave his side. Before leaving, however, he extracted from his purse two denarii,[29] that is, about twice as much as the laborers in the vineyard received for a day's labor (Mt 20:2). Entrusting these to the innkeeper, he charged him: "Take care of him, and whatever more you spend, I will repay you when I come again." And now the application: "Which of these three, do you think, proved to be a neighbor to the man who fell among the robbers?" The answer is easy enough. The law of love bound all three to perform the deed of mercy described, but only one of them did it. And he was a Samaritan. The lawyer was honest enough to answer the question correctly. But we should not commend him too highly. We might add that he was unwilling to take the hated name of the Samaritans on his lips and to give the whole detested nation credit for the kind deed of one. His answer was: "the one who showed him mercy." His paraphrase admitted well enough that a member of a schismatic nation had grasped and observed the true mandate of love. However, the very men whose official duty it was to interpret the Law and to lead in the worship of God had failed to do so. This, then, was the burden of our Lord's final reply: "You go, and do likewise." The Lord, who "knew what was in man" (Jn 2:25), desired to impress this much-needed lesson upon the lawyer. He had failed to show that love to his fellow men that the Samaritan had practiced. The lawyer learned that he did not, as he imagined, love his neighbor as himself; much less, then, did he love God above all things.[30]

10
"One Thing Is Necessary"
Lk 10:38–42

It is impossible to trace Jesus' movements in this period of His ministry. But between the Feast of Tabernacles and the Feast of Dedication and after His final departure from Galilee, His wanderings likely brought Him again to Judea, to the little town of Bethany,[31] hidden by the Mount of Olives, just a little east of Jerusalem. Here He found hospitality in the home of a certain woman named Martha, who received Him into her house. Whether she was the wife or the widow or some other relative of Simon the Leper (Mk 14:3; Mt 26:6), we do not know. The other known members of the household were a sister, Mary, and a brother, Lazarus. The latter, however, is not mentioned in this connection. He is not needed in this picture. Probably he was absent at the time. Martha had charge of the household and she is mentioned first, so we infer that she was the elder sister. We know that the sisters received general sympathy at a later, sad occasion (Jn 11:19, 33) and that Mary used costly ointment to anoint Jesus (Jn 12:3). So we assume that these disciples were "in easy circumstances and of sufficient dignity to attract the attention in their village as well as in Jerusalem."[32] We picture to ourselves a stir in this house as Jesus' arrival was probably announced by some of the Seventy-Two during their mission tour. And especially Martha, being a very kind hostess, was exceedingly busy. She was "distracted with much serving" and "anxious and troubled about many things" in her efforts to provide entertainment that would be both worthy of Jesus and to the credit of her house. Mary, too, was eager to give Jesus a proper reception. But the expression of her devotion was of a different kind. While Martha was all hustle and bustle and happily engaged in providing as best she could for the material comfort of her distinguished Guest, Mary dropped her work. She sat at Jesus' feet, as Martha thought, idly, and left all the troubles to fall on her sister. While Mary listened to Jesus speak, Martha was in no placid mood. Neither was she slow to express her mind. "Lord, do You not care that my sister has left me to serve alone? Tell her then to help me." In His answer, Jesus was both mindful of Martha's loving service and infinitely tender in supplying the needed correcting word. He would in no way "pain, but only purify, the faithful heart" to which He addressed His comments.[33] "Martha, Martha, you are anxious and troubled about many things"—this in grateful recognition of her loving concern for Him. "But one thing is necessary." After all, in His kingdom, the important thing is not food, but the Word; not the body and the house, but the soul and the kingdom of God. "Mary has chosen the good portion, which will not be taken away from her." Thus, Mary is defended, and yet Martha is not repelled. For "Jesus loved Martha and her sister" (Jn 11:5). Nor does the Lord discourage the Martha-like deeds of love done unto Him. That is not the point here. In this instance, well-meaning Martha permitted something to keep her from Jesus. Although we must place everything at the disposal of Jesus and His Word, there is nothing that should separate us from Him, be it time, money, or service. In the proper coordination and relation of values, first things must come first. "One thing is necessary." This is an absolute truth. For this there is no substitute. Otherwise, it would not be the "one thing . . . necessary."

In their wanderings through Perea, it was natural for the disciples to recall the activities of John. The scenes of his labor brought back to memory his message of repentance, his Baptism, his great earnestness and austere life, and especially also his life of prayer. Noticing how Jesus often resorted to prayer, one of His disciples raised a question. He was probably one of the outer circle, who had not been with Jesus when He preached the Sermon on the Mount, but had joined Him at a later period or came to Him from the company of John. He made the request: "Lord, teach us to pray, as John taught his disciples." Except for this notice, we would not have known that John gave his disciples particular instruction in prayer, although it might have been assumed (Lk 5:33). Jesus gladly consented and repeated in substance the Lord's Prayer, which He had already given at the time of the Sermon on the Mount.

11
Christ Again Gives the Lord's Prayer
Lk 11:1–4[34]

After Jesus had thus again taught His disciples to pray, He gave them the assurance that their prayers would be heard. They must, however, be persistent in prayer, as He explains in the parable of the impudent friend. While a certain man was sleeping in his house, he was roused out of his slumber by the unexpected arrival of a friend, who was engaged in a journey. To travel by night in a hot climate is probably "not unseasonable from the traveler's point of view, but a midnight arrival is unseasonable from the standpoint of the people at home."[35] Having "nothing to set before him," he in turn roused another friend out of his sleep with the urgent plea to lend him three loaves of bread. But the friend protested against this untimely request. The door had been barred for the night, the children had retired, and he did not wish to be bothered nor have the whole household disturbed for such a trifling cause. "I cannot get up and give you anything." But as the disturber suspected and the parable shows, it was not so much the inability as the unwillingness of the man to comply with the request of the troublesome friend. However, there was no rest for him as long as the knocking continued. We can picture the situation to ourselves as we seem to hear how the urgent pleas were repeated. And with this shameless disregard of his friend's private comfort and apparent indifference, the impudent disturber reached his goal. "I tell you, though he will not get up and give him anything because he is his friend, yet because of his impudence he will rise and give him" not merely the requested three loaves, but "whatever he needs." "The difficulty was not in the giving, but in the rising."[36] And this was overcome, if not because of the mutual friendship, but because of the impudence of the pleading friend. The point is clear, and the details of the parable need not be pressed. With that persistent knocking going on, the man could not sleep. And in order to be able to go back to sleep, he had to stop the noise. Now, if that slumber-loving sleeper could be forced to yield, how much more will our merciful Father in heaven grant the petitions we address to Him! So important is the lesson of unwearied perseverance in prayer, which may seem to verge on impudence, that the Lord repeats some of the sayings of the Sermon on the Mount (Mt 7:7–10). "Ask, and it will be given to you; seek, and you will find; knock, and it will be opened to you. For everyone who asks receives, and the one who seeks finds, and to the one who knocks it will be opened." Such a loving Father will, however, not only grant the requests of His children, but will also not deceive them as to the nature of His gifts. Which loving father would give his son a serpent when he has requested a fish? Or if he asks for an egg, will he offer him a scorpion? Now, if human parents, whose disposition by nature is evil, will show so much affection for their children, how much more will our heavenly Father grant good gifts, the best gifts, yes, even the Holy Spirit, to those who ask Him!

When Jesus healed a mute demoniac, which must be placed in this period of the Lord's ministry, accusers raised the same old blasphemous charge that the Savior drove out demons by the help of Beelzebul. This happened already in what we have called the second preaching tour, just before the parables by the sea. And the Savior made substantially the same reply: "If Satan also is divided against himself, how will his kingdom stand?" But repeated deeds and sayings in the life of our Savior need not surprise us. Like circumstances bring about like or similar actions, and similar objections are met, as they sometimes must be, with the same arguments. One part of this section, however, is new, though we are reminded of incidents of similar content generally (Mt 12:46–50; Mk 3:32–35; Lk 8:19–21). After Jesus defended Himself against the blasphemous accusation of being in league with the devil, a mother in the large gathering called out a blessing on His mother.[38] "Blessed is the womb that bore you, and the breasts at which you nursed!" The woman meant well. She thought and spoke like a mother who considers herself happy in the possession of a distinguished son. But Jesus pointed out to her that "true happiness, true blessedness, has a different basis, a different reason."[39] "The felicity of natural motherhood [is] entirely subordinate to that of discipleship."[40] Jesus addressed that woman in particular, but voiced a truth intended for the ears of all His hearers: "Blessed rather are those who hear the word of God and keep it!'"

13
The Healing of a Mute Demoniac
Lk 11:14–28[37]

The healing of the demoniac and Jesus' self-defense against the blasphemous Beelzebul theory caused multitudes to close in on Him from every side. Therefore, the Lord took the opportunity to address them all. His cue for the discourse was taken from the request of a sign from heaven.[42] As if miracles were not sign enough! As on the former occasion, Jesus made a veiled reference to His resurrection. He again pointed to the sign of Jonah and to what the queen of the South did, who on Judgment Day will condemn the Jews of Jesus' day (1Ki 10:1). From the extreme ends of the civilized earth, the queen of Sheba had traveled in search of the wisdom of a mere man, while here stood before them one greater than Solomon, whose wisdom they had rejected. Again, the inhabitants of Nineveh repented at the preaching of Jonah; "and, behold, something greater than Jonah is here." Instead of opposing and obscuring, His listeners should act as a light. Jesus explains this as He repeats the parable about placing the light on a candlestick and the parable of the eye. The reason why so many do not send forth a bright beam of light is because their "eye is bad"—they have no true understanding of God's Word, the heavenly light, in consequence of which their "body is full of darkness." In other words, all their works are contrary to the Word. The purpose of a light is to illuminate. And the function of a Christian is to be a light. But in order to serve this purpose, his whole body must be full of light.

14
The Sign of Jonah and the Parable of the Eye Repeated
Lk 11:29–36[41]

15
Jesus the Guest
of a Pharisee
Lk 11:37–41

While Jesus was still speaking to the people, He received and accepted a Pharisee's invitation to dine[43] with him. Why the invitation was extended is not stated. From the contents of the table-talk it seems that courtesy was not the only reason.[44] Jesus went into the house and sat down for the meal[45] without having previously washed[46] His hands. "The Pharisee was astonished," to say the least.[47] Although Jesus ordinarily kept the regulations of the people, it seems that He deliberately neglected them in this case. Deciding not to observe the ceremonial washings amounted to a confessional act for the very reason that Pharisees looked upon these washings as legally binding. Most people raised no direct objections, but from the disapproving hints and disgusted glances, Jesus must have noticed that the Pharisee and his company did not distinguish between the ceremonial and the moral law. In their insistence upon externals, the Pharisees lost a sense of right and wrong in things that really mattered. Therefore, the Lord[48] pointed out that they were most scrupulous about cleansing the outside of the cup and the platter, while the inside and the food were the product of wickedness and plunder. They stressed outside purity while the heart was filled with sin. By insisting upon strict adherence to external purification, they entirely overlooked that "He who made the outside [made] the inside also." So why put so much stress on the former? God is especially interested in the spiritual inside, in the purity of the heart. Now, if the Pharisees would give alms from a pure and generous heart instead of bothering so much about the outside, then all things would be clean for them.

16
Woes to the
Pharisees
Lk 11:42–54[49]

A number of woes followed this criticism of externalism. The Pharisees were scrupulously careful about paying the tenth (Gn 28:22; Dt 14:23) of every possible tithable commodity, even of aromatic seeds and fragrant herbs used as condiments or for medicinal purposes, such as mint, rue, dill, cumin, and "every herb."[50] They overlooked such very important matters as impartial and just judgment of their fellow men and love of God! Woe to them for their love of prominence and for their desire to occupy the place of elders and rulers in the synagogues and local courts and to receive the respectful greetings of the people in the marketplaces! Woe to them and also to the hypocritical scribes, for they were like graves without the distinguishing mark of whitewash;[51] those passing by could not help stepping on them and Levitically defiling themselves by a contact with the dead (see Nu 19:16; Ezk 39:15)! But in reality, the Pharisees with all their falsehood and hypocrisy ought to be whitewashed themselves, so as to warn the people who came into daily contact with them.

17
Woes to the Lawyers
Lk 11:45–54

As Jesus uttered these strong words in a blanket denunciation of the Pharisees, a professional member of the party, a lawyer (Lk 10:25) or a scribe, spoke up: "Teacher, in saying these things you insult us also." Up to this point, he had probably secretly enjoyed the fearful denunciations of the "silly pietists and woman Pharisees."[52] But now he began to feel that Jesus' attack condemned not only Pharisaic bigotry and practice, but also the whole system of traditionalism. This expert on canon law had guessed correctly, for Jesus had also called down woes upon the lawyers. As a result of their findings and interpretations of the Law, the lawyers imposed heavy burdens upon the people. "You load people with burdens hard to bear, and you yourselves do not touch the burdens with one of your fingers." They erected tombs to the prophets with the idea of honoring them, but in reality they continued the prophet-killing work of their fathers. In dealing with Israel, God had perfected a plan as Jesus, the personified Wisdom of God Himself, expressed it: "Therefore also the Wisdom of God said, 'I will send them prophets and apostles,'" holy men of God in the Old Testament and the apostles in the New Testament, whom He had appointed. But what happened? "Some of whom they will kill and persecute." And what is the divine judgment upon them? "This generation" had received greater grace than all previous generations of Israel. Therefore, "this generation" had also incurred greater guilt in rejecting Christ and His apostles. The blood of all the prophets and martyrs, "shed from the foundation of the world, may be charged against this generation, from the blood of Abel," the first martyr, who also was considered a prophet, "to the blood of Zechariah," the prophet mentioned in the last book of the Hebrew Bible, the Second Book of Chronicles, "who perished between the altar and the sanctuary."[53] For all these murders the present generation shall be held accountable. But the main responsibility must rest upon the lawyers. They were the teachers of the people and the interpreters of the Law. And this leads to the last woe. "Woe to you, lawyers! For you have taken away the key of knowledge. You did not enter yourselves, and you hindered those who were entering." The words of prophecy were so clear that the people might have gained the proper understanding themselves. But the leaders stepped in with their false and carnal interpretations and deprived the people of the knowledge of salvation. The words are hard, but true. Instead of leading the opposition to a true appraisal of its own deficiency, the scribes and Pharisees began to be furiously inflamed at Jesus. Jesus told them the truth, yet they treacherously lay in wait for Him, seeking for an opportunity to "catch Him in something He might say."

The scribes and Pharisees pressed upon the Lord vehemently with captious questions after He left the Pharisee's house. Thousands of people gathered,[54] insomuch that they trampled one another down in their desire to hear and see Jesus. Following His custom, the Savior took the opportunity to address the multitudes upon those subjects that best fit their needs. This He did by directing His remarks to His disciples, yet turning at times expressly to the people, so that all could receive the benefit of His teachings. We are unable to trace the trend of thought,[55] but the opening word is natural enough: "Beware of the leaven of the Pharisees, which is hypocrisy." This reminds us of the departure of Jesus from Dalmanutha when His

18
Former Sayings
Repeated
Lk 12:1–12

disciples forgot to take bread with them (Mt 16:6, 11).[56] The fact that Jesus repeated these subjects need not cause us any uneasiness, because Jesus repeated those things that He wanted to impress well upon the minds of His followers. The next sayings repeat words of comfort and encouragement, first given in connection with the mission of the Twelve (Mt 10:26–32).[57] The word of warning about the terrible sin against the Holy Spirit was already heard on that busy day in Capernaum preceding the parables by the sea (Mt 12:32).[58] And the final word about persecutions and the promised guidance of the Holy Spirit in defense of the truth was likewise included in the instructions given in the mission of the Twelve (Mt 10:19–20).[59]

19
Christ Refuses to Divide an Inheritance
Lk 12:13–15

One of the listeners momentarily interrupted Jesus' address of lofty content for the sake of a purely personal matter. A man who could speak with such authority, like Jesus, would certainly be of service in the one thing that this man regarded as the center of the universe at this time. There are always small people in quest of influence for personal reasons. In this case it was an heir in search of someone to help him settle an estate. "Teacher, tell my brother to divide the inheritance with me." Probably he was a younger brother, who had not received his share or was not satisfied with the prescribed division of one-third to the younger and two-thirds to the elder brother (Dt 21:17). But true to the principle that the spiritual must be strictly separated from the temporal, Jesus showed that He was not interested in the case. "Man, who made Me a judge or arbitrator over you?" He was neither a judge to pass on the merits of the case nor an arbiter to carry out the judgment He would be inclined to make.[60] Very likely the man was a miser at heart. At any rate, Jesus saw fit to add the moral: "Take care, and be on your guard against all covetousness." Instead of appealing to Jesus to help apportion his share of earthly goods, he ought to have applied to Him for a portion of the treasures in heaven. For a man's life does not consist in worldly treasures, however much he may possess.

20
The Parable of the Rich Fool
Lk 12:16–21

This thought received additional explanation in the parable of the rich fool.[61] The land of a certain man had "produced plentifully." But instead of turning to God in humble gratitude for His rich blessings, the rich man had thoughts only of his own future enjoyment of them, without regard to faithful stewardship before God and his duty to fellow men less fortunate than he, not to mention the possible loss of wealth and the uncertainty of the hour of death. He thought only of enlarged barns wherein to store up all his fruits and all his goods. "And I will say to my soul, 'Soul, you have ample goods laid up for many years; relax, eat, drink, be merry.'" But as he was thinking about the enjoyment of his possessions for many years to come, he did not even have the possession of days. In boasting of the morrow, he was blind to the possibilities of even the present day (Pr 27:1). In the midst of his godless meditations, there was a terrible echo from heaven: "Fool! This night your soul is required of you, and the things you have prepared, whose will they be?" And the lesson? "So is the one who lays up treasure for himself and is not rich toward God."[62]

The disciples again became the special audience of Jesus. But we suppose that the multitude also listened as Jesus repeated portions of the Sermon on the Mount. The section includes the warnings against anxiety about meat and clothing, in which Jesus points to the ravens; "for they neither sow nor reap," and to the lilies, "how they grow: they neither toil nor spin, yet I tell you, even Solomon in all his glory was not arrayed like one of these." And since it is God who "clothes the grass, which is alive in the field today, and tomorrow is thrown into the oven," the admonition is given to seek the kingdom of God, "and these things will be added to you." Here and there we find a slight variation in expression. And there is another gem added to the string of pearls, as, for instance, when the disciples are encouraged with the words: "Fear not, little flock, for it is your Father's good pleasure to give you the kingdom." To receive this Kingdom should be the object of all our desires, all is to be sacrificed for it, and its coming is to be eagerly awaited.

21
Repeating Former Sayings
Lk 12:22–34[63]

In watchful waiting for the Kingdom, "stay dressed for action and keep your lamps burning." That is, keep the robe lifted up and the hem fastened to the belt for instant service, and your lamps lit, as the Lord explains in the parable of the waiting servants. Be like faithful servants, waiting for their master, who has gone to his wedding feast and is expected to return with his bride. When the master returns and knocks at the door, every servant will be at his place and ready to receive him and give him joyful service. In a happy mood, the master will reward such faithfulness in an exchange of roles. Girding himself, he will reward his servants with portions brought from the wedding feast, especially if he will find them waiting in the second or third watch.[64] "Blessed are those servants." Thus, the Lord's disciples should be ready and wait for His return to judgment. This lesson of readiness is emphasized in another parable:[65] "If the master of the house had known at what hour the thief was coming, he would not have left his house to be broken into." To this, the lesson is added: "You also must be ready, for the Son of Man is coming at an hour you do not expect."

22
The Parable of the Waiting Servants
Lk 12:35–40

At this point, Peter raised the question of whether the parable and its lesson was meant for the disciples or for all. The Lord[67] did not answer directly, but the continuation of His discourse indicated that the reference was primarily to believing disciples. The master places the most faithful servants in positions of trust; for instance, he entrusts them with the administration of the household and the dealing out of portions of food. And "blessed is that servant whom his master will find so doing when he comes." His reward for faithful service is that "he will set him over all his possessions." But if the servant, trusting in the delay of the master's return, is found beating the male and female servants, eating and drinking, even becoming

23
The Parable of the Wise Steward
Lk 12:41–48[66]

drunk, at the moment when the master unexpectedly returns, he will receive the punishment that his unfaithfulness deserves. The master of that servant "will cut him in pieces"[68] and put him with the unbelievers. The punishment is severe, but it is according to the demands of responsibility and trust. The servant who knew his master's will but failed to do it "will receive a severe beating." But the offender "who did not know, and did what deserved a beating, will receive a light beating." Thus Peter receives his reply. A follower of Christ, especially the trusted disciple, must be alert at all times in the entire matter of sanctification. The general maxim, which metes out penalty according to responsibility and trust, applies also to the kingdom of heaven. "Everyone to whom much was given, of him much will be required, and from him to whom they entrusted much, they will demand the more."

24
"Do You Think That I Have Come to Give Peace on Earth?"
Lk 12:49–53

Great fidelity is required. And this becomes all the more difficult as the truth and the meaning of the Gospel become known. "I came to cast fire on the earth," the fire of a new faith, creating burning enthusiasm among some and fierce antagonism among others—deplorable, but inevitable, and the sooner kindled, the better. "Would that it were already kindled!" There will be fiery trials; but the disciples should be encouraged at the thought that the Lord Himself will not go out unscathed. "I have a baptism to be baptized with." The fiery baptism of His Passion looms up before Him with such threatening aspect that He feels Himself distressed on every side, both with a fervent desire of its accomplishment and with a natural dread of the great ordeal (Jn 12:27).[69] And do not misunderstand the reaction to the Gospel. "Do you think that I have come to give peace on earth?" Jesus is by no means a patron of war, and His Gospel is in every respect a message of peace; yet it will not be peacefully received. To His own question, He replies: "No, I tell you, but rather division." The preaching of the Word will always act as a separating force. Dissension, strife, and enmity will follow, even in the midst of the most close-knit family ties. "In one house there will be five divided," father, mother, son, daughter, and daughter-in-law, "three against two and two against three." The disciples should be forewarned about this saddest of conditions in religious life lest they be offended.

25
Interpreting the Signs of the Times
Lk 12:54–57[70]

This is a time of discord, conflict, and division, but a dawn of a new era nevertheless. And this period should be viewed in proper perspective, as the Lord points out again, directing Himself to the people. When the clouds came up black from the west, the region of the Mediterranean Sea, this meant rain. But if the winds blew from Arabia, across the burning deserts, it naturally meant withering heat. "This weather skill anyone in the audience might possess."[71] And still, "You hypocrites! You know how to interpret the appearance of earth and sky, but why do you not know how to interpret the present time?" The signs were here, the Messiah had come, and still the eyes of the nation had not discerned it. There was but one conclusion: they were unable to judge the signs. They were a shallow lot and without judgment in spiritual things.

It is necessary to be in harmony with the new day, as Jesus explains with a legal scene from everyday life. The lesson on reconciling the enemy given in the Sermon on the Mount is here described as an "effort"[73] in timely repentance, "lest he drag you to the judge, and the judge hand you over to the officer, and the officer put you in prison. I tell you, you will never get out until you have paid the very last penny."[74]

26
Conciliating the Adversary
Lk 12:58–59[72]

For the next teaching, the assumed setting is Judea, just before Jesus' visit to Jerusalem for the Feast of Dedication,[75] which was possibly even now in progress.[76] A report was brought to Jesus of "the Galileans whose blood Pilate had mingled with their sacrifices." These countrymen of Jesus may have offended the governor by revolt or protest, for which the Galileans were nationally known. We do not know the date of the event, and it might have happened at some other time. But it has been supposed[77] that they attempted an insurrection during the Feast of Dedication. This festival brought to memory the revolt of the Maccabees against the oppression of foreign masters and the eventual victory of the oppressed. For this, Pilate took fearful revenge. In the midst of their sacrifices, he caused the rioters to be slain in the temple, so that their blood mingled with the sacrifices that they intended to present. And this was not the first massacre in a holy place. Archelaus had slain three thousand Jews during a Passover disturbance thirty years before.[78] The news was brought to Jesus, presumably in the hope that He would be incensed at this outrage against His countrymen.[79] Instead of joining the nationalists in opposition to the hated rule of Rome, Jesus connects the report with a new admonition to repentance. Most people believed that so sudden a death in the midst of so sacred an act was evidence of a just divine punishment for especially wicked deeds that these victims committed (Jn 9:2–3). But Jesus corrects the notion. "Do you think that these Galileans were worse sinners than all the other Galileans, because they suffered this way?" He continues: "No, I tell you; but unless you repent, you will all likewise perish." And since He kept Himself informed on current events,[80] Jesus could point to another calamity that had taken place in Jerusalem, in which a "tower in Siloam" collapsed and killed eighteen people. Although we know of the Pool of Siloam near Jerusalem (Jn 9:7), our knowledge of this calamity is contained only in Jesus' question. The hearers probably supposed that the sufferers were sinners of exceptional guilt. But very emphatically, Jesus repeats the former statement: "No, I tell you." Contrary to popular expectation, some of the best minds in Israel might have been involved in these calamities. The main lesson, however, that Christ desired to teach was this: "Unless you repent, you will all likewise perish."

27
The Galileans Slain by Pilate
Lk 13:1–5

Repentance is needed for all. And there is time given for repentance. The Lord's long-suffering is great. But at last it will come to an end. This is the earnest lesson

28
The Parable of the Barren Fig Tree
Lk 13:6–9

Christ taught in the parable of the fig tree planted by a certain man of means in his vineyard, from which he naturally expected fruit. "And he came seeking fruit on it and found none." Finally, he gave it up. The tree had matured. In the ordinary course of nature, the time had fully arrived for it to yield a crop. However, three more years went by, and still there was no sign of fruit. "And he said to the vine-dresser, 'Look, for three years now I have come seeking fruit on this fig tree, and I find none. Cut it down. Why should it use up the ground?'" He had waited three years past the time of fruit-bearing to determine whether the fig tree would do the one thing for which it had been planted. It was not his purpose to raise it to be an ornament or to provide shade. But besides bearing no fruit, the tree occupied valu-able space that might be more profitably used. In the face of experience, it seemed useless to waste any more time on its cultivation. But the vinedresser interceded for the fig tree, pleading for a fourth year, when he would use all his arts, "dig around it and put on manure," in the hope that it might still be coaxed into bringing fruit. "Then if it should bear fruit next year, well and good." But if this last effort should also prove unfruitful, then "cut it down," remove it, and have another tree planted in its place. A few words of explanation. It has been thought that the three years pointed to the three-year public ministry of Jesus.[81] But the best interpretation seems to be to take the three years as the whole period of grace given to Israel in the Old Testament in which the chosen fig tree was expected to yield fruit acceptable to God.

> The fourth year, for which the Vine-dresser, Jesus, pleaded, was the special period of grace, which dawned with the ministry of John, burst into full brightness with the preaching of Jesus, and continued during the ministry of the apostles.[82]

"If it should bear fruit next year, well and good." But we know what happened. The extra time went by, and the fig tree was cut down, with the destruction of Jerusalem and the dispersion of the race.

29
The Crippled Woman Healed on a Sabbath
Lk 13:10–14

We have already called attention to the silence in the records about our Savior's teaching in the synagogues at this time as compared with His earlier ministry.[83] But here again we find Jesus teaching in a synagogue on a Sabbath day. If we are permit-ted to venture a guess, it was a Judean synagogue, probably in the neighborhood of Jerusalem,[84] and probably on the Sabbath before the Feast of Dedication or even on the Sabbath during the Dedication week of AD 32.[85] Among the worshipers in the synagogue, there was a poor woman "who had had a disabling spirit for eigh-teen years. She was bent over and could not fully straighten herself." The spirit of sickness that contracted her body was really a demon (v. 16),[86] who so paralyzed her muscular powers that she could not so much as raise her head. It held her down in a stooping position, as if bound by chains. The mere sight of her wretched condi-tion was sufficient appeal to the compassionate heart of Jesus. Calling her into His presence, He said to her, "Woman, you are freed from your disability." No sooner had He laid His hands on her than she straightened up and glorified God. Thus, there is a revelation of that Savior-glory as manifested in His usual healing ministry. But the praises of the healed woman were heartlessly cut short, because Jesus healed her on the Sabbath day. "In all the fussiness of official hypocrisy,"[87] the ruler of the synagogue sees fit to deliver a rebuke as he gets up and speaks "*to* the people"[88] about the crime of being healed on a Sabbath day. For they could just as well have been healed on any other day: "There are six days in which work ought to be done"—being healed is work!? "Come on those days and be healed, and not on the Sabbath day."

To this hopeless stupidity and purely mechanical observance of the Law, the Lord[89] replies with an argument that even this official is able to understand. This was not the first time that Jesus had to defend Himself against Sabbath infringements. And we notice that He constantly varied His arguments.[90] Here He appealed to the practice of the objector himself, as expressly permitted by rabbinic law.[91] "You hypocrites! Does not each of you on the Sabbath untie his ox or his donkey from the manger and lead it away to water it?" The Jewish elders permitted even the drawing of water, provided, however, that the water was not carried to the animal. And now the argument: A daughter of Abraham versus an ass. Bound by Satan for eighteen years versus the thirst of a few hours.[92] "Ought not this woman, a daughter of Abraham whom Satan bound for eighteen years, be loosed from this bond on the Sabbath day?" The argument was irresistible. "All His adversaries were put to shame," while "all the people rejoiced at all the glorious things that were done by Him."

Jesus took the joy of the people at the performance of the miracle on the crippled woman as a good sign for the future.[94] Although the rulers as well as the nation as a whole rejected Him, yet there would remain a "little flock" (12:32). Even in the face of persecutions, they would fearlessly receive Him with joyful acclaim. The joy of the people justified the hopes of the Savior on behalf of His kingdom, small and insignificant at first, but all-pervading and in the course of time growing into proportions of power. Thoughts such as these may have prompted Jesus to repeat the parables of the mustard seed "that a man took and sowed in his garden, and it grew and became a tree," and of the leaven "that a woman took and hid in three measures of flour, until it was all leavened." "This seems to be the only instance in which parables were connected with synagogue addresses as their occasion."[95]

30
"Ought Not This Woman Be Loosed from This Bond?"
Lk 13:15–17

31
Parables of Mustard Seed and Leaven Repeated
Lk 13:18–21[93]

22

AT THE FEAST OF DEDICATION IN JERUSALEM

LATE DECEMBER, AD 32

We have already stated our opinion that the events related in the preceding pages took place in the neighborhood of Jerusalem[1] and, we might add here, with Bethany as probable headquarters (Lk 10:38).[2] According to this arrangement, which fits in with the evangelist John,[3] there is no reason to conjecture a special journey to Jerusalem for the Feast of Dedication, which was celebrated at this time. It is indeed improbable that Jesus would otherwise have gone up simply because of this feast, because it was one of the minor festivals. Although many celebrated it in Jerusalem, He might have observed it anywhere else in the land as well.[4] But Jesus was the true Judas Maccabaeus and "trustworthy prophet" (1Macc 14:41)[5] for whose coming the royalty of the Maccabees was to be held in trust. Jesus was the true Deliverer from oppression and the Purifier of the temple of God from defilement as well as the true Light of Israel and the Lamp of David to shine into the darkness. So He gives His presence in Jerusalem, though probably only for one day, to this annual eight-day festival of patriotic yearning and national joy while also testifying to His divine Sonship, in which the visit resulted. The festival itself was not of biblical origin. Judas Maccabaeus instituted it in 164 BC, when the temple (which Antiochus Epiphanes had shamefully desecrated) was again dedicated to the service of God (1Macc 4:52–59).[6] The festival was also called The Lights,[7] from the custom of illuminating the temple and the private houses for the duration of the feast. There was also a chanting of the Hallel (Pss 113–18), the carrying of palm branches, and other characteristics of the Feast of Tabernacles. Although some of the ceremonies may have been taken over from Tabernacles, it seems that the illumination of the temple passed from Dedication into the observance of Tabernacles. Tradition has it that when Judas Maccabaeus restored temple services, the priests found that the oil was

1
The Feast of
Dedication
(Hanukkah)
Jn 10:22

desecrated. They discovered only one undefiled flagon that was sealed with the signet of the high priest. This supply was only sufficient to feed the sacred lampstand for one day, but a miracle replenished the flagon for eight days, when a supply of fresh oil was secured.[8] In memory of this, the temple was ordered to be illuminated the following year for eight days on the anniversary of its rededication. Hence the eight days, which were counted from the 25th of Chislev.

2
Solomon's Porch
Jn 10:23

At any rate, "the Feast of the Dedication[9] took place at Jerusalem. It was winter,[10] and Jesus was walking in the temple, in the colonnade[11] of Solomon." Because the weather was cold, He sought the sheltering columns on the east side of the temple, in front of the Beautiful Gate and facing the valley of the Kidron.[12] The name of Solomon clung to these columns either because they were an undestroyed relic of the old temple or because they were built of material that had formed part of the ancient structure.[13]

3
"If You Are the
Christ, Tell Us
Plainly"
Jn 10:24–26

At the anniversary of a splendid deliverance wrought by a handful of men, the air was mingled with memories of a glorious past and the fervent hope that a similar day, indeed a day of even greater deliverance, might soon arrive. As "the Jews"[14] noticed Jesus walking up and down between the marble columns, they rushed upon Him with the demand to relieve them of their suspense: "How long will You keep us in suspense? If You are the Christ, tell us plainly,"[15] even now and here in Solomon's Porch. As if He had not already done so! On many occasions He had testified to the fact by His messianic works (Jn 1:41; 4:26; 5:36; 8:42; 9:37). The trouble was not with Him, but with them. "He could not descend to their notions, nor would they rise to His."[16] Still others, who at the outset had probably shared the same false views, had accepted Him as the Christ of God. And yet, in spite of previous rejections and controversies, they would probably even now have acclaimed Him at once if only in a measure He would fulfill their unspiritual hopes. In His reply, Jesus first of all defends Himself against the charge that He had not told them the truth concerning Himself. And from His words, He appeals to the undisputed witness of the deeds that He had wrought in His Father's name. But their unbelief in view of all evidences was proof that they were not His sheep (8:47).

4
"My Sheep Hear
My Voice"
Jn 10:27–30

They would follow a shepherd like Judas Maccabaeus. But a voice that sounded the Gospel garnered no response. The reference to sheep in a figurative sense need not surprise us. He earlier made the same reference in this same place—and likely some of those who heard Him now had been present then—during the Feast of Tabernacles a few months before.[17] He spoke parables on the relation of the sheep and the shepherd. As He had stated then that it was the characteristic of sheep to recognize the voice of their shepherd (Jn 10:4), so He repeats here: "My sheep hear My voice, and I know them, and they follow Me." And lest through some carnal interpretation His hearers misunderstand the figure of speech, He adds that He is referring to spiritual things: "I give them eternal life." What He says here is a matter of the Word, the Father, the heart, divine promise, and absolute certainty and assurance of everlasting life. "No one will snatch them out of My hand." This statement can be so confidently made because the sheep of Jesus are a gift of the heavenly Father, who is "greater than all, and no one is able to snatch them out of the Father's hand." Neither is this a contradiction; for "I and the Father are one."[18]

A bit of history is helpful at this point. In the fourth century, Arian heretics would misinterpret Jesus' words about His unity with the Father. Yet, Jesus spoke "plainly, and there is no doubt about these words. And in their understanding of them the Jews were no Arians. In these words of Jesus the blind Jews saw more than the anti-Trinitarians see today."[19] And St. Augustine remarks[20] that the word *one* refutes Arianism, which denies the unity of essence, the *homoousion*. And the plural word *are* disproves Sabellianism, which denies the distinct persons in the Trinity. Again (see 8:59), the Jews, sensing blasphemy, stooped down to seize some of the scattered stones that the unfinished temple building supplied. They would have stoned Him. But the "undisturbed majesty of Jesus disarmed them"[21] with the words: "I have shown you many good works from the Father; for which of them are you going to stone Me?"

5
"I and the Father Are One"
Jn 10:30–32

In a reply that incidentally confirmed the miracles of Jesus, the Jews answered: "It is not for a good work that we are going to stone You but for blasphemy, because You, being a man, make Yourself God." They answered as they saw the situation.[22] In their ears, the claims of Jesus were nothing short of blasphemy (see Lv 24:10–16; Dt 18:20). But, as Jesus points out, it is even possible for ordinary men to be called gods.[23] "Is it not written in your Law, 'I said, you are gods'?" (see Ps 82:6). The argument is from the lesser to the greater. The reference is to magistrates, through whom the will of God was delivered to the people. If they, in their official capacity as God's representatives, are called gods, how much greater right has He, then, to be called the Son of God, whom the Father sanctified and sent to redeem the world! Jesus took His quotation from the Book of Psalms. He refers to it as "the Law," which in the Old Testament sense embraced all the canonical writings of the Old Testament.[24] As the divinely inspired Scriptures, they "cannot be broken." Returning now to His first argument, about His works, the Lord continues: "If I am not doing the works of My Father, then do not believe Me." If they would not credit His statements for His sake, they should at least accept the testimony of His undeniable deeds. He did not need glory. But through the testimony of His deeds, they might "know and understand that the Father is in Me and I am in the Father."

6
The Charge of Blasphemy
Jn 10:33–38

The argument was irresistible. They dared not stone Him. But upon His repeated reference to His personal, essential unity with the Father, "again they sought to arrest Him" (see Jn 7:30, 44). They would at least place Him under arrest and have Him

7
Retirement into Perea
Jn 10:39–42

examined by the proper authorities. But Jesus, escaping out of their hands, left the temple and the city and departed beyond the Jordan, to the place where John had begun His early ministry of Baptism.[25] Here he remained for the next few months. After the rejections in Galilee, Samaria, and Judea, Perea was the only region in the land of Israel still open for Him before His final presentation to the nation in Jerusalem at the Passover. Of this Perean period we know nothing, unless, as we assume, some of the chapters of St. Luke are to be assigned to this period (13:22–17:10).[26] The evangelist John reports that the stay in Perea was not exactly private. He tells us that many came to see Jesus there. John the Baptist was known to many of the inhabitants of this region. As they made comparisons between Jesus and His forerunner, they said: "John did no sign,[27] but everything that John said about this man was true." And although neither Jesus nor John was generally accepted in Jerusalem, the result of the ministry of Jesus in Perea was that "many believed in Him there."[28]

23

THE LATER PEREAN MINISTRY

AFTER THE FEAST OF DEDICATION TO THE RAISING OF LAZARUS

Probably January to February, AD 33

We remember that the final withdrawal of Jesus from Galilee after the Feast of Tabernacles, in the fall of AD 32,[1] was in reality the beginning of that final journey toward Jerusalem. He had the cross as His goal. That He visited Jerusalem itself or that He reached it again during the raising of Lazarus (Jn 11:17–44), does not change the fact that in this whole period, "He set His face to go to Jerusalem" (Lk 9:51). But as we have pointed out,[2] while His face was set toward Jerusalem, His mind was still occupied with other things. "He went on His way through towns and villages," presumably of Perea (Jn 10:40), "teaching and journeying toward Jerusalem."

Jesus' main occupation during this period was teaching, though a miracle also is recorded (Lk 14:1–6).[3] And in His teaching, He touched again and again on the theme of God's wrath,[4] admonishing people to prepare for the Day of Judgment and the return of the Son of Man. It was on this journey that someone addressed Him with the question: "Lord, will those who are saved be few?" But this was an idle question. Rather than calculating the number of those attaining salvation, one should be concerned about receiving salvation for himself, which is by far more important. Jesus had not "come into the world to gratify men's curiosity,"[5] but to save their souls. For the benefit, therefore, of the questioner and of others, Jesus repeated the saying in the Sermon on the Mount: "Strive to enter through the narrow door" (cf. Mt 7:13–14). Heaven is pictured as a house with but one door. And he that will not enter through this one door, the door of repentance and faith, will find himself shut out. Moreover, he who does not want to make his entry on the day of grace, while the door is still open, will likewise find himself shut out. As long

1
Journeying toward Jerusalem
Lk 13:22

2
"Lord, Will Those Who Are Saved Be Few?"
Lk 13:23–24

as the Gospel invitation is heard, the door is still open. It is definitely closed, however, for each individual in the hour of death and for the entire human race when the Lord returns for Judgment Day. This is explained in the parable of the master of the house.

3
The Parable of the Master of the House
Lk 13:25–30

When the master of a house entertains guests, he must wait for a certain time to receive his guests. When the appointed time has come and he deems that all the guests are, or ought to be, present, he at length rises up and shuts the door. After this, no one can be admitted (cf. Mt 25:11–12). They who have not heeded the invitation will receive the answer: "I do not know where you come from." And should they insist upon recognition, pointing out to the master of the house, as indeed the contemporaries of Jesus could do—"We ate and drank in Your presence, and You taught in our streets"—it will not help them. The reason of their exclusion was not because the door was too narrow, but because they would not come in. And now, seeing that the warning of Jesus was true after all, their Judgment Day repentance was too late. "I tell you, I do not know where you come from. Depart from Me, all you workers of evil" (cf. Mt 7:22–23). Thus the terrible words uttered against the false prophets in the Sermon on the Mount find a general application here. Judgment Day will be a day of surprise and of gnashing of teeth, when the prophets, the patriarchs, and all their true descendants, "Abraham and Isaac and Jacob and all the prophets," will be found sitting in the kingdom of God. But those who supposed themselves to be Abraham's sons and the prophets' followers will be thrust out. The Lord had already said in connection with the faith of the centurion at Capernaum that this would happen (see Mt 8:11–12): "And people will come from east and west, and from north and south, and recline at table in the kingdom of God." Thus, "some are last who will be first, and some are first who will be last" (cf. Mt 19:30; 20:16). The Jews thought there was little or no chance for heathen-born believers to enter the Kingdom. These unbelieving Jews, on account of their birth, thought themselves members of the first rank in the kingdom of the Messiah, but they would find no admission at all.

4
A Warning against Herod
Lk 13:31–33

While Jesus was still in the territory of Herod Antipas (presumably in Perea),[6] some of the Pharisees approached Him. They warned: "Get away from here, for Herod wants to kill You." It is impossible to decide whether they acted as the agents of Herod trying to intimidate Jesus, whether they stated a fact that had come to their knowledge, or whether they were acting in their own interest, anxious to get rid of the presence of Jesus. But Jesus seems to take the warning at its face value—namely, that they were friends warning against a foe. "Go and tell that fox, 'Behold, I cast out demons and perform cures today and tomorrow, and the third day I finish My course.'"[7] Although the fox does not appear elsewhere in Scripture as a symbol of cunning, it seems that Jesus here had the fox-like cunning and knavery of Herod

Antipas in mind.[8] As regards the three days, it seems that they are to be taken as a complete, albeit brief, period of appointed time.[9] Jesus had come into the world for a purpose, and He would accomplish this purpose. "Nevertheless, I must go on My way today and tomorrow and the day following." A termination of His activity is implied. Like John the Baptist, He would die a prophet's death. However, He would not die at the hand of Herod, and not at an improper place such as Machaerus. In accordance with the Father's purpose and will, He would die in Jerusalem. "For it cannot be that a prophet should perish away from Jerusalem."

The thought that He was even now on a journey that was to end at the cross caused Jesus solemnly to address the slayer of prophets: "O Jerusalem, Jerusalem,[10] the city that kills the prophets and stones those who are sent to it! How often[11] would I have gathered your children together as a hen gathers her brood under her wings, and you were not willing!"[12] Because of the city's obstinate resistance to Christ's gracious invitation, He pronounces a word of judgment upon the unrepentant inhabitants. The Lord would destroy the temple and leave the city desolate. There would be judgment for the obdurate, but blessings for the believers, when the true inhabitants of Jerusalem shall see Him again with the eyes of faith and on the day of the revelation of His glory. Jerusalem desolate, Israel dispersed—and still every believer, whether Jew or Gentile, will be able to say: "Blessed is He who comes in the name of the Lord!"

5
"O Jerusalem, Jerusalem!"
Lk 13:34–35

Again the Lord is engaged in a Sabbath controversy.[13] It was on a Sabbath day that Jesus was invited for a feast into the house of a prominent member of the Pharisaic party.[14] The Sabbath feast itself was not a violation of the Sabbath ordinance, provided the food had been previously prepared.[15] Jesus accepted the invitation, although He was aware of a rather strange situation: a great man among the Pharisees invited Jesus as a friend, as if to be held in honor, and yet Jesus was regarded with suspicion and carefully watched. Among those present was one—presumably an unbidden guest, yet there by arrangement—who had dropsy.[16] Because he was there in the plain sight of all and before Jesus, it was no doubt a trap set for Him. Jesus' opponents thought that Jesus would again venture to offend popular prejudice by curing the man on a Sabbath or that His miraculous powers might fail in dealing with this inveterate disease. Thus, heartless and unfeeling, the teachers cruelly make an object of mercy and his suffering a tool in their hands. But Jesus anticipated their charge of healing on the Sabbath. He submitted to the distinguished company a very simple question: "Is it lawful to heal on the Sabbath, or not?" But "they remained silent." They could not answer the question in the negative since there was no sound basis for that in the Law. They must have felt that it was not only lawful but also *right* to heal on the Sabbath;[17] and still, to admit this would have amounted to disloyalty to their whole system. So there was an awkward

6
The Man Afflicted with Dropsy
Lk 14:1–4

silence. But their very silence was sufficient justification for the merciful action of Jesus. "Then He took[18] him and healed him and sent him away."

And now a defense. "Which of you, having a son or an ox[19] that has fallen into a well on a Sabbath day, will not immediately pull him out?"[20] The argument was invincible. It was the appeal to a principle that they had always theoretically admitted. The healing of a man was far more important than the rescuing of a beast from a perilous situation. And besides, it involved less labor. The supreme law was the law of love. And where it was a question of love and mercy, the Sabbath ordinance did not prevent bodily labor. The plot had failed. There was not even an argument. Their very silence was complete proof of the refutation of their contention that they were too "ungenerous to acknowledge."[21]

The previous incident took place, we may believe, before the meal. Jesus healed the man and dismissed him, giving a lesson on true Sabbath observance. But noticing how the guests scrambled for preferred places at or near the head of the table, Jesus saw an opportunity to add another lesson. Not a lesson on table manners, but a lesson on humility on account of the lack of good table manners. Even among their own associates, it seems to have been impossible for the Pharisees to deny that they were Pharisees (Mt 23:6). In order to teach them a much-needed lesson, the Lord put forth a parable on proper behavior at a wedding feast. According to a "wiser and better principle of social courtesy,"[22] a guest at a wedding feast should not strive for the most-honored seat. It may easily happen that among those present there is one who is held in higher esteem by the host than someone who actually was—or assumed that he was—entitled to the seat of honor. What a humiliation it would be to a proud guest if the host compelled him to give up his place to the guest of honor and, since all the guests were now seated, to move to the lowest place! A better policy would be to sit down "in the lowest place, so that when your host comes he may say to you, 'Friend, move up higher.'" Thus true and sincere humility would be honored in the presence of all the guests. Obviously, the purpose of the parable is not to teach table manners or to show how in some clever way one may attain honor but to give a lesson on a great principle in the kingdom of God: "Everyone who exalts himself" (for instance, in pharisaical self-glorification) "will be humbled, and he who humbles himself" (that is, he whose humility is a fruit of true repentance) "will be exalted."

In the last analysis, the spirit of pharisaism—whether it be pride, ostentatious almsgiving, self-righteousness, long prayers, pretended sanctity, or even sham humility—was selfishness. And in accordance with the principle of unselfishness and true love of the neighbor, Jesus advises His host when making a dinner and inviting guests to not always select them according to the ordinary social standards of friends, brothers, kinsmen, rich neighbors, and those who might invite him or probably even outdo him in hospitality. With a kind and unselfish heart, a host should give attention to the poor, crippled, lame, and blind; then he would "be repaid at the resurrection of the just."

At this point, one of the guests who was deeply impressed by the words of Jesus, especially by the idea of a reward in heaven, made the remark: "Blessed is everyone who will eat bread in the kingdom of God!" Probably the expression was the result of momentary enthusiasm. At any rate, it served to call forth the parable of the great banquet. A certain man prepared an elaborate banquet and sent out invitations to a large number of guests. At the time of the feast, he ordered his servant to make the customary final call: "Come, for everything is now ready."

10
The Great Banquet
Lk 14:15-17

But as if by agreement, "they all alike began to make excuses." In every instance, those he invited named personal interests as excuses for not attending the feast. The excuses seemed reasonable. Here are a few examples: One had to manage a field recently purchased and had to go and look it over. "Please have me excused." Another was deeply engaged in an important business transaction, the purchase of five yoke of oxen, and, being now on his way to examine them, could not come. "Please have me excused." The mere statement of a third that he had married a wife seemed to be sufficient explanation for why he could not come. Thus the excuses ran in a general refusal. Of course, in the case of a real banquet, the offering of such excuses would have been most unusual, especially in view of the free offer, the quality and quantity of the refreshments, the host, and other considerations.[23] This parable depicts the bulk of the Jewish people as indifferent to the kingdom of Jesus and to the message of the Kingdom. So Jesus offered a sequel in the parable in accordance with the truth that He wished to impress upon the guest who had made the above remark.

11
"Please Have Me Excused"
Lk 14:18-20

A servant was obliged to report to his master a general rejection of the invitations and the almost unnatural behavior of invited guests. The master of the house was angry. And no wonder, since in the Middle East, and elsewhere for that matter, the failure to attend a banquet, even with apparently reasonable excuses, was a high insult. The fact remained that they did not come and they preferred their affairs to his. Being angry, the master sent out his servant again with the instruction to go quickly into "the streets and lanes of the city" and to bring in the poor, the crippled, the blind, and the lame. This was done, and many were led into the banquet hall. We might add that this was done in Israel when the spiritually poor, blind, and lame accepted the Savior's health and salvation while the scribes and Pharisees would not. But the servant reported to his master: "Still there is room." As a last resort, the master ordered his servant out into the country, along the highways and hedges, saying, "Compel people to come in, that my house may be filled." The details of the parables must not be pressed: it is not that those out in the country were "lower down socially"; rather, the host wanted to fill the house. These guests

12
"Go Out to the Highways and Hedges"
Lk 14:21-24

invited last represent the Gentiles.[24] No implication of a Jewish superiority as such is intended in the sequence of invitation. "For I tell you,[25] none of those men who were invited shall taste my banquet." The application was obvious to every guest who heard Jesus. God will have all men to be saved, and none will be rejected but those who exclude themselves. As applied to the kingdom of God—just as there will be surprises about those admitted, there will be even greater surprises about those who will find themselves cast out. Only recently the Lord had said: "In that place there will be weeping and gnashing of teeth, when you see Abraham and Isaac and Jacob and all the prophets in the kingdom of God and you yourselves cast out" (Lk 13:28).

13
The Cost of Discipleship
Lk 14:25–27

After the meal was over, Jesus again continued on the way that was finally to take Him to Jerusalem and to the cross. As formerly in Galilee, so here He was followed by great multitudes, to whom He spoke. The many around Him gave Him an occasion to repeat the demands He had made upon those who would follow Him in spirit and in truth (Mt 10:37–38). "If anyone comes to Me and does not hate[26] his own father and mother and wife and children and brothers and sisters, yes, and even his own life, he cannot be My disciple." Surprisingly strong words as compared with the words about the Twelve, where it was a question of loving less.[27] And still, how true! Love of other interests makes effective discipleship impossible: "He cannot[28] be My disciple." As compared with all other objects of natural love, even life itself, they must be hated so that Christ will be loved alone. True discipleship means the giving up of all else that is deemed precious. And more. Not only the denial of interests, but also actual sacrifice and suffering for the sake of Christ. "Whoever does not bear his own cross and come after Me cannot be My disciple" (cf. Mt 16:24; Mk 8:34; Lk 9:23).

14
Building a Tower
Lk 14:28–30

If that is discipleship, then certainly the costs must be counted. You must not only joyfully intend but also carefully consider, firmly resolve, and then follow through and carry out. It is just as with a man who wants to build a tower, a grand house, something to give credit to the builder and distinction to the community. Ordinary prudence will require that he first sit down and count the cost. Will he be able to carry it out? "Otherwise, when he has laid a foundation and is not able to finish, all who see it begin to mock him." In that event, instead of adding a point of interest to the community, he would have reared a monument to his shame.

15
A King Anxious to Fight
Lk 14:31–33

Or like a king who feels the urge of combat. Before he risks a battle with a neighboring king, he will first sit down and count how many of his subjects will be available for warfare.[29] Although it is possible for conquerors to overcome odds at the rate of two to one, it is unlikely. Therefore, if his army numbers only ten thousand, while the enemy is approaching with twenty thousand, common sense will prompt him to ask for peace, even though it means humiliation for him, rather than to risk miserable defeat. Thus they who would follow Jesus are required to count the cost. As to how the strong and conspicuous tower of sincere discipleship is to be built and where to gain the strength to overcome a two-to-one stronger enemy, that is a different matter.

The Lord is not so much interested in sudden gains as in the quality of discipleship. If a man is a disciple at all, he must show the characteristics of true discipleship. So the Lord repeats the illustration used in His Sermon on the Mount. "Salt is good"—that is, as long as it is salt (cf. Mt 5:13; Mk 9:50).[30] But if it has lost its saltiness, then it is good for nothing, not even "for the soil or for the manure pile." Mere outward conformity to the divine precepts of Christian living and sheer formality do not count in the kingdom of God. "He who has ears to hear, let him hear" (Mt 11:15; 13:9, 43; Mk 4:9; 4:23; Lk 8:8).

16
"Salt Is Good"
Lk 14:34–35

Now we come to a jewel in the Gospel account, which beautifully portrays God's love and grace toward a penitent sinner. In this period of the Lord's ministry as well as at other occasions, tax collectors and sinners approached Him "to hear Him." In accepting these and by telling the following parables, our Savior wished to emphasize the glorious truth that the love of God embraces every, even the greatest, sinner. But the professional guardians of Jewish morality objected to this intimate association of Jesus with the outcasts of society. "And the Pharisees and the scribes grumbled, saying, 'This man receives sinners and eats with them.'" It seems that it was this last particular fraternizing with them at table and thus winning their confidence that the Pharisees and scribes especially loathed. According to their opinion, this was carrying the matter of familiarity too far. But this narrow Pharisaic faultfinding served Jesus as an occasion for telling the three wonderful parables of the lost sheep, the lost coin, and the lost, or prodigal, son.

17
"Jesus Sinners Doth Receive"
Lk 15:1–2

Jesus previously told the parable of the lost sheep (Mt 18:12–14) at the close of His Galilean ministry and before His journey to the Feast of Tabernacles. At that time, His goals were to warn against offending the little ones and to restore the erring sinner. Here the point He wishes to emphasize is the joy of God and the holy angels over the conversion of a sinner in contrast to the ill will of the Pharisees. Rather than be offended at Jesus for receiving tax collectors and sinners, they should rejoice at their entry into the kingdom of heaven. Take, for instance, the case of a man who has a hundred sheep, but loses one of them. The shepherd is motivated not so much by the pain of diminished possession as by loss of, and concern for, the lost member of the flock. This man could easily have afforded to lose one sheep out of his herd; nevertheless, he leaves "the ninety-nine in the open country"—that is, in the unfenced pasture, and presumably under the care of an assistant. He takes immediate steps to find that one lost sheep. After he has found it, probably hungry and thirsty, with its strength practically spent but fortunately still alive and undevoured, "he lays it on his shoulders" and carries it to his home rejoicing. Coming home, he

18
The Lost Sheep
Lk 15:3–7

gives expression to his joy by calling together his friends and neighbors and saying: "Rejoice with me, for I have found my sheep that was lost." In like manner, there is "more joy in heaven over one sinner who repents than over ninety-nine righteous persons who need no repentance." The latter remark is for the special benefit of the Pharisees and scribes, who were like the rich who had need of nothing (Rv 3:17), and like the healthy, who needed no physician (Mt 9:12). They did not consider themselves lost and condemned sinners and therefore rejected Him who had come to seek and to save that which was lost.

19
The Lost Coin
Lk 15:8–10

Or think of a woman who has lost one of her ten drachmas, or pieces of silver. Now, a drachma in itself is of small value.[31] Yet to a poor woman who owned only ten drachmas in all, it was most valuable. How the woman lost the money is not stated, nor does it matter. But it is assumed that the loss occurred *in the house*, as compared with the sheep that had gone astray.[32] This is a point that the Pharisees and scribes might incidentally remember as homegrown Israelites. Immediately the woman lights a lamp, sweeps the house, peers into every nook and crevice, and seeks diligently till she finds the lost coin. Having found it, she calls her friends and neighbors and bids them rejoice with her over the recovery of a part of her possessions. Likewise, the Lord tells His adversaries, there is joy in the presence of God and of His "friends and neighbors" (the angels) "over one sinner who repents."[33]

20
The Prodigal Son
Lk 15:11–16

Now the most wonderful parable of all. "Never was there such a world of tenderness compressed into such few immortal words."[34] A certain man had two sons. The younger of them said to his father, "Father, give me the share of property that is coming to me." This was a demand for the property that would have fallen to him in due course of time, as founded upon the Jewish law of inheritance: two parts to the elder and one part to the younger son (Dt 21:17). "And he divided his property between them." Not that he was compelled to do so, but "that the story might go on."[35] The division of his property before his death was something that the father might, but did not have to do.[36] It seems that this father divided his property among both of his sons[37] in such a way as to reserve a sort of life lease on the portion of the elder son, who remained in his service. Not long afterward, the younger son gathered all he had and took his journey into an unnamed "far country" (for his purposes, the farther, the better) and "there he squandered his property in reckless living." This was the spurious independence of a son who was impatient with parental restraint and wished to do as he pleased. It was a sinner's love of the world. But the world "gives a miserable reward."[38] "And when he had spent everything, a severe famine arose in that country, and he began to be in need." Thus folly and sin are punished by the holy God. Not that the famine was especially created for the younger son; but had he not wasted his substance, he would have been able to weather the storm. "So he went and hired himself out to one of the citizens of that country," literally, he glued[39] himself to one who was not at all willing to engage the miserable wretch, but finally yielded by sending him "into his fields to feed pigs." A Jew could hardly imagine a more disgraceful lot. The heir of a proud race had become the caretaker of an animal whose very name was avoided and spoken of as "another thing."[40] And even in the foul infamy of this debasing service, the reward was so miserable that due to hunger, "he was longing to be fed with the pods[41] that the pigs ate, and no one gave him anything" (namely, anything better). His new master also felt the pinch of hard times, and "to get a meal of anything, even swine's food, was a treat."[42]

In this extremity of abject misery, the young man "came to himself."[43] Recklessness ended in misery and misery in reflection. He was the honored son of a respected father and then, for a brief spasm, the happy host of profligate friends. Now the pig-surrounded wretch began to meditate. "How many of my father's hired servants have more than enough bread, but I perish here with hunger!" And then the resolve, though it involved an effort and pained his pride: "I will arise and go to my father, and will say to him, 'Father, I have sinned against heaven and before you.'" Not that the possibilities that afterward occurred suggested themselves to his "befuddled" brain.[44] A reinstatement to sonship was too much to expect. Fully conscious that he had forfeited all claims as a son and keenly sensible of his husk-food and pig-surrounding, he wanted only to become a bread-fed servant in his father's house.

21
His Repentance
Lk 15:17–19

No sooner had the resolution been made than it was carried out. "And he arose and came to his father." What additional misery and privation was involved in his going back to his father as a beggar is not stated. The point is that true repentance must be revealed in deeds of repentance. "And now comes the never-to-be-equaled climax":[45] "But while he was still a long way off, his father saw him." No doubt he had been looking for him. No one would have recognized the ragged stranger as the rich man's son. "But the father's vision was sharpened by love."[46] The woeful sight awakened instant pity. "And [he] felt compassion, and ran"—walking was too slow—"and embraced him and kissed him." Thus the father is again introduced. All these actions were signs of love of a father who was ready to do anything to recover his loss. At this point, the son begins the speech that he had already rehearsed before the pigs and no doubt repeated along the way: "Father, I have sinned against heaven and before you. I am no longer worthy to be called your son." But it seems that the demeanor of his loving father repressed the last clause about making him one of the servants.[47] The mere fact that his son has returned is a proof to the father of his repentance. And immediately, he prepares to restore him to the rights and privileges of a son. We can picture to ourselves the scene: "Make haste!"[48] he calls to the servants who were attracted by the unexpected commotion. "Obliterate all traces of a wretched past! The lost son has returned!"[49] And so that they might understand the status of the new member of the household, he tells them: "Off with the rags

22
His Return
Lk 15:20–24

and get out the robes!" "Bring quickly the best robe, and put it on him, and put a ring on his hand, and shoes on his feet. And bring the fattened calf," he tells them, which is even now standing in the stall,[50] ready to serve at some future festal occasion. "Kill it, and let us eat and celebrate. For this my son was dead, and is alive again." And if there is joy in heaven at a sinner's return, so it is most fitting that the return of one as from the dead should be celebrated with feasting and "with music of angel harps."[51] "And they began to celebrate."

23
The Elder Brother
Lk 15:25–32

But the story has a sequel about the elder brother. It appears that he plays the role of the other lost son. In his attempt to throw a wet blanket over this gala affair, he represents the Pharisees in their chilling attitude toward Jesus' reception of tax collectors and sinners. While the festival was in progress, the elder son was "in the field." And, we might add, also while the younger son had been wasting his substance with riotous living, the elder son had been in the field. As he now returned to the house, he heard music and dancing. Naturally, he did not know what it was all about. The servant to whom he applied for information told him in simple language: "Your brother has come, and your father has killed the fattened calf, because he has received him back safe and sound." But with this news, the elder brother was not pleased, especially not with the manner in which the returning brother had been received. He was angry at what he considered the unfairness of the whole proceeding "and refused to go in." So "his father came out and entreated him." The elder son thought he had a good reason for complaint and made the most of it in a bitter speech. There was much on his mind. He did not like the sound of the music. He was angry with his father for his ready forgiveness of the profligate son. To show such a tender heart was a sign of weakness. Then there were other offenses too. For instance, he, the elder son, had never been rewarded for faithful service. In merciless judgment, saying "the worst in the coarsest way,"[52] the oldest brother dragged up again the forgiven sins of his repentant brother, whom he would not acknowledge as brother. "Look, these many years I have served you, and I never disobeyed your command, yet you never gave me a young goat, that I might celebrate with my friends. But when this son of yours came"—he would not call him brother—"who has devoured your property with prostitutes, you killed the fattened calf for him!" It was a son speaking to his father, but it was the language "of a servant"[53] and the expression of pharisaic conception of service and reward. But overlooking the self-righteousness of his elder son and justifying his own action of celebrating his younger son's return, the father tenderly replied: "Son, you are always with me, and all that is mine is yours." Have you forgotten? Why this uncharitable desire, this base touch, to make "the worst of sins repented of"?[54] And besides, not only the father's dealing with the younger son, but also his dealing with both of his sons was not a matter of service and reward but of grace and love. Therefore rejoice! "It was fitting to celebrate and be glad, for this your brother was dead, and is alive; he was lost and is found."—Both this and the two preceding parables were for the self-righteous Pharisees, who had expressed their dissatisfaction that Jesus had received spiritual prodigals, "tax collectors and sinners." These parables drove home the glorious truth that God's kingdom is a kingdom of divine grace, mercy, and love. He extends forgiveness freely to all who, having become ruefully conscious of their lost condition and of their awful plight in the face of a holy and just God, flee for pardon to Jesus. The Father had sent Him into the world to merit this free grace, whom they, however, spurned.

The disciples of Jesus had just heard the wonderful parable of the prodigal son. Jesus recruited them from those same tax collectors and sinners to whose reception the Pharisees and scribes objected. But lest the disciples become overly pleased that Jesus defended them and so neglect to perform their duty in the Kingdom, especially in the use of earthly possessions, Jesus sets forth the parable of the dishonest manager. A certain rich man had a manager who was accused of unfaithfulness in his duties. Calling the manager into his presence, he said to him: "What is this that I hear about you? Turn in the account of your management, for you can no longer be manager." There was no doubt, it seemed to him, as to the truth of the accusation and the justice of this discharge. But this sudden demand for an itemized account and the notice of his dismissal from a profitable post came to the manager like a thunderbolt from smiling skies. Immediately, he deliberated about a shrewd course of action. There was still some time to do so, and this he turned to good account. "The manager said to himself, 'What shall I do?'" By all means, something had to be done. There was no note of sorrow in his meditation, nor was there any desire to amend his ways. To his intensely practical mind, it was all a question of doing something to extricate himself from a very unpleasant situation. All possible schemes were rapidly reviewed, only to be as quickly dismissed, especially manual labor and begging. He was too weak to labor and too proud to beg. At last, however, he hit upon a feasible scheme, which would assure him willing reception into the houses of friends. Although his plan was dishonest and its whole execution based upon fraud at the expense of his master, it would secure his future. Remember that for the time being, the manager was still his master's representative, with all legal rights and authorities.[55] Possessing this authority, he was able to summon before him all of his master's debtors who either had bought goods on credit from him or were behind with their land rent. The security of his own future depended upon the successful outcome of a scheme with them. A few examples show how he insured their good will for his own best interests, involved them in his own deception and fraud, and secured his own future, all at the master's expense: "How much do you owe my master?" The reply was "a hundred measures of oil." The term used is *bath*, the largest

24
Parable of the Dishonest Manager
Lk 16:1–7

liquid measure among the Jews, corresponding to approximately six hundred gallons of olive oil.[56] The amount was not small.[57] But the manager told the debtor to take his bill[58] showing the amount of indebtedness and take off fifty percent. "Sit down quickly and write fifty." To another, who owed his master a hundred measures of wheat (about six hundred bushels[59]), he instructed him to deduct twenty percent. "Take your bill, and write eighty." In the same manner, he dealt with all the various debtors of his master. The diversity of deduction was merely to make the whole fraudulent proceedings look more like a true account.[60] There may be some questions asked, but it is assumed that after the day of reckoning, when the manager was shamefully dismissed, he had gained friends who were now themselves involved, and there was now no necessity for him to dig or beg.

25
The Application
Lk 16:8–13

"The master commended the dishonest manager for his shrewdness." The manager, whom he calls "dishonest,"[61] is not commended for his iniquity, but for his worldly prudence. "For," as Jesus explains, "the sons of this world are more shrewd in dealing with their own generation than the sons of light." From the false wisdom of the children of this world, how they deal with one another, and in regard to their own interests, the children of light should learn true spiritual wisdom. "And I tell you, make friends for yourselves by means of unrighteous wealth, so that when it fails they may receive you into the eternal dwellings," of course, not after the example of the dishonest manager but by making friends through deeds of charity. They should not do this as though by helping the poor they could earn salvation. Rather, they should secure witnesses at the portals of heaven who in the presence of the Judge will testify to their deeds of mercy and love (Mt 25:35–40). Jesus is not a teacher of immorality, as some have wrongly interpreted this parable. He that is a faithful manager of earthly possessions, great or small, will receive a gracious reward. He will be placed over greater things, oftentimes receiving greater earthly riches and honor but certainly, however, larger spiritual blessings. And he that is unfaithful as a manager of God in the use of his earthly wealth, great or small, has lost the faith. How, then, can he hope to obtain what had been his "own" as long as he stood fast in the faith, the heritage in heaven? Finally, repeating a saying of His Sermon on the Mount, Jesus said, "No servant can serve two masters, for either he will hate the one and love the other, or he will be devoted to the one and despise the other. You cannot serve God and money" (Mt 6:24).

26
The Law Has Not
Been Abolished
Lk 16:14–18

It seems that Jesus instructed His disciples in the hearing of all. Feeling the sting of the concluding saying, the Pharisees, who were lovers of money, showed their anger by turning up their noses,[62] by sneering, and by ridiculing Him. This childish behavior caused Jesus to chastise their self-righteousness.[63] As custodians of the Law, they justified themselves before men with their outward legality, but their self-righteousness was an abomination in the sight of God. In their proud aloofness from tax collectors and sinners, they overlooked the fact that the Law and the Prophets reached their goal and conclusion in John the Baptist (Mt 11:12–13). Since that time, the Gospel of the Kingdom has been preached, and penitent sinners have eagerly pushed forward and rushed into it, as it were, by force. Now, this does not mean that the Law has been abolished. The situation is rather this, that it is easier for heaven and earth to pass away than that the smallest turn or stroke of a Hebrew letter should fail (Mt 5:18). The commandments are still in force—for instance, the commandment against divorce. "Everyone who divorces his wife and marries another commits adultery, and he who marries a woman divorced from her husband commits adultery" (Mt 5:32; 19:9; Mk 10:11–12).

If they who appeal to the Law would only heed the Law, they would find that "the law and the prophets [are] a sufficient guide to a godly life."[64] In a most remarkable fashion, Jesus covers a number of points on the Law and the Prophets: worldliness, the service of money, the failure to secure the future, the neglect to make friends of the poor, and the like. In the striking parable of the rich man and Lazarus, a certain rich man is presented as clothed with the most expensive Egyptian white cotton and covered with the royal purple of Phoenician wool.[65] And his life was a daily feast; for he "feasted sumptuously every day." These details are given, not as if any blame were attached to the possession and enjoyment of wealth as such. For Abraham, who shortly afterward is introduced as presiding over heaven, was himself rich and yet God called Abraham His friend. However, from the language employed as well as from the trend of the whole story, the inference is justified that this particular rich man was of a worldly mind and chiefly concerned about the enjoyment of material things. Such was his manner of life. In contrast with this unnamed rich man,[66] Jesus presents a suffering beggar by the common name of Lazarus. The name itself probably means "God-help"[67] and is most likely introduced for the sake of convenience in telling the story, because he has to be referred to in the sequel.[68] Compared with the daily feasting of the rich man, Lazarus had a sorry lot. While servants would be carrying in food and drink for the master's table, friends would probably cast Lazarus down[69] at the gate of the rich man's estate, half-clothed and covered with ulcers. There, he might satisfy his hunger at least to a small extent and prolong his miserable existence by means of such scraps as would be cast from the rich man's table. Other creatures desired this position as well, the dogs of the street, who "came and licked his sores." Whether or not their visits alleviated or aggravated his misery, we do not know.[70]

The beggar died. No more of him here. But the angels came from heaven and carried him "to Abraham's side."[71] What happened to the soulless body is passed over in delicate reserve. But in due course of time, "the rich man also died and was buried." Brilliant was his life, his garments, his table, and even the arrangements that attended his death and burial. But here ends all his exaltedness before men.

27
The Rich Man and Lazarus
Lk 16:19–21

28
In the Hereafter
Lk 16:22–26

Death did not end all things in the case of poor Lazarus or in that of the rich man. But there was a difference. The soul of the rich man found itself in hell.[72] The experience is not a mere negative condition or state of death, but he was "in torment" and "with paradise dimly visible, yet within speaking distance."[73] Lifting up his eyes, the rich man could see "Abraham far off and Lazarus at his side." As to the various details, we must remember that they are not "dogmatic teaching, but popular description."[74] No doubt the rich man, a Jew and a son of Abraham, was greatly surprised to find himself in hell. The Pharisees among the listeners, for whose benefit Jesus told the story, were probably equally surprised on hearing Jesus make this statement. Although the rich man offers no furious resentment about a possible injustice because of his consignment to hell, when he sees and recognizes Abraham, he still hopes that the patriarch, his ancestor, can and will do something for him. In a strange dialogue, the tormented man calls out: "Father Abraham, have mercy on me, and send Lazarus to dip the end of his finger in water and cool my tongue, for I am in anguish in this flame." Firmly, Abraham replies: "Child, remember that you in your lifetime received your good things, and Lazarus in like manner bad things; but now he is comforted here, and you are in anguish." Not that the rich man was damned for the sake of his riches as such or that Lazarus was saved on account of his poverty and misery. Upon the rich man's request that his suffering be alleviated, Abraham tells him that because on earth he gave his heart to the things of this world and not to God, he is now getting his well-merited rewards by being tormented in hell. And besides, he must be reminded that "a great chasm has been fixed, in order that those who would pass from here to you may not be able, and none may cross from there to us." In those regions, there is a great chasm,[75] too wide to be bridged and too long to be outflanked. The disposition of all those entering either abode is fixed and final.

29
They Have Moses
and the Prophets
Lk 16:27–31

There is no use in pleading for himself. He must resign himself to his end. But as he sadly remembers former neglected duties, he continues the dialogue with the request: "Then I beg you, father, to send him to my father's house—for I have five brothers[76]—so that he may warn them, lest they also come into this place of torment." But even this request is denied. "They have Moses and the Prophets," the regular means of grace; "let them hear them." And here we have the answer to the question of why Lazarus was saved and the rich man awoke in hell. In misery, poverty, and suffering, Lazarus truly had "Moses and the Prophets." Without them and without true penitence and saving faith, regardless of his suffering on earth, he would have found himself alongside the rich man for continued suffering in hell. And the rich man was not rejected because he was rich or enjoyed life, but because he did not heed the Law and the Prophets in repentance and faith. Therefore, Abraham says about his five brothers, "Let them hear them." To this, the rich man objects: "No, father Abraham, but if someone goes to them from the dead, they will repent." However, without discussing whether Lazarus could go back to earth on this requested mission, the answer is given: "If they do not hear Moses and the Prophets, neither will they be convinced if someone should rise from the dead." If people will not hear and believe God's saving Word, they will never be saved "by ghosts."[77] Here, the parable as well as Christ's warning to the Pharisees is abruptly broken off.

There is a difference between giving and taking offense. The discussion of the foregoing chapters started when the Pharisees and scribes took offense at Jesus for receiving tax collectors and sinners (Lk 15:1–2). Yet Jesus had done no wrong. He had acted in accord with His messianic office. He had not *given* His revilers any offense, but they had unreasonably *taken* offense. The same was true when someone was offended at his neighbor's failure to observe fasting, ceremonial washings, and the like, which really was no sin because God did not command these things. They were only commandments of men. On the other hand, however, as Christ points out to His disciples, "Temptations to sin are sure to come, but woe to the one through whom they come!" There is a kind of offense that is extremely sinful—namely, that of scandalizing simple believers and especially children, causing them to trip and to fall away from Christ. It were far better for such an offender, as Christ says in a repetition of a former saying (Mt 18:6–7; Mk 9:42), "if a millstone were hung around his neck and he were cast into the sea."

30
Offenses
Lk 17:1–2

Followers of Christ must always guard against giving occasion to someone for stumbling. Moreover, a Christian should exercise brotherly love by admonishing the brother who has sinned against him (Mt 18:15). "And if he repents, forgive him." On account of the weakness of the erring brother, this process may have to be repeated. "And if he sins against you seven times in the day, and turns to you seven times, saying, 'I repent,' you must forgive him" (cf. Mt 18:21–22).

31
Forgiveness
Lk 17:3–4

What Christ here demanded of His followers required an unusual amount of love. And this unusual amount of love presupposes a correspondingly unusual amount of faith.[78] As matters stood, the apostles[79] were unequal to the task and said to the Lord:[80] "Increase our faith!" This request gave Jesus an opportunity to expand upon the favorite topic, that of the strength of faith. It is not so much a matter of quantity as of quality. "If you had faith like a grain of mustard seed, you could say to this mulberry tree,[81] 'Be uprooted and planted in the sea,' and it would obey you" (cf. Mt 17:20; 21:21; Mk 11:22–23).

32
The Great Power
of Faith
Lk 17:5–6

Faith will bring the disciples to such efficiency; but they should be warned against the idea of earning merit in the sight of God.[82] This is explained in the parable of the unworthy servants. A master who has servants—slaves in those days—plowing in the field or keeping sheep will not tell them at their return to the house to go

33
Parable of Unworthy
Servants
Lk 17:7–10

at once and eat their meal. He will rather make them serve him first. "Prepare supper for me, and dress properly, and serve me while I eat and drink, and afterward you will eat and drink." He does not thank the servant, does he? It is all in the day's work. So also it is in the kingdom of God. Even if it were possible for the followers of Christ to do their full duty, they would nevertheless in the sight of God be "unworthy servants." But is God a slave-driver? By no means. There is also a reward for faithful service. But that is not the point here. The purpose of Christ is not to teach in what spirit God deals with His servants, but in what spirit we should serve God.[83]

24

THE RAISING OF LAZARUS

AT BETHANY, NEAR JERUSALEM

Probably February, AD 33

While Jesus was in Perea, probably in February of AD 33, the news reached Him of a sick member of a household at Bethany, near Jerusalem, where He had been hospitably received on a former occasion (Lk 10:38–42). The sick man's name was Lazarus.[1] We do not know the nature of his sickness, except that he was in a critical condition, which caused his sisters, Martha and Mary, to send the message to Jesus: "Lord, he whom You love[2] is ill." This is evidently an urgent appeal for the helpful presence of Jesus, based not upon the worthiness (Lk 7:4) of Lazarus or of his sisters, but only upon the love of Jesus.[3] We have met the two sisters before: faithful, serving Martha and attentive Mary. The evangelist mentions an act of Mary that took place on a later occasion. "It was Mary who anointed the Lord[4] with ointment and wiped His feet with her hair."[5] Evidently, the sisters knew where to find Jesus and were confident that the mere notice of their brother's condition would bring Him to the rescue. They were assured of the love of Jesus because it is expressly stated that Jesus "loved[6] Martha and her sister and Lazarus." Jesus, however, gave a puzzling reply: "This illness does not lead to death. It is for the glory of God, so that the Son of God may be glorified through it." The Lord knew that the physical death of Lazarus was imminent, and still His words were true. He would let Lazarus die, so that He could restore him to life and manifest His glory. Instead of hastening to the bedside of His friend to effect his immediate restoration to health, He purposely decided to wait until Lazarus had breathed his last[7] and to remain "two days longer in the place where He was."

1
"Lord, He Whom You Love Is Ill"
Jn 11:1–6

2
"Lazarus Has Died"
Jn 11:7–16

Not until after the death of Lazarus, known to Jesus because of His omni-science, did Jesus announce His intention to His disciples to go to Judea. But the disciples received the announcement with astonishment. They reminded Jesus of His late experience both at the Feast of Tabernacles and at the Feast of Dedication (Jn 8:59; 10:31). "Rabbi, the Jews were just now seeking to stone You, and are You going there again?" But Jesus replies to this objection, saying that first of all it was still His day, appointed to Him by the Father, in which He must work. "Are there not twelve hours in the day?" And then, He continues in a parable: As long as the day lasts, a man may confidently go forward without stumbling, "because he sees the light of this world." But if a man walks around in darkness, he stumbles, "because the light is not in him." As long as His hour had not come in which He should suffer and die, no one would be able to harm Him. After quieting the disciples' fears about His safety, and incidentally also of their own (if they had been thinking about that), He speaks about Lazarus again: "Our friend Lazarus has fallen asleep, but I go to awaken him." Now, Jesus was speaking of the sleep of death. But the reference was misunderstood. "Lord, if he has fallen asleep, he will recover." Then Jesus told His disciples plainly: "Lazarus has died." Yes, He had permitted Lazarus to die. But in spite of the grief and pain this caused, and instead of grieving, He was glad for their sakes that He was not there when Lazarus died. In that case, Lazarus would not have died. But now it was His purpose to strengthen their faith by means of a miracle that He would perform. And so—"Let us go to him." But the disciples were still bewildered. No matter what Jesus intended by journeying to Judea, they were convinced that their Master was deliberately walking to His death. At least that was the view of Thomas, called Didymus ("Twin"),[8] who was the "pessimist" of the Twelve and later appears as the doubting Thomas (Jn 20:25). Yet despite what else might be said of him, Thomas was not a coward. To his mind, there was nothing left for Jesus but to die. His is such a sincere and affectionate loyalty that he cannot harbor the thought of allowing his Master to go alone. In addressing his fellow disciples, he expresses a fearless and undying loyalty in the words: "Let us also go, that we may die with Him." "In him unbelief and faith were contending with one another for mastery as Esau and Jacob in Rebecca's womb."[9]

3
"I Am the Resurrection and the Life"
Jn 11:17–27

We do not know from which point in Perea Jesus proceeded to Bethany nor how long it took Him to cover the distance. But because of the comparatively short distance between any point in Perea and Bethany[10] and on account of the following, we assume that Jesus was in no particular hurry. At any rate, when He reached Bethany, "He found[11] that Lazarus had already been in the tomb four days." According to the custom of the country, it is likely that they buried Lazarus the same day that he died. Since deep mourning lasted for seven days, Martha and Mary's house was still the center of the customary demonstration of grief and sorrow. That the family of Lazarus had some standing in the community can be seen from his burial in a tomb and from the visit of many Jews who had come from the nearby[12] capital city to express their condolences. As soon as Martha heard that Jesus was coming, she rushed out to meet Him, while "Mary remained seated in the house," immersed in grief. When Martha caught sight of Jesus, she called out to Him: "Lord, if You had been here, my brother would not have died." This was not said to blame Jesus for arriving too late; her words are merely a plaintive lament, issuing from the fullness of her grief-stricken heart. And even now, she goes on to correct her statement, as it were, in accordance with the message of Jesus.[13] She is convinced that "whatever You ask from God, God will give You." This is faith and hope. Still, there is something wrong with the statement. Jesus' deity was not yet living and real in Martha's consciousness. For the purpose of leading her to believe in Him as the One who could raise the dead by His own power, Jesus tells her: "Your brother will rise again." But it depends upon how these words are understood. "Martha ventures to take them as a consolatory word of promise relative to the resurrection at the Last Day."[14] It is a beautiful confession in itself: belief not merely in the immortality of the soul, but in the resurrection of the body.[15] But there is no resurrection at all (that is, to life) unless it is based upon Christ. "I am the resurrection and the life. Whoever believes in Me, though he die, yet shall he live, and everyone who lives and believes in Me shall never die." Jesus, and Jesus alone, is the resurrection and the life. "Do you believe this?" the Lord asks Martha. The believing heart of Martha answers: "Yes, Lord; I believe that You are the Christ, the Son of God."

This scene took place before the actual arrival of Jesus in Bethany.[16] After Martha had heard the Word of Life, she hastened back to Mary. The Jews were also present in her house, and she was aware of their enmity against Jesus. Because she wished to give her sister an opportunity to talk to Jesus alone, she said to her secretly: "The Teacher is here and is calling for you." In the conversation reported, Jesus had not expressed the wish to see Mary. But probably the whole conversation has not been reported, or Martha took it for granted that Jesus would gladly bring comfort to Mary also.[17] Immediately, Mary left her sister with the comforting visitors and rushed out to meet Jesus. The Jews thought an outburst of grief and sorrow had overcome Mary, and they intended to go to the grave and weep there. They were unwilling to leave her alone without words of sympathy and comfort. So they rose and followed her.[18] Consequently, when Mary reached Jesus, she had time only to fall down at His feet and to repeat the thought that undoubtedly had been the frequent refrain of her sorrow: "Lord, if You had been here, my brother would not have died." As Jesus noticed the tears of Mary and the wailing of the approaching Jews, He was filled with anger and displeasure in contemplation of the cause that has brought about all misery and suffering and finally death—sin. "He was deeply

4
"Jesus Wept"
Jn 11:28–37

moved in His spirit and greatly troubled." "His intense emotion prompts Him to end the scene."[19] He inquired about the location of the grave.[20] They told Him: "Come and see." He who possessed almighty power then disclosed human emotions in a burst of tears. "Jesus wept."[21] He is sorrowful with the sorrowful. Some of the Jews were touched at this manifestation of loving sympathy. "See how He loved him!" But others could make nothing of Jesus' tears; His weeping puzzled them. Why had He not healed Lazarus in the first place? Was it unwillingness or inability? It could have been neither. In a half-puzzled, half-mocking way, they asked: "Could not He who opened the eyes of the blind man [Jn 9:7] also have kept this man from dying?" If He was unable to raise a dead man, how about the other miracles? And if He was unwilling to do so, why the tears?

5
"Lazarus, Come Out"
Jn 11:38–46

The unkind attitude of the Jews toward Jesus (as revealed in their remark) caused Him to groan again as He approached the grave. This was a cave, whether natural or artificial we do not know, and a stone lay upon its mouth. What is supposed to be the tomb of Lazarus is still shown to travelers. Jesus said: "Take away the stone." But Martha, who had joined the gathering again, objected: "Lord, by this time there will be an odor, for he has been dead four days." But Jesus replied: "Did I not tell you that if you believed you would see the glory of God?" These words would rather recall what Jesus had said to His disciples in Perea (v. 4). But they must also have occurred in His conversation with Martha (vv. 23–26), though the account was probably abridged. Notwithstanding Martha's objection, possibly because they perceived that Jesus had some purpose in mind, "they took away the stone." Now Jesus speaks a brief prayer of thanksgiving, as if Lazarus had already been restored to life. "Father, I thank You that You have heard Me. And I knew that You always hear Me, but I said this on account of the people standing around, that they may believe that You sent Me." It was essential that the miracle Jesus was going to perform be credited to its real source—all should recognize that Jesus was in truth the Messiah sent by God. Crying now with a loud voice that all might hear Him, He gave the command: "Lazarus, come out." Scarcely were the words spoken when like a specter there issued from the rocky tomb a figure. "His hands and feet [were] bound with linen strips" (long linen wrappings) and with a broader cloth around the head, "which upheld the jaw that four days previously had dropped in death."[22] Lazarus was restored to life; indeed, as tradition has it,[23] to thirty more years of life and light and love. A dead man had returned to life. But since in the present condition he was unable to walk and was unfit for society, being wrapped in ghastly vestments, Jesus directed them: "Unbind him, and let him go." What a sight Lazarus must have presented as he returned to the village! And what an excitement his return to life must have caused as the miracle became known! How truly Quadratus (d. AD 129), an early apologist who heard the apostles preach, could write during the reign of Hadrian:

The works of our Savior were always present, for they were genuine:—those that were healed, and those that were raised from the dead, who were seen not only when they were healed and when they were raised, but were also always present; and not merely while the Savior was on earth, but also after his death, they were alive for quite a while, so that some of them lived even to our day.[24]

The effect of this stupendous miracle was twofold. Some of the Jews who had come to visit the sisters were convinced of the truth of Christ's words and of His divine power to perform true miracles. They "believed in Him." But others went to the Pharisees and told them what Jesus had done.

When the Pharisees received the information, they took action at once. They deemed the matter so important that they called an immediate meeting of the Council. The reality of the miracle could not be denied. But the members of this body refused to believe in Him who had performed it.[25] The general trend of the discussion was that something had to be done. If nothing is done, they assert, to change this impossible situation, then "everyone will believe in Him." Jesus would then head a messianic movement and make Himself king. And this would cause Rome to intervene and end the political existence of the Jewish leaders. While the members vainly raged, Joseph Caiaphas, "who was high priest that year,"[26] rose to address them. He was the son-in-law of Annas, who was one of his predecessors in the high-priestly office, and held his office from about AD 18 to 37, when Vitellius deposed him.[27] He contemptuously told the council: "You know nothing at all." There was only one thing to be done, and that was to select one person as their victim—whether innocent or guilty did not matter, as long as it was expedient for them—rather than to have the whole nation perish. Thus, murderous intention is presented under the guise of concern for the public welfare. No, he did not desire the death of Jesus! But the welfare of the nation made it necessary. The truth, however, was, as he and the members knew, that their own power and influence were at stake. The proposal was as selfish as it was unjust. And "what is morally wrong is politically inexpedient."[28] All things being equal, then, the well-being of the nation is worth more of course than the life of an individual. But this did not really apply. Here it was a case of public benefit, not of public danger. It was the life not of a disturber but of a benefactor. He was an innocent man, a popular teacher, a great healer, not to mention that He was the Messiah and the Son of God. And still, as the evangelist points out, in proposing the death of Jesus for the benefit of the people, Caiaphas unwittingly spoke a word of prophecy. In ancient days, the high priests communicated to the people the will and counsel of God by means of the Urim and Thummim (Ex 28:30; Nu 27:21), which may have been lost since the Babylonian exile. And so here once more, a Jewish high priest prophesied, albeit by the grace of the Romans and not by the grace of God. He unintentionally and

6
The Prophecy
of Caiaphas
Jn 11:47–52

unconsciously—like Balaam's donkey—revealed a sentence of the gracious will of God for the last time. It was indeed expedient that "one man should die for the people"; however, not in the sense of Caiaphas. "He did not say this of his own accord, but being high priest that year he prophesied that Jesus would die for the nation, and not for the nation only, but also to gather into one the children of God who are scattered abroad."

7
Retirement to Ephraim
Jn 11:53–54

This prophetic utterance of the "bilingual"[29] Caiaphas so influenced the perplexed members of the Council that "from that day on they made plans to put Him to death." But the hour of Jesus had not yet come. He was aware of the evil plan formulated against Him in the meeting place of the Council, the Hall of Hewn Stones. He withdrew once more so as not to precipitate matters further. For the last time, before the final Passover, He would become the true Paschal Lamb. He retired to "a region near the wilderness, to a town called Ephraim." There, He stayed with the disciples.[30] The place may be located a few miles northeast of Jerusalem, near Bethel, toward the Samaritan border.[31]

25

THE FINAL JOURNEY TO JERUSALEM

SHORTLY BEFORE THE PASSOVER OF AD 33

Jesus' public ministry had only a few weeks left. These were spent in quiet meditation in preparation for the ordeal before Him. He left His retreat at Ephraim (Jn 11:54),[1] in the wilderness of Beth-aven. A circuitous route took Him to Jerusalem. At first glance, it would seem that He was turning His back on Jerusalem for a journey that took Him northward through Samaria and then eastward "between Samaria and Galilee," between the two provinces and on the confines of both, toward the Jordan Valley and Perea.[2] He seems to have wished to join a caravan of Galilean pilgrims, probably at some appointed place, on their way to the Passover in Jerusalem. This apparently is confirmed by the later notice that His mother, Mary, as well as Mary Magdalene, Salome, and many other women went up with Him to Jerusalem (Mk 15:40–41; Lk 23:49).[3] And there was another reason for His journey through the borderlands of Samaria and Galilee: to bring healing to a band of unfortunates who "on the frontiers of two countries had been gathered like froth at the margin of wave and sand to share the misery of both."[4]

On the outskirts of an unknown village, Jesus met a company of ten lepers, "who stood at a distance." They dared not approach Him, since that would make Him unclean. In joyful and believing recognition of the great Stranger who had happened into their midst, they lifted up their voices and cried out: "Jesus, Master,[5] have mercy on us!" Jesus' heart was immediately thrilled with compassion. Quick as an echo, the words flashed back: "Go and show yourselves to the priests." The lepers knew the significance of the command. The local priests would not heal them, but they could confirm that the lepers were cured and certify their restitution to every privilege of social life (Lv 13:2; 14:2). "And as they went they were cleansed."

1
"Between Samaria and Galilee"
Lk 17:11

2
The Ten Lepers
Lk 17:12–14

3
The Grateful
Samaritan
Lk 17:15–19

Jesus bestowed a most wonderful blessing upon these unfortunate sufferers. For all practical purposes, since it was a case of real leprosy, it was the restoration to life. For if Jesus had not miraculously freed them from their dreadful malady, they could not have ever hoped to be cured. But only one, when he saw that he had been healed, turned back. He glorified God and "fell on his face at Jesus' feet, giving Him thanks." And then comes the significant sentence: "Now he was a Samaritan."[6] While the nine benefited Jews were coldly thankless, the Samaritan returned to Jesus. One would have expected that not even going through fire would have kept the nine from coming back. Jesus had frequently met ingratitude before, but He could not help being sadly affected by an instance so heartless and cruel. "Were not ten cleansed?[7] Where are the nine?" Jesus asks in sorrowful surprise. "He came to His own, and His own people did not receive Him" (Jn 1:11). A despised stranger must bring the recognition that He should have received from the children of the Kingdom. But be that as it may, the alien[8] shall not have returned in vain, nor shall his gratitude come short of the blessing it deserved: "Rise and go your way; your faith has made you well."

4
The Nature of the
Kingdom
Lk 17:20–21

It was clear, even to Jesus' enemies, that He had presented Himself as the Messiah and had proved it by His deeds. It was only their astounding blindness that made them fail to realize it. But because Jesus asserted that He was the Christ, the impatient and carnal-minded Pharisees wanted to know when the messianic *kingdom* would come. That is what they were interested in. "When is all this preaching and preparation to end and the *Kingdom*"—such as they expected of course—"to begin?"[9] But as in His many other encounters with the Pharisees, Jesus points out to them that, as usual, they were wholly mistaken in their point of view. The kingdom of God does not come in a vulgar, physical sense. "The kingdom of God is not coming in ways that can be observed." The word used[10] refers to the observation of heavenly bodies, from whose movements one can calculate when an expected phenomenon is to occur.[11] But all attempts at predicting the coming of the kingdom of God must fail. Since the Kingdom is spiritual, also its coming must be invisible. "Nor will they say, 'Look, here it is!' or 'There!' for behold, the kingdom of God is in the midst of you,"[12] for the Christ stood among them. If you receive through faith Him whom the Father has sent to build up this Kingdom in the hearts of men, you will also enter the Kingdom above.

5
The Day of the
Son of Man
Lk 17:22–37

Still, on the other hand, there will also be a glorious coming of the Son of Man. The kingdom of God does not come now with signs one can observe. However, there will be signs hereafter. For the present, there will be days when the disciples will desire the experience of just one day of joy and happiness with their Master, but they "will not see it." Deceivers and false christs will arise and cry: "'Look, there!' or, 'Look, here!'" But they are not to follow or go after them (Mt 24:23, 26–27; Mk

13:21). As for Christ, His final advent will take on the nature of lightning. But for the present, "He must suffer many things and be rejected by this generation." The day of glory for Christ and the Day of Judgment upon all unbelievers, however, will certainly dawn, just as the flood came in the days of Noah (Mt 24:37–39) and the destruction of Sodom in the days of Lot. As the waters of the flood covered the "sensualism in the days of Noah and the fire and brimstone from heaven streamed upon the busy wickedness of Sodom,"[13] so shall it also be in the day when the Son of Man will be revealed. And the disciples should be warned lest this day burst upon them unawares. When a hostile army makes a successful assault and the only safety is in sudden flight, there must be no looking back. "Remember Lot's wife." Thus the Lord incidentally confirms the historicity of the flood, the destruction of Sodom, and the transformation of Lot's wife into a pillar of salt (Gn 19:26). He who has in mind only the saving of earthly life and of his temporal goods on that day will lose both these and eternal life with God (Mt 10:39). Moreover, the Last Day is not only a day of judgment, but also a day of separation. Jesus explains this in a few examples. On that night,[14] there will be two people in one bed, but only one will be taken. Two women will be grinding at the same mill; one will be accepted, the other rejected. Two men will be in the field; one will be taken and the other will be left (Mt 24:40–41). Persons who were closely associated with one another in this life will be forever separated on the Last Day if one of them is a believer in Christ and therefore heavenly-minded, while the affections of the other during his lifetime were set on earthly things. The warning was not without effect upon the disciples. In awe and fear, they asked: "Where, Lord," will this separation take place? But the coming of the Lord is "as little geographical as it is chronological."[15] In a very fitting picture, the Lord replies that the Judgment will overtake the ungodly.[16] "Where the corpse is, there the vultures will gather" (Mt 24:28).

6
The Parable of the Persistent Widow
Lk 18:1–8

In listening to Jesus' words about His sudden reappearing and the possibility of their being unprepared, the disciples must have felt the need for divine protection and guidance. That is probably the connection between the foregoing and the present section, which speaks of prayer. To be instant and even persistent in prayer is certainly a necessity in the last days for all those who intend to heed the warnings about the coming of the Son of Man.[17] In order, now, to teach His disciples the necessity of diligent and unceasing prayer, Jesus tells them a parable about a judge in a certain city "who neither feared God nor respected man." Since the Jews had no one-man tribunals as such in those days, we are probably permitted to think of the type of judges that Herod or Pontius Pilate would appoint.[18] Now, there was a widow in that city with a case that required immediate adjustment. She went to the judge with the cry: "Give me justice against my adversary." What the grievance was is not stated, nor does it matter. Evidently, she had a right to demand justice. But the judge took no interest in the case in spite of the fact that she came again and again. Finally, for the selfish reason of ridding himself of a harassing annoyance, he said, "Because this widow keeps bothering me, I will give her justice," though he feared neither God nor man and did not act for the sake of justice. She was making life miserable for him. And if it was not the call of justice, it was the prospect of having the fists of an enraged woman placed below his eyes,[19] which moved his heart. Thus the shamelessly selfish and utterly unprincipled judge took action. The lesson: "will not God give justice to His elect," those whom He graciously predestined to eternal life, who stand in the closest relation to Him and "cry to Him day and night?" Though He delays His final intervention, yet He will avenge them shortly. But He wants them to cry to Him. However, with all the temptations surrounding them in the last days and from the standpoint of impotent man, "when the Son of Man comes, will He find faith on earth?"

7
The Pharisee and the Tax Collector
Lk 18:9–14

Among those in the presence of Jesus, if not in His direct following, there were some who thought like Pharisees, "who trusted in themselves that they were righteous, and treated others with contempt." To them, Jesus spoke a parable about two men, a Pharisee and a tax collector, who went up into the temple to pray. Incidentally, we notice that, while the worship in the temple was largely sacrificial, the house of God was also made the place of private prayer (Lk 2:37).[20] After taking his stand in the sacred enclosure, before God, the Pharisee offered up what was more an expression of self-congratulation than communion with God, prayer, and supplication: "God, I thank You that I am not like other men"[21]—that is, the common herd, "extortioners, unjust, adulterers, or even like this tax collector." Plainer words of a thankless thanksgiving could hardly have been spoken. Only one day of the year had been set aside for fasting, the Great Day of Atonement;[22] but he fasted twice a week, presumably on Mondays and Thursdays.[23] The Law required tithes of the herd and of the fruits of the field and trees (Lv 27:30, 32; Dt 14:22); but he gave the tenth of all that he possessed or acquired.[24] What, then, was he lacking? In his own mind, he was lacking nothing. In truth, however, he was lacking everything: the knowledge of sin, repentance, and realization of the fact that he needed a Savior. On the other hand, the tax collector, humbly standing aloof, not daring to lift up his eyes to heaven, and beating his breast in pungent remorse, penitently said: "God, be merciful to me, a sinner," literally, "*the* sinner."[25] What a contrast! In the Pharisee's mind, he was a saint before God and man; whereas the tax collector acknowledged himself in his heart as a sinner above all others. The judgment of Christ is clear and comprehensive. In the judgment of God, the tax collector, who sought refuge in the grace of God, was absolved. "I tell you, this man went down to his house justified, rather than the other." He received the forgiveness and justification that the other claimed. And the general principle, so often enunciated (Lk

14:11; Mt 23:12), also applies: "For everyone who exalts himself will be humbled, but the one who humbles himself will be exalted."

By this time, Jesus was again in Perea, on the journey already begun six months before, when He had definitely given up Galilee as a field of operations. This journey was now unquestionably leading Him to Jerusalem and to the cross. As He was approaching His final destination by way of Perea,[27] multitudes followed Him. He willingly administered to them the saving Word of Life, and He also performed healing deeds of love.

8
Returning to Perea
Mt 19:1–2;
Mk 10:1[26]

One of the burning questions of the day between the two rabbinic schools in Israel was the interpretation of the expression "matter of nakedness," or rather, the meaning of a single word, "indecency," or "nakedness," in the Mosaic marriage law.

9
Concerning Divorce
Mt 19:3–12;
Mk 10:2–12

> When a man takes a wife and marries her, if then she finds no favor in his eyes because he has found some indecency[28] in her, and he writes her a certificate of divorce and puts it in her hand and sends her out of his house, and she departs out of his house, . . . she [may go] and [become] another man's wife. (Dt 24:1–2)

A comparatively low estimate of woman may be noted in Hillel and his school. They explained the passage in the sense that a man might divorce his wife for almost any reason, while the stricter school of Shammai interpreted the passage as applying to moral delinquency. However, this was unreasonably extended to include, for instance, the supposed unchastity of appearing unveiled in the streets. "Hillel loosed what Shammai bound."[29] Shammai was right in so far as he permitted no divorce without legal basis in the most flagrant immorality. Hillel was right in that he left an opening for divorce. While the leaders disputed, the people were perplexed. And besides the theological and moral aspects, there was probably also a political aspect. The greatest of all prophets had lost his head for boldly expressing a view that was contrary to the practice of a royal adulterer (Mt 14:1–12). For Jesus to decide in favor of one school under the circumstances would, to say the least, have given mortal offense to the other.

The Pharisees submitted a tempting question, likely for the purpose of placing the Savior in the dilemma of either choosing the unpopular side of Shammai or of exposing Himself to the charge of laxity by siding with Hillel. "Is it lawful to divorce one's wife for any cause?" The latter clause seems to suggest that they expected Jesus to declare Himself in favor of the stricter view. In His response, Jesus safely placed Himself upon the authority of the Law. "What did Moses command you?" But that seems to be the opening that they were waiting for. The Mosaic precept is quoted: "Moses allowed a man to write a certificate of divorce and to send her away" (see Dt 24:1).[30] But without quibbling, Jesus appealed straight to the highest authority—God's institution of marriage. He who in the beginning "made them male and female" has said in His Word:[31] "Therefore a man shall leave his father and mother

10
"What Therefore
God Has Joined
Together"
Mt 19:3–6;
Mk 10:2–9

and hold fast to his wife." Thus marriage constitutes an alliance closer than that of parent and child. It is a union that is a unity. "What therefore God has joined together, let not man separate."

11
"Except for Sexual Immorality"
Mt 19:7–9;
Mk 10:10–12

But does not Jesus thus put Himself in opposition to Moses? "Why then did Moses command one to give a certificate of divorce and to send her away?" Jesus, however, corrected the misunderstanding. Moses did not command, but only permitted divorce, and this only under certain circumstances and as a concession to the hardness of their hearts. It was the introduction of a civil measure for the purpose of avoiding greater evils. "But from the beginning it was not so." Only adultery breaks the bonds of matrimony before death in the sight of God. Divorce obtained at the forum of the state is really no divorce, but merely a public declaration of a sinful condition that has already been established. A husband or a wife may not obtain a divorce unless the other party has committed adultery. "Whoever divorces his wife, except for sexual immorality, and marries another, commits adultery."

12
Celibacy
Mt 19:10–12

These words were intended as food for reflection for the Pharisees. What their reaction was the evangelists do not say. But the disciples were dismayed. If that is the meaning of Christ, that except in the case of adultery a man cannot rid himself of an utterly worthless and disagreeable wife, "it is better not to marry." Indeed, these matters must be considered before entering the state of matrimony. To this remark of the disciples, the Lord gives the somewhat dark reply: "Not everyone can receive this saying, but only those to whom it is given." He seems to refer to a person's abstaining from marriage. As to celibacy, there are three kinds of eunuchs:[32] those who are naturally unfit for wedlock; those who have been mutilated and made eunuchs by men; and finally, those who voluntarily make themselves eunuchs "for the sake of the kingdom of heaven." But not in the sense of the Church Father Origen, whose injudicious zeal for the kingdom of God drove him to be emasculated. These three classes differ from the way God established things in the beginning, even the last group. Yet there are extraordinary situations that impede marriage: persecution, great distress, and the like. At all times, even in wedlock, there must be a proper freedom of the heart and emancipation of the will for the service of Christ (1Co 7:26–29). As to celibacy, it is neither recommended nor forbidden. "Let the one who is able to receive this receive it." With this final word, Jesus again seems to indicate that not celibacy, but marriage, is the normal thing. At any rate, the doctrine that would make the unwedded state a higher degree of Christian perfection is in conflict with the Word of God: "It is not good that the man should be alone" (Gn 2:18).

13
"Let the Little Children Come to Me"
Mt 19:13–15;
Mk 10:13–16;
Lk 18:15–17[33]

As a touching commentary of divine blessing resting upon the institution of matrimony, the three Synoptists next related the account of Jesus blessing little children. "They"—presumably Perean mothers,[34] though fathers are not excluded[35]—"were bringing children to Him that He might touch them." The scene has inspired painters and poets of every Christian age. Was it possibly whispered around that a crisis was at hand and that Jesus would soon depart? At any rate, little children[36] were brought to Jesus so that He should touch them and bestow His blessings upon a generation yet to come. But the disciples rebuked those that brought them.[37] They did not want their Master to be needlessly troubled and disturbed. But Jesus was much displeased when He saw it and said to His disciples: "Let the children come to Me; do not hinder them, for to such belongs the kingdom of God." Children for the Kingdom. And in a deeper, spiritual sense: the Kingdom is also intended for them. They need it, and it belongs to them. For "Truly, I say to you, whoever does not receive the kingdom of God like a child shall not enter it." And conferring spiritual blessings upon the little children, "He took them in His arms and blessed them, laying His hands on them."

Jesus was again going forth "on His journey" that was to take Him steadily nearer to the cross. A young man of wealth and position, presumably a ruler of the local synagogue,[38] seems suddenly to have arrived at the conviction that he must by all means apply to the departing Jesus for direction in his quest of the highest good. Determined not to be too late, he came running. Breathlessly kneeling before Jesus, he addressed to Him an all-important question in sincerity and in terms of genuine respect: "Good[39] Teacher, what good[40] deed must I do to have eternal life?" From the standpoint of Jesus, the description *good* was perfectly proper, but it was wrong from the standpoint of the ruler. Jesus would not be reduced to a mere good rabbi, if indeed the rabbis were accustomed to such an address.[41] And even as on other occasions,[42] Jesus was unwilling to be called Christ indiscriminately. So He objects to the above title of honor, unless its implication is fully understood. As long as the ruler came to Jesus as to one who was no more than a man, the entire address, no matter how flattering, was a mistake. Therefore the correction: "Why do you call Me good? No one is good except God alone." It was evident that the youth was not ready to associate "good" with Jesus and God. As to the question itself, something good certainly must be done if by *doing* one would obtain everlasting life. The answer is found in the Law. "If you would enter life, keep the commandments." A most simple and logical answer, but it took the man by surprise. He did not expect to be directed to the commandments in general, but rather imagined that this Prophet would point to some new list of works. Something of this nature was in his mind when he asked, "Which ones?"[43] Since there was only one code in the moral law, and since the youth was determined to *do* something to gain salvation, Jesus directed his attention to the Ten Commandments and in particular for the purpose of His pedagogy to the precepts of the Second Table. "You shall not murder, You shall not commit adultery, You shall not steal, You shall not bear false

14
The Rich Young Ruler
Mt 19:16–19;
Mk 10:17–19;
Lk 18:18–20

witness, Honor your father and mother, and, You shall love your neighbor as yourself." As a true scholar of the Pharisees, the young man must have supposed these laws could be most easily kept.

15
"You Lack One Thing"
Mt 19:20–22;
Mk 10:20–22;
Lk 18:21–23

With the sincerity of an honest heart, the young man asserted: "All these I have kept from my youth." At least he thought he had, as would be expected from one who enjoyed, and very likely deserved, the honor and respect of his community. "What do I still lack?" There is an inward want. In spite of his outwardly exemplary life, there must have been some inward dissatisfaction. Otherwise, he would not have asked Jesus that question in the first place. "And Jesus, looking at him, loved him" for his sincerity and moral earnestness. He wanted to save his soul. But moral earnestness does not save; it does not suffice. The youth was deceiving himself. Even before the Law, which, he thought, he had kept ever since he became a "son of the Law," there was still much that he lacked. One might suppose that he did not love his neighbor as himself, he did not love God with all his heart, and he was not willing to leave all that he had to follow Christ. "You lack one thing." For the purpose of approaching perfection via the Law, there was one test that he might make: "Go, sell all that you have and give to the poor, and you will have treasure in heaven" (that is, inherit eternal life) and then "come, follow Me." Now, Christ was not teaching the purchase of salvation in exchange for voluntary poverty, as some have thought. This counsel was for an individual case and was given in order to impress upon the youth his deficiency; and it was not lightly given. Moreover, it was a commandment based upon the universal requirement of unconditional self-denial and willing surrender of all for the sake of Christ. The proposal was hopefully made. But the youth was not equal to the sacrifice demanded of him. It was too much. He lacked the knowledge of sin, the godly sorrow of repentance, and faith in the grace of God and Christ. There was a tender spot. With pain in his heart and a frown on his face, he walked away "sorrowful, for he had great possessions."

16
The Danger of Riches
Mt 19:23–26;
Mk 10:23–27;
Lk 18:24–27

The failure of the youth to meet the test saddened Jesus. Looking around at His disciples, He said: "How difficult it will be for those who have wealth to enter the kingdom of God!" The disciples were amazed. But Jesus repeated: "Children, how difficult it is[44] to enter the kingdom of God!" It was mildly, yet firmly spoken; it really is impossible for a man to enter heaven as long as he sets his heart upon earthly treasures. "It is easier for a camel[45] to go through the eye of a needle than for a rich person to enter the kingdom of God." At this proverbial saying, the disciples inquired with increased astonishment: "Then who can be saved?" They must have felt that Jesus' warning applied to rich and poor alike. Jesus replied that things impossible to human nature are possible to grace. "With God all things are possible." It is not the possession of wealth, whether great or small, that condemns, but the attitude of the heart to wealth; and this regardless of whether the man is or is not in the possession of wealth. Abraham and others were not only rich in goods, but also rich in God. On the other hand, Judas loved money, of which he did not even possess a great amount. Although we notice that Christ's tone is much more severe in reference to wealth than to wedlock (see Mt 19:10–12), His teaching concerning the possession of wealth is as "little Ebionite as His teaching concerning marriage is Essene."[46] In other words, Jesus set a unique course for interpreting and applying the Scripture to these controversial topics of the day, avoiding the extremes of other groups who urged poverty or celibacy.

The reaction of the disciples almost jars us. Peter, probably acting as spokesman for the rest of the apostles, speaks his mind: "See, we have left everything and followed You. What then will we have?" It was a gain-seeking question. But although Jesus rebuked His disciples on other occasions, this time He has no criticism to offer. Yes, there is a reward, not for the relinquishment of wealth as such, but for the surrender of wealth, home, family, friends, and all for His sake. There will be a harvest of hundredfold increase in the regeneration[47] of the Son of Man. Then shall the disciples "sit on twelve thrones, judging the twelve tribes of Israel,"[48] and share with their Master the eternal dominion of glory. And this reward is not only for the Twelve; but "there is no one who has left house or brothers or sisters or mother or father or children or lands, for My sake and for the gospel,[49] who will not receive a hundredfold now in this time, houses and brothers and sisters and mothers and children and lands, with persecutions,[50] and in the age to come eternal life." But the idea of merit must be excluded. Moreover, followers must remain faithful to the end, otherwise "many who are first will be last, and the last first" (cf. Lk 13:30).

17
Peter's Question
Mt 19:27–30;
Mk 10:28–31;
Lk 18:28–30

For the purpose of teaching His disciples that salvation is full and complete and that the standard of the Kingdom is not merit but grace, Jesus relates the parable of the laborers in the vineyard, also called the parable of the hours. It was probably in the busy season of grape-gathering that a certain "master of a house" went forth early in the morning to hire laborers for his vineyard. They agreed to work that day for a denarius. At that time, it was the ordinary wage for a day's labor. At the third, sixth, ninth, and eleventh hour, counting from six o'clock in the morning, the owner of the vineyard found "others standing idle in the marketplace." He likewise sent them out into the vineyard, without, however, stipulating the definite coin or sum—nothing but the promise: "Whatever is right I will give you." Up to this point, there was no hitch in the proceeding. When the evening arrived, the lord of the vineyard gave instructions to his steward to call the laborers and to pay them off, "beginning with the last, up to the first." This was a necessary part of the parable, because, as afterward appears, here is where the complications begin. The order was somewhat strange, but still stranger was the payment. "Each of them received a denarius," as though each of them had worked all day. To say the least, this

18
The Laborers in
the Vineyard
Mt 20:1–12

arrangement is not the one usually observed between master and men. Nothing is said about the workers who arrived later. But when the first workers came and saw what the last received—forgetting the contract, of course—they naturally expected that they would receive more. But "each of them also received a denarius." Evidently, the full amount that the eccentric master presented to the one-hour men was not a payment, but intended rather as a bonus or gift. However, those who had worked all day, not satisfied with this inept generosity, began to express their indignation. Their complaint was excellently put: "These last worked only one hour, and you have made them equal to us who have borne the burden of the day and scorching heat."

19
"Friend, I Am Doing
You No Wrong"
Mt 20:13–16

It is true that the workmen had forgotten the agreement. Still, our first impulse is to side with the grumblers. However, this is not a commentary on capital and labor, but a picture of the kingdom of heaven (v. 1). We must remember that, if we receive salvation at all, it is both a full salvation and is also given by grace. In the Lord's vineyard, work is our lifelong duty, and our faithful labors will be rewarded in heaven. But the bountiful reaping that will be our happy lot there will not be given as payment for services rendered, but will be a gift of the grace of God. There must be no jealousy among Christians nor a pointing to a greater or smaller amount of good works before God. As in other parables, we must not lose sight of the main point or press all details. Singling out one of the grumblers, the master reminded him of the agreement: "Friend,[51] I am doing you no wrong. Did you not agree with me for a denarius?" A man who insists upon right before God loses grace and receives judgment. "Take what belongs to you and go." As to this giving of a full and unstipulated denarius to each of the laborers, to which "the first" objected, that was both his distinct purpose and his own affair. "Am I not allowed to do what I choose with what belongs to me?" Instead of being a cause of offense, this act of kindness should have been an occasion for rejoicing. While the master of the house was good, the grumblers displayed a jealous heart. "Or do you begrudge my generosity?" In the Lord's kingdom, work is our duty and grace our reward. We should not be envious about those whom the Lord receives into His heavenly kingdom even if they came to Christ only in the eleventh hour, while we have served Him all our lives. Nor should we exhibit our good works before God to seek gain. The attainment of salvation is the same for both saint and sinner. And so Jesus repeats the lesson He had given Peter when he asked his question (Mt 19:27, 30), which suggested the parable, saying: "So the last will be first, and the first last." Indeed, "many are called, but few are chosen."[52] Many hear the Gospel. Few heed the call.

20
Death and
Resurrection
Again Foretold
Mt 20:17–19;
Mk 10:32–34;
Lk 18:31–34[53]

Again Jesus was on the way to Jerusalem, pressing forward and walking along the path into the deep valley of the shadow of death. His strange manner and His incessant pushing forward caused the disciples to be amazed and others that followed Him to be filled with fear. The very atmosphere seemed to be charged with a foreboding of evil. At last, Jesus paused. He beckoned His disciples to Himself and again told them about His impending betrayal, arrest, suffering, and death, and about His resurrection. The terrible details are all distinctly given: how all the things that the prophets wrote concerning the Son of Man will be accomplished. He will be betrayed[54] to the scribes and priests in Jerusalem, condemned by the Council, delivered to the Roman Gentiles, mocked, flogged, spit upon, and—for the first time, the terrible climax is clearly revealed—*crucified.*[55] But like a shining light comes also the comforting assurance of the resurrection: "And He will be raised on the third day." The words were clear, but false messianic hopes so filled the minds of the disciples that they passed the words by like an idle dream. "They understood none of these things. This saying was hidden from them, and they did not grasp what was said."

Soon after Jesus prophesied His death and resurrection, an unspiritual request revealed the disciples' ignorance about the nature of Christ's kingdom. The request came from James and John (the two sons of Zebedee) by means of[56] their mother Salome, the sister of the mother of Jesus.[57] We remember that these relatives of Jesus were among His most intimate associates and constant attendants. With an air of mystery, they approached Jesus and, kneeling, begged Him to do them a favor. But Jesus would not commit Himself before the wish was expressed. "What do you want?" The mother, speaking for her ambitious sons, requested that in His kingdom they might sit, the one on the right hand of His throne of glory and the other on the left. It was a carnal, selfish request, and it showed that the nature of Christ's kingdom was completely misunderstood. In a Middle Eastern kingdom, persons of the highest honor and men of the highest rank sat to the right and left of the throne.[58] Probably the two disciples had drawn a wrong conclusion from the promise of Jesus about sitting "on twelve thrones, judging the twelve tribes of Israel," given in connection with Peter's statement: "We have left everything and followed You" (Mt 19:27–28).[59] Jesus bore gently with their selfishness and error. "You do not know what you are asking." They did not know what Christ's glory was and how one could become a partaker of it. They sought exaltation and did not see the step leading to it. "Are you able to drink the cup that I drink, or to be baptized with the baptism with which I am baptized?" Jesus referred to His Passion, the cup of bitterness (Mt 26:39), and the billows of the dark waters of death (Ps 42:7; 88:7). However, the brothers were probably thinking of a cup of joy (Ps 23:5) or of the Epiphany glory on the banks of the Jordan (Jn 1:33–34). And if indeed by this time they were sufficiently aroused to grasp the reference to the Lord's greatest humiliation, they nevertheless imagined, due to an exaggerated trust in their own ability, that they were able to drink that cup. "They said to Him, 'We are able.'" Slowly, Jesus then lifted the veil and informed them that there would be suffering in store for them, but that thereby they could not *earn* glory. Glory would be theirs, not by

21
The Ambition of James and John
Mt 20:20–23;
Mk 10:35–40

way of merit as in the case of Christ, but by way of obedience as the lot of followers to share with Christ, to whom they were joined as Christians. "The cup that I drink you will drink, and with the baptism with which I am baptized, you will be baptized." The servant is not greater than his master (Jn 15:20). For all Christians, there will be more or less tribulation and persecution, in some instances even bloody martyrdom. But even this does not merit a seat of honor in heaven. There *are* degrees of glory in the realms of bliss; the disciples, however, had carnal conceptions regarding them. Jesus therefore tells them that they must discard these thoughts. The mighty of this earth, it is true, give places of honor to their favorites. Not so in His kingdom. Although James and John belonged to His intimate circle, they could not for that reason claim any special distinction in Jesus' kingdom, nor would He, in His present state of humiliation, give them any definite promise. In due time, sitting on His right and left hand "is for those for whom it has been prepared."

22
The Way to Glory in Christ's Kingdom
Mt 20:24–28;
Mk 10:41–45

James and John were corrected, and in a deeper sense their request was granted. As His true followers, they shared the bitter cup of Christ. James was the first martyr among the Twelve (Ac 12:2). And John became a partner of Christ's tribulation (Rv 1:9). In the kingdom of glory, they shine as "the brightness of the sky" and as "the stars forever and ever" (Dn 12:3). But the Ten, filled with the same ambition and jealousies, were indignant at the selfish request of James and John. They were incensed at their secret attempt to secure preeminence for themselves and seats of honor. The offense caused them to quarrel[60] in the presence of Jesus, who was obliged to call them aside and to calm their excited minds. In His kingdom, He told them, deepest humility won highest honor. The pyramid of honor was inverted: not the few lording it over the many, but the many, as it were, being lords of the few. In this respect, His kingdom differed from secular kingdoms. In this world, the man who reaches the height of his ambition has achieved greatness by appointing and employing great numbers of inferiors and by making his will their law. "You know that those who are considered rulers of the Gentiles lord it over them, and their great ones exercise authority over them." That was, as they could see from the long history of their own nation, the way of Egypt, Assyria, Babylonia, Persia, Greece, and Rome. "But it shall not be so among you." There is greatness also in the kingdom of Christ. But those who wish to be members of this kingdom here on earth must turn secular notions of greatness completely upside down. "Whoever would be great among you must be your servant,[61] and whoever would be first among you must be slave[62] of all." Thus a plan for the exercise of "ambition" is proposed that will not offend any of their fellow men. And for this there is the example of the Master. "For even the Son of Man came not to be served but to serve, and to give His life as a ransom[63] for[64] many.[65]

By this time, Jesus had left Perea, crossed the Jordan, and was approaching Jericho. In fact, it seems that He had already left the old Jericho and was approaching the Jericho that Herod the Great had rebuilt a generation before.⁶⁶ Jesus' disciples and a multitude of Passover pilgrims accompanied Him. Two blind beggars, one of whom was Bartimaeus,⁶⁷ acting as spokesman, heard that Jesus was passing by.⁶⁸ Immediately, they cried out, "Lord, have mercy on us, Son of David!" The multitudes resented the noisy clamor as showing disrespect to One who was about to present Himself in Jerusalem as the nation's Messiah. But the blind men cried all the more, "Lord, have mercy on us, Son of David!" The plea of Joshua caused heavenly bodies to halt in their orbits; these blind beggars caused the Sun of Righteousness to stand still. Jesus did not object to the messianic title with which they addressed Him. He ordered the blind men to be called into His presence. Suddenly the surrounding throng became most compliant and told Bartimaeus: "Take heart. Get up; He is calling you." He was probably so much more prominent than the other man that two of the writers do not even mention the other. At this, Bartimaeus jumped to his feet, threw off his cloak, and was led to Jesus. The heart of Jesus went out to him and to the other blind man. For the purpose of forestalling subsequent charges of fraud and to make the blind men express their faith, Jesus asked: "What do you want Me to do for you?" Had they been ordinary beggars, or had they believed that Jesus was an ordinary man, they probably would have asked Him to open His purse. But their reply, as formulated by Bartimaeus, was an expression of their faith. It gave Jesus the most reverential title: "Lord," Rabboni,⁶⁹ "let me recover my sight." Whereupon Jesus had pity on them and touched their eyes. "Immediately they recovered their sight," and amidst the rejoicing of the multitude, they followed Jesus, glorifying God.

23
Blind Bartimaeus and His Companion Healed at Jericho
Mt 20:29–34;
Mk 10:46–52;
Lk 18:35–43

Jesus continued on His way to Jericho, more particularly, the new Jericho, an important trade center and customs station. It was the home of Zacchaeus,⁷⁰ a wealthy "chief tax collector,"⁷¹ whose acquaintance we are about to make. Zacchaeus was anxious to see Jesus, the great Prophet of Nazareth, acknowledged by many as the promised Messiah, who was about to go up to Jerusalem and, in connection with the approaching Passover feast, to present Himself as Israel's King. But since Zacchaeus was small in stature, he was unable to look over the crowd. Running forward, he climbed into the low branches of a fig-mulberry, or sycamore, tree that stood by the road.⁷² This action must have exposed him to the ridicule of the bystanders, to whom no doubt he was well known, but by whom he was disliked. His purpose, however, was not curiosity alone. He was in spiritual distress. A secret resolve had come over him. He was in need of peace, which, he felt, he could not obtain by anything he might do. He was filled with a yearning for Him who did not despise tax collectors and sinners and who had even elevated one of his hated

24
Jesus Visits Zacchaeus
Lk 19:1–5

associates to the rank of an apostle. We are surprised that Matthew did not record this incident of Zacchaeus. But probably the very fact that Matthew had been a tax collector himself moved him to pass it by in silence. On the other hand, the glorious example of the Savior's love as found in the Gospel of Luke on other occasions (Lk 15) was something that this evangelist could not overlook. When Jesus passed under that tree, He paused, looked up, called the tax collector by name, and told him to come down.[73] "Zacchaeus, hurry and come down." Jesus was on His way to Jerusalem. There were still before Him about fifteen miles of arduous climbing. It was necessary for Him to find lodging for the night. He would not stay with one of the many priests who made their home at Jericho,[74] but rather chose to spend the night in a tax collector's house. "For I must stay at your house today." This was more than Zacchaeus could have expected even in his wildest dreams. But the Lord knew that a change had come over this formerly thievish tax collector and that he was penitent and was concerned about his soul's welfare.

25
"Today Salvation Has Come to This House"
Lk 19:6–10

Hastily, Zacchaeus climbed down the tree and joyfully received Jesus into his house, not caring for the muttering of those who objected that "He has gone in to be the guest of a man who is a sinner" (cf. Lk 15:2). In spite of Zacchaeus's name (which means "pure"), there is no doubt that Zacchaeus *was* a sinner in the popular sense. The tax collectors were notoriously dishonest. There was reason for popular hatred of them as a class and on account of some shady transactions in Jericho against Zacchaeus as an individual. In the collection of duties on balsam, for instance,[75] and imposts on products that passed between the province of Pilate and Herod Antipas, Zacchaeus was probably not innocent and pure. But listen to his penitent resolve: "Lord, the half of my goods I give to the poor." This was a general restitution of money or property fraudulently acquired from persons whom he could no longer specify. "And if I have defrauded anyone of anything, I restore it fourfold." The Mosaic Law (Ex 22:1–9; Lv 6:2–5) required a four- and even fivefold restoration. Jesus recognized the sincerity of this proposal, voluntarily and sincerely made. Here was a truly penitent and believing heart. Therefore, Jesus said to Zacchaeus, "Today salvation has come to this house." Others had made much of their physical descent from Abraham (see Jn 8:33); but here was one of Abraham's spiritual sons. And as to Jesus' going into Zacchaeus's house, that was in accordance with the purpose for which He had come into the world: "The Son of Man came to seek and to save the lost."

26
The Parable of the Minas
Lk 19:11–14

While Jesus rejoiced that He had converted a sinner and Zacchaeus rejoiced that he had found the Savior,[76] thoughts of the Kingdom occupied the disciples, which, they supposed, would now be revealed. There were many indications that a crisis was at hand. On the way to Jericho, Jesus had told His disciples that they were going to Jerusalem, where God would fulfill all the prophecies concerning the

Son of Man (Lk 18:31). In the hearing of multitudes and without any objection to it on the part of such as had heard it, Jesus permitted Himself to be addressed with the strictly messianic title "Son of David."[77] On other occasions, He had purposely discouraged messianic acclaim (Mt 9:27, 30; 12:16). Now the "Son of David" was near to Israel's religious center and the capital of David's ancient kingdom. In addition, the Passover was at hand, from which season the regnal years were counted.[78] There was no doubt that a crisis was coming. If only the disciples could get the idea of external messianic world power off their minds! Jesus wanted to teach them that the kingdom of glory, such as they imagined it to be, was not yet at hand. He must first leave the world and receive the royal insignia. Meanwhile, the disciples must faithfully "engage in business" until He would come again. So He taught them—most likely in the house of Zacchaeus, possibly at the evening meal—the parable of the minas. We need not enter into the discussion of a supposed confounding of this parable with a similar parable recorded later (Mt 25:14–30). In accordance with the practice of Herodian princes,[79] ever since Rome had entered into the history of Israel, "a nobleman[80] went into a far country to receive for himself a kingdom and then return." Before leaving, he called "ten[81] of his servants" and distributed among them "ten minas,"[82] with the instruction to do business and trade with them until his return.[83] No sooner had he left, however, than his countrymen sent a delegation after him with the message: "We do not want this man to reign over us." This actually happened in the case of Archelaus after the death of Herod.[84] Nevertheless, Archelaus came back from Rome successful, having attained his object, as did the nobleman in the parable. The only difference is that the people opposed Archelaus on just grounds, while King Jesus, in the interpretation of the parable, was rejected on unjust grounds.[85] And still He gained His kingdom in the end.

The nobleman in the parable, as stated, succeeded in his mission. He received the royal dignity. His first official act upon his return was to summon the servants before him to whom he had entrusted the silver coin. Modestly, the first one comes before him with the most successful report: "Lord, your mina has made ten minas more." For such increase and fidelity, there was a splendid reward of a decapolis,[86] or ten cities: "Well done, good servant! Because you have been faithful in a very little, you shall have authority over ten cities." In like manner, a second servant reports: "Lord, your mina has made five minas." He receives a similar reward: "five cities." There is nothing said about seven of the servants, nor is this necessary.

As a special warning against unprofitableness in the Lord's kingdom, a third servant is singled out. As he approaches his master with "slinking gait and whining voice,"[87] he returns the entrusted mina, tied up in a handkerchief.[88] He tries to excuse his failure by blaming the austerity of his master. He was unfaithful, inasmuch as he had not obeyed his lord's command, which was to increase the mina

27
"Have Authority over Ten Cities"
Lk 19:15–19

28
The Unprofitable Servant
Lk 19:20–24

entrusted to him, and therefore he was also unprofitable to him. And that was the point. "Here is your mina, which I kept laid away in a handkerchief." Fear of the master was advanced as an excuse for his failure. "For I was afraid of you, because you are a severe man. You take what you did not deposit, and reap what you did not sow." Out of his own mouth, he was condemned. Increase, not mere lazy safe-keeping, was the very purpose of the delivery and the only reason why the money had been entrusted to him. His behavior showed that he was unfit to serve in any administrative capacity. If he knew of his lord's exacting manner, why, then, did he not act in accordance with his convictions? And if he was afraid to invest the money on his own responsibility, why did he not at least put it in a bank?[89] Then he could have returned it with interest.[90] But he had done neither. And so he was punished: "Take the mina from him, and give it to the one who has the ten minas." This would at least give the king the best prospects for gaining a speedy increase.

29
The Lesson
Lk 19:25–28

"And they said to him, 'Lord, he has ten minas!'" But Jesus points to a truth previously expressed and variously applied (Lk 8:18; Mt 13:12; Mk 4:25): "I tell you that to everyone who has, more will be given, but from the one who has not, even what he has will be taken away." For the sake of his own best interests, the king was entirely justified in applying this principle. Jesus concluded the parable by telling His hearers what the nobleman commanded for those enemies who opposed his rule: "Bring them here and slaughter them before me." The meaning of the parable is this: there will also be a kingdom for Jesus. But first He must go into a "far country." In the meantime, the disciples, given "minas" as bearers of the Means of Grace, should faithfully "engage in business" until He returns. Upon His return on the Last Day, punishment will be meted out to His open enemies, and an account will be taken of those who according to their profession were His servants. There will be a reward of grace for the faithful and judgment upon those who have been lazy in their trust. Stewards must be found faithful (1Co 4:2). For such faithfulness, there was the example of the Lord. Having thus spoken, "He went on ahead," possibly on the next morning, and continued His journey to Jerusalem.[91]

26

ARRIVAL AT BETHANY

PROBABLY FRIDAY AFTERNOON BEFORE
THE WEEK OF PASSOVER, AD 33

March 27 and 28

Nisan (or Abib)									
7	8	9	10	11	12	13	14	15	16
March					April				
27	28	29	30	31	1	2	3	4	5
Fri.	Sat.	Sun.	Mon.	Tues.	Wed.	Thu.	Fri.	Sat.	Sun.

The Passover was at hand, and the roads were filled with Passover pilgrims. They would probably come to the Holy City a few days before the feast for the sake of purification, some features of which required a week, while others consisted only of trimming the hair and washing the clothes.[1] Since Jesus had aroused national attention, the main topic of conversation among those who stood about in groups in the courts of the temple was whether He would make His appearance at the feast. That there was room for differences of opinion was due to the fact that the "chief priests and the Pharisees," the Council, had given instructions that, if anyone knew where Jesus was to be found, he should "let them know," so that they might have Him arrested.

And now we must get our chronological bearing. According to the chronology that we have followed, it is the year AD 33, or 786 AUC. Here, we receive the notice that six days before the Passover Jesus arrived at Bethany. According to reliable astronomical calculations, the beginning of the Passover on the evening of the

[1]
"The Passover of the Jews Was at Hand"
Jn 11:55–57

[2]
"Six Days before the Passover"
Jn 12:1

fourteenth day of Nisan in the year of our Lord's crucifixion (that is, the year AD 33[2]) corresponded to Thursday evening, April 2,[3] of the Julian calendar. Counting back six days, we arrive at Friday, March 27, or the seventh day of Nisan. In covering the fourteen or fifteen miles between Jericho and Bethany, we assume that Jesus, after spending the night with Zacchaeus, left there early in the morning, so as to arrive at the home of His friends in Bethany before the sunset had commenced the Sabbath hours.[4]

3
The Anointment at Bethany
(Mt 26:6–7;
Mk 14:3);
Jn 12:1–3[5]

The Sabbath Day was spent in quiet. But the people of Bethany seem to have arranged an evening festive meal in Jesus' honor, and they enjoyed the privilege of attending the feast. The place of the banquet was the house of Simon the leper. Who this Simon was, whether he was the husband of Martha, the father of Lazarus, or a relative of the family, we do not know. From the expression "house of Simon the leper," we do not even know whether at the time he was alive or dead. But it is quite generally supposed that he was the host at the occasion and that the name "leper" still clung to him because of the malady from which Jesus had previously cleansed him. Among those present was the risen Lazarus, almost as much an object of curiosity as the Guest of Honor Himself. It was really a public affair. There were many people present, the disciples, the villagers, people from Jerusalem, and, as John says, "Martha served." Again she was in her peculiar province (Lk 10:40). Very likely she had the entire supervision of the feast. Of course, Mary was there too. John directs our particular attention to her. She must have sat and thought and gazed, until she finally jumped up to carry out her intention. She had an alabaster flask containing costly Indian nard.[6] She must have enjoyed both the possession and the use of wealth. Stepping softly to Jesus, she broke the narrow neck of the jar and poured the valuable contents of the pure and precious nard[7] first over His head and then over His feet and wiped the feet with the long tresses of her hair. In a few moments, a delicious odor filled the atmosphere of the whole house.

4
"Why This Waste?"
(Mt 26:8–9;
Mk 14:4–5);
Jn 12:4–6

It was a strange act. This unaccustomed exhibition of lavish luxury must have amazed many of those present. Even making an allowance for the eccentricities of society and wealth, many must have regarded the whole performance as of questionable taste. But what does the heart care about cold custom when love would have its way?[8] When the disciples saw it, they were filled with indignation toward Mary. "Why was the ointment wasted like that?" In their opinion, Mary might have devoted her lavish sacrifice to a better purpose. She might have converted her costly ointment into useful cash—an amount large enough to supply at least five thousand hungry people with a bite to eat.[9]

5
The Reaction of Judas
(Mt 26:8–9;
Mk 14:4–5);
Jn 12:4–6

The most vexed of the disciples was Judas. To his mind, there was perfect folly in the "perdition" of so much good money.[10] Money was his dearest treasure. For one-third of the amount (Mt 26:15),[11] this "son of perdition" was ready to sell the

Lord Himself. It is the first time that we hear him talk. "But Judas Iscariot, one of His disciples (he who was about to betray Him), said, 'Why was this ointment not sold for three hundred denarii[12] and given to the poor?'" But this little touch about giving to the poor was only a veil behind which he tried to conceal the baseness of his heart. He felt personally cheated. This act of Mary deprived him, the pilfering treasurer of the apostolic band, of the opportunity to get away with some of the common funds.[13] "He said this, not because he cared about the poor, but because he was a thief, and having charge of the money bag he used to help himself to what was put into it."

But Jesus defends Mary. "Leave her alone. Why do you trouble her?" Hers was a praiseworthy act. "She has done a beautiful thing[14] to Me." Even luxury and embellishment are permitted when the giver therewith seeks nothing but the glory of God.[15] As to the poor, they would always be found as objects of the disciples' love. "But you will not always have Me." And, whether Mary understood it or not, her act had a special significance. "She has anointed My body beforehand for burial." By anticipation, she actually succeeded to pay Him her last honors, which His body would otherwise not have received. Instead of being criticized for her deed, she should be praised, and her deed will be remembered to the end of days. "Wherever the gospel is proclaimed in the whole world, what she has done will be told in memory of her."

6
The Defense of Jesus
(Mt 26:10–13; Mk 14:6–9); Jn 12:7–8

In the course of the evening, visitors from Jerusalem arrived.[16] To them, it was a double attraction to see both the Raiser of the dead and the raised. "They came, not only on account of Him but also to see Lazarus, whom He had raised from the dead." The result was that many saw Lazarus—and believed in Jesus. This was as it should be. But the chief priests in Jerusalem, most of whom were resurrection-denying Sadducees, could not bear to have a living witness of life after death and a powerful testimony to the power of Jesus in their neighborhood. When the report reached them, they were moved toward the monstrous proposal to "put Lazarus to death as well."

7
The Reaction in Jerusalem
Jn 12:9–11

27

PALM SUNDAY: THE TRIUMPHAL
ENTRY INTO JERUSALEM

March 29, AD 33

Nisan (or Abib)									
7	8	9	10	11	12	13	14	15	16
March					April				
27	28	29	30	31	1	2	3	4	5
Fri.	Sat.	Sun.	Mon.	Tues.	Wed.	Thu.	Fri.	Sat.	Sun

From the visitors in Bethany on the evening before, it must have become known in Jerusalem that Jesus intended to make His appearance in the city on the following day. On the next morning, throngs of people streamed from the eastern gates of Jerusalem toward the Mount of Olives to meet Him on the way. According to their calendar, it was the ninth of Nisan, the day before the Passover lamb was to be selected (see Ex 12:3). But according to God's calendar, it was the day when Jesus was to come to Jerusalem as the true Paschal Lamb and to present Himself to the nation as the Redeemer King. "Behold, your king is coming to you." At the same time while crowds were streaming eastward on the road to Jericho, Jesus departed from Bethany. His disciples and a large following of friends accompanied Him. When He was about half-way and approaching the fig gardens of Bethphage ("the House of Figs"),[1] Jesus sent two of His disciples, possibly Peter and John,[2] with the instruction to proceed to the village. There, they would find a donkey tied and her unridden colt. "Untie them and bring them to Me." The underlying idea about the colt "on which no one has ever sat" was that for the intended sacred purpose, only an unused animal was to be employed (Nu 19:2; 1Sm 6:7). Taking into consideration

[1]
"Behold, Your King
Is Coming!"
Mt 21:1–3;
Mk 11:1–3;
Lk 19:29–31;
Jn 12:12

the possibility of objections to this requisition, Jesus said, "If anyone says to you, 'Why are you doing this?' say, 'The Lord[3] has need of it and will send it back here immediately."

2
"Mounted on a Donkey"
Mt 21:4–7;
Mk 11:4–7;
Lk 19:32–35;
Jn 12:14–16

The two disciples did as they were told. Everything happened as Jesus had said. They went and found a colt and his mother "tied at a door outside in the street."[4] When untying the animals, the disciples were challenged. They repeated the message of Jesus with satisfactory result. Then the disciples led the donkey and the colt to Jesus. They made a saddle of their upper garments and placed it upon the animals. Then, as Jesus indicated His choice of the mount, they lifted Him upon the colt. The triumphal procession began—not a triumphal entry into the city according to the fashion of a Roman conqueror, but a humble pomp, so to speak. The Savior rode unpretentiously into Jerusalem upon the foal of a donkey. The disciples recalled that this unostentatious procession, which supplied the Gentiles with material for stupid jests,[5] "took place to fulfill what was spoken by the prophet." "Say to the daughter of Zion,[6] 'Behold, your king is coming to you, humble, and mounted on a donkey, on a colt,[7] the foal of a beast of burden'" (Zec 9:9, prefaced by Is 62:11).

3
"Hosanna to the Son of David!"
Mt 21:8–9;
Mk 11:8–10;
Lk 19:36–38;
Jn 12:13, 17

No sooner had the procession started than the multitudes made a carpet of their upper garments for the path of Jesus. The Galilean Passover pilgrims, the townsmen of the risen Lazarus, and the approaching throng from Jerusalem made up the crowd, who had heard about Lazarus and many of whom had witnessed his resurrection. Enthusiasm was at its height. Many cut branches of palm and fig trees and spread them on the way. Then, in an outburst of exultation, the disciples began to shout, "Hosanna to the Son of David! Blessed is He who comes in the name of the Lord! Hosanna in the highest!" The multitudes joined in the strain that reechoed the great Hallel of Tabernacles and Passover (Ps 118:25–26), as also the Gloria of the angels (Lk 2:14).

4
"Look, the World Has Gone after Him!"
Lk 19:39–40;
Jn 12:18–19

In this happy mood, the procession moved onward to Jerusalem. But mingled with the crowd were also some of the Pharisees, to whom the joy of the multitude was as wormwood and gall.[8] Among themselves, they had to acknowledge their helplessness. "Look, the world has gone after Him!" What is the meaning of those messianic titles and jubilant cries? A few of them took it upon themselves to ask that Jesus rebuke His disciples. But His reply was "I tell you, if these were silent, the very stones would cry out."

5
"When He Saw the City, He Wept over It"
Lk 19:41–44

The joy of Jesus was soon turned into sorrow. As much as He rejoiced over the many sincere hosannas, He was nevertheless pained at the thought that much of the ecstasy was short-lived. Although the true believers would always acknowledge Him as the Son of David, He knew that Jerusalem was about to reject its King. And then the terrible consequences. As the awe-inspiring panorama of the ancient city—its surrounding walls, its splendid palaces, the marble pinnacles, and the gilded roof of the temple—suddenly burst into view, He was overcome with sadness and moved to tears. "And when He drew near and saw the city, He wept over it." A strange messianic triumph! Tears and lamentations interrupting the festal cries! If Jerusalem had only known and considered, even now, that day, the things that belonged to her peace! But now they were hid from her eyes. As matters stood, the period of grace for those who had hardened their hearts was already past. Days were to come when enemy hosts would cast a trench about the Holy City; surround her on every side; lay low her walls, her buildings, and the temple, in a destruction so thorough as not to leave one stone upon another; and slay her inhabitants. And all this "because you did not know the time of your visitation," as Jesus solemnly declared amid sobs and tears. "Sternly and fiercely, and in less than fifty years, these dire words were literally fulfilled."[9]

Progress was slow. As Jesus finally entered the city, the day was far spent. It was a memorable day. As the masses poured through the gates in an almost endless stream, excitement and alarm filled the whole city. What can this be? "Who is this?" is asked from the windows, the roofs, the streets, and the bazaars. Even Jerusalem, frozen with religious formalism, is stirred.[10] The answer is given: "This is the prophet Jesus, from Nazareth of Galilee." Thus the word is passed to the homes of the city, to the camps of the pilgrims, to the courts of the rulers, and to the palaces of Pilate, Herod, and Caiaphas. Thus ended the day, "as it was already late." After a brief visit in the temple, merely to look around, Jesus keenly observed the traffic going on within the sacred precinct and listened to the hum of bargaining voices and the clink of gold. But He postponed action and "went out to Bethany with the twelve."

6
Returning to Bethany
Mt 21:10-11;
Mk 11:11

28

MONDAY OF PASSION WEEK

March 30, AD 33

Nisan (or Abib)									
7	8	9	10	11	12	13	14	15	16
March					April				
27	28	29	30	31	1	2	3	4	5
Fri.	Sat.	Sun.	Mon.	Tues.	Wed.	Thu.	Fri.	Sat.	Sun.

As Jesus returned to the city on the next morning, He felt hungry. This seems to suggest that He had not spent the preceding night, at least not the latter part of the night, with His friends at Bethany, but rather under the canopy of heaven, in communion with His heavenly Father.[2] At any rate, as He walked along the road on Monday morning with His disciples, He beheld a solitary fig tree by the wayside. Seeing its green leaves and vigorous growth, "He went to see if He could find anything on it." But when He came, He found nothing but leaves. Although the ordinary season for the ripening of figs (June) had not yet arrived, we must not suppose that Jesus was ignorant of horticulture in Israel or unreasonable in being disappointed. Nor, for that matter, is the evangelist Mark wrong in remarking: "For it was not the season for figs." He probably was thinking of the spring or summer fig. We are told that at the time of Jesus, it was common to see figs and grapes ripening ten months of the year.[3] And modern writers tell us that early figs, called by the Arabs *taksh*, may be eaten as early as April.[4] But the tree that Christ approached was hopelessly barren. It was a fit emblem of a hypocrite. On it were neither the gleanings of the past nor the promise of the future.[5] Had it been fruitful the previous year, there would still have been a few of the figs hidden under its leaves. And

1
The Cursing of the Fig Tree (Mt 21:18–19a);[1] Mk 11:12–14

had it been fruitful that year, the untimely *taksh* would have appeared. Since, however, it was both deceptive and useless, the curse is loudly spoken: "May no fruit ever come from you again."

2
The Cleansing of the Temple
Mt 21:12–13;
Mk 11:15–17;
Lk 19:45–46[6]

Again the Lord of the temple entered into the temple of the Lord.[7] As in the beginning of His public ministry three years earlier, He would now, at the close of it, demand the purity of worship by forceful demonstration. Already on the day before, after His triumphal entry into the Holy City, He had briefly visited the temple and looked around. Again He had noticed that tradesmen for temple supplies—animals, oil, wine, and salt—and the exchangers of money had entrenched themselves in holy places. "Jesus entered the temple and drove out all who sold and bought in the temple, and He overturned the tables of the money-changers and the seats of those who sold pigeons." The whole worship had been commercialized, and this probably in the manner of modern concessions at fairs and places of amusement, to the advantage of the high priests. But Jesus cast out all the desecraters of His temple. In appealing to Scripture,[8] He defended His action with the words: "'My house shall be called a house of prayer,' but you make it a den of robbers." In His holy zeal, He would not even allow people passing to and fro with vessels and instruments to disturb the sacred courts, thus turning them into an ordinary thoroughfare. In this prohibition, He agreed with certain rabbinical expressions[9] as to the sacredness of holy places.

3
The Hosannas of the Children
Mt 21:14–17;
Mk 11:18–19;
Lk 19:47–48

In opposition to the temple traffic, Jesus manifested the spirit that shall obtain in His house by healing the lame and the blind who appealed to Him. But the leaders of Israel would not yield, neither listening to His Word nor acknowledging His deeds as divine miracles. When the very children of the temple, probably employed in the temple service, continued the hosannas of the day before, the scribes and priests were sorely displeased. They said to Him: "Do You hear what these are saying?" Again referring them to Scripture (Ps 8:2), Jesus replied: "Yes; have you never read, 'Out of the mouths of infants and nursing babies You have prepared praise'?" Jesus must have His praise. If the elders refuse to give it, then infants and nursing babies will do so. Yes, the very stones must then cry out (Lk 19:40). But the words of Jesus displeased the chief priests and the scribes all the more. They sought to kill Him; but they feared Him. They had to find a chance to arrest Him when a multitude of protecting friends did not surround Him. Unmolested and undisturbed, in spite of the rigorous manner by which He had interfered with their unhallowed gains, He passed another day. In the evening, He left the temple and the city and covered the two miles (Jn 11:18) to Bethany, where He stayed the night.[10]

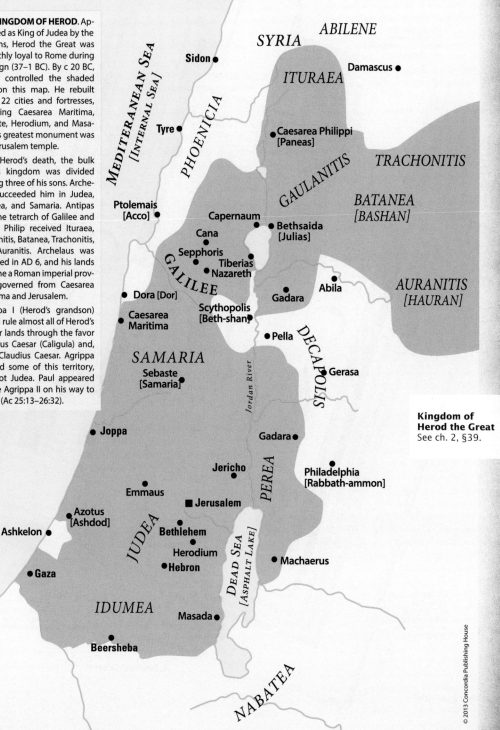

THE KINGDOM OF HEROD. Appointed as King of Judea by the Romans, Herod the Great was staunchly loyal to Rome during his reign (37–1 BC). By c 20 BC, Herod controlled the shaded area on this map. He rebuilt some 22 cities and fortresses, including Caesarea Maritima, Sebaste, Herodium, and Masada. His greatest monument was the Jerusalem temple.

After Herod's death, the bulk of his kingdom was divided among three of his sons. Archelaus succeeded him in Judea, Idumea, and Samaria. Antipas became tetrarch of Galilee and Perea. Philip received Ituraea, Gaulanitis, Batanea, Trachonitis, and Auranitis. Archelaus was deposed in AD 6, and his lands became a Roman imperial province governed from Caesarea Maritima and Jerusalem.

Agrippa I (Herod's grandson) would rule almost all of Herod's former lands through the favor of Gaius Caesar (Caligula) and, later, Claudius Caesar. Agrippa II ruled some of this territory, but not Judea. Paul appeared before Agrippa II on his way to Rome (Ac 25:13–26:32).

SYRIA

ABILENE

ITURAEA

Sidon

MEDITERANEAN SEA [INTERNAL SEA]

Damascus

PHOENICIA

Tyre

Caesarea Philippi [Paneas]

TRACHONITIS

GAULANITIS

BATANEA [BASHAN]

Ptolemais [Acco]

Capernaum

Cana

Bethsaida [Julias]

Sepphoris

Tiberias

Nazareth

GALILEE

Gadara

Abila

AURANITIS [HAURAN]

Dora [Dor]

Scythopolis [Beth-shan]

Caesarea Maritima

Pella

DECAPOLIS

SAMARIA

Gerasa

Sebaste [Samaria]

Jordan River

Joppa

Gadara

Jericho

Emmaus

PEREA

Philadelphia [Rabbath-ammon]

Jerusalem

Azotus [Ashdod]

Bethlehem

Ashkelon

Herodium

Hebron

DEAD SEA [ASPHALT LAKE]

Machaerus

JUDEA

Gaza

IDUMEA

Masada

Beersheba

NABATEA

Kingdom of Herod the Great
See ch. 2, §39.

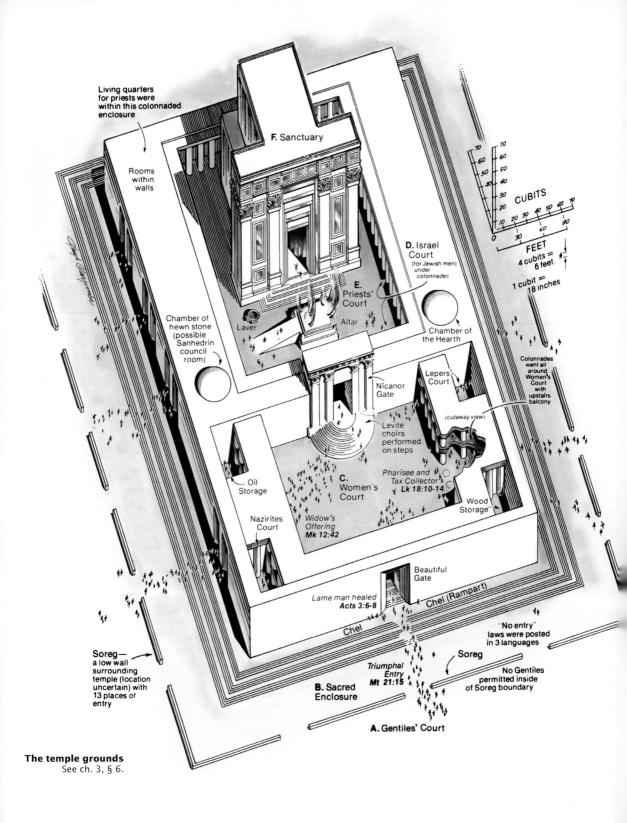

Living quarters for priests were within this colonnaded enclosure

Rooms within walls

F. Sanctuary

D. Israel Court
(for Jewish men) *under colonnades*

E. Priests' Court

Chamber of hewn stone (possible Sanhedrin council room)

Laver

Altar

Chamber of the Hearth

CUBITS

FEET

4 cubits = 6 feet.

1 cubit = 18 inches

Nicanor Gate

Lepers' Court

Colonnades went all around Women's Court with upstairs balcony

(cutaway view)

Levite choirs performed on steps

Pharisee and Tax Collector
Lk 18:10-14

Oil Storage

C. Women's Court

Wood Storage

Nazirites Court

Widow's Offering
Mk 12:42

Beautiful Gate

Lame man healed
Acts 3:6-8

Chel (Rampart)

Chel

"No entry" laws were posted in 3 languages

Soreg—
a low wall surrounding temple (location uncertain) with 13 places of entry

Triumphal Entry
Mt 21:15

Soreg

No Gentiles permitted inside of Soreg boundary

B. Sacred Enclosure

A. Gentiles' Court

The temple grounds
See ch. 3, § 6.

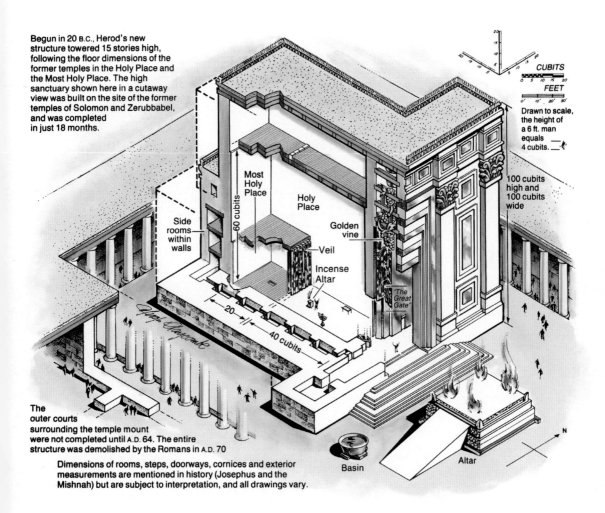

Begun in 20 B.C., Herod's new structure towered 15 stories high, following the floor dimensions of the former temples in the Holy Place and the Most Holy Place. The high sanctuary shown here in a cutaway view was built on the site of the former temples of Solomon and Zerubbabel, and was completed in just 18 months.

CUBITS
0 5 10 15 20

FEET
0' 10' 20' 30'

Drawn to scale, the height of a 6 ft. man equals 4 cubits.

100 cubits high and 100 cubits wide

Most Holy Place

Holy Place

Golden vine

Side rooms within walls

60 cubits

Veil

Incense Altar

"The Great Gate"

20

40 cubits

The outer courts surrounding the temple mount were not completed until A.D. 64. The entire structure was demolished by the Romans in A.D. 70

Basin

Altar

N

Dimensions of rooms, steps, doorways, cornices and exterior measurements are mentioned in history (Josephus and the Mishnah) but are subject to interpretation, and all drawings vary.

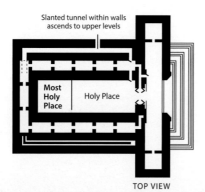

Slanted tunnel within walls ascends to upper levels

Most Holy Place

Holy Place

TOP VIEW

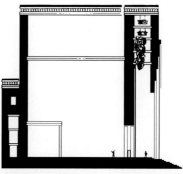

SIDE ELEVATION

TRAVELS OF THE HOLY FAMILY Mt 2:13–23 describes the flight of Jesus, Mary, and Joseph to Egypt. Only the endpoints of the journey are known: Bethlehem to Egypt; Egypt to Nazareth. One possible route to Egypt passed south over the Judean hills from Bethlehem to Beersheba. From there it went either by an inland route or via Gaza and then to Egypt on the main caravan route near the sea. Another route involved going to Ashkelon and thence on the caravan route to Gaza and Egypt. Perhaps Jesus and His family joined one of the Jewish communities in the Nile Delta or the Nile Valley. After leaving Egypt, Jesus' family settled in the Galilean town of Nazareth.

Gebal [Byblos]

Sidon

Damascus

Tyre

GALILEE

Nazareth

Caesarea
Maritima

Joppa

Jerusalem

Ashkelon
Gaza

Bethlehem

JUDEA

0   50   100 km.

0   50 mi.

MEDITERRANEAN SEA

Beersheba

Possible Travel Routes

Alexandria

Naucratis

Tanis

EGYPT

Heliopolis

Memphis

Nile R.

SINAI

**Joseph Flees with
Mary and Jesus**
See ch. 4, §28.

Mt. Sinai

Akhetaton
[Tell el-Amarna]

RED SEA

Thebes

© 2013 Concordia Publishing House

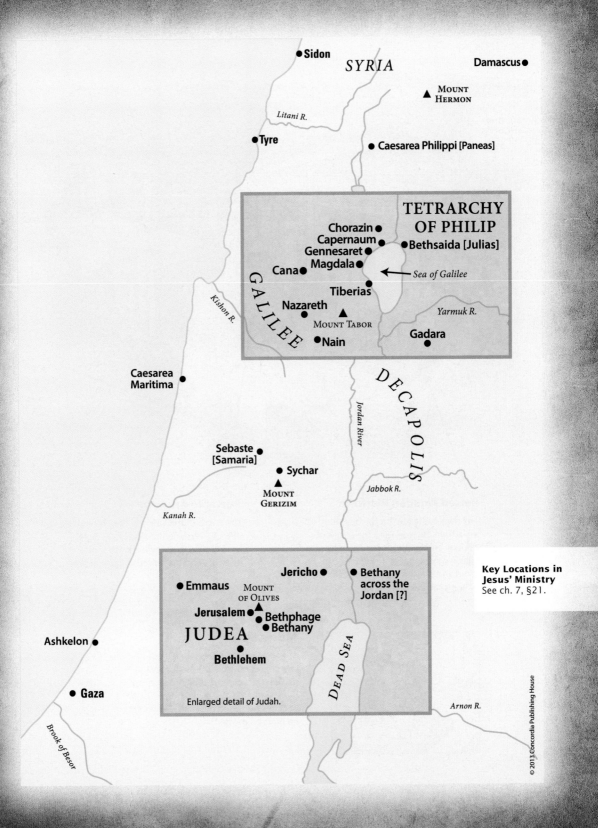

Sidon

SYRIA

Damascus

▲ Mount Hermon

Litani R.

Tyre

Caesarea Philippi [Paneas]

TETRARCHY OF PHILIP

Chorazin
Capernaum
Gennesaret
Magdala
Cana
Bethsaida [Julias]

GALILEE

← Sea of Galilee

Tiberias

Nazareth

Yarmuk R.

▲ Mount Tabor

Nain

Gadara

Kishon R.

Caesarea Maritima

DECAPOLIS

Jordan River

Sebaste [Samaria]

Sychar

▲ Mount Gerizim

Jabbok R.

Kanah R.

Jericho

Bethany across the Jordan [?]

Emmaus

Mount of Olives

Jerusalem
Bethphage
Bethany

JUDEA

Bethlehem

DEAD SEA

Ashkelon

Enlarged detail of Judah.

Arnon R.

Gaza

Brook of Besor

Key Locations in Jesus' Ministry
See ch. 7, §21.

© 2013 Concordia Publishing House

**Jewish Synagogues
in the Time of Christ**
See ch. 9, §4.

© CPH/Glenn Myers

Raised Wooden Platform

The religious leader for the day stood on
a platform. He read from the scrolls of
the Law and the Prophets. There was no
altar in a synagogue. Reading God's
Word and praying took the place of
offering sacrifices.

Portable Ark

The scrolls of the Law and the Prophets
(the Old Testament books of the Bible)
were kept in a portable ark. On special
days, the ark was carried in a procession.

© CPH/Glenn Myers

Moses Seat

After reading from the scrolls, the
teacher sat down in the Moses Seat to
explain the Scripture readings. Some of
those gathered at the synagogue sat on
benches that lined the walls. Others sat
on mats on the floor.

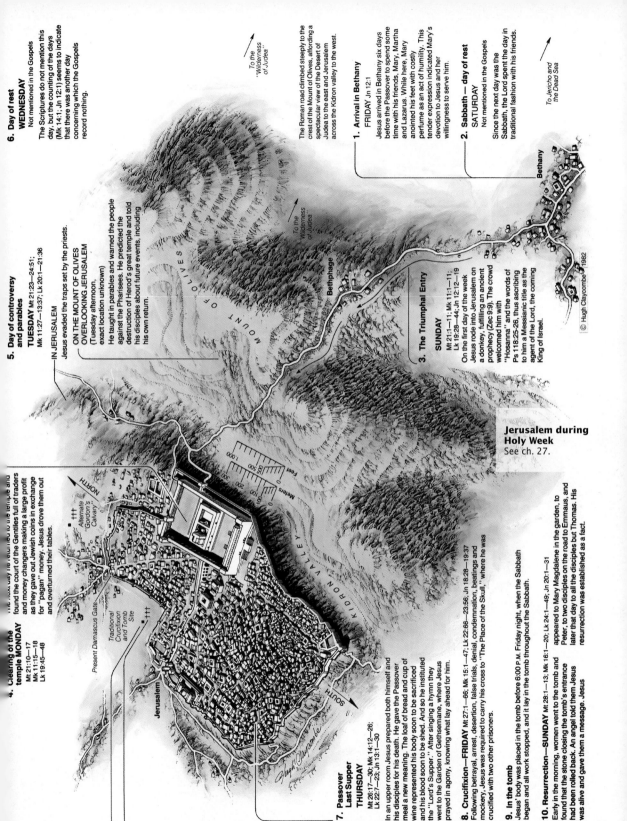

Jerusalem during Holy Week
See ch. 27.

6. Day of rest WEDNESDAY

Not mentioned in the Gospels

The Scriptures do not mention this day, but the counting of the days (Mk 14:1; Jn 12:1) seems to indicate that there was another day concerning which the Gospels record nothing.

The Roman road climbed steeply to the crest of the Mount of Olives, affording a spectacular view of the Desert of Judea to the east and Jerusalem across the Kidron valley to the west.

To the "Wilderness of Judea"

To the Wilderness of Judea

1. Arrival in Bethany

FRIDAY Jn 12:1

Jesus arrived in Bethany six days before the Passover to spend some time with his friends, Mary, Martha and Lazarus. While here, Mary anointed his feet with costly perfume as an act of humility. This tender expression indicated Mary's devotion to Jesus and her willingness to serve him.

2. Sabbath — day of rest SATURDAY

Not mentioned in the Gospels

Since the next day was the Sabbath, the Lord spent the day in traditional fashion with his friends.

To Jericho and the Dead Sea

Bethany

© Hugh Claycombe 1982

Bethphage

MOUNT OF OLIVES

5. Day of controversy and parables

TUESDAY Mt 21:23—24:51; Mk 11:27—13:37; Lk 20:1—21:36

IN JERUSALEM

Jesus evaded the traps set by the priests.

ON THE MOUNT OF OLIVES OVERLOOKING JERUSALEM (Tuesday afternoon, exact location unknown)

He taught in parables and warned the people against the Pharisees. He predicted the destruction of Herod's great temple and told his disciples about future events, including his own return.

3. The Triumphal Entry

SUNDAY

Mt 21:1—11; Mk 11:1—11; Lk 19:28—44; Jn 12:12—19

On the first day of the week Jesus rode into Jerusalem on a donkey, fulfilling an ancient prophecy (Zec 9:9). The crowd welcomed him with "Hosanna" and the words of Ps 118:25-26, thus ascribing to him a Messianic title as the agent of the Lord, the coming King of Israel.

4. Clearing of the temple MONDAY

Mt 21:10—17
Mk 11:15—18
Lk 19:45—48

The next day he returned to the temple and found the court of the Gentiles full of traders and money changers making a large profit as they gave out Jewish coins in exchange for "pagan" money. Jesus drove them out and overturned their tables.

NORTH

Alternate "Gordon's Calvary"

Present Damascus Gate

Traditional Crucifixion and Tomb Site

Feet
1,000
500
300
200
100
0

Meters
300
200
100
50
0

Jerusalem

KIDRON VALLEY

SOUTH

7. Passover Last Supper THURSDAY

Mt 26:17—30; Mk 14:12—26; Lk 22:7—23; Jn 13:1—30

In an upper room Jesus prepared both himself and his disciples for his death. He gave the Passover meal a new meaning. The loaf of bread and cup of wine represented his body soon to be sacrificed and his blood soon to be shed. And so he instituted the "Lord's Supper." After singing a hymn they went to the Garden of Gethsemane, where Jesus prayed in agony, knowing what lay ahead for him.

8. Crucifixion—FRIDAY Mt 27:1—66; Mk 15:1—47; Lk 22:66—23:56; Jn 18:28—19:37

Following betrayal, arrest, desertion, false trials, denial, condemnation, beatings and mockery, Jesus was required to carry his cross to "The Place of the Skull," where he was crucified with two other prisoners.

9. In the tomb

Jesus' body was placed in the tomb before 6:00 P.M. Friday night, when the Sabbath began and all work stopped, and it lay in the tomb throughout the Sabbath.

10. Resurrection—SUNDAY Mt 28:1—13; Mk 16:1—20; Lk 24:1—49; Jn 20:1—31

Early in the morning, women went to the tomb and found that the stone closing the tomb's entrance had been rolled back. An angel told them Jesus was alive and gave them a message. Jesus appeared to Mary Magdalene in the garden, to Peter, to two disciples on the road to Emmaus, and later that day to all the disciples but Thomas. His resurrection was established as a fact.

Possible diagram of the empty tomb
See ch. 37, § 6.

KOKH

KOKH

KOKH

KOKH

60in average

BENCH

PIT

ENTRANCE

EAST

24in

24in

Average width of burial bench was 24in all around the pit, according to E. L. Nitkow

29

TUESDAY MORNING OF PASSION WEEK

March 31, AD 33

Nisan (or Abib)							
9	10	11	12	13	14	15	16
March			April				
29	30	31	1	2	3	4	5
Sun.	Mon.	Tues.	Wed.	Thu.	Fri.	Sat.	Sun

On the next morning, Jesus and His disciples returned to the city. They passed by the fig tree that the Lord had cursed[1] and noticed that it had withered from its very roots. Most likely it was in the same condition on the previous evening, but it would have been too dark to examine it when they passed the spot. It was as if the hand of death had smitten it. The disciples marveled at the completeness of the judgment. Calling to mind what Jesus had said, they connected the present condition of the tree with the word that Jesus had spoken. Then Peter, acting as spokesman, expressed the surprise of the disciples: "Rabbi, look! The fig tree that You cursed has withered."

> **1**
> The Fig Tree
> Withered Away
> Mt 21:19b–20;
> Mk 11:20–21

In His reply, Jesus combined what the disciples needed to know: "Truly, I say to you, whoever says to this mountain, 'Be taken up and thrown into the sea,' and does not doubt in his heart, but believes that what he says will come to pass, it will be done for him."[2] These are mighty words that interpreters must not detract. Christians possess an instrument of divine power, regardless of whether or not they ever enjoy its use. Remember, however, that this power is not given to presumption, but to faith—absolute, simple, sincere, trustful faith, which gives all glory to God and seeks His glory and trusts in His promises. It is a faith that exercises itself

> **2**
> The Great Power
> of Faith
> Mt 21:21–22;
> Mk 11:22–26

in confident prayer: "Whatever you ask in prayer, believe that you have received it, and it will be yours." At all times, a true conciliatory spirit serves as a necessary background. "Whenever you stand praying, forgive, if you have anything against anyone, so that your Father also who is in heaven may forgive you your trespasses."[3]

3
The Authority of
Jesus Challenged
Mt 21:23;
Mk 11:27–28;
Lk 20:1–2

The last full working day of our Lord's public ministry to Israel had arrived. And what a day it was! To judge from the records, it was the busiest day of His life.[4] It was His last day in the temple, the last day of His teaching, the last warning He gave the Pharisees and Sadducees, and His last call to national repentance.[5] Scarcely had He entered the sacred courts after His discourse on the way as suggested by the withering of the fig tree, when an official delegation of the Jewish Council approached Him. The delegation consisted of (1) chief priests, probably members of the ruling high-priestly nobility and heads of the twenty-four priestly courses, mostly Sadducees; (2) scribes, that is, learned rabbis and prominent canonists, representing the teaching and legal profession, mostly Pharisees; and (3) rulers, men of wealth and leisure, who represented the laity. Surrounding Jesus on all sides, they asked the question: "By what authority are You doing these things, and who gave You this authority?" They demanded that He show them His commission authorizing Him to perform the duties of the public ministry, to assume the functions of a rabbi or prophet, to ride into Jerusalem amid messianic hosannas shouted and royal titles attributed to Him by attendant crowds, and to purge the temple of the traffickers (whom the leaders themselves had probably licensed) at whose presence in the temple courts they at least connived, and the like. The Council by no means exceeded its authority by sending a delegation of this kind. It was the duty of this body to watch over the morals and the worship of Israel, especially to pass on the credentials of a prophet, should one arise.[6] But here their purpose was evil, and they had already made their plans. They were not concerned about justice and the right of Jesus to act as He did. Their inquiry was a smoke screen behind which they could make preparations to carry out their murderous resolve. Most likely they thought that Jesus would appeal to His—as they would have it—unproved divine commission. Then they might easily pass legal judgment upon Him as a false prophet and blasphemer.

4
"Was the Baptism of
John from Heaven?"
Mt 21:24–27;
Mk 11:29–33;
Lk 20:3–8

Jesus' answer took them by surprise. It was a counter-question: "I also will ask you one question, and if you tell Me the answer, then I also will tell you by what authority I do these things. The baptism of John, from where did it come? From heaven or from man?" They were caught. Surely they, who had officially inquired into the commission of John (Jn 1:19–27), were able to answer the question.[7] But no answer came. Besides the fact that John had pointed out Jesus as *the* Prophet, the Messiah, there were the undisputed credentials of John himself. Not that they could not answer the question, but they would not. And why bring up this question of John's baptism now, after John was—as far as they were concerned, fortunately—dead? They were in a complete dilemma. So they reasoned among themselves that they would not say, "From heaven," because in their hearts they did not believe it. And besides, this would give Jesus the opportunity to ask, "Why then did you not believe him?" Still they could not speak derisively of John and say, "From man," because the people were persuaded, as even Josephus admitted,[8] that John was a prophet. To have stated this in the teeth of popular opinion would have endangered their personal safety: "All the people will stone us to death." Therefore, what they were unable to deny they were nevertheless unwilling to admit. So they answered, "We do not know."[9] What an admission by the "incorporate wisdom of Israel"! And what a death-blow to their pretensions! Jesus did not press them on this point. However, He would show them that He could not be caught off guard. He owed them no apology. Their failure to answer absolved Him from the necessity of explaining how He had His authority, for they admitted they were incompetent to judge the matter. Jesus replied, "Neither will I tell you by what authority I do these things." For the present, the defeated accusers withdrew to the background.

In spite of their pretended piety, it was clear that the leaders of Israel would not enter into the kingdom of God, for they would not receive the testimony of Jesus and John the Baptist. Jesus makes this clear in the parable of the two sons, the meaning of which both the multitudes and the members of the Council (who were still scowling in the background) could not fail to understand. "What do you think? A man had two sons." It appears from the lesson taught that the man in the parable is God, and both sons are members of the chosen race. "And he went to the first and said, 'Son, go and work in the vineyard today.'" The son flatly refused: "I will not." But then he changed his mind and went. Meanwhile, the father approached the second son and spoke likewise. With all due politeness, this son answered: "I go, sir," but then he "did not go." And now the question: "Which of the two did the will of his father?" The answer of the Lord's enemies was: "The first." Then Jesus pointed out to them the meaning of their reply. That is exactly what happened in His own ministry and in that of John. Despite their initial and open shamelessness and brazen-faced disobedience, it was the very tax collectors and prostitutes who, repenting went into the kingdom of heaven. "The tax collectors and the prostitutes go into the kingdom of God before you."[10] These despised and hated sinners are "streaming through the door which is not yet shut."[11] On the other hand, the professionally pious and the pretended holy legalists of the nation (as represented by the blandly promising, but non-performing second son) would not enter into the kingdom of heaven. Now, there was John the Baptist, who cultivated strict legal piety like themselves.[12] He stood for their own principles of strict righteousness and minute obedience to the Law; yet "you did not believe him." And even when the effect of his preaching was seen on the tax collectors and prostitutes, still "even when you

5
The Parable
of the Two Sons
Mt 21:28–32

saw it, you did not afterward change your minds and believe him." They were too proud to learn from tax collectors and prostitutes. The result was that these went into the kingdom before them.

This parable exposes the insincerity of the leaders in Israel, and it is followed by one that exposes their open revolt against divine authority and foreshadows the doom of Jesus. There was a master of a house who planted a vineyard, placed a fence around it to protect it from wild beasts, dug a winepress and a pit beneath it to receive the juices of the grapes, and built a tower for the laborers and for the storage of the fruit; in short, he did everything needed to make it a good vineyard and to insure a good yield of fruit (Is 5:2). Then he leased it out to tenants for a certain share of the annual crop as payment for the care and the general management of the vineyard. After he made all these provisions, he "went into another country." It is assumed that the reference is to a newly planted vineyard and that it would take a "long while," about two or three years, to raise a crop. At any rate, the parable conveys the total reasonableness on the part of the master. After a sufficient time had elapsed, and at the time agreed upon, he sent his servants to collect the rent. But what happened? The tenants treated the messengers in a most barbarous manner, beating and even stoning them or killing them in some other way. We might have expected the owner to take severe measures immediately; but instead, showing an extraordinarily high degree of good will and patience, he sent other servants and still others, all of whom, however, received the same brutal treatment. These things would hardly ever happen in ordinary life, but they can truly describe people's conduct in the spiritual sphere.[13] "For the vineyard of the LORD of hosts is the house of Israel, and the men of Judah are His pleasant planting" (Is 5:7). At last, "he had still one other, a beloved son. Finally he sent him to them saying, 'They will respect my son.' " But the result was the same.

> The appearance of the legal heir made them apprehensive of their tenure. Practically the vineyard was already theirs. By killing the heir, the only claimant to it would be put out of the way and so the vineyard [would] become in every respect their own.[14]

"Come, let us kill him, and the inheritance will be ours," thus they reasoned among themselves. They proceeded from the idea that the owner was in "another country" for an indefinite length of time. It seemed that he was unable to interfere, as indicated by his sending of servants successively. This plainly showed that his only chance of enforcing collection lay in the weak hope of the gentle power of persuasion. So they let the only son make his approach, who was unaware of the fate that would meet him. When he arrived, they pounced upon him, cast him out of the vineyard, and slew him.

The meaning of the parable is sufficiently clear. God planted the vineyard of the Old Testament theocracy. The fence is the Law and the covenant, which surrounded Israel and separated the Jew from the Gentile. The winepress is the temple with its rituals and sacrifices foreshadowing the supreme sacrifice of the promised Messiah for the sins of all mankind. A tower of civic order or of prophecy was constructed from which the prophetic watchmen could study the approach of messianic times (Mi 7:4; Is 52:8; 62:6). The vineyard was let out to tenants, even as the management of Israel was entrusted to rulers, teachers, and leaders. At the present time, these were the high priests and scribes. Jesus related this parable for their special benefit. And so forth. We need not go into details. In due season, God sent forth His servants, the prophets, from Moses to John the Baptist, to gather the fruits of love and obedience. But what happened? Jerusalem killed her prophets and stoned those who were sent to her (Lk 13:34; Mt 23:37); she became guilty of the blood of all the prophets shed on earth, from the blood of Abel to that of Zechariah (Lk 11:51; Mt 23:35), as well as of the blood of John the Baptist (Mk 9:13; Mt 17:12),[15] who died a prophet's death. At last, God sent His only Son, Jesus Christ. But His appearance made them fearful lest they fail to realize their unlawful desire of getting possession of the vineyard itself. "Everyone will believe in Him," and "the world has gone after Him" (Jn 11:48; 12:19). And so they cast Him out of His possession and killed Him.

> **7**
> The Meaning

There was no doubt as to the main drift of the parable. The hearers replied to Jesus' question about what the owner of the vineyard would do to these tenants when he returned. There could be only one answer: "He will put those wretches to a miserable death[16] and let out the vineyard to other tenants." From Jewish lips came the admission that, if God would take His Word and grace from them and give them to the Gentiles, this punishment would be well deserved. As a matter of fact, this very thing, as Jesus points out, had been prophesied in Scripture: "The stone that the builders rejected has become the cornerstone" (Ps 118:22).[17] This quotation contains the germ of another parable in which the rejected heir becomes the rejected stone of the builders—only, however, in turn eventually to become the accepted Cornerstone of God.[18] Against those who oppose Christ, the parable pronounced a general and an individual judgment. To the nation: "The kingdom of God will be taken away from you and given to a people producing its fruits." To individuals: "The one who falls on this stone will be broken to pieces; and when it falls on anyone, it will crush him." We are reminded of the words of Simeon: "This child is appointed for the fall and rising of many in Israel, and for a sign that is opposed" (Lk 2:34).

> **8**
> "The Stone that the Builders Rejected"
> Mt 21:40–44;
> Mk 12:9–11;
> Lk 20:15b–18

The scribes and the Pharisees, of course, saw through the veil of the parabolic language. They intended to ensnare Jesus, and now for the third time in rapid succession, He outsmarted them. The first time it was the implication—only too true—of their rejection of John (Lk 7:30). Then it was the charge of insincerity in the parable

> **9**
> "They Were Seeking to Arrest Him"
> Mt 21:45–46;
> Mk 12:12; Lk 20:19

of the two sons. And now in the parable of the tenants, it was the charge of open revolt, unsuccessful in the end and to be followed by the punishment and wrath of God. "They perceived that He was speaking about them" and intended to apprehend Him on the spot. "And although they were seeking to arrest Him, they feared the crowds, because they held Him to be a prophet."

10
The Parable of the
Wedding Feast
Mt 22:1–7

The threat that the kingdom of God would be "given to a people producing its fruits" (Mt 21:43) is followed by a parable that repeats the truth. Christ replies to the hostile thoughts and plans of His enemies, warning them that, unless they cease their enmity, judgment will come upon them. In its construction, this parable closely resembles that of the great banquet, spoken in the Pharisee's house in the later Perean ministry of Jesus (Lk 14:12–24). But it differs both as to details and as to the conclusion. The earlier parable was a parable of excuses and of rejected *grace*, while this is—with an addition—more directly a parable of *judgment* upon rejected grace.[19] The kingdom of heaven is compared to a king who gave a wedding feast for his son. His servants extend a preliminary invitation to the prospective guests and prepare an elaborate meal. At the appointed time, the king sends out a second invitation to the already invited guests:[20] "See, I have prepared my dinner,[21] my oxen and my fat calves have been slaughtered, and everything is ready. Come to the wedding feast." This second invitation seems to accord with Eastern custom (Est 6:14). Indeed, we are told[22] that, among the distinctions of the inhabitants of Jerusalem, none of them went to a feast until the invitation had been given twice. But in this banquet, no details of proper etiquette are overlooked, so as not to offend the most sensitive of the important, the rich, and the powerful of the invited guests. And a most attractive meal is prepared. But instead of showing the king how highly honored they felt at being invited by him and giving themselves the pleasure of being present at such a fine feast, they, making light of it, "went off, one to his farm, another to his business."[23] Some of them, probably the higher class of invited guests, added insult, even murder, to their indifference. "The rest seized his servants, treated them shamefully, and killed them." The kingdom of heaven is depicted. The King is God the Father. The Son is Jesus. The banquet is salvation. The guests are the members of the chosen race, the leaders and those led. The servants are the prophets, the disciples of Jesus, the apostles and evangelists included; and they are slain.[24] Then the parable merges into prophecy: "The king was angry, and he sent his troops and destroyed those murderers and burned their cities." This anticipates the Roman destruction of Jerusalem, when Vespasian and Titus led their armies to Jerusalem and burned the city in AD 70.

11
"Go therefore to the
Main Roads"
Mt 22:8–10

But the story must go on. The refusal of the Jews to accept Jesus' invitation shall not hinder the extension of the kingdom of God. The king said to his servants, "The wedding feast is ready, but those invited were not worthy. Go therefore to the main roads and invite to the wedding feast as many as you find." This was done. The servants went out on the Gentile roads and without regard to race, reputation, station, and social position, they swept the roads and the marketplaces and furnished the wedding with guests, "both bad and good." In like manner, the Gospel invitation was given: "Go into all the world and proclaim the gospel to the *whole* creation" (Mk 16:15).

Jesus then includes a sequel that warns all guests, Jews and Gentiles alike. The king was pleased with the success of his plan. As soon as the guests were placed, he entered the banquet hall. While he was passing down between the rows, his eye lighted upon a man without a wedding garment. There may have been others, but one serves to illustrate the principle. We do not know just how to understand this detail of the parable, whether all guests were supposed to come in special wedding garments or whether they were supplied with suitable vestments by the king. The latter is very probable if we suppose that the guests came in from the streets as they were.[25] But the historical accuracy of this assumption has been doubted.[26] At any rate, those invited were supposed to appear in festive attire, which was a matter of course and demanded by the rules of ordinary etiquette. How the vestment is acquired is not the point. It is the necessity of ownership that is stressed. Scripture teaches us elsewhere, and abundantly, that the righteousness of Christ is the only garment that is acceptable before God. In virtue of the suffering and death of Christ, it is a free gift, bestowed upon those who believe. However, this man had thrust himself into the company in rags, and, we might add, in the rags of his own righteousness. There is no answer to the question of the king: "Friend,[27] how did you get in here without a wedding garment?" The man was speechless. He had nothing to say. He had no excuse. Before men, we like to boast of our high moral standing, but before God, all our righteous deeds are like polluted garments (Is 64:6). He insults God's grace by demanding as a reward for his pretended piety that God receive him into heaven. We must remember that this is a parable of the Kingdom. Therefore, the man in the parable who appeared without a wedding garment was cast out. "Then the king said to the attendants, 'Bind him hand and foot and cast him into the outer darkness. In that place there will be weeping and gnashing of teeth.' " At the conclusion of the parable, the Lord Himself makes the transition to the spiritual sphere (Mt 8:11–12; 13:42, 50; 24:51; Lk 13:28–29). And again the warning is given: "Many are called, but few are chosen" (cf. Mt 20:16).[28] Many hear, but few heed, the Gospel call.

12
The Guest without the Wedding Garment
Mt 22:11–14

In their attempts upon Jesus' life, His enemies did not lack resourcefulness. Since they had failed in questioning His authority, they tried to drive Him into a collision with the civil powers. In evolving their plan, they first of all joined forces with the Herodians.[29] A strange alliance indeed. The Pharisees, as the representatives

13
The Question of Taxes
Mt 22:15–17;
Mk 12:13–14;
Lk 20:20–22

of the extreme Jewish nationalists and haters of Rome, made common cause with a political party that sought to strengthen the dynasty of Herod by cultivating the favor of Rome.[30] The purpose of this alliance was to spy on Jesus under the guise of an honest inquiry and, if possible, to entangle Him in His talk. They would do this by leading Him to make some incriminating statement against the government, whereupon they would deliver Him into the hands of the governor. In order to give the whole procedure an appearance of singleness of heart, the Pharisees would not come themselves, but would send a group of their keenest students together with the Herodians, who this time might be expected to come before Him without arousing in Him a suspicion of sinister motives on their part. The impression that they evidently designed to make was that a dispute had occurred between them and that they now desired to settle it by referring the matter to an authority such as Jesus was. Their plan was to put Him in a dilemma by asking Him to answer a question about paying taxes to Caesar. Ever since the birth of Christ and the days of Judas of Galilee (Lk 2:1; Ac 5:37), this had been a burning question in current politics and in theology. The Pharisees' disciples cunningly conceived the introduction of their speech. "Teacher, we know," everybody knows, "that You are true and teach the way of God truthfully." So that infamous accusation that Jesus was in league with Beelzebul was admittedly false (Mt 12:24)![31] The points that they stressed were His sincerity, His trustworthiness, His fearlessness, and His integrity. "You do not care about anyone's opinion, for You are not swayed by appearances." These were honeyed words. But they hid a forked tongue. And in a moment, a venomous fang appeared.[32] "Tell us, then," since You are so wise and courageous, "what You think." Thus they tempted Him to commit Himself, while they remained noncommittal. "Is it lawful to pay taxes[33] to Caesar?" And without playing a heroic part themselves, they seem to indicate the nature of their secretly desired reply in the final suggestion "or not?"[34] The trap was cleverly constructed. The question—whether for poll-tax or for state purposes—seemed to imply that paying such a tax conflicted with their duty to God as the only true Head of the nation (Dt 17:15). Did not the payment of taxes to the Roman emperor or to his representative virtually admit the sovereignty of a stranger over Israel, which in effect was denying the supremacy of God? No matter how Jesus answered the question, it seemed that He would certainly be caught. To answer it in Rome's favor—He had just been hailed as David's Son and Israel's King—would cost Him popular favor, and to answer it in favor of the people would get Him into serious trouble with Roman authorities, who would charge Him with disloyalty to Rome.

14
"Whose Likeness and Inscription Is This?"
Mt 22:18–22;
Mk 12:15–17;
Lk 20:23–26

But Jesus proved that He was indeed true, that He taught the way of God in truth, and did not fear any man. He knew their wicked scheme and said, "Why put Me to the test, you hypocrites? Show Me the coin for the tax."[35] Under the circumstances, as worshipers in the temple, they would probably only carry Jewish coins, without the hated images; but they could easily go to one of the money-changers squatted behind his low table by the pillars in the Court of the Gentiles and bring Him a current Roman coin. "And they brought Him a denarius."[36] It was the well-known Roman silver coin representing ten units of an earlier bronze standard, used to pay the annual tax. (This coin represented the average daily amount of a laborer's wages or a soldier's pay.[37]) On one side were stamped the haughty features of Tiberius, his Roman nose and scornful underlip, and the inscription: "Tiberius Caesar, son of the divine Augustus, Augustus,"[38] and on the other side "Pontifex Maximus,"[39] which title, "high priest" or "supreme bridge-builder," made him both the highest civil and the highest religious ruler of the land. The title itself surrounded the enthroned Caesar with his long scepter in his right hand and an emblem of honor in his left.[40] As Jesus looked at the coin, probably turning it in His hand, He asked the question: "Whose likeness and inscription is this?" They answered, "Caesar's." It is assumed that they could read the Latin lettering; if not, there is no doubt that they knew the meaning. Without evading in the least the question about the lawfulness of paying the tax, Jesus gave a real reply: "Render,"[41] give back, "to Caesar the things that are Caesar's." Yet even though they must acknowledge their political relationship to Caesar and observe the obligation that it implies (Jer 27:4–8; Rm 13:1; 1Pt 2:13–14), at the same time they must not disregard their theocratic duties. "And to God the things that are God's." There are duties to Caesar. But there are also duties to God. These must be strictly kept apart. It was their duty to obey and support the government that they (in a way) had chosen; for in the time of the Maccabees, the Jews themselves had sought the help of Rome (1Macc 8:17–20), and after the death of Herod, they themselves requested the removal of Archelaus and expressed the wish to be governed by a procurator.[42] Under these circumstances, the tax only represented the equivalent for the advantages that they received from Roman governance. To Tiberius they owed tax and submission; but at the same time, they owed themselves in uncompromised service to God. By the way, there was no intention on the part of Jesus to restore that former political status, the "kingdom of God" such as they hoped for. With His simple and true answer, Jesus pointed out the correct interrelation of Church and State.—In spite of His enemies' attempts, there was nothing in this guileless wisdom that they could attack. There was no way in which they could "entangle Him in His words." Amazed and humiliated, they left Him and went their way.

A number of Sadducees were present and had witnessed the crushing defeat of the Pharisees and the Herodians. These aristocratic rationalists of Israel welcomed this defeat because their faction opposed the others. But at the same time, they looked askance at the success of Jesus. Undiscouraged by the failure of their

15
The Question of the Sadducees
Mt 22:23–28;
Mk 12:18–23;
Lk 20:27–33

rivals, they came forward with the purpose of matching their strength with that of the Prophet of Galilee, with hopes of better success. Only on one occasion had Jesus come into public conflict with the Sadducees, when, characteristically, they had asked of Him a sign from heaven (Mt 16:1).[43] Representing the priestly and ruling classes, they contented themselves with material things, life upon earth. As long as they had wealth and an honorable position, they were perfectly satisfied with the present order of things. They opposed Jesus because in representing Himself as the Messiah and in teaching about the Kingdom, He threatened to disturb the Sadducean order. Like the Samaritans, they accepted only the five books of Moses. As materialists and cold Epicureans, they did not include the resurrection of the dead, the immortality of the soul, and the existence of angels and spirits in their theology (Ac 23:8). For the purpose of ridiculing the doctrine of the resurrection, known to them as being one of the tenets of Jesus and shared by the Pharisees, they came to Him with one of their stock conundrums and "stale pieces of casuistry" about the seven brothers and the one wife.[44] They introduced it by appealing to the ordinance of Moses regarding levirate marriage.[45] "Teacher, Moses said, 'If a man dies having no children, his brother must marry the widow and raise up offspring for his brother' " (cf. Dt 25:5–6). Then they submitted, as if it had actually happened, an odd case. An eldest brother died without having children. The six remaining brothers in succession had married his widow, but also had died without children, with the widow still surviving. And now, "in the resurrection," that is, if there is a resurrection,[46] "whose wife will she be? For they all had her." It was a very clever puzzle. The Pharisees, who had very materialistic views on the resurrection, some of them holding that a man would rise in exactly the same clothes in which he had been buried, had already to their own satisfaction conceded the wife to the first husband on account of the right of priority.[47] However, the Sadducees would not admit this in their disputes with others because to them, the fundamental question was still unanswered.

16
The Reply of Jesus
Mt 22:29–33;
Mk 12:24–27;
Lk 20:34–40

But if the Sadducees succeeded in baffling the Pharisees with their fairytales, they were not able to confuse Jesus. He heard their story to the end. Then He gave them an answer that will forever be remembered. Yes, there is a resurrection. But concerning its nature, "You are wrong, because you know neither the Scriptures nor the power of God." Marriage and the begetting of children is restricted to life in this world. Although love remains in that place of bliss beyond the grave, yet conditions in heaven supersede all that is earthly in human relationship.[48] In the resurrection and among those "*who are considered worthy to attain to that age* and to the resurrection from the dead,"[49] there is neither marrying for men nor being given in marriage for women. The relations of time will not apply to things eternal. The resurrected children of God will be like the angels, and matters belonging to the sphere of matrimony will no longer be of concern to them.[50] As to the question of the resurrection itself, this is plainly taught in Scripture, indeed, already in the very Books of Moses that they accepted and that they now marshaled against Him. In Jesus' argument, He refrains from quoting the prophetic books of the Old Testament in order to meet them on their own ground. For the purpose of showing their ignorance of Scripture, He calls their attention to that passage in the Book of Exodus relating to the burning bush, where God describes Himself to their great lawgiver as "the God of Abraham and the God of Isaac and the God of Jacob" (see Ex 3:6). At the time of Moses, these patriarchs had been dead a few hundred years, and still God calls Himself their God.[51] Now, personal existence does not cease with death, as the Sadducees had taught. The dead are absent from ongoing relationships with mankind, but in their relation to God, they continue to live. How unworthy would the title "God of Abraham, Isaac, and Jacob" have been had these fathers been but a handful of scattered bones and crumbling dust, now moldering in the Hittite's cave![52] "You are quite wrong." He who calls Himself the God of Abraham is not the God of dust. "He is not God of the dead, but of the living."—The Sadducees were crushed. "And when the crowd heard it, they were astonished at His teaching." Even the scribes were constrained to admit that Jesus had spoken well.

Although they were pleased to hear that Jesus had muzzled[53] the Sadducees, the Pharisees had not as yet added any luster to their achievement, so they gathered together to plan a new attack. They decided that one of their number, a legal expert, should act as their spokesman in tempting Jesus with one of the greatest problems of the day: "Teacher, which is the great commandment in the Law?" What must be its nature to determine the quality of greatness in the legal realm? Now, the rabbinic schools had spun a large accumulation of subtleties all over the Mosaic Law. They had come to the conclusion that there were at least six hundred and thirteen different ordinances: two hundred and forty-eight affirmative precepts, which corresponded to the parts of the human body, and three hundred and sixty-five negative precepts, as corresponding to the days of the year, the total being six hundred and thirteen, the number of Hebrew letters in the Ten Commandments. They reached the same result by other computations of equal value.[54] But of all these ordinances, the light and the heavy, those concerning the Sabbath, sacrifices, meat and drink, fasting, fringes, phylacteries, and ablutions, all equally binding, how was one to find the principle that establishes greatness? And "which commandment is the most important of all?"

Following the example of the legal expert in the introduction of the parable of the Good Samaritan (Lk 10:25–28),[55] Jesus points again to the Ten Commandments and the fundamental law of love: "You shall love the Lord your God with all your heart and with all your soul and with all your mind. This is the great and first

17
"Which Is the Great Commandment in the Law?"
Mt 22:34–36;
Mk 12:28

18
"You Shall Love the Lord Your God"
Mt 22:37–40;
Mk 12:29–31

commandment. And a second is like it: You shall love your neighbor as yourself" (see Dt 6:5; Lv 19:18). Love is the fulfilling of the Law (Rm 13:10). This does not mean the commandment of love should be counted as an individual precept but indicates the spirit that must underlie all obedience.[56] As referring to their object, God and the neighbor, the words might be divided into two commandments, but their essential demand is the same—love. Therefore, "On these two commandments depend all the Law and the Prophets."

19
"You Are Not Far from the Kingdom of God"
Mk 12:32–34

Again Jesus won the day. The scribe was intelligent enough to observe and fair enough to acknowledge: "You are right, Teacher." Then he repeated the twofold command of love. It is not the deed that counts, but the love that prompts the deed. That is "more than all whole burnt offerings and sacrifices." To obey from love is "better than sacrifice, and to listen than the fat of rams" (1Sm 15:22). When Jesus saw that this expert of Jewish Law had answered as one having sense,[57] He said to him, "You are not far from the kingdom of God." Again the Savior throws out the lifeline. But was the man won over? That is recorded in the yet "unread page of history."[58] At any rate, the Pharisees had received their answer. The result was that "no one dared to ask Him any more questions," that is, for the purpose of entangling Him in His talk. They were overcome, but apparently unconverted. There was one question that they should have asked: What must we do to be saved?

20
David's Son and David's Lord
Mt 22:41–46;
Mk 12:35–37;
Lk 20:41–44

The legalist is to be pitied. He seeks salvation in the Law and cannot find it there; he meets with salvation in the Gospel, but will not accept it. After the Pharisees question Him, Jesus turns the tables on His adversaries and questions them. Not for the purpose of plotting against them as they had done to Him, but in order to present to them a Gospel truth. For the last time during His public ministry, He calls their attention to the difference between the Messiah whom they expected and the Messiah of whom the Old Testament had prophesied. To convince them of His identity, He directs a question to them. And in order to make it easy for them to answer it, He bases His argument on their own principles of interpretation and supports it with a psalm that they regarded as distinctly messianic. Gently leading their thoughts from the region of precepts to the realms of promise, He asks them the momentous question: "What do you think about the Christ?" First generally and then particularly, as to His descent: "Whose son is He?" Their answer was expected. The Messiah must be David's son. That was the idea of the scribes, carrying along with it the hope of royal dignity and a restored kingdom. They said to Him: "The son of David." Jesus lets the answer stand. The Messiah was to be a true descendant of David. But at the same time, another side of the messianic relation must be brought out. How, then, does David call Him his Lord, which he does in Psalm 110? At the outset, both Jesus and His hearers agree that this psalm is of Davidic origin, that it is directly messianic, and that David spoke "in the Spirit" when writing it. The passage[59] reads as follows: "The Lord [*Yahweh*] said to my Lord [*Adonai*], 'Sit at My right hand, until I put Your enemies under Your feet.' " From this passage it is clear that the Messiah Lord is more than David's son, that He is almighty, and that the enemies at whom He strikes and over whom He exercises lordship are greater than earthly kings. And still He is David's son! Here is a puzzle: "If then David calls Him Lord, how is He his son?" Could Abraham have called Isaac, Jacob, or even the illustrious David himself his Lord? And if not, how did David come to do so? There could be but one answer: The Messiah is the Son of God and the Son of Man. According to His human nature, He is David's son, but according to the divine nature, He is David's Lord. But Jesus did not press the point. His believing followers and the "great throng," who heard Him gladly, may have understood. The adversaries, however, had hardened their hearts. "And no one was able to answer Him a word, nor from that day did anyone dare to ask Him any more questions." They did not dare to ask any more questions, because then the truth against which they rebelled would have been brought out. And they would not accept Jesus as the Messiah, the Christ.

By their inability to answer the question about David's Son and David's Lord, the pharisaic doctors had clearly demonstrated their incompetence as Israel's teachers. Turning again to His disciples, but "in the hearing of all the people" and with the Pharisees in the background, Jesus now hurls at them thunderbolts of denunciation. It was His solemn farewell address to all Israel, to its temple, and to its authorities.[60] The public preaching of Israel's great Prophet was rapidly drawing to its close. It was Tuesday morning of Passion Week. Much of the subject matter of this final temple discourse had been treated before in the Sermon on the Mount and especially at the meal in the Pharisee's house in Perea (Lk 11:37–54).[61] It begins with the words: "The scribes and the Pharisees sit on Moses' seat." They continued in the office of this great man of God, and in so far as they were actually engaged as interpreters of the Mosaic Law, they were right in demanding obedience. But the people should learn to distinguish between their words and deeds. In many instances, they exceeded the precepts of the Law. Like sheaves, they bound together heavy pack loads of rules and did not "move them with their fingers." And when they performed good works, they did so in order to be seen by other people. Taking various figurative injunctions literally, they would inscribe certain Bible texts (Ex 13:1–16 [v. 16]; Dt 6:4–8 [v. 8]; 11:13–21 [v. 18]) on pieces of parchment and place them in little boxes, or phylacteries,[62] and tie them to the left arm near the elbow, so that at the bending of the arm, they would rest over the heart. Or they would enclose them in frontlets and place them conspicuously on their foreheads between the eyes. In the same manner, so as to attract notice, they would lengthen the tassels, or fringes, of their outer garments, placed there as a reminder of the many commandments of

21
The Scribes and Pharisees Denounced
Mt 23:1–12;
Mk 12:38–40;
Lk 20:45–47

the Lord (Nu 15:37–40). This religious ostentation was followed by social vanity, the desire for seats of honor at tables and in the synagogues and for flattering titles. Long robes covered murderous hearts, and long prayers concealed covetous designs. They loved to be called "rabbi" and "father." With a side glance at His disciples, Jesus states that one is their Father, the Father in heaven, and one is their Teacher, "the Christ,"[63] and that they are all brothers. The way to greatness in Christ's kingdom is reached by humility and service; for "whoever exalts himself will be humbled" (see Mt 20:26; 18:4; Lk 14:11; 18:14).

22
"Woe to You, Scribes and Pharisees, Hypocrites!"
Mt 23:13–33

Now Jesus delivered His series[64] of denunciations. "Woe to you, scribes and Pharisees, hypocrites!" He says, pouring upon them His holy wrath for involving Jerusalem in common sin and causing God to visit His judgments upon it and them. Woe to them, hypocrites! And play-acting hypocrites they were. Of the ten kinds of hypocrisy in the world, nine were found in Jerusalem according to Jewish testimony.[65] (1) Woe to the scribes and Pharisees for shutting up the kingdom of God by their opposition to Christ! "You neither enter yourselves nor allow those who would enter to go in" (cf. Lk 11:52). (2) Woe to them for using their prayers as a cloak of maliciousness, especially covetousness! Some manuscripts include, "For you devour widows' houses and for a pretense you make long prayers." (3) Woe to them for their proselytism![66] Being hypocrites and self-righteous, they could not show the true way to heaven to those whom they gained as converts from heathenism with extraordinary zeal; indeed, their proselytes often outdid them in teaching and practicing works-righteousness, which made them twofold more children of hell than themselves. (4) Woe to them for their hair-splitting trivialities in the manner of oaths (see Mt 5:33–37)! It seems that they made the strangest distinctions between oaths and vows that they considered binding and other forms of oaths that were not due to some clever evasion. But Jesus stresses the sanctity of all proper oaths and vows. Specialization is not to be considered an indication of greater earnestness. People should be as much in earnest when they say "by the temple" as when they specify "by the gold of the temple." The best way is to be so truthful and trustworthy as not to be required to say either. Arbitrary trivialities as to form do not make the oath more or less binding. "Whoever swears by heaven swears by the throne of God and by Him who sits upon it." (5) Woe to them for extending the Law of tithing to mint, dill, and aromatic cumin[67] (see Lv 27:30–31) while disregarding weightier matters, such as justice, mercy, and faithfulness! Truly, this was a practice that reminded one of the proverbial straining of a tiny insect so as not to be defiled (Lv 11:41–43) and then choking in the attempt at swallowing an unclean camel. The smallest omission of some secondary rule hurt the consciences of the Pharisees while the infringement of some fundamental law made no impression upon them. On the topic of tithing, we are told that a certain rabbi had his donkey so well trained in piety that it would refuse grain from which its master had not yet collected the tithes.[68] (6) Woe to them for the external cleanness of the cup while the contents were the product of extortion and excess (see Lk 11:39–41)! (7) Woe to them for whitewashing the tombs before the Passover season to make them conspicuous, lest an inadvertent approach involve Levitical contamination, while they themselves—with all their outward righteousness—were full of uncleanness and dead men's bones! (8) Woe to them for erecting and maintaining memorials for murdered prophets and righteous men, lamenting the fact that their fathers were their murderers, while they perpetuated the same murderous spirit in their hearts (Lk 11:47–48). This prophet-killing practice resulted in the rejection and the murder of the great Prophet of God. Fill up the measure of your fathers, you serpents and offspring of vipers (Mt 3:7; 12:34; Lk 3:7)!

For the purpose of exhibiting this national impenitence, the murdered and rejected Messiah would again send them "prophets and wise men and scribes," the apostles and other messengers of the New Testament. But consistent with their attitude toward Christ, they would kill, crucify, scourge, and persecute also His messengers. Thus all the accumulated wrath of God would be visited upon them. As heirs of the guilt and partners of the sin of their fathers, all the blood of the martyred Abel (mentioned first in the Hebrew Bible) to the blood of Zechariah[69] (the prophet named in the last book of the Hebrew Bible) should come upon them. The well-deserved punishment will be swift and complete. "All these things will come upon this generation."

23
"The Blood
of Righteous Abel
to the Blood
of Zechariah"
Mt 23:34–36

In a final lament, Jesus addresses Himself to Jerusalem: "O Jerusalem, Jerusalem, the city that kills the prophets and stones those who are sent to it! How often would I have gathered your children together as a hen gathers her brood under her wings, and you were not willing!" (see Lk 13:34–35).[70] It was Christ's final invitation to Jerusalem to repent. But Jerusalem was "not willing." Punishment must therefore follow. "Your house is left to you desolate." It was a sad farewell of Israel's Messiah from Israel's city and its temple.[71] But it was a farewell that promised a coming again. "You will not see Me again, until you say, 'Blessed is He who comes in the name of the Lord.' " On the Last Day, even Christ's enemies will have to confess that He is the Lord, to the glory of God the Father (Php 2:11).

24
"O Jerusalem,
Jerusalem!"
Mt 23:37–39

After the great denunciation just related, it was only too clear that the rupture of Jesus with the leaders of Israel was final. But before Jesus left the temple for the last time, and while He sat down for a moment to rest His sad heart, an incident occurred that made it possible for Him to leave His Father's house with words of kindness and approval. In one of the courts of the temple, called the Court of the Women, or the Treasury, were placed thirteen brazen trumpet-shaped receptacles for the various kinds of temple offerings, as indicated by an inscription.[72] These offerings

25
The Widow's
Offering
Mk 12:41–44;
Lk 21:1–4

were contributions for wood, for sacrifices, for incense, and the like.[73] Into these were cast the offerings that helped to furnish the temple with its splendid wealth. We may calculate the amount of total contributions by recalling the circumstance at the time of Pompey and Crassus. The temple treasury at that time, after having defrayed every possible expenditure, still contained two thousand talents in money and eight thousand talents in precious vessels and gold.[74] Jesus seated Himself here at the depository of Israel's contributions, probably after He had ascended the flight of steps that led to the Beautiful Gate from the Court of the Gentiles to the Court of the Women. He "watched the people putting money into the offering box. Many rich people put in large sums." The average contributions very likely were of a moderate amount. But considering the large number of worshipers, the total amount that flowed into the temple treasury must have been enormous. Suddenly, the eyes of Jesus noticed a woman contributor. "A poor widow came and put in two small copper coins, which make a penny."[75] The terms used are two *lepta*. The value of such coins fluctuated over time, though the Gospel writers are certainly describing something with penny-like value. Although the contribution was too small to attract the attention of other contributors, it did not escape the notice of Jesus. Calling to His disciples, who were probably at the moment watching the noble and the rich, He pointed out to them the widow. "This poor widow has put in more than all those who are contributing to the offering box." What the others gave they never felt. They lightly flung in "out of their abundance"; "but she out of her poverty has put in everything she had, all she had to live on."

26
The Greeks Who
Wished to See Jesus
Jn 12:20–26

Probably at this point, while Jesus was still in the Court of the Women and was preparing to leave, a message was brought to the inner court from the Court of the Gentiles that certain Greeks "wish to see Jesus." They were probably proselytes from the Decapolis, Galilee, or some country more remote. They were of Greek extraction, still uncircumcised, and not yet fully admitted into the Jewish religion. But they attended services in the synagogue and participated in the worship of the temple on the occasion of the great festivals as "proselytes of the gate."[76] Struck by what they had seen or heard of Jesus, they came to Philip, very likely because he understood Greek or because they had seen him at Bethsaida in Galilee. They asked him to arrange for them a private interview with Jesus. It is always a good thing to know someone who knows Jesus. But Philip did not want to take the responsibility of introducing them and therefore first conferred with his fellow-townsman Andrew, the brother of Peter. Perhaps his hesitancy was due to the fact that in sending out the Twelve on their first mission, Jesus had said something about not going "among the Gentiles" (Mt 10:5).[77] If he had any misgivings on this point, they were removed. Together, Andrew and Philip told Jesus of the Greeks' wish. When Jesus was born, "Chaldeans from the East had sought His cradle, and now Greeks and sons of the

West came to His cross."[78] Whether they actually met Jesus is not stated. But, as Jesus told the disciples, perhaps in the hearing of the Greeks, He saw an indication of His glorification in this request, which consisted in His being acknowledged by men of all nations, as had been prophesied. The entrance to this glory, however, was reached through His death on the cross. Just as a kernel of wheat, before rising to life, must first fall into the ground and die, so also the road to His glory leads through humiliation. In a way, this rule also applies to His followers. "Whoever loves his life loses it, and whoever hates his life in this world will keep it for eternal life." As to "seeing" Jesus, this requires faith. Jesus must be viewed as a suffering Savior and as a living Lord. And it also entails love and service. "If anyone serves Me, he must follow Me." Then those who have sought and properly seen Jesus will be rewarded. "Where I am, there will My servant be also. If anyone serves Me, the Father will honor him."

But as Jesus contemplated the painful road to glory, His soul was troubled, and His heart shrank from the idea of death. Still it was His hour, and for this cause He had come into the world. Summoning courage in prayer, He cried: "Father, glorify Your name." And then for the third time in His life—at His Baptism, at His transfiguration, and now—came a voice from heaven, saying, "I have glorified it, and will glorify it again." The name of God had already been glorified on countless occasions, and He would glorify it again in the Passion of His Son. The mass of people standing by, presumably in the Court of the Gentiles, heard the sound, but did not recognize the voice. They thought it was thunder. Others, recognizing the voice, but not understanding the words, thought that it was an angel speaking to Jesus. He, however, explained that it was for their sakes that this voice had been heard. A critical time, an hour of trial for the world, had come. Now Satan, the prince of this world, was to be cast out, and this by the paradox of a victory through death on the cross. "And I, when I am lifted up from the earth, will draw all people to Myself." Death was to be a source of life. And a cross was to be the throne around which the believers would gather.[79] "He said this to show by what kind of death He was going to die."

The crowd apparently understood Christ's reference both to His death and to Himself as the Messiah. But they could not bring into agreement the idea of death with the prophecies concerning the Messiah and His unending kingdom. "We have heard from the Law[80] that the Christ remains forever (Ps 89:36; 110:4; Is 9:7; etc.). How can You say that the Son of Man must be lifted up? Who is this Son of Man?" This incidentally proves that the title "Son of Man" was associated with the Messiahship; although in this instance, Jesus had not, as reported,[81] referred to Himself as the Son of Man. Of course, Christ shall abide forever, but not in an earthly, physical kingdom. Without going into the details of the messianic relations, Jesus admonishes His listeners to use the brief respite during which the Light is still

27
The Voice from Heaven
Jn 12:27–33

28
"How Can You Say That the Son of Man Must Be Lifted Up?"
Jn 12:34–36

among them to yield to the influence of the Light, to believe in the Light, and to become the children of light (see Eph 5:8; 1 Th 5:5). His warning about the "little while" in which the Light would still be available was followed by His removal. "When Jesus had said these things, He departed and hid Himself from them."

29
Reflections on the
Unbelief of the Jews
Jn 12:37–43

Jesus had spoken the last word, a word of invitation and grace, in the temple. But just as those present had made His Father's house a den of thieves, so their blinded eyes were dull to the glorious truths and their hardened hearts were dead. "Though He had done so many signs before them,[82] they still did not believe in Him." Thus His whole ministry might be summed up in the complaint of Isaiah: "Who has believed what he has heard from us? And to whom has the arm of the LORD been revealed?" (Is 53:1). So few believed. Even this failure to accept their Messiah had been foretold. That they simply fulfilled a prophecy does not excuse the Jewish leaders before God and free them from divine punishment. This judgment for unbelief had already begun in the days of Isaiah and was consummated in the days of Christ. The Jews would not believe, and therefore they should not and could not believe (Is 6:9–10). Nevertheless, while the number of believers in Christ was not large, there were at least some. The inherent truth of Christ's teaching compelled response even in those least likely to be influenced. Even some of the rulers believed in Him, but they were afraid to confess Him on account of certain excommunication awaiting them. There were Nicodemus, Joseph of Arimathea, and no doubt others who were still afraid of criticism and "loved the glory that comes from man more than the glory that comes from God."

Jesus had left the temple (Jn 12:36b). But the evangelist concludes his report of the public teaching ministry of Jesus with a few quotations, statements spoken or repeated by Jesus during the last days of His life as they were addressed to the people in the temple. The evangelist distinctly calls to mind how Jesus on various occasions cried out and said: "Whoever believes in Me, believes not in Me but in Him who sent Me." Faith in Him may not be divorced from faith in the Father. After all, faith in Him is in accordance with the First Commandment of the Law. He is the Light of the world, and whoever believes in Him shall not remain in darkness. While it was not the purpose of His coming into the world to judge the world, yet he who rejects Him and His Word condemns himself. "The Word that I have spoken will judge him on the last day." It is not zeal for Himself and His honor that makes Him so insistent, but His eagerness to fulfill the commandment of His Father.[83] The Father's love prompted Him to send Jesus into the world. Since the Father's "commandment is eternal life," so during the past three years Jesus had told His hearers that He earnestly desired the salvation of all people through faith in Him, the world's Redeemer.

30

—

TUESDAY AFTERNOON OF PASSION WEEK

March 31, AD 33

Nisan (or Abib)							
9	10	11	12	13	14	15	16
March			April				
29	30	31	1	2	3	4	5
Sun.	Mon.	Tues.	Wed.	Thu.	Fri.	Sat.	Sun

As far as the temple in Jerusalem was concerned, the Messiah had come and gone. When Jesus left the temple after His denunciation of the religious authorities Tuesday morning of Passion Week, His disciples must have become aware that a terrible crisis had come and that their Master was leaving the temple forever. And so, leaving it, their thoughts still clung to it with understandable feelings of pride. It was a magnificent building, one of the showplaces of the ancient world. Herod the Great, an architectural genius, began its massive remodeling process, and forty-six years later, the builders were still working on it (Jn 2:20). However, because they had rejected God's Son, their work was "unblessed of God."[1] "Look, Teacher," one of the disciples exclaimed as Jesus was passing through the gates on the way to the Mount of Olives, "what wonderful stones and what wonderful buildings!" Look at the stones! Enormous blocks! Josephus tells us that the stones used in the temple were "white and strong, and each of their length was twenty-five cubits, their height was eight, and their breadth about twelve."[2] For building purposes, the length of the cubit was about twenty inches. Thus the blocks, measuring about forty-two by thirteen by twenty feet, must have exceeded anything found even today. The disciples wanted their Master to look with awe at the nine gates, which each had towers that were two stories high, with doors thirty by fifteen cubits, covered with

1
"There Will Not Be Left Here One Stone upon Another"
Mt 24:1–2; Mk 13:1–2; Lk 21:5–6

thick plates of silver and gold. The last gate to the east, in front of the holy house itself, was called the Beautiful Gate (Ac 3:2, 10), or Gate of Nicanor. It was made of solid Corinthian brass, was fifty cubits in height, and its forty-cubit doors were covered with plates of silver and gold.[3] The disciples call their Master's attention to the immense wealth with which the temple was filled, the rich votive offerings they had again seen, the donations of rulers and kings to the house of God: the large gold table and the two cisterns of gold from King Ptolemy Euergetes of Egypt;[4] the vast clusters of golden grapes, each cluster as large as a man, the gift of Herod the Great;[5] and many other costly gifts. They wanted Him to look at the rising terraces of courts, the Court of the Gentiles with its cloisters and porches, long rows of monolithic pillars of white marble, twenty-five cubits and more in height; above this the flight of fourteen steps that led to the Court of the Women; then the flight of fifteen steps that led to the Court of the Priests, with its immense altar of unhewn stones; and then, once more, the flight of twelve steps that led to the most sacred part of the temple, the entrance to which, without doors, was seventy cubits high and twenty cubits wide. This enclosed under a gold-covered roof the two chambers, separated by a large, heavily embroidered veil, called the Holy Place and the Most Holy Place. One side of the curtain contained the altar of incense, the table of the bread of the Presence, and the seven lamps; on the other side of the curtain stood the solitary stone upon which once a year the high priest sprinkled the blood on the great Day of Atonement.[6] This all the disciples would have Jesus behold, hoping perhaps to change His gloomy thoughts. Once more they turned around. It was a wonderful sight. As viewed under the bright skies of spring, the whole temple complex from the distance took on the appearance of a glorious mountain, whose snowy summit was gilded by the sun.[7] But Jesus said, "There will not be left here one stone upon another that will not be thrown down."

2
Prophetic Discourses, The Second Coming
Mt 24:3–14;
Mk 13:3–13;
Lk 21:7–19

By this time, they had reached the Mount of Olives across the valley of Kidron, and the walls of Jerusalem and the temple were in full view. There Jesus sat down for a moment, deeply absorbed in thought—no doubt over the words He had just spoken—and likewise His saddened band of faithful followers, who had been greatly touched by that discourse. There were questions in the minds of all, but the two pairs of brothers, Peter and Andrew, James and John, were more excited than the rest. "When will these things be," they ask with awestruck voices, "and what will be the sign of Your coming and of the end of the age?"[8] They had realized clearly that Jesus had been talking about Himself. It was also quite natural for them to connect the destruction of the temple with "the end of the age" and "the coming" of Christ. According to certain prophecies of the Old Testament, as well as in the light of the Savior's predictions, His final coming might be viewed together with the destruction of Jerusalem as the beginning of the end (Dn 9:26–27; 12:9–13;

Mt 16:27–28; 23:38–39; Lk 13:34–35; 17:23–24). Jesus tells His disciples there will be signs before the destruction of Jerusalem and the end of the world, and these will be of such a nature as to demand watchful minds and courageous hearts. False prophets will arise with the deceptive claim "I am the Christ" and will lead many astray. There will be wars and rumors of wars, nations rising against nations and kingdoms against kingdoms. There will be famines, plagues, terrifying events, signs from heaven, and earthquakes in various places. While these things introduce both the destruction of Jerusalem and Christ's second coming, these things are but "the beginning of the birth pains," because "the end is not yet."[9] This in general; and in particular, trials and tribulations will come upon the disciples of Christ. They will be hated, persecuted, excommunicated, arrested, called before governors and kings, tried, imprisoned, beaten, and killed. Some will be called upon to run the whole gamut; others will be allotted only a portion of these painful experiences. But in all these tribulations, they should remember that they will suffer all this "to bear witness" against the despisers of the Gospel and for the sake of Christ. And when they are called upon to give a witness of their faith, they should not be anxious beforehand; "but say whatever is given you in that hour, for it is not you who speak, but the Holy Spirit."[10] Trusting in the Lord, they should meet the test; for in spite of universal hatred, they would be in God's hand. "But not a hair of your head will perish" (cf. Mt 10:30; Lk 12:7). Even if they lose their life, they will gain their soul (cf. Mt 10:39; Lk 17:33; Jn 12:25). Therefore, "By your endurance you will gain your lives." Indeed, evil days are at hand. Brother will rise against brother, child against father, father against child (cf. Mt 10:21). The most intimate family ties will be severed. "You will be delivered up even by parents and brothers and relatives and friends, and some of you they will put to death." Iniquity will abound, and the love of many will grow cold. Faithfulness will be required. "The one who endures to the end will be saved" (cf. Mt 10:22). But in all this darkness, there will also be light—the Gospel will be preached.[11] "And this gospel of the kingdom will be proclaimed throughout the whole world as a testimony to all nations, and then the end will come."

Some signs are given that are especially to precede the final destruction: "When you see Jerusalem surrounded by armies, then know that its desolation has come near." And "Jerusalem will be trampled underfoot by the Gentiles, until the times of the Gentiles are fulfilled." Thus it was foretold by the prophet Daniel that "the abomination of desolation" would be seen standing in the Holy Place when the temple had fallen into heathen hands and the sacrifices to the living God had ceased (Dn 9:27; 11:31; 12:11). The literal fulfillment of this prophecy would be a premonition of the end of the world itself. Christians, of course, should not yet expect the final judgment—that is why the warning is given: "let the reader understand"—but

3
Signs Introducing Jerusalem's Destruction
Mt 24:15–22;
Mk 13:14–20;
Lk 21:20–24

when they see the Roman armies pouring into the Holy Land, carrying with them instruments of destruction foreshadowing the terrible execution of God's judgment upon Jerusalem, they should seek safety in sudden flight. "Let those who are in Judea flee to the mountains." Let those who are in the country not enter the city. Let those who are on top of their houses when the terrifying news comes not take time to carry things out of their dwellings. Without looking behind, let them descend and immediately run away from the city out into the countryside. Let him who is in the field not return to the house and get his coat. Terrible days of divine vengeance are at hand "to fulfill all that is written." Under these circumstances, woe to those women who are about to become mothers and those who are nursing infants! Christians should therefore pray that their flight will not occur in winter, when the weather conditions are unfavorable for sudden flight, or on the Sabbath, when those who are still binding themselves to Sabbath regulations needlessly endanger their lives. There will be great distress in the land, and God will execute His wrath upon this people. In fact, on account of its significance and effect as well as because of its severity, this tragic crisis of Israel will earn for itself a unique distinction as compared with all other calamitous experiences of the whole human race: tribulation "as has not been from the beginning of the world until now, no, and never will be."[12] It would be a case of God's mills grinding slowly, but with such terrible thoroughness that not one would escape. If the justice of God had not been mingled with mercy, if those days had not been shortened out of loving regard for those who are God's own, and if it had not been for the intercession of those in the mountains and of those who had found refuge beyond the Jordan, in Pella,[13] not one would have escaped the general destruction.

4
False Christs
Mt 24:23–28;
Mk 13:21–23

Jesus again refers to false Christs and false prophets. The Lord has in mind primarily the days preceding the destruction of Jerusalem, but the prophecies merge into warnings about the end of the world and the last days before then. What would people not give for a delivering Messiah in those days! Christ foresees the coming of such self-styled deliverers. But "if anyone says to you, 'Look, here is the Christ!' or 'There He is!' do not believe it." There shall arise false Christs and false prophets who shall show great signs and wonders, lying satanic wonders (Dt 13:1–3; 2Co 11:13–14; 2Th 2:9; Rv 13:13–14), to lead many astray, even, if that were possible, the very elect. "See, I have told you beforehand." Signs and wonders of such men will be no proof of their being true prophets if their teaching is contrary to the Word of God (Gal 1:8). True believers will not be deceived in the end, even though it be possible to confuse them for a time. Where Christ is, His elect are.[14] But they must be on their guard. Christ is to be found in His Word and Sacraments, among His people where they are gathered as His Church, not in the dreary wastes of asceticism or among those Christians who focus on emotion and a form of Christianity that drifts free from the purely taught Word of God. "If they say to you, 'Look, He is in the wilderness,' do not go out. If they say, 'Look, He is in the inner rooms,' do not believe it." As to Christ's final coming, it will not come to pass in such a way that men must search for Him. "For as the lightning comes from the east and shines as far as the west, so will be the coming[15] of the Son of Man." And His judgment upon the unspiritual cadavers of that day will be as inescapable as His appearance will be sudden. "Wherever the corpse is, there the vultures will gather" (cf. Jb 39:30; Lk 17:37).

The period from the destruction of Jerusalem to the final judgment is a drama with various interludes. The first disaster is merely the first act. When the last tribulations have reached their climax, the coming of the Lord Jesus Christ will be heralded by appalling signs. The powers of heaven will be shaken, the sun and moon will be darkened, and stars will fall. On the earth, among the nations, there will be distress, men fainting for fear and in expectation of the things to come—their fear caused also by the roaring noise of the billows of the sea. It seems that no ordinary eclipses and falling meteors are meant or storms and earthquakes acting in accordance with natural laws, but chaos and the subversion of all powers[16] as a premonition of the end of all things. Earlier signs, eclipses, comets, earthquakes, storms, wars, famines, floods, and the like, must be regarded as a preface to the final catastrophe. And then, amid the uproar of the universe, the great sign, the Son of Man Himself, clothed in majesty and power and accompanied by the heavenly hosts, will appear in the sky. "Then will appear in heaven the sign of the Son of Man." What this sign is, if indeed there is a reference to any distinctive sign, we cannot say. Whatever it is, it will be self-evidencing.[17] Nobody will miss it. Then "all the tribes of the earth will mourn," and the vast army of unbelievers and scoffers will tremble in fearful expectation of the descending doom. But all believers, seeing their redemption drawing nigh, will lift up their heads with joy when at the sound of the trumpet the angels will gather the elect from the four quarters of the globe. And of all this, the destruction of Jerusalem is but the initial act. As viewed by the Lord, with whom there is no time, the whole intervening period is a time of the coming of the Son of Man. That is why the Lord could in prophecy, without difficulty, pass from "immediately after the tribulation of those days" (the days of Vespasian and Titus) to the predictions of the tribulation in the latter days near the end of the world. With the destruction of Jerusalem, the curtain falls.[18] Infidels may still scoff at the despised Jesus of Nazareth. In certain respects, there has been no history since AD 70, only a long preparation for the end of all time.

At this point, Jesus continues His eschatological discourse in the form of a parable. With the appearance of young leaves and tender branches in spring, the observer does not require much intelligence to conclude that summer is near. "So also, when you see these things taking place," the signs preceding the destruction of Jerusalem,

5
Signs of the Second Coming
Mt 24:29–31;
Mk 13:24–27;
Lk 21:25–28

6
The Parable of the Fig Tree
Mt 24:32–35;
Mk 13:28–31;
Lk 21:29–33

the destruction itself, and the subsequent recurrence of similar signs, "you know that the kingdom of God is near." And as to the certainty of the fulfillment of "all these things," a final sign is solemnly given. "Truly, I say to you, this generation[19] will not pass away until all these things take place,"[20] or are accomplished. But if the Lord here includes, as He obviously does, His final parousia, how, then, is "this generation" to be understood? Was He mistaken? Did He share, or rather give rise to, the later mistaken apocalyptic misconceptions of the time in the belief of the nearness of the Lord? There is much dispute on this point. Most modern scholars insist that *generation* must be taken in the sense of a certain measure of time. But since the parousia of the Lord did not occur within the promised limits of time, unless included by anticipation in the judgment over Jerusalem, then Jesus must have been mistaken in His conviction that His reappearance would happen within the then living generation. Since this, however, is impossible, some other explanation must be found. Some have thought, for instance, that the prediction refers to the destruction of Jerusalem only, which, however, is obviously not the case; others, that with the destruction of Jerusalem all things have occurred, lacking only the final completion—a forced construction.[21] Other interpretations, associating another idea with the term *generation*, include either all humanity or the Christian Church as the generation of believers that the Lord has chosen. While it is true that the destruction of Jerusalem might be viewed as the beginning of the end[22] and as typifying the final destruction of the world, it seems that here a distinctive sign is definitely and solemnly given. It is the better choice to regard Jesus' mention of "generation" as a reference to sinful humanity, which continues to experience the judgment of God as signs of the coming end times.

7
Watchfulness Urged
Mt 24:36–42;
Mk 13:32–33

That Christ will return is certain. But the hour is not known. It is foolish to make any attempt to calculate or to speculate about the precise time of Christ's second coming. Many have tried and failed miserably in their attempts to do so. "Concerning that day and hour no one knows, not even the angels of heaven, nor the Son, but the Father only." The period preceding the final coming of Christ will resemble conditions at the time of the flood (cf. Lk 17:26–30, 34–36).[23] In those days, people were eating and drinking, marrying and giving in marriage, until the day that Noah entered the ark. No one knew when the threatened catastrophe would take place, indeed, no one believed what Noah said, until the flood came and took them all away. They cared for nothing but their material affairs. They closed their eyes to the signs of the time and their ears to the voice of the preacher of righteousness (2Pt 2:5). So also in the day of the parousia of the Son of Man. Two men will be in the field; one will be taken, and the other will be left. Two women will be grinding at the mill;[24] one will be taken, and the other will be left. "Stay awake, for you do not know on what day[25] your Lord[26] is coming."

Watchfulness presupposes sobriety. The disciples of Jesus should be on their guard lest at any time their hearts be distracted by drunkenness and the cares of this life. The pleasures of this life must not cloud our judgement or our watchfulness. The end will come like a trap for those who have not remained in a state of prayerful readiness and watchfulness. At all times, Christians should be spiritually awake, making supplication, so they will be ready joyfully to greet and meet the returning Lord.

Christ's exhortation to watch is enforced by a brief parable. The Son of Man is like a man, who, as he set out on a journey to distant parts, put his servants in charge, assigned to each of them a particular task, and commanded the doorkeeper to watch. During his absence each servant would have his particular duty to perform, and a certain responsibility would rest upon him. While it was the special duty of the doorkeeper to watch, yet this was the duty of all. "Stay awake[28]—for you do not know when the master of the house will come." Let no one scoff at the idea of return (2Pt 3:4). The return is certain while the hour is unknown. It may take place during the hours of the day (Mk 13:32) or "in the evening, or at midnight, or when the rooster crows," according to the Roman division of night watches (see Mt 14:25; Lk 12:38).[29] The disciples must watch not only one night, but every night. And what the Lord says to one, He says to all: "Stay awake!" (cf. Lk 12:41).

Watching for Judgment Day is just like guarding against thieves. If the master of the house had known when the thief was coming, he would have been on guard and would not have allowed his house to be broken into (cf. Lk 12:39–40).[30] Thus believers must constantly be on their guard. Their Master, the Lord of the Church, has placed them in positions of trust. "Who then is the faithful and wise servant?" (cf. Lk 12:42–46).[31] It is that rare servant who is steadfastly doing his duty. He is one of a thousand fit to be placed in charge over his master's estate. On the other hand, the servant who foolishly takes advantage of his master's delay, lording it over fellow servants, eating and drinking with drunkards, will receive due punishment when his master comes upon him when he least expects it. The master of that servant, on his return, "will cut him in pieces[32] and put him with the hypocrites. In that place there will be weeping and gnashing of teeth" (cf. Mt 13:42, 50; 22:13; 25:30).

While Jesus was still speaking to His disciples on the Mount of Olives on the last full day of His public ministry, He added two parables containing instruction and warnings. The first of the parables, that of the ten virgins, is immediately connected with the foregoing. "Then," namely, at His return for judgment, "the kingdom of heaven will be like ten virgins who took their lamps and went to meet the bridegroom." Again circumstances connected with Jewish marriage customs are used in the teaching of spiritual truths (cf. Lk 12:35–38; 13:25).[33] But here the marriage supper is not represented as taking place in the home of the bridegroom in accordance with the usual practice (cf. Mt 22:2–10)[34] but is conceived as being held in the

8
Warning against Dissipation and Drunkenness (Luke)
Mt 24:43–51;
Mk 13:34–37;
Lk 21:34–36[27]

9
Parable of the Doorkeeper (Mark)
Mt 24:43–51;
Mk 13:34–37;
Lk 21:34–36

10
Parable of the Master of the House and the Two Servants (Matthew)
Mt 24:43–51;
Mk 13:34–37;
Lk 21:34–36

11
The Parable of the Ten Virgins
Mt 25:1–11

home of the bride (cf. Jgs 14:10),[35] from which the bridesmaids set out in the evening for the purpose of meeting the groom. The parable proceeds from the assumption that the bridegroom is somewhere in the distance, so that the precise moment of his arrival cannot be known. But it is known that he will come that night and that the marriage, for which all preparations have been made, will take place. And so it is perfectly in order that all details for the customary marriage procession have been arranged. No mention is made of the bride, neither in this parable nor in that of the wedding guests (Mt 22), as unneeded for the purpose Jesus had in mind. Again we remind ourselves of the general principle to be used when interpreting parables: details must not be closely pressed. Ten virgins of the bride chamber, a round number, probably determined by the wealth of the parents, are represented as going forth to meet the bridegroom. "Five of them were foolish, and five were wise." Not as if the equal numbers were intended to represent the proportion in the spiritual realm; they are merely to show for reasons that will soon appear, that there were prudent and imprudent, thoughtful and thoughtless among them. In setting out to meet the bridegroom, all of them took their lamps,[36] consisting of a wooden staff held in the hand, with a receptacle on top, in which was placed a clay dish or saucer, with an opening for pouring oil and a vent for air and a spout for the wick. Now, "When the foolish took their lamps, they took no oil with them." But the wise had oil in their lamps and had taken an extra supply with them. As appears in the sequence, this was a necessary precaution, as for some unknown reason, the bridegroom hesitated and therefore proved their prudence. This point is used to admonish believers to be ready. "As the bridegroom was delayed, they all became drowsy and slept," presumably in some house along the way,[37] in order to await there the approach of the bridegroom. They all slept. This was perfectly natural on account of the long waiting and the extended delay of the bridegroom; and it was perfectly harmless as far as the wise virgins were concerned, because they were ready. But it was fatal for the foolish virgins. At length, in the middle of the night, the cry was raised by someone not asleep: "Here is the bridegroom! Come out to meet him." Immediately the virgins rose and proceeded to trim their lamps by pulling the wicks from the spout so that they might burn with full brightness in the joyous wedding-feast pageant. At this point, a startling surprise forced the foolish virgins to make a sad request: "Give us some of your oil, for our lamps are going out." But the wise answered, prompted by sheer necessity and sound prudence: "There will not be enough for us and for you." Not as if the wise virgins were selfish or ungenerous. You cannot enter heaven on the merits of others. The wise virgins have only the one advice to offer, if indeed it was not—as it seemed it was—too late: "Go rather to the dealers and buy for yourselves." By this time, the oil merchants were fast asleep, even as at the moment of the Lord's coming, the dispensers of grace will have closed their shops. "While they were going to buy, the bridegroom came." In a panorama of lights and in the midst of festal joy, the bridegroom was escorted to the waiting bride. "Those who were ready went in with him to the marriage feast." The happy moment had arrived. Naturally, in view of all the opportunities given for making definite arrangements, with plenty of time and warning to do so, all guests were supposed to be inside by now. "And the door was shut."

When it was too late, the other virgins came. Whether or not they succeeded in obtaining oil is of no importance. If they did, it was no longer of any possible use to them, since it could no longer serve the purpose for which it was purchased. The urgent, desperate appeal: "Lord, lord, open to us!" is met with a solemn "Truly, I say to you, I do not know you." The period of eleventh-hour repentance cannot be extended. Professing to be members of the bridal party, they ought to have been in the bridal procession. Lapsed membership in the kingdom of grace—which has ceased to exist with the coming of Judgment Day—does not entitle one to membership in the kingdom of glory. Without going into details, we might give a brief interpretation of the parable. The bridegroom is Jesus. The feast is heaven. The virgins are the members of the visible Church. The lamps are faith, fed by the oil of the Means of Grace. Naturally the wise virgins are those who continued in faith to the end and therefore were members of the invisible Church, as contrasted with the foolish virgins, who, being without faith, were not. No special significance attaches to the numbers 10 and 5, the cry, the procession, and the like. Neither is the falling asleep to be represented as a moral shortcoming, for it happened to the wise as well as to the foolish. There is a delay in the bridegroom's coming, even as there is a delay in, but not a failure of (2Pt 3:3–9), the Lord's return. All the more reason for watchful waking. And that is the point that Jesus makes: "Watch therefore, for you know neither the day nor the hour," night or day, week, month, or year, "wherein the Son of Man cometh" (KJV).[38]

Continuing with the same thought of His parousia, but linking it up with the duty and work of His disciples during His absence, Jesus tells a parable similar to the one spoken in the house of Zacchaeus at Jericho shortly before His arrival at Bethany in the preceding week.[39] The situation in the kingdom of heaven is, as Jesus points out, like that of a man going abroad who called his servants and gave his goods into their charge. In leaving his money with them, he did the best thing he could do under the circumstances, unless he wanted to entrust it to strangers. To one of his servants he delivered five talents, to another two, and to still another one, according to the ability[40] of each. And then he set out on his journey. The amount of money entrusted to these servants was considerable: a talent was a monetary unit worth about twenty years' wages for a laborer. Immediately after his master's departure, the first servant, who had received five talents, lost no time in investing his share.

12
"Lord, Lord, Open to Us!"
Mt 25:11–13

13
The Parable of the Talents
Mt 25:14–18

He gained another five talents. Likewise the second, who had received two talents, gained two more. But the third servant, who had received one talent, buried his silver in the ground. The reference, of course, is to the various commissions in the Kingdom, the wider or narrower fields of activity, and the diverse abilities and gifts.

14
"Well Done, Good and Faithful Servant"
Mt 25:19–23

After a long time, the master returns. Immediately he arranges a conference with his servants for the purpose of checking over their accounts. The first of them submits his report: "Master, you delivered to me five talents; here,"[41] as if inviting him to count the money, "I have made five talents more." A gain of one hundred percent! "Well done, good and faithful servant," the master replies. "You have been faithful over a little; I will set you over much." It is not the money that is stressed, but faithfulness. A rich master is speaking, to whom a few talents more or less are as little things. But seeing the capacity[42] of the servant, he would make more extensive use of his faithful efforts in what he considered a limited sphere. "Enter into the joy[43] of your master." With this expression, the Savior directs the earthly-minded disciples to heavenly things. The second servant submits a similar report and receives a corresponding reward.

15
"You Wicked and Slothful Servant!"
Mt 25:24–30

The third servant now steps up and makes his speech. "Master, I knew you to be a hard man." Guided by this opinion of a master who was hard to please, who struck a hard bargain, who reaped where he had not sown and gathered where he had not reaped, and fearing lest he lose the talent itself and displease the master all the more, the servant had hidden his talent in the ground. No, he was not dishonest! "Here," behold,[44] as if likewise inviting him to count the money, "you have what is yours." Just as if the mere safe return of the money were the sole purpose for which the master had entrusted the funds to him! But the servant's own words condemned him. We are rather surprised at this servant. He was a disappointment. From him, as judged by the yield frequently returned by such of his class in the Kingdom, the unfavored and those handicapped by the lack of fortune and opportunity at the outset, we should have by comparison expected a return of—let us say—an additional talent and one half or a gain of at least one hundred and five percent, just to show that he was not to be outdone. But instead, he had proved himself a small man in every respect. This kind of person, however, sad to say, is also found in the Kingdom. If that was the idea he had of his master, whose character he had altogether misjudged in that he spoke of him as one who reaped where he had not sown and let his servants slave without offering them any inducement, and if he himself was too much afraid to risk trading with his master's money, then why did he not, without trouble for himself and with profit to his master, put it in the bank? "You ought to have invested my money with the bankers."[45] Now he was not only useless to his master as a servant, but what he said in defense of his conduct was preposterous. "Take the talent from him and give it to him who has the ten talents." This would at least give the master some prospects of a speedy return. In this manner of dispensing justice, the general rule applies: "To everyone who has will more be given, and he will have an abundance. But from the one who has not, even what he has will be taken away" (cf. Lk 8:18; Mt 13:12; Mk 4:25). The general lesson is clear. The whole Kingdom with all its reward will come to faithful servants. The *Kingdom* for servants. But *servants* for the Kingdom. In the end, the useless and unprofitable servant, like the fruitless fig tree, "use[es] up the ground" (Lk 13:7). He will be cast out into outer darkness, where "there will be weeping and gnashing of teeth" (Mt 24:51; 8:12; 13:42, 50; 22:13). This parable is a stern rebuke to those who think that the Christian is simply a person who merely assents intellectually to the doctrines of the faith, which is to reduce faith to an empty husk, rather than understanding the Christian life to be one of joyful service in thankful response to the gifts of forgiveness, life, and salvation.

With an illuminating word picture of the final judgment, the Lord closes His prophetic discourse on the Mount of Olives, leaving an urgent exhortation impressed upon the hearts and minds of His disciples to be ever watchful and faithfully waiting for the coming of the Son of Man. As time passes into eternity, the Son of Man, accompanied by the host of holy angels, shall return in the fullness of His heavenly glory. Immediately there shall be assembled in perfect attendance all the members of the human race, "the living and the dead" (Apostles' Creed), the willing and the unwilling, those who were prepared and those who were not prepared to meet their Judge. At the same time, a separation will be made—not according to sex, age, color, birth and rank, and the like, but "as a shepherd separates the sheep from the goats." Evidently the reference is to the sheep that hear His voice (Jn 10:27) and the proverbially stubborn goats. In other words, the separation will be according to whether a person was a believer or an unbeliever in this life. "And He will place the sheep on His right, but the goats on the left." With this separation, in which the believers will receive the place of honor, being placed at "His right," the judgment is already rendered, and the subsequent sentence is only the confirmation of an act already in the past.

16
The Final Judgment
Mt 25:31–33

A hearty welcome is extended to the righteous by the Son of Man, who now speaks of Himself as King: "Come, you who are blessed by My Father, inherit the kingdom prepared for you from the foundation of the world." The promise of a glorious inheritance, which excluded every consideration of merit, made by the one-time lowly Jesus of Nazareth to His once despised and persecuted little flock, is true after all! Come nearer and enjoy glory and the blissful state of the Kingdom! And what is the reason of this wonderful gift? All this as a gracious reward for everyday, simple little deeds of love. "For I was hungry and you gave Me food, I was thirsty and you gave Me drink, I was a stranger and you welcomed Me, I was naked and you clothed

17
"Come, You Who Are Blessed by My Father"
Mt 25:34–40

Me, I was sick and you visited Me, I was in prison and you came to Me." Not as if the believers were saved by these deeds; these deeds of love are mentioned because by them their faith was attested. In surprise, the righteous reply: "Lord, when did we see You hungry and feed You, or thirsty and give You drink? And when did we see You a stranger and welcome You, or naked and clothe You? And when did we see You sick or in prison and visit You?" Surely the King must be mistaken! Of such high honor of personal service they had been altogether unaware. But, as Jesus points out, all deeds of love performed in faith are considered as done to Him. "Truly, I say to you, as you did it to one of the least of these My brothers, you did it to Me."

From those on His right, the King turns to those at the left. By the way, He had placed the sheep at *His* right hand[46] and the goats at the left.[47] Then He had turned to those on *His* right. And now He addresses those on the left. Before God, there is no predetermined "left hand," meaning eternal damnation, but only a "right hand," signifying life everlasting. It is really an upsetting of God's plan that "any should perish" (2Pt 3:9). Since, however, men willfully transgressed His commandments, would not heed His warnings, but defied Him and despised His Word of Grace, punishment became necessary; justice must be executed. Sternly the Judge addresses Himself to those at the left: "Depart from Me, you cursed, into the eternal fire prepared for the devil and his angels." It is an awful sentence. The Judge takes no pleasure in its pronouncement, and He is most particular in the choice of His words. He does not say, "Cursed of My Father"; for they brought the curse upon themselves. Neither does He say, "Prepared from the beginning of the world." God's original plan did not call for the damnation of anyone. The "left hand" was a later addition, prepared only for the devil, but in time was reserved and kept ready for occupation by such as followed his leading. According to the same standard by which those at the right hand were judged to be blessed of the Father, those at the left are now condemned. As in the case of the righteous, nothing was said of martyrdom and heroic acts, so in this case, by contrast, there is no mention of murder or heinous crimes. Nor is there a chance given for many of them to point with pride to the erection of hospitals and institutions, to the creation of funds, endowments, and memorials to the honor and glory of their name. This was not discussed. It was the neglect of true charity and the small deeds of Christian love that testified to their lack of faith and love of Christ. Of course, there is a chorus of protests: "When did we see You hungry or thirsty or a stranger or naked or sick or in prison, and did not minister to You?" But Jesus replies, "Truly, I say to you, as you did not do it to one of the least of these, you did not do it to Me." There was no faith, and therefore there could be no outflow of faith—love, love of Christ and of their fellow men for Christ's sake. Such love as they showed did not spring from faith, but was unsanctified love such as is found in natural man. "And these will go away into eternal punishment, but the righteous into eternal life." Everlasting life for the believers, unending torment for the damned. There is no happy last-minute reversal of judgment in a supposed restoration of all things. Neither is there an annihilation of the wicked. The words are clear. The absolute idea of eternity with respect to the punishment in hell cannot be removed by toning down the force of the word *eternal*[48] to age-long, but not everlasting, and *punishment*[49] to pruning, so as to leave room for hope of an ultimate delivery from "the eternal fire." Scripture is Scripture.

From the Mount of Olives, it was but a short distance to the home of Jesus' friends at Bethany, where He spent the night. It was from this place, as we have seen, that He started early in the morning to instruct the waiting multitudes in the temple. With His departure from the temple on that memorable Tuesday, however, and His prophetic discourses on the Mount of Olives, this glad ministry had at this particular point already come to an end.

The Lord's public work was finished. With His arrival in Bethany, He saw fit to repeat the sad announcement of His impending death, at the same time giving the exact time and manner of its occurrence. According to the Jewish calendar it was the twelfth day of the month of Nisan, two days before the Feast of Passover, or the seven days of Unleavened Bread, which began on the evening of the fourteenth day of Nisan (Ex 12:1–27; Lv 23:5–6). This Passover was to be distinguished as no Passover ever celebrated before. It was to be the Passover in which the Lamb of God was presented, and all the Old Testament types of Christ—the sacrifices, the Passover, the lamb without blemish, the sprinkling of blood, the passing over—and all the ceremonies of the Old Testament worship were to be fulfilled. This Jesus knew. And therefore, before dismissing His disciples for the night after what would seem according to the records the most crowded day of His public life,[51] He turned to them with the prediction: "You know that after two days the Passover is coming, and the Son of Man will be delivered up to be crucified."[52]

As Jesus was talking, the betrayal process had already begun. An important meeting was being held in Jerusalem. In unholy assembly, the members of the Council were gathered in the palace[53] of Caiaphas, the high priest. It was Caiaphas who had already settled the fate of Jesus with these words: "It is better for you that one man should die for the people" (Jn 11:50). The events of the last few days seemed to make it clear that he was right. Under his leadership, Pharisees, Sadducees, Herodians, priests, scribes, rabbis, lawyers, and elders were all united in an alliance of destruction. Of the meeting itself and of the discussions, we know nothing. However, we have some information as to the conclusions reached. These included a number of points: Jesus must be put to death; there must be no delay; He must be arrested at a time when He would not be surrounded by a protecting crowd; the whole thing must be slyly handled; and on account of His popularity, the murder had best be

19
Return to Bethany
Lk 21:37–38[50]

20
Jesus Again Predicts His Death
Mt 26:1–2

21
The Rulers Plot Jesus' Death
Mt 26:3–5; Mk 14:1–2; Lk 22:1–2

postponed until immediately after the Passover in order to give the multitudes a chance to disperse and especially to give the enthusiastic Northern pilgrims a chance to return to their homes. But after all, in spite of their determination, one point still remained unsettled, and that was *how* they might put Him to death. While they were still discussing ways and means, an event occurred that at once altered their conclusions and made possible the immediate capture of Jesus without the tumult they feared (see Mt 26:6–13; Mk 14:3–9; cf. Jn 12:1–11).[54]

22
Judas Bargains for the Betrayal of Jesus
Mt 26:14–16;
Mk 14:10–11;
Lk 22:3–6

While the members of the Council were still deliberating on ways and means of ridding themselves of the hated Jesus of Nazareth, Judas Iscariot, one of the Twelve, came with an offer to betray his Master. Ever since the rebuke administered to him by Jesus in connection with the anointing at Bethany, related by Matthew and Mark at this juncture, there had been something on his mind. But was it only the loss of the three hundred denarii,[55] which, he claimed, might have been "given to the poor," but upon which he would have laid his hands, that prompted him to commit that most awful crime? Was it the nearly irresistible attraction of the prospects of making a paltry gain? Was it in a fit of uncontrolled passion for the purpose of seeking revenge because Jesus had called him to task? Was it the petty jealousy of small circles that deeply resent even the smallest inequality in the distribution of favors? Or was it that as almost the only true Judean among the apostles, he was sorely disappointed at the failure of Jesus to fulfill the Jewish messianic hopes? Or was it his purpose to force Jesus, if He really was no pretender, to prove His messianic claims? And if He was no pretender, could He not easily save Himself by a miracle and give him a chance to make a little money besides? But to account for the conduct of Judas is like trying to determine the depth of the universe itself. Satan had entered into his heart. This statement of our Lord best explains his awful state. Otherwise it would have been unthinkable for one of the twelve chosen apostles to present himself to the sworn enemies of Jesus with an offer to betray Him and to deliver Him into their hands.[56] Naturally there was some discussion among the members of the Council when Judas approached them. There were questions. Who was Judas? Just what did he know about Jesus? How long had he been in His company? Was it really true that Jesus made the claim that He was the Messiah? And where did He keep Himself when He was not surrounded by protecting hands, or rather, when and where could they come upon Him when He was not surrounded by a multitude of friends? But Judas was not willing to talk just yet. "What will you give me if I deliver Him over to you?" There was some more discussion. Finally an agreement was reached. We can picture to ourselves the scene—hushed tones, pleased gestures, devious smirking smiles, flickering lights. The plan appealed to the scribes and the officers of the temple police, the captains,[57] whose aid would be needed to carry out the plan. And the price? "They paid him," or rather they placed or deposited,[58] "thirty pieces of silver,"[59] the price of a slave.[60] It was the amount that, for instance, was collected as a fine when an ox had wounded a slave (Ex 21:32). If the money was taken from the temple treasury, as seems likely, then the payment was made in shekels, probably even carefully weighed out, true to form—the most iniquitous thing done in the most orthodox way.[61] For a miserable purse, Judas sold his Lord. For a sack of jingling coins, he sold his soul. The sum represented at that time at least four months of a working-man's pay—it was enough to attract the avarice of Judas. As a pledged traitor, a chosen apostle of Jesus left the assembly under the agreement to inform the members of the Council of the first opportunity to arrest Him in the absence of the usual circle of protecting friends.

31

THURSDAY AFTERNOON TO THURSDAY NIGHT OF PASSION WEEK

PASSOVER AND THE INSTITUTION OF THE LORD'S SUPPER

April 2, AD 33

AUC	782	783	784	785	786
AD	29	30	31	32	33
Approx. Age of Jesus	30	31	32	33	34
Passovers		I	II	III	IV

Nisan (or Abib)							
9	10	11	12	13	14	15	16
March			April				
29	30	31	1	2	3	4	5
Sun.	Mon.	Tues.	Wed.	Thu.	Fri.	Sat.	Sun

We have no records of Jesus' movements on Wednesday of Passion Week. No doubt even on this day the people in Jerusalem waited for His appearance in the temple (Lk 21:38). Since their agreement with Judas, the priests and Pharisees looked out for Him with sinister aims. But He did not come. During this day, the Lord most likely remained in seclusion in Bethany, probably once more seeking quiet solitude in prayer with his heavenly Father, which He had so earnestly sought in the midst of His active ministry, in order to strengthen Himself for the ordeal of His suffering and death.

1
Wednesday

2
The Preparation of
the Paschal Meal
Mt 26:17; Mk 14:12;
Lk 22:7–9

It was some time during the next day, Thursday, the thirteenth of Nisan, or Abib, probably in the afternoon, that the disciples came to Jesus with the question: "Where will You have us prepare for You to eat the Passover?" Strictly speaking, the Passover Festival began that evening (the beginning of the fourteenth day of Nisan, which began at sundown[1]). But because by noon of this day, all traces of yeast had to be removed from the houses and no leavened bread was to be eaten until the evening of the twenty-first (Ex 12:18; Dt 16:1), it was already called "the first day" of the feast. At this point, we remind ourselves that the Passover Festival was instituted to commemorate the deliverance of the Israelites from the destroying angel when all the firstborn of the Egyptians were killed (Ex 12:27). It was distinguished chiefly by the eating of a roasted male Passover lamb, one year old, without blemish, between the evenings of the fourteenth and fifteenth of Nisan (Ex 12:6) by one or two families (Ex 12:4)—according to the size,[2] for none of the meat was to be left over (Ex 12:10)—with unleavened bread and bitter herbs. Originally the lamb to be sacrificed, which was selected on the tenth of the month, was slaughtered at home by the father of the household or the servant appointed for this task. But later it was slain by the worshiper in the temple under the supervision of priests, by whom the blood was caught up in a golden bowl and in one jet was emptied upon the altar.[3] While this was going on, there was a threefold blast from the silver trumpets of the priests, and the "Great Hallel" or "Praise the LORD" (Pss 113–18) was chanted by the Levites, with responses by the people. The fat, kidneys, liver, and tail were burned as sacrifices to the Lord. Bound up in its skin, the rest of the lamb was then carried to the house where the feast would be prepared. The number of animals slain each Passover was enormous; and from the number of sacrifices we can make an estimate of the immense throng gathered in Jerusalem for the annual Passover. In the time of Nero, who held the Jewish nation in contempt, the governor of Syria, Cestius, tried to convince the emperor of the city's strength. He instructed the chief priests, if by any means possible, to take a census of the population. They simply counted the lambs slain at a Passover Feast—256,500—and multiplied the number by ten. Thus they were able to report that during the observance of Passover, the population there was over 2.5 million in the city and surrounding villages.[4]

3
The Passover
Festival

In a heated oven, the lamb was roasted intact over a glowing fire. Not a bone of it should be broken. And at sundown on April 2, the beginning of the fourteenth of Nisan,[5] the roasted lamb was placed on the table. Other parts of the menu included unleavened bread, bitter herbs, probably a salad of cucumbers and lettuce, besides a dish containing vinegar and salt water, with a sauce prepared of various fruits, and wine mixed with water, in proportion of one to two.[6] On the next day, still the fourteenth, there were special sacrifices, the second *chagigah*, in which thank-offerings from the flock and herd were made and eaten.[7] On the third day, the sixteenth of Nisan, the firstfruits of the barley harvest were brought to the temple and waved before the Lord to consecrate the harvest.[8] Thus the first few days. And the last day of the Passover, the same as the first, was again a day of holy convocation and was observed as a Sabbath. The intervening days were minor festivals, for which, however, minute rules as to the kind of labor allowed were laid down.[9]

This, then, was the holy festival for which they had made the pilgrimage to Jerusalem. It was one of the three holy festivals on which all male Israelites were commanded to appear before the Lord (Ex 23:14, 17). And since the disciples did not know where Jesus desired to eat the Passover, they asked for instructions as to the place where preparations should be made. Under the circumstances, the supper could have been held in Bethany; for it seems that for ecclesiastical purposes, Bethphage and Bethany were included by the rabbis as parts of Jerusalem.[10] But it was Jesus' intention to eat the Passover in Jerusalem. Two disciples, Peter and John, were singled out and given definite instructions—one of the pair known for deepest feelings and the other as a man of very quick action. And Judas was listening. "Go into the city, and a man carrying a jar of water will meet you. Follow him." If the purpose of this mysterious instruction was to keep the knowledge from Judas[11]—lest the last meal with the institution of the Holy Supper be interrupted and Jesus' last retreat betrayed before all had been said and done, even down to the last prayer in Gethsemane—then these words are a wonderful combination of foreknowledge and prudence. It is not that Jesus had made arrangements previously with some friends in Jerusalem. The Lord is here giving His disciples a most remarkable proof of His omniscience and omnipotence. To carry water in the East is commonly considered a woman's work. While a man might be seen with a water pitcher, the chances were extremely rare.[12]

Jesus' instruction continues: "And wherever he enters, say to the master of the house, 'The Teacher says, Where is My guest room, where I may eat the Passover with My disciples?' " The time of the Master was at hand—for the celebration of the Passover and also in a larger sense. The man, who evidently was a believer, would understand. He would place at the disposal of Jesus and His disciples a large upper room,[13] a spacious hall, from which all leaven had been removed, large enough to accommodate a number of guests and furnished with tables and couches.[14] Who he was, Joseph of Arimathea or the father of John Mark (Ac 12:12) or a disciple of Christ unknown to us, is not stated. The two disciples went forth and found everything as Jesus had said and did as they had been told. In the city they met a man, most likely a servant, carrying a water pitcher, and they followed him to the house where he was going. Then they talked with the landlord, delivered the message, secured the room, provided themselves with the lamb, went up to the temple, offered

4
"Where Will You Have Us Prepare?"
Mt 26:18a;
Mk 14:13; Lk 22:10

5
"The Teacher Says, Where Is My Guest Room?"
Mt 26:18b–19;
Mk 14:14–16;
Lk 22:11–13

the necessary sacrifices,[15] joined in the hallelujahs and responses, carried the lamb back to the Upper Room, and made all arrangements for the Passover.[16]

6
Jesus on the Way to
the Passover Meal
Mt 26:20; Mk 14:17;
Lk 22:14

It was that evening at sundown when, according to Jewish reckoning, the fourteenth of Nisan began and Jesus, accompanied by the Twelve, made His way to Jerusalem. After completing the arrangements for the Passover supper, Peter and John seem to have rejoined their Lord. Nothing is said of the mother of Jesus, the mother of James and John, and other women, although on the following day, we meet them again. They belonged to the party of the Galilean Passover pilgrims, but probably because His hour of suffering had come, Jesus had tenderly left them behind. As the party climbed up to the city, it was already growing dark. From the rear, bright and full, the Passover moon was rising in the star-sown sky. Soon they came to the designated house, where an outside staircase led to the Upper Room. Lighted lanterns hung from brackets on the wall. They went in, took off their sandals, and left them by the wall near the door. The door was closed. And the Passover supper began.

7
The Ritual of the
Passover Feast

According to the later rituals, the Passover meal followed a certain order. Yet the evangelists do not state which of the details Jesus observed. The characteristic features of the feast, however, are known from the Gospel account. The meal was opened by the head of the house, who filled a goblet of wine, took it in his hands, and consecrated it with words of thanksgiving and prayer. "Blessed art Thou, Jehovah, our God, who hast created the fruit of the vine." The first cup of wine was then drained, and each washed his hands. On this particular evening, the washing of the disciples' feet was evidently connected with the washing of hands. Then the table was brought forward, on which were placed the unleavened bread, the bitter herbs, the side dishes, the paschal lamb, and—if for a larger company the flesh of a small Eastern lamb did not suffice for a complete meal—the flesh of an additional sacrifice, which was called the first *chagigah*. In order that the guests might not be disturbed, the divans, or couches, were placed on three sides of the table only. One side was left open. As the eating began with a benediction, a second cup of wine was poured out. A very interesting ceremony then took place. The youngest member present inquired into the meaning of the feast. Then followed the *haggadah,* or instruction, by the father or the host regarding the meaning of the feast. The first part of the Hallel (Pss 113–14) was then sung, a blessing repeated, the Passover lamb was eaten, a third cup, "the cup of blessing," was drained, the rest of the Hallel was sung (Pss 115–18), a fourth cup of wine was drunk, and the ceremony ended with the singing of a hymn of praise (Ps 136). The meal had to be concluded by midnight, and what remained of the lamb was burned (Ex 12:10).[17]

8
"I Have Earnestly
Desired to Eat This
Passover with You
before I Suffer"
Mt 26:20; Mk 14:17;
Lk 22:14–18

This was really the first Passover, and also the last, of which Jesus participated together with the full number of His apostolic band. At the first Passover of His ministry, His twelve apostles had not yet been gathered,[18] neither at the second, if the Unnamed Feast was indeed a Passover.[19] And the third Passover Jesus did not attend. At that time, after the death of John the Baptist, He was in the utmost parts of Galilee, in the borders of Tyre and Sidon, where of course no sacrifices could be made.[20] And so it is with peculiar significance that Jesus opened the feast with the announcement: "I have earnestly desired to eat this Passover with you before I suffer." No more festival dinners would He enjoy with His disciples until the perfection of the Kingdom was attained. Again the reference to suffering, which, of course, the disciples did not understand. They had ears only for the Kingdom, concerning which, however, they continued to entertain conceptions of their own. As the Host of the day, Jesus opened the feast by filling a goblet of wine, over which the customary prayers were spoken, and passed it along with the same thought: "Take this, and divide it among yourselves. For I tell you that from now on I will not drink of the fruit of the vine until the kingdom of God comes."[21]

Imagination loves to reproduce the probable details of the solemn scene. And if we compare the notices of ancient Jewish customs with the fashions still existing in the changeless East, we can feel quite confident as to the general nature of the arrangements. The scene is not as we see it in paintings from the Middle Ages, such as by Da Vinci, the apostles all sitting at a long table.[22] The couches, or cushions, each large enough to hold three persons,[23] were arranged in the form of an elongated horseshoe around three sides of one or more low wooden tables, each one scarcely higher than a stool. The seat of honor was probably the central position on the first couch, to the right of the servants as they approached the open end of the table.[24] The Talmud formulates the position of guests as follows: The worthiest lies down first, on his left side, with his feet stretching back. The next worthiest reclines behind him at his left hand. The third worthiest lies beside the one who had lain down first (at his right), so that the chief person is in the middle (between the worthiest guest at his left and the less worthy one at his right hand).[25] From the Gospel narrative we know that John occupied a place to the right of Jesus, so that his head could at any moment be placed upon the breast of his Friend and Lord (Jn 13:23). He would therefore have received the second place of honor among the guests. At the left and back of Jesus lay Judas Iscariot, as we infer from a few details of the meal, namely that he dipped his hand into the dish with Jesus, received the bread dipped in the dish directly from Him, and other indications that point to a position close to the Lord. According to the arrangement prescribed by the Talmud, it seems that he really occupied a place at the Passover table first in honor. It is probable that he boldly claimed and obtained the chief seat at the table next to the Lord. His place was at the end of the row. It was called among the Romans the *locus consularis*, as it was a place of honor at the head of the table next to the host. Since it

9
The Arrangement of the Paschal Table

was on the open side of the couch, it was chosen in order that, if a consul happened to be present, he might be able to receive communications, sign documents, or transact business without the least inconvenience. This arrangement explains how Jesus, beginning at the end, could hand the bread to Judas first without attracting the particular attention of the others. It also accounts for the circumstance that no one—except John and probably Peter across the table—knew what had been said when Judas, wanting to ascertain whether his treachery was known, dared to ask, "Is it I?" and the Lord answered in the affirmative.[26] Peter, we assume, in accordance with his character, after the Lord had rebuked the disciples for striving to be uppermost, claimed for himself the place across from John, at the *foot* of the table. From there he could easily give a hint[27] to John across the table to ask Jesus who the traitor was (Jn 13:24).[28]

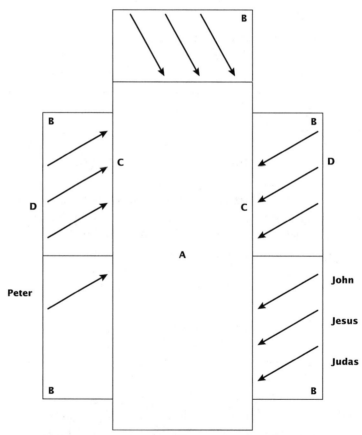

A. The table

B. The *triclinia*, or divans, on which the guests reclined on their left side, with their

C. Heads pointing towards the table and their

D. Feet stretching back towards the floor.

It may be that the very act of taking their seats started the contention among the disciples as to their respective places. In hearing the reference to the Kingdom, they had thoughts only of the trappings of royalty and of the order of precedence observed at kingly courts. The question had been brought up and settled before.[30] Gently the Lord tells them that it was the custom of Gentile kings to exercise lordship and to give themselves flattering titles, such as *Euergetes*, which means "The Benefactor."[31] "But not so with you. Rather, let the greatest among you become as the youngest, and the leader as one who serves." He points to His own example: His whole life has been one not of being served but of serving. However, since as His disciples they have faithfully shared His trials, He graciously promises them that they shall share His glory in the kingdom that His Father has appointed to Him. They are to participate in His messianic glory, eat and drink at His table in His kingdom, and sit on twelve thrones, judging the twelve tribes of Israel.[32]

For the purpose of teaching His disciples a lesson of humility, Jesus performed for them a service that otherwise would have been the task of the lowliest of servants. He knew that His hour had come. He also knew what Judas had in mind and that His glorification was by way of suffering and death. But since love had been the keynote of His whole life, He decided to display this love to those who had been His particular friends to this very hour. It was while this meal was in progress, at supper time (v. 2),[34] that Satan had taken full possession of Judas Iscariot, Simon's son, prompting him, likely after he had overheard a remark made by Jesus as to His intention after the Passover meal, to betray Jesus by bringing this information to the high priests. Nevertheless, without interfering with his plan, though He had full knowledge of all these things, and obediently submitting Himself to the humiliation and pain that the next few hours would bring, Jesus rose from the supper, which had just begun with the first cup, and did a most peculiar thing. Quarreling about their respective places at the table, the disciples had failed to wash their feet, or rather to have them washed, as befitted men of rank about to enjoy, as they supposed, a royal banquet! This was the work of slaves! Since no one, therefore, in this small assembly of expectant rulers and generals volunteered to perform this service, the King Himself left His couch, put aside His outer garments, wrapped a towel around His waist, poured water into a basin, and without a word, probably starting with Judas,[35] stepped up behind the couches, and, as though He were the lowliest servant, began to wash the feet of His disciples and to dry them with a towel. Awe and shame sealed their lips until Jesus came to Peter, who had probably drawn up his feet and could hardly repress his emotions. To the half-indignant question: "Lord, do You wash my feet?" Jesus replied: "What I am doing you do not understand now, but afterward you will understand." But Peter persisted: "You shall never," till the end of time, "wash my feet!" But here Jesus revealed to Peter the harm he

10
Contention among the Disciples as to Rank
(Lk 22:24–30)[29]

11
Washing the Disciples' Feet
Jn 13:1–11[33]

would do his soul by false humility: "If I do not wash you, you have no share with Me." Clearly here we have an allusion to Holy Baptism in which we are washed and made clean with the water connected to the powerful Word of God. Even as Jesus had spoken many parables, so now, in the washing of His disciples' feet, He, as it were, performed a parable. It was clear to Peter that Jesus was pointing to some connection not conditioned by mere external washing of feet. These words of Jesus suddenly changed the whole current of Peter's thoughts. Have no share with Jesus? Heaven forbid! And then he shot to the other extreme. In that case, if that is what Christ meant, then, Peter said, "Lord, not my feet only but also my hands and my head!" Once more, however, Jesus must correct His impulsive disciple. Correctly understood, "The one who has bathed does not need to wash, except for his feet, but is completely clean." In other words, as a believing disciple and by virtue of the redemption of Christ, Peter was clean already, and he was in need only of daily spiritual cleansing, daily sanctification, corresponding to the daily washing of feet in physical life. Otherwise the disciples were entirely clean, only that the sanctification of their lives must continue as symbolized by the washing of feet. In making this declaration, however, Jesus made an exception: "But not every one of you." Jesus knew who would betray Him. And he who rejects Christ, refusing to be washed of his sins by Him, and therefore is not justified before God naturally excludes himself from sanctification.

12
The Washing Explained
Jn 13:12–17

After Jesus had finished His lowly task, He again slipped into His outer garments and went back to His place at the table as the Head of the household. The disciples were still watching in questioning silence as He explained His action: "Do you understand what I have done for you?" They regarded themselves as privileged persons and therefore desired to occupy seats of honor in the Kingdom—and now the King had washed their feet! As their Lord and Master, He tells them, He has given them an example, namely, an example of humble service and brotherly love. As their Lord has done for them, so they should do for others. Not in literal imitation, as if the disciples should now make it a daily or yearly practice to wash one another's feet. That would be a pharisaic interpretation of their Master's example. No; they should make a general application of this divine exemplar: love and serve one another. "Truly, truly,[36] I say to you, a servant is not greater than his master, nor is a messenger greater than the one who sent him."[37] This important principle of Christianity applies to every follower of Christ as well as to His apostles. And "if you know these things, blessed are you if you do them."

13
An Allusion to Judas
Jn 13:18–20

The discourse continues with another allusion to Judas, who, though one of the chosen Twelve, was, sad to say, not one of the elect. To him the words of blessing do not apply. Not that he had been preordained to be "the son of destruction"— no one is predestinated to eternal damnation; he was lost only because he rejected

Christ. By his betrayal of the Savior, he assisted in bringing about the fulfillment of Scripture. This is what Jesus now refers to as He quotes the following prophecy: "Even My close friend in whom I trusted, who ate My bread," that is, who enjoys the distinction of utmost intimacy and friendship, "has lifted his heel against Me" (Ps 41:9). The choice of Judas as an apostle had been made in good faith, but at the same time with full knowledge of what would happen. It is not for us to dispute with the omniscient God because of His inscrutable ways, which are past finding out (Rm 9:20; 11:33). And now, since that most heinous crime would be committed and had been divinely predicted, Jesus makes an announcement of it for the very purpose of strengthening the faith of His disciples in His messiahship. "I am telling you this now, before it takes place, that when it does take place you may believe that I am He." But treason perpetrated by one of their number should not discourage them from performing their duty. In spite of the defection of one, they have the most glorious promise for their apostleship: "Truly, truly, I say to you, whoever receives the one I send receives Me, and whoever receives Me receives the one who sent Me" (cf. Mt 10:40; Mk 9:37; Lk 9:48).

The presence of a traitor at His table caused the Lord to become troubled in spirit. Even as David's heart was filled with sadness when his nearest friend and trusted counselor became his bitterest foe,[39] so it was with David's Son. "Truly, I say to you, one of you will betray Me, one who is eating with Me." While it is true that "the Son of Man goes as it is written of Him," still that does not relieve the instrument of wickedness of his responsibility. "Woe to that man by whom the Son of Man is betrayed! It would have been better for that man if he had not been born." At these words, the eyes of the disciples fell and their hearts misgave them. None of them felt safe now. Glancing from one to another, they could read shame and self-distrust in one another's eyes. Each was not thinking of his fellow disciple, but only of himself as he sadly asked, "Is it I?" Still leaving the special person undetermined, Jesus said, "It is one of the twelve, one who is dipping bread into the dish with Me." The reference very likely was to the dish of bitter herbs, the *charoseth*, a gravy-like sauce of a muddy color, made of figs, dates, vinegar, and spices, in which the cakes of unleavened bread were dipped to remind the Passover celebrants of the burning of bricks in Egypt.[40] Into this common dish Jesus may have dipped a morsel of bread and passed it along. But this sign would not make the matter sufficiently clear to the anxious questioners, unless Judas, who occupied the first place at the table, was the first one to receive the bread dipped in the dish, for which, however, we have no certain proof. At any rate, the disclosure was not generally evident, even as we are not certain of the detailed sequence of events. It may have been at this point that Peter, who was probably reclining across the table from John, motioned to the disciple "whom Jesus loved," who was "reclining at table at Jesus' side," that is, to the

14
The Traitor is Revealed
Mt 26:21–25;
Mk 14:18–21;
(Lk 22:21–23);[38]
Jn 13:21–30

right of the Master, to find out from Him who the betrayer was. We assume that this disciple, who does not name himself, was John. Quietly Jesus gave the sign: "It is he to whom I will give this morsel of bread when I have dipped it."[41] This He proceeded to do. Very likely already before this, when the rest had raised their voices, Judas also, to keep up an appearance of innocence, had joined in the question: "Is it I, Rabbi?"[42] Then came the reply, no doubt made in a low voice: "You have said so." It was another effort of the loving Jesus to save the soul of the traitor. "So when he had dipped the morsel, He gave it to Judas, the son of Simon Iscariot." In giving the betrayer's full name and parentage, John, as it were, made a formal arraignment. Jesus knew. Judas knew; but he was dead to the final warning of Christ; Satan had entered his heart. Likewise Peter and John knew. But not the rest. For when Jesus, seeing that the fate of Judas was sealed, began to direct events Himself by telling Judas: "What you are going to do, do quickly," the other disciples did not know what it was about. This final word was spoken loud enough for all to hear; the disciples, however, thought Jesus was giving Judas some instructions as the company's treasurer for tomorrow's sacrifices or that he was to make some offering for the poor.[43] When Judas had received the bread, he slipped off from his couch, an appalling figure, and rushed out into the night.

15
Upon the Departure of Judas, Jesus Indicates His Glorification
Jn 13:31–35

With Judas's departure, the atmosphere seemed cleared. It was a critical moment. The hour of the Lord's Passion had now arrived. The betrayal was the first step, which led down into the deepest humiliation; but it was also the first step to glorification. "Now is the Son of Man glorified, and God is glorified in Him." After the accomplishment of His life work, the Son of Man would soon be glorified by His Father. Only a little while longer the Master would remain with those whom He affectionately addressed as "little children," or boys.[44] Soon the intimate association they had all enjoyed would cease. As Jesus had told the Jews at the Feast of Tabernacles that they would seek Him when it was too late and that where He went they could not go (Jn 7:34; 8:21, 24), so also the disciples, He said, would seek Him after His departure with a sad and longing heart. Still they should not be discouraged. He would leave, but they would follow. He would go, but He would come again. And in the meanwhile: "Love one another."

16
The Institution of the Lord's Supper
Mt 26:26–29;
Mk 14:22–25;
Lk 22:19–20;
1Co 11:23–26

We now come to the most solemn part of the night, the institution of the Lord's Supper. It is beyond the limits of this present work to delve into all the questions and controversies that, sad to say, have gathered around the plain and simple words of this sacred institution. And still it would not be quite honest if we were to pass them by altogether. It was in the same night in which Jesus was betrayed, and "after supper,"[45] when the Passover meal as such had come to a close. The reporters are the Synoptists Matthew, Mark, and Luke, while the absence of John is made up by the narrative of St. Paul, who vouches that he "received from the Lord"[46] that which he relates. From the expression "cup of blessing"[47] some have thought that the institution of the Lord's Supper came after the third cup, when the Passover meal as such had been brought to a close, while others think that it came after the fourth cup, which preceded the singing of the final hymn.[48] This does not matter. While there was a connection with the Old Testament Passover, still there is the indication that the Lord's Supper was the inauguration of a new covenant, or testament,[49] and that the Old Testament Passover had forever ceased.[50] Even as with the sacrifice of Christ, all other sacrifices ceased, so also the Lord's Supper was not a sacrifice, but a feast, an eating and drinking. It is important here to make it very clear that the Lord's Supper is not a continuation of the Passover, nor should it ever be regarded as a "Christian Passover meal." It is not. In the four accounts of the first Lord's Supper, we notice that Mark follows Matthew and Luke follows St. Paul. But in calling attention to this particular, we are not suggesting that or showing how the evangelists copied from one another. The Words of Institution used in our churches do not strictly follow any of the four separate versions but are an adaptation from the fourfold account of an ancient liturgy. While it is true that none of these versions gives us the words of Christ in the original language He spoke (Aramaic), we are sure and certain that they are an accurate record of what Christ said, since the words were given by the inspiration of the Holy Spirit to the writers of Scripture. And what do the records state?

As the disciples were still sitting and eating at the Passover table—the meal having naturally been interrupted by the discussion about Judas, but now resumed—Jesus took bread. The reference is evidently to unleavened bread; but since in the fourfold account the term is simply *bread*,[51] it is quite clear that for future practice, the unleavened nature of the bread used in the Lord's Supper is not a major issue. Next, Jesus gave thanks to God and invoked a blessing upon the bread.[52] The ancient Jewish prayer over the bread was: "Blessed are You, Lord, our God, King of the universe, who brings forth bread out of the earth."[53] Then He broke the bread, for the purpose of distribution. Beyond this, there is no significance to be attached to this action; for even if the expression "which is broken for you" (KJV), considered by many an early gloss, is authentic, we must remember that no bone was broken either of the prototype, the paschal lamb (Ex 12:46), or of the antitype, Jesus (Jn 19:36).[54] Then Jesus gave the consecrated bread to the disciples with the command: "Take, eat."[55] A remarkable statement, however, is added. "This," namely, that which you are to take and eat, "is My body, which is given for you." The reference was clearly to the body that was to die on the cross and to the unspeakably great benefit that was to come to them through His vicarious suffering and death and then His resurrection. The words are clear, and yet their meaning has been questioned in many different ways. Does the little word *is*,[56] which in every language under the sun stands for

17
"This Is My Body"
Mt 26:26; Mk 14:22;
Lk 22:19;
1 Co 11:23–24

Matthew (26:26–29)	Mark (14:22–25)	Luke (22:19–20)	Paul (1Co 11:23–26)
			For I received from the Lord what I also delivered to you, that the
Now as they were eating, Jesus	And as they were eating, He	And He	Lord Jesus on the night when He was betrayed
took bread,	took bread,	took bread,	took bread,
and after blessing it	and after blessing it	and when He had given thanks,	and when He had given thanks,
broke it	broke it	He broke it	He broke it,
and gave it to the disciples,	and gave it to them,	and gave it to them,	
and said,	and said,	saying,	and said,
"Take, eat; this is My body."	"Take; this is My body."	"This is My body,	"This is My body
		which is given for you.	which is for you.
		Do this in remembrance of Me."	Do this in remembrance of Me."
And He took a cup,	And He took a cup,	And likewise the cup	In the same way also He took the cup,
		after they had eaten,	after supper,
and when He had given thanks	and when He had given thanks		
He gave it to them,	He gave it to them,		
	and they all drank of it.		
saying,	And He said to them,	saying,	saying,
"Drink of it, all of you			
for this is My blood	"This is My blood	"This cup that is poured out for you	"This cup
of the covenant,	of the covenant,	is the new covenant in My blood."	is the new covenant in My blood.
which is poured out for many for the forgiveness of sins.	which is poured out for many.		
			Do this, as often as you drink it, in remembrance of Me."
I tell you	Truly, I say to you,		
I will not drink again of this fruit of the vine until that day when I drink it new with you in My Father's kingdom."	I will not drink again of the fruit of the vine until that day when I drink it new in the kingdom of God."		For as often as you eat this bread and drink the cup, you proclaim the Lord's death until He comes.

real existence, here suddenly acquire a symbolic significance, or did the Lord really mean to invite His disciples, while physically sitting in their presence, to partake of His body? What did the disciples think? The disciples were simple believers, not much given to speculation. And even if they had been, it does not matter what they thought. We do not know how much or how little they were able to grasp. Nor does it concern us in the least. Our faith is not based upon what fallible men may think, but upon the Word of Christ. According to the highest critical standards, the truthfulness of the record cannot be questioned. It is clear from the account that in the Holy Supper, Christ has promised that His true body and blood are present and are received by all who partake of this Sacrament—not just by those who believe His body and blood are present, but by both believing and unbelieving alike, by worthy and unworthy alike. This is crucial because Paul warns, "For anyone who eats and drinks without discerning the body eats and drinks judgment on himself. That is why many of you are weak and ill, and some have died" (1Co 11:29–30). For this reason, we take great care to assure that those who are receiving the body and blood of Christ know what they are receiving, believe it to be so, and understand why they come to the Lord's Supper—so it will not harm them, but benefit them. Thus, to say that the word *is* denotes only a symbolic existence is to juggle with the language. Even in figurative language, for instance, in "The Lord *is* my Shepherd," the word *is* does not lose its force. But, on the other hand, to say that the bread has been changed into Christ's body, and is no longer bread, is going beyond the Words of Institution as explained by Paul: "For as often as you eat this bread." The bread is still bread. One cannot prove from the Words of Institution that the consecrated bread is changed into the body of Christ (transubstantiation) or that the bread and the body form a third substance (consubstantiation). Without speculating, simple faith believes that both the bread and the true body of the Lord are received with the mouth, the former in a natural, the latter in a supernatural manner. That in this gift of Christ a new order of things is intended and at the same time the establishment of an inseparable, most intimate, relation between Him and the partaker is effected is indicated in the words "Do this in remembrance of Me."

The taking and the blessing of the cup followed the distribution of the bread. The usual word of blessing spoken over the cup, as transmitted to us, was as follows: "Blessed is He who created the fruit of the vine."[57] The expression *cup*[58] naturally refers to the contents of the cup. The history of the Jewish Passover makes it clear that there was real wine in the cup, not simply grape juice.[59] The wine in the cup is the means of conveying the atoning blood of Christ, at the point of being shed. And because through the shedding of His blood a new covenant is to be established, Jesus calls the cup, by virtue of its contents, the new testament in His blood. This cup He now offers to His disciples with the invitation to drink its consecrated

18
"This Is My Blood of the Covenant"
Mt 26:27–28;
Mk 14:23–24;
Lk 22:20;
1Co 11:25a

contents. "Drink of it, all of you"—which they did (Mk 14:23)—"for this is My blood of the covenant." What has been said before about the term *is* in connection with bread and body applies also to wine and blood.—With the next words, as reported by Matthew, the purpose and the benefit of the shedding of Christ's blood is already given: "which is poured out for many for the forgiveness of sins."[60] The expression *for many* is not to be understood as if the Lord desired to say that He would not die for all; He merely emphasizes that His work is not done for a few, but for many, all mankind constituting a mighty host. From the words *for you*,[61] *poured out for you, poured out for many for the forgiveness of sins*,[62] it is certainly clear that the Lord's Supper is in a special sense a Sacrament and a Means of Grace. It is not a mere ceremony, a solemn memorial, but it actually gives and imparts to the believing, worthy communicant the forgiveness of sins. And where there is the forgiveness of sins, there is life and salvation.

19
"For as Often as You Eat This Bread and Drink The Cup"
Mt 26:29; Mk 14:25;
1 Co 11:25b–26

In the concluding words as reported by Paul, two truths are stressed. "Do this, as often as you drink it, in remembrance of Me." In the first place, unlike Baptism, this Sacrament is to be received not only once; it is to be received often. The Lutheran Confessions indicate that the standard practice of the Lutheran Church is to make the Sacrament of the Altar available to all who desire it on every Sunday and any other feast or festival day, or whenever there are those gathered who ask for it (AC XXIV 34).[63] In the second place, at each celebration of it, until Judgment Day, there is an inseparable relationship between the partaking of Holy Communion and its being a witness and testimony of the atoning death of Christ. Not that the Lord's Supper is a repeated, or "represented" sacrifice. "For as often as You eat this bread and drink the cup, you proclaim the Lord's death until He comes." As the Passover of the Old Testament was a remembrance of the exodus of Israel from Egypt and a testimony to the protecting hand of God, so this Paschal Feast of the New Testament is to be a testimony of the Lord's redeeming death and a reminder of His coming to judgment. And as the Passover strengthened Israel for its long journey through the wilderness, so the Lord's Supper cheers and comforts the children of God in the New Testament on their pilgrimage through this vale of tears, incidentally pointing to the end of the journey and to the happy reunion and the marriage supper of the Lamb in the heavenly kingdom. "I tell you I will not drink again of this fruit of the vine[64] until that day when I drink it new with you in My Father's kingdom."[65]

32

Thursday Night of Passion Week—
Farewell Discourses

April 2, AD 33

Nisan (or Abib)							
9	10	11	12	13	14	15	16
March			April				
29	30	31	1	2	3	4	5
Sun.	Mon.	Tues.	Wed.	Thu.	Fri.	Sat.	Sun

AUC		782	783	784	785	786
AD		29	30	31	32	33
Approx. Age of Jesus		30	31	32	33	34

After the singing of the paschal hymn,[1] or, in this case, the first Christian Communion hymn, Jesus and His disciples went out of the Upper Room to the streets of Jerusalem, across the brook of Kidron, to the Garden of Gethsemane, on the slopes of the Mount of Olives. While the hour cannot be determined, it was most likely quite late at night. But at some point between the departure from the guest chamber and the actual arrival at Gethsemane, Jesus announced the dispersion of the Twelve and three denials of Peter and delivered the great farewell discourse as recorded in the Gospel of John, the precise order of which, however, cannot really be determined.[2] Before the institution of the Holy Supper, Jesus made a reference to His departure. "Yet a little while I am with you." And then the disciples would seek Him. But "where I am going you cannot come" (Jn 13:33). The statement had left a question in Peter's mind. And now, to prepare His disciples for the matter at

1
"Strike the Shepherd"
Mt 26:30–33;
Mk 14:26–29;
Jn 13:36–37

hand, Jesus gives the warning: "You will all fall away because of Me this night." In the next few hours, events would happen that would cause all the disciples to become offended by Jesus or afraid to be seen with Him. His great humiliation would not at all agree with their messianic conception. The result would be the fulfillment of the prophecy: "Strike the shepherd, and the sheep will be scattered" (Zec 13:7). A bright future, however, is added to dispel the gloom: "After I am raised up,[3] I will go before you to Galilee." But Peter did not agree with his Master. He resented the implication of general apostolic weakness. "Where are You going?" The Lord would not needlessly excite His disciples by plainly telling them of His death, for He still had much to tell them to which He wished them to listen undisturbed.[4] "Where I am going you cannot follow Me now, but you will follow afterward." Thus the Lord pointed out to Peter in a veiled manner His future martyrdom (Jn 21:19). But Peter answered: "Why can I not follow You now?" Suppose his Master *did* refer to death, could he not also say with Thomas: "Let us also go, that we may die with Him" (Jn 11:16)? And he added: "I will lay down my life for You." As to being offended, or scandalized, Peter was willing to concede that such a thing could happen to the rest, but not to him.[5] "Though they all fall away because of You, I will never fall away."

2
"Before the Rooster Crows Twice"
Mt 26:34–35;
Mk 14:30–31;
Lk 22:31–34;
Jn 13:38

Peter thought he knew himself. But the heart is a deceitful thing. And the Lord, who loved him and knew his weakness, had made him the object of special prayer. "Simon, Simon, behold, Satan demanded to have you,[6] that he might sift you like wheat." Satan was not satisfied with Judas only; if at all possible, he would have them all. In the process of sifting, where that which is not wheat is cast out, Satan would have Peter and his companions. "But I have prayed for you that your faith may not fail." There would be an onslaught; but Satan's victory would not be final. "And when you have turned again (Mt 18:3), strengthen your brothers." Peter's fall and repentance are both foretold, the latter being necessary before he could again become an apostle of Jesus. But Peter still objects: "Lord, I am ready to go with You both to prison and to death." Peter was willing, but he did not know himself. He was ignorant both of his own weakness and the exact nature of his Master's fate. The reference to dangers ahead is quite definite, but there is a big difference between prison and death. Without arguing the point, Jesus gives Peter a definite warning: "Truly, I tell you, this very night, before the rooster crows twice, you will deny Me three times."[7] But Peter vehemently protested the announcement: "If I must die with You, I will not deny You." And in this he was joined by the other disciples.

3
"Let the One Who Has No Sword Buy One"
Lk 22:31–39

But in their overconfidence, the disciples had probably overlooked one thing. Their previous safety from vicious attacks and temptations lay in the protecting hand of the Lord. But other times were now at hand. When the Lord had previously sent them forth without provisions and means of defense, "Did you lack anything?" Their reply: "Nothing." But now the relation was changing. Jesus tells

His disciples that they would need supplies and means of defense. "Now let the one who has a moneybag take it, and likewise a knapsack," or bag. "And let the one who has no sword sell his cloak and buy one." Bitter enmity would have to be expected. Preparation was necessary. "The sword is the one thing needful."[8] If their Master is a "crucified Criminal—what could His followers expect?"[9] As for Him, the words of prophecy—"And He was numbered with the transgressors" (see Is 53:12)—must be fulfilled. This cannot be changed now. He desired to carry out His Father's loving decree to save all mankind through His own vicarious suffering and dying (Ps 40:7–8). But once more the words are understood in a grossly material sense. After the manner of their countrymen, these Galileans had provided themselves with two swords, which were "concealed under their upper garment."[10] And Peter carried one of them. "Look, Lord," they call out, "here are two swords." Jesus' reply is brief: "It is enough." In fact, too much for the purpose He had in mind. But there is no use going into this matter again. Enough for the present of misunderstanding and attempts at disenchantment![11] Events will soon teach where instruction has failed.

The hearts of the disciples were troubled on account of their Master's repeated references to His departure; for this departure was incompatible with their worldly messianic views. Therefore Jesus comforted them in an extended farewell discourse. While it was true that He would depart to the Father in order to prepare a place for them, still He would come again. This the disciples knew, for they had been sufficiently instructed; but for the present "they did not know that they knew," inasmuch as for the moment it had slipped their minds.[12]

4
Jesus Comforts His Disciples in an Extended Farewell Discourse
Jn 14:1–4

That this was the case was clear from the way Thomas spoke: "Lord, we do not know where You are going. How can we know the way?" Just like Thomas. He was willing to believe, but he wanted to be shown. His difficulty was that not knowing the goal, the destination, he could not know the way. What was Christ driving at? What was the goal? And which was the way to it? In Jesus' reply, He disclosed both the way and the goal. "I am the way, and the truth, and the life. No one comes to the Father except through Me." Believing in Christ is both seeing and approaching the Father. He Himself was the Jacob's Ladder to heaven, on the top of which stood the Father.

5
Interrupted by Thomas
Jn 14:5–7

These words interested the practical-minded Philip. Immediately he made some calculations. He considered the possibility of actually receiving a physical glimpse of God. "Lord, show us the Father, and it is enough for us." Thus he uttered the universal human craving for faith that is based upon the evidence of physical sight. Always there persists the feeling that something more might be done to make God known. But as Paul tells the Corinthians, "We walk by faith, and not by sight" (2Co 5:7).[13] Jesus gently points out to Philip that to have seen Him as manifested in His words and works is to have seen the Father. If the disciples were tempted to doubt

6
Interrupted by Philip
Jn 14:8–21

His works, faith might have the evidence of greater works in personal experience. By preaching the Gospel, they would cure the spiritually sick and awaken the spiritually dead to everlasting life. It is not that Jesus had not converted men by His preaching, "but the great work of the New Testament, the gathering of the Christian Church through the preaching of the Gospel and administration of the Sacraments, did not really begin until after Pentecost."[14] Then there is also the evidence of unlimited power in the promised answer to prayer. Of course, this power is qualified by faith and by obedience to His commandments. Finally, there is the evidence of the Holy Spirit, the other Helper, the Paraclete, or Advocate,[15] even the Spirit of truth, whom the Father will send. The Son was sent into the world. But, not so the Holy Spirit; He is sent to believers. This the disciples know because He dwells in them. And in view of His promised coming as a representative of Christ, the disciples would not be left comfortless or orphans in this world. While it is true that the unbelieving world, which only saw what fell within the range of outward vision, would henceforth see Jesus no more—supposing that He had been permanently removed when He was laid in the grave—the disciples would see Him on account of this comforting presence and enjoy with Him the fellowship of life. And not only on the day of the advent of the Holy Spirit, on Pentecost, but throughout the whole Christian era, the believers would enjoy His blissful indwelling in their hearts.

7
Interrupted by Judas
Jn 14:22–31

At this point in the discourse, which we will discuss only briefly and which, even if we tried to enter upon it more fully, we could not hope to fathom, Jesus was again interrupted. This time by Judas, "not Iscariot." On the roster of apostles, he appears as Judas, Thaddaeus, Lebbaeus (KJV), and "Jude of James."[16] Yet, although he has many names, we know little about him. By this time, it was clear that the manifestation referred to was not along the expected messianic lines. What arrested the attention of Judas was that the manifestation was not to the world, but to believers only. In expressing his thought, which was no doubt also the thought of the rest, he asks, "How is it," what is the reason, what has happened, "that You will manifest Yourself to us, and not to the world?" He still held to the opinion that messianic glory would somehow be in the nature of a great demonstration and with much display of temporal power. Once more, Jesus patiently explains. Together with the Spirit, He Himself and the Father will dwell in those who love Him. When He is no longer bodily present with them, the Helper, the Holy Spirit, whom the Father will send in His name, will bring all these things to their remembrance. He will be His Representative. The Lord's messianic mission was not to bring temporal power, but spiritual peace. To bring His work to conclusion, He was going to the Father by means of suffering and death. He would have to meet the last onslaught of the prince of this world and ruler of death; but on account of His sinless nature, Satan would have no claim on Him. Still He would go out to meet him in battle and submit to his sting of death. Not as if He were crushed by the machinations of Satan; He would go voluntarily in order that the world might know that He was doing it out of love and in obedience to the gracious and saving will of God. Since this was the purpose of His coming into the world, there was not at all, as Judas thought, a change in His messianic program. And thinking about it, and since the hour of His suffering was rapidly drawing near, the summons was given: "Rise, let us go from here."

Just what the occasion was that prompted the Lord to continue His discourse by presenting Himself as the true Vine, whether it was the fruit of the vine in the paschal meal or a vine growing in the courtyard or the symbol of the vine on one of the temple gates, we do not know. In the Old Testament, Israel is represented as a vineyard planted by God to bring forth fruit (Is 5:1–7; Ps 80:8–14). But Christ represents Himself as the true Vine, the Father as the Vinedresser, and the disciples as the branches. The most intimate relationship exists between Christ and all those who believe in Him. By accepting His Word, His saving Gospel, the believers cling to Christ as a branch does to the vine. His Word brings them in close communion with Him—"if . . . My words abide in you." And as the branches receive sap and vigor from the vine, so that they can grow and bring fruit, so the believers, who without Christ can do nothing pleasing to God, through His Word obtain spiritual strength and willingness to bear fruit, yes, much fruit, to abound and be fruitful in every good work, to the glory of the Father. Moreover, if they abide in Christ, they have the glorious privilege of asking of the Father in prayer what they will and may be assured that it shall be done to them.—The Lord then reminds His disciples of the unspeakable love He has shown them and will show them by laying down His life for them and all men. This should prompt them to keep His commandments, particularly to love one another as He loves them.

> **8**
> Christ the True Vine
> Jn 15:1–17

From the relation of the disciples to one another Christ now turns to their relation to the world. Because He has chosen them out of the world, they will be hated by the world. This is to be expected. "A servant is not greater than his master" (cf. Mt 10:24; Lk 6:40). "If they persecuted Me, they will also persecute you." The mere fact that Jesus' disciples afterwards professed their faith in Him constituted a capital offense in the eyes of His enemies. To speak the very name was a crime in the eyes of the law.[17] "But all these things they will do to you on account of My name,[18] because they do not know Him who sent Me." And that was their own fault. If Jesus had not proved to them by His preaching and by His astounding miracles that He was the Son of the Father and the promised Redeemer of the world, if He "had not done among them the works that no one else did," they could not have been faulted for not believing in Him. "But now they have no excuse for their sin" of unbelief. However, by rejecting and hating Him, they also hated the Father who had sent Him into the world. It was an almost incredible blindness and

> **9**
> The Relation of the Disciples to the World
> Jn 15:18–27

stubbornness. This hatred and rejection was foretold in the Old Testament. "But the word that is written in their Law must be fulfilled: 'They hated Me without a cause.' "[19] And, therefore, they would persecute His disciples and followers too. But there is also an encouraging note. The Helper will come and testify, in whose effective witness the apostles are to join. "You also will bear witness, because you have been with Me from the beginning."

10
Persecution
Jn 16:1–15Jesus comes back to the subject of persecution. As viewed in the light of fulfillment, one such prediction would have been sufficient. It was, however, in order to save His disciples from falling away that these repeated predictions were made. Not only would they be excommunicated, or put out of the synagogue,[20] but whoever killed them would deem this a religious service to God. This fanatical blindness was of course due to ignorance of Christ and of God; but the disciples were forewarned lest they be taken unawares. There had been suggestions of persecutions before (Mt 10:17–18; Mk 13:9; Lk 21:12–13; etc.), but Jesus had not previously made definite and full predictions regarding the experiences the apostles would have when they no longer would enjoy His visible presence because until this eventful day, He had not considered it necessary. But now the time for His departure had come. The apostles, however, were so sadly absorbed in the thought of separation from their beloved Master and its consequences to them that they did not pause to inquire: "Where are You going?" That is, they thought only of the fact of His departure and did not inquire into the purpose, and the benefit to them and the world, of His going to the Father, of His suffering and death, His resurrection, and finally His ascension. Viewed from that angle, it was certainly to their advantage that Jesus go away; for otherwise they would not have a Savior, there would have been no pouring out of the Holy Spirit, no coming of the Helper, and there would have been no Christian Church. As regards the advent of the Helper, that will be an event of supreme importance; for "He will convict the world concerning sin and righteousness and judgment." This the Lord explains. The world stands accused of sin, namely, of the one chief sin, the rejection of the Gospel and therefore its refusal to believe in Christ as the Redeemer; and the Holy Spirit convicts it of this damning sin. He will convict it also of righteousness; that is, He will cause it to be proclaimed in all the world that by His fulfillment of the Law in the sinners' stead and by the shedding of His holy, precious blood, Christ has merited for all people the righteousness that alone avails before God, and that therefore he who spurns this righteousness has no hope of salvation. Lastly He convicts the world of judgment, "because the ruler of this world is judged." Since Christ has destroyed the works of Satan, this archenemy of mankind is condemned, his doom is sealed, and all who nevertheless follow him will be equally doomed.—Many things remained to be said, but due to their present depression of spirits and insufficient measure of spiritual knowledge,

the disciples could not bear them now. The Holy Spirit, however, the Spirit of truth, who would soon be poured out upon them and whose essential function was to guide them, would lead them into all truth, which would make them infallible teachers of the Church.

Only a little while, Jesus continues, during the few hours of darkness in the tomb, He would be hidden from them. But the disciples did not understand. "What does He mean by 'a little while'? We do not know what He is talking about." Jesus therefore explains what He means. They will weep and lament at the supposed loss of their Master, but the world, His enemies, will rejoice. "You will be sorrowful, but your sorrow will turn into joy." An illustration is added of the pain suffered by a mother at the birth of a child; upon the delivery of the child, her anguish is turned into joy. So the sorrow of the disciples because of His announced departure, His suffering and death, will after "a little while"—after His resurrection—be turned into joy that no one will be able to take from them; for they will rejoice over the heavenly treasures He will bring from the grave. And "in that day," after the outpouring of the Holy Spirit, all the questions they would like to ask Him now will be answered. Then, after fully understanding His person and His work, they will address all their prayers to the Father in His name, which they have not done until now; and since they will receive what they ask for in His name, their joy will be full. They will pray all the more confidently when He, through the Holy Spirit, will no longer speak in parables to them but will make God's entire wonderful counsel of salvation fully clear to them. Jesus moreover assures them that He need not first conciliate the Father in order that He may be willing to listen to their petitions, since in consequence of His work of redemption, He is already reconciled to them, indeed, loves them.—After these enlightening and comforting words of the Lord, the disciples not only reaffirmed their faith in Him as the Son of the Father but also intimated that they now understood all He had ever taught them. Jesus, however, forewarned them that their faith would be put to a severe test. When His hour of suffering would come, they would all be scattered and, what is worse, they would cowardly desert Him. This dark hour of the beginning of Jesus' Passion was to be a warning of the manifold tribulation they and all His followers would have to suffer throughout their lives, yet with this comfort to sustain them, that they have peace with God through Him who has overcome the world and Satan.

After Jesus had finished His great farewell discourse, He lifted up His eyes to heaven and poured out His soul to God in words of infinite tenderness and love. The seventeenth chapter of the Gospel of John has been called the great high priestly prayer,[21] because the Lord on the very threshold of His Passion presents Himself to the Father as the true High Priest, making intercession for His disciples and for all who would at some future time be joined to Him in faith. Where the words were

11
"A Little While"
Jn 16:16–33

12
The Great
Intercessory Prayer
Jn 17:1–26

spoken, whether in the Upper Room or in the courtyard or in some retreat on the way to Gethsemane—hardly in the temple—the evangelist does not indicate.[22] It is quite possible that the whole farewell discourse was spoken as the disciples rose from the table, strapped on their sandals, stepped out on the balcony, and were standing in the courtyard; very likely, "He came out and went, as was His custom, to the Mount of Olives" (Lk 22:39). A party of twelve could not have conveniently talked together in the streets.[23] We can scarcely imagine that the discourse was uttered while they were passing through the narrow streets of Jerusalem,[24] and surely the prayer was not spoken then. As to the prayer, no more blessed or exalted voice was ever heard in earth or heaven. "Plain and simple as it sounds, so deep, rich, and wide it is, that none can fathom it."[25] "Spener," a devout preacher, "never ventured to preach upon it, because he felt that its true understanding exceeded the ordinary measure of faith; but he caused it to be read to him three times on the evening before his death."[26] It naturally divides itself into three parts.

13
For Himself
Jn 17:1–5

In the first place, Jesus prays for Himself. It is at the culmination of His whole life's work and at the hour in which He went forth to suffering and death that He approaches the throne of heaven with the words: "Father, the hour has come." He asks the Father to glorify His Son that the Son may glorify Him. The work of redemption that the Father gave Him to perform can now be considered accomplished, and He asks the Father to lead Him through to glory and permit Him again to enjoy the undiminished glory that He shared with Him in heaven before the world began. It is a prayer for His own glorification as man, which glorification, however, will also redound to the benefit of men.[27] It is glorification linked up with the salvation of men. "This is eternal life, that they know You the only true God, and Jesus Christ whom You have sent."[28]

14
For His Disciples
Jn 17:6–19

In the second place, Jesus prays for His believing disciples who have accepted Him as the Messiah sent by the Father. Setting aside the unbelieving world, He makes the disciples the object of His prayer, because they are His own. "I am praying for them. I am not praying for the world but for those whom You have given Me, for they are Yours." Not as if He were praying against the world. For afterwards (v. 20), He prays for all who to the end of the world will be brought to faith in Him by means of the Word. But since God's work has already been manifested to His disciples, He feels a certain responsibility for them. Viewing Himself as already gone from the world, thus depriving His disciples of His visible presence, He realizes that they are in need of His protection. In praying for them, He has two important objects in mind. "Holy Father, keep them in Your name, which You have given Me, that they may be one, even as We are one." That is, keep them in true faith and in the confession of the saving truth that in no way the spiritual union may be disturbed. While He was with them, He personally kept them in the faith. "I have guarded them, and not one of them has been lost except the son of destruction, that the Scripture might be fulfilled" (cf. Jn 18:9; 13:18; Ps 69:4; 109:8; Ac 1:20). We have already pointed out that Judas was not deliberately chosen for the purpose of playing the role of traitor.[29] He was chosen in good faith, but he turned traitor, and thus Scripture was fulfilled.[30] He utters this prayer on behalf of the disciples while He is still in their presence to assure them of His interest in them. They will now be left in the world. The world will hate them because they are not of the world. His prayer is not that the Father would take them out of the world, but that He would keep them from the evil one.[31] "Sanctify them in the truth; Your word is truth." All the more should they be separated from all that is impure and consecrated to God and His service because as His apostles they are to be sent out into the world. As He brought the sacrifice by which He made atonement for their sins, sanctified and consecrated Himself for them in His divine office of Savior, so they must dedicate themselves to the task of being His witnesses.

Finally, the Lord includes all future believers in His prayer. "I do not ask for these only, but also for those who will believe in Me through their word." He prays that they may be one in the Father and in Him and in loving union and communion with one another. There should be no disruptions and discord among them, already for the reason that Christian testimony and unity may serve as a visible testimony that Jesus was sent of God. The very existence of the Christian Church and the sincere love and godly walk of the Christians should act as a missionary agency, "so that the world may know that You sent Me and loved them even as You loved Me." And as Christ has received glory from the Father, so there shall be glory for all those who believe in Him. "Father, I desire that they also, whom You have given Me, may be with Me where I am." All the greater is His boldness in making this request because the believers are a gift of God's love and because the Father loved the Son before the foundation of the world. In conclusion, He appeals to the justice of the Father as the basis of His assurance. The world does not know God, but the believers know that Christ was sent by God to redeem the world, and they accept Him as their Savior. According to God's justice, therefore, the believers must not share the fate of the unbelieving world; but as the Father loves the Son, so He cannot but love those who believe in Him and let them dwell with Him forever and behold His glory. And as Christ has made known the name of God during His three-year public ministry, so He will continue to do, even after the withdrawing of His visible presence, namely, by the Spirit of truth, whom He will send. Thus the end and crown of all will be "that the love with which You have loved Me may be in them, and I in them." This was the final amen. As the last tones of this divine prayer were dying away, the Lord led His disciples into the "moonlit silence of the night"[32] in quest of that place of final seclusion that was to precede His willing death.

15
For All Believers
Jn 17:20–26

33

THURSDAY NIGHT TO FRIDAY MORNING OF PASSION WEEK

AGONY IN GETHSEMANE, BETRAYAL, ARREST, AND TRIAL BEFORE JEWISH AUTHORITIES

April 2 and 3, AD 33

AUC	782	783	784	785	786
AD	29	30	31	32	33
Age of Jesus	30	31	32	33	34

Nisan (or Abib)							
9	10	11	12	13	14	15	16
March			April				
29	30	31	1	2	3	4	5
Sun.	Mon.	Tues.	Wed.	Thu.	Fri.	Sat.	Sun

It was the night in which Jesus was betrayed. We do not know through which gate the Savior left the city of Jerusalem on His way across the brook of Kidron[2] to His retreat on the slopes of the Mount of Olives—perhaps it was one of the eastern gates, north or south of the temple area. But the place to which He retreated was called Gethsemane, or Oil Press, and probably was a small garden or orchard connected with some nearby olive press, from which it received its name. What today is pointed out as the site of the sacred spot, a walled-in enclosure containing eight old olive trees, is about seventy steps square. The location is probably approximately correct, although the gnarled old olive trees can hardly be those of the time of Jesus.[3]

1
The Agony of Jesus in Gethsemane
Mt 26:36–37;
Mk 14:32–33;
Lk 22:39–40;
Jn 18:1[1]

From the expression "as was His custom" (Lk 22:39), we assume that it was a spot Jesus frequently used as a retreat and that it was the property of an unknown man who was a friend of the Lord. It was a quiet resting place, very appropriate for retirement and prayer, perhaps also for sleep, used as such before this and known to the disciples, including Judas, who was soon to make his appearance. After Jesus had passed through the entrance of the garden, He pointed out a certain spot for eight of His disciples to sit and rest, while He Himself advanced with Peter, James, and John a stone's throw farther in order to pray. It was fit that the three disciples who had been witnesses of His glory—when He raised the daughter of Jairus (Mk 5:37–43) and when He was on the Mount of Transfiguration (Mt 17:1)—should now become witnesses of, and a source of comfort in, His agony,[4] but also because Peter had vehemently assured Him of his loyalty (Mt 26:35) and the sons of Zebedee had so confidently professed their ability to drink His cup (Mt 20:22).

2
"Father, If You Are Willing, Remove This Cup"
Mt 26:38–39;
Mk 14:34–36;
Lk 22:39–44

It was the hour of trial. As a real man, Jesus felt the need for a few intimate friends. Anticipating the pain of the coming struggle, He announced: "My soul is very sorrowful, even to death" (cf. Ps 42:6). But soon the society of His most trusted friends was more than He could bear. Before Him was a struggle in which He must engage alone. Withdrawing from them a little, but being still in their hearing and asking them to watch with Him in this bitter hour, He fell upon His knees and prayed: "Abba, Father, all things are possible for You. Remove this cup from Me. Yet not what I will, but what You will." The three evangelists here, as so often, supplement one another. Obedient to the will of the Father, yet trembling with fear, the holy Son of God shudders as He comes in close contact with death. And there was also the onslaught of Satan, the power of darkness (Lk 22:53). It was a terrible struggle, in which our salvation was at stake. But we must not intrude too closely upon the awful scene. The Father heard the Savior's prayer because He was satisfied with His beloved Son's submissive obedience. During His agony, there came an angel from heaven, strengthening Him and encouraging Him to carry out the work of redemption, probably by picturing to Him the glorious result of His substitutionary suffering. But for the present, the struggle went on.[5] When He was in great agony, "His sweat became like great drops of blood falling down to the ground." It is Luke, the physician, who reports the rare phenomenon of the bloody sweat. When one is under the pressure of supreme agony or fear, not only the waters of perspiration, but also blood ooze through the pores. It is reported that under certain psychological or physical conditions, other such actual cases of bloody sweat have occurred.[6] And even if there were no instances of bloody sweat in the medical records, the historical character of this phenomenon would nevertheless come under the same category as that of the angelic strengthening.

Rising from prayer, the Savior returned to His three disciples and found them asleep. To have heard one word of encouragement from their lips would have been music to His soul.[7] There was pain in His heart when He shook the slumberers, addressing Himself especially to Peter: "Simon, are you asleep? Could you not watch one hour?" It seems that the term "one hour" is a proverbial expression, without reference to the particular time. The disciples were aroused, but hardly sufficiently to heed the admonition: "Watch and pray that you may not enter into temptation." The "fiery Sons of Thunder" and the would-be-valiant Peter were fast asleep. What the other eight disciples were doing is not stated. Most likely they, too, were asleep.[8] The hour was late, and the disciples were tired. Of course, they were as compassionate, tender-feeling, and sad as they could be under the circumstances; but deep grief is apt to relax the tension of the nerves, with the result that such a person involuntarily falls asleep. And that is exactly what happened; they were "sleeping for sorrow," as Luke states. It is true that children cry themselves to sleep; but sleep in this case was also a mark of indifference and a result of disregard of warnings, although the loving Lord put the best construction upon the behavior of His disciples by saying: "The spirit indeed is willing, but the flesh is weak." Again Jesus retired and prayed: "My Father, if this cannot pass unless I drink it, Your will be done." Once more, the devil had made his onslaught but failed. And in spite of the chilly evening (Jn 18:18), the disciples were sleeping again. Their eyes were heavy with untimely sleep, and they knew not how to excuse themselves. For the third time, Jesus left them and prayed. And for the third time, He returned, this time completely strengthened and triumphant. He now aroused His disciples with the words: "Sleep and take your rest later on."[9] No longer was He in need of their watchful interest. Still, "it is enough."[10] Arise! Awake! "The hour has come. The Son of Man is betrayed into the hands of sinners. Rise, let us be going; see, My betrayer is at hand."

While Jesus was still speaking, Judas approached with a crowd composed of Roman soldiers from the cohort[11] stationed in the garrison of the castle of Antonia, members of the temple guard,[12] Jewish leaders, and private citizens. It was a motley band. The Roman soldiers of course were regularly armed with swords, but also, as at other times, with staffs,[13] for the purpose of keeping order against possible Passover disturbances. The temple guard was unarmed, but probably in this case these members of the Levitical police were deputized to assist in Jesus' arrest—to resist possible interference—and were supplied, if not with swords, with clubs and, in spite of the full moon, with torches and lanterns. As to the exact progress of events, there is some diversity of opinion.[14] Whether the multitude mentioned by the Synoptists was in addition to the arresting party, itself a large number, or not, is of little importance. Since Judas had brought the word earlier in the evening, there had been hasty conferences in Jerusalem. Messengers were sent to and fro, from the

3
The Sleeping Disciples
Mt 26:40–46;
Mk 14:37–42;
Lk 22:45–46

4
Judas's Betrayal
Mt 26:47–48;
Mk 14:43–44;
Lk 22:47; Jn 18:2–3

palace of Caiaphas to the hall of Pilate. Orders were issued and dispatched to the castle of Antonia and to the temple guard. The forces of darkness were busy. Rumor was naturally very active in throwing out hints about a riot that would be ready to break out at any moment. And all this while the suspected rioters, the disciples of Jesus, were fast asleep. Soon a band of mixed forces was making its way to the Mount of Olives. A signal had been agreed upon for establishing the identity of Jesus. As soon as He would be singled out, the guard was to seize Him and lead Him away; and Judas had said "safely" (KJV).[15] He might slip out of your hands! This He had done at other times (Lk 4:30; Jn 8:59). Here we have one of the involuntary traces of the secret terror and misgivings of Judas.[16]

5
"Judas, Would You Betray the Son of Man with a Kiss?"
Mt 26:49–50a;
Mk 14:45; Lk 22:48

We picture the scene as follows. Judas is ahead of the crowd. He hastily approaches Jesus. He is in sight of the armed band, a short distance in the rear. He is a traitor. His part is to play the hypocrite, to deceive Jesus and the disciples, perhaps coming in the nick of time to warn Jesus of the danger that was even now threatening at his heel. He advanced and greeted Jesus with "Greetings, Rabbi!" so as to be heard by the rest. "And he kissed Him." Not only did he give Him the customary Eastern greeting, which included a kiss, but he actually covered Him with kisses.[17] In all innocence—apparently. But it was a signal to those now at his heels. Jesus suffered the indignity. But He showed that He was not ignorant of the meaning of what would otherwise have been the usual greeting. "Friend," comrade, "do what you came to do."[18] "Judas, would you betray the Son of Man with a kiss?" Judas had betrayed Jesus to His enemies, but he had also betrayed himself.

6
"Whom Do You Seek?"
Mt 26:50b;
Mk 14:46;
Jn 18:4–9

At this point, it seems, the passage from John comes in. The signal had been given in plain sight of the advancing band. But Jesus Himself took matters in hand. "Whom do you seek?" They answered: "Jesus of Nazareth." To the title by which He was commonly known, Jesus responded: "I am He." By this time, Judas was standing with the party to which he actually belonged. Struck by the majesty of the word "I am He," they fell to the ground. While they were still "cowering and struggling,"[19] Jesus, permitting them to rise, again asked them: "Whom do you seek?" Once more they replied: "Jesus of Nazareth." Thus Jesus forced them to make their mission public. He would not suffer Himself to be taken and put away, as it were, on the sly. But He stated the terms of His arrest. "I told you that I am He. So, if you seek Me, let these men go." Jesus would permit Himself to be taken, but the disciples must go free, and this in fulfillment of the High Priestly Prayer: "I have guarded them, and not one of them has been lost" (Jn 17:12). Then they laid their hands on Jesus and took Him.

7
Peter's Untimely Zeal
Mt 26:51–54;
Mk 14:47; Lk 22:49–
51; Jn 18:10–11

This was too much for Peter, who by this time was wide awake. When he and the others saw the enemies step forward to lay unholy hands on Jesus, they cried out: "Lord, shall we strike with the sword?" They had only two swords (Lk 22:38), but they would not have their Lord delivered into the hands of His captors without a blow. Without waiting for Jesus' reply, Peter drew forth his sword and with an ill-timed blow slashed off the right ear of a man named Malchus, who happened to be the servant of the high priest. Peter thought he was able to protect Jesus with physical force, and it was his intention no doubt to cleave the servant's head. But in resorting to violence, he made an ordinary rioter of himself besides making the case look bad for Jesus. Jesus could not afford to implicate Himself in this rash deed of an impassioned disciple. Peter did not realize what he was doing. In offering resistance to those who were on the point of arresting Jesus, he was blocking salvation for himself. Jesus reprimanded him by saying: "Put your sword into its sheath; shall I not drink the cup that the Father has given Me?" The sword has its place, but not here. By his action, Peter had provided a just cause for the sword to be turned against him. "For all who take the sword will perish by the sword." Jesus did not need this kind of assistance, especially not in this case, when it meant resistance to lawful government. If it were God's will that His Son should be rescued, it could be done in different ways. "Do you think that I cannot appeal to My Father, and He will at once send Me more than twelve legions of angels?" Not merely two protecting swords for twelve disciples, but for each of the twelve disciples more than six thousand angels, according to the standard of the Roman army. "But how then should the Scriptures be fulfilled, that it must be so?" By his rash act, Peter would harm the cause of Christ besides frustrating salvation for himself. The damage must be repaired. With the words "No more of this!"[20] meaning probably, "Just a moment, please!" or, "Forget about this single act of resistance!" Jesus touched the ear of Malchus and healed him.

After Jesus had called His combative disciple to order, He turned to the crowd that closed in on Him to make the arrest. Already some of the elders, chief priests, and temple officials in the crowd were coming forward to gaze on Him with "insulting curiosity."[21] But Jesus had one more word to say before He permitted His holy and unresisting hands to be placed into disgraceful bonds: "Have you come out as against a robber, with swords and clubs?" Was He one of those Sicarii (Jewish zealots) who infested the country in the final struggle with Rome?[22] Neither was He a robbing bandit, nor was He hiding from justice. "When I was with you day after day in the temple, you did not lay hands on Me." The point is not that they did not make the attempt, but that His behavior and speech were without reproach and that He did not have to slink into hiding like a common thief. But this—namely, His submission to the present disgrace—is done "that the Scriptures of the prophets might be fulfilled." And even as their nature agreed with the hour of the night, so it was their hour and the power of darkness.

8
"Have You Come Out as against a Robber, with Swords and Clubs?"
Mt 26:55–56a;
Mk 14:48–49;
Lk 22:52–53;
Jn 18:12

9
The Disciples Flee
Mt 26:56b;
Mk 14:50–52

These fatal words to His captors quenched the last hope in the minds of the disciples. They realized that Jesus' announcements about His capture had to be literally understood. So they all—including the fiery Peter, the loving John, the unemotional Thomas—left Him and fled. Another drop was added to the bitter cup.[23] And still, for the present, Jesus was not entirely alone. There remained an unknown and interested witness, a certain young man, as some think, the evangelist Mark, who recorded this incident. It is like a "monogram in the corner of the picture."[24] When the band went to the Mount of Olives, he was for some reason or other found in the crowd. Assuming that he was a disciple of Jesus, he had received notice of the movement to arrest Him and was apparently aroused from sleep, for he had nothing but a linen sheet[25] cast about his naked body. This curious guise attracted attention and aroused suspicions. He was seized, causing the terrified stranger to leave the linen cloth in the snatching hands and flee away naked. After this, Jesus, with His hands tied to His back, was left absolutely alone.

10
Jesus First Brought
before Annas
Jn 18:13–14[26]

Surrounded by Roman soldiers and followed by Jewish emissaries, Jesus once more went forth into the night, but this time like a sheep led to the slaughter, over the Kidron, through one of the eastern gates, and up the slopes of the city. The strange procession reached its destination at the palace of Caiaphas, the high priest, which at this time seems to have been occupied by the two "prime movers in the black iniquity,"[27] Annas and his son-in-law Joseph Caiaphas. We are bearing in mind that Judea was under Roman rule and administered by Pontius Pilate, who usually resided at the seaport Caesarea[28] but during the annual Passover found it expedient to establish his headquarters in the ancient palace of Herod.[29] It was the policy of Rome to flatter its conquered nations with a semblance of self-government and to be tolerant, especially in matters of religion.[30] In general, there were but two rules that had to be strictly obeyed: proper regard for the *pax Romana* and the payment of taxes. Thus, in Judea, the ancient religious tribunal—the honorable Jewish Council[31]—was still permitted to try all religious offenses and to punish offenders. In the matter of serious offenses and where the verdict was a sentence of death, the case had to be retried by the governor; and the carrying out of the sentence of the Council, if it was confirmed, passed on to him. In the present case, it was at the request of the Council, as led by Caiaphas, the acting high priest, that Jesus was arrested. But as a matter of fact, Caiaphas's father-in-law, Annas, a man of seventy, who had been high priest himself twenty years before and after him five of his sons and one son-in-law, was still the power behind the throne.[32]

11
The House of Annas

In ancient days, the high priesthood was an office for life (Ex 29:9, 29); but since the days of Herod and the Roman rule, the dignity had been degraded from a permanent and sacred religious office to a "temporary secular distinction."[33] Josephus tells us that from the days of Herod the Great to the taking of Jerusalem, there were twenty-eight high priests in 107 years.[34] No longer did the high priests rule by the grace and in the fear of God, but by the grace of the Romans and in their own interest. As to Caiaphas, it was he who, being used by the Lord as His instrument to speak a divine prophecy, had given the counsel "that it is better for you that one man should die for the people" (Jn 11:49–50). Both he and Annas, including their families, were cold, haughty, and worldly Sadducees,[35] an able but ambitious and arrogant race.[36] The Talmud preserves a sort of street ballad that characterizes the popular hatred against this infamous house: "Woe is me for the house of Annas! Woe is me for their whisperings!" (snakelike hissings and secret denouncements). "For they are the high priests and their sons the treasurers; their sons-in-law are temple officers, and their servants beat the people with their staffs."[37] Jealous of their power and fearful of losing it, they were filled with deadly hatred against the great Miracle Worker and popular Teacher, who a few days before had for the second time cleansed the temple and "interfered with their illicit and greedy gains."[38] And there was good reason why Annas, who is remembered by his own people as the head of "a viper brood," should strain to the utmost his cruel power to "crush a Prophet whose actions threatened to make him and his family wholly contemptible and comparatively poor."[39]

Jesus was brought to Annas first. This gave him a chance to subject the Savior to an initial investigation, and it allowed time for the Council to assemble. Of course, this session was not quite legal. The midnight meetings of the Council, which were illegal, and other features of the Passion history recorded by the Gospel writers are sometimes pointed to as proofs that not all the statements of the Gospel writers are historically correct. But in the proceedings against Jesus, which were a mockery and a shameful perversion of all justice, such an illegal course of action is rather to be expected. Since there was an opportunity to get rid of Jesus before the Passover Sabbath,[40] the members of the Council were in trouble and in haste. Imagine what might happen if Jerusalem awoke in the morning and found the popular Teacher in the hands of His unpopular enemies! At all events, He had to be accused, tried, condemned, and delivered into the strong hands of the Romans before morning and before the multitudes had learned what it was all about. While messengers scoured the city for an urgent midnight meeting, Annas asked Jesus about His disciples and His teaching.[41] The purpose of the question was to ensnare Him into some incriminating statement and to advance some charge of secret sedition and unorthodox teaching. Jesus replied—and for all His calmness His answer contained a stinging rebuke: "I have spoken openly to the world. . . . Why do you ask Me? Ask those who have heard Me what I said to them." Thereupon, a miserable underling, probably seeing an indignant blush on the high-priestly face, struck Jesus in the mouth, saying, "Is that how You answer the high priest?" The face that angels behold in wonder

12
Preliminary
Investigation
Jn 18:13–14, 19–23

is struck by a contemptible slave![42] But without a trace of temper, Jesus reproved this shameless lawbreaker: "If what I said is wrong, bear witness about the wrong; but if what I said is right, why do you strike Me?" Jesus was well aware that the high priest was a "ruler of [the] people" (Ex 22:28), and He had only given him, respectfully but firmly, a reply such as his questioning deserved.

13
Jesus Led before the Council[43]
Mt 26:57, 59–60a;
Mk 14:53, 55–56;
Lk 22:54a; Jn 18:24

In the meantime, the Council had been assembled. Jesus was led into its majestic presence, the members seated in a semicircle around the high priest, Joseph Caiaphas, and his two clerks, whose duty it was to count the votes.[44] The seventy members themselves, with the high priest as the seventy-first, were made up of Sadducean priests, nonprofessional elders, and Pharisaic rabbis or scribes. Ordinarily, in judicial trials, witnesses are on hand. But in this case, witnesses had to be found. And though many witnesses came, their witness did not agree. Many were called to testify against Jesus, but the fiasco grew worse and worse. This would not do! If incriminating evidence could not be obtained in any other way, false witnesses must be sought, whose accusations would be of such a nature as to justify the High Council to pass a verdict of death upon Jesus.

14
False Witnesses
Mt 26:60b–61;
Mk 14:57–59

Finally, two witnesses were brought into approximate agreement, out of which it was hoped a successful charge could be constructed. As this was a religious court, Jesus had to be charged with having taught false doctrine and at the same time having offended the moral law, so as to make it a criminal offense punishable by the civil court. Thus the testimony against Jesus centered upon a statement made in the early days of His public ministry about destroying the temple and in three days building it again (Jn 2:19). But while one witness twisted the words to refer to the physical temple, the other possibly testified that the reference was made to a temple built without hands. Just how the statement should constitute a criminal offense, except if it was argued that Christ had spoken of demolishing a public building of the city, is not stated. The fact of the matter was that the words of Jesus were neither a command to destroy nor a promise to restore the temple of Jerusalem after its destruction, but a veiled reference to His death and resurrection. At any rate, it was as clear as day, even to the high priest, that out of these words a successful charge of blasphemy named against the Prisoner before them could not be constructed. Jesus looked on in absolute silence while His disunited enemies confuted one another's testimonies. Mark these silences of Jesus! There will be more as the trial proceeds. As the carefully prepared "arrows of perjuries" fell at the Savior's feet,[45] it looked as if the enemies would fail for the lack of a few consistent lies.

15
"Tell Us If You Are the Christ, the Son of God"
Mt 26:62–66;
Mk 14:60–64

Overcome with an explosion of anger lest, after all, his thirst for blood go unquenched, the high priest sprang to his feet. "Have You no answer to make? What is it that these men testify against You?" But Jesus held His peace. Reduced almost to utter despair and fury, the high priest now took one more arrow from his quiver of unrighteousness. It was not what the Defendant had done that concerned the sphere of the court, but what He was, at least what He claimed He was, as had been consistently reported to the high priest and as he most likely had himself ascertained in his interview with Judas (Lk 22:4). "I adjure You by the living God, tell us if You are the Christ, the Son of God." As this concerned a holy and eternal truth, this question had to be answered. Apparently Jesus recognized the right of the high priest to put Him under oath. At least He saw that silence at this point would have been construed as a withdrawal of His claims. Decidedly and solemnly, He therefore answered: "You have said so."[46] For the moment, His accusers were His judges. But some day, He would be theirs. For He adds: "From now on you will see the Son of Man seated at the right hand of Power and coming on the clouds of heaven." What was that? "Power"? "Clouds of heaven"?[47] Even from the standpoint of their false conception, there could be no mistaking these messianic references. It has often been stated that Christians claim for Christ what He did not assert of Himself. But here we have a straightforward, properly witnessed affirmation of the deity of Christ.[48] If Jesus was the Messiah, then He was the Son of God. And if He was the one, He was the other *ipso facto* (by the very fact). If He was the Son of God, then He was also God. This clearly, incontrovertibly, follows. But what appears as the most glorious truth to the believing heart was as blasphemy in the horrified ears of the Council. The cry of "Blasphemy!" reverberated through the sacred hall. In holy horror, the high priest tore his robes.[49] "What further witnesses do we need? You have heard His blasphemy. What is your decision?" he exclaims. Obviously it was not blasphemy for a man to call himself the Messiah in a country where a Messiah was expected, unless of course he did so falsely. And that was the point that here at the outset was taken for granted. "He deserves death." He is a *ben maveth*, a son of death! was their impassioned reply.[50]

Now we come back to what happened in the meantime. After the first panic of Christ's capture in the Garden of Gethsemane and the flight of the disciples, two of them—Peter and another—had so far recovered as to trail along behind the moving mass.[52] It was only when the band was nearing its destination, the palace of the high priest, that they pushed forward—a disciple, presumably John, entered with Jesus into the courtyard, while Peter, however, remained behind until someone could secure him admission. Let us try to picture the scene. Whereas typical Western houses today look out into the street, an Eastern house looks upon an open yet enclosed inner court, which is reached through an arched passage that is usually guarded and watched. When the arresting party arrived with their Prisoner, the gate was opened, the whole party admitted, including the disciple whom we may surmise to have been John, who was acquainted with the high priest. But Peter was shut out. As the sequel shows, it would have been better had his exclusion been final. It seems

16
Peter Denies Jesus[51]
Mt 26:58; Mk 14:54;
Lk 22:54c–55;
Jn 18:15–16

that John occupied a higher social level than the rest of the Twelve. Since the Gospel of John is rich with details of the Judean ministry of Jesus, it has been claimed with a good degree of likelihood that he had spent quite a bit of his time previous to his discipleship in Jerusalem, perhaps as the youthful representative of his father's prosperous fish business in the capital city.[53] At any rate, the disciple in question was known to the high priest, also to the servants at the gate, because shortly after he had entered the palace, he went out to the maid who kept the door and brought Peter in. It was a friendly act. And still it was an ill turn that he did his fellow disciple. Neither of these two disciples had any business to be there. John did not enter as the disciple of Jesus, but as the friend of the high priest. And as to Peter, it was his purpose to see the end; but this led him into temptation. After he had been admitted, it seems John hurried across the court into the hall where Jesus was in order to witness the proceedings. Not Peter. He did not feel at home in that strange, big house. He felt more at ease among the servants; but even there he was out of place.

17
The First Denial
Mt 26:69–70;
Mk 14:66–68a;
Lk 22:56–57;
Jn 18:17–18

It was long past midnight by this time, and the spring air was cold and chilly. In the center of the court, the servants had built a fire to warm themselves and were now standing with others around the coals of fire. It was this miscellaneous group that Peter resolved to join. But he did not "belong." He was in danger, though in another sense than he had supposed. It was not bodily peril; his fiery nature would have been able to cope with that eventuality. No, what he did not anticipate was danger to his soul. Yet that was the very danger lurking in the shadows at the fire. No doubt the fireside rang with jests about the Prisoner who had been captured. Peter was silent. He did not interrupt their conversation. He simulated disinterest and indifference. It is when least expected that temptation like a wild animal sneaks up and strikes a sudden blow. Already in the darkened archway, Peter's pretended indifference and betraying restlessness had attracted the gate-keeping maid by whom he had been admitted. As a hypocrite, Peter was a failure. When the gate-keeper was relieved by another maid, she stepped closer to the fire to verify her suspicious intuition concerning Peter. She fixed upon him an earnest gaze. No, she was not mistaken! With a flash of recognition, she exclaimed: "You also were with the Nazarene, Jesus." What an honor! To what greater praise could mortal man ever aspire? What better inscription could be engraved on the tombstone of a Christian's grave than the words: "He was also with Jesus of Nazareth"? At another time, Peter himself would have desired none better. But here he was taken off guard. A mask had suddenly been torn from his face. But instead of taking himself in hand, since the mask did not fit him anyhow, and confessing before all, he denied, lamely saying: "I do not know what you mean." How easily, how quickly, Peter glided and fell!

18
The Second Denial
Mt 26:71–72;
Mk 14:68b–70a;
Lk 22:58; Jn 18:25

For a while, Peter was at rest. No one pursued the subject brought up by the maid. No one bothered him. But he felt uneasy and warm. There was a fire burning within him. Quietly, he slunk away from the glowing embers to the arch-covered entrance of the open court. He suddenly felt in need of refreshing air. Just then, the crowing of a rooster "smote unheeded on his guilty ear."[54] But it did not occur to him that Christ had said, "Truly, I tell you, this very night, before the rooster crows twice, you will deny Me three times" (Mk 14:30). If he only had heeded the warning! But he did not. That is the way of sin and, since the fall, our miserable human nature. A second maid replaced Peter's first accuser. At that moment, she probably was talking with a number of men. Pointing Peter out to them, she came forward and said, "This man was with Jesus of Nazareth." Poor Peter! Again he was knocked to the ground by the gentle touch of a "woman's hand." How often a woman's "saucy tongue and jeering laugh" have made a man feel ashamed of his highest and holiest possessions![55] This time, it took more than a mere denial to set Peter straight in the eyes of those servants. "He denied it with an oath: 'I do not know the man.'" This was the second denial.

No sooner had this false oath passed Peter's lips than cold shivers rushed down his back. By this time, an hour had passed. Turning on his heels, he returned to the fire. He was now completely wild. He was boiling with conflicting emotions, and his mouth was out of control. Before he had been silent, but now he would talk. Assuming an air of defiance, he threw himself into the conversation, outdoing all the rest in coarse and noisy talk. He would show them that he had not been with Jesus of Nazareth. But before he knew it, he was fatally betrayed by his rough "Galilean burr."[56] "Certainly you too are one of them," the scoffing fire-siders insisted, "for your accent betrays you." Galilean speech was defective in pronouncing certain sounds. But Peter would show them! He would also be very careful lest his *sh* sound like a *th*.[57] As an old proverb goes, "When you are with the Romans, you must do as the Romans." But the more Peter tried, the less he succeeded. A Christian cannot twist his mouth to speak the language of the devil. The more he tries to do so, the more he becomes a laughingstock for the devil. In spite of his oaths and denials, Peter was utterly despised. A kinsman of the previously wounded Malchus, whose ear Peter had slashed off in the garden, stoutly asserted that Peter had been with Jesus in the garden. In the face of such evidence, how could Peter deny? And still he made one more awful effort. "Then he began to invoke a curse on himself and to swear." This was the third denial. How easily, how quickly, and how deeply Peter had fallen! If he could not bear to be teased and vexed by maids, how could he defend himself when an overpowering group of ruffians would pile in on him? And immediately as his shameless curses were still quivering in the air, the rooster crowed, and the word of Jesus had been fulfilled: "Before the rooster crows, you will deny Me three times." But repentance for Peter? Not yet. To his denials, he had added curses and oaths. As far as he was concerned, he had done his part and tried his best to fill the

19
The Third Denial
Mt 26:73–75a;
Mk 14:70b–72b;
Lk 22:59–61;
Jn 18:26–27

whole courtyard with foul and infernal fumes. He had for the time being thoroughly lost his faith. "Like a raging bull in the arena he was stabbed from every side."[58] He became blind with fury, rage, and shame.

20
"And He Went Out and Wept Bitterly"
Mt 26:75b;
Mk 14:72c;
Lk 22:62

But there is a sequel. It was the Lord Himself who brought about Peter's return. "I have prayed for you that your faith may not fail" (Lk 22:32). Not even the second crowing of the rooster, which ought to have struck into his conscience like a charge of dynamite, brought Peter to his senses. Peter called to mind the word that Jesus had said to him. And it was the look that the Lord employed for this purpose. "And the Lord[59] turned and looked at Peter," likely as He was conducted across the court from Annas to Caiaphas. But what a look! It was as if an "arrow had pierced His" fallen favorite's "inmost soul."[60] *Then* Peter remembered, but not before. There was pain in that look, along with disappointment and reproach, but also understanding, kindness, grace, forgiveness, and unspeakable love. With his heart filled with unbearable pain, Peter cast down his tear-stained eyes, and flinging the fold of his mantle over his shame-flushed face,[61] like Judas he rushed out into the night. Gone, forgotten, were his foolhardiness, his fears, enemies, denials, curses, oaths, and perjuries, and something else had filled his heart. He rushed out into the night, but not into the "unsunned darkness of miserable remorse,"[62] the midnight of hopeless despair, but into the "darkness of repentance" preceding the morning dawn.[63] "And he went out and wept bitterly."

21
Jesus Mistreated during the Night[64]
(Mt 26:67–68);
(Mk 14:65);
Lk 22:63–65

And now let us return to Jesus. The foul work of the night had been accomplished. It needed but the technicality of a few hours' adjournment to make the sentence entirely legal and binding. According to Jewish law, an acquittal could be immediately made, but a capital sentence could not be definitely pronounced until the following day.[65] A court of law is supposed to be a place of dignity, where even the condemned is treated with respect. But in this court, all forces of evil were united to cover Jesus with shame. During the remaining hours of the night, He was left in the coarse and cruel hands of the guard. To make play of their victim and to while away their time, masters and servants alike beat Him with sticks, struck Him with the palms of their hands, and spat in His face. So fertile was their infernal imagination that they even invented some sort of game to scoff and mistreat Him. In allusion to His claim of being the messianic prophet, they slapped Him and spit on Him, sneering again and again, "Prophesy to us, you Christ! Who is it that struck You?" Yes, there are terrible things in the heart of man. We can hardly conceive how such shameless insults could be borne so meekly and patiently by our Savior. "The claw of the dragon was in His flesh and its foul breath in His mouth."[66]

22
Formally Condemned by the Council
Mt 27:1; Mk 15:1a;
Lk 22:66–71

After a brief reassembly of the whole Council in an early-morning official session, the tentative sentence of the nightly meeting was speedily confirmed. Again the question was asked: "If You are the Christ, tell us." And again Jesus gave an answer, somewhat indirectly, but still in the affirmative: "If I tell you, you will not believe, and if I ask you, you will not answer [nor let Me go]."[67] What is the use of extending the argument? But again Jesus pointed to a speedy change of position from humiliation to exaltation. "From now on the Son of Man shall be seated at the right hand of the power of God." The reference was only too clear. Eagerly grasping at the handle offered by these words, they pressed Jesus for a direct answer: "Are You the Son of God, then?" Jesus answered this question with an affirming formula: "You say that I am." The judges were satisfied with the reply. "What further testimony do we need? We have heard it ourselves from His own lips." The chairman raps for order. "What do you think?" The votes are taken and counted. Beginning with the youngest, each judge stands up in turn.[68] With the noble exception of Joseph of Arimathea (Lk 23:50–51)[69] and Nicodemus, possibly also of Gamaliel, the votes are all for condemnation. "He is a *ben maveth*! He is guilty of death!"

34

FRIDAY OF PASSION WEEK

"SUFFERED UNDER PONTIUS PILATE"

April 3, AD 33

AUC	782	783	784	785	786
AD	29	30	31	32	33
Approx. Age of Jesus	30	31	32	33	34
Passovers		I	II	III	IV

Nisan (or Abib)							
9	10	11	12	13	14	15	16
March			April				
29	30	31	1	2	3	4	5
Sun.	Mon.	Tues.	Wed.	Thu.	Fri.	Sat.	Sun

"Suffered under Pontius Pilate." With these words, the Christian Creed forever not so much places the whole blame for the suffering of Jesus on Pontius Pilate as fixes the time when this supreme event of the world's history took place. For if anyone was very anxious, if not to spare the agony of Jesus, at least to save His life, it was that Roman—Pontius Pilate. The sentence of death had been passed on Jesus by the Council, the highest ecclesiastical court in the land. These Jewish judges would have gladly carried out their sentence, presumably by stoning (Lv 24:11–16), but it was not in their power. A capital sentence had to be confirmed by the provincial governor, in this case Pontius Pilate. And this he did in the end. Thus he was indeed guilty of the death of Christ, though, as Christ said (Jn 19:11), not

1
Jesus Brought
before Pilate
Mt 27:2; Mk 15:1b;
Lk 23:1; Jn 18:28a

in the same measure as the Jews, especially the chief priests and rulers. The beginning of Pilate's governorship coincided approximately with the beginning of John the Baptist's ministry. He had been in office long enough to become thoroughly acquainted with the most difficult race the experienced officials of Rome ever had to manage. Neither did he like his subjects nor they him. And so there was no love lost between them. His usual residence was at sea-washed Caesarea (Ac 23:33), itself a little Rome.[1] But the pomp and the perils of the Passover Festival, when the heaving lava of glowing patriotism was ever apt to leap into eruption, yearly summoned him to the "capital of a nation which he detested and the headquarters of a fanaticism which he despised."[2] At such times, especially when accompanied by his wife, he would occupy the gorgeous palace that the architectural genius of the first Herod had reared.[3] It was a luxurious abode, overlooking Jerusalem to the southwest of the hill on which the temple was built.[4] In front of it extended a broad pavement, locally called Gabbatha (Jn 19:13), flanked by porticoes and columns of marble. And here, in the open and from a raised platform, the trials were conducted on account of the prejudice of the Jews against entering the Gentile ruler's house. Besides, now, in the season of Passover, when every trace of yeast had to be removed, there was all the more reason to guard against ceremonial defilement. In this, Pilate had to yield to his subjects' scruples, though secretly, in his heart, he cursed them. But before proceeding with the account of the civil trial of Jesus, a terrible thing is related, which happened about the same time that Jesus was led to Pilate.

2
Remorse and Suicide of Judas
Mt 27:3–5; (Ac 1:18)

When Judas saw Jesus being led away to Pilate, he realized the Savior's fate was sealed, and his brain reeled at the thought of what he had done. He "changed his mind."[5] It was not godly grief, however, which works repentance to salvation, but worldly grief, which works death (2Co 7:10), being without faith in Him who can save to the uttermost. Instead of prostrating himself at the feet of his Savior, Judas despaired and went to the associates of his crime. The miserable thirty silver pieces in which his heart had delighted were now like thirty serpents in his bag. With wild eyes, a haggard face, and an indescribable pain in his heart, he brought back the silver, "the reward of his wickedness" (Ac 1:18), to the partners of his crime. At least that was his intention, and he wanted to remove as far as possible the terrible divine curse laid upon his atrocious crime: "Cursed be anyone who takes a bribe to shed innocent blood" (Dt 27:25). With a wild cry, he broke into a confession of his sin: "I have sinned by betraying innocent blood." Here we have out of the mouth of the traitor a confession of his treachery as well as incidentally a testimony to the innocence of Jesus. But the guilty priests were not interested in a sinner's return. "What is that to us? See to it yourself." The bargain had been made, the money had been paid, and they owed him nothing, not even sympathy. Judas now had no friends, no partners, no Savior, no peace—only thirty pieces of silver. And the sight of them filled him with utter disgust. Where Judas's interview with the priests and elders took place, whether in the Hall of Polished Stones or in the palace of Caiaphas, we do not know. But we surmise that with fire in his eyes, he rushed forward to the Sanctuary, through the Court of the Women, up the flights of stairs, through the Court of Israel, as far as—if not into—the Court of the Priests.[6] There he stopped. He bent forward and with all his might hurled the silver pieces into the Holy Place.[7] And then, with the empty bag still in his hands, he rushed out of the temple, out of the city, across the Valley of Hinnom,[8] up the slopes of the mountain, and straight into the gnarled branches of a tree overhanging a rock, "and hanged himself." "Falling headlong," the branch probably breaking from the weight, "he burst open in the middle and all his bowels gushed out."

In the meantime, there was staged in the temple a piece of hypocrisy in its most repulsive form. In certain respects, the heirs of Judas, the priests and elders in the temple, were scrupulous men. While the murder of an innocent man was not against their code, the possible infraction of a legal statute filled their hearts with dread. They were not interested in Judas's remorse. "What is that to us? See to it yourself!" they cried out when their partner in sin confessed his crime. They would not accept those silver pieces from Judas. Of course, they were forced to pick them up; however, they would not return the coins to the sacred treasury, or corban; for—this much they admitted—it was blood money. "It is not lawful to put them into the treasury, since it is blood money."[9] Finally, they decided to use the money for some charitable purpose. A parcel of ground was purchased, perhaps a worked-out clay pit still called the potter's field, and used as a burying ground for pilgrims who happened to die in Jerusalem. On account of the association, another name afterward clung to it: Akeldama, or the Field of Blood. In a remarkable way, there was also a prophetic correspondence: "And they took the thirty pieces of silver, the price of Him on whom a price had been set by some of the sons of Israel, and they gave them for the potter's field, as the Lord directed me" (see Zec 11:13; Jer 18:2; 19:2; 32:6–15).[10]

It may have been about six o'clock on that memorable April morning when a dignified procession, no doubt followed by a thrill-seeking throng, was seen approaching Pilate's palace at an unusual hour. The matter was urgent and had to be completely dispatched before sundown on the day that had just begun. The long-bearded and wise-looking judges, probably headed by Caiaphas himself, would not enter the governor's headquarters, or praetorium,[11] "so that they would not be defiled, but could eat the Passover";[12] and so Pilate went out to them. They were afraid of coming in contact with yeast, which in this season would be found in a Gentile's house; but they did not shrink from the shedding of holy and innocent blood. Disturbed in that early hour, Pilate was in no pleasant mood, although he knew that disturbances might be expected at the Passover Festival. In a half-necessary

3
The Potter's Field
Mt 27:6–10;
(Ac 1:19)

4
Jesus before Pilate
the First Time
Jn 18:28b–29

condescension, he accommodated himself to what he considered the puzzling super-stition of a hated race. As he ascended the tribunal, no doubt accompanied by secretaries and guarded by bronzed representatives of the power of Rome, he cast one haughty look over the priestly notables and the turbulent mob. Noticing also a bound victim in their midst and observing, in spite of the bonds, some unexplain-able glint of glory, he immediately demanded, "What accusation do you bring against this man?"

5
"Judge Him by Your Own Law"
Jn 18:30–32

The question took the Jews by surprise. It almost seems as if they had expected Pilate to accept their verdict and to sign the bill of execution, as we would say, sight unseen. This manner of dispensing justice was sometimes observed by provin-cial governors, either out of indolence or in blind reliance upon the native courts. Especially, as in this case, in religious matters, which a foreigner was not expected to understand, it was not always the unreasonable course to pursue.[13] "If this man were not doing evil, we would not have delivered Him over to you," is the some-what offended reply. But this morning, Pilate was in no yielding mood. He would not give the sanction of his tribunal to their dark decree. He would not be the exe-cutioner where he had not been the judge.[14] Very well, "Take Him yourselves and judge Him by your own law." If you do not want me to take up the case, you must be satisfied with what the law allows. This meant that they would have to impose excommunication, fines, imprisonment, forty lashes less one (Dt 25:3; 2Co 11:24), or other punishments. This, however, would not at all have satisfied their thirst for blood, and the sentence upon which they had agreed would not have been executed. Revealing their infernal desires as well as acknowledging the power of Rome, they were forced into the humiliating confession: "It is not lawful for us to put anyone to death."[15] Even if they had had the right to inflict capital punishment, it was decreed in the counsel of God as well as foretold by Jesus Himself that He was to die, not by stoning or by strangulation, but by the Roman mode of executing a criminal, by crucifixion: "And deliver Him over to the Gentiles to be mocked and flogged and crucified" (Mt 20:19).

6
The Charges against Jesus
Lk 23:2

Therefore, since Pilate was determined to retry the case, the accusers were forced to formulate definite charges, hoping that by doing so, their sentence would be confirmed. Witnesses poured out a flood of vehement but unprovable accusations, out of which at last three distinct charges emerged. First, this Jesus of Nazareth was misleading the nation. Second, He was forbidding the giving of tribute to Caesar. Third, He set Himself up as Christ the King. The fourth charge, blasphemy, for which the Council had really pronounced the death sentence upon Him, was not even mentioned. They knew too well that if they had advanced this charge here, they would have been sneered out of court. The first, a rather vague charge, "We found this man misleading our nation," Pilate passed by. If they had told the truth, they would probably have stated that He was making too many disciples and that they were afraid the whole nation would accept His false teaching. Pilate knew perfectly well "that it was out of envy that they had delivered Him up" (Mt 27:18; Mk 15:10). Likewise, the second charge, "forbidding us to give tribute to Caesar," Pilate ignored. If it had been true, that would have been a crime. But Pilate's government was too well organized not to know that this accusation was a flagrant lie. Jesus had taught the very opposite. There must have been a smile on the governor's face at the prospect of this sudden zeal for the paying of the Roman tribute. Could it really be true that the *pax Romana* was actually becoming popular on this Palestinian soil? It was the third charge that attracted his attention: "Saying that He Himself is Christ, a king." Discounting the ungrasped messianic reference for the present—if it was true that He was setting Himself up as king, a possible rival to gloomy Tiberius, this accusation certainly had to be investigated. Not as if Pilate had any particular worries in this respect; but it must not be charged against him that he was sleeping on the job.

Just how much Pilate was acquainted with Jesus' career we do not know. It is certain that he was not altogether ignorant of it. On the previous evening, he had granted a Roman guard to assist in His arrest.[16] Then there was the dream of his wife, Procula, which seems to show that there had been a conversation in his house about that "young enthusiast who was bearding the fanatic priests."[17] Now there was the charge that He was "Christ, a king." We assume that during these proceedings, Jesus was within the walls of the praetorium, probably with a guard. Leaving the impatient Council and the raging crowd, Pilate retired into his headquarters. There he stood face-to-face with Almighty Power veiled in human flesh. "Are You the King of the Jews?" he asked. But that depends upon how the royalty of Jesus is understood. In His reply, the Savior was cautious. "Do you say this of your own accord, or did others say it to you about Me?" "Am I a Jew?" was Pilate's disdainful reply. "Your own nation and the chief priests have delivered You over to me. What have You done?" What a shame—and what a charge! Israel's own people had rejected Israel's King. And what had He done? Done? He had done all things well, performed works of mercy, love, power—and still He was now a prisoner, standing at the bar of justice. A just judge should not ask that question. A prisoner ought to be considered innocent until his guilt is proven. In answering Pilate, Jesus reverts to his first question. Yes, He is a king. But no rival of Tiberius. For if that were the case, His servants would fight for Him. And still a king. But His kingdom "is not of this world." In giving the explanation, He had used the word *kingdom*. At this point, Pilate broke in and said, "So You are a king?" "Yes," Jesus answered, "You say that I am a king. For this purpose I was born and for this purpose I have come into the world—to bear witness to the truth. Everyone who is of the truth listens to My voice." So that's it—a king! However, not a king of men, but a king of hearts and of

7
The King of Truth
Mt 27:11; Mk 15:2;
Lk 23:3–4;
Jn 18:28b–38

428 / CHAPTER 34

the truth. Truth! Truth? But "what is truth?" What has he, a "busy, practical Roman governor, to do with such abstractions"![18] At this, almost persuaded, like Agrippa (Ac 26:28), Pilate rushed out. So near the fountain and yet so far from the life-giving stream. This idea of nonearthly royalty he set aside as completely unreal. Too bad, he thought, "What a high-souled, but altogether impractical dreamer!" But this much was certain: whatever He was, He was not guilty of death. Pilate went out to the impatient Council and pronounced an emphatic and unhesitating acquittal. "I find no guilt in Him."

8
The Weakness of Pilate

The judge had arrived at his conclusion. He was satisfied that Jesus was no dangerous character. To his mind, He was probably only a man with a fixed idea. And now, what ought to have followed? The unjust verdict of the Council ought to have been reversed, the Prisoner released, and, if necessary, protected by a Roman guard. And why was this not done? Leaving out of consideration for the moment the "determinate counsel" of divine mercy that Jesus should die for the sins of the world, we cannot but say that Pilate, with all his bold swagger, was a coward and did not have the courage to resist the bold and influential accusers. This they knew. They were confident that, if they would insist that their verdict be upheld, they would see the fulfillment of their foul design. An incident in the previous official life of Pilate may best explain.[19] Some years before, as recently arrived governor, with a supply of new ideas, Pilate resolved to move the headquarters of the Roman army from Caesarea to Jerusalem. Resolved and done. Roman legions with clanking swords, shining helmets, armored breastplates, and military ensigns, to which were affixed the Roman eagles and the effigy of the imperial master, were seen in Jerusalem. And who was there to resist? But to the popular mind, it was sanctioning idolatry to permit these images in the Holy City and was considered a gross insult and desecration. There was no objection to the image of Tiberius on the denarius, especially if sufficiently multiplied. Neither was there resistance to the blades on the end of the hilt and the spears on the shaft. But there was serious objection to the gilded ornaments on the tip of the military ensigns. Soon a noisy delegation rushed down to Caesarea with well-spiked protests against the introduction of idolatrous images into the Holy City. And besides, what was the idea of sneaking them in at nighttime, as had been done? Furthermore, the delegation reminded Pilate that, when former governors made their entry into the city, it was without those idols on the top of the poles. Pilate refused to listen. He was still a new governor, and he had to learn. For five days, he refused. Finally, he was so irritated that he gave the order to disperse the noisy mob and, if necessary, to cut off their heads, since there was no other way of silencing their mouths. "All right!" they cried and stretched forth their necks, saying that they would rather die than have their city defiled. In the end, Pilate had to have the images of his imperial master carried out of Jerusalem and stored in a warehouse at Caesarea. Such was the governor, and such were the people with whom he had to deal. For the sake of a principle and the effigy of his master, he could not afford to arouse a revolution and to wreck the revenues of a tribute-producing province.

The words "I find no guilt in Him" were but a signal for the release of an angry clamor. Charges and accusations were hurled from every direction. "And the chief priests accused Him of many things." Pilate, hopelessly in the air, weakly turned to Jesus Himself: "Have You no answer to make? See how many charges they bring against You." But Jesus, with His life at stake, was the only calm person in the assembly,[20] and He "made no further answer, so that Pilate was amazed." Suddenly, however, in the midst of the confusion, a way out of the difficulty seemed to open itself to Pilate. He heard the word *Galilee.* "He stirs up the people, teaching throughout all Judea, from Galilee even to this place." The mention of Galilee was intended to excite prejudice against Jesus, because Galilee was a hotbed of insurrection. But to Pilate's mind, there was suggested a way of ridding himself of the terrible responsibility in the present case and at the same time of flattering Herod, who was present in Jerusalem for the Passover. This he could do in accordance with Roman law by transferring the Prisoner to him, because Jesus of Nazareth, as a resident of Galilee, belonged to Herod's jurisdiction.[21] Glad to get rid of this detestable business, he sent the Prisoner and His accusers down the hill to the nearby ancient Maccabean palace in which Herod used to reside on his visits to the capital city. It lay lower down on the eastern slope of the southwest hill, where at a later time, as Josephus expressly says, Herod Agrippa II and his sister Bernice were living.[22]

In order to understand the following, we must briefly review a bit of Herodian family history.[23] After the death of Herod the Great, his dominions were divided by Rome among three of his sons, so as thus more effectually to keep the country under control. Archelaus received Judea, soon to be taken from him at the request of the people themselves and to be administered by Roman governors, of whom Pontius Pilate was fifth in line. Philip received Iturea and the northern regions. And Antipas received Galilee and a strip of land east of the Jordan; and at this time, after thirty years, Philip and Antipas were still enjoying their possessions. Like his father, Herod Antipas was a builder. Also corrupt. But otherwise, he lacked his father's ability, and his reign was drowned in debauchery and blood. He took a fatal step when he married Herodias, his niece and the former wife of his brother Herod Philip. This marriage brought about the death of John the Baptist and a war with Aretas of Arabia and in the end cost him his tottering throne.

When that stern wilderness preacher of repentance, John the Baptist, began to set fire to the country, Herod Antipas was interested and invited him to his palace and heard him gladly until John said, "It is not lawful for you to have her," Herodias (Mt 14:4; Mk 6:18). That was carrying the matter of repentance too far.

9
"He Stirs Up the People"
Mt 27:12–14;
Mk 15:3–5;
Lk 23:5–7

10
Herod Antipas

11
The Death of John the Baptist

And especially did Herodias "have it in" for him. We know what happened. On the king's birthday, Herodias's daughter by a former marriage, Salome, danced before a drunken crowd. The king was pleased with her unchaste performance and promised to give her anything that she might ask, up to one half of his kingdom. And "he promised with an oath" (Mt 14:7). The "young witch, well drilled by her mother in the craft of hell,"[24] asked for the head of John the Baptist on a platter and was not refused. The executioner was sent to John in the dungeon. "No time for preparation is given nor needed."[25] A few minutes, and it was all over. The guard returned, and Herodias received her "ghastly dish."[26] This awful crime filled the country with horror. Herod's own mind was haunted by the specters of an impenitent remorse. When the fame of the great Galilean Prophet reached him, he thought it was none other than John the Baptist risen from the dead. Feeling the hatred of his subjects, he turned more and more to foreign customs. His court was distinguished for Roman and Greek imitations and pretensions. And especially the professional conveyors of pleasure, the charlatans and fakers of the day, jugglers, and the like, were welcome at his court.[27] His annual visit to the Passover at Jerusalem was altogether conventional and was not inspired by devotion, but by hope of amusement.

12
Jesus and Herod
Lk 23:8–9

"When Herod saw Jesus, he was very glad." It was an excitement. And then, because Jesus was sent to him by the proud Pilate, it was a compliment. Indeed, we are told that as a result of this unexpected attention, the former enemies became friends. But most of all, his delight was increased by the hope that this great Galilean miracle worker would entertain him with two or three choice miracles for his particular benefit. And why not? This was a prisoner's chance to influence him, a king, in his favor. No doubt he thought Jesus would grasp the opportunity to show, as he regarded it, His skill. Thus he revealed his estimate of the person of Christ. At once, he addressed Jesus in the friendliest manner and "questioned Him at some length." We can imagine his welcoming smile. In his eagerness, he altogether forgot the purpose for which Pilate had sent Him. But Jesus "made no answer." Herod exhausted himself, waiting for Christ to speak. He waited. But Jesus never uttered a word. Silence continued. At last, the old chatterer grew angry.

13
Treated with
Contempt and
Mocked
Lk 23:10–12

The king is through speaking. And now the accusers begin. "The chief priests and the scribes stood by, vehemently accusing Him." The same old charges were poured out, and this time, it seems, into receptive ears. Then the corrupt satellites around the debased throne chimed in. "And Herod with his soldiers treated Him with contempt." Mocking Jesus' harmless innocence and ridiculing His candidacy for the messianic throne, they threw a shining robe over His holy shoulders. And in the midst of offensive laughter and cruel insults, Herod sent Him back to Pilate, for which he then became Pilate's friend. Just what the cause of the previous enmity had been cannot be ascertained. Most likely it was the jealousy of a native prince harbored against a foreign ruler. Some commentators think that it was on account of the Galileans whose blood Pilate had mingled with their sacrifices (Lk 13:1). But the records do not state that the friendship brought about by such unholy circumstances endured for a long time. Enmity against Christ and His Church does make strange bedfellows and friends. It would have been a thousand times better for both Pilate and Herod had they sought and retained the friendship of Jesus.

Pilate's hope of disposing of the case by sending Jesus to Herod was in vain; for before long, the Prisoner was brought back to the royal palace. While Herod had treated Jesus with shameless disdain, Pilate still treated Him with genuine respect. Yet he could plainly see that Herod's verdict agreed with his own; namely, that whatever views might be held as to the teaching and person of the Galilean Prophet, He at least was not guilty of death. This point was now definitely established by Pilate's own observation and confirmed by expert advice, for that was the only way to interpret the action of Herod, a native prince.[28] If Jesus was guilty, Antipas would have condemned Him. For Pilate, there was now absolutely no excuse for a delay of favorable action. But what did he do? He still followed the policy of all weaklings, that miserable policy of stalling for time. When Jesus' fate was once more placed into his unhappy hands, he called together the chief priests and the rulers and the people for the purpose of making an important announcement, always probably hoping that something, he knew not what, might turn up. At last, he began his speech. "You brought me this man as one who was misleading the people. And after examining Him before you, behold, I did not find this man guilty of any of your charges against Him. Neither did Herod, for he sent Him back to us." He could have added, "By the way, there is nothing to the rumor at all that Herod and I are not on speaking terms. Herod examined Him. And the result is the same. And therefore," he could continue, still thinking hard, "therefore,"—therefore what? "And therefore," you would expect him to say, "I am going to release Him; and I warn you by the power of Rome and the terrible anger of Tiberius not so much as to disturb a single hair of His head." But instead, he offered a proposition in defiance of all logic and justice: "I will therefore punish and release Him." Was there a more unjust proposal ever made: to inflict a severe punishment as a "concession to their rage" and then to release Him as a tribute to justice?[29] And yet this proposal was thoroughly characteristic of the man who made it and the system that he represented. The spirit of Imperial Rome was ever the spirit of compromise, so as ultimately to gain its end. And nine times out of ten, it worked. Scores of officials throughout the empire were even then successfully conducting their administration along these very lines. "Only to Pilate fell the sinister distinction of applying the base system to an altogether unexpected exception to the rule."[30] In proposing to have Jesus, though innocent, chastened, Pilate cut himself loose from all principles of justice. But he hoped by

14
Returned to Pilate
Lk 23:13–16

doing this to guide his course safely to the point at which he aimed. In this, he was fatally deceived. The impulse of his own false beginning could end only in his own wreck and ruin. Only by means of right can you achieve right. You cannot do one thing wrong in the hope of making another thing right. It cannot be done.

15
"Barabbas, or Jesus?"
Mt 27:15–18;
Mk 15:6–10;
Jn 18:39

It seems that in Pilate's eager pursuit of stalling measures, another avenue of hoped-for escape opened. Up to this point, the actors assembled on the stage of Christ's trial were still comparatively few compared with the masses that now appeared on the scene. And it was just by means of this mob of Jerusalem as against the leaders with whom he had been dealing that Pilate hoped to extricate himself from a dilemma. He hoped to turn his knowledge that it was for envy that Jesus had been delivered by the leaders to good account. It was the custom of the Roman governors, as a contribution to the Passover joy of the people, to release a prisoner whom they wanted. There were generally plenty of political prisoners on hand, rebels against the detested power of Rome, but for that reason popular heroes.[31] And for once, the annual demand to have a prisoner released was welcome to Pilate. Here was the plan: he would give them the choice of freeing either Barabbas,[32] a robber and leader of sedition who in a late uprising had committed murder, or Jesus, who but a few days before had been the hero at a popular demonstration. As an aspirant to messiahship, he imagined, Jesus would be the very person they should want. It was seemingly a good plan. He thought he could not go wrong. And still, taking into consideration the Person and the issue, failure was the only outcome in which this plan could result. You cannot gamble with justice. It was an utterly unjust thing for Pilate to do because the proposal treated Jesus as if He were guilty and already condemned, which was not the case. And furthermore, it staked the life of an innocent man upon the voice of the people in the hope that the *vox populi* would be *vox Dei*, the voice of the people would be the voice of God, which is not always the case.[33]

16
The Message from Pilate's Wife
Mt 27:19

Not that Pilate did not know better nor that he was unwarned. It was about this time that a distinct warning came to him from Procula,[34] his loving wife. As a good wife of a husband who was in need of sound advice, she sent a messenger to tell him of a terrifying dream she had had about the Prisoner and to warn him not to have anything to do with that righteous Man. How she knew about Him is not stated. But we must remember that Jesus was nationally known and no doubt had been the subject of many a conversation in the palace. On the evening before, Pilate had put a Roman guard at the disposal of the high priest to assist in His arrest. Perhaps he mentioned this matter to his wife, and with thoughts of Jesus, Procula went to sleep. Now, we are not going to talk about dreams. But we can be assured that the hand of God was in this dream and that in the message, the hands of both God and a loving wife were outstretched to save Pilate from a doom to which he was hastening.[35] Pilate, who as an educated Roman would have remembered Caesar's death and Calpurnia's dream,[36] must have been impressed. Gladly would he have yielded if it had not been for that secret streak of cowardice.

There was a brief interval, which was put to good use by the priests and the scribes: since Pilate had appealed to the mob, they, too, would appeal to it. And they knew the mob better than Pilate. They persuaded the people and moved the mob to do their bidding. All they had to do was employ a simple political trick, as old as politics, and pass the word on as to which of the two was Pilate's choice. And then, as far as the mob was concerned, the matter was safe. Picture the scene: the holy, undefiled, sinless Son of God standing with a scowling thug on that high tribunal! Words fail to describe the contrast, as great as heaven and the bottom of hell. "For the Holy, the Harmless, for Him whom a thousand hosannas had greeted five days before, not a word of pity is heard."[37] And then, as the choice is made that is to decide the fate of the Redeemer and forever confirm the tragic truth of the natural depravity of the human heart, ten thousand hands are pointed, and ten thousand voices raise the cry of "Barabbas!"

And so, in spite of manipulations, the matter had come to the worst. After a last brief moment of hopeful suspense, the choice of Barabbas must have been a staggering blow to Pilate. He had staked all on the choice of the people and lost. His testimony to the innocence of Jesus, his repeated appeals to the people's conscience, his outrageous strategy of having Him whom he had pronounced innocent cruelly scourged to satisfy His bitter enemies in order to save Him from crucifixion—all had been in vain. "What shall I do with Jesus who is called Christ?" he asked in helpless despair. This is a question that every believer asks and properly answers. Probably Pilate had hoped for the answer "release Him too." How willingly would he have complied with such a request! "What shall I do with the man you call the King of the Jews?" The appeal to their messianic as well as to their national aspirations left them untouched. Quick as an echo, the answer was flashed back: "Crucify Him!" As with wild vehemence, the hideous yells rent the air, and Pilate now became fully aware that this pack of accusers was deadly earnest in their clamor for blood. What the governor had considered "a loophole for escape was a noose into which he had thrust his neck."[38] He was lost. There was no use of his pleading any longer.

When Pilate saw that he could not prevail, he did a most unusual thing. Calling for a basin of water, he washed his hands before the multitude and said, "I am innocent of this man's blood; see to it yourselves." In itself, it was a most impressive act,[40] but in the case of Pilate, it was a farce. Blood and guilt are not washed off so easily. And Pilate's hands were covered with blood. Instead of washing his hands, he ought to have used them;[41] he ought to have refused to perform a deed of which he himself disapproved. Pilate was guilty. Still, behind it all was the sinner-saving will of God. Pilate, coward that he was, was afraid of heaping guilt upon his soul. But the people

17
Barabbas Is Chosen
Mt 27:20–21;
Mk 15:11; Lk 23:17–19; Jn 18:40

18
"What Shall I Do with Jesus?"
Mt 27:22–23;
Mk 15:12–14;
Lk 23:20–23

19
Pilate Washes His Hands
Mt 27:24–25[39]

were not. His pitiful plea of mercy for Jesus—for that is what it was—was met with a hideous howl of hell. "His blood be on us and on our children!" Madder cries were never uttered, and profaner curses were never heard. But a short time later on a hill outside Jerusalem, Jesus took their guilt and punishment upon Himself, praying, "Father, forgive them, for they know not what they do" (Lk 23:34).

20
Barabbas Released
and Jesus Scourged
Mt 27:26; Mk 15:15;
Lk 23:24–25;
Jn 19:1

Pilate's various attempts to save Jesus had completely failed. There was now no other course open to him than to hand Him over to the tormentors. In presenting the intense suffering of our Savior, it is not necessary to dwell upon every detail until each sentence drips with blood, as used to be the custom in a more realistic age, as long as we remember that it was a real suffering, a vicarious suffering, and we in true penitence meditate on the cause—our sins. The people had spoken, but the voice of the people is not always the voice of God. Now Pilate had to yield to the popular storm. He released Barabbas and delivered Jesus to be scourged.[42] This terrible punishment, from which Roman citizens were exempt (Ac 22:25), was ordinarily done in preparation for crucifixion and other forms of capital punishment. Woe to him upon whom it was inflicted! It meant that he was doomed to die. It was a punishment so terrible that the mind revolts even at the description of it.[43] The victim was stripped and tied in a bent position to a pillar; then blows were laid on the naked back with leather thongs, weighted with jagged edges of bone and lead. Scourging as practiced by the Romans[44] was so merciless and fierce that the victim generally fainted and often died.[45] The reason why Pilate tolerated this torture before the last and deciding word had been finally spoken apparently was that he was still hoping to save Jesus, thinking that by causing Him to undergo so much suffering he would arouse the pity of the previously furious mob; and then he would set Him free. But if these were his hopes, they were as futile as his measures were heartless and unjust.

21
The Crown
of Thorns
Mt 27:27–31a;
Mk 15:16–20a;
Jn 19:2–3

Assuming that Jesus was condemned and that He was their victim, whom they might treat as they pleased, the soldiers now took Him in hand. They led Him away within the court and called together the whole battalion.[46] In civilized countries, all possible measures are taken—and sometimes this is even overdone—to spare the suffering of a murderer condemned to death. But with the Roman soldiers, who were hardened to bloodshed and delighted in the bloody sports of the arena, the opposite was the case. If they had not been permitted to treat a condemned criminal roughly, so as to cause him additional pain and humiliation, they would have considered themselves deprived of their greatest fun. Jesus' trial was over. The Passover celebrated in Jerusalem meant nothing to these soldiers. Therefore, they would have a Roman holiday of their own. Somehow the fact had penetrated their barrack-schooled brains that the drift of the charge against Jesus was that He pretended to be a king. Thus, their horseplay took the form of a mock coronation.[47] In staging their heartless ceremony, the hardened ruffians treated Jesus as if they were creating a successor to Emperor Tiberius, the aged and suspicious incumbent of the purple who at the time was hiding his gloomy features at Capri.[48] A king must wear the purple, so they tore Herod's gift, the shining robe, from His bleeding shoulders and threw over Him a cast-off officer's coat.[49] He must have a crown. Therefore, one of them pulled a few sharp-needled twigs off a nearby bush and plaited them into a crown of thorns.[50] He must also have a scepter. And thus a reed[51] was thrust into His rope-tied hands. The royal outfit was finally complete. Now their newly made king must be duly saluted. As to the proper royal address, the only time when they had seen that made was at Rome in the circus, when they had seen gladiators approach the imperial presence with the greeting "*Ave, Caesar, morituri te salutant!*" "Hail, Emperor, those who are about to die salute you!" So they advanced, one after the other, and, bending low, said: "Hail, King of the Jews!" Then, passing from unshamed mockery to savage cruelty in the midst of outbursts of coarse laughter, they struck Him over the head with the cane that His hand was unable to hold. And—must we repeat it?—they covered His face with spit.[52]

What a spectacle! Putting an end to this misery for the present, Pilate led Jesus out. Hoping the sight of the scourged Prisoner would satisfy the Jews, he brought Him out that they might see Him and that the governor might have another opportunity to pronounce Him guiltless. Pointing to Jesus, who was still wearing the mock symbols of royalty and was covered with blood, he burst out into that famous "involuntary exclamation which has thrilled untold millions of hearts":[53] "Behold the man!" Painters have chosen this moment of extreme humiliation when Jesus came forth, bleeding from cruel stripes, His back lacerated, wearing the scarlet robe and the crown of thorns, the weariness of deathly agony pictured in His sleepless eyes, as the one to portray the Man of Sorrows.[54] And many a priceless canvas bears the title "*Ecce Homo*! Behold the man!" Two phrases fell from Pilate's lips that the world will never forget: "What is truth?" (Jn 18:38) and "Behold the man!" One may be taken as the answer to the other. "What is truth?" Heavenly truth, the will of the Father, and the way to life may be beheld only in the man Christ Jesus. Let the whole world turn to Him and with a truly penitent and believing heart "behold the man." It was an outcry to move the hard hearts to mercy; but it only awakened a fierce uproar of bloodthirsty screams: "Crucify Him, crucify Him!" The mere sight of the suffering Jesus, even in these unspeakable depths, seemed only to add fuel to their infernal flames. Pilate pleaded with them. But again he missed his guess. There was no voice of compassion, but only the "howling refrain of their wild liturgy of death."[55] At his wit's end, Pilate cried out in utter disgust: "Take Him yourselves and crucify Him, for I find no guilt in Him." What an admission from a Roman judge, and what a wretched dishonesty to attempt to escape the responsibility by shifting the blame to the Jews! Now the enemies felt safe. They saw that they had

22
"Behold the Man!"
Jn 19:4–7

the governor completely in their power. Now they could even come out boldly with their real charge against Jesus, which until now they had kept carefully concealed. "We have a law,[56] and according to that law He ought to die because He has made Himself the Son of God."

23
"Where Are You From?"
Jn 19:8–11

What was that? "Son of God"? When Pilate heard these words, terror filled his superstitious soul. Immediately, he left the howling multitude and took Jesus with him to the interior of his headquarters. There he asked Him with a mixture of awe and terror: "Where are You from?" For the fourth time since the trial began, Jesus retired into majestic silence.[57] We can but guess at the purpose. He could not say that He was not the Son of God. And in this connection, to have said that He was would have been interpreted by Pilate in a grossly pagan sense.[58] So, He said nothing. Besides, it was too late now. Pilate had heard enough. Almost angrily, he broke out: "You will not speak to me? Do You not know that I have authority to release You and authority to crucify You?" But Jesus soon set him straight on this point. Talk about power! In reality, he had none except the governmental powers given to him from above. And he should be very careful not to abuse this power. Of course, he had been compelled to conduct this trial; yet he would not be excused for the miscarriage of justice. He would still be guilty, although the prosecutors, Caiaphas— "he who delivered Me over to you"—and the members of the Council, had "the greater sin." Thus with "infinite dignity and yet with infinite tenderness did Jesus judge His judge,"[59] who just a few minutes before had given Him over to be tortured.

24
"Behold Your King!"
Jn 19:12–15

Pilate returned. He was still intent upon releasing the Prisoner. For the third[60] and last time since the beginning of that memorable trial on that early Good Friday morning, from about 6 to 7 a.m.,[61] Pilate ascended the tribunal erected on the pavement called Gabbatha. This time, he was determined to carry out his purpose at all hazards. A crisis had come, and the frantic rioters could plainly see that there was fire in his eyes. But in his speech, he never got beyond his opening words. For once, he was willing to assent to their guilty and ill-concealed royalistic aspirations. "Behold your King!" But again he failed. For once, the enemies of Rome would not have their disloyalty to the dearly beloved government of Rome flung into their face! Loyalty? Patriotism? Why, they even threatened Pilate with his! "If you release this man, you are not Caesar's friend. Everyone who makes himself a king opposes Caesar." Pilate could not take Jesus' side and retain Caesar's friendship. This was plain language. "Shall I crucify your King?" The reply is: "We have no king but Caesar." If Tiberius had only heard this! How was that for patriotism as coming from that hotbed of insurrection? That settled it for Pilate, for the priests, for the people, for one and for all. Nothing would stop the crucifixion now. That *was* the last straw. "If you release this man, you are not Caesar's friend." At the terrible name of Caesar, Pilate trembled. At all events, there must be no complaint lodged against him in Rome. Rather the loss of an innocent life, yes, a thousand lives, than the loss of Caesar's friendship. And what about that hypocritical loyalty to Caesar? "We have no king but Caesar." Indeed, how true! Pilate took them at their word; henceforth they would have no Savior, no Redeemer, no Friend, no King—but Caesar!

35

FRIDAY OF PASSION WEEK

"CRUCIFIED"

April 3, AD 33

AUC	782	783	784	785	786
AD	29	30	31	32	33
Approx. Age of Jesus	30	31	32	33	34
Passovers		I	II	III	IV

Nisan (or Abib)							
9	10	11	12	13	14	15	16
March			April				
29	30	31	1	2	3	4	5
Sun.	Mon.	Tues.	Wed.	Thu.	Fri.	Sat.	Sun

Jesus' trial was over. The death warrant was signed. Once more, the Savior was "unrobed and robed."[1] The mock purple was torn from His wounded shoulders, and with the order "*Ibis ad crucem!* Away to the cross!" or some similar phrase,[2] Jesus was immediately led away. Crucifixion was not a Jewish mode of punishment. In Rome, it became deplorably common after the time of Julius Caesar. It particularly seems to have characterized the government of Rome in Judea. Rome had a merciful law that required two to ten days to pass between a capital sentence and its execution; but either it did not extend to the provinces, or it did not apply to Jesus "because He had made Himself king."[3] Because of the approaching Passover Sabbath, there was no time to be lost. The terrible preparations, the cross, the hammer, and the

1
Jesus Led to
the Cross
Mt 27:31b;
Mk 15:20b;
Lk 23:26a;
Jn 19:16–17a

nails were soon made. Naturally, the Roman soldiers were in charge. According to all appearances, it was a perfectly proper public Roman execution. As always, the cross was carried to the place of execution by Him who was to suffer on it. The procession was led by a centurion[4] and preceded by one who carried an inscription proclaiming the nature of the crime. The cross itself appears in varied form. As an instrument of torture, it first was a single pole (|), the *crux simplex*, after which it assumed the following forms: the so-called St. Andrew's cross (X), the *crux decussata*; the Egyptian, or St. Anthony's, cross (T), the *crux commissa*; the later Greek cross (+), the *crux quandrata*; and the Latin cross (†), or *crux immissa*.[5] It was the latter on which, we believe, the Savior died.[6] This form would most readily permit the threefold inscription of the accusation on the cross to be attached above Jesus' head.

2
The Via Dolorosa

Jesus is now on His way to be crucified. In modern Jerusalem, there is a street—running roughly northeast to southwest, from the castle Antonia on the northwestern corner of the temple complex to the Church of the Holy Sepulcher—that is said to be the authentic Via Dolorosa ("Way of Sorrows") along which the procession passed. But many investigators doubt this. We must remember that ancient Jerusalem, even more than ancient Rome, is buried beneath the rubbish of centuries.[7] We begin with our assumption that Jesus was buried outside of the present city walls and somewhere near the traditional holy sepulcher. If the praetorium where Jesus stood trial before Pilate was at Herod's palace, as we take it, the way to the crucifixion site ran north and south and not roughly east and west. But, of course, if the praetorium is to be identified with the castle Antonia (which many refuse to admit), then the street ran southwest along the traditional way. One problem with the traditional site of Christ's crucifixion and death, over which the Church of the Holy Sepulcher is built, is that it lies inside the present walls. This does not agree with the requirement that Jesus, condemned as a criminal, had to, and did, suffer crucifixion outside the city gates (Lv 24:14; Nu 15:35–36; Dt 17:5; Jn 19:17; Mt 28:11; Heb 13:12). But this argument is met with the claim that at the time, the place was outside the walls. The opinions are about equally divided. There are also those who place the site of the crucifixion to the south, across the Valley of Hinnom. But there is a rapidly growing agreement that the place was on the northern end of the temple hill, near the Damascus Gate, and outside the city wall. On the southern face of this hill, there are holes in the rock, making it look much like a skull. This place at least fulfills all conditions,[8] but after all, it does not matter. The important consideration is not the place, but the cause and purpose of Christ's death and the truth of His resurrection. The straining endeavors of ages have found locations for a number of events that are said to have taken place on the Via Dolorosa: the place where the fainting Jesus made an impression with His shoulder in the stone wall when He fell; the house of St. Veronica, who wiped Jesus' bleeding brow with a handkerchief; and the like.[9] We can discard these incidents as later disturbing embellishments. Two incidents, however, are recorded in the Gospel history as having occurred on the way to the cross.

It will be readily understood that Jesus, after the agony and tortures of a sleepless night, collapsed under the load of the cross.[10] Even if pity did not move the Roman soldiers, they naturally would object to hindrance and delay. They helped themselves out of the difficulty by making a military requisition. An inhabitant of Cyrene, a city in North Africa, south of Crete, who presumably was in Jerusalem on a Passover pilgrimage[11] and at the moment was coming into the city from the country, was pressed into service and compelled to bear Christ's cross. His name was Simon, and afterwards, most likely on account of his Christian connection, he was familiarly known to Mark and other Christians as the father of Alexander and Rufus.[12] But there can be little doubt that the connection of the whole family with the Christian Church was the result of this incident in the father's life.

> **3**
> Simon of Cyrene
> Mt 27:32; Mk 15:21;
> Lk 23:26b

While Jesus was betrayed by Judas, denied by Peter, forsaken by the disciples, accused by false witnesses, condemned by the Council, struck by the servants, reviled by Herod, lashed by the soldiers, sentenced by Pilate—all men—He was now lamented by at least one section of the community. We have not forgotten the part that women played in the denials of Peter, but it is quite significant that there is no instance in the Gospel records of women being directly hostile toward Jesus. Women followed Him, served Him, remembered His sayings, sat at His feet, called after Him, ministered to Him out of their substance, washed His feet with tears, anointed His head with oil, testified to His innocence during His trial, stood under His cross, and later went to embalm His body. And now, while their husbands, brothers, and fathers were hounding Him to death, they bewailed and lamented Him.[13] All this, of course, is a strong testimony to Jesus' character as well as a credit to the so-called weaker sex. Yet, though women were, and still are, some of the most faithful followers of Jesus, and though their tears were natural and in some respects a genuine expression of their sympathy, Jesus would have none of them. Mere sympathy with the condemned Christ almost certainly involves a presumption that He was guilty. And shedding tears without repentance implies a view of Him and His Passion that is essentially the opposite of what His innocent suffering for us sinners should create in us. The weeping of those women was at best an emotional outburst. Turning to them, Jesus says, "Daughters of Jerusalem, do not weep for Me, but weep for yourselves and for your children." He warns them of the wrath that awaits them and their children and their race. When the day of punishment will come to strike an impenitent race, it will strike men, women, and children alike. In those days, childlessness will be a blessing and barrenness an advantage. "Blessed are the barren and the wombs that never bore and the breasts that never nursed!" So

> **4**
> The Lamentation
> of the Daughters
> of Jerusalem
> Lk 23:27-31

terrible will be the affliction of those days that the people will call upon the mountains and hills to fall upon them to hide them from the wrath of almighty God. "Then they will begin to say to the mountains, 'Fall on us,' and to the hills, 'Cover us' " (cf. Hos 10:8; Is 2:19). For if such terrible punishment as they are now about to witness is administered upon One who is Himself innocent, but upon whom the Lord has laid the iniquity of us all that He might atone for the sins of the world, what will happen to the guilty if they themselves are exposed to the burning fire of the wrath of God? "For if they do these things when the wood is green, what will happen when it is dry?"

5
The Arrival at Golgotha
Mt 27:33; Mk 15:22;
Lk 23:32–33a;
Jn 19:17b[14]

At this point, we are informed that there were also two others, criminals, led[15] with Jesus to be put to death. They were rebels and thugs of the lowest character. As far as the Romans were concerned, it was all in a day's work. There were always prisoners on hand, robbers, bandits, and—as dissatisfaction toward the powers that be grew—especially those who rebelled against the government of Rome.[16] If the crowds had not chosen him, no doubt Barabbas would also have been included in the procession. It is true that Pilate had been more than usually interested in the case of Jesus. But, after all, He was only one of many. His execution could be made part of that of other victims scheduled for the day. And so it happened that three condemned prisoners were marched out to the fatal spot. It was called Golgotha, or, in its Latin form, Calvary—that is, The Skull. Whether or not it had received its name from the fact that it was the usual execution ground, we do not know. Presumably it was called this on account of its skull-like shape. It is constantly referred to as the hill of Golgotha or Mount Calvary, though the Gospels speak of it merely as a place. While we picture it off the highway to the north of Jerusalem, just outside the Damascus or St. Stephen's Gate, near Jeremiah's Grotto, nothing definite is known. All that we know of Golgotha, and all that God willed us to know, is that it was outside the city gate (Heb 13:12). The representation in pictures of a skull at the foot of the cross refers to an old legend that the cross of Jesus rested on Adam's grave.[17]

6
The Myrrh Mingled Cup
Mt 27:34; Mk 15:23

It was a merciful custom to give those led to crucifixion a medicated cup of sour wine mixed with some narcotic like wormwood or myrrh to deaden consciousness. This charitable practice is said to have been performed at the cost of wealthy ladies in Jerusalem.[18] The intoxicating potion was probably freely taken by the two criminals. It was offered also to Jesus. But as soon as He had tasted it and noticed its character and the purpose for which it was offered Him, He would not drink of it. Just as He declined the tears of the daughters of Jerusalem, so He now refused their cup. He preferred "to look death straight in the face."

7
Crucified
Mt 27:35a, 38;
Mk 15:24a, 27;
Lk 23:33b–34a;
Jn 19:18

"And when they had crucified Him"—this is the way one evangelist, and the other three in an equally passing manner, relate the terrible deed. We turn our heads in horror as the huge nails "tear their way through the quivering flesh."[19] It was a terrible death. "Let it never," says Cicero,[20] "come near the body of a Roman citizen; nay, not even near his thoughts or eyes or ears!" As a method of dispatching condemned criminals from life to death, it was a most inhuman means of execution. Its only purpose must have been to strike horror into the hearts of witnesses, to torture the victims, and to make death as painful and lingering as was humanly endurable. The crosses were erected so that the cross of Jesus was reared in the middle, and those of the criminals were placed one on the right hand and the other on the left. Thus was the prophecy of Isaiah fulfilled that "He was numbered with the transgressors" (Is 53:9, 12; Lk 22:37; Mk 15:28[21]). And in the midst of this infinite horror, a voice cries out; it was not a cry of agony, as might have been expected, nor a cursing scream, but a fervent petition of the suffering Savior for His enemies, His first word on the cross: "Father, forgive them, for they know not what they do."

Mark informs us that Jesus' crucifixion took place at the third hour, that is, nine o'clock in the morning.[22] According to Roman custom, the clothes of the unrobed victims were divided among the four squads of soldiers (Ac 12:4) whose duty it was to guard each of the crosses. This precaution was taken to prevent the possibility of rescuing the crucified. In the last Jewish war, Josephus requested that Titus allow three men who had been crucified to be taken down alive. But in spite of all possible efforts to save them, two of them died.[23] The soldiers at the cross of Jesus decided to divide His headgear, outer garment, belt, and sandals among themselves. But for the more valuable seamless inner garment, or *chiton*, which was woven in one piece from top to bottom, they decided to cast lots. If they tore it, they would have ruined it. "Let us not tear it," they said to each other, "but cast lots for it to see whose it shall be." We do not know how this was done, probably by casting dice. Without realizing it, they perfectly fulfilled a Scripture prophecy: "They divided My garments among them, and for My clothing they cast lots" (Ps 22:18).[24]

An inscription was placed above each of the crosses stating the charge for which the sufferers had been condemned. The title could be plainly seen, and it was indeed read by many because the crosses were conspicuously placed off the highway and near the city. In the case of Jesus, the title, it seems, had been drawn up under the special direction of Pilate. It ran in the three languages of the ancient civilized world. One of these was certain to be known to everyone in the assembled multitude: local Hebrew, or Aramaic, the common language of the Eastern world; popular Greek, the language of culture throughout the Roman Empire; and official Latin, the language of camp and court. The title was supposed to state the charge, but at the same time it made public a sacred truth: JESUS OF NAZARETH, THE KING OF THE JEWS.[25] Officially, Jesus was crucified as a rebel, the judicial verdict being that He was executed because He had made Himself king of the Jews. But as the chief priests and leading Jews studied the superscription, it suddenly occurred to them that in

8
The Parting of
Christ's Garments
Mt 27:35b;
Mk 15:24b–25;
Lk 23:34b;
Jn 19:23–24

9
I.N.R.I
Mt 27:37;
Mk 15:26;
Lk 23:38;
Jn 19:19–22

using this particular wording in the charge against Jesus, Pilate and the Roman government were really heaping an insult upon the Jewish nation. King of the Jews? And crucified? It was as clear as day that Pilate and Rome were serving public notice that this is what would happen to everyone who would become a Jewish king. Why this insult? Had they not that very day professed their loyalty to Rome? And besides, they had not even acknowledged Jesus as their king! Immediately, they rushed to Pilate and demanded a change in the obnoxious title. "Do not write, 'The King of the Jews,' but rather 'This man said, I am King of the Jews.' " A slight change, but still in agreement with Pilate's sentence and—understanding "King" as the "Messiah" and "Son of God"—in accordance with the finding of the Jewish court. But this was Pilate's chance to get even with them for having forced him that morning to act against his will. His courage, which had so rapidly melted away at the mention of Caesar, had now returned. He dismissed the priestly notables with a curt and contemptuous reply: "What I have written I have written." And Jesus was indeed in the true sense the King of the Jews, the promised Messiah, and the Son of God.

10
Mocked and Ridiculed by Passersby
Mt 27:39–44;
Mk 15:29–32;
Lk 23:35–37, 39[26]

The people stood there and gazed. But some of them, probably some of the many false witnesses of the previous night, as they passed by the cross, ridiculed Jesus, wagged their heads (Ps 22:7), and said: "You who would destroy the temple and rebuild it in three days, save Yourself! If You are the Son of God, come down from the cross." Likewise the scribes, chief priests, elders, and rulers were not ashamed to disgrace themselves with taunting cries: "He saved others; He cannot save Himself. He is the King of Israel; let Him come down now from the cross, and we will believe in Him. He trusts in God [Ps 22:8]; let God deliver Him now, if He desires Him. For He said, 'I am the Son of God.' " If these unholy priests did not consider it beneath their dignity to heap insults upon a silently suffering and dying man, no wonder that the soldiers, probably as they sat down to their midday lunch, in coarse brutality drank to Him as they gulped down their cheap sour wine and even mockingly asked Him to pledge them in return (Lk 23:36).[27] It was the basest mockery of His royalty when they flung at Him the taunt: "If You are the King of the Jews, save Yourself!" Yes, even the poor wretches who were crucified with Him joined in this shameful abuse. Reproachfully, they demanded Him to save Himself and them if He were really the Christ.

11
The Penitent Thief
Lk 23:39–43

The priests, the scribes, the rulers, the soldiers, and, as a class, even the robbers on the cross joined in the mockery of Jesus. But there was an exception. One of the criminals, whom tradition remembers as Dysmas, first joined in the ridicule, but soon the Spirit of God worked in him a true and sincere sorrow of heart on account of his sins. Turning to the other criminal, whom tradition has given the name Gestas,[28] the "good robber"[29] rebuked him for his blasphemous remarks: "Do you not fear God, since you are under the same sentence of condemnation?" And then followed the wonderful confession: "And we indeed justly, for we are receiving the due reward of our deeds; but this man has done nothing wrong." These words are a testimony to the innocence of Jesus and also a dying thief's confession of faith in the crucified Christ, for he adds, "Jesus, remember me when You come into[30] Your kingdom." In spite of death, You are going to Your kingdom, and may I go there to be with You at the resurrection of the dead! To this intense appeal, the Lord replies, "Truly, I say to you, today"—not tomorrow or the following day or on the Last Day, at My second coming, but today—"you will be with Me in paradise."[31] Death is a door through which he must pass; but as to his soul, his last day upon earth is to be his first day in heaven.

Many voices were raised to mock Jesus, and still there were hearts in the crowd that painfully beat in sympathy and deepest sorrow. Conspicuous among this heart-stricken group were the women who had followed Jesus from Galilee (Mt 27:55). While the disciples were in hiding, at least most of them, these women followers exposed themselves to attack and shame. First of all, there was the mother of Jesus, the Virgin Mary, a sword now passing through her soul at this horrible sight (Lk 2:35). Then there was Salome (Mk 15:40; Mt 27:56), the sister of Mary. It is quite consistent for John to refer to this second member of the small congregation under the cross of Jesus, his own mother Salome, only indirectly as "His mother's sister"; for in speaking of himself, he never mentions his name and even does not mention his brother.[32] The third member of the group is Mary, the wife of Clopas, or, as we suppose, Alphaeus, the brother of Joseph.[33] And, besides John, the reporter, Mary Magdalene, out of whom the Lord had cast out seven demons (Lk 8:2),[34] completes the group.[35] If our identification is correct, then not only Salome, the sister of Mary, but also Mary, the wife of Clopas, Joseph's brother, would in a certain sense have been the aunts of Jesus and their sons His cousins. Thus we notice among the twelve apostles five cousins of the Lord: James and John, the sons of Salome and Zebedee; and the three sons of Alphaeus, or Clopas, and Mary—James, Judas, and Simon. Jesus was filled with loving concern for His own even in death. When His eye fell upon His mother and the disciple "whom He loved," He entrusted His mother to him as a sacred charge. "Woman,"[36] He said to her, "behold, your son!" Henceforth John was to take His place as a providing son. And to John, He said, "Behold, your mother!" If John was His mother's nephew, as we feel confident he was, then it was only natural that Jesus would entrust her to him rather than to one of the sons of His foster-father's brother. The charge was accepted. Immediately, John led her away from this scene of unutterable horror to the shelter of his home.[37] Except the notice that Mary continued with the early Christians in Jerusalem in prayer and supplication (Ac 1:14), this really completes the story of Mary, the mother of Jesus. A few hours later, we do not find her with the group consisting of Mary Magdalene; Mary,

12
Jesus Commends
His Mother to John
Jn 19:25–27

the mother of James and Joses; Salome, the mother of James and John; and other women, "looking on from a distance" (Mt 27:55–56; Mk 15:40–41).

It was high noon by this time, and now an unnatural darkness swept over the guilty world. It cannot have been an ordinary eclipse of the sun because of the full Passover moon.[39] Neither was it a sandstorm, for it was a darkness[40] as if the sun were actually eclipsed,[41] without the phenomenon of the moon passing in front of the sun. The darkness continued from the sixth to the ninth hour,[42] from noon until three o'clock, and extended, if not over the whole earth, at least far over Judea and adjoining lands. Scripture tells us nothing about the last three dark hours. "The awful darkness of the bright noonday sun in spring may well have overawed every heart into an inaction respecting which there was nothing to say."[43]

It was as if the voice of heaven were making itself heard through nature. A silent gloom made it appear as if even the earth and the sun were bewailing the disgraceful death of the Son of God. Jesus drank the deepest dregs of the cup of humiliation and sank into the "fathomless depth of suffering, into which we cannot enter."[44] It was a suffering beyond all human endurance; it was possible for Him to endure it only because He is the Son of God. At the end of the third hour, He broke the silence He had maintained during that dread darkness by bursting forth into that awful, mysterious cry: "*Eli, Eli, lema sabachthani?*" that is, "My God, My God, why have You forsaken Me?" (Ps 22:1). The Suffering Savior was made to feel the full weight of the sins of the world. Even God, whom in the last fearful moments of His extreme agony He addressed in His own familiar Aramaic, had forsaken Him. God forsaken by God! It is a mystery that eternity alone will solve. Christ felt the full measure of the wrath of God against sin and all the pain and anguish of hell deserved by every sinner. But He did not despair. Nor did He succumb. There was strength and glory in His suffering. This can be inferred from His very words, a quotation from a prophecy that contains a picture of His whole Passion, from extreme distress to supreme glory at the completion of the work of redemption. It was in His most intense anguish that His thoughts turned to that great messianic psalm, the twenty-second, which begins with a cry of deepest agony and ends in praise.

Amid the darkness and the muffled noise of the milling mass, the words were not understood. Even if they had been, they would have been misunderstood. Some, very likely catching only the first word of the cry, thought that Jesus was calling upon Elijah for help. And indeed, from their standpoint, it did seem as if the forerunner of the great and terrible day of Jehovah (Mal 4:5) were in some way connected with this marvelous phenomenon. At the very moment, the bright spring sun was shrouded in an impervious dark veil. According to a view held at that time, Elijah's coming again was intricately mingled with the coming of the Messiah. So revelations of divine wrath were to be expected. "The sun shall be turned to darkness, and the moon to blood, before the great and awesome day of the LORD comes" (Jl 2:31). The heavens would come down and touch the mountains, and in some awful form, Elijah—who went up by a whirlwind into heaven (2Ki 2:11)—would make his reappearance, riding upon pillars of smoke; or something similar would happen. Of course, these vague anticipations were unfulfilled. Both Elijah (Mt 11:14; Mk 9:13) and the Messiah had already come. And the latter was at that very moment hanging on the cross.

At the cry of Jesus, someone thinking to help ran to the vessel containing the posca, or sour wine, of the Roman soldiers. The mouth of the vessel was filled with a sponge, which served as a cork.[45] It was probably also at this moment that Jesus, "knowing that all was now finished," in order that the Scripture, a word of prophecy (Ps 69:3, 21), might be fulfilled, broke into His only cry expressing physical suffering: "I thirst." Instantly, the sponge soaked up the wine, was placed upon the end of a hyssop reed,[46] and was raised to the parched lips of the dying Savior. But even this simple act of pity, which Jesus did not refuse, was the occasion of mocking remarks. All right! Let Him be refreshed! they said. "Wait, let us see whether Elijah will come to take Him down." It seems that even he who performed the act of mercy joined the rest in uttering these unloving words (Mk 15:36).

Elijah did not come! There was no *deus ex machina*,[47] no Elijah, no angel, no deliverer! It was the will of God that the Savior should drink the cup and be made perfect through sufferings (Heb 2:10). Jesus had taken the drink, not on account of a phony thirst for the sake of fulfilling an old prophecy; on the contrary, a real need contributed to a true fulfillment. Afterward, Jesus announced to the world the completion of His work. It was not the gasp of a dying man, but as a proclamation of victory, Jesus uttered the exultant cry: "It is finished." Finished was His suffering for the sins of mankind, finished was His redeeming work! All the things that were written in the Old Testament Scriptures concerning the Messiah were now fulfilled (Lk 24:44; Ac 3:18). The nearly unending mockery and endless shame were at an end at last. All things were now accomplished. The battle had been fought, the serpent had been crushed, sin had been conquered, redemption was effected, and the walls of separation between man and God were removed.

And then, once more crying out with a loud voice, not in the manner of a dying man,[48] with the words of a psalm on His lips (Ps 31:5), the Savior commended His spirit into the hands of God. "Father, into Your hands I commit My spirit!" Death did not come to Jesus, but Jesus came to Death.[49] Even as He had come forth from the Father and gone into the world, so He here for "a little while" (Jn 16:16) cut Himself off from physical life and went to the Father.

16
"I Thirst!"
Mt 27:48–49;
Mk 15:36;
Jn 19:28–29

17
"It Is Finished"
Jn 19:30a

18
"Father, into Your Hands I Commit My Spirit"
Mt 27:50a;
Mk 15:37a;
Lk 23:46a

36

FRIDAY OF PASSION WEEK

"DEAD AND BURIED"

April 3, AD 33

AUC		782	783	784	785	786
AD		29	30	31	32	33
Approx. Age of Jesus		30	31	32	33	34
Passovers			I	II	III	IV

Nisan (or Abib)							
9	10	11	12	13	14	15	16
March			April				
29	30	31	1	2	3	4	5
Sun.	Mon.	Tues.	Wed.	Thu.	Fri.	Sat.	Sun

With these words, the evangelists describe the death of the Savior. They do not use the word *died*, which would describe a passive condition, but instead use a phrase that distinctly asserts an act. Indeed, the Savior died. "O sorrow dread! Our God is dead" (*LSB* 448:2). It was a true death in every respect. But at the same time, Christ's death was a voluntary resignation of His life in accordance with His own words: "I lay down My life that I may take it up again. No one takes it from Me, but I lay it down of My own accord. . . . I have authority to take it up again" (Jn 10:17–18). It was a distinctly voluntary sacrificial act, but still it was death. Indeed, there is real sorrow when a noble life is softly and peacefully pillowed in death; but there never was such a pitiful sight as when this great Sufferer, whose life had been spent

1
"And Gave Up His Spirit"
Mt 27:50b;
Mk 15:37b;
Lk 23:46b;
Jn 19:30b

in perfect obedience to His Father's will and in loving service of man and who suffered and died for the redemption of sinful mankind, bowed His head on the cross. Dead. But He died that we might live.

Strange phenomena attended the death of Christ. "Behold, the curtain of the temple was torn in two, from top to bottom." This is the first event spoken of because it was most significant, especially to Israel. The curtain was the veil that separated the holy from the Most Holy Place in the temple. It was made "of blue and purple and scarlet yarns and fine twined linen" (Ex 26:31). From a rabbinic source, we learn that its dimensions were sixty by thirty feet and that it was of the thickness of a palm. In the exaggerated language of the time, it was so heavy that it required three hundred priests to handle it.[2] This veil was now torn in two, exposing the Most Holy Place to the common eye. Here was a clear indication that the Old Testament with its high priests and exemplifying sacrifices was now a thing of the past. There was now no more need of an intervening screen and mediating high priests; for by virtue of the atoning blood of Christ, all sinners have free access to the throne of God (Heb 9:8–15; 10:20). The tearing of the curtain must have taken place about the time when the priests in the temple were making preparations for their evening sacrifice. How it happened we do not know. But all of a sudden, the priests were able to gaze into that awful emptiness of the most holy enclosure into which previously the high priest alone had been permitted to enter, and that but once a year. For a priest to gaze on the dwelling place of God without special rights must have seemed a terrible sign. Indeed, we are told of strange omens that appeared forty years before the destruction of Jerusalem. The mysterious extinction of the chief light in the golden lampstand, the supernatural opening of the great temple gates by themselves, and the shattering of a vast beam over a temple threshhold[3] may have been distorted versions of the strange phenomena attending the death of Christ.

And there were other signs. "The earth shook, and the rocks were split." As a result, graves were opened, and dead bodies of departed saints returned to life. This does not mean that in the confusion of an unnatural darkness, to which was added the terror of an earthquake, bewildered minds imagined that they saw the disimprisoned spirits of the dead, as some have proposed. There was an actual restoration to life of departed saints. Through His death, Christ "abolished death and brought life and immortality to light" (2Tm 1:10). The evangelists do not state who these were. Whether they had recently died or had been long dead does not matter. "Many bodies of the saints who had fallen asleep were raised, and coming out of the tombs after His resurrection[4] they went into the holy city and appeared to many." In spite of its monstrous wickedness, Jerusalem was still called the "holy city" (Is 48:2; 52:1; Ne 11:1; Mt 4:5)[5] because it harbored the temple of God. Of these resurrected saints, nothing further is known.

The long darkness, the loud voice, the Savior's sudden death, and the earthquake were not without effect. The leader of the executioners and of the Roman guard, the centurion, whom tradition remembers as Longinus,[6] now came forward with a wonderful confession. He must have seen many sad scenes of horror in his day—it was a cold and an inhuman age—but none like this. It is assumed that he had witnessed all, from the trial before Pilate, probably even from the arrest in the garden, to the end. He could only arrive at one conclusion. Jesus was not guilty, even as Pilate had repeatedly stated, and He was actually what He professed to be, the profession for which He was condemned. "Certainly this man was innocent"[7] and "the Son of God."[8] It was a Christian confession, and it was the truth. And not only the centurion was impressed, but also "those who were with him, keeping watch over Jesus," the Roman guards, who had previously derided Jesus, "were filled with awe" and joined in the confession. Likewise all of the crowds, when they saw what had taken place, returned home beating their breasts. We may hope that as a result, many of them afterward embraced the Christian faith.

Only a small congregation of faithful followers remained. "All His acquaintances" who followed Him from Galilee stood far off. But only women followers are named, such as had ministered to Him and followed Him from Galilee to Jerusalem. Among these was Mary Magdalene. Then there was Mary, the mother of James the younger and Joses.[9] Also Salome, the wife of Zebedee and mother of James and John. And there were others. Mary, the mother of Jesus, who appeared with Salome and the two Marys—the wife of Clopas and Mary Magdalene—under the cross (Jn 19:25), is not mentioned. It is assumed that John, who is silent at this point, had removed her from this scene of horror and himself left the cross for a few minutes after Jesus had committed His mother to John's charge.

As the darkness receded from the completed sacrifice on Calvary, the reappearing April sun was fast approaching the evening of the Sabbath, which began at six o'clock. In general, there was a law that the body of a criminal should not be left hanging unburied overnight (Dt 21:23). And now, since it was the Day of Preparation, that is, Friday, and the next day was both a Sabbath and the second Paschal Day and therefore a high day and the day when the sheaf of the firstfruits of the harvest was waved as an offering to the Lord (Lv 23:11–14),[10] there was all the more reason to have the corpses removed. Those who had not considered the murder of the Messiah a defilement of the Passover were now concerned about the sanctity of the Passover Sabbath. Official application was therefore made to Pilate for an order to have the legs of the crucified victims broken and their bodies taken down. Ordinarily, according to Roman custom, the bodies would have decayed on the cross. And if the bodies were taken down, precaution was taken by means of the so-called crurifragium (the breaking of the legs) to make sure the crucified were not

4
"Truly This Was the Son of God!"
Mt 27:54; Mk 15:39;
Lk 23:47–48

5
The Women Followers
Mt 27:55–56;
Mk 15:40–41;
Lk 23:49

6
The Breaking of the Bones
Jn 19:31–33

still alive when their bodies were taken down. Now, crucifixion was a slow death, the sufferers living at least twelve, sometimes as long as forty-eight hours before death set in. Thus by means of a club or hammer, followed probably, as some think,[11] by the stroke of a sword or the thrust of a spear, an end was quickly put to what remained of life. Pilate had no objection to the request and therefore granted it. The soldiers came, probably from both sides, and broke the legs of the criminals first; but when they came to Jesus, they found that He had already died. Unwittingly, they observed a regulation of the Passover lamb (Ex 12:46; Nu 9:12), which pointed to Jesus, and contributed to the fulfillment of a prophecy: "Not one of His bones will be broken" (Ps 34:20).

7
The Spear Thrust
Jn 19:34–37

But in order to make certain of the death of Jesus, one of the soldiers forced the head of his spear into His side. "At once," says St. John, attesting the truthfulness of his account, "there came out blood and water." This puzzling outpouring has caused much discussion.[12] It is said that this phenomenon would naturally take place, but only if a crucified person died of a rupture to the heart. But it is best not to make an attempt at a physiological explanation. Why speak of the physical cause of the death of Christ? What happens and ordinarily does not happen with corpses can hardly be applied to the sacred and uncorrupted (Ps 16:10) body of Christ. John himself offers no explanation. He merely stresses the remarkable fact, assures the reader that his is a truthful account, and points to a fulfillment of Scripture: "They will look on Him whom they have pierced" (Zec 12:10). "He who saw it has borne witness—his testimony is true, and he knows that he is telling the truth—that you also may believe." Quite naturally, the passage lends itself to symbolical interpretation. From the lacerated side of Jesus there springs forth the cleansing water and the redeeming blood (Jn 7:38; 1Jn 1:7). The beautiful saying has come down from the Fathers that from the side of Jesus, as from the open door to life, has flowed the Holy Sacraments of the Church.[13] At any rate, there is no doubt that Jesus truly died.[14]

8
Joseph of Arimathea
Mt 27:57–58a;
Mk 15:42–43;
Lk 23:50–52;
Jn 19:38a

For the present, the members of the Council were not concerned about the burial of Jesus. As long as His dead body was removed from the cross so as not to defile the land (Dt 21:22–23), especially in this sacred season, they would have been satisfied if together with the bodies of the criminals it had been cast into some nameless grave. But someone else was interested in His burial, one whose strange attention in the matter could not be easily brushed aside. On that memorable pre-Sabbath afternoon, one of their aristocratic associates came out boldly before Pilate and "asked for the body of Jesus." His name was Joseph of Arimathea. The place from which he came, a Jewish city, is otherwise unknown.[15] He was a man of wealth and high character and a distinguished member of the Council of Jerusalem. In the trial of Jesus, he had not consented to the Council's wicked decision, he himself looking for the kingdom of God. In fact, he was a secret disciple, but before this had failed to openly profess his faith on account of his fear of the Jews. But now, in a bold declaration of his love, he asked for permission to bury the body of Jesus.

Two things must have curiously impressed Pilate. In the first place, that this man of position, whom an apocryphal Gospel[16] even calls a "friend of Pilate," should make this request. Did he not belong to those very religious leaders who had so urgently insisted upon the death of Christ? And in the second place, Pilate was astonished that Jesus was already dead. Calling the centurion, he asked him "whether He was already dead." The centurion assured him that Jesus was certainly dead; for otherwise he and his guard would still be out there watching the crosses. And when Pilate had learned that all was in order, he immediately assigned the body of Jesus, probably with some degree of satisfaction, to this "respected member of the council" (Mk 15:43).

9
Pilate Gives Permission to Bury Jesus
Mt 27:58b;
Mk 15:44–45;
Jn 19:38b

The time was growing short. Joseph wasted no time; while he still had a chance, he purchased a long, fine piece of linen cloth before the shops closed. And immediately another man came forward. We have met him before, another member of that distinguished body that had passed sentence upon Jesus. It was none other than the Pharisee who had come to Jesus by night—Nicodemus (Jn 3:1).[17] It was he who at a later time had asked the unholy plotters: "Does our law judge a man without first giving him a hearing and learning what he does?" (Jn 7:50–51). If he was present at the trial of Jesus, we may hope that he likewise dissented from the death sentence. He made his appearance with a costly compound of myrrh and aloes (Ps 45:8) for embalming Jesus. The supply was bountiful, "about seventy-five pounds in weight,"[18] testifying both to his riches[19] and to the great measure of his love of Jesus.

10
Nicodemus
Mk 15:46a;
Jn 19:38c–39

Whether these two Jewish dignitaries had previously been closely associated we do not know. But deeds of love and charity are in need of no introduction. Close by the place of crucifixion was[20] a court or garden belonging to Joseph. In this garden, he had a new and unused tomb, hewn out of the solid rock for his own future use, "where no one had ever yet been laid" and which therefore was fresh and clean. The Sabbath was so near at hand that the embalmment could be only temporary and hasty. Joseph and Nicodemus wrapped the limbs and body, from which the vital organs had not been removed, in the long strips of linen cloth with the spices, according to *Jewish* burial customs.[21] And likewise, a face cloth was wrapped around the head. The sun was sinking behind the western hills. As the Day of Preparation, that is, Friday, came to a close and Sabbath dawned,[22] they rolled a great stone in front of the entrance to the tomb and departed.

11
Jesus Laid in Joseph's Tomb
Mt 27:59–60;
Mk 15:46b;
Lk 23:53–54;
Jn 19:40–42

For the moment, nothing more could be done. Only a few of the faithful women who had followed Jesus from Galilee to Jerusalem remained in the neighborhood to see where His body was laid. They could hardly be expected to come forward when they observed that two distinguished members of the Council had

12
Women Followers Witness the Burial
Mt 27:61; Mk 15:47;
Lk 23:55

taken matters in hand. They noticed, however, that the body had not yet been properly and completely embalmed. Among them were the same women who have previously been mentioned:[23] Mary Magdalene and the other Mary—the wife of Alphaeus, or Clopas, and the mother of James and Joses (Mk 6:3; Mt 13:55)—and a few other women.

13
The Guard at the Tomb of Jesus
Mt 27:62–66;
Lk 23:56b

And now it was the Sabbath and time for rest—rest for all except the enemies of Christ. Because of their uneasy consciences, they were troubled with awful misgivings in spite of the Savior's death on the cross, especially since they had likely seen two of their own number attend to the burial of the slain Jesus of Nazareth. This aroused harassing suspicions within them. And there was no rest for Pilate either. From the standpoint of the Jewish recorder, it was already "the next day, that is, after the day of the Preparation." But according to our division of time, it was probably still the same day, that is, Good Friday, the evening of the Sabbath that had just begun. Again Pilate was disturbed by a delegation. Whatever else we might say about this representative of the power of Rome, it must be stated to his credit that at all hours of the day, he was on the job. From the early hours of the morning to late at night, he was in his office in the interest of a disliked *pax Romana* on this unthankful Palestinian soil. The relentless enemies of the slain Jesus were still persecuting the object of their unspent venom even after death. With a contemptuous reference to the unnamed object of their hatred, they said, "Sir, we remember how that imposter[24] said, while He was still alive, 'After three days I will rise'" (Mt 12:40). Of course, there was no danger of His returning to life, but the attempt might be made to supply a fictitious fulfillment of His prediction. "Order the tomb to be made secure until the third day, lest His disciples go and steal Him away and tell the people, 'He has risen from the dead,' and the last fraud will be worse than the first." In a contemptuous manner, Pilate gave them permission to do anything they liked in the matter. "You have a guard of soldiers.[25] Go, make it as secure as you can." A guard was placed at their disposal. The stone was sealed. This was probably done by stretching a cord across the stone at the mouth of the tomb and then fastening it to the rock on both ends by means of sealing clay.[26] And all precautions were taken to prevent theft—and resurrection.

14
Saturday
Mt 28:1; Mk 16:1;
Lk 23:56a

The disciples spent the next day, Saturday, in a sad and miserable silence. They were as a flock of scattered sheep whose shepherd had been slain. Not until late in the afternoon,[27] when the Jewish Sabbath verged on the first day of the week, that is, Saturday evening, did the two Marys—Mary Magdalene and the other Mary, the mother of James and Joses—venture out for a brief glimpse of the guarded grave, after which, together with Salome, they completed the purchase and preparation of spices and ointment for the task they intended to perform early the following day.

37

THE RISEN AND EXALTED SAVIOR

RESURRECTION TO ASCENSION

From Sunday, April 5 (Nisan 16), to Thursday, May 14, AD 33

APRIL, AD 33

Sun.	Mon.	Tue.	Wed.	Thur.	Fri.	Sat.
			1	2	3	4
5	6	7	8	9	10	11
12	13	14	15	16	17	18
19	20	21	22	23	24	25
26	27	28	29	30		

We have now arrived at the most important chapter of this book. If this chapter is not true, then all the rest might as well have been left unwritten. St. Paul says, "If Christ has not been raised, your faith is futile and you are still in your sins. Then those also who have fallen asleep in Christ have perished" (1Co 15:17–18). If the Christian religion applies only to this life, then those who profess it "are of all people most to be pitied" (v. 19). Then the Christian religion would have value only as a philosophy of life, and a sorry one at that, as compared with a looser moral standard, which would make the most out of enjoying material things. "Behold, these are the wicked; always at ease, they increase in riches" (Ps 73:12). Make a list of a half dozen of the most distinguished men living in the world today, and hardly one of them is distinguished for his Christian faith. "But in fact Christ has been raised from the dead" (1Co 15:20). The most comforting "but" in all Scripture. Everything depends on it, our hope of heaven, and from it everything follows. And

1
The Resurrection
of Jesus

since our faith is based upon the biblical account of Christ's resurrection, we can proceed with our story. We do not need to be ashamed of this faith either. Every honest and unprejudiced scholar has had to confess that the resurrection of Christ is a fact. Judged merely from the standpoint of authenticity, the Gospels have proven themselves thoroughly reliable and trustworthy records of history in every respect. The writer is here not quoting the opinion of others. This very book is the result of an extended and detailed study on the historicity of Jesus. But we cannot enter into the subject here. The whole life of Jesus is a proof of His resurrection. Then there is the transformation of the disciples at the outpouring of the Christ-sent Holy Spirit and the existence and preservation of the Christian Church.

2
The Earthquake and the Rolling Away of the Stone
Mt 28:2–4

Apparently the sealed and guarded grave of Jesus had been left undisturbed until the first faint streaks of that great Easter dawn. Even then, without thoughts of a possible resurrection of Him whom they loved, a group of pious mourners were on their way to do the last sad honors to a highly esteemed man. But in the meantime, wonderful things had happened at the grave of Christ. There was another earthquake, a great shaking of the earth, coinciding with an angel of the Lord coming down from heaven, who rolled away the stone and sat upon it as the guardian of an opened and empty grave. The appearance of his face was as lightning and his clothing as white as snow. At this dazzling appearance, the frightened and trembling guards became as dead men, and when they recovered from their fainting, they turned and fled.

3
Women Going to the Grave
Mk 16:2–4; Lk 24:1–2; Jn 20:1

It was very early on Easter Sunday morning, while it was still dark, when a band of grief-stricken followers left their quarters in Jerusalem or Bethany on their way to the tomb in order to complete the embalmment. These included Mary Magdalene; the other Mary, the mother of James; Salome; Joanna, the wife of Chuza (Lk 8:2–3),[1] and others, whose names have not passed into history but are recorded in the Book of Life. The grief-stricken mother of Jesus is not mentioned. Probably her very sorrow caused her to be left behind. It seems that Mary Magdalene played the same part among the women that Peter assumed among the men. For the moment, however, stormy Peter and the leaderless group were still in hiding. As this devoted band of women with their burden of precious spices made their way through the glimmering dawn, they anxiously asked among themselves: "Who will roll away the stone for us from the entrance of the tomb?" After all, they were only weak women, and the slab may have weighed from three to five hundred pounds. But as they approached the grave, probably as the first rays of the rising sun were breaking over their shoulders, they could see that the stone had already been rolled away. It was probably at this point, without going any farther and fearing the worst, that Mary Magdalene rushed back to inform Peter and John of what she had seen.

4
"Why Do You Seek the Living among the Dead?"
Mt 28:5–7; Mk 16:5–7; Lk 24:3–8

As the perplexed women pushed forward, they indeed found the stone removed, but, what was more, the grave was empty and the body gone. Moreover, looking up, they found that they were not alone. Luke tells us, "Two men[2] stood by them in dazzling apparel." They were struck with a nameless fear as they looked upon first one and then the other. The latter, who probably acted as spokesman, had apparently seated himself "on the right." Pointing to the empty tomb, he preached the first Christian Easter sermon. It concerned the dying Savior and the living Lord. "Why do you seek the living among the dead? He is not here, but has risen. Remember how He told you, while He was still in Galilee [Mk 8:31], that the Son of Man must be delivered into the hands of sinful men and be crucified and on the third day rise." And "See the place where they laid Him. But go, tell His disciples and Peter that He is going before you to Galilee. There you will see Him, just as He told you."

Trembling with fear and joy and probably forgetting all about the precious ointment that was no longer needed, the women fled from the tomb. They said nothing to anyone along the way because they were afraid. But before they reached the city, Jesus Himself met them and said, "Greetings!" Immediately, they "took hold of His feet and worshiped Him." They were overawed by His sudden appearance. But Jesus said, "Do not be afraid" and added what they had already heard from the angel: "Go and tell My brothers to go to Galilee, and there they will see Me." With their hearts and minds bursting with news of such paramount importance, they went to the Eleven[3] and to the circle of waiting friends. But to these the extremely strange news appeared as an idle tale.

By this time, Mary had already brought her report to Peter and John: "They have taken the Lord out of the tomb, and we[4] do not know where they have laid Him." For how else could she explain it? This startling news was too much for Peter and John. It caused them to run off at once. Now followed an extraordinary race to the grave of Christ. At first, the disciples ran together, side by side. But soon the younger and nimbler John outran Peter and won the race. He came first to the grave. But there he hesitated. He could not make up his mind to enter, but, stooping down and peeping in, he noticed the linen cloths that had been wound around Christ's body, but did not go in. By this time, the impulsive Peter had arrived. There was not a moment's hesitation. He entered and examined. And what he saw was significant. He saw the linen cloths lying there, but found that the face cloth that had been wrapped around Jesus' head was not with the other linen, but was lying by itself and was fallen together, as it were, in itself. Peter's remarkable discovery was communicated to John, who now entered and saw and believed. Just what did Peter see that caused him to wonder? What did John see and believe? What is there so significant about these linen cloths[5]—in three verses they are mentioned three times—that was to these disciples an indisputable proof that no one had removed Jesus' body, as Mary had feared, but rather that a resurrection had taken place?

5
Jesus Appears to the Women
Mt 28:8–10;
Mk 16:8; Lk 24:9–11

6
Peter and John Rush to the Grave of Christ
Lk 24:12;
Jn 20:2–10

7
The Linen Cloth and
the Face Cloth
Lk 24:12;
Jn 20:2–10

Most commentators of this passage satisfy themselves with the explanation that it was the *order* found in the grave that convinced the disciples that the body had not been stolen by friends nor removed by enemies, but that a resurrection had taken place. Without trying to force my views on others, the present writer is of the opinion that John says much more. Christ had risen with a glorified body, not only freeing Himself from the linen cloths, but passing through them, even as He afterwards passed through closed walls and doors (Lk 24:36; Jn 20:19), leaving the linen cloths as an empty shell fallen together and undisturbed. This agrees with what John says in particular about the face cloth.[6] He saw it lying, not on the heap with the other linen, as you would expect to find it when a man had taken off his clothes, but "by itself," in its own place—namely, on that particular place that had been occupied by the head, but the head was gone. We are told that it was "folded up in a place by itself," literally, in *one* place by itself.[7] That is, it was now still wrapped together just as it had been wound around the face and head, but the head was gone. In other words, the grave clothes—the linen cloths and the face cloth—had not been touched or unwound or disturbed since they had been placed about the sacred body of our Lord by Joseph and Nicodemus and were still lying there in the same place, but crumpled together like an empty shell. But the body was gone. Lazarus could not rise that way. He came out, bound hand and foot with linen strips, his face bound with a cloth, so that Jesus had to say, "Unbind him, and let him go" (Jn 11:44). We have here a most wonderful proof of the bodily resurrection of our Lord.[8] Standing and gazing at the evidence before their very eyes, Peter and John came to the knowledge of the truth. It certainly is a remarkable fact, which aids in making the story trustworthy, that it was not the belief based on Old Testament Scripture or on Christ's own prediction that He would rise from the dead that led them to expect it—in a way preparing the ground for resurrection stories—but the evidence that He had risen from the dead led them to the Scriptures, to a right understanding of the messianic prophecies as well as to a recollection of what Jesus had taught them. The resurrection of the Lord! We are not dealing with an invention or a delusion, with a vision or a fraud, but with history, written by eyewitnesses, yes, a fact that was unexpected and a startling surprise to the eyewitnesses themselves. It was not that the hope that they had entertained in their hearts had paved the way for a belief in the resurrection of the Lord; rather, what they had beheld with their own eyes, the empty grave and the crumpled linen, convinced them that their beloved Master had taken up His life again, as He had told the Jews He would and as had been prophesied in Scripture, all of which had previously been an enigma to them.

8
The Appearance
to Mary
Mk 16:9–11;[9]
Jn 20:11–18

In the meantime, Mary, who had followed Peter and John to the grave, stood outside, hopelessly weeping. But to her, from whom had been cast out seven demons (Lk 8:2), was to go the honor of the first private interview with the risen Lord. As she peered into the tomb with tear-filled eyes, she beheld the figures of two angels in white. They were sitting, one at the head and the other at the feet, where the body of Jesus had lain. To their question "Woman, why are you weeping?" she replied, "They have taken away my Lord, and I do not know where they have laid Him." At that moment, probably hearing a footstep, she turned back and saw Jesus.[10] But so altered was His appearance from the suffering figure she had last seen stretched on the cross that she did not know it was Jesus, not even when He addressed her: "Woman, why are you weeping? Whom are you seeking?" Supposing Him to be the gardener or caretaker, as the only one likely to be present on the premises in that early hour, Mary said to Him, "Sir, if you have carried Him away, tell me where you have laid Him, and I will take Him away." It almost seems as if she thought the body had been removed because Joseph of Arimathea changed his mind about letting his tomb be used for a stranger. Jesus addressed her with one word: "Mary." Recognizing the Master, she demonstrated her great surprise in an exclamation indicating highest respect: "Rabboni!"[11] "Oh, my Teacher!" She may have moved forward as she said this,[12] but Jesus halted her. "Do not cling to Me," He said, "for I have not yet ascended to the Father." Not as if Jesus could not be touched. He had just permitted Mary's friends to touch His feet in adoration. He later offered His body to the touch of the doubting disciples in proof that He was no spirit (Lk 24:39). But that was different. The prohibition in this case was because His resurrection did not mean He was returning to visible fellowship with His disciples.[13] This was reserved for a later time; and even then He would no longer hold long discussions with them in the same manner as in His former state of humiliation. "But go to My brothers and say to them, 'I am ascending to My Father and your Father, to My God and your God." Patiently wait for the time when, in heaven, all who believe in Me will forever enjoy a most intimate, blissful communion with Me. With a cry of joy, Mary added her testimony to that of her friends: "I have seen the Lord!" But as yet, the weeping disciples disbelieved.

While the women delivered the message of the risen Lord, a few of the guard reported what had happened at the tomb of Jesus to the Council, because Pilate had made them responsible to the chief priests. "Some of the guard went into the city and told the chief priests all that had taken place." This report included the shaking of the earth, the appearance of the angel, the moving of the stone, their being seized with a paralyzing fear, and the empty tomb. The matter was considered important enough to be deliberated upon at a session of the highest Jewish court. The matter was solemnly discussed, and the only way that seemed open to them to save their reputation and to prevent the people from believing in Jesus was to resort to a lie. Thoroughly understanding the value of silver,[14] these worthy judges were not slow in spreading it with a free and easy hand. The distribution was accompanied with the

9
The Report of
the Guard
Mt 28:11–15

instruction: "Tell people, 'His disciples came by night and stole Him away while we were asleep.' " Of course, in spreading this report, the soldiers incriminated themselves. It was well known that the ordinary military punishment for falling asleep on the watch was death. But aid was promised if the story should lead to complications. "And if this comes to the governor's ears, we will satisfy him and keep you out of trouble." The soldiers took the money. They might then have submitted a true report to the governor. But it seems that they did as they had been told. And whatever else might be said of the theft theory, we know that ever since those days, it has not failed to make its threadbare rounds.

10
The Two Disciples on the Way to Emmaus
Mk 16:12;
Lk 24:13–24

On that same Sunday afternoon, "two of them," not of the Twelve, but of the larger circle of disciples, were on their way to a village named Emmaus, which was situated sixty stadia, or seven miles, from Jerusalem. The two disciples were having a lively discussion about the happenings of the last two days when Jesus drew near. He asked them why they looked so sad and talked about matters that seemed to trouble them very much. "But their eyes were kept from recognizing Him." One of them was Cleopas, otherwise unknown.[15] Many commentators have thought of Luke himself as the other. If this was the case, then each of the four Gospels would, like a picture, bear in some obscure corner the indication of its author:[16] Matthew, who alone among the evangelists uses the epithet "the tax collector" in mentioning his name (Mt 10:3); Mark, the young man who "ran away naked" (Mk 14:52); John, "the disciple whom Jesus loved" (Jn 21:20); and the other disciple on the way to Emmaus (Lk 24:18). It was the companion of this unknown disciple who turned to Jesus with a touch of surprise: "Are you the only visitor to Jerusalem who does not know the things that have happened there in these days?" Jesus asked them, "What things?" And then they told Him. The one supreme topic of the hour was concerning Jesus of Nazareth, a prophet mighty in deed and word, whom the chief and popular rulers had condemned to death and crucified. But they had hoped, evidently misunderstanding the messianic prophecies, that He would redeem Israel. They had probably dreamed of the overthrow of the Romans and the reestablishment of David's throne; but all their hopes had come to nothing. He was dead. And besides all this, it was now the third day since these things had come to pass. And still a story was making the rounds; some women talked of an empty tomb, of visions of angels, and told them that He was alive. Certain of the brothers had made an investigation at the tomb and had found that what the women had reported about the tomb's being empty was true. "But," the speaker added, probably with a significant shrug, "Him they did not see."

11
"O Foolish Ones, and Slow of Heart to Believe!"
Mk 16:12;
Lk 24:25–32

The Stranger listened in silence until the speaker had finished. Now it was His turn to speak. He reproached the two men for their dull intelligence and slowness of heart to believe all that the prophets had spoken. "Was it not necessary that the

Christ should suffer these things and enter into His glory?" And then, beginning with Moses and all the prophets, He led them to a true understanding of Scripture's prophecies concerning Himself. By this time, they had reached Emmaus. But Jesus "acted as if He were going further." They pressed Him to stay, stressing the late hour, which, however, was not their real reason. "Stay with us, for it is toward evening and the day is now far spent." His teaching had impressed them, and they were anxious to learn more. "So He went in to stay with them," at least for the evening meal. "When He was at table with them, He took the bread and blessed and broke it and gave it to them." This is not a reference to the Lord's Supper. It was when He acted as their host, saying the table prayer and distributing the food, which they had so often seen Him do before, that "their eyes were opened, and they recognized Him." But when this point was reached, which included positive identification, the truth and proof of His resurrection, and, incidentally, the opening of Scripture and comprehension of the true significance of His messianic work, "He vanished from their sight." As soon as they recognized Him, He was gone. Looking at each other in questioning surprise, they could read in each other's eyes the same question together with its answer: "Did not our hearts burn within us while He talked to us on the road, while He opened to us the Scriptures?"

That same day, but in circumstances and in a manner unknown to us, the Lord appeared to Peter. He is the first of the apostles mentioned to whom was given the privilege of looking upon the risen Lord. And he needed this interview, for he was burdened by a deep sorrow over a grievous sin. It was a special interview, certainly not intended to stir jealousy[17] in the hearts of the other disciples; it was granted to him by the risen Savior because of His loving concern for him, as shown in the words that He spoke to him not many hours before his denial: "I have prayed for you that your faith may not fail" (Lk 22:32), on account of which the angel at the tomb had received the divine charge to say to the women, "Tell His disciples *and Peter*" (Mk 16:7, emphasis added).

12
The Appearance to Peter
Mk 16:13; Lk 24:33–35; (1Co 15:5)

It was impossible for the two disciples at Emmaus to keep the good news to themselves. Rising from their unfinished meal, they hurried to inform their brothers in the city. When they arrived, they found the Eleven[18] and those gathered with them and heard of the risen Lord's appearance to Peter. The doors were closed for fear of the Jews (Jn 20:19). The subject of their conversation of course was the risen Lord. We can imagine Peter surrounded by nine of his colleagues and engaged in a lively debate. The two pilgrims who had gone from Jerusalem to Emmaus and had just returned immediately added their testimony to that of Peter: "The Lord has risen indeed." But Thomas was not the only doubter. Even as the two rehearsed their story, the others disbelieved.

13
The Two Disciples Report to the Eleven
Mk 16:13; Lk 24:33–35

14
The Appearance on
Sunday Evening
Mk 16:14;[19]
Lk 24:36–43;
Jn 20:19

That Sunday evening, as the disciples were still discussing the happy news about the risen Lord, Jesus Himself appeared with the greeting "Peace to you!" But the disciples were terrified and supposed that they were looking at a spirit. Jesus rebuked them for their unbelief and their hardness of heart because they had not believed those who had brought the joyous report of His resurrection. "Why are you troubled?" He asked them. "And why do doubts arise in your hearts? See My hands and My feet, that it is I Myself. Touch Me, and see. For a spirit does not have flesh and bones as you see that I have." Jesus was able to prove that He had certainly risen from the dead. Even while He spoke, He showed them His hands and His feet. And while joy and doubt were still struggling in their hearts, He asked them, "Have you anything here to eat?" Since His resurrection, He was no longer in the state of humiliation, but in the state of glory; but in order to assure them that He still had a true human body (Lk 24:39 ["flesh and bones"]; Jn 20:27; Php 3:21), He ate a piece of broiled fish and some honeycomb (KJV)[20] in their presence.

15
"If You Forgive the
Sins of Any"
Jn 20:20–23

"Sir, we wish to see Jesus." With this request, certain Greeks had approached Philip a few days before Jesus' crucifixion (Jn 12:21). This same request was in the minds of the disciples. "Then the disciples were glad when they saw the Lord." Their sorrow was turned into joy (16:20). To the proof of His resurrection, Jesus now adds a sermon. Again He addresses them, "Peace be with you" and prepares them for their mission of peace: "As My Father has sent Me, even so I am sending you." Even as He had become the Father's Apostle, so they should become the apostles of Christ. The purpose of His labors on earth was to secure the forgiveness of sins. The blessings of the completed work of redemption should now be brought to others in the proclamation of the Gospel. He then bestowed upon them the Holy Spirit, with whom He had been anointed without measure (Ps 45:7; Is 61:1; Ac 10:38). In order to symbolize the transmission and passing on to them of the Spirit of God, He breathed on them and said, "Receive the Holy Spirit. If you forgive the sins of any, they are forgiven them; if you withhold forgiveness from any, it is withheld." Not until Pentecost, however, when the Holy Spirit would be poured out upon them and they would be clothed with power from on high, were they definitely and publicly to begin their work of peace. Nor is the Office of the Keys an authority conferred on only certain individuals, a privileged class, or to be an arbitrary power,[21] but it accompanies, rather, is an outflow of, the Gospel; absolution is "the application of the general Gospel promises of forgiveness to individual persons."[22] By the preaching of the Gospel and the administering of the Sacraments, heaven is opened and sins are forgiven to all who believe; but the sins of those who reject the Means of Grace are retained.

16
Thomas Is Absent
Jn 20:24–25

On this Sunday evening, Thomas, called Didymus, or Twin,[23] one of the Twelve, "was not with them when Jesus came." We do not know why. When the other disciples told him, "We have seen the Lord," he would not believe them. It was not willful rejection of a divine truth on his part, but he feared that his fellow apostles had become victims of hallucination. Nothing short of the testimony of his own physical senses would convince him. He was willing to believe—under certain conditions. And he stated the terms: "Unless I see in His hands the mark[24] of the nails, and place my finger into the mark of the nails, and place my hand into His side, I will never believe."

A week had passed and with it the Passover festival and the Days of Unleavened Bread.[25] But the disciples were still in Jerusalem. Although they continued to assemble privately, the expression "for fear of the Jews" no longer appears. For the present, that apprehension had passed away. Once more, Jesus appeared with the greeting "Peace be with you." This time Thomas was present. He had not entirely separated himself from the "apostolic band." Nor had he become an outright agnostic; for otherwise his associates would not have tolerated his presence. Immediately, the Lord directed Himself to His doubting disciple. Thomas had demanded proof. And proof could be given. "He said to Thomas, 'Put your finger here, and see My hands; and put out your hand, and place it in My side. Do not disbelieve, but believe.' "

17
The Appearance after Eight Days
Jn 20:26–27

We do not know if Thomas actually availed himself of the opportunity to satisfy his physical senses. At any rate, he was convinced. He burst forth into that most wonderful confession: "My Lord and my God!" Thomas no longer doubted. His confession has become the confession of the Christian Church: "My Lord and my God!" Many years later, in Pliny's letter to Trajan, the Christians are described as singing hymns to Christ as God.[26] But Thomas was also corrected. "Do not disbelieve, but believe." He should have believed the testimony of the other disciples, of his Master, and of Scripture.[27] "Have you believed because you have seen Me? Blessed are those who have not seen and yet have believed." This does not mean that we should close our eyes and believe anything and anybody (1Jn 4:1; Mt 24:4–5). Faith must be based on reliable testimony. But it is wrong to say, as the rationalists do, that the testimony of the Word of God is not a sufficient basis for our religious teachings, that these teachings, to be acceptable, must be approved by our reason or be confirmed by the verdict of our own senses and observation. Even in the natural sphere, it is unreasonable to reject the testimony of witnesses. Most of us have not seen the regions of the North Pole and the land of the midnight sun, where, so we are told, the sun does not set for weeks and months. Yet it would be foolish for us to deny—just because we have not seen—that this is actually the case. How much less should we refuse to accept the unerring testimony of the Word of God!

18
"My Lord and My God!"
Jn 20:26–29

Here follows the first close of John's Gospel, in which we are informed that Christ performed many unrecorded miracles. "Now Jesus did many other signs in the presence of the disciples, which are not written in this book." Such as have been

19
Unrecorded Miracles
Jn 20:30–31

recorded are "written so that you may believe that Jesus is the Christ, the Son of God, and that by believing you may have life in His name."

A pause must have occurred in the appearances of the risen Savior, which may have caused the disciples to return to Galilee, where He had promised to see them (Mt 28:7; Mk 16:7). In the group of disciples gathered by the Sea of Galilee, we find Peter, Thomas,[28] Nathanael (who we are informed was from Cana), James, John, and two others whose names are not given. For the moment, they were without a final commission and without a common moneybag.[29] For three years they had followed Jesus, going on their errands without moneybag and knapsack, never, however, lacking anything (Lk 22:35); but now we may suppose they were in difficult circumstances. Quite naturally we can imagine them discussing ways and means of earning a livelihood and finally joining Peter when he said, "I am going fishing." This for the present seemed to them the only way of making an honest living. But they did not succeed in catching any fish. After getting their boats and nets, probably long unused, in order and setting out one evening, they toiled all night, but caught nothing. The next morning, Jesus stood on the beach; but they did not know it was Him. He called to them: "Children,[30] do you have any fish?"[31] It was as if a fish merchant was asking them about their catch. "No," was their despondent reply. The voice came back: "Cast the net on the right side of the boat, and you will find some." They probably supposed that the Stranger had been making observations from the shore and had noticed a shoal or signs of fish.[32] They followed the direction and dropped their net. "And now they were not able to haul it in, because of the quantity of fish." It was a miracle. The incident was so remarkable that the miraculous catch of fish of earlier days was called to their minds (Lk 5:1–11). Immediately, the beloved disciple, John, whispered to Peter: "It is the Lord!" Instantly, though only half dressed,[33] Peter threw on his outer garment and jumped into the sea. He swam the hundred yards or so[34] to the shore, leaving the disciples to drag the fish. On the shore, preparations for a meal were already found: a charcoal fire, bread, and broiling fish. When the disciples approached, Jesus called out: "Bring some of the fish that you have just caught." There was to be a meal for all. Slowly, they dragged in the strained, but unbroken net, containing exactly one hundred and fifty-three good-sized fish. We need not seek a mystical meaning in this number.[35] It simply means that the fish were large, that the catch was remarkable, that the net was unbroken, and that Simon and John were real fishermen, who would not make a haul without noticing the size and counting the number of the fish. Assuming the part of host, Jesus now invited the disciples: "Come and have breakfast." As they gathered around the fire for their morning meal, with Jesus breaking the bread and distributing the fish, they could not help realizing that it was the Lord. But none "dared ask Him, 'Who are You?' They knew it was the Lord." This was the third time since His resurrection that Jesus appeared to a group of disciples.

After the meal, Jesus took up a discussion with Peter, whom, however, He addressed by his original name: "Simon, son of John, do you love[36] Me more than these?" There was a painful reference in the words "more than these" (Mt 26:35; Mk 14:29). Peter replied, "Yes, Lord; You know that I love You."[37] Jesus said to him, "Feed My lambs." For the second and third time came the same question: "Do you love Me?" and likewise Peter's answer: "Lord, You know that I love You," and now both times the Lord's command: "Feed My sheep." When the Lord asked the question the third time, evidently wishing to remind Peter of his triple denial, Peter was grieved. Deeply humbled and greatly distressed, he replied, "Lord, You know everything; You know that I love You." By commanding Peter to feed both His lambs and His sheep, the Lord reinstated him in the apostleship and commissioned him to preach the Gospel to young and old. But His threefold question showed him as well as his fellow apostles that loving Him is essential for the proper performance of the ministry. And their love would be put to a severe test. In the case of Peter, the statement was made: "Truly, truly, I say to you, when you were young, you used to dress yourself and walk wherever you wanted." Formerly his will was his law, limited only by his ability to carry it out. But in the service of Christ, not the principle of will and choice, but the principle of obedience and submission applies. "When you are old, you will stretch out your hands, and another will dress you and carry you where you do not want to go." What the Lord here alluded to is explained by the evangelist: "This He said to show by what kind of death he was to glorify God." Tradition has it that during the reign of Nero, Peter died on the cross.[38] With the words "Follow Me," Peter was again officially called to be the Lord's apostle. He was not made the highest incumbent of the apostolic office, with supreme authority and dominion over all the other apostles or with the right to fleece the herd, but with the duty laid upon him to join the other shepherds in the work of feeding the lambs and sheep of Christ. "Feed My lambs. . . . Feed My sheep. . . . Follow Me."

As Peter rose to follow Christ, thinking probably about the pangs of his predicted martyrdom, he turned and noticed John, his own intimate companion and the disciple whom Jesus loved, slowly following them. Curiosity prompted him to ask the question: And what about him? "Lord, what about this man?" In seeking to know the future of another disciple, Peter was clearly overstepping his ground. Mysteriously, Jesus replied, "If it is My will that he remain until I come, what is that to you? You follow Me!"[39] *Your* business is to follow Me, not to meddle in the affairs or others.[40] The answer led to the wide misunderstanding prevalent in the Early Church that John was not to die until the second coming of Jesus. Quietly, the evangelist corrects the error by quoting the exact words of Jesus. He points to

21
"Feed My Lambs. . .
Feed My Sheep"
Jn 21:15–19

22
Prediction
Concerning John
Jn 21:20–23

the hypothetical form of the remark. "Jesus did not say to him that he was not to die, but, 'If it is My will that he remain until I come, what is that to you?' " John *did* outlive all the other apostles. In fact, he lived to see the destruction of Jerusalem and the terrible overthrow of the Jewish nation, which might be taken as the beginning of Christ's return.[41]

23
The Close of
John's Gospel
Jn 21:24–25

At this point, we may as well bring the account of John to a close. In a final note, the apostle defends the truthfulness of the record he has offered. He has not written on the basis of questionable sources, but he knows, and others who join him in this certification know with him,[42] that his testimony is true. When he had attained to a very old age, living probably in Ephesus,[43] there were still other Christians of venerable age and of highest integrity who were able to certify the truth of his account. Incidentally, he affirms that, if all the sayings and miracles of Jesus were to be recorded, the world, as one might say, could not contain the books.

24
The Great
Mission Command
Mt 28:16–19a;
Mk 16:15;
(1Co 15:6)

It may have been in connection with His appearance by the Sea of Galilee that Jesus designated the particular mountain in Galilee where He would meet all those who loved Him for a final general assembly. We do not know where the mountain was. Most likely it was a place, such as the Mount of Beatitudes or some other height, made familiar by former occasions. If we may bring in the testimony of St. Paul at this place, it was a large assembly. "He appeared to more than five hundred brothers at one time, most of whom are still alive, though some have fallen asleep" (1Co 15:6).[44] When Jesus made His appearance, some worshiped Him, while others still doubted. And it seems that the reference is to some of the Eleven. When Jesus made His appearance in Jerusalem, it was Thomas who doubted. But Thomas was cured of all his doubts. We are expressly told that he was with the seven assembled at the Sea of Tiberias (Jn 21:2). But on the occasion under discussion, some of the others expressed doubt. The disciples did not doubt the resurrection of Jesus, but the doubt seems to have concerned the identity of Him who stood before them. The doubt of the disciples is rather a testimony to the truth of the inspired record. The disciples were not easily convinced, and the very fact that Jesus had to remove their doubts proves beyond a doubt that He truly rose from the dead.[45] As Jesus came closer to them, however, He removed all fear and uncertainty. It was a most solemn occasion; for now He issued His great mission command, the Great Commission: "All authority in heaven and on earth has been given to Me. Go therefore and make disciples of all nations."

25
The Institution of
the Sacrament of
Holy Baptism
Mt 28:19b–20a;
Mk 16:15

According to this great mission command, disciples are made by two Means of Grace: by "baptizing [all nations] in the name of the Father and of the Son and of the Holy Spirit" and by "teaching them to observe all that I have commanded you"; in other words, by "proclaim[ing] the gospel to the whole creation" and administering the Sacraments as the Means of Grace. Here we have the institution of the *sacramentum initiationis*, the Sacrament of Initiation, of the Christian Church. In the Great Commission of our Lord, "baptizing" is mentioned previous to "teaching," or "preaching." But this is not to be taken as a command that Baptism must at all times precede instruction. Still less reason is there to conclude that instruction must always precede Baptism, for instance, in the case of children. And these are not excluded, because the Lord says, "Make disciples of all nations, baptizing them."

Likewise the way of gaining salvation is briefly shown. "Whoever believes and is baptized will be saved, but whoever does not believe will be condemned." When a sinner hears the Gospel of Christ, he must accept it as true, as meant for him, and he must appropriate its promises to himself. Since this is impossible for fallen humans, the Holy Spirit graciously operates on the heart of the hearer through the Gospel and kindles this faith. He kindles it also through Baptism; for Baptism is "the washing of regeneration and renewal of the Holy Spirit, whom He poured out on us richly through Jesus Christ our Savior, so that being justified by His grace we might become heirs according to the hope of eternal life" (Ti 3:5–7). But Jesus does not say, "Whoever does not believe *and is not baptized* will be condemned"; therefore it is only unbelief that damns. In other words, an unbaptized person may be saved. But though saving faith may exist with lack of Baptism, it cannot exist with the contempt of it.[46]

26
Way of Salvation
Mk 16:16

And miraculous signs are to follow. "And these signs will accompany those who believe: in My name they will cast out demons; they will speak in new tongues;[47] they will pick up serpents with their hands; and if they drink any deadly poison, it will not hurt them; they will lay their hands on the sick, and they will recover." These signs are given not only to the apostles or other preachers of the Gospel, but to "those who believe." And all these miracles actually were performed within the Christian Church. But a few points must be remembered. In the first place, these signs were given for a purpose, as a testimony, to prove the truth of the Gospel and to establish it in this or that locality, especially in the early days when the Christian Church was being established. In the second place, the words of Jesus are by no means a promise that each individual believer will be able to perform a sign whenever he feels the urge.[48] In the great mission command, the disciples were not primarily commissioned to become, as it were, miracle-workers, but were commanded to baptize and to teach. And if necessary for their work, for the establishment of the Gospel and for the glory of God, miracles would follow. In making this statement, we are on safe ground. An appeal to Mark 16:17–18 cannot be made for all kinds of healings and speaking in tongues. And if the particular signs are more uncommon in our day than they were, for instance, in the Early Christian Church, it is partly due to insufficient faith, partly, or rather largely, also to the circumstance that they are no longer needed; after all these centuries of Christian preaching in all the world,

27
Signs
Mt 28:20b;
Mk 16:17–18

there is no particular need of signs confirming the Word. We have "Moses and the Prophets." And "let them," all men, "hear them." "If they do not hear Moses and the Prophets, neither will they be convinced if someone should rise from the dead" (Lk 16:29–31). But at the same time, Christians always have this promise of divine protection: "Behold, I am with you always, to the end of the age." And this promise concludes the Gospel of St. Matthew.

28
Appearances to James and Paul
(1 Co 15:7–9)

There were appearances of the risen Christ in addition to those recorded in the Gospels. St. Paul relates that after the appearance to the five hundred, "He appeared to James." But he does not tell us which James it was. Positive identification is impossible. Yet it is believed that it was not the brother of John and son of Zebedee, who met a tragic death by the sword at the hands of Herod Agrippa I as early as AD 41.[49] The reference is likely to that James whose mother, Mary, is called the mother of James and wife of Clopas, or Alphaeus, and also called the brother of our Lord (Lk 24:10; Jn 19:25; Gal 1:19).[50] This James, also called the younger, in order to distinguish him from James, the son of Zebedee, is quite generally identified as the head of the church of Jerusalem in the apostolic age (Ac 12:17; 15:13; 21:18; etc.). And it was probably the circumstance of his future high position that accounts for the fact that the risen Lord granted him a special interview.[51] Likewise Paul, the great apostle to the Gentiles, had the honor of a special appearance. Modestly, Paul refers to this appearance[52] with the words: "Last of all, as to one untimely born, He appeared also to me. For I am the least of the apostles, unworthy to be called an apostle, because I persecuted the church of God" (see Ac 9:3–6; 26:14–18).

29
The Last Appearance in Jerusalem
Lk 24:44–49;
(Ac 1:3–5)

MAY, AD 33

Sun.	Mon.	Tue.	Wed.	Thur.	Fri.	Sat.
					1	2
3	4	5	6	7	8	9
10	11	12	13	**14**	15	16
17	28	19	20	21	22	23
24	25	26	27	28	29	30
31						

Forty days had passed since the resurrection of Jesus on Easter morning. Referring again to our calendar, this would bring us to Thursday, May 14, AD 33. The day had arrived for Jesus to be taken up into heaven.[53] It seems that Jesus had directed His disciples in Galilee to return to Jerusalem. At any rate, we find the Eleven assembled in Jerusalem and Jesus with them. It is as if the former days had returned. Jesus is in the midst of an address.[54] It is a farewell discourse. The Savior is speaking as though He were already parted from His disciples. "These are My words that I spoke to you while I was still with you." He reminds them that all the things they had witnessed, His entire work, His suffering, death, and resurrection on the third day, were necessary that the entire Scriptures, the Law of Moses, the Prophets, and the Psalms, should be fulfilled in Him. And pointing to the prophecies, He opened their understanding of Scripture. This was necessary because they were to be His witnesses. The contents of their testimony among all nations, beginning at Jerusalem, was to be repentance and the remission of sins. A glorious message, but also a staggering task. It is true, what the injunction demanded of them was beyond their strength; but the Holy Spirit would make them equal to the task. When He "breathed on them" (Jn 20:22), He had already conferred on them a portion of their required spiritual equipment; but they were soon to receive the full measure of the Father's promise (Is 44:3; Jl 2:28). "Stay in the city until you are clothed with power from on high." A spiritual baptism was soon to take place. "For John baptized with water, but you will be baptized with the Holy Spirit not many days from now."

It was in this way that Jesus, not only on this occasion, but also on others in the period of the glorious forty days, spoke to His apostles of the things pertaining to the kingdom of God. But previously they had cherished a mistaken messianic hope. Again they had heard something about the Kingdom, and now the Lord spoke also of the Baptism with the Holy Spirit, which they correctly, but still in a false interpretation, had connected with messianic times.[55] Linking the promise of the Spirit and the reference to the Kingdom with earthly dominion, the disciples asked: "Lord, will You at this time restore the kingdom to Israel?" Jesus had not been speaking of the "kingdom of Israel," but of the "kingdom of God." Immediately, He halted their nationalistic hopes: "It is not for you to know times or seasons that the Father has fixed by His own authority." They were always thinking of power,[56] authority, dominion, and glory. But the power that the Lord had in mind for them was the power[57] of the Holy Spirit. "You will receive power when the Holy Spirit has come upon you." That was the power they were to receive—the ability to become effective witnesses for the Gospel of Christ. "You will be My witnesses in Jerusalem and in all Judea and Samaria, and to the end of the earth."

30
"You Will Be My Witnesses"
(Ac 1:6–8)

Read that last sentence once more. Was there a more sublime utterance ever made? Under any other circumstances, the words could be disposed of as sheer boastful speech, but here they were uttered by the One whom we have followed from the manger to the regions beyond the grave and of whom it can be truly said that not once "was deceit found in His mouth" (1Pt 2:22). And besides, they are the heritage of Him whom we are about to behold ascending to the portals of heaven. "You will be My witnesses in Jerusalem and in all Judea and Samaria, and to the end of the earth." And after He had said this, He led His disciples out until they were opposite

31
The Ascension
Mk 16:19; Lk 24:50–51; (Ac 1:9)

Bethany—past the scene of His triumphal entry into the city of Jerusalem, past Gethsemane and the site of His suffering, to one of the slopes of the Mount of Olives overhanging the village of His no-longer-to-be-visited friends. There was nothing more to be done beyond saying good-bye to His disciples. The work He had come to do was accomplished. And the future of the Church was provided for. "But the Helper, the Holy Spirit, whom the Father will send in My name, He will teach you all things and bring to your remembrance all that I have said to you. Peace I leave with you; My peace I give to you. . . . Let not your hearts be troubled, neither let them be afraid" (Jn 14:26–27). And He lifted up His hands and blessed them. And it came to pass, while He blessed them, He was taken up, the eyes of the disciples following Him higher and higher, until a cloud received Him out of their sight. It was the ascension of Christ into heaven, the coronation of the heavenly King, who "has gone up with a shout, the LORD with the sound of a trumpet" (Ps 47:5). He sat down[58] at the right hand of God, there to assume the rule, also according to His human nature, over all creatures and especially to govern and to protect His Church and finally to lead it to glory.

32
Conclusion
Mk 16:20; Lk 24:52–53; (Ac 1:10–12)

We have come to the close of the Gospel records and to the end of our book. But the complete story of Christ has not been told. The ascension of our Lord was followed by the founding of the Christian Church, whose Head was and is and ever will be the ascended and ever-living Lord. There is another chapter, still incomplete, of the life of Christ, which takes us to Judgment Day, to be followed by the chapter on the eternal joy and glory of all the saints with Christ in heaven. With worshiping hearts, the disciples gazed at what seemed to them a disappearing Lord. Luke states, "And while they were gazing into heaven as He went, behold, two men[59] stood by them in white robes, and said, 'Men of Galilee, why do you stand looking into heaven? This Jesus, who was taken up from you into heaven, will come in the same way as you saw Him go into heaven.' " And since that is the case, the separation from their departed Master was not a cause for sorrow, but an occasion of great and undiminished joy. The disciples returned to Jerusalem. Joyfully they went forth and preached everywhere, praising and blessing God.

There are many "Lives of Christ." As we lay aside our books and finish our task of love and joy, we hope that the reader also will finish reading these pages with a sense of joy. Lift up your heads with joy. "This Jesus, who was taken up from you into heaven, will come in the same way as you saw Him go into heaven."

"TO WHOM BE GLORY FOREVER!"

Appendixes

The Distinctive Miracles of Jesus

Besides this list, Jesus performed numerous miracles that have not been particularly described. The chapter column refers to the chapters in *The Life of Christ*.

	MATTHEW	MARK	LUKE	JOHN	CHAPTER
1. The water made wine. Cana				2:1–11	6, §§ 21–23
2. The healing of the official's son. Cana				4:46–54	7, §§ 22–24
3. The healing of the invalid at the Pool of Bethesda. Jerusalem				5:2–9	8, §§ 3–5
4. The miraculous catch of fish. Capernaum			5:1–11		9, § 12
5. The healing of a demoniac. Capernaum		1:21–28	4:31–37		9, §§ 14–19
6. The healing of Peter's mother-in-law. Capernaum	8:14–15	1:29–31	4:38–39		9, § 20
7. The healing of a leper. Galilee	8:2–4	1:40–45	5:12–15		10, § 7
8. The paralytic healed. Capernaum	9:2–8	2:1–12	5:17–26		10, §§ 11–14
9. The man with a withered hand. Galilee	12:9–14	3:1–6	6:6–11		10, §§ 29–30
10. The centurion's servant. Capernaum	8:5–13		7:1–10		11, § 43
11. The raising of the widow's son. Nain			7:11–17		12, § 1
12. The blind and dumb demoniac. Capernaum	12:22–37				12, § 13
13. The stilling of the storm. Sea of Galilee	8:23–27	4:36–41	8:23–25		13, §§ 5–6
14. The Gadarene demoniacs	8:28–34	5:1–20	8:26–40		13, §§ 7–12
15. The raising of Jairus's daughter. Capernaum	9:18–26	5:22–43	8:41–56		13, §§ 13, 16
16. The woman with the issue of blood. Capernaum	9:20–22	5:25–34	8:43–48		13, §§ 14–15
17. Two blind men healed. At or near Capernaum	9:27–31				13, § 17
18. The mute demoniac. At or near Capernaum	9:32–34				13, § 18
19. The feeding of the five thousand. Bethsaida	14:15–21	6:35–44	9:12–17	6:3–13	16, §§ 2–3
20. Jesus walking on the water. Sea of Galilee	14:24–33	6:47–52		6:16–21	16, §§ 5–6

	MATTHEW	MARK	LUKE	JOHN	CHAPTER
21. The daughter of the Syrophoeni-cian woman. Tyre	15:21–28	7:24–30			17, §§ 2–4
22. The healing of the deaf man. Decapolis	15:30–31	7:32–37			17, § 6
23. The feeding of the four thousand. Decapolis	15:32–38	8:1–9			17, § 7
24. The blind man. Near Bethsaida		8:22–26			18, § 2
25. The demoniac boy. At Mount Hermon	17:14–18	9:14–27	9:37–43		18, § 11
26. The temple tax miraculously provided. Capernaum	17:24–27				19, §§ 3–4
27. The man born blind. Jerusalem				9:1–41	20, §§ 21–26
28. The healing of the mute demo-niac. Perea			11:14–28		21, § 13
29. The crippled woman. Perea or Judea			13:10–17		21, §§ 29–30
30. The man with the dropsy. Perea			14:1–4		23, § 6
31. The raising of Lazarus. Bethany				11:1–46	24, §§ 1–5
32. The ten lepers. Border of Samaria and Galilee			17:12–19		25, §§ 2–3
33. Blind Bartimaeus and his com-panion. Jericho	20:29–34	10:46–52	18:35–43		25, § 23
34. The fig tree cursed. Near Jeru-salem	21:18–20	11:12–20			28, § 1; 29, § 1
35. The healing of the ear of Mal-chus. Gethsemane			22:50–51		33, § 7
36. The second miraculous catch of fish. Sea of Galilee				21:1–14	37, § 20

"Now Jesus did many other signs in the presence of the disciples, which are not written in this book" (John 20:30). Compare: Mt 4:23; 9:35; 11:21; Mk 6:56; Lk 4:40; 5:15; 6:18; 7:21; 10:13; Jn 2:23; 3:2; 4:45; 20:30; 21:25.

The Parables of Our Lord

The limits between parable, simile, and metaphor are not strictly defined. Often there is scarcely any difference. In a technical sense, the word *parable* ordinarily signifies a complete, howbeit imaginary, story. But etymologically, the word signifies the placing of two or more objects together for the sake of comparison. In a wider sense, the public preaching of our Lord assumed the general characteristic of speaking in parables. "All these things Jesus said to the crowds in parables; indeed, He said nothing to them without a parable" (Mt 13:34). The following list does not confine itself to parables in the strictly technical sense, nor does it exhaust the parabolic sayings of our Lord.

	MATTHEW	MARK	LUKE	JOHN	CHAPTER
1. The friends of the bridegroom	9:15	2:19–20	5:34–35		10, § 23
2. A new patch on an old garment	9:16	2:21	5:36		10, § 24
3. New wine in old wineskins	9:17	2:22	5:37–39		10, § 25
4. The blind leading the blind			6:39		11, § 35
5. The speck and the log	7:3–5		6:41–42		11, § 35
6. The light of the world	5:14–16	4:21–22	8:16–17		11, § 20; 12, § 22
7. The salt of the earth	5:13	9:50	14:34–35		11, § 20; 19, §§ 8; 23 § 16
8. The wise and foolish builders	7:24–27		6:47–48		11, § 41
9. The children in the market-places	11:16–17		7:31–32		12, § 4
10. The two debtors			7:40–42		12, § 10
11. Satan's kingdom	12:25–29	3:23–27			12, § 14
12. The return of the evil spirit	12:43–45				12, § 16
13. The sower	13:3–9	4:3–9	8:5–8		12, § 19
14. The seed growing of itself		4:26–29			12, § 23
15. The weeds	13:24–30				12, § 24
16. The mustard seed	13:31–32	4:30–32	13:18–19		12, § 25
17. The leaven	13:33		13:20–21		12, § 26
18. The hidden treasure	13:44				12, § 29
19. The pearl of great value	13:45–46				12, § 30
20. The net	13:47–50				12, § 31
21. The master of the house	13:51–53				12, § 32
22. Things defiling a man	15:10–20	7:15–23			16, §§ 16–17
23. The unforgiving servant	18:23–35				19, § 13
24. The Good Shepherd				10:1–21	20, §§ 27–29
25. The good Samaritan			10:30–37		21, § 9

	MATTHEW	MARK	LUKE	JOHN	CHAPTER
26. The impudent friend			11:5–13		21, § 12
27. The rich fool			12:16–21		21, § 20
28. The waiting servants			12:35–40		21, § 22
29. The wise steward			12:41–48		21, § 23
30. The barren fig tree			13:6–9		21, § 28
31. Seats at a wedding feast			14:7–11		23, § 8
32. Feast for the poor			14:12–14		23, § 9
33. The great banquet			14:15–24		23, § 10
34. Building a tower			14:28–30		23, § 14
35. A king anxious to fight			14:31–33		23, § 15
36. The lost sheep	18:12–14		15:3–7		23, § 18; 19, § 9
37. The lost coin			15:8–10		23, § 19
38. The prodigal son			15:11–32		23, §§ 20–23
39. The dishonest manager			16:1–13		23, §§ 24–25
40. The rich man and Lazarus			16:19–31		23, §§ 27–29
41. The unworthy servants			17:7–10		23, § 33
42. The persistent widow			18:1–8		25, § 6
43. The Pharisee and the tax collector			18:9–14		25, § 7
44. The laborers in the vineyard	20:1–16				25, §§ 18–19
45. The minas			19:11–27		25, §§ 26–29
46. The two sons	21:28–32				29, § 5
47. The wicked tenants	21:33–41	12:1–9	20:9–16		29, §§ 6–7
48. The rejected building stone	21:42–45	12:10–11	20:17–18		29, § 8
49. The marriage of the king's son	22:1–14				29, §§ 10–12
50. The fig tree	24:32–35	13:28–31	21:29–33		30, § 6
51. The doorkeeper		13:34–37			30, § 9
52. The master and the thief	24:43–44				30, § 10
53. The two servants	24:45–51				30, § 10
54. The ten virgins	25:1–13				30, §§ 11–12
55. The talents	25:14–30				30, §§ 13–15
56. The sheep and the goats	25:31–46				30, §§ 16–18

THE GENEALOGY OF CHRIST

OLD TESTAMENT	MATTHEW 1:1–17		LUKE 3:23–38 (IN REVERSED ORDER)	
Adam (Gn 5:3ff.; 1Ch 1:1ff.)			v. 38	1. Adam, the son of God[1]
Seth				2. Seth
Enosh				3. Enos
Kenan			v. 37	4. Cainan
Mahalelel				5. Mahalaleel
Jared				6. Jared
Enoch				7. Enoch
Methuselah				8. Methuselah
Lamech			v. 36	9. Lamech
Noah				10. Noah
Shem				11. Shem
Arpachshad (Gn 11:10ff.)				12. Arphaxad
---				13. Cainan (inserted in LXX and in Luke)
Shelah			v. 35	14. Shelah
Eber				15. Eber
Peleg				16. Peleg
Reu				17. Reu
Serug	v. 1	The book of the generation of Jesus Christ, the Son of David, the Son of Abraham		18. Serug
Nahor			v. 34	19. Nahor
Terah				20. Terah
Abraham	v. 2	Abraham		21. Abraham
Isaac (1Ch 1:34)		Isaac		22. Isaac
Jacob		Jacob		23. Jacob
Judah (1Ch 2:1ff.)		Judah and his brothers	v. 33	24. Judah
Perez	v. 3	Perez and Zerah by Tamar		25. Perez
Hezron (Ru 4:18ff.)		Hezron		26. Hezron
Ram		Ram		27. Arni
---				28. Admin
Amminadab	v. 4	Amminadab		29. Amminadab
Nahshon		Nahshon	v. 32	30. Nahshon
Salmon		Salmon		31. Sala
Boaz	v. 5	Boaz by Rahab		32. Boaz
Obed		Obed by Ruth		33. Obed
Jesse		Jesse		34. Jesse
David	v. 6	David the king	v. 31	35. David
Solomon (1Ch 3:1ff.)		Solomon by the wife of Uriah		36. Nathan
				37. Mattatha
				38. Menna
Rehoboam	v. 7	Rehoboam		39. Melea

OLD TESTAMENT		MATTHEW 1:1–17	LUKE 3:23–38 (IN REVERSED ORDER)	
Abijah		Abijah	v. 31	40. Eliakim
Asa		Asaph/Asa		41. Jonam
Jehoshaphat		Jehoshaphat		42. Joseph
Joram	v. 8	Joram		43. Judah
Ahaziah		---		44. Simeon
Joash		---	v. 29	45. Levi
Amaziah		---		46. Matthat
Azariah, or Uzziah (Is 1:1)		Uzziah		47. Jorim
Jotham		Jotham		48. Eliezer
Ahaz	v. 9	Ahaz		49. Joshua
Hezekiah		Hezekiah	v. 28	50. Er
Manasseh		Manasseh		51. Elmadam
Amon	v. 10	Amos/Amon		52. Cosam
Josiah		Josiah		53. Addi
Jehoiakim (2Ki 24:6)		---		54. Melchi
Jeconiah, or Coniah (Jer 22:24)	v. 12	Jechoniah	v. 27	55. Neri
Pedaiah (Shealtiel)[2] (1Ch 3:17)		Shealtiel (Gk Salathiel) (Ezr 3:2; 5:2)		56. Shealtiel (Gk Salathiel)
Zerubbabel (1Ch 3:19)		Zerubbabel		57. Zerubbabel
Meshullam = Rhesa? (Hananiah = Joanan?)				58. Rhesa
	v. 13	Abiud = father or grandfather[3] of Jud or Joda = ?		59. Joanan
			v. 26	60. Joda[4]
				61. Josech
				62. Semein
				63. Mattathias
				64. Maath
			v. 25	65. Naggai
				66. Esli
				67. Nahum
		Eliakim		68. Amos
		Azor		69. Mattathias
	v. 14	Zadok	v. 24	70. Joseph
		Achim		71. Jannai
		Eliud		72. Melchi[5]
	v. 15	Eleazar		73. Levi
		Matthan m. = Estha (?) m. =		74. Matthat
		Jacob = step-brothers? =	v. 23	75. Heli (m. Anna?)
	v. 16	Joseph the husband of Mary, of whom		76. (Mary) = Joseph[6]
		JESUS was born,[7] who is called Christ		77. JESUS[8]

TIME RECKONING IN THE BIBLE

For the Israelites, reckoning time was more than a matter of business or convenience. Because a calendar would guide the celebration of religious festivals, reckoning time was a matter of devotion, which became hotly disputed during the Intertestamental Era. Below are different calendar systems that affected life for the people of Judea during the Intertestamental and New Testament eras.

Annual Reckoning

	TEMPLE JUDAISM CALENDAR	MACEDONIAN CALENDAR	QUMRAN JUDAISM CALENDAR	ROMAN (JULIAN) CALENDAR
Natural Basis	Lunar	Lunar	Solar	Solar
Form	12 months of 29/30 days each, totaling 354 days	12 months totaling c. 354 days	12 months of 30 days, adjusted to make 52 weeks (364 days)	12 months totaling 52 weeks (365 days)
Adjustments (due to different annual cycles of the sun and moon)	Extra month (Second Adar) added every 36 months	Extra month added every other year	A "remembrance day" added once per quarter	One day added to February every fourth year
Notes	The calendar found in the OT; see p. 262 in *TLSB*	Spread by Alexander the Great; adapted by Seleucid and Ptolemaic rulers of Syria and Egypt (including Judea)	Known from the Dead Sea Scrolls; a similar calendar appears in Jubilees and 1 Enoch	The basis of the modern Western calendar

Day Reckoning

Services for the morning and evening sacrifices were offered at the temple after dawn and before sunset. (On hours of prayer, cf. Ps 55:17; 119:164; Ac 3:1; 10:9; 16:25.) The Sabbath began at sunset on Friday and continued 24 hours until sunset on Saturday. Jews often regarded part of a day as if it were a full day (e.g., the "three days" Jesus was in the tomb, from Friday evening to Sunday morning). The nights were divided into watches, when guards patrolled city streets. Hours could be discerned from one another using water clocks and sundials. Roman-civil reckoning began from midnight.

OLD TESTAMENT RECKONING	ROMAN-CIVIL RECKONING	COMMON RECKONING OF NEW TESTAMENT ERA
Dawn, c. 6 a.m.	6 a.m.	1st hour, c. 6 a.m.–7 a.m.
	7	2nd hour
	8	3rd hour
Morning	9	4th hour
	10	5th hour
	11	6th hour
Midday	12 p.m./Noon	7th hour
	1	8th hour
	2	9th hour
	3	10th hour
	4	11th hour
Evening/Sunset, c. 6 p.m.	5	12th hour
1st watch of the night 6 p.m.–10 p.m.	6	1st watch of the night 6 p.m.–9 p.m.
	7	
	8	
	9	2nd watch 9 p.m.–midnight
2nd watch 10 p.m.–2 a.m.	10	
	11	
	12 a.m./Midnight	3rd watch Midnight–3 a.m.
	1	
3rd watch 2 a.m.–6 a.m.	2	
	3	4th watch 3 a.m.–6 a.m.
	4	
	5	
	6	

THE FAMILY OF JESUS

The purpose of this graph is not to pretend wisdom where Scripture is silent, but to help us picture the life of Him who became incarnate for our salvation and lived among men. This family tree assumes that the genealogy in Matthew traces Jesus' legal genealogy through Joseph while Luke traces His actual genealogy through Mary. Notice Joseph's genealogy runs through David's son Solomon, while Mary's runs through David's son Nathan.

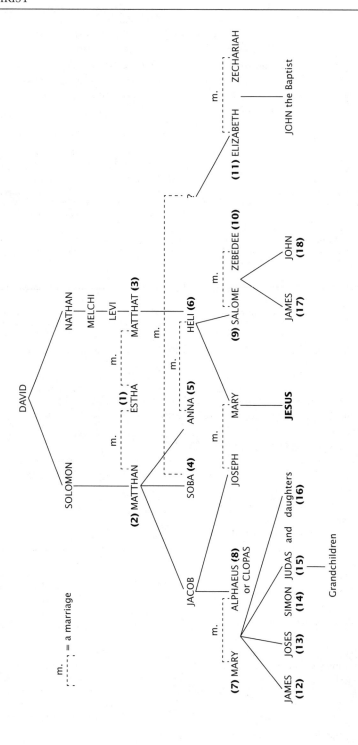

m. ----- = a marriage

DAVID

SOLOMON — NATHAN
MELCHI
LEVI
(2) MATTHAN — m. — (1) ESTHA — m. — MATTHAT (3)
SOBA (4) — ANNA (5) — m. — HELI (6)
JACOB — JOSEPH — m. — MARY — JESUS
(7) MARY — m. — ALPHAEUS (8) or CLOPAS
(9) SALOME — m. — ZEBEDEE (10)
? — (11) ELIZABETH — m. — ZECHARIAH
JOHN the Baptist
JAMES (17) — JOHN (18)
JAMES (12) — JOSES (13) — SIMON (14) — JUDAS (15) and daughters (16)
Grandchildren

Notes

1. Estha. "By Estha then (for this was the woman's name according to tradition) Matthan, a descendant of Solomon, first begat Jacob" (Eusebius, *NPNF*2 1:92).
2. Matthan. See ch. 3, n. 82.
3. Matthat. Eusebius, quoting Africanus, says that Estha, after the death of Matthan, married Melchi. But it seems Matthat is meant. He refers to him as Melchi, the third from the end. But in the present texts of Luke, Melchi is given as the fifth from the end. It is suggested (see Westcott and Hort's *Greek Testament*, Appendix, p. 57) that Levi and Matthat were missing in the text of Africanus. "It is impossible to suppose that Africanus in such an investigation as this could have overlooked two names by mistake if they had stood in his text of the Gospels" (*NPNF*2 1:91 n. 112).
4. Soba, the mother of Elizabeth and sister of Anna, the mother of Mary. See note for Matthan.
5. Anna, the mother of the Virgin Mary (Apocryphal Gospel of the Birth of Mary 1:1; Gospel of James 2:1). Of Bethlehem. Married to Heli, or Joachim, of Nazareth in Galilee.
6. Heli. Of Nazareth. According to the Gospel of the Birth of Mary 1:1 and the Gospel of James 1:1, his name was Joachim. The name God, Jahve, was substituted for Elohim. Joachim = Eliachim = Eli or Heli. Anna and Heli were the parents of Mary.
7. Mary. The Mary in the Gospels, called the wife of Alphaeus or Clopas (Jn 19:25). Mary, the mother of James and Joseph (Mt 27:56).
8. Alphaeus, or Clopas, the brother of Joseph (Eusebius, *NPNF*2 1:146, 199; see also ch. 4, § 43).
9. Salome, sister of Mary (Jn 19:25 as compared with Mt 27:56 and Mk 15:40).
10. Zebedee. The father of James and John.
11. Elizabeth, cousin to Mary (Lk 1:36).
12. James. The apostle James the Younger. See ch. 11, § 13. Early head of the Jerusalem Church.
13. Joses/Joseph (Mk 6:3; Mt 13:55). Otherwise unknown.
14. Simon. The apostle Simon the Zealot. "Became bishop after James the Just, and fell asleep and was buried there at the age of 120 years" ("Hippolytus on the Twelve Apostles," *ANF* 5:255); likewise Eusebius (*NPNF*2 1:164) says, "Symeon, the son of Clopas, . . . suffered martyrdom, at the age of one hundred and twenty years, while Trajan was emperor."
15. Judas, the apostle Thaddaeus, or Lebbaeus (KJV). See ch. 11, § 14. His grandchildren were brought before Domitian (Eusebius, *NPNF*2 1:149).
16. Daughters. The sisters of Jesus (Mk 6:3).
17. James. The well-known apostle James. Killed by Herod Agrippa (Ac 12:2).
18. John, the apostle and evangelist.

THE PHYSICAL APPEARANCE OF JESUS

In Psalm 45:2, we read: "You are the most handsome of the sons of men," and in Isaiah 53:2: "He had no form or majesty that we should look at Him, and no beauty that we should desire Him." But from these or other passages of Scripture, which refer either to the glory or shame of Christ in His work of redemption, we must not infer great physical beauty nor exceptional deformity in the external appearance of our Lord.

Aside from the consideration of His divine nature, there is no doubt as to the superior intelligence, the attractive personality, the commanding figure, and the oratorical ability of Jesus. He who could attract and hold the attention of multitudes and minister to them, especially in His work of healing, must have enjoyed certain favorable physical qualities, at any rate, a voice that could make itself heard and understood in an audience of thousands. Yet, in spite of the supreme distinction of His person and office, the external appearance of Jesus was in every respect that of a fallen and sinful man. That there was really nothing remarkable about His appearance may probably be gathered from the fact that a betrayer was engaged to point Him out, that—in addition to other reasons—Mary Magdalene mistook Him for the gardener, and that the disciples on the way to Emmaus as well as the apostles at a later occasion failed to recognize Him. As a true human being, He endured the common, or general, infirmities of men. He lived and walked. He was hungry, thirsty, tired, happy, or sad just as other men. But of any personal illness, such as a siege of sickness or of any physical deformity or defect in body or limbs, there is no record.

Precious works of art may stimulate the imagination, but as to height, weight, and other details of the physical appearance of Jesus, nothing definite is known. The earliest pictorial representations, such as the Vine, or the Lamb and the Fish in the catacombs, are purely symbolic. On account of their largely Jewish extraction, the first Christians and witnesses of Palestine were not much given to pictorial representation. An ancient brass figure, however, erected at Caesarea Philippi, attracted considerable attention as the supposed representation of Christ's healing of the woman with the discharge of blood (Mt 9:20). This is the statue that Eusebius saw and that Julian the Apostate is said to have destroyed (Eusebius, *NPNF2* 1:304; Sozomenus, *NPNF2* 2:342). Eusebius also speaks of likenesses of Peter and Paul as well as of Christ Himself, said to have been painted by St. Luke. Of these, not a trace, not even an early description, has remained. The apocryphal accounts of the miraculous impression on the napkin of Veronica, the likeness of Christ sent with the famous letter to Abgarus, the ruler of Edessa, and the like, must be considered unreliable tradition.

A detailed description of the appearance of Jesus, though not older than the twelfth century, is of considerable interest for the history of Christian art. It is in the form of a letter supposed to have been composed by a certain Roman officer, Publius Lentulus, and is addressed to the senate of Rome. While the remarkable document is no doubt based upon earlier tradition, it can hardly be accepted as genuine. None of the Church historians from Eusebius (fourth century) to Evagrius (sixth century) mention it. The first time it appears in the pages of history is in the *Historia Ecclesiastica* of Nicephorus, who flourished in Constantinople about AD 1325. "There has appeared in our times," he quotes from that letter, "a man of great virtue, named Jesus Christ. . . . He is a man of lofty stature, beautiful, having a noble countenance, so that they who look on Him may both love and fear. He has wavy hair, rather crisp, of the colour of wine, and glittering as it flows down from His shoulders, with a parting in the middle of the head after the manner of the Nazarenes." (It seems that Nazarites, or Nazirites, is meant. But Jesus was no Nazirite.) "His forehead is pure and even, and His face without any spot or wrinkle, but glowing with a delicate flush. His nose and mouth are of faultless beauty; He has a beard abundant and of the same hazel-colour as His hair, not long, but forked. His eyes are blue and very bright. He is terrible in rebuke, calm and loving in admonition, cheerful but preserving gravity. He has never been seen to laugh, but oftentimes to weep. His stature is erect, and His hands and limbs are beautiful to look upon. In speech He is grave, reserved, and modest; and He is fair among the children of men."[9]

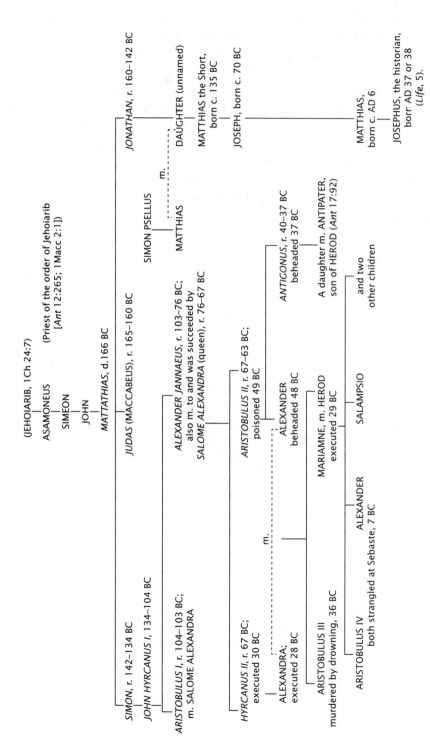

THE MACCABEAN FAMILY

(JEHOIARIB, 1Ch 24:7)

ASAMONEUS (Priest of the order of Jehoiarib [*Ant* 12:265; 1Macc 2:1])

SIMEON

JOHN

MATTATHIAS, d.166 BC

JUDAS (MACCABEUS), r. 165–160 BC

JONATHAN, r. 160–142 BC

SIMON PSELLUS   DAUGHTER (unnamed)

SIMON, r. 142–134 BC

MATTHIAS the Short, born c. 135 BC

MATTHIAS — m. —

JOHN HYRCANUS I, 134–104 BC

JOSEPH, born c. 70 BC

ARISTOBULUS I, r. 104–103 BC; m. SALOME ALEXANDRA

ALEXANDER JANNAEUS, r. 103–76 BC; also m. to and was succeeded by *SALOME ALEXANDRA* (queen), r. 76–67 BC

MATTHIAS, born c. AD 6

JOSEPHUS, the historian, born AD 37 or 38 (*Life*, 5).

HYRCANUS II, r. 67 BC; r. 67–63 BC; executed 30 BC

ARISTOBULUS II, r. 67–63 BC; poisoned 49 BC

ALEXANDER — m. — ALEXANDRA; executed 28 BC

ALEXANDER beheaded 48 BC

ANTIGONUS, r. 40–37 BC beheaded 37 BC

ARISTOBULUS III murdered by drowning, 36 BC

MARIAMNE, m. HEROD executed 29 BC

A daughter m. ANTIPATER, son of HEROD (*Ant* 17:92)

ARISTOBULUS IV

ALEXANDER both strangled at Sebaste, 7 BC

SALAMPSIO

and two other children

The names of the Maccabean rulers are in italics.

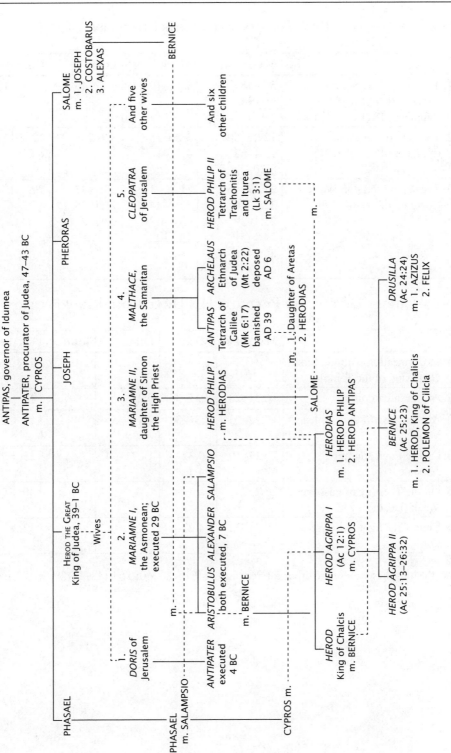

THE HERODIAN FAMILY

ANTIPAS, governor of Idumea

ANTIPATER, procurator of Judea, 47–43 BC
m. CYPROS

PHASAEL

PHASAEL
m. SALAMPSIO

CYPROS m.

HEROD THE GREAT
King of Judea, 39–1 BC
Wives

1.
DORIS of
Jerusalem

2.
MARIAMNE I,
the Asmonean;
executed 29 BC

ANTIPATER
executed
4 BC

ARISTOBULUS ALEXANDER SALAMPSIO
both executed,
7 BC
m. BERNICE

HEROD
King of Chalcis
m. BERNICE

HEROD AGRIPPA I
(Ac 12:1)
m. CYPROS

HEROD AGRIPPA II
(Ac 25:13–26:32)

BERNICE
(Ac 25:23)
m. 1. HEROD, King of Chalcis
   2. POLEMON of Cilicia

DRUSILLA
(Ac 24:24)
m. 1. AZIZUS
   2. FELIX

HERODIAS
m. 1. HEROD PHILIP
   2. HEROD ANTIPAS

SALOME
m.

3.
MARIAMNE II,
daughter of Simon
the High Priest

HEROD PHILIP I
m. HERODIAS

4.
MALTHACE,
the Samaritan

ANTIPAS
Tetrarch of
Galilee
(Mk 6:17)
banished
AD 39
m. 1. Daughter of Aretas
   2. HERODIAS

ARCHELAUS
Ethnarch
of Judea
(Mt 2:22)
deposed
AD 6

5.
CLEOPATRA
of Jerusalem

HEROD PHILIP II
Tetrarch of
Trachonitis
and Iturea
(Lk 3:1)
m. SALOME

And five
other wives

And six
other children

JOSEPH

PHERORAS

SALOME
m. 1. JOSEPH
   2. COSTOBARUS
   3. ALEXAS

BERNICE

For a greater number of details, see: (1) *Ant* 14:121; *War* 1:181. Parents, brothers, and sisters of Herod. (2) *Ant* 17:19–22; *War* 1:562–63. Wives and children of Herod. (3) *Ant* 18:130–42; 19:354–55; *War* 2:220–22. Descendants of Mariamne.

BUSY DAYS IN THE LORD'S MINISTRY

	MATTHEW	MARK	LUKE	CHAPTER
1. The Day of the Sermon on the Mount (Number of verses: 155)	5:1–48 6:1–34 7:1–29	3:13–19	6:13–49	11, §§ 18–42
2. The Day of the Parables (Number of verses: 171)	12:22–50 13:1–53 8:20–27	3:20–35 4:1–41	8:4–25	12, § 12 to 13, § 6
3. Tuesday of Passion Week (Number of verses: 399)	21:19–46 22:1–46 23:1–39 24:1–51 25:1–46 26:1–5	11:20–33 12:1–44 13:1–37 14:1–2	20:1–47 21:1–38 22:1–2	29, § 1 to 30, § 21

CHRIST DISTINCTLY PREDICTS HIS DEATH AND RESURRECTION

	MATTHEW	MARK	LUKE	JOHN	CHAPTER
1. In Connection with the First Cleansing of the Temple				2:19–22	7, § 3
2. At Caesarea Philippi	16:21–23	8:31–33	9:22		18, § 6
3. At the Close of the Galilean Ministry	17:22–23	9:31–32	9:43–45		19, § 2
4. On the Final Journey to Jerusalem	20:17–19	10:32–34	18:31–34		25, § 20
5. On the Tuesday of Passover Week (Death)	26:1–2				30, § 20
6. Thursday Night (Resurrection)	26:31–32	14:27–28			32, § 1

Besides these, there are other references: Mt 9:15; 12:40; 16:4; Lk 11:29; Jn 3:14; 6:51.

Sabbath Controversies

	Matthew	Mark	Luke	John	Chapter
1. The Invalid at the Pool of Bethesda—Christ appeals to His own authority and at a later occasion to the practice of circumcision on the Sabbath. Compare Jn 7:21–24.				5:10–19	8, §§ 6–9
2. The Disciples Plucking Grain on the Sabbath—Christ appeals to precedents in Scripture and to temple service.	12:1–8	2:23–28	6:1–5		10, §§ 26–27
3. The Man with a Withered Hand—Christ appeals to common sense. The sheep fallen into a pit	12:9–14	3:1–6	6:6–11		10, §§ 29–30
4. The Man Blind from His Birth—"We must work the works of Him who sent Me while it is day; night is coming, when no one can work."				9:1–34	20, §§ 21–25
5. The Crippled Woman Healed on a Sabbath—The watering of an ox or ass on a Sabbath			13:10–17		21, §§ 29–30
6. A Man Healed on the Sabbath Who Had Dropsy—The ox fallen into a well			14:1–6		23, §§ 6–7

THE INNOCENCE OF JESUS

As Brought Out during His Trial and Death on the Cross

Judas. (When he returned the thirty pieces of silver.)
"I have sinned by betraying innocent blood." (Mt 27:4)

Pilate. (At the beginning of the trial, after he had asked the question: "What is truth?")
"I find no guilt in Him." (Jn 18:38; Lk 23:4)

Pilate. (After Jesus returned from Herod.)
"And after examining Him before you, behold, I did not find this man guilty."
(Lk 23:14)

Herod. (As reported by Pilate.)
"Neither did Herod." (Lk 23:15)

The Wife of Pilate. (While the people were considering the choice of "Barabbas or Jesus?")
"Have nothing to do with that righteous man." (Mt 27:19)

Pilate. (After the choice of Barabbas.)
"Why? What evil has He done? I have found in Him no guilt deserving death."
(Lk 23:22)

Pilate. (Washing his hands.)
"I am innocent of this man's blood." (Mt 27:24)

Pilate. (Twice; immediately before and after speaking the words: "Behold the man!")
"See, I am bringing Him out to you that you may know that I find no guilt in Him." (Jn 19:4)
"Take Him yourselves and crucify Him, for I find no guilt in Him." (Jn 19:6)

The Penitent Thief. (On the cross.)
"This man has done nothing wrong." (Lk 23:41)

The Centurion. (After the death of Christ.)
"Truly this was the Son of God!" (Mt 27:54)
"Truly this man was the Son of God!" (Mk 15:39)
"Certainly this man was innocent!" (Lk 23:47)

CONFESSING CHRIST

John the Baptist
"Behold, the Lamb of God!" (Jn 1:29, 36)

Andrew
"We have found the Messiah." (Jn 1:41)

Philip
"We have found Him of whom Moses in the Law and also the prophets wrote."
(Jn 1:45)

Nathanael
"You are the Son of God!" (Jn 1:49)

The Disciples
"Truly You are the Son of God." (Mt 14:33)

Peter
"You are the Holy One of God." (Jn 6:69)
"You are the Christ, the Son of the living God." (Mt 16:16; Mk 8:29; Lk 9:20)

Thomas
"My Lord and my God!" (Jn 20:28)

Two Blind Men
"Have mercy on us, Son of David." (Mt 9:27)

A Canaanite Woman
"Have mercy on me, O Lord, Son of David." (Mt 15:22)

Two Other Blind Men near Jericho
"Lord, have mercy on us, Son of David!" (Mt 20:30, 31)

Palm Sunday Crowds
"Hosanna to the Son of David!" (Mt 21:9, 15)

Bartimaeus, a Blind Beggar
"Jesus, Son of David, have mercy on me!" (Mk 10:47, 48)

A Blind Man near Jericho
"Jesus, Son of David, have mercy on me!" (Lk 18:38, 39)

ENDNOTES

INTRODUCTION

1   See Gibbs, *Matthew 1:1–11:1*, 64.
2   See Gibbs's analysis in *Matthew 1:1–11:1*, 12–30.
3   See, e.g., Maier's comments at the beginning of *In the Fullness of Time*, 3–4.
4   See Just's introduction to *Luke 1:1–9:50*, 16–19.
5   See Gibbs's analysis in *Matthew 1:1–11:1*, 12–30.
6   Gk *psyche kosmou*; Lat *anima mundi*.

CHAPTER 1
THE STATE OF THE WORLD

1   Milman, *History of Christianity*, 21. For a detailed look at the succession of empires and Israelite history, read Raymond F. Surburg's "The Historical Setting of the Apocrypha" in *ALEN*, xliii–xc.
2   See "Roman Empire" in *ABD* 5:801–6. The article notes that the Jews in Israel were an exception, since the Romans had difficulty understanding their religious zeal for monotheism, which led to major conflicts.
3   Charles Merivale in Myers, *General History*, 200.
4   Gibbon, *Rome* 1:55.
5   Agrippa's speech against Roman war describes the subjugation of so many nations. Cf. *War* 2:378–80.
6   Gibbon, *Rome* 1:2–3.
7   Tacitus, *Annals* 1.11.
8   Suetonius, *Augustus* 22. They had been closed but twice before in the seven hundred years since the founding of Rome.
9   Graetz, *History of the Jews* 2:103; *War* 1:397.
10 *Ant* 17:198; *War* 1:672.
11 *War* 2:376–77.
12 Gibbon, *Rome* 1:46.
13 *Graecia capta ferum victorem cepit.*
14 *ALEN*, lvii.
15 Myers, *General History*, 178.
16 The Decapolis.
17 The Septuagint, LXX.
18 The apocryphal books: Additions to Daniel and Esther, 2 Maccabees, Wisdom of Solomon, and others.
19 Deissmann, *Licht vom Osten*, 63.
20 Deissmann, *Licht vom Osten*, 50.

21 Gibbon, *Rome* 1:47.
22 Suetonius, *Julius* 7.
23 Suetonius, *Julius* 82.
24 "More haste, less speed." "Better a safe commander than a bold." Suetonius, *Augustus* 25.
25 Suetonius, *Tiberius* 21.
26 Suetonius, *Caligula* 22.
27 Suetonius, *Nero* 38. Tacitus, *Annals* 25.39.
28 The *Kyrie eleison* has survived to the present day.
29 Tertullian in Carthage. Milman, *Hist. of Lat. Christianity* 1:55. Cf. Engelbrecht, *Church from Age to Age*, 12.
30 Founded by Greeks in 600 BC.
31 *NPNF*2 43:287.
32 From papyri, ostraca, and inscriptions. Deissmann, *Licht vom Osten*, 53ff.
33 Cremer, in his *Biblico-Theological Lexicon of the N.T. Greek*. See also Deissmann, *Licht vom Osten*, 55: "*Streit der Puristen und Hebraisten.— Dass die Heilige Schrift allermindestens in das klassische Sprackgewand eines Demosthenes und Plato gekleidet sein muesse, das erschien vielen als selbstverstaendlich, und gegenteilige Behauptungen empfand man als ein Attentat auf den Heiligen Geist. Wir unsererseits stehen auf seiten derer, die den wilden Rosenstrauch nicht deshalb fuer unschoen halten, weil er keine gloire de Dijon traegt.*"
34 *Ant* 12:7.
35 *Ant* 12:147–49.
36 Cf. *Ant* 14:77–79; *War* 1:152–54, 157–58.
37 Already in the time of Jeremiah, and against the will of the prophet (Jer 43:1–7).
38 Graetz, *History of the Jews* 2:201. See also Schama, *Story of the Jews*, 99–100.
39 Schürer, *Jewish People* 2.2:220. See Schama, *Story of the Jews*, 89.
40 Cf. *Ant* 11:133; Graetz, *History of the Jews* 2:203.
41 Graetz, *History of the Jews* 2:223. See *ALEN*, lxii–lxiii.
42 Suetonius, *Julius* 59.
43 Gibbon, *Rome* 1:63.
44 Suetonius, *Julius* 57; *Augustus* 49.

45 For an interesting itinerary from York to Jerusalem (3,740 miles), see Gibbon, *Rome* 1:63 n. 85.

46 See photograph of a Roman bridge over upper Jordan River in *ISBE* 4:2602.

47 Lat *numina*, not *dei*.

48 Lat *lares et penates*. The hearth as symbolizing the family and home and the pantry, or cupboard, as symbolizing food and provisions.

49 Janus, probably as a symbol of peace and safety.

50 Mars.

51 Milman, *History of Christianity*, 22.

52 Lat *religio licita*. Among these was also the Jewish religion. See *ALEN*, lxxxi.

53 Gibbon, *Rome* 1:34. Augustus rebuilt eighty-two heathen temples in Rome.

54 Tacitus, *Annals* 15.45; Rm 1:24–31.

55 Suetonius, *Vespasian* 4, at the time of the last Jewish war: "There had spread over all the Orient an old and established belief that it was fated at that time for men coming from Judea to rule the world. This prediction, referring to the emperor of Rome, as afterwards appeared from the event, the people of Judea took to themselves."

56 Tacitus, *History of the Jews* 5.13, also referring to the last Jewish war: "The greater part had a firm belief that it was contained in the old sacerdotal books, that at this very time the east would prevail, and that some that came out of Judea should obtain the empire of the world, which obscure oracle foretold Vespasian and Titus; but the generality of the common people, as usual, indulged their own inclinations."

57 *War* 6:312–13, likewise referring to the last Jewish war: "But now, what did the most elevate them [the Jews] in undertaking this war, was an ambiguous oracle that was also found in their sacred writings, how, 'about that time, one from their country should become governor of the habitable earth.' The Jews took this prediction to belong to themselves in particular, and many of the wise men were thereby deceived in their determination. Now this oracle certainly denoted the government of Vespasian, who was appointed emperor in Judea." Thus Josephus proves that he knew of the true messianic expectations of his people, but that he himself did not share them and was base enough to deny and betray them.

58 3.652–6. In its oldest part, 170 BC, there occurs the brief prediction of a king whom God shall send from the sun, "who shall cause the whole earth to cease from wicked war, killing some and exacting faithful oaths from others." The general picture of messianic times presented is generally admitted to have formed the basis of Virgil's dream of the Golden Age. See Edersheim, *Life and Times of Jesus*, 1:172, 203.

59 This *Eclogue* (4) of Virgil (70–19 BC) celebrates the birth of a child, though there was no agreement as to who this child was whose birth was to be coincident with the advent of a new era and who, after filling the other great offices of state, was to "rule with his father's virtues the world at peace." On account of this supposed prophecy of the coming Christ, Virgil became so popular in the Middle Ages as to be almost considered an unwitting instrument of the Holy Spirit.

CHAPTER 2
THE STATE OF THE JEWS

1 Or still later, when the destruction of Jerusalem brought final proof that the Savior had come.

2 *Erets Israel* (Hbr) is the territory from the "Brook of Egypt" to "Lebo-hamath" (as promised by Moses in Nu 34:5–8) and from the Lebanon to Tadmor (the Roman Palmyra, the city that Solomon built in the wilderness [2Ch 8:4]).

3 Robinson et al., *Palestine in General History*, 3.

4 Robinson et al., *Palestine in General History*, 3. See also "Census Figures," *TLSB*, 213.

5 See Blunt, *Israel in World History*, 9ff.

6 Notice the remarkable boundary line of mountains and highlands between the present rulers of the world and the world rulers of the past. A high fence extends in an almost unbroken line: the Himalayas, Pamir Mountains, Hindu Kush, Alborz, Caucasus, the Kurdish and Armenian Highlands; and in Europe: the Balkans, the Carpathians, the Alps, and the Pyrenees (Shepherd, *Historical Atlas*, 2–3).

7 The Scythian invasion in the latter half of the seventh century BC. This marks the first of a long series of invasions: Parthians, Turks, Mongols, Goths, Vandals, and Huns, until the barbarians themselves took a hand in ruling the world.

8   Alluded to in Zep 2:4–6; Jer 1:14. See Stanley, *Jewish Church* 2:432ff. Breaking through the barriers of the Caucasus, the Scythians swept down like a swarm of locusts upon Media and Assyria, turned fruitful fields into deserts, and, pushing across Mesopotamia, ravaged Syria, crossed Israel, and penetrated to the borders of Egypt, where they were bought off by Psammetichus I. For twenty-eight years, they remained in Western Asia, but only one trace of their passage remained. The name of the old Canaanite city of Beth-shean (Jgs 1:27) was changed into Scythopolis, that is, the city of the Scythians (one of the cities of the Decapolis; see Schama, *Story of the Jews*, 109). Ezekiel may associate them with the Scythian tribe called "Rus" that dwelt in the northern Taurus Mountains. However, the Scythian Rus must not be associated with Russia, a much later title that does not occur in the Bible. See Hummel, *Ezekiel 21–48*, 1106–07.

9   The Syrian, Libyan, and Sahara deserts.

10   Breasted, *Conquest of Civilization*, 117.

11   Both the cause of their prosperity and the source of their protection. They did not live on the international highway and so for the most part could afford to be careless "after the manner of the Sidonians" and were "quiet and unsuspecting" (Jgs 18:7).

12   Jared Diamond offers a description of the remarkable role of the Fertile Crescent in the development of agriculture, trade, and civilization in *Guns, Germs, and Steel: The Fates of Human Societies* (New York: W. W. Norton & Company, 2005). See, e.g., p. 182 of his book.

13   See "The Press of Mighty Empires," *TLSB*, 1205.

14   From Elath (at the northern extremity of the Red Sea) to Tiphsah (at the Euphrates; 1Ki 4:24) an area of sixty thousand square miles, as compared with the seven thousand square miles of the tribal possession (Hurlbut, *Bible Atlas*, 69). Tiphsah was known as Thapsacus and Amphipolis in classical times.

15   Cf. *War* 7:252–406 concerning Masada.

16   The following summarizes the history of the kingdoms. (1) *The kingdom of Israel*, or of the Ten Tribes. It secured allegiance of all the tribes east of the Jordan. Nineteen kings ruled over this kingdom, from Jeroboam I to Hoshea, representing several dynasties, with intervals of anarchy and frequent change, until its fall in 722 BC and the deportation of the ten tribes into Assyria. (2) *The kingdom of Judah*, including Judah, Simeon (subsumed within Judah), Benjamin, and the Levitical cities. The latter, thirteen in number, were all located in the tribes of Judah, Benjamin, and Simeon—a most remarkable arrangement (Jsh 21:9–19). This kingdom remained loyal to the house of David during all its history and was ruled by twenty-one kings, from Rehoboam to Zedekiah, until the Babylonian captivity, 587 BC. (3) *The kingdom of Syria*, north of Dan and Palestine proper, with Damascus as its capital. This kingdom, small at first, soon rose to power under Ben-hadad I and II, and at the height of its power, under Hazael, it was the leading nation in Asia west of the Euphrates. In c. 732 BC Assyria subjugated it. (4) *The kingdom of Moab*, lying east of the Dead Sea, between the river Arnon and the brook Zered. It was usually subject to Israel, but at times it revolted and set up a government of its own. Eventually it also had to bow to Assyria and Babylonia. Later in history, it was overrun by the Arabians, with whom the Moabites were afterwards confounded (*Ant* 13:374). Machaerus, the scene of the tragic death of John the Baptist (*Ant* 18:119), was located in Moab. (5) *The kingdom of Edom*, south of the Dead Sea. It held about the same relation to Judah as Moab held to Israel. Its conquest opened to Solomon the ports of the Red Sea. But like all the fragments of Solomon's empire, it also fell under the rule of Nebuchadnezzar. This country was to be a particular curse to Judah in the declining days of its history. As Idumea, it was taken by Judas Maccabeus in 165 BC (1Macc 4:29–35); but it revenged itself upon its conquerors when the Idumean Herods finally succeeded in placing themselves on the Jewish throne. See Hurlbut, *Bible Atlas*, 78.

17   Blunt, *Israel in World History*, 57.

18   The latter half of the seventh century BC. Blunt, *Israel in World History*, 77.

19   Breasted, *Conquest of Civilization*, 179, 405.

20   Jehoiakim's successor.

21   See *Crossway ESV Bible Atlas*, 175.

22 The "lost" ten tribes have definitely passed out of history.

23 Called "holy city" in Ne 11:1; Is 48:2; 52:1.

24 Breasted, *Conquest of Civilization*, 164, 198.

25 By way of Israel and the Hellespont.

26 Blunt, *Israel in World History*, 96.

27 See "The Hellenistic Era," *Crossway ESV Bible Atlas*, 187–95.

28 *Ant* 11:336–39.

29 Particularly in Samaria. Afterwards organized by Pompey into the Decapolis. Schürer, *Jewish People* 2.1:123.

30 *ABD* 1:150.

31 *Perata tēs oikoumenēs.*

32 See *ALEN*, 160.

33 The kingdom of the Ptolemies in Egypt began in 323 BC with Ptolemy I, who declared himself king in 305 BC, and the Ptolemies ruled Egypt for almost three centuries. In 30 BC, the year that marks the death of Cleopatra, it became a Roman province. Seleucus Nicator, famous as the builder of cities, founded the Syrian kingdom, which his successors subjected to harassing vicissitudes. The Roman Republic dissolved the kingdom in 63 BC and incorporated its lands into their territory.

34 From Hellenist, a non-Greek who adopts the Greek language as well as Greek customs and manners.

35 The story is as follows: King Ptolemy II Philadelphus (285–246 BC) was induced by his librarian to have the laws of the Jews translated into Greek for his library. At his request, the Jewish high priest Eleazar sent him seventy-two able men, six out of each of the twelve tribes of Israel, who finished their task in seventy-two days (Schürer, *Jewish People* 2.3:159; see also Schama, *Story of the Jews*, 95).

36 Schürer, *Jewish People* 2.3:159.

37 Schürer, *Jewish People* 2.1:59; Schama, *Story of the Jews*, 111. See also note on 1Macc 1:9 in *ALEN*, 160. The Syrian supremacy lasted from 198 to 166 BC.

38 Schürer, *Jewish People* 1.1:203.

39 Schürer, *Jewish People* 1.1:201; Schama, *Story of the Jews*, 114. See also note on 1Macc 1:10 in *ALEN*, 160. *Epiphanes* means "the Evident God"; but he was also called Epimanes, "the Madman."

40 *History of the Jews* 5:8.

41 The original Pharisees; the party of the "Pious," or Hasideans. See 1Macc 2:42 and note in *ALEN*, 164.

42 See "The Maccabean Era," *Crossway ESV Bible Atlas*, 197–203.

43 *Ant* 12:265–78; 1Macc 2:23–48. Mattathias was of the house of Hasmoneans and of the order of Joarib (Jehoiarib; see 1Ch 24:7).

44 Maccabean, from Judas Maccabeus, "the Hammerer," son of Mattathias.

45 On the 25th of Chislev, 164 BC.

46 In the battle at Beth-zechariah, 100,000 foot soldiers, 20,000 riders, and 32 wine-crazed elephants were engaged (1Macc 6:30–47).

47 The office was hereditary. Only twice had the line been broken in Jewish history: when Eli superseded the elder house of Eleazar and when Zadok replaced Abiathar (Stanley, *Jewish Church* 3:314; see also Schama, *Story of the Jews*, 120). Cf. Schürer, *Jewish People* 2.1:223–24.

48 Schürer, *Jewish People* 1.1:264–65; Schama, *Story of the Jews*, 121.

49 Cf. Schürer, *Jewish People* 1.1:3.

50 *Ant* 13:171–73.

51 The *Chasidim*, or Hasideans (1Macc 2:42; 3:13). See Schürer, *Jewish People* 1.1:287; Schama, *Story of the Jews*, 125–26.

52 *Sadducee* is likely a Greek form of the Hebrew name *Zadokite*. See Schürer, *Jewish People* 1.1:287.

53 Schürer, *Jewish People* 2.2:42; Schama, *Story of the Jews*, 125.

54 In the time of Alexander Jannaeus, a Sadducean prince (103–76 BC), eight hundred Pharisees were crucified in Jerusalem (*Ant* 13:380). This was the first appearance of the cross in the hills of Israel.

55 *Ant* 13:257–58.

56 *Ant* 14:8. It was in accordance with his own ambitious schemes to have a weak overlord placed on the Judean throne.

57 *Ant* 14:37.

58 *Ant* 14:64.

59 *Ant* 14:72; Tacitus, *History of the Jews* 5.9.

60 *Ant* 14:73, 79

61 In fact, eighty years.

62 Alexander and Antigonus.

63 *Ant* 14:99.

64 By defeating Pompey at Pharsalus, August 9, 48 BC.

65 Caesar permitted Antipater to choose the principality he desired and allowed him to select the title he wished to bear. Antipater, returning the compliment, left the decision to Caesar, and Caesar made him procurator of Judea, while Hyrcanus received honor, but no power (*Ant* 14:143).

66 See Lv 21:17–24. It was Antigonus who slashed off his uncle's ears (*Ant* 14:366). According to one report, he bit them off with his teeth (*War* 1:270)!

67 *Ant* 14:365. Antigonus was the last surviving son of Aristobulus. He with Hyrcanus were the last of the Maccabean princes, except Aristobulus III, young son of Alexander.

68 *Ant* 14:386–87.

69 Sossius was the Roman general sent by Antony to assist Herod. He hurried Antigonus off in chains to Antony at Antioch, and a bribe from Herod to Antony sealed his fate. Thus with Mattathias, the Hasmonean dynasty began, and with Antigonus, who was also called Mattathias, it came to an end (*Ant* 14:487–90).

70 According to Josephus, Herod was a descendant of an honorable Idumean family (*War* 1:123). Eusebius says that Herod was an Idumean on his father's side and an Arabian on that of his mother, and quoting Julius Africanus, he adds that he believed him to be descended from a Philistine slave (*NPNF*2 1:89; see also Schürer, *Jewish People* 1.1:314, n. 3). This explains the epithet "Edomite Slave." On account of the enforced Idumean conversion, he was also called a "half Jew" (*Ant* 14:403). In the Talmud, he is referred to as "the slave of King Jannaeus" (Stanley, *Jewish Church* 3:361; Schama, *Story of the Jews*, 133).

71 Schürer, *Jewish People* 1.1:416–19.

72 *Ant* 15:373.

73 The title "Great" was bestowed upon him by his Greek flatterers.

74 Schürer, *Jewish People* 1.1:419–26.

75 *Ant* 14:403–4.

76 *War* 1:358; *Ant* 15:5. Schürer, *Jewish People* 1.1:420.

77 *Ant* 15:55–56.

78 Territory along the coast and an especially valuable district around Jericho.

79 *Ant* 15:97–98.

80 *Ant* 15:194.

81 *Ant* 15:20.

82 *Ant* 15:179–82; Schürer, *Jewish People* 1.1:427–28.

83 Schürer, *Jewish People* 1.1:428; *Ant* 15:217.

84 End of 30 BC. *Ant* 15:218.

85 Stanley, *Jewish Church* 3:376.

86 End of 29 BC. *Ant* 15:237–45.

87 Sometime around 28 BC. *Ant* 15:251.

88 Schürer, *Jewish People* 1.1:432–37; Schama, *Story of the Jews*, 134–35; *Ant* 17:306–7.

89 "These vestments king Herod kept in that place" (*Ant* 15:404).

90 *Ant* 15:331–32.

91 A Greek word corresponding to the Latin *Augustus*: venerable, august.

92 *War* 2:84–92.

93 At Ascalon, Damascus, Tyre, Sidon, Tripoli, Ptolemais, even at Athens and Lacedemonia, he built gymnasia, walls, halls, porticoes, temples, marketplaces, theaters, aqueducts, baths, fountains, colonnades, playgrounds, and polished-marble street pavements (*War* 1:422).

94 Stanley, *Jewish Church* 3:384.

95 Not a new building. The Temple of Herod was regarded as identical with that of Zerubbabel.

96 *Ant* 15:380. Schürer, *Jewish People* 1.1:409 gives AUC 734 as the date.

97 *Ant* 15:425. But the building process carried on for the next eighty years, during the entire life of Christ, and was only completed in the time of Albinus (AD 64), a few years before its final destruction (AD 70).

98 Schürer, *Jewish People* 1.1:438.

99 *Ant* 15:424.

100 Klausner, *Jesus of Nazareth*, 151; Schürer, *Jewish People* 1.1:445.

101 *War* 1:400; *Ant* 15:361; Stanley, *Jewish Church* 3:413.

102 Schürer, *Jewish People* 1.1:448.

103 *Ant* 15:365; 16:64.

104 *Ant* 15:306–7.

105 *Ant* 15:308.

106 Schürer, *Jewish People* 1.1:454–67.

107 *Ant* 17:14, 19–21; cf. Dt 21:15–17; 25:5–10.

108 *Ant* 15:342.

109 Schürer, *Jewish People* 1.1:457.

110 *Ant* 16:81–86.

111 *Ant* 16:356.

112 Probably 7 BC. *Ant* 16:362–72, 392–94.

113 *Ant* 17:65–69.

114 *Ant* 17:93–98.

115 *Ant* 17:196–99.

116 Edersheim, *Temple*, 176.

117 Klausner, *Jesus of Nazareth*, 145.

118 *War* 2:90–91.

Chapter 3
The Threshold of the New Testament

1   Roman Catholic critical scholar Raymond E. Brown writes that Jesus' birth is not the subject of early apostolic preaching (*Birth of the Messiah*, 33). Although it is certainly true that the apostles focused especially on Jesus' death and resurrection in their preaching and teaching, they did not neglect to mention Jesus' birth. In Galatians, one of the earliest New Testament documents, Paul argued for our adoption as God's children through "His Son, born of woman, born under the law" (Gal 4:4). Paul later alluded to Jesus' birth in his great Christological hymn when he spoke of Christ Jesus "taking the form of a servant [Gk *doulos*], being born in the likeness of men" (Php 2:7). A comparable title appears in the apostolic prayer of Ac 4:27, 30, which refers to Jesus as a servant/child (Gk *paidos*). In any event, Paul agreed with Matthew and Luke that Jesus' conception was an act of God.

2   The name of the city of Judah in which they lived is not given. Hebron has been suggested on account of Jsh 21:11.

3   Schürer, *Jewish People* 2.1:222–24; Edersheim, *Life and Times of Jesus* 1:141.

4   8,580 Levites in the time of Moses (Nu 4:48); 38,000 in the time of David (1Ch 23:3). Josephus speaks of 20,000 priests, *Against Apion* 2:108.

5   Schürer, *Jewish People* 2.1:273; *Ant* 7:365–67. The act of the worship proper and the sacrifices were in the hands of the officiating priests. The Levites acted as assistants, temple servants, guards, gatekeepers, singers, musicians, and the like. See also Edersheim, *Temple*, 63.

6   According to Ezr 2:36–39, it was the children of Jedaiah, Immer, Pashhur (who was the son of Malchijah), and Harim—corresponding to the second, third, fifth, and sixteenth families in the order of 1Ch 24:7–19.

7   *Life*, 2–5; Edersheim, *Life and Times of Jesus* 1:135; Schürer, *Jewish People* 2.1:222.

8   For the financial advantages of the priesthood see Schürer, *Jewish People* 2.1:235–49. See also Schama, *Story of the Jews*, 106–7.

9   No fewer than 142 disqualifying bodily defects were counted. However, a priest who for any reason was debarred from exercising the functions of his office was still entitled to his share of the benefits belonging to those of the priesthood (Schürer, *Jewish People* 2.1:214).

10 See Ware, *When Was Jesus Really Born?*, 103.

11 Dionysius concluded that AD 1 corresponded with the year 754 of the building of Rome (*ab urbe condita*, or AUC). Since Jesus was born before Herod died, He could not have been born in AD 1, as historians today (e.g., Steinmann *From Abraham to Paul*, 230–34) ascertain that Herod died shortly before the Passover of 1 BC.

To obtain the years of Rome corresponding to the AD system, we must add 753 to the number in question: Thus the year of Jesus' death, AD 33, would correspond to 786 AUC. If we would obtain the year of Rome before the birth of Christ, we must subtract the number in question from 754. Thus if Christ was born two years before the Christian Era, or 2 BC, then, subtracting 2 from 754, we arrive at 752 AUC.

12 The remains of Robinson's Arch may mark the spot where this bridge or staircase connected to the temple complex.

13 See maps in *ESV Bible Atlas*, 233, as well as the north facing diagram, 230–31.

14 Stanley, *Jewish Church* 3:389.

15 The gate through which the scapegoat or Azazel was led on the Day of Atonement was on the eastern wall (Edersheim, *Temple*, 278).

16 There was even supposed to have been a temple synagogue within the bounds of the sacred building, although Edersheim considers this "quite untenable" (*Life and Times of Jesus* 1:246; 2:742).

17 Edersheim, *Temple*, 22.

18 For a description of Herod's temple see Schürer, *Jewish People* 2.1:280ff.; Edersheim, *Temple*, 22ff.; Hurlbut, *Bible Atlas*, 137ff.

19 *War* 6:125; Deissmann, *Licht vom Osten*, 63. A fragment of this wall with its inscription was found in Jerusalem in 1871. In the Slavonic version of Josephus, there is an interesting addition concerning the temple inscription and also incidentally concerning Jesus: "And in it there stood equal pillars, and upon them there were titles in Greek and Latin and Jewish characters, giving warning of the law of purification that no foreigner should enter within; for it was called the inner sanctuary, being approached by fourteen steps and the upper area being built in quadrangular form. And above these titles was hung a fourth title in the same characters, announcing that Jesus [the] King did not reign, [but was] crucified [by the Jews] because He prophesied the destruction of the city and the devastation of the Temple" (Thackeray, *Selections from Josephus* 3:657). At one time, Paul was arrested because it was asserted that he had led Greeks into the Sacred Enclosure (Ac 21:28).

20 *Against Apion* 2:104.

21 See Schürer, *Jewish People* 2.1:282f.

22 Edersheim, *Temple*, 33f.

23 *War* 5:224.

24 Schürer, *Jewish People* 2.1:282.

25 The lampstand is sometimes incorrectly called a "candlestick," though it burned oil rather than candles.

26 See note in Schürer, *Jewish People* 2.1:281.

27 See ch. 2, § 30.

28 Stanley, *Jewish Church* 3:384.

29 The first mention of Herod's name in connection with the rebuilding of the temple occurs in the Babylonian Talmud, and then neither gratefully nor graciously (Edersheim, *Temple*, 36).

30 Edersheim, *Life and Times of Jesus* 1:135.

31 Schürer, *Jewish People* 2.1:278; Edersheim, *Temple*, 122.

32 Schürer, *Jewish People* 2.1:276; *Ant* 3:151–58.

33 Schürer, *Jewish People* 2.1:293.

34 Fahling wrote that, according to Josephus in *Against Apion* 2:119, the services of two hundred men were required every time the temple gates were closed. However, updated editions of the Whiston translation have just twenty men, noting that the Greek incorrectly has two hundred, which conflicts with *War* 6:293: "The eastern gate of the inner [court of the] temple, which was of brass, and vastly heavy, [was] with difficulty shut by twenty men." The creaking of the gates is said to have been heard as far as Jericho! (Schürer, *Jewish People* 2.1:267). In all, two hundred forty Levites and thirty priests were on duty every night and fifty priests every day (Edersheim, *Life and Times of Jesus* 1:134, note; *Temple*, 119).

35 The Shema was a collection of three passages: Dt 6:4–9; 11:13–21; Nu 15:37–41.

36 Edersheim, *Life and Times of Jesus* 1:134.

37 Besides the three ingredients mentioned in Ex 30:34, stacte, onycha, and galbanum, there were added in rabbinic times myrrh, cassia, spikenard, saffron, costus, mace, cinnamon, salt, and an herb which had the property of causing the smoke to ascend vertically. See Thackeray's note to *War* 5:218 in *Selections from Josephus* 3:266, n. a.

38 Edersheim, *Temple*, 141f. Schürer, *Jewish People* 2.1:296.

39 This was the public sacrifice. However, day by day, numerous victims were slaughtered and their flesh burned upon the altar; at all the high festivals so many sacrifices were offered that the officiating priests were kept extremely busy (Schürer, *Jewish People* 2.1:298).

40 See Schürer, *Jewish People* 2.1:290, 273–97; Edersheim, *Temple*, 121–44.

41 Edersheim, *Life and Times of Jesus* 1:138.

42 Which was the right side? From the standpoint of the angel, who probably made his appearance from the direction of the Most Holy Place, it was on the south side of the altar, between the altar and the lampstand; from that of Zechariah it was on the north side, between the altar and the table of the bread of the Presence.

43 Edersheim, *Temple*, 139–40.

44 *John* in Hebrew means "God is gracious."

45 There were two kinds of Nazirite vows according to Nu 6:2–8 and 30:2—a positive and a negative vow, a *Neder* and an *Issar*. In the former, "A man vowed a vow unto Jehovah" in which He consecrated unto God himself, some person, or a certain thing; in the latter, he "swore

an oath to bind his soul with a bond," that is, he renounced the use of certain things. The keeping of the vow of a lifelong Nazirite, or Nazirite from birth, entailed (1) complete abstinence from wine and the fruit of the vine; (2) keeping hair and beard unshorn; (3) guarding against touching a dead body; (4) refraining from eating Levitically unclean food. Only three lifelong Nazirites are mentioned in the Bible: Samson, Samuel, and John the Baptist. (See Edersheim, *Temple*, 322ff.) Tradition adds James the Just (Eusebius, *NPNF2* 1:125). Temporary Nazirites vowed to consecrate themselves to the Lord for a specified time (Nu 6:1–21).

46 Gk *euangelisasthai*. For the first time we meet with the beautiful word *euangelion*, that is, the Gospel.

47 Gabriel appeared also in Dn 8:16; 9:21.

48 Since negative views are not testimonies, it will be unnecessary always to mention the holders of such views and to quote the respective titles and pages of their books.

49 Meyer, *Commentary on the N.T.*, on Lk 1:21.

50 As suggested by Ebrard on account of Lk 1:63 (*Gospel History*, 164).

51 Edersheim, *Life and Times of Jesus* 1:134.

52 From Lk 1:60 we see that Zechariah, now mute, in some way communicated to Elizabeth all that had happened to him in the sanctuary.

53 *Cabul*, according to Josephus, means "what does not please" (*Ant* 8:142).

54 105–104 BC. See Schürer, *Jewish People* 1.1:294.

55 *War* 3:41–43, 301–5. Much is made by some writers (for instance, Emil Ludwig in *The Son of Man* and by those whom he has followed) of the carnal and political messianic hopes and revolutionary tendencies of the Galilean zealots in explanation of the Galilean success and supposed purpose of the Lord's public ministry. But since we can see no particular connection of these thoughts—or facts—with the history of Christ's work, except probably to explain Jn 6:66; 7:3, and similar passages, we are giving them only this passing notice.

56 Quoted by Edersheim, *Life and Times of Jesus* 1:223. It was here in Galilee that Asher "dip[ped] his foot in oil" (Dt 33:24). The rabbis themselves said that it was easier to rear a forest of olive trees in Galilee than one child in Judea (Edersheim, *Life and Times of Jesus* 1:224).

57 Some derive Nazareth from *notser*, to guard or keep (Edersheim, *Life and Times of Jesus* 1:146), others from *nezer*, to separate, and Jerome says it means a flower: "Let us go to Nazareth and see the 'Flower of Galilee'" (*Epistola*, 46, Ad Marcellam; quoted by Andrews, *Life of Our Lord*, 105). But since Mt 2:23 is not a direct quotation, it is also possible that a comparison was intended with the messianic picture in Is 53, on account of the low esteem in which Nazareth was held. But, as applied to Jesus, under no condition is it permissible, thus charging Matthew with confusion, to derive the term from *nazir* in the attempt to make a Nazirite out of Jesus, which is contrary to the promises and facts of the life of the Savior. See Klausner in *Jesus of Nazareth*, 230.

58 Neither is it apparently mentioned by any Christian writer prior to Eusebius, in the fourth century (*NPNF2* 1:93). But after that, it became one of the most famous of holy places.

59 We can no longer trace the source of popular prejudice against it.

60 See Guthe, *Bibelatlas*, 13. However, Edersheim, (*Life and Times of Jesus* 1:147), Andrews (*Life of Our Lord*, 106), MacCoun (*The Holy Land* 2:86), and others suppose the *Via Maris*, the ancient caravan route between Acco (Accho) and Damascus, to have passed through Nazareth.

61 The Plain of Esdraelon, a Y-shaped region, 250 feet above sea level, surrounded by mountains, is situated between Mounts Carmel, Tabor, Gilboa, and the Hill of Moreh. More battles are said to have been fought on this plain than on any other field in the world. Some historians count thirty-four major battles, such as Eric H. Cline in *The Battles of Armageddon: Megiddo and the Jezreel Valley from the Bronze Age to the Nuclear Age* (Ann Arbor: University of Michigan Press, 2000). In the Old Testament, it is called the Valley of Jezreel, from the city on its eastern end, its Greek name Esdraelon being a modification of Jezreel. It is also called the Valley of Megiddo, from the city on its western edge. Armageddon or Harmageddon (Rv 16:16) is transliterated into Greek to refer to the Mountain of Megiddo (Hurlbut, *Bible Atlas*, 15).

62 Each writer on Israel tries to paint a picture of the splendid panorama: Klausner, *Jesus of Nazareth*, 236; Weiss, *Life of Christ* 1:211; Andrews, *Life of*

Our Lord, 107; Edersheim, *Life and Times of Jesus* 1:145; Farrar, *Life of Christ* 1:100; and others.

63 Neubauer, *Sketches of Jewish Social Life*; quoted by Edersheim, *Life and Times of Jesus* 1:147, and Andrews, *Life of Our Lord*, 106.

64 According to Klausner, a Jewish writer from Jerusalem, in *Jesus of Nazareth*, 229.

65 We do not suppose that they made their home away from their ancestral seat in despised Galilee and in an obscure village in order not to arouse the jealousy of Herod. Of this there is no proof. It is rather to be explained as a sign of the fallen estate of that once royal house. See Andrews, *Life of Our Lord*, 66.

66 According to one tradition, Joseph had been previously married to Melcha (or Escha or Salome), by whom he had two daughters and four sons, of whom the youngest was James the Less, "the Lord's brother." His marriage to Mary is placed a year after his wife's death. (See *Catholic Encyclopedia* 8:505, which does not assume the reliability of the legends. In the *New Catholic Encyclopedia*, the legends are played down further, 7:1108.)

67 The Greek Church affirms that the Annunciation took place at the village fountain, at present marked by the Church of the Annunciation. The Latins believe that the angel found the virgin in a grotto, where a church has been erected, which, after that of the Holy Sepulchre, is said to be the most beautiful in Israel. Bengel thinks that the appearance was at evening (Andrews, *Life of Our Lord*, 68). According to an ancient tradition, which merits small credence, there were other members of David's family living in the same territory.

68 While it is true that the grammatical construction of this particular passage, Lk 1:27: "betrothed to a man whose name was Joseph, of the house of David. And the virgin's name was Mary," favors the reference to Joseph only, there is no doubt about the Davidic descent of Mary, even if both genealogies are taken as those of Joseph. Meyer, *Commentary on the N.T.*, commenting on Lk 1:26–27, claims that "the descent of Mary from David cannot at all be proved in the New Testament." He should rather have said that the proof is too evident to be denied. Luke 1:27 and

69 prove her Davidic descent beyond the shadow of a doubt. And besides, there are the inescapable inferences in Ac 2:30; Rm 1:3; 2Tm 2:8; and Heb 7:14.

69 Andrews, *Life of Our Lord*, 57.

70 Ephiphanius and the *Historia Iosephi* both give his age as eighty years (Andrews, *Life of Our Lord*, 56).

71 Prolonged intervals between betrothal and marriage were deemed undesirable for many reasons. See *ISBE* under "Marriage."

72 Edersheim, *Life and Times of Jesus* 1:149.

73 Depending upon the order in which the action of Joseph is placed (Mt 1:24), before or after the three months' visit of Mary to Elizabeth (Lk 1:56); most likely after. See Andrews, *Life of Our Lord*, 68; Meyer, *Commentary on the N.T.* 2:244; Ebrard, *Gospel History*, 172.

74 Edersheim, *Life and Times of Jesus* 1:150.

75 No interpretation of the name here as in Mt 1:21.

76 If Jesus is to be *her* son and David is called *His* father, then surely Christ's Davidic descent through Mary is granted at the outset (cf. Lk 1:69).

77 Compare Zechariah, Lk 1:18.

78 Meyer, *Commentary on the N.T.*, on Lk 1:34; Ebrard, *Gospel History*, 167.

79 Edersheim, *Life and Times of Jesus* 1:152. "*Inquirendo dixit, non desperando*" (Augustine). Meyer argues that "I know not a man" (KJV) should not be understood as a vow of perpetual virginity or a resolution to that effect (Meyer, *Commentary on the N.T.*, on Lk 1:34).

80 Edersheim, *Life and Times of Jesus* 1:152.

81 Bruce, *Synoptic Gospels*, on Lk 1:34–35; Meyer, *Commentary on the N.T.*, on Lk 1:35. See also statements from other Fathers in the Catalog of Testimonies, *Concordia*, 623–48; Pieper, *Christian Dogmatics* 1:550; 2:73.

82 There are different traditions about Mary's parents and grandparents. According to the apocryphal gospel of James (second century), the parents of Mary were Joachim and Anna. Sometimes Hebrew names change out titles for God, such as Joachim changing to Eliachim, which then might be shortened to Eli. This would correspond with the rabbinical tradition that Mary was the daughter of Eli. Anna, her mother, was supposed to

have been of priestly stock (*Catholic Encyclopedia*, under "Virgin," 15:464E). According to another (late) tradition, Matthan had two daughters, Anna and Soba, and a son, Jacob. Anna was the mother of Mary and Soba the mother of Elizabeth (quoted by Andrews, *Life of Our Lord*, 57; also in *New Catholic Encyclopedia* 5:280). The source of this tradition is Nicephorus Callistus, quoting Hippolytus, *Historia Ecclesiastica* 2.3.

83 See Meyer, *Commentary on the N.T.* 2:249, 259.

84 In *Synoptic Gospels*, 465, Bruce translates "*en tais hēmerais tautais*" as "in these days," not "in those days" (*ekeinais*), as in many Bible translations. This really seems the best view on the subject in opposition to Ebrard (*Gospel History*, 172) and others, who would place Mary's visit with Elizabeth *after* her marriage to Joseph, because "virgins were *never* allowed to travel." (Alone?) If any such law was in force at that time—rabbinical authorities are quoted—then Mary may have journeyed with friends, under the protection of a servant, or with neighbors and friends going to the Passover (Andrews, *Life of Our Lord*, 69; Meyer, *Commentary on the N.T.* 2:244). After her three-month visit, it is said (Lk 1:56) that she returned to her own house, which also seems to imply that she was not yet married (Andrews, *Life of Our Lord*, 69).

85 Tatian's *Diatessaron*, c. AD 150, has her travel to Judea right after the angel's announcement (*ANF* 10:44; Hill, *The Earliest Life of Christ*, 44).

86 Edersheim, *Life and Times of Jesus* 1:152.

87 Commentators discuss the connection between maternal excitement and the quickening of the child, but these and other details should be passed over in respectful silence (Bruce, *Synoptic Gospels*, 465).

88 Edersheim, *Life and Times of Jesus* 1:153.

89 Stöckhardt, *Biblische Geschichte*, 7.

90 The hymn naturally divides itself into four parts: (1) the singer's joy, vv. 46–48a; (2) the cause of gladness, vv. 48b–50; (3) the new order of the Gospel in Christ's kingdom, vv. 51–53; (4) the birth of Christ as a deed of God's mercy and grace, vv. 54–55. See also Luther's commentary in AE 21:295–355.

91 Weiss, *Life of Christ* 1:236. Although Mary's return is mentioned before the delivery of Elizabeth, the Gospel writer, they explain, wanted to finish the passage concerning Mary first before proceeding with the account of John's birth. There is no reason, however, to assume a "historical anticipation" at this place (Ylvisaker, *Gospels*, 72).

92 The traditional day for the nativity of John is June 24. The discoveries of certain mythologists, according to which the Gospel stories are supposed to have "astronomical correspondence," do not merit our attention.

93 Gk *emegalyne*.

94 Edersheim, *Life and Times of Jesus* 1:157.

95 The naming of Isaac was connected with the circumcision on the eighth day.

96 Gk *ekaloun*, the imperfect.

97 Ancient commentators, Origin and Ambrose, but also Meyer, supposed a divine revelation. But Ebrard, Weiss, Stöckhardt, and others disagree with them.

98 John Hyrcanus II, 30 BC.

99 For this seems to be the implication of the Gk *eneneuon*, "made signs to" him (used only here in the New Testament), that he was stricken both deaf and mute, although various suggestions have been made to evade the conclusion: Meyer and others, that only a sign was needed, Zechariah having heard all that was said, etc. See Meyer, *Commentary on the N.T.*, on Lk 1:62.

100 Edersheim, *Life and Times of Jesus* 1:158.

101 How did he ask? Likewise through a sign. For even if he was able to hear, as some think, he at least could not speak.

102 Gk *egrapsen legōn*, "He wrote, saying." While it is to be admitted that the explanation "He wrote and at the same time said" fits beautifully into the story, it seems that the speech of Zechariah did not return until v. 64 and that the word *legōn* is used here in true Hebrew fashion—to the effect, he said by writing (Bruce, *Synoptic Gospels*, 468).

103 It is best divided into two parts: (1) Vv. 68–75. A prayer of thanksgiving for the messianic deliverance and blessing already accomplished. Notice the past tense. (2) Vv. 76–79. Prophecies concerning John the Baptist. Notice the future tense.

104 Edersheim, *Life and Times of Jesus* 1:158.

105 Gn 3:15; 22:16–18; Dt 18:15; 2Sm 23:1–5; etc.

106 Figurative designation of the Messiah. *Anatolē* is taken by some as the Greek equivalent for

"Branch" in the Septuagint rendering of Jer 23:5; Zec 3:8; etc. But see Meyer, *Commentary on the N.T.*, on Lk 1:78.

107 Bruce, *Synoptic Gospels*, on Lk 1:80. See ch. 15, endnote 9 in this volume.

108 Brown concludes that Matthew and Luke wrote independently, being unaware of each other's accounts (*Birth of the Messiah*, 34). He lists a variety of differences to make his point. However, since Matthew's account is dominated by concern to show fulfillment of the Old Testament and Luke's account focuses on the temple, it would be natural for the accounts to differ. One might also see Luke supplementing the sparse account recorded by Matthew (cf. Lk 1:1–4), providing details as they served his narrative goals. Differences in accounts are not necessarily evidence for contradiction. Brown ultimately concludes that the evangelists share a common understanding of the Messiah's birth (p. 497).

109 How did Joseph find out? Perhaps from "suspicious women," the so-called *pronubae* (Lat), through whom the bride and bridegroom before their marriage had to make their communication (Ebrard, *Gospel History*), or from Mary herself (Edersheim, *Life and Times of Jesus*), or by observation? And did he, as "the first Ebionite" (denying the virgin birth), refuse to believe her (Lange, quoted in Meyer, *Commentary on the N.T.* 2:244)? We simply do not know.

110 Dt 22:23–24 does not apply.

111 According to Dt 24:1. This also applies to betrothed persons. See Meyer, *Commentary on the N.T.*, on Mt 1:19.

112 Joseph's intent was to divorce her quietly (Gk *lathrai*). However, a dismissal by a letter of divorcement, even under arrangements providing for secrecy, would have to be handed her in the presence of two or three witnesses (Edersheim, *Life and Times of Jesus*).

113 Gk *eboulēthē*, he made the resolution.

114 Gk *apolysai autēn*, to put her away.

115 The angel addressed Joseph in this way because he was bringing tidings of the coming of the Messiah. The fact that he called him son of David confirms the view that the genealogy of Matthew's Gospel is that of Joseph, while Luke, writing the account of the infancy of Jesus from

the standpoint of Mary, was apparently supplied with the genealogy of her family in writing his Gospel.

116 Ylvisaker emphasizes that "your wife" is in apposition to "Mary," so one should not translate it as "Mary as your wife" (as in the ESV), but rather "Mary, your wife." See Ylvisaker, *Gospels*, 77 n. 101.

117 Gk *autos gar*.

118 "His people"; these first, but also the Gentiles (Jn 4:22; Rm 1:16). "From their sins," Gk *apō tōn hamartiōn*, not merely "from sinning."

119 Gk *hē* (emphatic) *parthenos*.

120 *Ha'almah*. Also here *the* virgin.

121 There is no contradiction in the fact that Mary is still called Joseph's betrothed in Lk 2:5. This expression must be read in connection with Matthew. It likely protects Mary's virginity, since "wife" would normally imply sexual relations.

122 Edersheim, *Life and Times of Jesus* 1:155.

123 Whatever view may be taken of the brothers and sisters of the Lord, whether they are regarded as the children of Joseph from a former marriage or as his children with Mary, or as the cousins of Jesus, an appeal cannot be made to this verse in support of the "perpetual virginity" of Mary. Really, it does not matter. The chief consideration is not, "What do you think of Mary?" but, "What do you think of Christ?" See also Pieper, *Christian Dogmatics*, 2:308–9.

CHAPTER 4
THE BIRTH AND CHILDHOOD OF JESUS

1 Quoted by Edersheim, *Life and Times of Jesus* 2:751.

2 See ch. 1.

3 Gk *apographesthai*. Notice the present tense in Lk 2:1, 3. Not a single census, but the introduction of a new system. But notice also the change to the aorist in v. 5, *apograpsasthai*, to indicate one definite occasion.

4 The following material cannot be appealed to: (1) The *Breviatium Imperii*, a booklet of Augustus in his own handwriting, which contained accounts of the number of soldiers, taxes, imposts, and the like (Tacitus, *Annals* 1.40). It concluded with the advice never to aim at an extension of empire. It

is also mentioned by Suetonius, *Augustus*, 101, *Breviarium totius imperii*, to be cut upon bronze tablets and set up at the entrance to the mausoleum of Augustus. The original of this inscription is lost, but the greater part of a copy inscribed in Greek and Latin on marble has been preserved at Ancyra, Asia Minor, and is known as the *Monumentum Ancyranum* (Wieseler, *Synopsis*, 79ff.). While it gives much information on the reign of Augustus, it does not mention the detail in question, a general census. (2) A passage of Dio Cassius, 54:35: "Augustus set on foot a census, to which he allowed his own private property to be submitted, just as if he were a private person, that he might avoid all possible cause of offense." (3) A few passages of a later (Christian) period, in the words of Cassiodorus and others. Cassiodorus, *Variarum* 3:52: "The Augusti at various times wrote out a census of the *orbis Romanus terrarum*." Isidorus, *Etymologiarum* 5:36, which Schürer calls a confused rigmarole: "An era inaugurated by Caesar Augustus, the first to institute a census and to write up the *orbem Romanum*." (Isidorus was a Spanish encyclopedist and historian, c. 560–636.) Suidas (Greek lexicographer, tenth century), *Lexicon, s. v. apographē* and *Augoustos*: "Caesar Augustus conducted this first census, and twenty men of high character were appointed to carry it out in the provinces." Not much stress, however, is laid on these passages, because it is supposed that they rest only upon the narrative of Luke. All of the above references may be found in Schürer, *Jewish People* 1.2:114ff., and Wieseler, *Synopsis*, 68ff.

5   Inscriptions (Ramsay, *Was Christ Born at Bethlehem?*, chs. 8 and 11) and the papyri found in the rubbish piles and graves of ancient Egypt (Ramsay, *Was Christ Born at Bethlehem?*, x, 148, and 170) demonstrate the process. See also Maier, *In the Fullness of Time*, 3–10. The notice in Luke is a chronological tag for Syria, to which the province Judea belonged. Luke omits the story of the flight into Egypt, which a writer connected with Egypt would be most unlikely to do, thus hinting that Luke did not construct his story after the conditions in Egypt (Ramsay, *Was Christ Born at Bethlehem?*, 149). The governorship of Quirinius formerly offered a real problem. It was thought by

many that Luke was mistaken or that he confused the decree of Augustus with the days of the census in AD 6 (Ac 5:37). Josephus writes about this in *Ant* 17:354; 18:1–2. But since 1764, it has been known, due to the famous Quirinius stone discovered at Tivoli, Italy (Ramsay, *Was Christ Born at Bethlehem?*, 227; Schürer, *Jewish People* 1.1:354), that Quirinius was governor of Syria twice: AD 6–9 and at some previous time. The problem, however, was when to place this earlier tenure of office without conflicting with Josephus and with other known facts of history. Zumpt, Mommsen, and Schürer (Andrews, *Life of Our Lord*, 78) proposed that the first governorship of Quirinius was placed somewhere between 4–1 BC. Another proposed solution holds that the census began with C. S. Saturninus (9–6 BC), continued with P. Q. Varus (6–4 BC), and concluded with Quirinius (3–1 BC). See also Ramsay, *Was Christ Born at Bethlehem?*, chs. 6–11, and *Bearing of Recent Discovery*, chs. 19–21; Deissmann, *Licht vom Osten*, 4–5 n. 1; 231 n. 10; Robertson, *Luke the Historian*, ch. 9.

6   Schürer, *Jewish People* 1.1:449.

7   Wieseler, *Synopsis*, 87. See also Edersheim, *Temple*, 122. When in the counting of the assembled priests the lot was taken in the temple, the priests held up their hands to be counted, considering it unlawful to count persons.

8   *Ant* 16:290. It seems that Herod was falsely accused. It is uncertain when this letter was written, but Schürer (*Jewish People* 1.1:414) is inclined to date it 8 BC.

9   The chief city of Syria and third city of the empire (*War* 3:29; *Ant* 17:132: "palace of the Syrians").

10   Sylleus had a motive in casting aspersions on Herod before Augustus. Herod had refused to give him permission to marry his sister Salome unless he submitted to circumcision and accepted Judaism, which he refused to do (*Ant* 16:225, 275).

11   Augustus was probably even now thinking of reducing Judea to a Roman province, but not until after Herod's death.

12   Ramsay, *Was Christ Born at Bethlehem?*, 188.

13   Ramsay, *Bearing of Recent Discovery*, 274; *Was Christ Born at Bethlehem?*, 133–34, 185, 222, 224.

14 If the census had to be completed according to the Roman year, then December 31 was the last day. But if an exception was made also in this particular, then the time was extended to about the 17th of April, the close of the Syrian year. After the Babylonian captivity, until the first century AD, the Jewish year began with Nisan (April), but later—and this holds good to the present time—the ancient 7th of Tishri, in autumn, was revived for the beginning of the Jewish New Year.

15 Deissmann, *Licht vom Osten*, 231; Robertson, *Luke the Historian*, 126.

16 Schürer, *Jewish People* 2.1:223.

17 Schürer, *Jewish People* 2.1:357.

18 Farrar, *Life of Christ* 1:9; Schürer, *Jewish People* 2.1:360.

19 Nine thousand denarii.

20 Eusebius, *NPNF2* 1:149.

21 Cf. Eusebius, *NPNF2* 1:93.

22 *TLSB* color map 4.

23 Beginning from Bethlehem, Gibbs provides comment on the harmonization of the accounts in Matthew and Luke. See *Matthew 1:11–11:1*, 145–50.

24 The promise was known.

25 We see no reason why, without weighty arguments to the contrary, the universally accepted traditional date of December 25 should be discredited. While there are earlier references, it has been established that Pope Julius I (337–52) definitely fixed the celebration of Christmas for December 25. For a discussions on the matter see Steinmann, *From Abraham to Paul*, 251–54; Maier, *In the Fullness of Time*, 29–31; Ware, *When Was Jesus Really Born?*, 11–36. Edersheim has an interesting Talmudic tradition which strengthens us in our supposition that December 25 is the true date (*Life and Times of Jesus* 1:187 n. 3, a fast day; reasons not stated). The Eastern Church, which had previously favored January 6, gradually adopted the same date.

26 Whatever view may be taken as to the genealogies of Matthew and Luke with respect to Mary, even as regards her Davidic descent, there is every reason to suppose that Joseph, expecting the confinement of Mary, as a true son of David and in obedience to divine command, wanted the expected child of Mary entered in

the public registers of Bethlehem as his legitimate son (Weiss, *Life of Christ* 1:252).

In reply to the objection that it was not necessary for Mary to accompany Joseph for the enrollment it may be said that in an Egyptian census, in the time of Commodus, twenty-seven persons were enumerated in one paper by a householder (Ramsay, *Was Christ Born at Bethlehem?*, 146; see also p. 101; Deissmann, *Licht vom Osten*, 233; Ramsay, *Bearing of Recent Discovery*, 273; Robertson, *Luke the Historian*, 125, 127; Robertson, *Harmony of the Gospels*, 266). Besides, Luke does not say that Mary had to go along.

27 See Lk 2:24 (and cf. Lv 12:8), which conclusively proves that Mary was not an heiress, with property in Bethlehem, which made necessary her personal appearance.

28 High authorities are inclined to regard a cave southeast of the town—now covered by a Latin convent, on the floor of which is seen the inscription *"Hic de virgine Maria Iesus Christus natus est"*—as the very place where the Virgin gave birth to Jesus. The evidence in its favor is given by Farrar, *Life of Christ* 1:1ff. See also Edersheim, *Life and Times of Jesus* 1:185; Andrews, *Life of Our Lord*, 85; etc. However, in contrast see Mathews, *Life of Jesus*, 3. On account of the shepherds, who hardly could have been expected to examine all the caves in the neighborhood, we believe it to be best to connect the birthplace with the inn and with the town of Bethlehem itself. At any rate, the Magi found the child in a *house* (Gk *oikia*; Mt 2:11).

29 This term is used by Luke as a historian. It is not opposed to the view that Mary did not have other sons; but neither can it be used as an argument that she did. See Meyer, *Commentary on the N.T.*, on Lk 2:7; Mt 1:25.

30 Andrews, *Life of Our Lord*, 14.

31 Edersheim, *Life and Times of Jesus* 1:186, 187.

32 Edersheim, *Life and Times of Jesus* 1:187, 188.

33 The birth of Christ redounds to the glory of God. The "peace" on earth is not a chronological note, as taken by some writers, on account of the general civil peace existing at the time, but refers to the peace that the Lord has established in Christ. As regards "good will toward men" (KJV; ESV

has "with whom He is pleased") the variants are divided between *eudokia* and *eudokias*. One may follow the *textus receptus* and interpret it: Not that the Lord has shown grace to men who are of good will, but that, regardless of their intentions towards Him, He has shown good will towards them. A better alternative is to see "men of good pleasure" as a Semitic reference to God's election, as appears in Qumran hymns.

34 Edersheim, *Life and Times of Jesus* 1:188.

35 The Greek has the particle *dê*, which occurs only a few times in the New Testament, but always with marked expressiveness. See Bruce, *Synoptic Gospels*, on Mt 13:23.

36 Farrar, *Life of Christ* 1:19.

37 Called *Iēsou* (Gk) in Ac 7:45.

38 Farrar, *Life of Christ* 1:20.

39 Only those of non-Levitic descent had to be redeemed. This, therefore, Edersheim says (*Life and Times of Jesus* 1:194), disposes of the idea that Mary was of direct Aaronic or Levitic descent. The redemption money went to the priesthood.

40 Seven plus thirty-three days (Lv 12:3–4).

41 Some interpreters hold that there were seventy weeks from the announcement of John's birth to Jesus' presentation in the temple. See Just, *Luke 1:1–9:50*, 57–58.

42 Bonaventura, quoted in Farrar, *Life of Christ* 1:21.

43 Legend gives Simeon an age of 113 years at the time and tries to identify him with Simeon the father of Gamaliel I and son of Hillel, for which, however, there is no historical basis (Bruce, *Synoptic Gospels*, on Lk 2:28; Farrar, *Life of Christ* 1:23ff.).

44 Gk *Christos Kyriou*. A beautiful expression. See Lk 9:20.

45 This tradition is attributed to Nicephorus in Farrar, *Life of Christ* 1:22ff.

46 Gk *goneis*. This expression, procreators, while not appropriate to the bodily sonship of Jesus as applied to Joseph, has lost its etymological significance and is not at all a disavowal of the virgin birth of Christ.

47 Bengel, quoted by Meyer, *Commentary on the N.T.*, on Lk 2:25.

48 Edersheim, *Life and Times of Jesus* 1:200.

49 See Herod's enrollment by tribes and the genealogies of Christ, Farrar, *Life of Christ* 1:23.

50 Edersheim, *Life and Times of Jesus* 1:200.

51 This seems to be the best interpretation of *heōs*, etc. (Lk 2:37). Otherwise her age would be about 107. Married, say, at sixteen, a widow at twenty-three, and a widowhood of eighty-four years—in all 107 years. See Meyer, *Commentary on the N.T.*, on Lk 2:36.

52 This refers to the fervency of her service and does not mean that she actually lived in the temple. "No one, least of all a woman, permanently resided in the Temple" (Edersheim, *Life and Times of Jesus* 1:200).

53 According to Herodotus (*History* 1:101), one of the six Median tribes.

54 Dn 2:2, 48: "chief prefect over all the wise men of Babylon."

55 See Meyer, *Commentary on the N.T.*, on Mt 2:1.

56 Eastern lands, *apo anatolōn* (Gk), Mt 2:1; 8:11; 24:27.

57 Which some have done on account of Ps 68:31; 72:10; Is 49:7; 60:3.

58 Tertullian, *Contra Marcionem*.

59 Augustine and Chrysostom.

60 Farrar, *Life of Christ* 1:27.

61 Farrar, *Life of Christ* 1:28.

62 See ch. 1, § 22; Tacitus, *History of the Jews* 5.13; Suetonius, *Vespasian*, 4; *War* 6:312; and the famous Fourth Eclogue of Virgil, on account of which supposed Messianic prophecy Virgil gained such popularity in the Middle Ages as to be considered almost inspired.

63 Farrar, *Life of Christ* 1:29.

64 Schürer, *Jewish People* 2.3:277; Edersheim, *Life and Times of Jesus* 1:203.

65 Ramsay, with true historical instinct, thinks of the East struggling against the West (Rome) and believes that the Magi shared the Oriental interpretation of the Messiah as an Oriental delivery from European domination. That there was a struggle is a historic fact. "Mithridates received support from being champion of Asia against Europe. He had been destroyed." But that was only one stage of the struggle, and another deliverer was sought.—This may all be true, but it is a misconception of the messianic promise and of Christ's mission and work. See Ramsay, *Bearing of Recent Discovery*, 145.

66 Dividing the zodiac into trigons, each of which denoted a particular country, while the sign of the fish, Pisces, is supposed to have denoted Judea (Wieseler, *Synopsis*, 57). The statement of the learned Rabbi Abarbanel, AD 1547, as to a much later belief, which makes Pisces the special constellation of the Israelites, is hardly sufficient, yet still it is accepted by many. See Wieseler, *Synopsis*, 59. In contrast, see Andrews, *Life of Our Lord*, 96; Meyer, *Commentary on the N.T.*, on Mt 2:2.

67 Bar Kokhba, the pseudo-Messiah in the time of Hadrian, who called himself "Son of the Star" and caused a star to be stamped on his coinage (Wieseler, *Synopsis*, 55).

68 The reference to Balaam has this in its favor, that he also came from the East (Nu 23:7), *apo anatolōn*, according to the LXX. But the silence of Matthew in *not* referring to this star as a fulfillment of prophecy is significant.

69 Even in the Targumim it is interpreted in no other way.

70 Weiss, *Life of Christ* 1:266.

71 Wieseler, *Synopsis*, 58; Edersheim, *Life and Times of Jesus* 1:209.

72 See Mt 1:23; 2:6, 15, 23, etc. We agree that an argument from silence is weak.

73 Edersheim, *Life and Times of Jesus* 1:212; Wieseler, *Synopsis*, 56ff.

74 The view of Farrar and others (*Life of Christ* 1:35).

75 Edersheim, *Life and Times of Jesus* 1:210.

76 By Ideler, see Andrews, *Life of Our Lord*, 9.

77 Andrews, *Life of Our Lord*, 8.

78 The view of Kepler, Ebrard, and others, based on a brilliant periodical star of the first magnitude which appeared in connection with the conjunction of Jupiter and Saturn and the close of approximation of Mars in 1604 (Ebrard, *Gospel History*, 178).

79 Chinese records preserve the appearance of one or two comets in 5 and 4 BC (according to French astronomer Pingré). Wieseler combines the conjunction of planets in 7 and 6 BC with the appearance of a new star or comets in 5 and February, 4 BC, and accounts for the difference of time by the setting out of the Magi after the first appearance, and followed by the second

appearance after their departure from Jerusalem (Wieseler, *Synopsis*, 63).

80 Andrews, *Life of Our Lord*, 8.

81 See Robertson, *Harmony of the Gospels*, 263.

82 A star not by nature, but by appearance. Chrysostom: Not *physei* but *opsei monon* (Bruce, *Synoptic Gospels*, on Mt 2:2).

83 The view of Augustine, some of the Fathers, Chemnitz, and others. Not one of the heavenly orbs, properly so called, but some extraordinary luminous starlike appearance (Andrews, *Life of Our Lord*, 10).

84 Probably corresponding to Mt 2:12.

85 The usual assumption is that a tradition was kept alive based on a prophecy as to the coming of a star.

86 Henry, *Commentary*, on Mt 2:9–12.

87 Gk *ho techtheis* ("has been born"), implying that the birth had already taken place.

88 Bengel and Meyer, *Commentary on the N.T.*, on Mt 2:2.

89 See ch. 2, §§ 34–40.

90 Eusebius, *NPNF*2 1:93.

91 *Ant* 14:9.

92 Edersheim, *Life and Times of Jesus* 1:204.

93 Compare Jn 11:47–50.

94 Not necessarily the Council, as shown by Meyer (*Commentary on the N.T.*, on Mt 2:4), Edersheim (*Life and Times of Jesus* 1:215), etc., if indeed that body had anything more than a shadowy existence under Herod.

95 Also according to common knowledge (Jn 7:42).

96 According to this view, the first appearance of the star did not coincide with the exact moment of the birth of Christ, but rather with the Annunciation, or one might say, it took place at any time before the Nativity, not exceeding two years. It is not stated that the Wise Men started immediately. The distance, too, and the time the journey would consume must be taken into account.

97 When? In daytime? At night? We do not know.

98 Not into a well, seeing the reflection of the star in the water, as told in the Legend of the Well.

99 "Really, in the view of the evangelist, went before and stopped over the house" (Bruce, *Synoptic Gospels*, on Mt 2:9).

100 If the Christ Child was born in a cave, now at least He was found in a house.

101 It does not at all seem to us "a strange conceit" that the gold enabled the poor parents to make a hasty journey to Egypt (Meyer, *Commentary on the N.T.*, on 2:11).

102 Bruce, *Synoptic Gospels*, on Mt 2:11.

103 Farrar, *Life of Christ* 1:36.

104 Edersheim, *Life and Times of Jesus* 1:214.

105 Stöckhardt, *Biblische Geschichte*, 7.

106 Tradition has it that Joseph traveled by way of Hebron, Gaza, and the desert, which, as the most direct way, is likely correct. The traditional place of refuge in Egypt is usually given as the village of Metariyeh, not far from Heliopolis, on the way to Cairo. See Meyer, *Commentary on the N.T.*, on Mt 2:13; Andrews, *Life of Our Lord*, 100; Farrar, *Life of Christ* 1:38.

107 Quoting directly from the Hebrew text of Hosea 11:1 and not from the LXX, which has *ta tekna autou* (his [Israel's] children).

108 Not a misunderstanding, but an antitype to the historical meaning of the words of Hosea, in order that the words of the prophet—not a prediction— might receive their messianic fulfillment. In the flight of Jesus to Egypt, a believing reader of the Old Testament cannot but see a correspondence to a type provided by God. See Meyer, *Commentary on the N.T.*, on Mt 2:15.

109 "Tricked," fooled. He no doubt regretted now that he had permitted the Wise Men to leave Jerusalem without even a guide to make sure that his crafty designs would be carried out.

110 See, however, Suetonius, *Augustus*, 94:3; Farrar, *Life of Christ* 1:41.

111 Andrews, *Life of Our Lord*, 101; Farrar, *Life of Christ* 1:41; Edersheim, *Life and Times of Jesus* 1:214. According to an extravagant legend the number was 14,000!

112 Josephus is silent. Probably he had a motive: his own opinion about nascent Christianity, not to say anything about Christ—in Rome (Andrews, *Life of Our Lord*, 101). And still Rome knew about it, as reflected by the pun of Macrobius. In a confused narrative, which included Herod's son among the slain Syrian children, Augustus is quoted as commenting: "It is better to be Herod's swine (Gk *hyn*, Lat *porcum*) than to be his son (Gk *hyion*, Lat *puerum*). Swine were safe before Herod, but not children! Macrobius lived about AD 400 (Farrar, *Life of Christ* 1:44).

113 Edersheim, *Life and Times of Jesus* 1:214. The flowers of martyrdom, or *flores martyrum.*

114 Stöckhardt, *Biblische Geschichte*, 18; Edersheim, *Life and Times of Jesus* 1:214.

115 See ch. 2, §§ 47–48. Briefly reviewed here for the purpose of connecting the events before us.

116 *Ant* 17:66.

117 *Ant* 17:93.

118 Farrar, *Life of Christ* 1:47.

119 *Ant* 17:169.

120 The only one mentioned by Josephus and important for its chronological value. March 13, 4 BC, according to Whiston in *Works of Josephus*, 462 n. c. However, Steinmann argues for January 10, 1 BC (*From Abraham to Paul*, 230–34).

121 *Ant* 17:171–78.

122 *Ant* 17:182.

123 *Ant* 17:183–87.

124 Before the Passover.

125 *Ant* 17:191.

126 *Ant* 17:193.

127 At least according to Edersheim, *Life and Times of Jesus* 1:219; *Temple*, 176. For comments on this tradition see also Schürer, *Jewish People* 1.1:467.

128 *Ant* 17:197–99.

129 Ituraea and Trachonitis (Lk 3:1). See also *Ant* 17:317–19.

130 Drachmae. See *Ant* 17:190.

131 After the complications connected with Herod's death, the kingdom was divided as indicated. Of the four quarters of the kingdom, Archelaus received two, with the title ethnarch, which was to be exchanged for the title of king should he prove worthy of it (*Ant* 17:317). Antipas and Philip received each a fourth of the kingdom with the corresponding title tetrarch.

132 Not fled, but returned.

133 Gk *ēlthen eis gēn Israēl.*

134 Gk *hoi zētountes.*

135 Bruce, *Synoptic Gospels*, on Mt 2:20.

136 Bruce, *Synoptic Gospels*, on Mt 2:20. Something like the word of the Lord to Moses: "Go, return into Egypt, for all the men are dead which sought thy life" (Ex 4:19), although it was *Pharaoh* from whom Moses fled.

137 Archelaus is charged with having had merry meetings the same night in which his father died, with shedding tears in the daytime and making mirth at night for having succeeded him on the Jewish throne (*Ant* 17:234–35). He was afraid he would not be deemed Herod's true son; but he soon led the nation to recognize his true Herodian descent. As an illustration of his future virtues and as an example of his good rule, Josephus scornfully remarks that he caused three thousand of his own countrymen to be killed at the Passover gathering in the temple a few days after Herod's death (*Ant* 17:313).

138 Gk *basileuei*. The word can also be used of another rule than that of a king (to rule, *regnare*; Meyer, *Commentary on the N.T.*, on 2:22). But Archelaus actually did reign as king for a short time until he came to Rome for confirmation of his royal title. Augustus permitted him only the title of ethnarch until he would make himself worthy of the assumptions and trappings of royalty (*Ant* 17:228–49). Josephus calls him king and also ethnarch (17:210, 339). Farrar says (*Life of Christ* 1:50) it is remarkable how near the evangelists often seem to be to an inaccuracy, while a closer inspection shows them to be, in these very points, minutely accurate.

139 Probably he chose a route along the coast, avoiding Judea altogether.

140 But of which prophecy? Of all pertinent prophecies (Is 11:1; 53:2–3; Zec 6:12, etc.), it is probably best to derive the term Nazareth from the Hebrew *netzer* (Is 11:1), branch, a lowly and despised branch. Probably *we* should not have seen the prophetic correspondence before the fulfillment; but "the prophecies are the music; the key is the history," the fulfilment (Bruce, *Synoptic Gospels*, on Mt 2:23).

141 Omitting the flight into Egypt and the slaughter of the innocents altogether, Luke passes from Bethlehem and the presentation immediately to Nazareth. But there is no contradiction. We must bear in mind the respective purpose of the two evangelistic accounts: of Luke (from the standpoint of Mary), to explain how Jesus, whose home was Nazareth, was born in Bethlehem; of Matthew, to show how it came about that Jesus, who was born in Bethlehem, lived in Nazareth.

142 As found in the *Proto-Evangelium*, the *Pseudo-Matthew*, and the *Arabic Gospel*. See Schneemelcher, *New Testament Apocrypha*, vol. 1; *ANF* 8.

143 At the same time that Archelaus sailed to Rome to have Herod's testament confirmed (*Ant* 17:314).

144 The defense of Nicolaus of Damascus—the old friend of Herod, his own friendship for Herod, or that clause in Herod's will about the ten million coins?

145 *Ant* 17:317.

146 A part of the regular income was confiscated for the imperial treasury by the order of Augustus.

147 Fifty ambassadors, supported by the more than eight thousand Jews living in Rome (*Ant* 17:300).

148 *Ant* 17:344.

149 *Ant* 17:354.

150 *War* 2:117. Often titled "the consensus view," it is the commonly accepted view of Ramsay and others. But Lodder, after an examination of Josephus (*Die Schaetzung des Quirinius*), was inclined to identify the taxing of the Acts with the first census and the rioting of Judas as immediately following the death of Herod.

151 Founder of the party of the Zealots (*Ant* 18:4).

152 And when he did lose them in AD 39, it was on account of his wife, the ambitious and envious Herodias. See, e.g., *Ant* 18:253–55.

153 An "innumerable multitude" of people (*War* 2:10). In a report made to Nero, who was anxious to learn the defensive strength of the city, it is stated that no fewer than 256,500 lambs were slaughtered for the Passover Feast. If we count no fewer than ten participants for each Passover meal, whereas there were sometimes as many as twenty, we arrive at a figure of over two and a half million worshipers, exclusive of foreigners and those who were ceremonially unclean (*War* 6:423–27; Farrar, *Life of Christ* 1:72).

154 Meyer, *Commentary on the N.T.*, on Lk 2:41.

155 Schürer, *Jewish People* 2.2:52. See also Farrar, *Life of Christ*.

156 Square capsules, covered with leather, containing on small scrolls of fine parchment the following Bible passages: Ex 13:1–10, 11–16; Dt 6:4–9; 11:13–21 (Schürer, *Jewish People* 2.2:113).

157 Gk *goneis*. See § 14.

158 Farrar, *Life of Christ* 1:70ff.

159 Nisan, AD 10. See also Andrews, *Life of Our Lord*, 108; Farrar, *Life of Christ* 1:70.

160 Schürer, *Jewish People* 2.1:198.

161 Schürer, *Jewish People* 2.1:359ff.; Edersheim, *Life and Times of Jesus* 1:239.

162 Edersheim, *Temple*, 189ff.

163 Some texts have "Joseph and Mary"; other texts "parents," as in v. 41. The change was probably made for dogmatic reasons.

164 Tradition says at El Bireh, north of Jerusalem (Andrews, *Life of Our Lord*, 109).

165 Edersheim, *Life and Times of Jesus* 1:246.

166 As the *Arabic Gospel* of Jesus' infancy depicts it (Farrar, *Life of Christ* 1:74).

167 Anything like forwardness in boys was peculiarly distasteful to the Jews (Farrar, *Life of Christ* 1:75), as, for instance, the almost incredible immodesty of Josephus: "When I was a child, and about four-teen years of age, I was commended by all for the love I had to learning; on which account the high priests and the principal men of the city came then frequently to me together, in order to know my opinion about the accurate understanding of points of the law" (!) (*Life*, 9).

168 Farrar, *Life of Christ* 1:77.

169 Earlier at 2:29, Luke used the term *despota*, "Lord, All-highest, Sovereign," for God; here he has the dearer term: *Father*.

170 See Farrar, *Life of Christ*, ch. 6.

171 See Farrar, *Life of Christ*, ch. 6.

172 Cf. 2 Tm 1:5; 3:15; Dt 6:6–7. Edersheim, *Life and Times of Jesus* 1:231.

173 A Semitic form of speech related to the Hebrew, but differing from it in vocalization and in a num-ber of grammatical forms (Schürer, *Jewish People* 2.1:8ff.). See Mk 15:34.

174 See Farrar, *Life of Christ*, ch. 7, for this section.

175 On one occasion He wrote in the sand (Jn 8:6; see Farrar, *Life of Christ* 1:90). But it is to be admitted that this writing may have been merely a tracing of symbolic figures. Compare also the alleged corre-spondence of Christ with Abgar, King of Edessa, related by Eusebius, *NPNF2* 1:101.

176 Weiss, *Life of Christ* 1:283. Jesus grew up near Sepphoris, which was a thoroughly Hellenized city.

177 For instance, *modius*, Mt 5:15; *quadrans*, Mt 5:26; *legio*, Mt 26:53.

178 Klausner, *Jesus of Nazareth*, 233; Andrews, *Life of Our Lord*, 110.

179 Mt 13:55; Mk 6:3: "And are not His sisters here with us?"

180 *ANF* 8.

181 Possibly children of Joseph by his first wife (Andrews, *Life of Our Lord*, 118).

182 The Epiphanian Theory.

183 According to an early tradition (Chrysostom), Alphaeus and Clopas were the same person. Married to Mary, sister to Mary (Stöckhardt, *Biblische Geschichte*, 33)? See Mt 10:3; Lk 6:15; Mk 15:40; Mt 27:56; Jn 19:25.

184 The Hieronymian Theory.

185 The Helvidian Theory. (All three theories named after their original or at least chief advocate.)

186 *Adelphoi* and not *anepsioi* or *syngeneis*?

187 See "Mary, Blessed Virgin," pt. 3, in *Catholic Encyclopedia*.

188 The Helvidian Theory.

189 This was not really unbelief, but only "relative" unbelief, shared also by His chosen Twelve (Mt 17:17, 20).

190 These terms, however, prove nothing absolutely as to what did or did not happen afterwards.

191 See Andrews, *Life of Our Lord*, 111f.; Farrar, *Life of Christ* 1:95f.; Weiss, *Life of Christ* 1:281f.; Pieper, *Christian Dogmatics* 2:309–10.

192 Quoted by Eusebius, *NPNF2* 1:146, 199.

193 See Pieper, *Christian Dogmatics* 2:309–10.

194 Delicately alluded to, but unnamed, in Jn 19:25 as compared with Mt 27:56 and Mk 15:40. (Four women at the cross?) If Salome was a sister of Mary, it does not surprise us that her sons were at first disciples of John the Baptist, whose mother and the Virgin were related (Lk 1:36), and that Jesus entrusted His mother to John, who conse-quently would be her nephew. See Farrar, *Life of Christ* 1:99.

195 Suetonius, *Augustus*, 23.

196 Suetonius, *Augustus*, 97, and *Tiberius*, 21; Tacitus, *Annals* 1.3.

197 Schürer, *Jewish People* 2.1:198–99. See also Steinmann, *From Abraham to Paul*, 281.

198 Schürer, *Jewish People* 1.2:81.

199 *Ant* 18:172–77.

Chapter 5
The Period of John

1   *Life*, 11–12.

2   The Essenes were an obscure ascetic Jewish order of men of monastic tendencies, numbering about four thousand members at the time of Christ. Their favorite dwelling place was in the desert of Engedi on the Dead Sea, although they had "houses" in various cities of Israel, notably in Jerusalem, where indeed one of the city gates was named after them. Their repeated washings were symbolic of inward purity, prompted by the desire to live a life of Levitical purity, being extremists in this respect. They were people of puritanical tendencies and peculiar customs. Since they were always dressed in white and their vestments were made of fine linen, they would not have presented themselves in other clothes, nor would they have eaten locusts like John the Baptist, as they abstained from all animal food. Like the Sadducees, they denied the resurrection of the body and other fundamental doctrines of Scripture and therefore were outside the pale of the Church of God (*Ant* 18:18–22; *War* 2:119–61; Schürer, *Jewish People* 2.2:190–218; Edersheim, *Life and Times of Jesus* 1:324–35, 264 and note).

3   According to Nu 4:3, etc.

4   Schürer, *Jewish People* 2.1:215.

5   *Ant* 18:88–89.

6   Schürer, *Jewish People* 1.2:10.

7   *Ant* 18:106–8.

8   Bruce, *Synoptic Gospels*, on Lk 3:1.

9   Schürer, *Jewish People* 1.2:338; Meyer, *Commentary on the N.T.*, on Lk 3:1–2.

10 Farrar, *Life of Christ* 1:111.

11 Appointed by Quirinius and holding office from c. AD 6 to 15.

12 Schürer, *Jewish People* 2.1:198–99. Compare also Jn 18:13–24; Ac 4:6; Mt 26:3, 57; Jn 11:49.

13 Mark cites both Malachi and Isaiah but mentions Isaiah only. This is not an error, however, but rather an indication that he had the quotation from Isaiah chiefly in mind.

14 Edersheim, *Life and Times of Jesus* 1:272.

15 Still the food of the poor in the East. See Bruce, *Synoptic Gospels*, on Mt 3:4.

16 Opinion is divided between bee honey and tree honey, i.e., honey made by wild bees in trees or holes in the rocks or a liquid exuding from palms and fig trees. See Meyer, *Commentary on the N.T.*, on Mt 3:4.

17 Gk *Iōannēs ho baptistēs*. John was well known by this epithet and referred to under that designation by Josephus, *Ant* 18:116.

18 Edersheim (*Life and Times of Jesus*, Appendix 12) states that among the Jews, proselytes of righteousness (such as adopted Judaism in its entirety) were obliged to accept, besides circumcision, the initial rite of a certain baptism, which, however, "only implied a new relation to God and to Israel" and was not divinely commanded. See also Schürer, *Jewish People* 2.2:319ff. Proselyte baptism may or may not have existed at this time (Bruce, *Synoptic Gospels*, on Mt 3:1).

19 Cf. Pieper, *Christian Dogmatics* 3:288.

20 As Wieseler thinks (*Synopsis*, 186); Andrews, *Life of Our Lord*, 145; Edersheim, *Life and Times of Jesus* 1:278; and others. See Lv 25:1–7.

21 Gk *epi*. Mt 3:7.

22 The war Herod waged against Aretas was later. The words "And we" (Lk 3:14) may connect these soldiers to the aforementioned tax collectors (Lk 3:12).

23 See ch. 15.

Chapter 6
The Beginning
of Christ's Public Ministry

1   Some hold the tradition that our Lord was baptized on January 6 or 10 (Edersheim, *Life and Times of Jesus* 1:278 n. 4; Andrews, *Life of Our Lord* 1:31).

2   See Meyer, *Commentary on the N.T.*, and Bruce, *Synoptic Gospels*, on Jn 1:28. Robertson, *Studies in the Text of the N.T.*, 34, 73.

3   Beth-nimrah, on a small stream east of the Jordan.

4   The apocryphal gospel to the Hebrews says that Jesus was urged to the Baptism of John by His mother and brothers (Klausner, *Jesus of Nazareth*, 251). But cf. Mt 3:13–15, from which we see that our Lord came to John of His own accord and why He desired to be baptized by him.

5   Ezekiel prophesied about baptizing through sprin-
     kling (Ezk 36:25–27). Romans 6:4 implies the use
     of immersion. Didache 7 refers to Christians using
     various methods for applying the water.

6   Compare Ezk 1:1; Ac 7:56; Rv 4:1; Is 64:1.

7   Compare Lk 9:35; Jn 12:28.

8   Edersheim, *Life and Times of Jesus* 1:291.

9   The question is about the peccability or impec-
     cability of His human nature, and whether His
     sinlessness sprang from a *peccare non posse* or
     a *posse non peccare* (inability to sin or an abil-
     ity not to sin, like Adam; Farrar, *Life of Christ*
     1:123; Edersheim, *Life and Times of Jesus* 1:298).
     "Capable of not sinning, but not incapable of
     sinning."

10   See also Is 53:9; Lk 1:35; Jn 8:46; 1Pt 1:19; etc.

11   Pieper, *Christian Dogmatics* 2:75–77.

12   Farrar, *Life of Christ* 1:123.

13   Andrews, *Life of Our Lord*, 155. See *ISBE* under
     "Temptation of Christ."

14   Edersheim, *Life and Times of Jesus* 1:300 n. 2, and
     others.

15   Absolute, if the words of Luke "He ate nothing"
     are to be taken in the strictest literal sense.

16   Lat *Lapides Iudaici*. Farrar, *Life of Christ* 1:129.

17   Stöckhardt, *Biblische Geschichte*, 26.

18   This seems to be the order, following Matthew:
     "*Then* the devil," etc. (v. 5). Luke transposes the
     second and third temptations, but does not state
     a definite order of sequence.

19   Already called holy at the time of Isaiah (48:2) and
     Nehemiah (11:1), it is still called Al-Quds, that is,
     the Holy City, by the Arabians. See also Mt 27:53.

20   Edersheim, *Life and Times of Jesus* 1:303 n. 2. Cf.
     Ant 15:411–12. Anderson writes that it was 326
     feet above the bottom of the Kidron valley (*ISBE*
     under "Temptation of Christ").

21   Edersheim, *Life and Times of Jesus* 1:304.

22   Stalker, *Life of Jesus Christ*, 44. In contrast, see
     Weiss, *Life of Christ* 1:346.

23   Farrar, *Life of Christ* 1:134.

24   Historically there is no record that Jesus was later
     tempted again in like manner. There were other
     temptations, clearly satanic, but in these Satan was
     indirectly engaged, e.g., Jn 8:4–11; 13:2, 27; Mt
     16:23. See Meyer on Lk 4:13.

25   Though we may assume that they brought Him
     food, their chief ministration perhaps consisted

in comforting Him after the fiery trial He had
endured.

26   Andrews, *Life of Our Lord*, 155 n. 1; Schürer,
     Jewish People 2.1:186; Dods, *Gospel of St. John*,
     on Jn 1:19.

27   Edersheim, *Life and Times of Jesus* 1:310.

28   Edersheim, *Life and Times of Jesus* 1:344f.;
     Andrews, *Life of Our Lord*, 161.

29   Thursday the interview. Friday "the next day"
     (v. 29). Saturday "the next day again" (v. 35).
     Sunday "the next day" (v. 43). Monday. Tuesday.
     Wednesday "the third day," the wedding at Cana
     (2:1).

30   Dods, *Gospel of St. John*, on Jn 1:20.

31   Dods, *Gospel of St. John*, on Jn 1:21. Schürer,
     Jewish People 2.2:157.

32   Gk *ho prophētēs*.

33   Schürer, *Jewish People* 2.1:185. But compare Ac
     9:2.

34   Edersheim, *Life and Times of Jesus* 1:344.

35   Gk *pros auton*.

36   Farrar, *Life of Christ* 1:144. Gk *emblepsas* (cf. Mk
     14:67). The Lord looked upon Peter, *eneblepse* (Lk
     22:61).

37   Farrar, *Life of Christ* 1:144.

38   Farrar, *Life of Christ* 1:145.

39   Lenski, *Eisenach Gospel Selections*, 241.

40   Cf. Dods, *Gospel of St. John*, on Jn 1:39.

41   Thus: Jn 1:39 the "tenth hour" is equal to our
     4 p.m.; 4:6, "sixth hour," noon; 4:52, "seventh
     hour," 1 p.m.; 11:9, "twelve hours," one day, from
     the rising to the setting of the sun; but 19:14,
     "sixth hour," 6 a.m. (compare 18:28: "It was early
     morning"). See "Time Reckoning in the Bible"
     in the Appendices. For 4 p.m., Jewish reckon-
     ing, see Farrar, *Life of Christ* 1:146; Weiss, *Life of
     Christ* 1:365; Dods, *Gospel of St. John*, and Meyer,
     Commentary on the N.T., on Jn 1:39; etc.; for 10
     a.m., Roman reckoning, see Andrews, *Life of Our
     Lord*, 159; Robertson, *Harmony of the Gospels*,
     286; Wieseler, *Synopsis*, 376; Ebrard, *Gospel
     History*, 210; Edersheim, *Life and Times of Jesus*
     1:346; etc. The various methods of reconciling
     the statements are well given by Andrews, *Life of
     Our Lord*, 159ff., 545ff.

42   The name is of Greek origin, *Andreas*, "manly";
     but it was in use among the Jews (Lightfoot,
     quoted by Farrar, *Life of Christ* 1:152 n. 1). It also

occurs in the Jerusalem Talmud (Klausner, *Jesus of Nazareth*, 260 n. 4).

43 Weiss, *Life of Christ* 1:367.

44 Extended to the members of his family, his brother James, and his mother Salome. The third of the women named by Mark in 15:40, Salome, is the sister of Mary, the mother of Jesus, in Jn 19:25 (Weiss, *Life of Christ* 1:366 and n. 1).

45 Gk *heurēkamen ton Messian*. See Farrar, *Life of Christ* 1:147.

46 *ISBE* under "Peter, Simon."

47 Farrar, *Life of Christ* 1:147.

48 Gk *prōtos*. See Meyer, *Commentary on the N.T.*, on Jn 1:41–43.

49 Weiss, *Life of Christ* 1:366.

50 It quite answers to John's method not to refer to his own mother directly; for in speaking of himself, he never tells us his name and never even mentions his brother. Weiss, *Life of Christ* 1:366 n. 1.

51 We notice that in all the four lists Philip takes fifth place: Mk 3:16–19; Mt 10:2–4; Lk 6:14–16; Ac 1:13.

52 "Lover of horses." See note on Andrew, § 16.

53 See *ESV Bible Atlas*, 227.

54 See ch. 3, § 32.

55 Mt 10:2–4; Mk 3:16–19; Lk 6:14–16. Only in Ac 1:13 he is given seventh place.

56 Farrar, *Life of Christ* 1:152.

57 See articles in Bible dictionaries.

58 Weiss, *Life of Christ* 1:375; Farrar, *Life of Christ* 1:156; and others.

59 Gk *amēn, amēn*. Used in this form twenty-five times in John (always single in the Synoptic Gospels) and well rendered "truly, truly." Christ Himself is the faithful and true Witness and called Amen in Rv 3:14. See Meyer, *Commentary on the N.T.*, and Dods, *Gospel of St. John*, on Jn 1:52.

60 Books have been written on Jesus' own designation of Himself as the Son of Man. For a true interpretation of it, see Peter's answer to Christ's question: "Who do people say that the Son of Man is?" Mt 16:13, 15–19, an answer of which the Lord approved (cf. Dn 7:13–14). See Pieper, *Christian Dogmatics* 2:74–75; Kretzmann, *Popular Commentary* 1:47.

61 Counting from 1:43. The Greeks reckoned thus: *sēmeron aurion tēi tritēi hēmerai*—today, tomorrow, the day after tomorrow (Lk 13:32).

62 Edersheim, *Life and Times of Jesus* 1:344f.; *Jewish Social Life*, 151ff.

63 Though possibly, according to a legend, he was involved as paranymph, whose duty it was to escort the bride. See Farrar, *Life of Christ* 1:162.

64 Edersheim, *Life and Times of Jesus* 1:355.

65 Cana, "Place of Reeds." The name of a stream on the borders of Ephraim and Manasseh (Jsh 16:8; Kanah). A city in Asher (Jsh 19:28). Cana of Galilee is mentioned also by Josephus (*Life*, 86; *War* 1:334) to distinguish it from Cana in Coelesyria (*Ant* 15:112). The Kehf Kennah, accepted by the Greek and Latin churches, is in the proximity of Nazareth and on the direct road to Lake Gennesaret (Andrews, *Life of Our Lord*, 163f.).

66 They each contained twenty or thirty gallons.

67 Cf. Jn 19:26 and Lk 13:12. Dods, *Gospel of St. John*, on Jn 2:4.

68 Farrar, *Life of Christ* 1:168ff.

69 Gk *architriklinos*.

70 Dods, *Gospel of St. John*, on Jn 2:8.

71 Edersheim, *Life and Times of Jesus* 1:362.

72 They begin their account with the later Galilean ministry.

73 Gk *sēmeia*.

74 The little party actually went *down* (Gk *katebē*) from the higher lands around Nazareth and Cana to the lower levels of the lakeside, 680 feet below the Mediterranean Sea. On account of recent archeological discoveries it seems that Tell Hum, nearly two and a half miles southwest of the mouth of the upper Jordan, has the better claim as the site of Capernaum. At Tell Hum, pottery of the Roman period abounds, exactly the period of the glory of Capernaum. On the extensive finds, see *ABD* 1:866–69.

75 Not yet as apostles. First as occasional companions, then as constant attendants, and finally as chosen apostles.

76 Capernaum is not mentioned in Scripture outside of the Gospels, but it is twice mentioned in Josephus: *Life* 403; *War* 3:519. The meaning of the name is doubtful.

77 Farrar, *Life of Christ* 1:182.

78 On account of Lk 4:23. Unless reference is there made to Jn 4:46–54.

Chapter 7
The Early Judean Ministry

1 Ch. 5, § 1.
2 Ch. 6, § 1.
3 See Meyer, *Commentary on the N.T.*, on Mt 23:27. Edersheim, *Life and Times of Jesus* 1:367.
4 See ch. 4, § 37.
5 Gk *anebē*.
6 St. Bonaventura, quoted in Farrar, *Life of Christ* 1:21.
7 See ch. 3, § 8.
8 Edersheim, *Life and Times of Jesus* 1:368. Farrar, *Life of Christ* 1:185.
9 Schürer, *Jewish People* 2.1:250.
10 Two thousand talents in pure gold, eight thousand talents in other articles of value (*Ant* 14:105). A talent weighed c. 75 pounds or 34 kilograms.
11 Edersheim, *Life and Times of Jesus* 1:371.
12 Lat *flagellum*. Not of rushes, but of ropes made of rushes (Gk *phragellion ek schoiniōn*).
13 Dods, *Gospel of St. John*, on Jn 2:12–22.
14 *Ant* 20:219.
15 See Steinmann, *From Abraham to Paul*, 262.
16 Stöckhardt, *Biblische Geschichte*, 35. See AE 43:120; cf. 1Co 3:2.
17 Edersheim, *Life and Times of Jesus* 1:381 n. 1. Meyer, *Commentary on the N.T.*, on Jn 3:1–2.
18 *ISBE* under "Nicodemus."
19 Farrar, *Life of Christ* 1:197.
20 Meyer, *Commentary on the N.T.*, on Jn 3:3.
21 The plural form seems to include other members of the ruling class upon whom the ministry of Jesus in Jerusalem had made a favorable impression.
22 Chrysostom, quoted by Meyer, *Commentary on the N.T.*, on Jn 3:3.
23 Gk *anōthen*, from above or again? The latter; Nicodemus himself so understands it.
24 Notice that Christ recognized the effectiveness of the Baptism of John.
25 Farrar, *Life of Christ* 1:199.
26 From the expression *ho didaskalos tou Israēl*, Farrar has argued (*Life of Christ* 1:199) that Nicodemus was the third member of the Council: (1)

Nasi-president (king); (2) Ab-beth-din, vice-president (father of the house of judgment; presiding judge); (3) Chakam (wise man). But it seems that the designation "teacher" refers to Nicodemus as an individual, an acknowledged teacher of the people (Meyer, *Commentary on the N.T.*, on Jn 3:9–10). Of this term in an official sense, Schürer knows nothing (*Jewish People* 2.1:184).
27 Kretzmann, *Popular Commentary* 1:422.
28 Probably because the words "which is in heaven" (KJV) were not understood, they were omitted in certain ancient texts.
29 This He did because of the paramount importance of His suffering and death as the ransom paid for mankind's redemption. In the case of Nicodemus, this enigmatic germ then sown bore fruit at the foot of the cross, Jn 19:39 (Meyer, *Commentary on the N.T.*, on Jn 3:14–15).
30 The words are Christ's and continue His address to Nicodemus (through v. 21). They are not, as some have thought, an explanatory meditation of the evangelist. The latter view is an assumption justified neither by anything in the text nor by the use of the Greek word *monogenēs*, although nowhere else used by Christ. See Meyer, *Commentary on the N.T.*, on Jn 3:16.
31 Luther, quoted by Meyer, *Commentary on the N.T.*, on Jn 3:18.
32 On account of v. 26, "All are going to Him," which seems to imply a considerable period of time.
33 On account of Jn 4:35. The saying will be considered there.
34 See Meyer, *Commentary on the N.T.*, on Jn 3:22–23.
35 (1) On the *southern* border of Judea. Evidently out of the question. (2) Near Shechem. In the very heart of Samaria? Hardly possible. (3) Eight miles south of Scythopolis, in the corner, bordering on Samaria, Galilee, Decapolis, and Perea. Not far off are seven copious fountains, which might well be called Aenon, place of springs. And there is reason to believe that this district did not belong to Samaria, but was included in the Decapolis. See *ESV Bible Atlas*, 225.
36 On account of v. 26, where Bethany is spoken of as across the Jordan.
37 Edersheim, *Life and Times of Jesus* 1:393.
38 Some texts (including the ESV) have "a Jew."

39 They are mentioned first.

40 Edersheim, *Life and Times of Jesus* 1:391.

41 Farrar, *Life of Christ* 1:203.

42 The *paranymphios* (Gk), who was employed to arrange the marriage. For marriage customs and festivities see Edersheim, *Life and Times of Jesus* 1:353ff.

43 Edersheim, *Life and Times of Jesus* 1:392.

44 Notice the expression *ho kyrios* that appears in early manuscripts (the early witnesses are divided over whether John uses Jesus' name or His title). Compare 6:23; Lk 7:13; etc. Possibly the evangelist, writing later, unconsciously departs from contemporary speech and speaks for himself as a believer.

45 See § 12.

46 Namely, in consequence of the many people who flocked to Him.

47 See Meyer, *Commentary on the N.T.*, under Jn 4:1–3 n. 1.

48 See Ylvisaker, *Gospels*, § 29. Without this period of retirement, the calling of the disciples in Mt 4:18–22; Mk 1:16–20; and Lk 5:1–11, or rather the recalling of the disciples as compared with Jn 1:35–51, is hard to explain in the arrangement of various Gospel harmonies: Robertson, *Harmony of the Gospels*, §§ 34–41; Cadman, *Critical Harmony*, §§ 28–32; Broadus, *Harmony of the Gospels*, §§ 23–27; Stevens and Burton, *Harmony of the Gospels*, §§ 24–38; Kerr, *Harmony of the Gospels*, §§ 27–33.

49 In other words, the events of Jn 4 and 5—the Samaritan ministry, the healing of the ruler's son, and the unnamed feast—are to be inserted before Mt 4:12 and parallels. In deciding upon this chronological order, we are following Wieseler, Andrews, and Stöckhardt and no less a historical authority than Eusebius in his *Church History* 3.24. For a full discussion see Wieseler, *Synopsis*, 147ff., and Andrews, *Life of Our Lord*, 179ff., 188, 215.

50 *Ant* 20:118.

51 The distance from Galilee to Jerusalem could be covered in three days.

52 Jews living in Judea. Edersheim, *Life and Times of Jesus* 1:394.

53 Ch. 2, § 10.

54 From the city built by Omri as the capital of the Kingdom of Israel (1Ki 16:24). It was destroyed by John Hyrcanus c. 109 BC, rebuilt by Herod, and named Sebaste in honor of Augustus.

55 Edersheim, *Life and Times of Jesus* 1:395.

56 Unencumbered by pharisaic tradition.

57 As asserted by the rabbis and, following them, by the Fathers (Edersheim, *Life and Times of Jesus* 1:402).

58 They asserted that their roll of the Pentateuch was the only authentic copy.

59 On the ground of a passage from the Torah (Dt 18:15).

60 Farrar, *Life of Christ* 1:210 n. 1. *Ant* 9:291; 11:340–41; 12:257.

61 167 BC. See ch. 2, § 22.

62 Edersheim, *Life and Times of Jesus* 1:399.

63 Farrar, *Life of Christ* 1:206.

64 See "Jacob's Well" in *ABD* 3:608.

65 We suppose that John used the ordinary Jewish reckoning of time throughout except in 19:14, where he quoted the time in the language of the Roman court. See ch. 6, § 15. It could hardly have been six o'clock in the morning. While noon was not the hour for general resort to the well, the fact that the woman at the well was alone and held so long a private conversation uninterrupted, seems to favor our assumption. Also, Jesus apparently had no intention of halting here for the night, as He would have had, had it been evening (Andrews, *Life of Our Lord*, 186; Dods, *Gospel of St. John*, on Jn 4:1–16).

66 Edersheim, *Life and Times of Jesus* 1:402.

67 That is, a Samaritan woman, not a woman of the city of Samaria, which was two miles distant from the well.

68 Farrar, *Life of Christ* 1:208.

69 The difference in pronunciation concerned chiefly the vowel sounds. Among the consonants, the letter *s*, for instance, was sometimes pronounced *s* and sometimes *sh* by the Hebrews; but the Samaritans always pronounced it *sh* (Edersheim, *Life and Times of Jesus* 1:409 n. 3).

70 The diameter of the traditional well is about seven feet. See "Jacob's Well" in *ABD* 3:608. Andrews, *Life of Our Lord*, 185.

71 Gk *Kyrie*.

72   Both terms, *pēgēi* (v. 6) and *phrear* (v. 11), are used, the former meaning the spring of the well of water, the latter the dug and built pit, or well.

73   Farrar, *Life of Christ* 1:210.

74   Not *andra*, but *andras*; not man, but men; not husband, but husbands.

75   Dods, *Gospel of St. John*, on Jn 4:17–26.

76   Farrar, *Life of Christ* 1:212.

77   See Meyer, *Commentary on the N.T.*, on Jn 4:27; Farrar, *Life of Christ* 1:214; etc.

78   On the chronological value of this passage see Wieseler, *Synopsis*, 194ff.; Meyer, *Commentary on the N.T.*, on Jn 4:35; Andrews, *Life of Our Lord*, 182ff.

79   Past tense. Not prophetic; with their calling as disciples, their mission was already involved. See Meyer, *Commentary on the N.T.*, on Jn 4:37–38.

80   § 13.

81   And afterwards (Lk 4:24; Mt 13:57; Mk 6:4).

82   Compare v. 48 with v. 41. After considerable study of this most "perplexing passage" (Meyer, *Commentary on the N.T.*) of John, the above is the interpretation that we finally have decided upon to offer. The trouble is in the little word "for" in v. 44 and in the last two words of the same verse, "own hometown." A number of different explanations have been advanced for the particle "for," none of which, however, fully satisfy. In bringing the "for" into direct connection with v. 43 (as we must), compared with vv. 1–3, we approximate the view of Dods (*Gospel of St. John*), with the exception of the "threatened collision with the Pharisees" in vv. 1–3. And as to the "own hometown" of Jesus, a number of homes are proposed: Judea as opposed to Galilee in general, or vice versa, or Nazareth and Capernaum in particular as opposed to Galilee in general.

83   Chapter 6, § 25. Farrar, *Life of Christ* 1:233.

84   But Weiss, *Life of Christ* 1:378; 2:44, and Andrews, *Life of Our Lord*, 189, think that the family of Jesus now resided at Cana.

85   Farrar, *Life of Christ* 1:231.

86   Edersheim, *Life and Times of Jesus* 1:424.

87   The common reckoning of time. See § 15; ch. 6, § 15.

88   If there were any unrecorded miracles during the brief stay at Capernaum (Jn 2:12 as compared with Lk 4:23), then this is the correct

understanding. But since the "What we have heard You did at Capernaum" might possibly (though hardly) refer to this particular miracle performed at Cana from a distance, the understanding might also be: the second Galilean miracle. Weiss (*Life of Christ* 2:45) thinks that this miracle is the same as that narrated in Mt 8:5–13; but the differences are so evident that his view hardly deserves serious consideration.

CHAPTER 8
THE UNNAMED FEAST

1   This may explain the intervening silence in the Synoptists' account as also the supplementary character of the Gospel of St. John.

2   Because in 6:4 a Passover is mentioned as still approaching, Keppler, Meyer, Wieseler, and others, have argued that reference is here made to a festival between the December of Christ's return and the Passover of AD 31, deciding upon Purim, the Feast of Lots, celebrated in March in commemoration of the national delivery from the bloody designs of Haman, Est 9:21–22. But the Passover of Jn 6:4, which Jesus most likely did *not* attend, may just as well have been the Passover of AD 32. While the annual Passover was a festival that Jesus would *naturally* attend unless prevented by open hostility (none as yet appeared), Purim was more of a secular or patriotic holiday, accompanied with hilarity, feasting, and the exchange of gifts. Edersheim, placing Jesus' return from Judea in the middle of May and inclined to identify the unnamed feast with either the Ingathering of Wood or the Feast of Trumpets (August and September), "can scarcely conceive our Lord going up to a feast observed with such boisterous merriment as Purim was, while the season of the year in which it falls would scarcely tally with the statement . . . that a great multitude of sick people were laid down in the porches of Bethesda" (*Life and Times of Jesus* 1:460; 2:768). The question cannot be definitely decided. Nearly all the Jewish festivals have been mentioned as being the unnamed feast of Jn 5:1; but the opinions are chiefly divided between Purim and Passover. Steinmann (*From Abraham to Paul*, 263), however, argues for the Feast of Tabernacles.

Fortunately, for the understanding of the passage it matters little which festival one believes it to have been. In our choice of the Passover in AD 31 we are unconscious of a "most glaring arbitrariness in placing a *spatium vacuum* of a year between it and 6:1–4" (Meyer, who argues for Purim) because we remember that, whether the interval was a month or a year, John's apparent purpose in writing his Gospel was not to present a complete outline, but to supplement the Synoptists' accounts of the life of Christ. There is no need of entering deeper into the discussion. For a more detailed examination of the problem see Andrews, *Life of Our Lord*, 189ff.; Meyer, *Commentary on the N.T.*, on Jn 5:1; and Robertson, *Harmony of the Gospels*, 267ff.

3   John's Gospel was written after the destruction of Jerusalem, but that does not oppose the use of the present tense *estin*. What John represents is that the bath was still existing at his time. Compare his use of *hēn* in 11:18: "Bethany *was* near"; 18:1: "where *was* a garden" (Gethsemane); 19:41: "there *was* a garden" (at Golgotha).

4   See Meyer, *Commentary on the N.T.*, on Jn 5:2–3; Dods, *Gospel of St. John*, on Jn 5:1–14.

5   Andrews, *Life of Our Lord*, 200; McRay, *Archaeology*, 123–24, 187.

6   Edersheim, *Life and Times of Jesus* 1:463.

7   Farrar, *Life of Christ* 1:372.

8   Stöckhardt, *Biblische Geschichte*, 46.

9   Kretzmann, *Popular Commentary*, 434; Dods, *Gospel of St. John*, on Jn 5:1–14.

10 Members of the Council. The particular Jews are quite regularly so named by John because of their hostility to Jesus (Jn 5:15, 18). See also Jn 6:41, 52 (in Galilee) and ch. 16, § 10.

11 Farrar, *Life of Christ* 1:375.

12 Farrar, *Life of Christ* 1:376.

13 By Farrar, *Life of Christ* 1:378.

14 Farrar, *Life of Christ* 1:378.

15 The *hēn* naturally refers to something in the past, but it does not, as some think, necessarily refer to the death of John, which did not occur until later.

16 Meyer, *Commentary on the N.T.*, on Jn 5:39–40.

17 Ch. 7, §§ 11–12.

18 At one time named as successor of Herod the Great, but then dropped in his will and apparently living as a private man of means in Rome (*Ant* 17:53; 18:109–15; *War* 1:600).

19 *War* 2:182.

20 *Ant* 18:118.

21 By Josephus (*Ant* 18:119).

22 Stöckhardt, *Biblische Geschichte*, 51.

CHAPTER 9
THE BEGINNING
OF THE GREAT GALILEAN MINISTRY

1   Andrews, *Life of Our Lord*, 209ff.

2   In spite of the many Phoenician, Arabian, Syrian, and Greek inhabitants (Schürer, *Jewish People* 1.1:192; Andrews, *Life of Our Lord*, 214).

3   Schürer, *Jewish People* 2.1:185. The Council had no judicial jurisdiction over Jesus so long as He remained in Galilee. In a certain sense, no doubt, it exercised such jurisdiction over every Jewish community in the world and in that sense over Galilee as well. But it was only within the limits of Judea proper that it exercised any *direct* authority. However, compare Ac 9:2.

4   In spite of the fact that he caused the arrest of John. Indeed, we know that for a considerable time he took no notice at all of the Lord and His work; and if he heard of Him, he regarded Him as one of the rabbis, who was gathering disciples around Him and believed His work to be without political significance. Not until after the Baptist's death did he desire to see Him; and thus the Lord, unmolested by the authorities, could visit all parts of the province and teach openly in all places (Andrews, *Life of Our Lord*, 214).

5   Some harmonists make this visit parallel with Mt 13:53–58 and Mk 6:1–6, which apparently, however, happened later. Although there are points of similarity, the points of difference are more numerous and more plainly marked. For discussion, see Andrews, *Life of Our Lord*, 218; Meyer, *Commentary on the N.T.*, on Lk 4:16 and Mt 13:53; and Wieseler, *Synopsis*, 258.

6   Ch. 6, § 1.

7   Ch. 4, § 43.

8   For a more detailed discussion, see *ABD* 6:252; Schürer, *Jewish People* 2.2:58ff.; *ISBE* under "Synogogue"; Edersheim, *Life and Times of Jesus* 1:431ff.; Farrar, *Life of Christ* 1:222ff.

9   Edersheim, *Life and Times of Jesus* 1:432.

10 Targum, targuming. The Scripture read in Hebrew and repeated in the vernacular, the Aramaic.

11 Edersheim, *Life and Times of Jesus* 1:434. Not towards the east, i.e., the consecrated direction of Mohammedan worship.

12 Also spelled Hazzan (Hbr "cantor"). See *The New Standard Jewish Encyclopedia*, 7th ed., Geoffrey Wigoder, ed. (New York: FactsOnFile, 1992), 422–23.

13 This would popularly have been considered authoritative. Only the Hebrew original could be regarded as final.

14 The collecting had to be done by at least two and the distributing by at least three.

15 Edersheim, *Life and Times of Jesus* 1:433f.

16 Only in the temple was the name of God pronounced as written (Schürer, *Jewish People* 2.2:82 n. 143).

17 Edersheim, *Life and Times of Jesus* 1:442.

18 The Pentateuch was divided into 154 pericopes, so that the whole Law could be read in regular order in the course of three years. There was also a lectionary for the prophetical books.

19 Edersheim, *Life and Times of Jesus* 1:445.

20 Called also *Sheliach Tsibbur*, or delegate of the congregation.

21 Farrar, *Life of Christ* 1:222. From this passage it has been argued that the Sabbath was on the Great Day of Atonement, because in later times Is 61 was the lesson to be read on that day. But Edersheim and Meyer both contend that the modern lectionaries from the Prophets did not exist in the times of Jesus (Edersheim, *Life and Times of Jesus* 1:444, 452 n. 2; Meyer, *Commentary on the N.T.*, on Lk 4:18–19).

22 Bruce, *Synoptic Gospels*, on Lk 4:16–21.

23 Farrar, *Life of Christ* 1:223.

24 See Meyer, *Commentary on the N.T.*, on Lk 4:18–19; Farrar, *Life of Christ* 1:223 n. 2.

25 Meyer, *Commentary on the N.T.*, on Lk 4:20–21.

26 Words about the grace of God in the Pauline sense, whereby the prophecy was fulfilled (Bruce, *Synoptic Gospels*, on Lk 4:22–30).

27 Farrar, *Life of Christ* 1:224.

28 This reflects a literal translation of the Greek, which is footnoted in the ESV translation.

29 See also ch. 8, § 9.

30 Farrar, *Life of Christ* 1:226.

31 This reference implies an antecedent ministry there. See ch. 6, § 25. Jn 2:12 ("for a few days").

32 Meyer, *Commentary on the N.T.*, on Lk 4:23–24.

33 Farrar, *Life of Christ* 1:226.

34 Three and a half years in accordance with Jas 5:17 and universal Jewish tradition is the exact time as compared with the round number, three years, in 1Ki 17:1; 18:1.

35 It is said that the ancient city stood higher on the slope than the modern. The Mount of Precipitation, a conspicuous object from the Plain of Esdraelon, which for many years has been pointed out as the place where the attempt was made on the Lord's life, lies some two miles from the village. Its distance from the village is sufficient proof that it cannot have been the real scene of the event. The cliff that travelers have generally fixed upon as best answering the narrative lies just back of the Maronite church and is some thirty or forty feet in height (Andrews, *Life of Our Lord*, 221).

36 Farrar, *Life of Christ* 1:227.

37 The altitude of Nazareth is given as 1,602 feet above sea level and Capernaum as 682 feet below the level of the Mediterranean Sea. In twenty miles a difference of over 2,200 feet.

38 Until Passover. See ch. 6, § 25.

39 Ch. 8, § 1.

40 Compare Andrews, *Life of Our Lord*, 164, 239; Wieseler, *Synopsis*, 155 and n. 5. See ch. 7, § 22. It cannot of course be stated with certainty. (Weiss thinks that the family of Jesus resided in Cana [*Life of Christ* 1:378; 2:44].) The reason of the "stayed there for a few days" in Jn 2:12 is explained by v. 13: "The Passover of the Jews was at hand." And even if Mary had returned to Nazareth, the "dreadful insult which Jesus had received would have been alone sufficient to influence His family to leave the place, even if the other members did not directly share in the odium and persecution which His Word had caused" (Farrar, *Life of Christ* 1:234). Alford: "The change of abode seems to have included the whole family, except the sisters, who may have been married at Nazareth." Greswell: "The incident respecting the tribute-money established that Jesus was a legal inhabitant

of Capernaum." Quoted in Andrews, *Life of Our Lord*, 240.

41 On account of Mk 6:3, "Are not His sisters here with us?"

42 Andrews, *Life of Our Lord*, 239.

43 The quotation in Mt 4:15–16 freely follows the original (Is 9:1–2), with glances at the Septuagint (Bruce, *Synoptic Gospels*, on Mt 4:14–16).

44 Ch. 2, § 10

45 Edersheim, *Life and Times of Jesus* 1:458.

46 The parentheses indicate that the passage has been taken out of its own true order. Except in cases in which there is no chronological sequence involved, we for the first time are leaving the natural order of the individual Gospels. And until the account of the death of John the Baptist there will be other transpositions, especially in Matthew, whose Gospel, it seems, was in part based on topical rather than a strictly chronological arrangement. In spite of the ingenious arrangement of some older harmonists, for instance, A. Osiander (1537) and E. D. Hauber (1740), they cannot be avoided. For the purpose of constructing a harmony that leaves each Gospel in its own undisturbed sequence the present author made the same attempt, but after a concentrated effort, in which neither thought, labor, nor paper was spared, he was forced to give it up. In the present instance, although there are still a number of harmonists who do *not* consider the above passages parallel, it seems to us that on account of the unexpected nature of the miracle, as evidenced in the reaction of Peter, Luke himself does not insist upon an order that places this miracle *after* the miraculous healing of Peter's mother-in-law. Weiss thinks that in the sudden introduction of the sons of Zebedee in v. 10, Luke himself seems to indicate that what is related in the story is from the same time as what is recorded Mt 4:18–22 and Mk 1:16–20 (*Life of Christ* 1:56 n. 1).

47 Weiss, *Life of Christ* 2:59.

48 This is the first time that we meet with James, although it is generally accepted that he was with his brother John at Bethany beyond the Jordan (Jn 1:40–42). See ch. 6, § 18.

49 Edersheim, *Life and Times of Jesus* 1:473.

50 Weiss, *Life of Christ* 1:366.

51 Edersheim, *Life and Times of Jesus* 1:472.

52 Farrar, *Life of Christ* 1:242.

53 Bruce, *Synoptic Gospels*, on Lk 5:5.

54 The Greek word *Epistata* is used instead of the usual Hebrew for rabbi. Occurs only in Luke, Peter does not yet address Jesus as his teacher (Meyer, *Commentary on the N.T.*, on Lk 5:5).

55 Farrar, *Life of Christ* 1:243.

56 The name Peter is here introduced for the first time without explanation, presumably to mark the great crisis in his history.

57 But possibly the phrase "when they had brought their ships to land" also includes the disposal of the fish.

58 When Jesus told a scribe who wanted to follow Him that He had "nowhere to lay His head" (Mt 8:20), He meant to say that He had no home of His own.

59 Eusebius, *NPNF2* 1:173.

60 Ch. 6, § 25.

61 "The sixth hour . . . at which hour our laws require us to go to dinner on Sabbath days" (*Life*, 279).

62 The scribes (*Sopherim*, lawyers, or Scripturists) date as a distinct body from the period of Ezra, himself a scribe. Their functions were to copy, read, explain, defend, and preserve the Law. In their zeal to protect the Law, they invented the "fences," which under the title "Words of the Scribes" formed the nucleus of the "tradition of the elders," or oral law, as distinguished from the written Law. Any transgression of the oral law was declared to be more heinous than the transgression of the words of the Bible itself. Originally the priests and Levites were the teachers and guardians of the Law (Lv 10:11; Dt 33:10; 2Ch 15:3). Gradually, however, this was changed, especially during the exile and after, when no longer primarily the temple worship, but the Law served to keep a largely dispersed people united. The higher the Law rose in the estimation of the people, the more did its professional study and explanation become an independent calling. It was the Law of God, in which every member of the nation, and not only the priests, had an individual interest. Hence, *non-priestly Israelites* more and more occupied themselves with its scientific study. The professional occupation of these real

rabbis and masters of Israel may be summed up as follows: (1) The theoretic development of the Law. What was clearly binding in principle was mechanically developed by continuous methodical labor into endless subtle casuistic details. And the more the credit of the scribes increased, the more did their theory become valid Law. (2) The teaching of the Law, that is, the written Law, as delivered by Moses, as well as their own gratuitous oral embellishments. The ambition of every scribe was to create popular professional acquaintance with the Law and to "bring up many scholars." (3) The passing of sentence in the courts of justice. In Jewish communities, anyone might be appointed judge through the confidence of his fellow citizens. But since confidence is usually placed in proportion to the knowledge and ability displayed, it was only natural that scribes were usually appointed to the office of judges. The same held true with regard to delivering the lectures in the synagogues. Though this was open to all, the choice usually fell upon a local scribe. (4) Guardians and preservers of the written text of Scripture. Although as a class, the scribes at the time of Christ were His implacable enemies, we owe them—rather, their successors of a later period—a great debt because of their extremely conscientious labors for the unadulterated preservation of the sacred text. See Schürer, *Jewish People* 2.1:312–328; Farrar, *Life of Christ* 1:265.

63 For synagogue sermons, see Edersheim, *Life and Times of Jesus* 1:448ff.

64 Gk *Ea*—a cry of horror.

65 Gk *ti hēmin kai soi*; What is there in common between us? (Jn 2:4).

66 The diseased man speaks for the demon in him and the demon for the entire infernal host, as having all the same interest (Bruce, *Synoptic Gospels*, on Mk 1:24).

67 *Ant* 8:46–48. Cf. *War* 7:180–85.

68 Edersheim, *Life and Times of Jesus* 1:480.

69 As is actually claimed by some writers.

70 Gn 3:1 (cp. Rv 12:9); Jb 2; Mt 4:1–11; 1Pt 5:8; Jas 4:7; Jude 6; etc.

71 What is called demon possession is familiar today in parts of Asia and Africa (Mathews, *Life of Jesus*, 504). See Robert Bennett, *I Am Not Afraid:*

Demon Possession and Spiritual Warfare (St. Louis: Concordia, 2013).

72 Edersheim, *Life and Times of Jesus* 1:483.

73 See ch. 1.

74 So long as the usual definition for demoniac is given as a person who is *supposed* to be under the influence of a demon, it is clear why most of the articles under this subject are not satisfactory. For a positive discussion, see Weiss, *Life of Christ* 1:76–88; Edersheim, *Life and Times of Jesus* 1:479–84; and the few sentences in Pieper, *Christian Dogmatics* 1:615.

75 Edersheim, *Life and Times of Jesus* 1:485.

76 Transposed. See remarks on previous transposition (§ 11). This is the first time that we are leaving the natural order of Matthew. And not without good reason. In comparing Matthew with Mark and Luke, it seems that the events of the first Gospel up to the death of John the Baptist are not related in strict chronological sequence, but are given in topical order for didactic purposes. With all due respect to the learning and labor of the keenest minds, we are convinced that the problem of the chronological sequence of the various events of the life of Jesus, in particular those now under consideration, cannot be solved by criticism nor in a mathematical or mechanical way. (1) *Criticism.* The "synoptic problem." According to this theory, an original and now lost written or oral source (commonly called Q for *Quelle* [source] or *Logia* [oral tradition], upon the basis of which the first Gospel, for instance, Matthew or Mark, was written) is presupposed. Using the material at hand, editing, revising, changing, or supplying, the other Gospels followed. Each of the three synoptic Gospels was in turn placed first in order. But of late, Mark is enjoying the greatest favor. In the words of Robertson: "It is plain as a pikestaff that both our Matthew and Luke *used* practically all of Mark and followed his general order of events" (*Harmony of the Gospels*, 255). There is truth in the statement with respect to the *order* of Mark. But in accepting the *principle*, questions naturally arise, and conclusions follow. Without entering into the controversy, we merely wish to state that we cannot accept any theory that exalts any one Gospel at the expense of another, as all are equally inspired. The more we study the matter,

the more we are convinced that the evangelists wrote *independently* of one another and that in finding the true order of the respective events, (a) the natural order of the individual Gospels must be followed, but (b) unless it is expressly stated, a consideration of the purpose for which the events are grouped or of the circumstances in which they are introduced is permitted. We agree with Prof. M. B. Riddle: "The writer may be pardoned for alluding to his own experience in connection with this point [origin and relation of the synoptic Gospels]. In the exegetical labors of some years he found himself accepting the theory that the three Synoptists wrote independently of one another. Afterwards, when the task of editing Dr. Robinson's *Greek Harmony* compelled him to compare again and again every word of each account, the evidence of independence seemed to him to be overwhelming" (introductory essay to *St. Augustine's Harmony of the Gospels* [*NPNF*2 6:68 n. 1]). (2) A *mathematical* solution was attempted by Ebrard in his *Gospel History* but with unsatisfactory result. (3) Neither can a solution be found in a *mechanical* way. For a study of the synoptic problem the student is referred to the *Introductions* of Zahn and Weiss.

77 *Life*, 279; Edersheim, *Life and Times of Jesus* 1:455.

78 Or "Him," according to some manuscripts of Matthew.

79 Transposed, but in order.

80 Farrar, *Life of Christ* 1:238.

81 Edersheim, *Life and Times of Jesus* 1:488.

Chapter 10
From the First Galilean Circuit to the Choice of the Twelve

1 As seems likely on account of "again" in the Greek of Mk 2:1.

2 *War* 3:41.

3 Gk *selēniazomenous*.

4 Here follows the miraculous catch of fish in the order of Luke (Lk 5:1–11). See ch. 9, §§ 11–12.

5 See previous notes on transpositions, ch. 9, §§ 11, 20–21. The healing of the leper cannot have taken place after the Sermon on the Mount—for "great crowds followed Him" then (Mt 8:1)—but privately, which is evident from the command of silence given the healed leper (v. 4); although he nevertheless "began to talk freely about it, and to spread the news" (Mk 1:45). That this healing is not placed chronologically by Matthew appears also from the whole arrangement of chs. 8, 9, and 11, successive miracles recorded after 8:2 without regard to the exact order of time—from here to the parables.

6 Some writers believe that the disease called *lepra* by the Greeks and the plague of Lv 13—*tsara'ath*—are not identical. The disease mentioned in Scripture seems to have been curable, whereas the leprosy of the Greeks—elephantiasis graecorum—was not, except in the early stages. The former is now usually identified with psoriasis, dry tetter, a noncontagious, irritating skin disease in which white scales form on the body ("a leper white as snow"). These scales spread until they become the size of a quarter or half dollar, by which time they fall from the central part of the circle, leaving it red. Perhaps the Hebrew term *tsara'ath* was generic, and elephantiasis and psoriasis were two of its species. See Mathews, *Life of Jesus*, 504; Davis, *Dictionary of the Bible*, on "Leprosy."

7 A punitive miracle.

8 Biblical accounts use "leprosy" in a more general way for diseases of the skin. See articles on leprosy in *ABD* 4:277–82; *ISBE*; and *Encyclopedia Britannica*. Edersheim, *Life and Times of Jesus* 1:491ff. Weiss, *Life of Christ* 2:163ff.

9 The lining of the cavities leading to the exterior of the human body.

10 Edersheim, *Life and Times of Jesus* 1:493.

11 Edersheim, *Life and Times of Jesus* 1:491.

12 Weiss (*Life of Christ* 2:164) thinks that it was in a synagogue, on account of Mk 1:39. Bruce (*Synoptic Gospels*, on Mk 1:43) points out that the Gk *exebalen*, "cast him out," in v. 43 could indicate casting out of a synagogue, but this may also refer to being sent out of a city or a crowd.

13 Farrar, *Life of Christ* 1:275.

14 Gk *Thelō, katharisthēti*.

15 Farrar, *Life of Christ* 1:275.

16 A cure through human agency was never contemplated by the Jews (Edersheim, *Life and Times of Jesus* 1:492). Josephus speaks of the possibility of

a cure in answer to prayer (*Ant* 3:264). Compare also 2Ki 5:7.

17 Only clean persons were allowed to offer sacrifices (Lv 14:9–10).

18 Not necessarily in Jerusalem, but to the priest in the province whose business it was to attend to this duty (Bruce, *Synoptic Gospels*, on Lk 5:14).

19 Meyer, *Commentary on the N.T.*, on Mt 8:4.

20 Stöckhardt, *Biblische Geschichte*, 106.

21 Farrar, *Life of Christ* 1:277.

22 Compare ch. 9, § 19.

23 Gk *ton logon*, the report of the healing word.

24 It is interesting to note that Luke constantly refers to the prayers of Jesus: 3:21; 5:16; 6:12; 9:28; 11:1; 23:34; 23:46.

25 Transposed. Chronologically this section, Mt 9:1–17, including the call of Matthew, and 12:1–21, belong before the Sermon on the Mount.

26 The presence of Pharisees and scribes from Jerusalem, the charge of blasphemy, the word to the paralytic "Rise, take up your bed and walk" (cf. Jn 5:8), and the reference of Jesus to the authority given Him by the Father (cf. Jn 5:27) convince us that this miracle took place *after* the encounter at the unknown feast rather than as shown in the usual chronological arrangement, by which Jn 5 is placed immediately before the plucking of grain on a Sabbath day, Mk 2:23–28 and parallels.

27 Gk *di' hēmerōn*.

28 Bruce, *Synoptic Gospels*, on Mk 2:1.

29 If the house was, as we suppose, Peter's home, it must have been one of the better dwellings of comfortable income, since it contained, besides a large family room for friends and guests, accommodations for Peter and his wife, for Peter's mother-in-law, and for Jesus as the honored Guest (Edersheim, *Life and Times of Jesus* 1:502).

30 Edersheim, *Life and Times of Jesus* 1:501.

31 The Word *par excellence*, the Gospel. The phrase reminds us of the Apostolic Church (Bruce, *Synoptic Gospels*, on Mk 2:2).

32 Gk *paralytikos*.

33 Gk *teknon*, child, affectionately (see also Mk 10:24; Lk 16:25). Meyer, *Commentary on the N.T.*, on Mt 9:2.

34 Cf. Jesus' command in Mt 24:17, which may imply an external staircase or withdrawing over

the flat roofs of the adjoining houses. "The road of the roofs" (Edersheim, *Life and Times of Jesus* 1:503).

35 Edersheim, *Life and Times of Jesus* 1:503.

36 Gk *pistin autōn*. We see no reason why the faith of the sick man should not be included in the *autōn*.

37 Edersheim, *Life and Times of Jesus* 1:504.

38 Ch. 9, § 13.

39 Gk *kathēmenoi*.

40 Gk *dialogizomenoi*.

41 The term *Son of Man* occurs here for the first time in Mark. Cf. Dn 7:13–14; Jn 1:51; Mt 8:20. Pieper, *Christian Dogmatics* 2:74–75. See also ch. 6, § 20.

42 Weiss, *Life of Christ* 2:233.

43 Farrar, *Life of Christ* 1:346.

44 Farrar, *Life of Christ* 1:346.

45 Gk *paradoxa*, paradoxes (Lk 5:26). The only place in the New Testament where this word occurs.

46 Transposed. If Levi is the same as Matthew and to be identified with the evangelist St. Matthew, of which there is hardly any doubt, then it seems that the writer of the first Gospel does not insist upon placing his call *after* the Sermon on the Mount, which he has reported at length. The feast spoken of in Mt 9:10–13 may have been given later, before the healing of Jairus's daughter (Mk 5:22–24; Lk 8:41–42) on account of the words "while He was saying these things" (Mt 9:18), but is here related in order to gather in a group all that concerned Levi-Matthew personally. Or the call of Matthew may have occurred earlier, according to the arrangement of many Gospel harmonies, e.g., that of Tatian (c. AD 160–75), who, however, seems to have considered Levi and Matthew as two different persons. Compare Hill's edition of Tatian's *Diatessaron*, 7:9 and 5:25.

47 Schürer, *Jewish People* 1.2:68.

48 Schürer, *Jewish People* 1.2:7; *Ant* 17:317–18. The salary of Herod Antipas (200 talents) was vast.

49 *Ant* 18:172–73; Schürer, *Jewish People* 1.2:82. See also ch. 4, § 44.

50 *Ant* 14:201.

51 Schürer, *Jewish People* 1.2:79.

52 *Publicanus* (Lat), *telōnēs* (Gk).

53 Edersheim, *Life and Times of Jesus* 1:517.

54 Walking sticks with a secret place for pearls (Schürer, *Jewish People* 1.2:71).

55 By Edersheim, *Life and Times of Jesus* 1:517.

56 "Little mokhes," or *douanier*.

57 See *Oxford Bible Atlas*, 27.

58 A confusion that actually arose in very early times, the consequence of which was that in some manuscripts we find the reading James (instead of Levi) in Mk 2:14. See Meyer, *Commentary on the N.T.*, on Mk 2:14.

59 Meyer, *Commentary on the N.T.*, Introduction to Matthew, 1. The *legomenon* in Mt 9:9 seems to imply a change of name.

60 Farrar, *Life of Christ* 1:248, n. 1.

61 Farrar, *Life of Christ* 1:248, n. 1.

62 See Eusebius, *NPNF2* 1:152, 171; Bruce's and Meyer's introductions to Matthew, etc.

63 Edersheim, *Life and Times of Jesus* 1:519.

64 On Capernaum, see ch. 6, § 25. The intersection of the trade routes would be south of Capernaum. See Smith, *Atlas of Historical Geography*, 20.

65 Weiss, *Life of Christ* 2:25.

66 Nicoll, *Expositor's Greek Testament*, 498.

67 Farrar, *Life of Christ* 1:348

68 Edersheim, *Life and Times of Jesus* 1:519.

69 Farrar, *Life of Christ* 1:348.

70 Edersheim, *Life and Times of Jesus* 1:520.

71 Farrar, *Life of Christ* 1:349.

72 Edersheim, *Life and Times of Jesus* 1:662. On account of Mk 2:18: "were fasting." These days were Mondays and Thursdays; for Moses was supposed to have gone up the Mount for the second tables of the Law on the fifth day of the week and to have returned on a Monday (Farrar, *Life of Christ* 1:349 n. 3). Only one day of fasting was divinely appointed for the entire year, the Day of Atonement (Lv 16:29; Nu 29:7). But it appears that in the period of the captivity, four annual fasts had sprung up (Zec 8:19; 7:1–12), which in the time of Jesus had increased to two a week (Lk 18:12).

73 Farrar, *Life of Christ* 1:349.

74 Bruce, *Synoptic Gospels*, on Mt 9:15.

75 Edersheim, *Life and Times of Jesus* 1:663.

76 Literal translation of the Gk *hoi huioi tou nymphōnos*, which is translated as "wedding guests" in the ESV.

77 Farrar, *Life of Christ* 1:351.

78 Compare Jn 2:19; 3:14. Jesus knew His death to be divinely appointed from the very beginning; He did not only gradually attain to this knowledge, after experiencing such opposition as He did.

79 Bruce, *Synoptic Gospels*, on Mt 9:16.

80 Matthew and Mark.

81 Luke.

82 For a critical discussion see Nicoll, *Expositor's Greek Testament*, or Meyer, *Commentary on the N.T.* At any rate, the verbal variations of the Synoptists in recording this saying of our Lord present the strongest internal evidence against the theory of dependence on one another or on an earlier written source.

83 Bruce, *Synoptic Gospels*, on Mt 9:16.

84 Bruce, *Synoptic Gospels*, on Lk 5:39.

85 At this point, many harmonists insert Jn 5:1–47, the unnamed feast. For a discussion of it, see ch. 8.

86 A new transposition. Chronologically this section (Mt 12:1–21) must be placed before the Sermon on the Mount.

87 On account of the words "*Again* He entered the synagogue" in Mk 3:1, that is, the synagogue already mentioned in 1:21, called "their synagogue" in Mt 12:9, where the Pharisees who put a reproachful question to the disciples are spoken of as members of that synagogue.

88 That is, we suppose it to have been wheat. For chronological reasons, many—placing the event after the unnamed feast of Jn 5—have supposed that it was barley. But barley, besides being the usual feed for horses—though barley bread was eaten by the poorer classes (Edersheim, *Life and Times of Jesus* 1:681), also by Jesus and His disciples in Jn 6:9—is not so readily rubbed in the hands for immediate consumption. See Andrews, *Life of Our Lord*, 259.

89 The ESV includes the textual note "Some manuscripts *On the second first Sabbath* (that is, on the second Sabbath after the first)." This mysterious *deuteroprōtei*, "second first" of Luke, missing in some of the best manuscripts, has caused considerable discussion. Meyer and Bruce do not accept its authenticity. For a possible explanation of the term and its appearance in the manuscripts, see Metzger, *Textual Commentary*, 139.

90 Farrar, *Life of Christ* 1:436.

91 A Sabbath day's journey (Ac 1:12), reckoned at 2,000 cubits, was the assumed distance from the tents of the children of Israel to the tabernacle during their sojourn in the wilderness and the distance they had to keep from it while crossing the Jordan (Jsh 3:4).

92 Edersheim, *Life and Times of Jesus* 2:56.

93 *Ant* 6:261.

94 According to the principle that danger to life (the life of an Israelite) superseded the Sabbath law. Quoting Lv 18:5, "It was argued, that a man was to keep the commandments that he might live— certainly not, that by so doing he might die" (Edersheim, *Life and Times of Jesus* 2:57).

95 Farrar, *Life of Christ* 1:438.

96 Gk *meizōn*. A reference not to the work, but to the person of Jesus. Meyer, *Commentary on the N.T.*, on Mt 12:6.

97 Bruce, *Synoptic Gospels*, on Mt 12:6.

98 Bruce, *Synoptic Gospels*, on Mt 12:4.

99 Bruce, *Synoptic Gospels*, observes on Mk 2:27: "For this saying alone, and the parable of gradual growth (4:26–29), his Gospel was worth preserving."

100 Concerning the term *Son of Man* see above, § 13, and ch. 6, § 20. This designation of Jesus as the Messiah occurs eighty-four times in the New Testament. A mere "ideal" man is certainly not Lord of the Sabbath. It evidently refers to His person as the Messiah: "True God, begotten of the Father from eternity, and also true man, born of the Virgin Mary, . . . my Lord" (SC, Second Article). See also Kretzmann, *Popular Commentary*, 47–48.

101 Following Lk 6:4 in Codex D (Bezae), now at the University Library, Cambridge.

102 Somewhat like Ac 20:35, which, however, is recorded in a canonical book.

103 And Heb 11:6: "Without faith it is impossible to please Him."

104 Lk 6:6: *en heterōi sabbatōi*.

105 Inferred from the progress of the story and the Gk *palin*, "again," in Mk 3:1. The synagogue previously mentioned in Mk 1:21: "synagogue"; "Capernaum" in 2:1; "in his house" in 2:15; "synagogue" in 3:1.

106 *Zēra*, possibly a familiar expression in Hebrew pathology.

107 Hebrew Gospel of Nazarenes and Ebionites (Farrar, *Life of Christ* 1:439).

108 Edersheim, *Life and Times of Jesus* 2:59.

109 Bruce, *Synoptic Gospels*, on Mk 3:4.

110 The Gk here is *tis . . . anthrōpos*, "man." One is tempted to put emphasis on *man*. "Humanity was what was lacking in pharisaic character" (Bruce, *Synoptic Gospels*, on Mt 12:11).

111 They held it to be permissible to pull a sheep out of a pit if it was in danger of drowning. In less extreme cases, planks could be put in and food furnished (Farrar, *Life of Christ* 1:440 n. 1).

112 Andrews, *Life of Our Lord*, 261.

113 The case of John the Baptist.

114 Mentioned only here in the New Testament. The country of the Edomites, Hebron and the surrounding territory, belonging to Judea.

115 Gk *mastigas* (Mk 3:10).

116 "*Er wollte mit seinen Wundern keinen Rumor machen*" (Stöckhardt, *Biblische Geschichte*, 85).

117 See ch. 9, §§ 19, 21. Compare also Lk 4:41; Mk 1:34.

118 Freely quoted by Matthew from the Hebrew with side glances at the Septuagint (Bruce, *Synoptic Gospels*, on Mt 12:15–21).

CHAPTER 11
CHOOSING OF THE TWELVE AND THE SERMON ON THE MOUNT

1 Gk *exēlthen* (Luke), probably suggesting Capernaum, as compared with Lk 7:1: *eisēlthen eis Kapharnaoum*.

2 Compare Mk 1:33 and various passages in Luke. See also ch. 10, § 2.

3 Cf. Mt 4:13; 8:5 as suggested by David P. Scaer, *The Sermon on the Mount* (St. Louis: Concordia, 2000), 61.

4 See Andrews, *Life of Our Lord*, 269.

5 Or 1,083 feet above the Mediterranean Sea.

6 Farrar, *Life of Christ* 1:250. It is called by western Christians the Mount of Beatitudes, and it overlooks the spot where the army of Crusaders, in AD 1187, made its last memorable stand and was almost utterly annihilated by the hosts of Saladin. (W. W. Smith, *Historical Geography of the Holy Land*, 10). In presenting our preference we admit that there is no certainty in the matter.

The tradition does not date farther back than the twelfth or thirteenth century. Robinson contends that there are a dozen other mountains in the vicinity of the lake that would answer the purpose as well (Andrews, *Life of Our Lord*, 269). And Edersheim says that Kurn Hattin for many reasons is unsuitable (*Life and Times of Jesus* 1:524).

7   Farrar, *Life of Christ* 1:250.

8   Gk *epoiēse*. Bruce, *Synoptic Gospels*, on Mk 3:14.

9   Eusebius, *NPNF2* 1:129, 132. For a recent, extensive article on Peter, see *ABD* 5:251–63.

10   Davis, *Dictionary of the Bible*. See also *ABD* 1:242–43.

11   See ch. 4, § 43. On James, the son of Zebedee, see *ABD* 3:617.

12   There is also a tradition stating that Zebedee was of the house of Levi. And Eusebius (*NPNF2* 1:163) quotes an *Epistle of Polycrates*, Bishop of Ephesus, to Victor, Bishop of Rome, in which it is claimed that John was a priest.

13   See also ch. 6, § 18.

14   Zebedee was of the house of Levi and Salome of the house of Judah, according to apocryphal tradition. On John the son of Zebedee, see *ABD* 3:883–86.

15   By Brandes in *Jesus: A Myth*.

16   Farrar, *Life of Christ* 1:256.

17   Weiss (*Life of Jesus* 1:92) credits Irenaeus with this tradition and cites Eusebius, *NPNF2* 1:238–39; 242.

18   On Philip the disciple, see *ABD* 5:311.

19   Clement of Alexandria, *Stromata* 3:4 (*ANF* 2:385).

20   Kretzmann, *Popular Commentary* 1:296. Eusebius says (*NPNF2* 1:242) that he died in Hierapolis, that he had two aged virgin daughters, and another daughter, who was laid to rest at Ephesus.

21   See ch. 6, § 20. On Bartholomew, see *ABD* 1:615.

22   Eusebius, *NPNF2* 1:225.

23   Ch. 10, § 18. On Matthew, see *ABD* 4:618–22.

24   Eusebius, *NPNF2* 1:173.

25   Notice his quotations from the Old Testament and translation of Hebrew and Aramaic words and phrases in Mt 1:23; 27:33, 46.

26   Primitive Gospel and original source theories.

27   Fuerbringer, *Einleitung*, 23.

28   Kretzmann, *Popular Commentary* 1:296; Meyer, *Commentary on the N.T.*, Introduction to Matthew.

29   On Thomas, see *ABD* 6:528–29.

30   *ZPBD* 849.

31   Farrar, *Life of Christ* 1:251. On James the younger, see *ABD* 3:617–18.

32   It is inferred that *Klōpas* and *Alphaios* are two slightly varying forms of the same name: *chalphay*. See both Meyer (*Commentary on the N.T.*) and Dods (*Gospel of St. John*) on Jn 19:25.

33   Ch. 4, § 3. Some think that this Mary was a sister of the mother of our Lord.

34   Weiss, *Life of Christ* 2:270.

35   Stöckhardt, *Biblische Geschichte*, 87.

36   Kretzmann, *Popular Commentary* 1:297; Fuerbringer, *Einleitung*, 94.

37   Eusebius, *NPNF2* 1:126–27; *Ant* 20:200.

38   Robertson, *Harmony of the Gospels*, 273. *Leb* means heart in Hebrew. *Thad* means a mother's breast in Aramaic. Fuerbringer, *Einleitung*, 99. On Thaddeus, see *ABD* 6:435.

39   Gk *Ioudan Iakōbou* (Lk 6:16).

40   Meyer (*Commentary on the N.T.*) says on Lk 12:14: "'The brother of James' is without foundation in exegesis." Edersheim (*Life and Times of Jesus* 1:522): "Less probably the son of James."

41   Eusebius, *NPNF2* 1:148–49.

42   On account of the term Canaanite, *Kananitēs* or *Kanaios*. Possibly a piece of information based on an independent, yet seemingly reliable source as referring to the name of a place (Cana?); or an interpretation of a Hebrew word, *qan'aniy*, for *zēlōtēs*, zealot. See Bruce (*Synoptic Gospels*) or Meyer (*Commentary on the N.T.*) on Mt 10:4.

43   See "The Revolutionaries and Jesus" in *ABD* 6:1052.

44   Eusebius, *NPNF2* 1:146, 163–64, 199.

45   Judas, the son of Simon Iscariot (Jn 6:71; 13:2). See *ABD* 3:1091–96.

46   Probably near Hebron.

47   Farrar, *Life of Christ* 1:254.

48   Farrar, *Life of Christ* 1:252.

49   Farrar, *Life of Christ* 1:258.

50   Here we have come back to the natural order of Matthew. He makes topical arrangements and apparent chronological inversions of events in his Gospel, such as placing the call of the apostles,

including his own call, after the Sermon on the
Mount. See notes in ch. 9, §§ 11, 20, and ch. 10,
§ 4.

51 Gk *katabas . . . epi topou pedinou.*

52 For a discussion, see Andrews, *Life of Our Lord,*
268–73; Tholuck, *Bergpredigt Christi,* 1ff.

53 Farrar, *Life of Christ* 1:258, n. 2.

54 "A great crowd of His disciples and a great multitude of people" (Lk 6:17).

55 Jn 13–17 may include more words from Jesus but
reads as a dialogue, where actions described by the
narrator, questions, and statements from the disciples precede sayings from Jesus.

56 Ludwig, *Son of Man,* 130; Klausner, *Jesus of
Nazareth,* 384.

57 Although the oral rabbinical traditions are of
ancient origin, it must be noted that they were not
collected and edited until toward the end of the
second century after Christ. See *ALEN* 354–55.

58 At the first glance we would count eight, viewing
Mt 5:11 and 12 as an enlargement of v. 10. The
traditional number, however, is seven, vv. 10–12
being regarded as a transition to a new topic. In an
attempt to establish an analogy with the Decalog,
ten have been counted (Bruce, *Synoptic Gospels,* on
Mt 5:3).

59 The reference of Jesus is not exclusively or chiefly
physical wealth.

60 Notice the all-embracing "earth" and "world." And
even if *gē* is to be restricted to the Jewish soil, you
still have the universal *kosmos.*

61 See Mk 9:50; Lk 14:34, 35. The Lord often
repeated His sayings.

62 Edersheim, *Life and Times of Jesus* 1:146; Meyer,
Commentary on the N.T., on Mt 5:14.

63 Cf. Mk 4:21; Lk 8:16; 11:33: Gk *modios,* a Latin
word, *modius.* See note in ch. 4, § 42.

64 Gk *kala erga.* "Nice" works are good works.

65 Jesus had previously called God His Father (Jn
5:17). But here, quite naturally and as a matter
of course, He introduces God to His disciples as
"your Father who is in heaven."

66 Gk *Amēn,* often used by Jesus. Used iteratively by
John (Jn 1:51). See ch. 6, § 20.

67 See Lk 16:17. *Iōta* is the smallest letter in the
Hebrew alphabet: ʼ. And *keraia,* horn, is a little
projecting point or base line distinguishing certain letters from another, similar one: ב-כ , ד-ר.

See Meyer's footnote on Mt 5:18 in *Commentary
on the N.T.*

68 The first "until" is a strong way of saying never.
The second "until" implies the adequate fulfillment made by Christ.

69 The view of Luther and others. See Meyer
(*Commentary on the N.T.*) and Bruce (*Synoptic
Gospels*) on Mt 5:19.

70 The scribes were the acknowledged teachers of
the people, and the Pharisees were a sect, to which
many of the scribes belonged. See note in ch. 9,
§ 14.

71 Bruce, *Synoptic Gospels,* on Mt 5:20.

72 "Without cause," *eikē,* missing in many manuscripts. "But whether genuine or not, this word
expresses the true sense. Eph 4:26" (Farrar, *Life of
Christ* 1:261 n. 1).

73 The fire of Hinnom, the valley where the refuse
of Jerusalem was burned—a figure often used
by Jesus in speaking of the punishment of hell
fire (Kretzmann, *Popular Commentary* 1:27).
Notice: "Judgment" means a local court of seven;
"Council" means the court of seventy, the Jewish
Council, the Supreme Council; "hell fire" means
the highest court.

74 Gk *hraka,* empty head!

75 "You fool," *mōre,* expressing contempt for
someone.

76 Gk *kodrantēs,* a Latin word, *quadrans,* worth about
3/10 cents. See note in ch. 4, § 42.

77 Mentioned here in Mt 5. Another ground for
divorce, mentioned by St. Paul, is malicious
desertion, when one's spouse simply leaves (1Co
7:15); indeed, "desertion is in itself divorce" (Fritz,
Pastoral Theology, 181).

78 Nicoll, *Expositor's Greek Testament,* 111.

79 Bruce, *Synoptic Gospels,* on Mt 5:41. Gk *Milion,*
another word derived from the Latin (*milia,* plural
of *mille,* meaning a thousand). The term signifies
a thousand paces, equal to 1,618 English yards.

80 Kretzmann, *Popular Commentary* 1:30.

81 Kretzmann, *Popular Commentary* 1:30.

82 *ZPEB* 2:696.

83 Kretzmann, *Popular Commentary* 1:30.

84 To be understood metaphorically. The word *hypocrite* is derived from the Gk *hypokritēs,* stage actor.

85 A person could intentionally be in public at the
appointed time for *prayer* and so gain an audience

86 for his piety (Bruce, *Synoptic Gospels*, on Mt 6:5–6).

86 See also Lk 11:2–4. Ch. 21, § 11.

87 Phrases from Luther's Catechism appear throughout this paragraph. See SC, The Lord's Prayer.

88 Daily, Gk *epiousion*, only here and in Lk 11:3. An apparently simple, yet puzzling term. A *Volkswort*, says Deissmann (*Licht vom Osten*, 61). It reminds us of the word *homoousios*. Jerome, in Mt 6:11, translates: *supersubstantialis*, while in Lk 11 he renders the word as *quotidianus*. The problem is to account for an undoubtedly simple and at the time well-understood term. Whether it is qualitative, needful, or temporal, daily, depends upon whether it is derived from *epeinai* or *epienai*; however, as far as grammar, at least as far as interpretation, is concerned, the temporal interpretation has most in its favor. For discussion, see Bruce (*Synoptic Gospels*) and Meyer (*Commentary on the N.T.*) on Mt 6:11 (Tholuck, *Bergpredigt Christi*, 407–26).

89 The old translation "trespasses" used in Lutheran churches is that employed in the translation of Luther's catechism in the confessional writings.

90 Bruce, *Synoptic Gospels*, on Mt 6:12.

91 Some Bible translations render *ponērou* "from the evil one," referring to the devil.

92 SC, The Lord's Prayer, Seventh Petition.

93 The closing words of the Lord's Prayer are regarded by most modern critics as an ancient liturgical insertion. They are not included in the Vulgate, St. Jerome's officially adopted Latin version—hence the omission in the Latin churches. They are also not found in the three leading and most ancient existing manuscripts of the Greek New Testament—hence their omission in some leading printed editions and also in more recent versions of the Bible. But on the other hand, the words appear in the *textus receptus*, the traditional text, and upon it Luther's translation and also the King James Version are based.

94 Tertullian.

95 See ch. 10, § 22.

96 Gk *haplous*, sound, healthy; generous.

97 Gk *ponēros*, evil.

98 Bruce, *Synoptic Gospels*, on Mt 6:22–24.

99 Riches personified. Gk *Mamōnas*, Plutus, a Chaldee, Syriac, and Punic word (Bruce, *Synoptic Gospels*, on Mt 6:22–24).

100 Gk *hēlikia* means both stature and age; *pēchys* means cubit, six handbreadths, or 1 ½ feet. There is much difference of opinion as to whether Jesus referred to height of body or length of life. Most recent interpreters favor the latter. See also Ps 39:5; Jb 14:5. The adoption of either the one or the other view leaves the thought unchanged.

101 Gk *krina tou agrou*. The *lilium Persicum* (Lat), emperor's crown, or *Kaiserkrone* (Grm), according to some; the red anemone, growing luxuriantly under thorn bushes, according to others. We don't know. All flowers as represented by the lily is probably the best view. The reference points to the season of spring when the flowers are in bloom.

102 Bruce, *Synoptic Gospels*, on Mt 6:28–30.

103 Hay was used to heat clay ovens (Meyer, *Commentary on the N.T.*, on Mt 6:30).

104 Gk *karphos*, chaff.

105 Gk *dokos*, wooden beam, joist.

106 Kretzmann, *Popular Commentary* 1:37.

107 Kretzmann, *Popular Commentary* 1:38.

108 Gk *ophis*, serpentlike fish found in the Sea of Galilee, three feet long, often caught in the nets, and of course thrown away like the dogfish in our waters (Bruce, *Synoptic Gospels*, on Mt 7:7–11).

109 Gk *ponēroi*, a strong word, morally evil. "Such a mean spirit is considered unnatural even among men, from whom one might, according to the natural depravity of the hearts, possibly expect a behavior of that kind" (Kretzmann, *Popular Commentary* 1:38). Or "evil" as compared with God (Meyer, *Commentary on the N.T.*, on Mt 7:11).

110 Transposed.

111 Negative in Tob 4:15. See Meyer, *Commentary on the N.T.*, on Mt 7:12. "The negative confines us to the reign of justice, which is still far from the positive, which takes us into the region of generosity and grace and so embraces the Law and the Prophets" (Bruce, *Synoptic Gospels*, on Mt 7:12). Edersheim, *Life and Times of Jesus* 2:236.

112 *ZPEB* 2:409.

113 Gk *pseudoprophētai*.

114 Bruce, *Synoptic Gospels*, on Mt 7:24.

115 *LSB* 575, refrain.

116 With regard to the scribes, see ch. 9, § 13.

117 Kretzmann, *Popular Commentary* 1:41.

118 Lk 7:3: *presbyterous*. Bruce (*Synoptic Gospels*) thinks that the reference to the elders is probably to the elders of the city rather than to the rulers of the synagogue. According to Schürer (*Jewish People* 2.1:150), in strictly Jewish communities the same men would be the elders of the community and the rulers of the synagogue.

119 Gk *paralytikos*. See Mt 9:2. Probably inflammatory rheumatism (Andrews, *Life of Our Lord*, 644). See ch. 10, § 11.

120 Andrews, *Life of Our Lord*, 274.

121 Edersheim, *Life and Times of Jesus* 8:434; McRay, *Archaeology*, 67–72.

122 See ch. 7, § 22.

123 Gk *hikanos*, "I am not worthy," not fit, Levitically or Judaistically speaking, and therefore not worthy spiritually, morally, religiously (Edersheim, *Life and Times of Jesus* 1:548).

124 Farrar, *Life of Christ* 1:281.

125 Edersheim, *Life and Times of Jesus* 1:550.

126 Bruce, *Synoptic Gospels*, on Mt 8:12.

CHAPTER 12
A SECOND PREACHING TOUR, INCLUDING THE PARABLES BY THE SEA

1 Gk *en tēi hexēs* (*hēmerai* understood). Farrar, *Life of Christ* 1:284 n. 1.

2 Farrar, *Life of Christ* 1:284.

3 Andrews, *Life of Our Lord*, 277.

4 Gk *ho kyrios*, the heavenly Christ and Lord of the Church (Bruce, *Synoptic Gospels*, on Lk 7:13).

5 Edersheim, *Life and Times of Jesus* 1:557.

6 See ch. 10, § 7.

7 Farrar, *Life of Christ* 1:286.

8 Eusebius, *NPNF2* 1:175.

9 Probably since the autumn of AD 30. See ch. 8, § 11. He seems to have enjoyed a measure of freedom and intercourse with his disciples even during his confinement.

10 See ch. 10, § 22.

11 Luther, quoted by Kretzmann, *Popular Commentary* 1:61.

12 Notice the "Me." By changing a general to a personal statement, Jesus plainly identifies Himself with the promised Christ.

13 Kretzmann, *Popular Commentary* 1:303.

14 On account of his embassy to Christ (Jn 1:19–28).

15 Without any authority from the Hebrew, the LXX here reads *Elian ton Thesbitēn*.

16 A proverbial form of speech often used by Jesus after an important utterance, here for the first time.

17 When and where this was said has not been recorded by any of the evangelists.

18 Compare also Lk 10:13–16.

19 In Luke's arrangement, the woes are placed in the time when the Lord sent out the Seventy-Two, in which connection, at the final withdrawal of Jesus from Galilee, they are also perfectly in order. Useless difficulties in the historical arrangement can be avoided by remembering that Jesus found need and occasion to repeat many of His sayings (Andrews, *Life of Our Lord*, 280; Kretzmann, *Popular Commentary* 1:64).

20 Compare also Lk 10:21–22.

21 On this and the following, this perfect pearl of the sayings of Jesus in Matthew, one of splendor like those in John's Gospel, see Meyer, *Commentary on the N.T.*, on Mt 11:22ff.

22 "Take My yoke upon you, and learn from Me" expresses the relation of master and pupil.

23 It is futile to make the attempt to identify Simon the Pharisee with Simon the leper and identify the unknown sinner who anointed Jesus with Mary of Bethany, who anointed Him during Passion week (Mt 26:6–13; Jn 12:2–8; Mk 14:3–9). See Meyer, *Commentary on the N.T.*, on Lk 7:37–38; Robertson, *Harmony of the Gospels*, 187.

24 Farrar, *Life of Christ* 1:297.

25 Edersheim, *Life and Times of Jesus* 1:564.

26 St. Gregory, quoted by Edersheim, *Life and Times of Jesus* 1:563.

27 Farrar, *Life of Christ* 1:305. For a discussion, see Andrews, *Life of Our Lord*, 285, and Meyer, *Commentary on the N.T.*, on Lk 7:37–38.

28 For instance, Mathews, *Life of Jesus*, 242, and Ramsay, *Was Christ Born at Bethlehem?*, 74.

29 See ch. 7, § 22. Cf. Lk 23:55; 24:10.

30 Edersheim, *Life and Times of Jesus* 1:573.

31 Now they come back to the house, Gk *eis oikon* (home), namely, in Capernaum, as in 2:1, to which also the subsequent *palin* points back (Meyer, *Commentary on the N.T.*, on Mk 3:20).

32 Those "with Him" (*sui* in the Vulgate), relatives coming from Nazareth or the outer circle of disciples (Bruce, *Synoptic Gospels*, on Mk 3:21).

33 Compare also Lk 11:14–23, which brings the repetition of a similar blasphemous accusation uttered against the Lord in Judea.

34 Enough time had elapsed since the event recorded in Lk 7:11–17.

35 For a recent review of the name, see *ABD* 1:638–40.

36 Bruce, *Synoptic Gospels*, on Mt 12:26.

37 Bruce, *Synoptic Gospels*, on Mt 12:27.

38 The sin is unpardonable not on account of its greatness, but on account of its nature. Compare Mt 12:31–32. See ch. 21, § 18.

39 Mueller, *Christian Dogmatics*, 233.

40 See article in Kretzmann, *Popular Commentary* 1:179. Mt 12:33–37 compared with Lk 6:43–45.

41 Compare Lk 11:29–32.

42 "The expression means little more than the *nychthēmeron* of 2Co 11:25. Compare 1Sm 30:12–13; 2Ch 10:5, 12." The popular method of computation by which parts of a day were counted as whole days (Meyer, *Commentary on the N.T.*, on Mt 12:40; Farrar, *Life of Christ* 1:461 note).

43 Bruce, *Synoptic Gospels*, on Mt 12:40.

44 Kretzmann, *Popular Commentary* 1:70.

45 Luke's placing of this incident after the parables by the sea is evidently topical (Bruce, *Synoptic Gospels*, on Lk 8:19–21).

46 Evidently none of those of His brothers, if indeed there were such, who now belonged to the apostolic band. See ch. 4, § 43.

47 Edersheim, *Life and Times of Jesus* 1:577.

48 There are two other groups. One in Luke only, chs 14–16; another group during the last week in Jerusalem, Mt 21–22; 24–25, and parallels.

49 According to his custom, Matthew points this out.

50 In His answer to the question, "Why do You speak to them in parables?" (Mt 13:10).

51 Andrews, *Life of Our Lord*, 293.

52 Kretzmann, *Popular Commentary* 182.

53 The Gk is *hina* in Mk 4:12 and Lk 8:10; *hoti* in Mt 13:13.

54 If we regard the quotation from Is 6:9–10 as words of Christ and not of Matthew.

55 Compare Lk 10:23–24.

56 Gk *synientos*, Mt 13:19, translated in the ESV as "understand it."

57 Cf. Mt 5:15; Lk 11:33; Mt 25:29; Lk 19:26; etc.

58 "He put another parable before them," Gk *autois*, to the multitudes. Compare Mt 13:3, 10, and 34. Meyer, *Commentary on the N.T.*, on Mt 13:24.

59 *Zizania*, bastard wheat, darnel, which grew in Israel.

60 Augustine, quoted by Meyer, *Commentary on the N.T.*, on Mt 13:30.

61 Compare also Lk 13:18–19. Ch. 21, § 31.

62 This explains our Lord's phrase, "faith like a grain of mustard seed" (Mt 17:20; Lk 17:6).

63 Compare also Lk 13:20–21. See ch. 21, § 31.

64 § 18.

65 Bruce, *Synoptic Gospels*, on Mk 4:34.

66 Meyer, *Commentary on the N.T.*, on Mt 13:35.

67 The same house referred to in v. 1.

68 Gk *phrason*, here and 15:15.

69 Bruce, *Synoptic Gospels*, on Mt 13:45.

70 Kretzmann, *Popular Commentary* 1:76.

71 Adapted from Bruce, *Synoptic Gospels*, on Mt 13:51–52.

72 Here follows in the order of Luke: "Jesus is called by His mother and brothers" (Lk 8:19–21). See § 17: "Interfering Kinsmen." Luke's placing of the incident after the parables by the sea is evidently topical.

CHAPTER 13
THE GADARENE JOURNEY

1 A return to the natural order of Matthew. See note under next section.

2 See ch. 12, § 12.

3 See ch. 12, § 17.

4 Probably without food or other preparation for the trip across the lake.

5 See also ch. 21, § 3.—The multitude from which Jesus escapes in Mark's narrative is that gathered on the shore in connection with the parable discourse. In agreement with Matthew and Luke this is followed by the crossing of the lake, the

calming of the storm, and the Gerasene journey. From this it seems to follow that the whole sections in Mt 11:2–30; 12:22–13:53 have been related out of chronological order, and we therefore now return to Mt 8:18ff. The placing of the present incident in Luke seems to indicate a loose arrangement, though what is related here may have happened again, at a later time. See Farrar, *Life of Christ* 1:327; Stöckhardt, *Biblische Geschichte*, 176.

6   Farrar, *Life of Christ* 1:327.

7   As assumed by Meyer on account of the expressions *heis grammateus* that is, *one* (disciple), a scribe (v. 19), and *another* disciple (v. 21).

8   Bruce, *Synoptic Gospels*, on Mt 8:19.

9   Gk *kataskēnōseis*, that is, roosts. For the birds do not live in nests.

10   This term appears for the first time here in Matthew = the Messiah. Compare Ac 7:55–56. See ch. 6, § 20.

11   Farrar, *Life of Christ* 1:328 n. 1.

12   Judas Iscariot, Thomas, and Matthew, according to Lange, *Matthew*, 160. Assuredly those applicants for discipleship were none of the Twelve (Lk 6:13–16). See Meyer, *Commentary on the N.T.*, on Lk 9:57–60.

13   Kretzmann, *Popular Commentary* 1:45.

14   Bruce, *Synoptic Gospels*, on Mt 8:19–22.

15   Making the incident in Luke parallel.

16   Something like Luther, who, upon entering the monastery at Erfurt, invited his friends for a farewell feast. See Martin Brecht, *Martin Luther: His Road to Reformation, 1483–1521* (Minneapolis: Fortress Press, 1993), 50.

17   Bruce, *Synoptic Gospels*, on Lk 9:61–62.

18   St. Augustine, quoted by Farrar, *Life of Christ* 1:328.

19   Bruce, *Synoptic Gospels*, on Lk 9:62.

20   He was in "*the* boat" (Mark), the well-known boat of the sons of Jonas or of Zebedee, both of which were always at His disposal.

21   Farrar, *Life of Christ* 1:329.

22   Andrews, *Life of Our Lord*, 294.

23   Edersheim, *Life and Times of Jesus* 1:601.

24   Gk *epetimēse*, chided.

25   Gk *siōpa, pephimōso* (from *phimoō*).

26   Farrar, *Life of Christ* 1:331.

27   Farrar, *Life of Christ* 1:331.

28   Because the demoniac saw Jesus from afar (Mk 5:6). Daytime—as against the view (Edersheim, *Life and Times of Jesus* 1:606) that the arrival of Jesus from Capernaum after the stilling of the storm took place the same evening and that the healing of the demonized at Gerasa was a night scene.

29   There has long been a controversy regarding both site and text, due in part to spelling variants as well as general and specific uses of terms. The identification of the site clears up the "discrepancy" of the text. It cannot have been the Greek city Gerasa, in the eastern extremity of Perea, in Gilead, about thirty-six miles from the Galilean Sea (*ABD* 2:991). It cannot have been Gadara, another city of the Decapolis, lying about seven miles southeast of Gennesaret, unless—which is likely—as the chief city in the region it lent its name to the district as that of the Gadarenes. The latter view explains the matter with respect to the reading "Gadarenes." And it seems that there was another Gerasa (Kersa, Chersa, Gersa, or Gergesa) to account for the readings "Gerasenes" or "Gergesenes." The latter was located on the shore of Galilee. As regards the term *Gergesenes*, it is found in eight uncials, most cursives, and (among others) in the Coptic and Ethiopic versions. It is to be remembered that Matthew lived on the shore of the lake and was likely to know its minute topography (Farrar, *Life of Christ* 1:333, n. 1). See also Nicoll, *Expositor's Greek Testament* 1:144; Barton, *Archaeology and the Bible*, 214; Kretzmann, *Popular Commentary* 1:186; Ylvisaker, *Gospels*, 189.

30   Farrar, *Life of Christ* 1:334.

31   See Jn 2:4. Edersheim, *Life and Times of Jesus* 1:610.

32   Bruce, *Synoptic Gospels*, on Mk 5:9.

33   Farrar, *Life of Christ* 1:336.

34   Bruce, *Synoptic Gospels*, on Mk 5:9.

35   Kretzmann, *Popular Commentary* 1:187.

36   Rosenmueller, quoted in Nicoll, *Expositor's Greek Testament*, 146.

37   Farrar, *Life of Christ* 1:341. The Jews, we know, were not allowed to have pigs.

38   Farrar, *Life of Christ* 1:341.

39   Here follows in the order of Matthew: The paralytic healed (9:2–8); Matthew called (9:9–13);

John's disciples' question about fasting (9:14–15); the parable of new wine and fresh wineskins (9:16–17). All in order, but transposed as compared with Mark and Luke. See ch. 10, § 11ff. There are some difficulties as to the proper sequence of events on account of the words "while He was saying these things" in Mt 9:18, which seems to compel a connection with v. 17. However, since Matthew is not chronological in this part of his Gospel, it is best to follow the order of Mark and Luke, but to bear in mind that the feast previously referred to and probably there related to bring together everything that concerns Levi-Matthew personally, may have taken place at this time. See ch. 10, § 15. Gibbs points out that this portion of Matthew emphasizes Jesus' authority through the various miracles in his ministry (Gibbs, *Matthew 1:1–11:1*, 43). Perhaps this thematic goal overshadowed chronological interests.

40 Farrar, *Life of Christ* 1:353. See ch. 11, § 43: *presbyterous*, but here *archōn*. In strictly Jewish communities the same men would be officers of the city and of the synagogue (Schürer, *Jewish Church* 2.1:150).

41 The passage has created work for the harmonist, because Mark and Luke say "dying" and Matthew says "dead." The latter was actually the case when the final report came (Mk 5:35). For the sake of brevity, it seems, Matthew contracts the whole narrative into the briefest possible summary.

42 Farrar, *Life of Christ* 1:355. According to a legend, it was Veronica (that is, *vera icon* [*eikōn*], "true image"), a woman from Caesarea Philippi, at the foot of Mount Hermon. Eusebius tells us that in commemoration of her cure by Jesus, she erected a statue of Jesus in bronze. It represented her in the act of touching the robe of Christ. This alleged statue of Jesus was the earliest of which we seem to have any record. It was destroyed by Julian the Apostate (Eusebius, *NPNF2* 1:304; Sozomenus, *NPNF2* 2:343; Farrar, *Life of Christ* 1:356 n. 2).

43 Farrar, *Life of Christ* 1:354.

44 The *chitōn* (Gk).

45 Gk *himation*.

46 Edersheim, *Life and Times of Jesus* 1:624.

47 Bruce, *Synoptic Gospels*, on Mk 5:28.

48 Farrar, *Life of Christ* 1:356.

49 Bruce, *Synoptic Gospels*, on Mt 9:23; Farrar, *Life of Christ* 1:357; Ylvisaker, *Gospels*, 205.

50 Special witnesses of His "greatest exaltation and most abject humiliation" (Ylvisaker, *Gospels*, 205). Compare the Transfiguration and the suffering in Gethsemane (Mk 5:37; 14:33).

51 Bruce, *Synoptic Gospels*, on Mk 5:41.

52 Bruce, *Synoptic Gospels*, on Mt 9:27.

53 Gk *enebrimēsato* (v. 30).

CHAPTER 14
A THIRD PREACHING TOUR, INCLUDING THE MISSION OF THE TWELVE

1 Transposed. In the order of events we follow Mark rather than Luke. Matthew relates this visit to Nazareth immediately after the parables by the sea. Chronologically, however, the departure in Mt 13:53 was not to Nazareth, but across the sea to Gergesa (Mk 5:1). We must therefore place the Gerasene journey, the healing of the demoniacs, the raising of Jairus's daughter, the healing of the woman with the discharge of blood, the healing of the two blind men, and the healing of the mute man possessed with an evil spirit between Mt 13:53 and 54. This brings us to the last visit Jesus made at Nazareth. And taking up the broken thread in Mt 9:35, we have returned to the synoptic order. (Next section.)

2 Robertson, *Harmony of the Gospels*, 77.

3 See ch. 4, § 43.

4 Ch. 4, § 43.

5 Unknown. The *History of Joseph* supplies the names of Anna and Lydia; the Coptic apocryphal gospels mention Lysia and (or) Lydia (Harris, *Twelve Apostles*, 50).

6 Cf. Jn 2:12; see ch. 6, § 25. Cf. also Lk 4:31; see ch. 9, § 10. It seems that the "sisters" of Jesus, now mentioned as residing at Nazareth, probably married, did not accompany Him and His "brothers" to Capernaum.

7 Cf. Lk 4:24. A repetition of Jn 4:44, with a changed reference and in a different connection. This brings to our mind a Logion of Jesus as found in the Oxyrhynchus Papyri I, lines 31–36 and the Gospel of Thomas, Logion 31: "A physician does not work cures on them that

know him." See Schneemelcher, *New Testament Apocrypha* 1:109.

8   Bruce, *Synoptic Gospels*, on Mt 9:36.

9   The image used again in Mk 6:34.

10   Bruce, *Synoptic Gospels*, on Mt 9:36.

11   The saying is repeated in connection with the sending out of the Seventy-Two (Lk 10:2).

12   Bruce, *Synoptic Gospels*, on Mt 10:1.

13   Up to this time it has not been mentioned that the Twelve performed any miracles, nor is it recorded that they did so after they rejoined the Lord. However, even then the power was not absolutely withdrawn; the exercising of it depended upon their faith (Andrews, *Life of Our Lord*, 312).

14   Ch. 11, § 4–17.

15   On account of this command it is likely that the disciples did not reach Judea.

16   This clause is well attested in the best manuscripts. But it is unlikely that the apostles used this power before Christ Himself rose from the dead (Bruce, *Synoptic Gospels*, on Mt 10:8; Kretzmann, *Popular Commentary* 1:55).

17   From a comparison of the three evangelists we infer this to be the meaning of this injunction (Farrar, *Life of Christ* 1:363 n. 2).

18   Incidentally this is a proof of the one-time existence of the doomed cities as well as of the resurrection of the wicked.

19   Farrar, *Life of Christ* 1:367.

20   Compare Lk 10:2–12; 12:2–9; 21:12–19; Mk 13:9–13.

21   Ylvisaker, *Gospels*, 317.

22   Plural. Not the Council, but the local courts.

23   Ch. 21, § 18.

24   Bruce, *Synoptic Gospels*, on Mt 10:19.

25   The view of Edersheim, *Life and Times of Jesus* 1:646, and Ylvisaker, *Gospels*, 319.

26   Compare Lk 12:2–9. See ch. 21, § 18.

27   See Engelbrecht, *Church from Age to Age*, 65; Robert Louis Wilken, *The Christians as the Romans Saw Them*, 2nd edition (New Haven: Yale University Press, 2003), 21–22.

28   Tacitus, *Annals* 15.44, 45.

29   Gk *assarion*, a Roman coin equal to about one cent.

30   Bruce, *Synoptic Gospels*, on Mt 10:30.

31   Compare Lk 12:8–9.

32   Kretzmann, *Popular Commentary* 1:59.

33   This is not necessarily an allusion to the death of Jesus by crucifixion. The Roman custom condemning a doomed criminal to carry his cross was known (Bruce, *Synoptic Gospels*, Mt 10:38).

34   Ylvisaker (*Gospels*, 322) thinks that the procedure, being not directly enjoined by Jesus, was employed of their own accord. The passage has nothing to do with the *unctio extrema*.

35   Here follows in the order of Matthew:

1. The message from John the Baptist (11:2–19; see ch. 12, §§ 2–4).

2. Woes to the unrepentant cities (11:20–30; see ch. 12, §§ 5–7).

3. The disciples plucking grain (12:1–8; see ch. 10, §§ 26–28).

4. The man with a withered hand (12:9–14; see ch. 10, §§ 29–31).

5. Jesus teaches and heals by the Sea of Galilee (12:15–21; see ch. 10, §§ 32–33).

6. Jesus defends Himself against a blasphemous accusation (12:22–37; see ch. 12, §§ 13–15).

7. Scribes and Pharisees demand a sign (12:38–45; see ch. 12, § 16).

8. Jesus is sought by His mother and His brothers (12:46–50; see ch. 12, § 17).

9. The parables by the sea (13:1–53; see ch. 12, §§ 18–32).

10. The last visit at Nazareth (13:54–58; see ch. 14, §§ 1–2).

With the exception of a few details, the account of the death of John the Baptist marks the end of the transpositions. Henceforth, to the end of the combined account, the fourfold Gospel unfolds itself in a truly remarkable parallel account.

CHAPTER 15
THE DEATH OF JOHN THE BAPTIST

1   Schürer, *Jewish People* 1.2:32.

2   Schürer, *Jewish People* 2.1:136f., 143f.; 1.2:19f.

3   Schürer, *Jewish People* 2.1:141.

4   *Ant* 18:119.

5   Mark, writing for the Roman world.

6   Bruce, *Synoptic Gospels*, on Mt 14:1.

7   Farrar, *Life of Christ* 1:384.

8   Summer, AD 31. Ch. 12, § 2.

9 Writing later, Matthew, as one of the Twelve, was both a reporter and a witness to the reports. It is possible that Luke received some of his information from the family of Chuza, Herod's household manager, whose wife, Joanna, followed Jesus (Lk 8:3; ch. 12, § 11), as well as from a certain Manaen, "a lifelong friend of Herod the tetrarch," who appears as a leader in the church of Antioch (Ac 13:1). The same applies to Mark (Ac 12:25). But the assumption that makes this Manaen an Essene and a son of the Essene Manaen, who foretold the future dignity of Herod the Great, as told by Josephus (*Ant* 15:373–79), and then to connect John the Baptist with the Essenes, is without historical foundation. See ch. 3, § 45, and Farrar, *Life of Christ* 1:394.

10 The Greek terms used by Josephus are *baptismos* and *baptisis*.

11 Thackeray's translation is used (*Selections from Josephus*, 80–81).

12 *Ant* 18:109–12.

13 *War* 1:562.

14 *War* 1:600.

15 *Ant* 18:136.

16 Gk *eneichen*.

17 The Herods were Idumeans.

18 The Maccabees traced their ancestry to Jehoiarib (1Ch 24:7; 1Macc 2:1).

19 Edersheim, *Life and Times of Jesus* 1:673.

20 *War* 2:183; *Ant* 18:252–55.

21 Farrar, *Life of Christ* 1:388.

22 Farrar, *Life of Christ* 1:389.

23 *Ant* 15:423. See Meyer, *Commentary on the N.T.*, or Bruce, *Synoptic Gospels*, on Mt 14:6.

24 Edersheim, *Life and Times of Jesus* 1:672.

25 Edersheim, *Life and Times of Jesus* 1:672.

26 *Ant* 18:136.

27 *Ant* 18:137; Schürer, *Jewish People* 1.2:342–343; Farrar, *Life of Christ* 1:390. The Herodian princesses were famed for their beauty. Legend makes Salome die a retributive death in consequence of a fall on the ice (Edersheim, *Life and Times of Jesus* 1:673; Farrar, *Life of Christ* 1:394). The tradition is mentioned by Jerome and Nicephorus.

28 Farrar, *Life of Christ* 1:391.

29 Farrar, *Life of Christ* 1:392.

30 Bruce, *Synoptic Gospels*, on Mk 6:23.

31 Farrar, *Life of Christ* 1:393.

32 Edersheim, *Life and Times of Jesus* 1:674.

33 Farrar, *Life of Christ* 1:393. Gk *apekephalise*, a very expressive word.

34 Edersheim, *Life and Times of Jesus* 1:674.

35 Other examples: Cicero's head and hands were sent to Rome and nailed to the rostra after Fulvia, wife of Antony, had thrust a hairpin through his tongue. After the execution of Paulina Lollia, the raging Agrippina—mother of Nero—examined her head.

36 Farrar, *Life of Christ* 1:387.

37 To the omniscient Jesus the fate of His forerunner was prophetic of His own. Compare Mk 9:12–13.

CHAPTER 16
THE PERIODS OF RETIREMENT AND SPECIAL TRAINING OF THE TWELVE

1 See ch. 8. An interval of one year, assuming that the unnamed feast in Jn 5 was the Passover of AD 31. All four evangelists mentioned the following incident of the feeding of the five thousand. Since the time is given as near a Passover (John), which also agrees with the "grass" in the account of Matthew, Mark, and John, we have here an important chronological notice.

2 Ch. 9.

3 Farrar, *Life of Christ* 1:399.

4 Kretzmann, *Popular Commentary* 1:79. Christ's time had not yet come. The following year He would present Himself to the nation as the promised King.

5 We assume that this was a Passover that Jesus did not attend.

6 The Sea of Galilee here also called by John (6:1) the Sea of Tiberias.

7 If, as seems probable, the discourse of Jn 6:26–59 was on a Sabbath ("in the synagogue, as He taught at Capernaum" [v. 59]), then it is possible to fix the days of these events with a certain degree of probability: Thursday: the crossing of the lake and the feeding of the five thousand. Friday: the reception at Gennesaret. Saturday: the sermon on the bread of life. See Edersheim, *Life and Times of Jesus* 2:4; also Andrews, *Life of Our Lord*, 330, who thinks that it was on a Sabbath, but points out that the synagogue was

used for teaching also on other days (Mondays and Thursdays).

8   Mathews, *Life of Jesus*, 248.

9   Lonely and deserted.

10   Farrar, *Life of Christ* 1:400.

11   Mt 14:15, early evening (afternoon); v. 23, the second or later evening. See Edersheim, *Life and Times of Jesus* 1:681.

12   Gk *pothen* may mean either "from which village?" or "from what money?"

13   Cyril, quoted by Dods, *Gospel of St. John*, on Jn 6:5.

14   Gk *dēnarion*, denarius. A Roman silver coin, 25 of which made an *aureus*, the standard gold coin of the empire in the time of Augustus. The denarius was the ordinary daily wage of a laborer or soldier. See *ABD* 1:1086.

15   If one denarius would feed ten persons and 200 would provide a day's ration for 2,000, then upon this basis 200 denarii would supply 4,000 with a most meager ration.

16   Who the "*one* (*hen*) little boy" was, whether a lad of their own company guarding the boat or a shepherd boy of the neighborhood with his food in his pouch, we do not know. The *hen* brings out the meagerness of the supply.

17   Farrar, *Life of Christ* 1:401.

18   "As much as they wanted." Luther's translation, "As much as *He* would," rests upon an unsupported reading in Erasmus (Meyer, *Commentary on the N.T.*, on Jn 6:11). *Opsarion* for fish in John is whatever is eaten with bread as a side dish, hence preeminently fish (Dods, *Gospel of St. John*, on 6:9).

19   Farrar, *Life of Christ* 1:402.

20   Kretzmann, *Popular Commentary* 1:440.

21   Probably there were not many in that lonely spot.

22   Gk *kophinos*, a large wicker basket, our "coffin" or "coffer." In ancient times it always identified the Jew, who on account of special food regulations would, when traveling in non-Jewish communities, always carry his basket with provisions for a day or two (Dods, *Gospel of St. John*, on Jn 6:12; Mathews, *Life of Jesus*, 248).

23   It has been suggested that the number twelve is accounted for by the individual disciples. But we do not know why they would have been carrying twelve empty baskets with them.

24   Lk 9, between vv. 17 and 18.—At this point occurs "the great gap" in the narrative of Luke as compared with Matthew and Mark, all of Mt 14:22 to 16:12 and of Mk 6:45 to 8:27 being omitted: from the feeding of the five thousand to Peter's wonderful confession at Caesarea Philippi. Various explanations are offered: accidental loss due to some unknown casualty; loss of a portion of original manuscript; mistake of the eye (of the writer in following Mark?), passing from the second feeding as if it were the first; etc. See Bruce, *Synoptic Gospels*, on Lk 9:18–27. All unsatisfactory. These and other explanations imply that the omission was unintentional and that Luke's Gospel is not complete in its present form, for which theory there is no proof. A close examination will show that, as far as Luke is concerned, there is no omission at all. It was the purpose of Jesus to retire (v. 10). But it was some time before He could be alone (v. 18). The fact that Luke does not relate intervening events certainly proves a great stumbling block to the theory of his dependence on Mark. The proponents of the dependence theory are usually quite silent at this point.

25   Dods, *Gospel of St. John*, on Jn 6:14.

26   Farrar, *Life of Christ* 1:405.

27   There was more than one site called "Bethsaida." Archaeologists distinguish (1) the older fishing village on the northeast end of the lake (*el-Araj*), and (2) Bethsaida Julias (*et-Tell*), built by Herod Philip more than a mile north of the older site (*ABD* 1:692). Mark writes that Jesus sent the disciples toward Bethsaida (Mk 6:45); John writes that their destination was Capernaum (Jn 6:17). Because of this, some scholars propose that there was a third site called Bethsaida that was near Capernaum, though such a location is not known from ancient sources or archaeology. Mark writes that the disciples would go "to the other side/ shore" (*eis to peran*) where Bethsaida was located, which does not have to mean that they would make a long crossing from one side of the lake to the other. Jesus may have intended that the disciples would sail from the desolate place to spend the night at the fishing village of Bethsaida where He would rejoin them for the longer voyage to their ultimate destination, Capernaum. At

any rate, the storm blew them off course, into the midst of the sea, so that they never reached Bethsaida (Voelz, *Mark 1:1–8:26*, 433).

28 On account of Jn 6:17.

29 When they saw Jesus retire into the mountain, they probably hoped to renew their efforts to make Him king when He reappeared the following day.

30 Compare Mt 14:15. A later hour.

31 In ancient days the Jews divided the night into three watches (Jgs 7:19), but later the Roman division of four watches between 6 p.m. and 6 a.m. was generally adopted. See "Time Reckoning in the Bible" in the Appendices.

32 25 or 30 stadia. A stadium was a Greek measure equal to about 600 feet. There were between eight and nine to a mile. Josephus says that the lake is about forty stadia wide (*War* 3:506).

33 Gk *oupō*.

34 At some appointed rendezvous (Andrews, *Life of Our Lord*, 327).

35 682 feet below sea level. Cold air always rushes downwards.

36 "My experience in this region enables me to sympathize with the disciples in their long night's contest with the wind. The wind howled down every way from the northeast and east, with such fury that no efforts of rowers could have brought a boat to shore at any point along the coast" (Thomson, quoted by Andrews, *Life of Our Lord*, 327f.). According to the view of Farrar, Godet, and others it was the intention of Jesus to join the disciples somewhere along the northwestern coast between Capernaum and the eastern and western Bethsaida, and now the disciples were driven *away* from the shores. At any rate, the winds were "against them."

37 Farrar, *Life of Christ* 1:406 n. 3.

38 Gk *peripatōn epi tēs thalassēs*. Not "on the land above the sea level" or "along the shoreline" or "by the sea," but *on the water*.

39 Gk *epi ta hydata*.

40 Gk *periepatēsen epi ta hydata*.

41 Bruce, *Synoptic Gospels*, on Mt 14:30.

42 Peter could swim (Jn 21:7).

43 There is no contradiction in Jn 6:21. "They were glad to," and of course did, "receive Him into the boat" (Farrar, *Life of Christ* 1:407).

44 "Princely Gardens." Not a city, but a district, which may also have included Capernaum and the western Bethsaida, about four miles long and two miles wide. Josephus calls it "the ambition of nature," with grapes and figs hanging on the branches ten months of the year. The boundaries are given as thirty furlongs long and twenty in breadth (*War* 3:516–21).

45 These verses at the same time may also sum up the Galilean ministry as a whole.

46 Mathews, *Life of Jesus*, 259.

47 See above, § 4.

48 A city about six miles south of Capernaum, on the western shore. Herod the tetrarch had recently rebuilt it and named it after the reigning Roman emperor Tiberius Caesar (*Ant* 18:36; *War* 2:168). Later it served as the capital of Galilee. After the destruction of Jerusalem it became the virtual metropolis of the Jewish nation.

49 Here we have an incidental confirmation of the truth that a gale had been blowing the night before (Dods, *Gospel of St. John*, on Jn 6:23).

50 See § 1. Edersheim, *Life and Times of Jesus* 2:4.

51 Kretzmann, *Popular Commentary* 1:442.

52 Ylvisaker, *Gospels*, 338

53 Farrar, *Life of Christ* 1:413; or of false messianic hopes. According to the legends of their nation the Messiah was to crown and enrich them; He was to banquet them on pomegranates from Eden, serve them with red wine, and feed them upon the flesh of Behemoth and Leviathan and of the great bird Bar Juchne (Farrar, *Life of Christ* 1:412).

54 "Truly, truly," John repeats the "truly." See also vv. 47 and 53.

55 Compare this with what the woman of Samaria said (Jn 4:15).

56 It was by this name that the "Rabbi" (v. 25) was popularly known.

57 In the popular sense. Jesus passed by His miraculous birth lest by removing one stumbling block He interpose another (Euthymius, quoted by Dods, *Gospel of St. John*, on 6:36). "Whose father and mother *we* know"—Galileans. This seems to confirm our arrangement as compared with others in linking up the sermon on the bread of life immediately with the miraculous feeding and the following (Mt 14:36; Mk 6:56). The dispute with

the Pharisees and scribes from *Jerusalem*, Judeans, will be treated in the next section.

58 See Jn 6:65 and 14:6.

59 Not in the usual sense of John, as referring to the Jerusalem party, but with the same hostile implication in the use of the term. See Dods, *Gospel of St. John*, on Jn 1:19 and ch. 8, § 6.

60 The "disciples" as distinct from the Twelve.

61 We should like to think that there is a significance in the words (1) "we have believed" and (2) "have come to know." Compare Augustine: "*Credimus ut intelligamus*" (Dods, *Gospel of St. John*, on Jn 6:69). And surely, first we must accept with a believing heart, and then comes the better understanding. There are many truths that are first believed and then understood. But it seems from 1Jn 4:16 ("We have come to know and to believe") that we cannot here press the order. Compare also Jn 10:38.

62 Iscariot (Hbr *Ish Kerioth*) = "the man of Kerioth." Kerioth was in the tribe of Judah (Jsh 15:25).

63 Schürer, *Jewish People* 2.1:185.

64 See Dods, *Gospel of St. John*, on Jn 1:19. "The judgment of the case of a false prophet is specially named in the Mishna as belonging to the Council of the Seventy One" (Watkins, *Gospel According to St. John*).

65 Mathews, *Life of Jesus*, 256.

66 Compare ch. 12, § 13.

67 They would hardly leave Jerusalem until after the Passover.

68 Gk *koinais chersi*, "with common hands."

69 As Edersheim suggests (*Life and Times of Jesus* 2:8).

70 Farrar, *Life of Christ* 1:443.

71 Gk *paradosis*. Founded on Dt 4:14; 17:10, which could be interpreted as describing unwritten laws.

72 See *ABD* 6:638–39.

73 Gk *pygmēi nipsōntai*, to wash with the fist, that is, diligently, or to prevent the soiling of one hand with the palm of the other (Edersheim, *Life and Times of Jesus* 2:11).

74 It was contended that to eat with unwashed hands was just as sinful as to commit adultery (Ylvisaker, *Gospels*, 354).

75 Gk *baptismous*.

76 Gk *chestōn*, sextus or sextarius (containing about 1½ pints), another one of Mark's Latinisms.

(Compare 6:37, *dēnariōn*, denarii.) Here used without reference to contents.

77 Defiled earthen vessels would have to be broken, not washed (Lv 15:12).

78 Couches for meals, *triclinia*.

79 Farrar, *Life of Christ* 1:445.

80 The order in Mk 7:9–13 is inverted as compared with Mt 15:3–6.

81 Moses in Mark. Which amounts to the same since Moses wrote by inspiration of God.

82 Gk, *dōron*; Hbr, *qarban* (Lv 1:2; 2:1; 3:1). To say this word, however rashly and inconsiderately, involved a vow, and some of the rabbis had expressly taught that this vow superseded the necessity of obedience to the Fourth Commandment (Farrar, *Life of Christ* 1:445; Edersheim, *Life and Times of Jesus* 2:18).

83 Gk *hypokritai* (Mt 6:2, 5, 16; 7:5). Here, it seems, for the first time applied directly to the Pharisees. To describe the character of the Pharisees, Epiphanius (*Haeres.* 16:34) invented a very forcible expression, *etheloperissothrēskeia*, that is, voluntary, excessive, external service. An example of their hypocrisy: According to their self-imposed obligation, a Sabbath day's journey must not exceed 2,000 yards. Now, it was their custom to meet for banquets on a Sabbath. But suppose the distance was greater than 2,000 yards? Here is how they got around the difficulty: On the evening before the Sabbath they deposited some food at a distance of 2,000 yards. This created a fictitious home. From this fictitious home they would go 2,000 yards farther to the place of meeting. And in order to make sure, they could put doorposts and lintels at the end of various streets, so that all intervening space might be regarded as one large house (Farrar, *Life of Christ* 2:472)!

84 Farrar, *Life of Christ* 1:448.

85 Some manuscripts add the phrase, "If anyone has ears to hear, let him hear"—a proverbial form of speech and a common rabbinical expression. See ch. 12, § 3.

CHAPTER 17
THE SECOND AND THIRD RETIREMENTS

1 Bruce, *Synoptic Gospels*, on Mt 15:2.

2 Schürer, *Jewish People* 2.1:157, 185.

3 The passage Lk 13:31 will be examined later.

4 About the time of the Passover week, April 17–24 (Wieseler, *Synopsis*, 434).

5 Gk *eis*, towards or into. Opinion is much divided. Since there was no reason why He should not enter heathen territory on account of ceremonial defilement—compare, for instance, the ministry in Samaria and in the practically heathenish Decapolis—we are inclined to the view that *eis* should be rendered "into." This especially on account of the reading of notable manuscripts in Mk 7:31: "He returned from the region of Tyre and went *through* Sidon to the Sea of Galilee."

6 The region is so called on account of the two chief cities, separated by about twenty-five miles of Mediterranean shore.

7 See ch. 2, § 5.

8 See *ABD* 5:354.

9 After the building of the temple, Solomon gave Hiram twenty cities in the northern part of Galilee to recompense him for the skilled labor and the building material furnished him. When Hiram came out to view the cities, "they did not please him," and he called them "the land of Cabul to this day," that is, displeasing or dirty (1Ki 9:12–13). This section was mostly inhabited by Gentiles and for that reason was called "Galilee of the nations" (Is 9:1), a title extended later on to the whole province; for after the ten tribes had been led into the Assyrian Captivity, the majority of the inhabitants of Galilee were heathen until about 150 BC, when Galilee became thoroughly Jewish.

10 How did she know this? See Mk 3:8; Lk 6:17—people from Tyre and Sidon were among those who listened to Jesus and witnessed His miracles. The title was used (and heard) in Mt 9:27 and 12:23.

11 Farrar, *Life of Christ* 1:474.

12 Bruce, *Synoptic Gospels*, on Mt 15:23.

13 Gk *kynaria*. Bruce, *Synoptic Gospels*, on Mt 15:26.

14 Gk *gar*—not dissent, but eager assent. Stronger than "yet."

15 Gk *psichia*, the smallest crumbs, illustrating her humility.

16 Farrar, *Life of Christ* 1:476.

17 Bruce, *Synoptic Gospels*, on Mt 15:28.

18 See critical note on Mk 7:31 in Bruce, *Synoptic Gospels*: "Came through Sidon unto the Sea of Galilee."

19 Or Magadan (Mt 15:39).

20 See ch. 13.

21 The historians do not entirely agree on the names of the Ten Cities. We shall give them here as follows: (1) Scythopolis (Beth-shean), the only one west of the Jordan (ch. 7, § 11); (2) Gadara; (3) Gerasa; (4) Canatha; (5) Abila; (6) Raphana; (7) Hippos; (8) Dion; (9) Pella; (10) Capitolias. To these may be added (11) Philadelphia (Rabbath-ammon) and (12) Damascus.

22 Ch. 2, § 2.

23 A site is suggested in the neighborhood of the ravine nearly opposite to Magdala, which is now called Wady Semak (Andrews, *Life of Our Lord*, 337).

24 Ylvisaker, *Gospels*, 360.

25 Compare ch. 10, §§ 9, 32.

26 There is no reference to lilies and flowers, as when He preached the Sermon on the Mount, and to the green grass, as at the feeding of the five thousand at the "desolate place."

27 Matthew and Mark relate the feeding of both the five and the four thousand. The same evangelists report Jesus as referring to both incidents (Mt 16:9–10; Mk 8:19–20). In the face of these data, how can anyone speak of confusion in the claim that both feedings are the same?—not to mention the difference of time, place, number, details, and results.

28 Gk *epi tēn gēn*.

29 Gk *spyridas* this time, not small *kophinoi*, as in the previous miracle, the same kind of basket in which St. Paul was let down the wall of Damascus (Ac 9:25).

30 The ESV reads "region of Magadan," *horia Magdala*, in Matthew and "district of Dalmanutha," *merē Dalmanoutha*, in Mark, while the KJV has "coasts of Magdala" and "parts of Dalmanutha." Some of the best manuscripts in Matthew have "borders of Magadan," which is considered by most authorities the better reading on the ground that early copyists, ignorant, just as we are, of the existence of Magadan, changed the name to the more familiar Magdala. It is likely that both readings refer to the same place.

Identification with Magdala is made probable by the frequent interchange of *l* for *n*, e.g., Nathan (Hbr) for Nethel (Aramaic). For more on the text issues, see *ABD* 4:463–64.

31 Edersheim (*Life and Times of Jesus* 2:68) shows that the demand for a sign was in accordance with rabbinic thought and practice.

32 It seems that the devil had this same thought in mind in tempting Jesus to cast Himself from the temple (Mt 4:6).

33 Schürer, *Jewish People* 2.2:29f.

34 Herod was all the Messiah they cared for or believed in (Bruce, *Synoptic Gospels*, on Mt 16:1). Cf. the reference of Jesus to the "leaven of Herod" in Mk 8:15 as compared with the "leaven of the Pharisees and Sadducees" in Mt 16:11. They were well-disposed to the government, local and Roman in general, as well as to the ruling high-priestly party.

35 Farrar, *Life of Christ* 2:3.

CHAPTER 18
THE FOURTH RETIREMENT, INCLUDING THE TRANSFIGURATION

1 Cf. Lk 12:1; ch. 21, § 18. Matthew: "Watch and beware of the leaven of the Pharisees and Sadducees." The worldly-minded Sadducees adhered to the party of Herod. The morally vile views entertained by him and accepted by those who adhered to him are "the leaven of Herod." See Meyer, *Commentary on the N.T.*, on Mk 8:15.

2 Gk *oligopistoi*. Compare Mt 8:26.

3 Gk *kophinous*. Compare Mt 14:20.

4 Gk *spyridas*. Compare Mt 15:37.

5 V. 25: "again."

6 At this point Luke again joins the synoptic account. See ch. 16, § 4 note 24.

7 On the sources of the Jordan, see *ISBE* under "Jordan."

8 McRay, *Archaeology*, 171–72. *ISBE* under "Caesarea."

9 *Ant* 18:28; *War* 2:168.

10 "Into the *district* of Caesarea Philippi."

11 Farrar, *Life of Christ* 2:11. See Mal 4:5.

12 On the legend, see Edersheim, *Life and Times of Jesus* 2:79.

13 Compare previous confessions: John the Baptist (Jn 1:29), Andrew (Jn 1:41), Philip (Jn 1:45), Nathanael (Jn 1:49), the disciples (Mt 14:33), the disciples (Peter; Jn 6:69).

14 Bruce, *Synoptic Gospels*, on Mt 16:20.

15 Compare 1Co 12:3.

16 Gk *petros*.

17 Gk *petra*.

18 Gk *ekklēsia*. The new Israel. Not an anachronism, as if borrowed by a later order of things and put back into the mouth of Jesus. It is a familiar term for the congregation of Israel, found in Dt 18:16; 23:2; Ps 22:25 (Bruce, *Synoptic Gospels*, on Mt 16:17).

19 Bruce, *Synoptic Gospels*, on Mt 16:18. Bengel lists examples of why Peter was fittingly mentioned: he converted many Jews (Ac 2), he first welcomed the Gentiles (Ac 10), and the Lord commanded him to strengthen the brothers and feed the sheep (Lk 22:32; Jn 21:15–19).

20 The announcements are in order as follows: (1) Jn 2:18–22; (2) Mt 16:21–23; Mk 8:31–33; Lk 9:22; (3) Mt 17:22–23; Mk 9:31–32; Lk 9:43–45; (4) Mt 20:17–19; Mk 10:32–34; Lk 18:28–30; and (5) Mt 26:1–2; Mk 14:1–2; Lk 22:1–2. Other references may include Jn 3:14; Mt 9:15; Jn 6:51; Mt 16:4.

21 The three constituent parts of the Jewish Council. (1) Chief priests, Gk *archiereis*. As a rule named first. Probably the presidents of the twenty-four classes of priests or members of the reigning high-priestly family. Mostly of the Sadducean nobility. (2) Scribes, Gk *grammateis*. Jewish canonists, learned councilors, mostly pharisaic doctors, who represented the teaching profession. (3) Elders, Gk *presbyteroi*. Nonprofessional members. Priests and laymen alike who did not belong to classes 1 and 2. See Meyer, *Commentary on the N.T.*, on Mt 2:4; Schürer, *Jewish People* 2.1:178. The latter are also called *archontes* (Lk 23:13; 24:20).

22 Probably intimated in Mt 16:24.

23 Gk *hileōs soi*. (God) have mercy on You, God forbid! A sort of expletive, like *Gott bewahre!* in German (Farrar, *Life of Christ* 2:19).

24 Gk *skandalon*.

25 Gk *phroneis*, mindset.

26 Punishment by crucifixion was well known. An intimation of the cross of Jesus, but at the same

time a common phrase to denote extreme torment and disgrace (Bruce, *Synoptic Gospels*, on Mt 16:24).

27 Matthew and Mark have "six" days, and Luke has "about eight" days, most likely including the day of Peter's confession and the night of the transfiguration of Christ (Edersheim, *Life and Times of Jesus* 2:92).

28 Ch. 13, § 16.

29 To be more exact, "the" mountain, according to St. Luke, the one outstanding elevation in that particular region.

30 Farrar, *Life of Christ* 2:26.

31 At the time of the transfiguration, the summit of Tabor was occupied. Afterwards, it was fortified by Josephus (Schürer, *Jewish People* 1.2:215; *War* 4:1, 54–61; Andrews, *Life of Our Lord*, 358; and others).

32 We are not told of His new location until Mk 9:30.

33 9,200 feet high; 16 to 20 miles long from north to south.

34 Farrar, *Life of Christ* 2:25.

35 Indirectly, Mount Horeb (Ex 3:5) and the "Zion, my holy hill" (Ps 2:6). Farrar, *Life of Christ* 2:25.

36 According to His custom (Mk 6:46; Lk 6:12). Also Lk 9:32, compared with v. 37.

37 Edersheim, *Life and Times of Jesus* 2:96.

38 Gk *metemorphōthē*.

39 Gk *gnapheus*, the bleacher, who was usually also the dyer. Before the woven cloth could be properly dyed, it had to be freed from the oily and gummy substances in the raw fiber. White clay, the ashes of certain desert plants, and other aids were used. Compare Mk 2:21: *agnaphou*, new, that is, unshrunk, cloth.

40 Edersheim, *Life and Times of Jesus* 2:97.

41 Stöckhardt, *Biblische Geschichte,* 147.

42 Gk *ekbasis*, departure, exodus. His "outgoing," but also including His "incoming," resurrection and ascension.

43 Edersheim, *Life and Times of Jesus* 2:97.

44 Matthew: Lord. Mark: Rabbi. Luke: Master or Teacher.

45 Gk *kalon estin hēmas hōde einai*. Not as if it had been Peter's intention to say that it was good for himself and for other disciples to be present on this occasion—for then he would have used the

expression *kalon estin hēmin*—but the meaning is: It is fortunate that we are here, for we can attend to the erection of tents (Ylvisaker, *Gospels*, 411).

46 Some texts have "I will make."

47 Gk *skēnas*, tents, or booths, of branches, shrubs, etc.

48 Farrar, *Life of Christ* 2:29.

49 But here the words are added: "Listen to Him," indicating that Jesus was indeed that Prophet who was to come. Compare Mt 3:17; Dt 18:15; Ps 2:7; Is 42:1.

50 Farrar, *Life of Christ* 2:29.

51 Edersheim, *Life and Times of Jesus* 2:102. The Feast of Transfiguration was anciently celebrated on August 6 (Andrews, *Life of Our Lord*, 359).

52 Gk *horama* (Mt 17:9). This word is found only here in the Gospels; in Ac 7:31, etc.

53 Bruce, *Synoptic Gospels*, on Mt 17:9.

54 Farrar, *Life of Christ* 2:31.

55 When John disclaimed his being Elijah (Jn 1:21), he only wished to state that he was not Elijah of old come back in person, according to the popular superstition. "Without any authority from the Hebrew, the LXX renders Mal 4:5 Elijah the Tishbite" (Farrar, *Life of Christ* 2:31).

56 Farrar, *Life of Christ* 2:32.

57 Bruce, *Synoptic Gospels*, on Mt 17:15. Mt 4:24: "epileptic"; "lunatic" (KJV).

58 Bruce, *Synoptic Gospels*, on Mk 9:14.

59 Gk *exethambēthēsan*. The amazement of joyous surprise on account of His appearance at the critical moment. See Meyer, *Commentary on the N.T.*, on Mk 9:15. The term is used by Mark here, in 14:33, and in 16:5 in connections that demand a strong expression.

60 Farrar, *Life of Christ* 2:33.

61 Some manuscripts (KJV) include "believe."

62 Gk *mēketi eiselthēis*. Enter not again! "This was the essential point in a case of intermittent possession. The spirit went out at the end of each attack, but returned again" (Bruce, *Synoptic Gospels*, on Mk 9:25).

63 Relative unbelief (Pieper, *Christian Dogmatics* 2:368). There is no particular need for toning the *apistian* in Mt 17:20 down to *oligopistian*.

64 Edersheim, *Life and Times of Jesus* 2:109.

65 The whole verse of Mt 17:21 and "and fasting" in Mk 9:29 are omitted in the best uncials and, in consequence, also by editions of the Greek New Testament.

CHAPTER 19
THE CLOSE OF THE GALILEAN MINISTRY

1 Compare ch. 18, § 6.

2 Bruce, *Synoptic Gospels*, on Mt 17:24.

3 Gk *didrachma*. The only place in the New Testament where we meet with this word. Frequent in the LXX for the Hebrew shekel.

4 Edersheim, *Life and Times of Jesus* 2:112; Schürer, *Jewish People* 2.1:250.

5 *War* 7:218.

6 The commentators explain a certain passage in the Mishna and the Talmud as implying that the Jews in Palestine had to pay the temple tribute at Passover, that those of the neighboring lands might bring it at the Feast of Weeks and those of remote countries, such as Babylon and Media, as late as the Feast of Tabernacles (Edersheim, *Life and Times of Jesus* 2:111).

7 Meyer, *Commentary on the N.T.*, on Mt 17:24.

8 Farrar, *Life of Christ* 2:44.

9 Gk *proephthasen*, anticipated him.

10 Gk *telē*, indirect taxes on wares.

11 Gk *kēnson*, census, direct taxes on persons. Since the evangelist used neither of these two terms but *ta didrachma* instead, it is clear that the tax demanded was the temple tax, rather than a Roman tax, as some have tried to make out.

12 Gk *skandalisōmen*.

13 Gk *ankistron*, a fishhook, not a net. The only place in the Gospels in which mention is made of fishing with a hook.

14 Gk *anti emou kai sou*, "instead of," because the money was redemption money. "For Me and for yourself," not "for us," because the money was paid differently for each (Farrar, *Life of Christ* 2:45).

15 Kretzmann, *Popular Commentary* 1:97.

16 Gk *statēr*.

17 Lk 9:46: "which of them."

18 Bruce, *Synoptic Gospels*, on Mt 18:4.

19 Bruce, *Synoptic Gospels*, on Mt 18:2. See also Ylvisaker, *Gospels*, 421; Eusebius, *NPNF2* 1:149,

166. For all we know, the little child may have been Peter's little son.

We shall not see Matthew, Mark, and Luke together again in a threefold account until the blessing of little children in Perea, six months later (ch. 25, § 12).

20 Gk *tachy*, quickly. He will do it neither now nor later.

21 Compare Mt 10:42. There is no reason to suppose that Mk 9:41 has been taken over from, or introduced into, Mt 10:42. Jesus repeated some of His sayings, sometimes in a different connection and with different application.—Note that Jesus here calls Himself Christ.

22 Gk *mylos onikos*. Not the small house-mill, which could be placed on a table and turned by hand (Bruce, *Synoptic Gospels*, on Mt 18:6).

23 Gk *eis tēn geennan tou pyros*. The fires of the Valley of Hinnom, near Jerusalem, where the refuse of the city was burned, were commonly taken as a type of the fires of hell.

24 Compare Lk 15:4–7.

25 Some English translations of *elegxon* may cause confusion of practice. For example, translations such as "show him his fault" (NASB, NET) and "point out [his] fault" (NIV, NRSV) try to capture the more complex sense of the verb, which means "to reprove," so that the brother is convicted of his sin. However, these translations may also mislead people into assuming that they don't actually have to discuss the issue with the brother, that they can handle the matter by hinting at it or alluding to it by illustration. Such an approach to the passage totally violates the immediate context, which is filled with words of speaking and hearing ("Tell . . . listen . . . listen . . . charge . . . listen . . . tell . . . listen"; vv. 15–17). Jesus' teaching is also rooted in the broader biblical context of courtroom justice since His wording derives from Lv 19:15–18, especially v. 17 (cf. the setting in Dt 19:15–21). Without a clear statement of the fault, the entire process fails and, in fact, does more harm than good since matters are left unclear, which could lead to ongoing sin and conflict. For these reasons, the simple translation, "Tell him his fault" (ESV, KJV) is superior, especially when tempered with the apostle Paul's teaching, "Brothers, if anyone is caught in any

transgression, you who are spiritual should restore him in a spirit of gentleness" (Gal 6:1).

26 Gk *ekklēsia*.

27 Gk *eis to emon onoma*. Literally, "to My name," that is, to the honor of His name.

28 Looking into the future—"am I." Christ's presence is certain even with reference to the future (Bruce, *Synoptic Gospels*, on Mt 18:20).

29 See § 6 above.

30 Based on Am 1:6 (Bruce, *Synoptic Gospels*, on Mt 18:21).

31 Some translations say "seventy-seven times."

32 Bruce, *Synoptic Gospels*, on Mt 18:23.

33 Gk *talantōn*.

34 Gk *dēnaria*.

CHAPTER 20
AT THE FEAST OF TABERNACLES IN JERUSALEM

1 Following the Feast of Weeks, or Pentecost, the day of firstfruits.

2 Gk *skēnopēgia*, the fixing of tents, or booths.

3 Probably based on the list in Gn 10.

4 13 + 12 + 11 + 10 + 9 + 8 + 7 = 70.

5 Notice the recurrence of the holy number *7*, a symbol of completeness, and its multiples.

6 Farrar, *Life of Christ* 2:48. Observed on the 10th of Tishri (Lv 16). By the way, if "afflict yourselves" (Lv 16:29; 23:27; Nu 29:7) means fasting, then this was the only fast day prescribed by the Law. Compare Ac 27:9.

7 On the issue of whether these were half brothers or cousins of Jesus, see ch. 4, § 43.

8 Pieper, *Christian Dogmatics* 2:368.

9 "To the Jews there was only one kind of learning, that of theology, and only one road to it, the schools of the Rabbis. Their major was true, but their minor false; and Jesus hastened to correct it" (Edersheim, *Life and Times of Jesus* 2:151).

10 Dods, *Gospel of St. John*, on 7:20.

11 Farrar, *Life of Christ* 2:54.

12 Dods, *Gospel of St. John*, on Jn 7:27.

13 Possibly on a Thursday. There is some difference of opinion as to whether this last day was the seventh or the eighth. Most commentators maintain that the eighth was the day when the great feast as a whole was brought to a termination. See Andrews, *Life of Our Lord*, 345.

14 Edersheim, *Temple*, 244.

15 And also on the eighth day (Farrar, *Life of Christ* 2:56, and others).

16 Siloah, meaning "sent," or "conducted" (by means of an aqueduct). It was an ancient, deep-walled pool, less than a half mile south of the temple area, where the Tyropeon and Kidron valleys meet. For many hundred years before the days of Jesus, the waters had come through an ancient tunnel from the fountain of Gihon, now called the Virgin's Fount, outside the city wall, in the Kidron Valley, through more than a thousand feet of rock, till it issued on the other side of the hill, inside the city wall. There the water ran into the oblong Pool of Siloam, hewn in the rock. It is flowing to this day, the only spring, or living water, in Jerusalem. See McRay, *Archaeology*, 191–92; *ABD* 2:1018; 6:23–24. Mathews writes (*A Life of Jesus*, 298) that he "waded through the tunnel from end to end. It was cut by masons, who began with hammer and chisel, from both ends, as can clearly be seen and as described on a Hebrew inscription (the oldest Hebrew inscription in the world) cut in Phoenician characters, discovered in the tunnel and now in the Constantinople Museum. After many windings, totaling over seventeen hundred feet, the masons met in the middle. The height of the tunnel varies from three to fourteen feet, but for a good part of the distance a man must stoop."

17 To show that it was actually poured out.

18 There was some dispute on this point as well as on others between the Pharisees and Sadducees, the latter holding that the pouring of water upon the altar was not an ordinance instituted by Moses. To give expression to his views, the high priest Alexander Jannaeus, instead of pouring the water on the altar, poured it on the ground. The Pharisees in their fury hurled at his head the citron fruits that they were carrying—Lv 23:40: "the fruit [KJV: "boughs"] of splendid trees"—in their left hands. Alexander called his mercenaries to his aid, and a riot ensued, in which about 6,000 people were killed in the temple (*Ant* 13:372–73; Schürer, *Jewish People* 1.1:300).

19 Is 44:3; 58:11. Not direct quotations. Christ alludes to passages in which the Spirit, whom God would send in the days of the Messiah, is compared to streams of water (Dods, *Gospel of St. John*, on Jn 7:38).

20 Gk *ek tēs koilias autou*. As represented in the metaphor, these rivers take their rise from the water that has been drunk; so the effect referred to flows forth in an oral effusion. The divine grace and truth that a believer has received out of Christ's fullness into his inner life does not remain shut up within, but will communicate itself abundantly as a life-giving stream to others (Meyer, *Commentary on the N.T.*, on Jn 7:38).

21 Compare 1Macc 14:41; Jn 1:21; 6:14.

22 Farrar, *Life of Christ* 2:59.

23 Gk *epikataratoi*. Compare Gal 3:10, 13.

24 Edersheim, *Life and Times of Jesus* 2:162. The people of the soil, the *'Am ha Aretz*.

25 Farrar, *Life of Christ* 2:59.

26 Farrar, *Life of Christ* 2:59. Elijah, Hosea, Nahum? (Capernaum = Caper Nahum, according to some.)

27 Farrar, *Life of Christ* 2:60.

28 For a standard review of the text critical issues, see Metzger, *Textual Commentary*, 219–22. The story may be taken as a genuine, independent account from the life of Jesus that later scribes added to the Gospel of John and to a few manuscripts of Luke.

29 Lk 10:38; Jn 11:18; 12:1; Mk 11:11; Mt 21:17, as compared with Lk 21:37–38.

30 Compare Mk 9:14; 8:11; 7:1. As a rule, the scribes were Pharisees. Some of them were members of the Council. But we assume that the opponents in this instance were not members of that august body.

31 Farrar, *Life of Christ* 2:66. Edersheim, who rejects the passage (*Life and Times of Jesus* 2:163 n. 1): "Farrar has devoted to the illustration of this narrative some of his most pictorial pages."

32 Gk *tas toiautas*—contemptuously.

33 Farrar, *Life of Christ* 2:68.

34 Under the circumstances, the natural thing. If He would actually have written words, these presumably would have been recorded.

35 This explanatory addition in the King James Version is not in the *textus receptus*, which we have been following throughout.

36 A command: *baletō*.

37 As the first and chief witness. Thus the Law: Dt 17:7.

38 Farrar, *Life of Christ* 2:69.

39 Farrar, *Life of Christ* 2:71.

40 The rebuilding of the temple was not completed until shortly before its destruction (*Ant* 20:219). It was not the intention of Jesus that stones should be actually hurled at the woman. Besides, according to the Mosaic Law, the execution would have taken place outside the city (Dt 22:24).

41 See ch. 3, § 9.

42 Edersheim, *Temple*, 246.

43 Edersheim, *Life and Times of Jesus* 2:166.

44 See ch. 3, § 10. Edersheim, *Life and Times of Jesus* 2:165.

45 V. 22, compared with v. 13.

46 Ylvisaker, *Gospels*, 385.

47 Gk *ou chōrei en hymin*, "finds no place in you," does not move forward, progress, advance. Compare v. 30 with v. 33.

48 Gk *anthrōpon*, simply used as we might say "person," without reference to the deity of Christ, *sine praeiudicio deitatis* (Bruce, *Synoptic Gospels*, on Jn 8:40).

49 Dods, *Gospel of St. John*, on Jn 8:42.

50 Dods, *Gospel of St. John*, on Jn 8:42.

51 Dods, *Gospel of St. John*, on Jn 8:45.

52 Dods, *Gospel of St. John*, on Jn 8:50.

53 Notice again that John repeats the *amēn*. Compare 1:51; 3:5, 11; 8:51, 58.

54 Gk *tērein*, in the sense of accepting by faith. Compare Jn 14:15–24.

55 A round number, sufficiently exact for their purpose and not used to indicate the age of Jesus (Dods, *Gospel of St. John*, on Jn 8:57).

56 Dods, *Gospel of St. John*, on Jn 8:58.

57 See § 15 above. *Ant* 20:221.

58 It is impossible to determine the exact date. But the definite mention that it was a Sabbath (v. 14) rather indicates that it was not the same day on which the Jews tried to stone Jesus (Dods, *Gospel of St. John*, on Jn 9:1).

59 At the Beautiful Gate, the eastern gate of the temple leading into the treasury, or Court of the Women. However, the blind man was not begging, because it was the Sabbath day (Edersheim, *Life and Times of Jesus* 2:178).

60 There was no direct mention of them in John since the sermon on the Bread of Life in Capernaum (6:67). But it is only natural to suppose that they had accompanied the Savior to the Feast of Tabernacles.

61 Dods, *Gospel of St. John*, on Jn 9:3.

62 Gk *hēmas dei*. Some manuscripts have *eme dei*.

63 Or covered.

64 For in other cases of blindness, He did not employ it, e.g., Mk 10:46–52. Compare also Mk 8:23, the healing of the blind man at Bethsaida.

65 See § 8 above.

66 *Apestalmenos* (Gk), *shaluach* (Hbr), *missus* (Lat). Compare Is 8:6–10. Dods, *Gospel of St. John*, on Jn 9:7.

67 Gk *aneblepsa*, looked up.

68 Edersheim, *Life and Times of Jesus* 2:182; Farrar, *Life of Christ* 2:83.

69 Not the Jewish Council, but an informal, yet apparently responsible (v. 34), group of a local authority.

70 Gk *schisma ēn en autois*.

71 Gk *aposynagōgos genētai*, unsynagogued, or put out of the synagogue.

72 See Edersheim, *Life and Times of Jesus* 2:183–84, or Dods, *Gospel of St. John*, on Jn 9:22.

73 Dods, *Gospel of St. John*, on Jn 9:22.

74 Farrar, *Life of Christ* 2:85.

75 Dods, *Gospel of St. John*, on Jn 9:27.

76 Gk *touton*.

77 Gk *su*.

78 Gk *hēmas*.

79 The word here used is *exebalon*. Compare Lk 6:22; Jn 16:2.

80 Gk *prosekynēsen*, used in the sense of divine worship.

81 Gk *eis krima*. Not the act of judging, *krisis*, but the result, *krima*. Lk 2:35: "that thoughts from many hearts may be revealed."

82 Meyer, *Commentary on the N.T.*, on Jn 9:39. For the figure, see 1Co 1:18ff.

83 Edersheim, *Life and Times of Jesus* 2:188.

84 Edersheim, *Life and Times of Jesus* 2:189.

85 It was exceptional with Him to begin His discourse with a repeated "amen."

86 Dods, *Gospel of St. John*, on Jn 10:2.

87 Gk *paroimia*, more exactly, not parable, *parabolē* of the Synoptists (because it is not a history), but allegory.

88 Dods, *Gospel of St. John*, on Jn 10:7.

89 Gk *ho poimēn ho kalos*. "Good" probably in the sense in which we speak of a "good" painter or a "good" architect (Dods, *Gospel of St. John*, on Jn 10:11).

90 Bengel (quoted by Edersheim, *Life and Times of Jesus* 2:229) points out a fourfold parallelism in the words of Christ, but of an antithetic character, and with descending and ascending climax.

91 Gk *entolē*, authorization as embracing the *exousia* both to die and to rise again.

CHAPTER 21
JESUS' FINAL WITHDRAWAL FROM GALILEE AND THE LATER JUDEAN MINISTRY

1 There is an interval of about two months between verses 21 and 22 in Jn 10, Tabernacles to Dedication, unless (which seems unlikely) this interval is to be placed between Jn 8:59 and 9:1. Although John does not mention the fact, there is little doubt that after Jesus' visit to the temple at the Feast of Tabernacles, He returned to Galilee and shortly afterward took His final departure southward, returning to Jerusalem for the Feast of Dedication, retiring to Perea, returning to Bethany for the raising of Lazarus, withdrawing to Ephraim, and then making His final journey to Jerusalem in the spring of AD 33. The intermission between Tabernacles and Dedication seems to be filled in by Lk 9:51–13:21.

John speaks of four journeys of Christ to Jerusalem: for the feasts of Tabernacles and Dedication, for the raising of Lazarus, and for the final visits at Bethany. Likewise it seems that there are corresponding breaks in Luke, to be arranged as follows:

Tabernacles—Jn 7:10–10:21, followed by Lk 9:51–13:21.

Dedication—Jn 10:22–10:42, followed by Lk 13:22–17:10.

Raising of Lazarus—Jn 11:1–54, followed by Lk 17:11–19:28 and parallels.

Arrival at Bethany—Jn 11:55–12:11, followed by Lk 19:29 and parallels.

(But for the sequence of this portion of the Lord's ministry, there seem to be as many arrangements as there are inquirers. See Andrews, *Life of Our Lord*, 365–85. After repeated comparisons, we have come to the conclusion that the order we have adopted is preferable.)

2 Gk *analēpsis*. The term occurs in the New Testament only here. However, since *analambanō* is the customary term for reception into heaven (Mk 16:19; Ac 1:2, 11, 22; 1Tm 3:16), this word ought to offer no particular difficulty. For harmonistic reasons, Wieseler offers this explanation: when the days drew to an end in which He found a taking up, reception, in Galilee, He journeyed to Jerusalem to work there (*Synopsis*, 297).

3 In the conception of John, the glorification of Christ included the Passion. In the conception of Luke, the assumption into heaven included the crucifixion.

4 *Ant* 20:118.

5 See Meyer, *Commentary on the N.T.*, on Jn 4:25 and Lk 9:53.

6 Whether they were the messengers, as has been thought by some, is not apparent from the text.

7 See ch. 11, § 7.

8 Compare ch. 13, § 2.

9 Gk *en tōi hodōi* does not mean on the way to the next village, but in the general period that has been introduced by Luke as the death journey to Jerusalem.

10 Ch. 14, §§ 5–10.

11 Ch. 12, § 5.

12 Compare Mk 16:18.

13 Farrar, *Life of Christ* 2:133.

14 Bruce, *Synoptic Gospels*, on Lk 10:22. See ch. 12, § 6.

15 See ch. 12, § 20.

16 Edersheim, *Life and Times of Jesus* 2:234.

17 The lack of direct references to our Savior's teaching in the synagogues as compared with His earlier ministry is striking. In the light of Jn 9:22, Jesus had in all probability been placed under the ban of excommunication, but the exclusion from one synagogue did not involve exclusion from all or from the temple, where a separate door was provided for the excommunicate. The Synoptic Gospels last mention Him teaching in a synagogue at Mt 13:54; Mk 6:2; Lk 13:10 (though cf. Jn 18:20). Compare Farrar and authorities quoted by him, *Life of Christ* 2:86, 113. It is also possible that the size of the crowds attending Him prevented Him from teaching in small, enclosed public buildings.

18 Edersheim, *Life and Times of Jesus* 2:235.

19 And the rabbis were never weary of quoting the saying of Hillel, who summed up the whole Law in negative form (as compared with the positive statement of Jesus [Mt 7:12]): "What you hate, do not do to anyone" (Tob 4:15). See ch. 11, § 38. Cf. Edersheim, *Life and Times of Jesus* 2:236.

20 In a false interpretation of Dt 6:6.

21 Bruce, *Synoptic Gospels*, on Lk 10:27.

22 From 2,593 above to 820 feet below sea level.

23 Then and afterward infested with marauders.

24 Bruce, *Synoptic Gospels*, on Lk 10:30.

25 If Jericho was no priestly city (Meyer, *Commentary on the N.T.*), as has usually been taken for granted (since Joseph Lightfoot), it was at least the residence of a large number of priests (Edersheim, *Life and Times of Jesus* 2:351).

26 According to the Jewish view that sickness and misfortune are always the punishment for some grievous sin.

27 Edersheim, *Life and Times of Jesus* 2:239.

28 Bruce, *Synoptic Gospels*, on Lk 10:33, "Fully equipped." Also see v. 35.

29 Gk *duo dēnaria*. One denarius was ordinarily the daily wage of a soldier or laborer.

30 Did the Lord here relate a true happening? The story could have happened, but it is usually regarded as a parable. The parable is clear in itself as to both content and purpose.

31 Compare Jn 11:1.

32 Farrar, *Life of Christ* 2:140. See Jn 12:9–10, 17.

33 Farrar, *Life of Christ* 2:142.

34 Compare Mt 6:9–13. See ch. 11, § 29.

35 Bruce, *Synoptic Gospels*, on Lk 11:5.

36 Edersheim, *Life and Times of Jesus* 2:241.

37 Compare Mt 12:22–30, 43–45. Ch. 12, §§ 13, 16.

38 Bruce, *Synoptic Gospels*, on Lk 11:27–28.

39 Kretzmann, *Popular Commentary* 1:330.

40 Bruce, *Synoptic Gospels*, on Lk 11:27–28.

41 Compare Mt 12:38–42; ch. 12, § 16; Mt 5:15; ch. 11, § 20; Mt 6:22–23, ch. 11, § 32.

42 Compare also Mt 16:1–4; Mk 8:11–12 (ch. 17, § 8); Lk 11:16.

43 Gk *aristan, ariston*. The first of the two customary chief meals of the day.

44 Compare Lk 14:1.

45 Gk *anepesen, anapiptein*, recline at the table.

46 Gk *ebaptisthē*, baptized.

47 Compare Mt 15:2; Mk 7:2, the disciples eating with unwashed hands. See ch. 16, § 13.

48 Gk *ho kyrios*. Again, as often in Luke.

49 Compare Mt 23:1–36; Mk 12:38–40; Lk 20:45–47: Tuesday during Passion Week.

50 Compare Mt 23:23. Mint, peppermint, flourished all over the mountains in Israel. Rue was a small shrub with a strong odor. The seeds of dill have an aromatic flavor and are used as a condiment in cooking and as a carminative in medicine. Cumin, resembling caraway in form and flavor (Grm, *Kuemmel*), also has carminative qualities and was used for flavoring various dishes, especially during feasts.

51 The whitewashing of graves was done every year on the fifteenth of Adar (Meyer, *Commentary on the N.T.*, on Mt 23:27).

52 Edersheim, *Life and Times of Jesus* 2:212.

53 According to the arrangement of our Bible, the book of the prophet Malachi is the last book in the Old Testament. But the Hebrew arrangement is as follows: Genesis to 2 Kings; Isaiah, Jeremiah, Ezekiel; the twelve minor prophets, Hosea to Malachi; Psalms, Proverbs, and the remaining books to 1 Chronicles and 2 Chronicles. Since the phrase "from the blood of Abel to the blood of Zechariah" is evidently a designation for the blood of the martyrs of the whole Old Testament canon, we have from the mouth of Jesus an implied argument against the apocryphal books of the Old Testament.

In Mt 23:35, Zechariah is called "the son of Barachiah." Since Berechiah appears as the father of the *prophet* Zechariah (Zec 1:1, 7), it has been contended that Barachiah is a gloss, which through confusion has crept into the text. But the best explanation is that the Barachiah of Matthew was either the father or the grandfather of the Zechariah in 2Ch 24:20. According to the

latter explanation, Barachiah would have had two names, Jehoiada Barachiah.

54 Gk *myriadōn*, an "innumerable multitude." These words are not to be taken "hyperbolically." We have only a fragmentary account of probably the "largest crowd mentioned anywhere in the gospels" (Bruce, *Synoptic Gospels*, on Lk 12:1). The Gospels do not contain a complete life of Christ as one of the Gospel writers himself admits in his concluding word: "Now there are also many other things that Jesus did. Were every one of them to be written, I suppose that the world itself could not contain the books that would be written" (Jn 21:25).

55 Most likely the address has not been reported in full.

56 Ch. 18, § 1.

57 Ch. 14, § 8.

58 Ch. 12, § 15.

59 Ch. 14, § 7.

60 Bruce, *Synoptic Gospels*, on Lk 12:14.

61 Compare Ps 49:16–18; Ecclus 11:18–19; 1Sm 25:11.

62 Gk *eis theon ploutōn*. Rich with respect to those treasures laid up with God.

63 Compare Mt 6:25–34; ch. 11, § 34; vv. 19–21; ch. 11, § 31.

64 See Mt 14:25. According to ancient Jewish custom, the night was divided into three watches, as compared with the Roman division of four. Compare Mk 13:35.

65 Compare Mt 24:43–44.

66 Compare Mt 24:45–51; ch. 30, § 10.

67 Gk *kyrios* again used by Luke instead of the usual Jesus.

68 Gk *dichotomēsei*, cut asunder with a saw. For this cruel mode of punishment, see 2Sm 12:31; 1Ch 20:3; Heb 11:37.

69 Kretzmann, *Popular Commentary* 1:388.

70 Compare Mt 16:2–3.

71 Bruce, *Synoptic Gospels*, on Lk 12:54–59.

72 Compare Mt 5:25–26. See ch. 11, § 22.

73 Gk *dos ergasian*, a Latinism: *operam da* (Bruce, *Synoptic Gospels*, on Lk 12:58).

74 Gk *lepton*, half of a *kodrantēs*, Matthew's word (5:26), *quadrans*, the smallest Roman coin, equal in value to about ¼ cent. Compare Mk 12:42 (Bruce, *Synoptic Gospels*, on Lk 12:59).

75 See next chapter.

76 Wieseler, *Synopsis*, 435.

77 See Ylvisaker, *Gospels*, 476.

78 *Ant* 17:213–18. Compare also the Pentecost disturbance shortly afterwards under Sabinus (*Ant* 17:254–64). And on one occasion, Pilate actually disguised his soldiers as peasants and sent them to use their daggers freely on the mob (*War* 2:176).

79 Some scholars have seen the cause of the enmity between Pilate and Herod (Lk 23:12) in this event (Andrews, *Life of Our Lord*, 394; Kretzmann, *Popular Commentary* 1:339).

80 Bruce, *Synoptic Gospels*, on Lk 13:4.

81 Wieseler, *Synopsis*, 235.

82 Kretzmann, *Popular Commentary* 1:340.

83 See above, § 8.

84 Possibly at or near Bethany. See next chapter.

85 In Lk 10:38, we have traced Jesus to Bethany. This is followed by the teaching of chs. 11 and 12 in "a certain place" (11:1). There is no movement in these sections. A report is brought of the apparently fresh massacre of the Galileans in Jerusalem in 13:1. And as we have pointed out (§ 1 note 1, above), reasons exist for inserting the Dedication between vv. 21 and 22 of Lk 13. As to the suggestion, "even on the Sabbath during the Dedication week," attention is called to the fact that Jesus, for instance, did not spend the whole of the Feast of Tabernacles week in Jerusalem (Jn 7:14). Of course there is no certainty. We are merely trying to picture the events to ourselves without taking undue liberties.

86 Even as in the last analysis all sickness and suffering is caused by sin, which was first brought into the world by the devil.

87 Farrar, *Life of Christ* 2:114.

88 Bruce, *Synoptic Gospels*, on Lk 13:14.

89 Again *kyrios*.

90 Farrar, *Life of Christ* 2:115. For Sabbath controversies, see (1) Jn 5:10–17; compare Jn 7:21–24 about His own authority as well as circumcision on the Sabbath; (2) Mt 12:1–8; Mk 2:23–28; Lk 6:1–5, appealing to precedents in Scripture and to temple service; (3) Mt 12:9–14; Mk 3:1–6; Lk 6:6–11, appealing to common sense; sheep fallen into pit; (4) Jn 9:1–34 about a man born blind: "We must work the works of Him who sent Me while it is day; night is coming when no one can work"; (5) Lk 13:10–17 about watering donkeys on Sabbath day; and (6) Lk 14:1–6 about an ox fallen into a pit.

91 Edersheim, *Life and Times of Jesus* 2:225.

92 Bruce, *Synoptic Gospels*, on Lk 13:16.

93 Compare Mt 13:31–33; Mk 4:30–32. See ch. 12, § 25.

94 Bruce, *Synoptic Gospels*, on Lk 13:18–21.

95 Bruce, *Synoptic Gospels*, on Lk 13:18–21.

Chapter 22
At the Feast of Dedication in Jerusalem

1 See ch. 21, § 29.

2 See ch. 21, § 10.

3 Between vv. 21 and 22 in chapter 10.

4 Andrews, *Life of Our Lord*, 398.

5 See ch. 2, § 25.

6 See ch. 2, § 23. For a general account, see Schürer, *Jewish People* 1.1:207ff, 217. The temple was rededicated precisely the same day on which three years before, for the first time, the altar had been desecrated by the offering up of heathen sacrifices. A new altar was built of unhewn stone (Ex 20:25), while the stones of the earlier altar were laid aside until there would "come a prophet" to show what should be done with them (1 Macc 4:46).

7 Gk *ta phōta*. *Ant* 12:325.

8 Edersheim, *Life and Times of Jesus* 2:227.

9 Gk *ta egkainia*, the feast of renewal.

10 Gk *cheimōn ēn*. Not stormy weather, but the season is meant. Inserted probably for Gentile readers and to explain why Jesus was teaching under cover (Dods, *Gospel of St. John*, on Jn 10:22).

11 Gk *stoa*, portico, cloister.

12 Compare ch. 3, § 7ff.

13 *Ant* 20:221; Farrar, *Life of Christ* 2:144.

14 A standing term for the party of opposition.

15 Gk *parrhēsiai*, in so many words, devoid of all ambiguity (see Jn 16:29; Dods, *Gospel of St. John*, on Jn 10:24).

16 Farrar, *Life of Christ* 2:149.

17 Ch. 20, §§ 27–29.

18 Gk *egō kai ho patēr hen esmen*. Bengel (quoted by Edersheim, *Life and Times of Jesus* 2:229) points out a triplet of double parallelisms in ascending climax:

Ascending		Ascending
My sheep hear My voice	parallel	And I know them
And they follow Me		I give them eternal life
And they will never perish		And no one will snatch them out of My hand

19 Bengel, quoted by Dods, *Gospel of St. John*, on Jn 10:30. See also Farrar, *Life of Christ* 2:147.

20 As quoted by Meyer (*Commentary on the N.T.*) and Edersheim (*Life and Times of Jesus*).

21 Farrar, *Life of Christ* 2:147.

22 Kretzmann, *Popular Commentary* 1:470.

23 Dods, *Gospel of St. John*, on Jn 10:34.

24 Dods, *Gospel of St. John*, on Jn 10:34. Compare Jn 12:34; 15:25; Rm 3:19; 1Co 14:21.

25 Gk *prōton*, "at first" (Dods, *Gospel of St. John*, on Jn 10:39). See Lk 3:3 and ch. 5, §§ 2ff., compared with Jn 1:28 and ch. 6, §§ 1ff.

26 See next chapter.

27 Thus it seems that Jesus did perform some miracles in Perea.

28 See Dods, *Gospel of St. John*, on Jn 10:39.

CHAPTER 23
THE LATER PEREAN MINISTRY

1 See ch. 21, § 1.

2 Ch. 21, § 1.

3 Note also the implication in Jn 10:41: "John did no sign," implying that Jesus did.

4 Compare Lk 12:40, 59; 13:9.

5 Ylvisaker, *Gospels*, 481.

6 "At that very hour."

7 *Teleioumai* (Gk). *Ad finem pervenire* (Lat), to come to an end. See Meyer's note on Lk 13:31 in *Commentary on the N.T.* To come to a conclusion in the way appointed by the Father through death on the cross.

8 Bruce, *Synoptic Gospels*, on Lk 13:32. As a destructive force in the Lord's vineyard, many commentators point to "the little foxes that spoil the vineyards" (Sg 2:15).

9 Like the three years of Lk 13:7. Compare Hos 6:2. Not to be taken as a chronological tag, as Wieseler does (*Synopsis*, 235), who from these words makes the inference that Jesus was still a three days' journey from Bethany.

10 In the Greek text, the word *Jerusalem* appears three times in immediate succession: *Hierousalēm* (v. 33). *Hierousalēm, Hierousalēm.*

11 Luke reports only one journey of Jesus to Jerusalem during His public ministry. But this word shows that the Synoptists knew of the various journeys John records, although they are not reported in their writings (Ylvisaker, *Gospels*, 484).

12 Compare Mt 23:37–38.

13 (1) The lame man at the Pool of Bethesda (Jn 5:10). (2) The disciples in the grainfield (Mt 12:2; Mk 2:24; Lk 6:2). (3) The man with a withered hand (Mt 12:10; Mk 3:2; Lk 6:7). (4) The man born blind (Jn 9:13–14). (5) The crippled woman (Lk 13:14). (6) The man afflicted with dropsy (Lk 14:1–4).

14 Gk *archontōn tōn Pharisaiōn*. Probably a member of the local Jewish Council. As such, the Pharisees had no rulers. This Pharisee may have occupied a position of honor on account of great learning. Hardly a member of the Council of Jerusalem if the scene is to be placed in Perea.

15 Ylvisaker, *Gospels*, 486. Cf. Ne 8:10.

16 Gk *hydrōpikos* (*hydrops*). Swelling caused by water pockets collecting in body tissue. The only place in the New Testament where the disease is mentioned.

17 Farrar, *Life of Christ* 2:120.

18 Gk *epilabomenos*. Compare Mk 8:23. The impressive means employed. Stronger than *hapsamenos*, "touched him" (Mt 8:3). See Meyer, *Commentary on the N.T.*, on Lk 14:4.

19 Many manuscripts have *huios ē bous*, a son or (even) an ox, etc. (Bruce, *Synoptic Gospels*, on Lk 14:5, with text note).

20 Compare Mt 12:11.

21 Farrar, *Life of Christ* 2:121.

22 Farrar, *Life of Christ* 2:122.

23 This implied business folly, as though the field and the oxen had been purchased, as it were, sight unseen. The view of Wetstein, De Wette, and

24 Bruce, *Synoptic Gospels*, on Lk 14:23.
25 Plural *hymin*, you (v. 24), as compared with the singular, *autōi*, you, in v. 16.
26 Gk *misei*.
27 Bruce, *Synoptic Gospels*, on Lk 14:26.
28 Gk *ou dynatai*.
29 Some have seen in these words a reference to the war of Herod with Äretas of Arabia as the result of the repudiation of the Arabian king's daughter by Herod and his marriage of Herodias. But this is unlikely. The date given by Schürer (*Jewish People* 1.2:30) for this war is AD 36 (after the death of Christ). It seems that the time of the public ministry of Jesus was a period of peace. This, of course, does not prevent the Lord from referring to war.
30 Ch. 11, § 20.
31 Gk *drachmē*. Used in the LXX as the rendering of "half-shekel." Commonly taken as the equivalent of the Roman denarius, equal to the ordinary daily wage of a soldier or laborer.
32 Edersheim, *Life and Times of Jesus* 2:257.
33 Bruce, *Synoptic Gospels*, on Lk 15:10.
34 Farrar, *Life of Christ* 2:135.
35 Bruce, *Synoptic Gospels*, on Lk 15:12.
36 Edersheim, *Life and Times of Jesus* 2:258.
37 Gk *dieilen autois*.
38 Ylvisaker, *Gospels*, 494.
39 Gk *ekollēthē*.
40 Hbr *dabhar acheer*. Farrar, *Life of Christ* 1:427 n. 1.
41 Gk *keratia*, the long, bean-like pods of the carob tree.
42 Bruce, *Synoptic Gospels*, on Lk 15:16.
43 Gk *eis heauton elthōn*.
44 Ylvisaker, *Gospels*, 494.
45 Farrar, *Life of Christ* 1:428.
46 Bruce, *Synoptic Gospels*, on Lk 15:20.
47 Although it appears in some manuscripts.
48 Some manuscripts prefix an expressive *tachy* after "said to his servants": "[Make haste,] bring quickly," etc.
49 Bruce, *Synoptic Gospels*, on Lk 15:22.
50 Meyer, *Commentary on the N.T.*, on Lk 15:23: "The well-known one, which stands in the stall."
51 Farrar, *Life of Christ* 1:428.
52 Bruce, *Synoptic Gospels*, on Lk 15:28.
53 Edersheim, *Life and Times of Jesus* 2:263.
54 Farrar, *Life of Christ* 1:429 n. 1.
55 Edersheim, *Life and Times of Jesus* 2:267.
56 Gk *batos*. A *bath* equals approximately 6 gallons (see *TLSB*, cx). But the expositors are not agreed as to the exact amount. It does not matter. It seems that the size varied in different sections of Palestine, Judea, and Galilee (Edersheim, *Life and Times of Jesus* 2:268).
57 Edersheim, *Life and Times of Jesus* 2:269.
58 Gk *ta grammata*.
59 Gk *koros*. A cor was about 6 bushels (*TLSB*, cx).
60 Bruce, *Synoptic Gospels*, on Lk 16:6.
61 Gk *oikonomon tēs adikias*.
62 Bruce, *Synoptic Gospels*, on Lk 16:14; *exemyktērizon* is *ek* and *myktēr*, the nose. See Lk 23:35.
63 Kretzmann, *Popular Commentary* 1:355.
64 Bruce, *Synoptic Gospels*, on Lk 16:19–31.
65 A probable rendition of *bysson* and *porphyran*.
66 Remembering that the Lord is evidently stating a parable (although some, following Tertullian, think that He is relating history), there is no sense in a tradition that provides a name, Nineue (Sahidic version: "*Cuius erat nomen Nineue*") for the rich man. See Meyer, *Commentary on the N.T.*, on Lk 16:19.
67 *Gotthilf* (Grm), from *'ela'azar* (Hbr), although some have seen in it a "No Help God" from *lo''ezer*. See Meyer, *Commentary on the N.T.*, on Lk 16:20–21.
68 Bruce, *Synoptic Gospels*, on Lk 16:20.
69 Gk *ebeblēto*.
70 Dogs are otherwise in Scripture not represented as symbols of pity and compassion (Ylvisaker, *Gospels*, 501).
71 Gk *eis ton kolpon tou Abraam*. Symbolic language for the blessed abode of departed souls.
72 Gk *en tōi haidēi*.
73 Bruce, *Synoptic Gospels*, on Lk 16:23.
74 Bruce, *Synoptic Gospels*, on Lk 16:23.
75 Gk *mega chasma*.
76 A random number, large enough to make the interest in their eternal well-being on the part of a deceased member very intelligible (Bruce, *Synoptic Gospels*, on Lk 16:27).
77 Farrar, *Life of Christ* 2:127.
78 Kretzmann, *Popular Commentary* 1:358.
79 Gk *hoi apostoloi* instead of the usual *mathētai*.

80 Luke's frequent *Kyrios.*

81 Gk *sykaminōi* = *sykomorean* of Lk 19:4. The fig-mulberry tree. A tree here, a mountain in Matthew and Mark.

82 Meyer, *Commentary on the N.T.,* on Lk 17:7–10.

83 Bruce, *Synoptic Gospels,* on Lk 17:7–10.

CHAPTER 24
THE RAISING OF LAZARUS

1 The traditional tomb of Lazarus is still shown in a village on the southeastern slope of Olivet, nearly two miles from Jerusalem, on the way to Jericho, now called El Aziriyeh, after Lazarus.

2 Gk *phileis,* Lat *amas.* Affectionate love. Natural human affection. Love as expressed in marks of affection.

3 The sisters do not say: "He who loves You." This, of course, is also implied.

4 Recorded by St. John in the following chapter (12:3).

5 Also recorded by Mk (14:3–9) and Mt (26:6–13). We notice that John presupposes an acquaintance with the synoptic Gospels (Ylvisaker, *Gospels,* 513).

6 Here the term *ēgapa* is used; from *agapaō* (Gk), *diligo* (Lat). A higher type of love, involving will and judgment.

7 Contrary to the common view that Lazarus died at the time of the arrival of the messenger and that the two days of waiting and two days of travel made up the four days of v. 17. We agree with Ebrard, *Gospel History,* 353.

8 *Thōmas* (Gk) is the transliteration of *Toma'* (Hbr), and *didymos* means twin (Dods, *Gospel of St. John,* on Jn 11:16).

9 Dods, *Gospel of St. John,* on Jn 11:16.

10 From twenty to seventy-five miles.

11 Presumably by inquiry. A proof of the true human nature of Jesus, corresponding to the proof of His omniscience in v. 14.

12 Gk *hōs apo stadiōn dekapente.* A stadium (furlong) is equal to 606¾ feet and is thus somewhat less than a furlong, which is 660 feet. Fifteen stadia are about 3,030 yards or about two miles as in the ESV translation.

13 Assuming that the messenger had returned with the message (Ylvisaker, *Gospels,* 517).

14 Meyer, *Commentary on the N.T.,* on Jn 11:23–24.

15 Gk *anastēsetai en tēi anastasei.*

16 Martha had rushed out to meet Jesus (v. 20).

17 Kretzmann, *Popular Commentary* 1:474.

18 Ylvisaker, *Gospels,* 519.

19 Dods, *Gospel of St. John,* on Jn 11:34.

20 Either because He wanted those present to accompany Him or because according to His human nature He did not know, voluntarily abstaining from the use of the divine omniscience communicated to His human nature.

21 The shortest verse in the English Bible.

22 Farrar, *Life of Christ* 2:171.

23 Farrar, *Life of Christ* 2:171.

24 Quoted by Eusebius, *NPNF2* 1:175. See ch. 12, § 1.

25 Farrar, *Life of Christ* 2:174.

26 This is not said to imply that the Jews had a new high priest every year, but simply to point out that he was the high priest in that memorable year when Jesus was to die (Ylvisaker, *Gospels,* 523).

27 Steinmann, *From Abraham to Paul,* 281, 300.

28 Farrar, *Life of Christ* 2:175 n. 2.

29 Dods, *Gospel of St. John,* on Jn 11:51.

30 That He spent a few weeks in secrecy is implied in the statement that, if anyone knew where He was, he was to inform the chief priests and the Pharisees (v. 57).

31 *Oxford Bible Atlas,* 87. About thirteen miles northeast of Jerusalem, in the wilderness of Bethaven. The present village of Taiyibeh. See also Wieseler, *Synopsis,* 291 n. 7.

CHAPTER 25
THE FINAL JOURNEY TO JERUSALEM

1 Dods, *Gospel of St. John,* on Jn 11:54.

2 This seems to be the meaning of the disputed *dia mesou* of the *textus receptus* or the *dia meson* or *ana meson* or *meson* alone of other readings. See Andrews, *Life of Our Lord,* 412.

3 Confirmed also by Mt 20:20.

4 Farrar, *Life of Christ* 2:111.

5 Gk *epistata,* a "Lucan expression" (see Lk 5:5; 8:24, 45; 9:33, 49; 17:13).

6 Compare Lk 10:33.

7   The word for healing lepers is *cleanse*. To a certain extent, being afflicted with this disease also involved ceremonial defilement.

8   Gk *allogenēs*.

9   Farrar, *Life of Christ* 2:136.

10 Gk *paratērēsis*.

11 Bruce, *Synoptic Gospels*, on Lk 17:20.

12 Gk *entos hymōn estin*. For this reason, there can be no "coming" of the Kingdom, because, correctly understood, the Kingdom is already here.

13 Farrar, *Life of Christ* 2:137.

14 Hitherto "day." The reference to night suits the illustration (Bruce, *Synoptic Gospels*, on Lk 17:34).

15 Farrar, *Life of Christ* 2:138.

16 Kretzmann, *Popular Commentary* 1:362.

17 Kretzmann, *Popular Commentary* 1:362.

18 Edersheim, *Life and Times of Jesus* 2:287.

19 Gk *hypōpiazēi*, from *hypōpion*—hypo and ōps.

20 Edersheim, *Life and Times of Jesus* 2:289.

21 The *hoi loipoi* (Gk). The *Am ha Aretz* (Hbr), the people of the soil, from whom he as a Pharisee would be separated.

22 If that was the meaning of "afflict yourselves" (Lv 16:29; 23:27).

23 Edersheim, *Life and Times of Jesus* 2:291.

24 Gk *ktōmai*.

25 Gk *tōi hamartōlōi*.

26 Matthew and Mark link up the following with the discourses in Capernaum, after the transfiguration. But the notice of the departure from Galilee does not prevent the insertion of intervening visits to Jerusalem before this final journey, as supplied by John and introduced between corresponding sections of Luke:
   1. Tabernacles, Jn 7:10ff., followed by Lk 9:51ff.
   2. Dedication, Jn 10:22ff., followed by Lk 13:22ff.
   3. Raising of Lazarus, Jn 11:1ff., followed by Lk 17:11ff.
   4. Final journey, Mt 19:1ff.; Mk 10:1ff., joined by Lk 18:14ff. As we have seen (§ 1), from Ephraim, Jesus went northward, then eastward across the Jordan, and then south through Perea to Jericho, to Bethany, to Jerusalem. See Robertson, *Harmony*, 141, note, and 276–79.

27 The reading of the *textus receptus* in Mk 10:1 is *Eis ta horia tēs Ioudaias dia tou peran tou Iordanou*.

28 Hbr *'erwath dabar*, "matter of nakedness," "some indecency," *aliquam foeditatem* (Lat), *Bloesse in irgend etwas* (Grm).

29 See Edersheim, *Life and Times of Jesus* 2:333; Farrar, *Life of Christ* 2:152; Ylvisaker, *Gospels*, 444.

30 Since there is a great difference between the term *command* in the question of Jesus and the *allowed* in the reply, this was really a begging of the question.

31 "And said"—that is, God said, speaking through the mouth of Adam (see Gn 2:24).

32 Gk *eunouchos*, the keeper of the bedchamber in a harem.

33 Here, Luke again joins Matthew and Mark, whom he had left at the close of the Galilean ministry, before the Feast of Tabernacles, six months previously. From this point, the Synoptic Gospels will be parallel more frequently than they were even during the great ministry of Christ in Galilee. See ch. 19, § 5.

34 On account of *brephē* (Gk) in Luke. Sucklings, *infantuli ab uberibus pendentes* (Lat). See Ac 7:19; 1Pt 2:2. Ylvisaker, *Gospels*, 447.

35 On account of *autois*, masculine (Mt 19:13; Mk 10:13).

36 Gk *paidia* in Matthew and Mark.

37 Compare the remark of the disciples concerning the Syrophoenician woman (Mt 15:23).

38 Gk *archōn*—Luke.

39 Some manuscripts omit "good." We have followed the *textus receptus*. For critical remarks, see commentaries.

40 Omitted by Mark and Luke.

41 Edersheim, *Life and Times of Jesus* 2:339; Farrar, *Life of Christ* 2:160. The title was unknown among the Jews.

42 See Mt 16:20; compare also Mt 9:30; 12:16.

43 Gk *poias* (*entolas*); what sort of commandments?

44 Some manuscripts include "for those who trust in riches" here as well.

45 Not Gk *kamilos*, a rope, but *kamēlos*, a camel, the largest animal in use among the Jews, as the eye of a needle, *rhaphis*, was the smallest known opening. The explanation that makes a small side gate of a city through which a laden camel

might enter with difficulty called "a needle's eye" lacks confirmation (Farrar, *Life of Christ* 2:163). For the origin of the expression, it has been suggested that a camel-driver leaning against his camel and failing to thread a needle with which to sew his sacks might say in comical exaggeration: I might as well try to put the camel through the eye (Bruce, *Synoptic Gospels*, on Mt 19:24). Similar expressions, however, are also found in rabbinic writings: an elephant passing through the eye of a needle (Edersheim, *Life and Times of Jesus* 2:342).

46 Farrar, *Life of Christ* 2:163.

47 Gk *en tēi palingenesiai*. A new word in the Gospel vocabulary, pointing to a general renewal at the end of days (Bruce, *Synoptic Gospels*, on Mt 19:28).

48 Not to be taken literally. Stöckhardt (*Biblische Geschichte*, 218): "The saints made perfect, the great company of the elect."

49 In Mark only.

50 In Mark only.

51 Gk *hetaire*, comrade. Friendly, but firmly.

52 This phrase was included in the KJV but is missing in many manuscripts. Compare Mt 22:14. Gk *eklektoi*, chosen, not in the sense as though some were predestined or preordained to damnation. There is no foreordination to damnation; but salvation is by the grace of God and damnation through man's own fault. Those who have been chosen from eternity are during their life on earth called by the Means of Grace. Those who do not heed the Gospel call are not among the elect of God.

53 Compare: (1) Jn 2:18–22. In connection with the first cleansing of the temple. (2) Mt 16:21–23; Mk 8:31–33; Lk 9:22. At Caesarea Philippi. (3) Mt 17:22–23; Mk 9:30–32; Lk 9:43–45. At the close of the Galilean ministry. (4) Mt 20:17–19; Mk 10:32–34; Lk 18:31–34. In Perea. (5) Mt 26:1–5; Mk 14:1–2; Lk 22:1–2. At Bethany on Tuesday evening of Passion Week.

54 Gk *paradothēsetai*. The word is used thirty-six times in the New Testament for the betrayal of Jesus Christ and in addition only three times (Mt 24:10; Mk 13:12; Lk 21:16) of kinsmen delivering up one another to prosecution See *ISBE* under "Betray."

55 Gk *staurōsai*. Mock, flog, crucify, all new features.

56 This seems to be the combination of Matthew and Mark. In Mark, it is the sons who petition Jesus, whereas in Matthew it was their mother. The request was made by the mother, who was the intercessor; but in truth it was the request of the two disciples, and therefore Jesus directs His reply, even in Matthew, to them and not to their mother.

57 See ch. 4, § 43.

58 Ylvisaker, *Gospels*, 529.

59 See § 17 above.

60 Compare Mk 9:33–34, after the transfiguration.

61 Gk *diakonos*, helper, servant.

62 Gk *doulos*, slave.

63 Gk *lytron*. The symbolism is that of prisoners who are liberated upon the payment of a price. Thus the blood of Christ is a ransom (Col 1:14; 1Tm 2:6; Ac 20:28). This ransom was not paid to the devil, but to divine justice.

64 Gk *anti*, in place of, instead of—vicarious suffering and death. Compare *antilytron hyper pantōn* in 1Tm 2:6.

65 Gk *pollōn*. Not restrictive, as if Christ did not die for all, but used in special reference to the great number in whose behalf the sacrifice was made. See Ylvisaker, *Gospels*, 530.

66 The old and the new Jericho were not quite two miles apart. This seems to be the best explanation of the age-long controversy concerning the "discrepancy" between Matthew and Mark as compared with the account of Luke. Matthew says "out of Jericho" and Mark says "leaving Jericho"—the old Jericho; Luke has "near to Jericho," the new Jericho, which Herod had rebuilt and named Cypros in honor of his mother (*Ant* 16:143; *War* 1:407, 417; see also *Ant* 17:340). Zacchaeus had his home, naturally enough, at the customs station in New Jericho. Matthew writes for the Christians among the Jews. It was necessary for him to designate the place just as we find it in his Gospel. Luke writes to Gentile Christians, particularly to those in the Middle East. When they spoke of Jericho, it was the Jericho of the customs station. In order to point out the place where the blind men were healed, he had to say that Christ came to Jericho. Mark, however, drawing his material from Peter,

naturally would speak like the apostle Matthew. Thus there is perfect harmony where a dis-agreement would seem to exist. See Macknight, *Harmony* 2:569–70; Ylvisaker, *Gospels*, 533–34; Robertson, *Harmony of the Gospels*, 149; Andrews, *Life of Our Lord*, 418; Farrar, *Life of Christ* 2:181.

67 The son of Timaeus.

68 Matthew mentions two blind men, while Mark and Luke speak of only one, who probably was, and continued to be, the better known of the two.

69 Gk *Rabbouni* in Mark. Compare Jn 20:16. Farrar says in *Life of Christ* 2:183, that the steps of honor in the title are Rah, Rabbi, Rabban, Rabboni.

70 Zacchaeus, a Jewish name, from Hbr *zakkai*, meaning pure, as if describing a particular char-acteristic. Probably a headman, or overseer, over the local collectors of taxes.

71 Gk *architelōnēs*. Nowhere else in the New Testament (Bruce, *Synoptic Gospels*, on Lk 19:1).

72 Gk *sychomoraia*, a fig-mulberry tree.

73 Jesus, who had followed Nathanael to the place where he stood, beneath the fig tree (Jn 1:48), was not ignorant of anything that was going on.

74 Edersheim, *Life and Times of Jesus* 2:351.

75 *Ant* 14:54.

76 According to tradition, Zacchaeus later became the bishop of Caesarea (Andrews, *Life of Our Lord*, 420).

77 See § 23 above.

78 Ylvisaker, *Gospels*, 537.

79 It is assumed that Jesus and His hearers were familiar with the practice. "A nobleman went into a far country to receive for himself a king-dom" would be an utterly unintelligible sentence if we did not know that this was actually done both by Archelaus and Antipas in applying for royal dignity in Rome after the death of Herod (*Ant* 17:222, 224). Here, we have one of those unexpected indications of the authenticity and truthfulness of the Gospel account (Ylvisaker, *Gospels*, 537; Farrar, *Life of Christ* 2:186 n. 3).

80 Gk *eugenēs*, well-born man.

81 A round number.

82 Gk *deka mnas*. The value is less important com-pared with the importance placed upon fidelity

and increase. That there is a reference to a silver standard seems to be indicated in the expression *money*, Gk *argyrion*.

83 Gk *pragmateusasthe heōs erchomai*. The for-mer verb used only here in the New Testament (Bruce, *Synoptic Gospels*, Lk 19:13).

84 *Ant* 17:230–39.

85 Bruce, *Synoptic Gospels*, on Lk 19:14.

86 Gk *deka poleōn*. See Bruce, *Synoptic Gospels*, on Lk 19:17.

87 Kretzmann, *Popular Commentary* 1:369.

88 Gk *en soudariōi*. Cf. Jn 11:44; 20:7.

89 Gk *epi tēn trapezan*, upon a (banker's) table.

90 Gk *syn tokōi*. Such transactions were forbid-den among Israelites, but were allowed with Gentiles. Interest rates were from 1 to 4 percent, per month, or from 12 to 48 percent, per year (Edersheim, *Life and Times of Jesus* 2:463).

91 As a note of time, the expression *eipōn tauta* is rather vague. We do not know how much time intervened between the telling of the parable and the commencement of the ascent to Jerusalem. It is one of Luke's formulas of transition (Bruce, *Synoptic Gospels*, on Lk 19:28).

CHAPTER 26
ARRIVAL AT BETHANY

1 According to the general principle of appearing before the Lord ceremonially pure (Gn 35:2; Ex 19:10–11; Nu 9:6–14; 2Ch 30:17–22).

2 See Ware, *When Was Jesus Really Born?* 77–79.

3 "14 Nisan ran from sundown Thursday to sun-down Friday" (Steinmann, *From Abraham to Paul*, 273 n. 433). See also Steinmann's chart "The Chronology of Holy Week and Easter" in the same book, pp. 288–89, and Ware, *When Was Jesus Really Born?* 76.

4 This seems to be the simplest and most natural course of events. While Jesus told the Jewish rab-bis that deeds of mercy and emergency acts were not forbidden on the Sabbath, we do not read that He used the Sabbath for ordinary journeys (Ylvisaker, *Gospels*, 542).

5 This anointing has nothing in common with that recorded by Luke (7:36–50; second preach-ing tour in Galilee; see ch. 12, §§ 9–10), except that in each passage, a woman anointed the

Savior's feet and the name of the host, Simon, which was borne by many Jews, was the same. The account of Matthew and Mark seems to have been brought in parenthetically. It is not to be connected with the "two days" before the Passover (Mt 26:2; Mk 14:1), but with the words "Now when Jesus was at Bethany" (Matthew) and "while He was at Bethany" (Mark). The exact time when the anointing took place is not stated (Andrews, *Life of Our Lord*, 426). And even in John, the time is given only in a general way: between Jesus' arrival at Bethany and His entry into Jerusalem.—The following considerations have moved us to place the anointment on Saturday evening: (1) It was the day before Christ's entry into Jerusalem, Palm Sunday (Jn 12:12). (2) The supper was an *evening* meal, Gk *deipnon* (v. 2). (3) Some time must be allowed for preparations and for the coming of people from Jerusalem, which on account of the Sabbath regulations regarding labor and travel would have been out of the question between the sunsets from Friday to Saturday. It is natural to suppose that the report of the arrival of Jesus at Bethany reached Jerusalem on Friday evening and that the people came out on Saturday evening.

6 "It was made from the root and the lower stem of a plant, with spikes of purple four-stamened flowers, that grows only on mountain heights in North India. Found there with great difficulty, the nard was carried on camelback up through the passes of Afghanistan and across Persia into the Roman Empire and there regarded as the choicest of all elements in the most perfect ointment" (Mathews, *Life of Jesus*, 380).

7 Gk *alabastron myrou nardou pistikēs polytelous* (Mk 14:3).

8 Ylvisaker, *Gospels*, 545.

9 300 denarii, as compared with the 200 denarii in Jn 6:7, which were estimated by Philip as required to supply 5,000 persons with a meager meal (Edersheim, *Life and Times of Jesus* 2:358).

10 Farrar, *Life of Christ* 2:192. Gk *eis ti hē apōleia hautē* (Mt 26:8).

11 Thirty pieces of silver.

12 Gk *triakosiōn dēnariōn*. Three hundred denarii would equal about a laborer's wages for three hundred working days, or one year.

13 Gk *ta ballomena ebastazen*. Made away with what was put therein (Bruce, *Synoptic Gospels*, on Jn 12:6).

14 Gk *kalon ergon,* a lovely deed. A "nice" deed is a good deed.

15 Ylvisaker, *Gospels*, 546.

16 After sundown, when the regulation regarding the "Sabbath Day's journey" was lifted. Compare Ac 1:12. The distance from Jerusalem to the Mount of Olives is from 1,000 to 1,200 yards, 5 to 6 stadia, whereas the distance to Bethany is about 15 stadia.

CHAPTER 27
PALM SUNDAY: THE TRIUMPHAL ENTRY INTO JERUSALEM

1 Otherwise unmentioned in the Bible. From several Talmudic references, it may be inferred that it was near the Mount of Olives and at the Sabbatical-distance limit east of Jerusalem (*ABD* 1:715).

2 Compare Lk 22:8.

3 Gk *ho kyrios* in the same sense as used of Christ in the Gospels otherwise—Mt 8:25, etc. (Bruce, *Synoptic Gospels*, on Mt 21:3).

4 Gk *dedemenon pros tēn thyran exō epi tou amphodou*. Tied to the gate or door outside or on the path that leads from the road or the meeting of the road.

5 The Romans indulged in all kinds of sneers against the Jews in connection with the donkey—worshipers of a donkey's head, and the like—and the Christians came in for their share of them. In the East, the donkey is not a despised animal. The rabbis believed that if the Messiah would not appear floating upon a cloud, He would come riding on a donkey as a sign of their faithlessness (Farrar, *Life of Christ* 2:197).

6 The believing citizens of Jerusalem in general.

7 This has caused much trouble as some translations use the word "and" (see KJV). Obviously Jesus did not ride on both animals. It has been explained why He rode the colt. Luke gives the answer when he stresses "on which no one has ever sat." It seems that "a donkey *and* a colt" is a parallelism, or it is epexegetic—"and," in the

sense of "and that upon" or "and, to be explicit, upon" (Ylvisaker, *Gospels*, 549).

8 Farrar, *Life of Christ* 2:203.

9 Farrar, *Life of Christ* 2:201.

10 Gk *eseisthē*, as if rocked by an earthquake.

CHAPTER 28
MONDAY OF PASSION WEEK

1 Mark indicates that the incident of the cursing of the fig tree and the discussion on the matter took place on two different days, Monday and Tuesday morning (Mk 11:12–14, 20–21). In Matthew, the story of the two days is compressed into one, Tuesday morning.

2 Ylvisaker, *Gospels*, 553.

3 *War* 3:519.

4 When the young leaves newly appear in April, every fig tree that is going to bear fruit at all will have some *taksh* ("immature figs") on its branches, even though "it was not the season for figs"—that is, for the ordinary crop, either early or late. "This *taksh* is not only eaten today, but it is sure evidence, even when it falls, that the tree bearing it is not barren" (*ISBE* under "Fig").

5 Farrar, *Life of Christ* 2:214.

6 Not to be confused with the cleansing of the temple at the beginning of our Lord's ministry at the Passover of AD 30 (Jn 2:13–21). See ch. 7, §§ 1–3.

7 See ch. 4, § 13 and ch. 7, § 2.

8 Is 56:7, from the LXX, with omissions; and Jer 7:11. See Bruce, *Synoptic Gospels*, on Mt 21:13.

9 Bruce, *Synoptic Gospels*, on Mk 11:16.

10 Gk *ēulisthē*, from *aulizesthai*. To remain in the *aula*, to spend the night (Mt 21:17).

CHAPTER 29
TUESDAY MORNING OF PASSION WEEK

1 See ch. 28, § 1.

2 Compare Mt 17:20; Lk 17:6.

3 Compare Mt 6:14–15.

4 He had another busy day in Galilee, the day of the parables. See ch. 12, §§ 18–32.

5 Edersheim, *Life and Times of Jesus* 2:380.

6 Schürer, *Jewish People* 2.1:186.

7 Farrar, *Life of Christ* 2:218.

8 *Ant* 18:116–19.

9 Gk *ouk oidamen*.

10 Gk *proagousin*. With the words "before you," Christ still leaves the door open to them for repentance.

11 Farrar, *Life of Christ* 2:221.

12 Bruce, *Synoptic Gospels*, on Mt 21:32.

13 Bruce, *Synoptic Gospels*, on Mt 21:35.

14 Edersheim, *Life and Times of Jesus* 2:424.

15 See ch. 18, § 10.

16 Gk *kakous kakōs apolesai*, badly destroy bad men.

17 From the Septuagint. Bruce, *Synoptic Gospels*, on Mt 21:42.

18 As in the case of Joseph, when men thought evil against him, but God meant it for good (Gn 50:20), so here, "This was the Lord's doing, and it is marvelous in our eyes" (Ps 118:23).

19 Bruce, *Synoptic Gospels*, on Mt 22:1–14.

20 Gk *kalesai tous keklēmenous*, to invite the invited. Bruce, *Synoptic Gospels*, on Mt 22:3.

21 Gk *ariston*, midday meal.

22 Edersheim, *Life and Times of Jesus* 2:427.

23 Gk *eis tēn emporian*, store.

24 Compare Mt 21:35.

25 Bruce, *Synoptic Gospels*, on Mt 22:12.

26 See Meyer, *Commentary on the N.T.*, on Mt 22:11.

27 Gk *hetaire*, a mild way of introducing a rebuke (Meyer *Commentary on the N.T.*, on Mt 20:12).

28 Ch. 25, § 19.

29 Gk *hēroidianoi*, a Latinism (Mk 3:6). See ch. 10, § 31.

30 See ch. 17, § 8.

31 See Bruce, *Synoptic Gospels*, on Mt 22:16.

32 Farrar, *Life of Christ* 2:230.

33 Gk *kēnson, censum*. Another Latinism. *Phoron* in Luke.

34 *War* 2:345–401. The speech of Agrippa against the final war. Populous, wealthy, and vast Alexandria does not disdain to submit to Roman domination, yet "it pays more tribute (Gk *phoros*) to the Romans in one month than you do in a year" (*War* 2:386).—Gk *Exestin hēmin Kaisari phoron dounai; . . . deixate moi dēnarion* (cf. Lk 20:22, 24). The Jews, when accusing the Lord before Pilate, falsely accused Him of "forbidding us to give tribute, *phorous*, to Caesar" (Lk 23:2). *Kēnsos* (Gk) was

a poll tax and *phoros* a payment for state purposes (Madden, *History of Jewish Coinage*, 247).

35 Gk *nomisma*. Latinism, *numisma*. The current coin in which the tax was paid. A denarius (Mark).

36 Gk *dēnarion*, Lat *denarius*. From *as* (*aes*), the original bronze standard. Ten of them, *decem asses*, amounted to one silver denarius. The fourth Latinism: *Hecodiani, numisma, census, denarius*.

37 Compare Mt 20:2.

38 *TI(berius) CAESAR DIVI AUG(usti) F(ilius) AUGUSTUS.*

39 *PONTIF(ex) MAXIM(us).*

40 For illustration, see Bible dictionaries under "Denarius." Deissmann, *Licht vom Osten*, 214; Madden, *History of Jewish Coinage*, 247; Williamson, *Money of the Bible*, 70.

41 Gk *apodote.*

42 *Ant* 17:313–14.

43 See ch. 17, § 8; 18, § 1.

44 Farrar, *Life of Christ* 2:234.

45 To perform the part of a *levir*, brother-in-law, by marrying a deceased childless brother's widow.

46 "When they rise again" (Mark).

47 Farrar, *Life of Christ* 2:235; Edersheim, *Life and Times of Jesus* 2:398ff.; Bruce, *Synoptic Gospels*, on Mt 22:28.

48 Cf. Farrar, *Life of Christ* 2:236.

49 Luke: *anastasis ek nekrōn* (Gk). Not merely a vague immortality of the soul.

50 Jesus does not state that they become angels, but that they are *like* the holy angels in relation to the estate of marriage (Ylvisaker, *Gospels*, 576).

51 The point is not in the Gk *eimi*, "am," for which there is no Hebrew or Aramaic equivalent, but in the relation implied in the title (Bruce, *Synoptic Gospels*, on Mt 22:32).

52 Farrar, *Life of Christ* 2:236.

53 Gk *ephimōsen*, from *phimos*, a muzzle. Cf. Dt 25:4.

54 Farrar, *Life of Christ* 2:239; Ylvisaker, *Gospels*, 578.

55 See ch. 21, § 8.

56 Bruce, *Synoptic Gospels*, on Mt 22:38.

57 Gk *nounechōs*, "wisely, discreetly."

58 Edersheim, *Life and Times of Jesus* 2:405.

59 Exactly reproduced from the LXX (Bruce, *Synoptic Gospels*, on Mk 12:36).

60 Edersheim, *Life and Times of Jesus* 2:406.

61 See ch. 21, §§ 15–16.

62 Gk *phylaktērion*, "guard."

63 Jesus refers to Himself. And Matthew, reporting the discourse, refers to the speaker as Christ.

64 Eightfold in the *textus receptus*; sevenfold if, according to some leading manuscripts, Mt 23:14 is to be omitted, the contents of which are found in Mk 12:40.

65 Farrar, *Life of Christ* 2:245 n. 1.

66 That the Jews were zealous in making converts is the testimony of Josephus and the complaint of classical writers (*Ant* 18:81–82; 20:34–48; *Against Apion* 2:10, 39; Tacitus, *History of the Jews* 2.5; *Annals* 2.85).

67 Gk *hēdyosmon, anēthon, kyminon*, garden herbs: mint (literally, sweet-smelling), dill, also aromatic cumin (Grm, *Kuemmel*) with aromatic seeds. Used as condiments or for medicinal purposes. Cf. Lk 11:42. Bruce, *Synoptic Gospels*, on Mt 23:23.

68 Edersheim, *Life and Times of Jesus* 2:413.

69 See ch. 21, § 17, n. 53.

70 See ch. 23, § 5.

71 Edersheim, *Life and Times of Jesus* 2:414.

72 Bruce, *Synoptic Gospels*, on Mk 12:41.

73 Edersheim, *Life and Times of Jesus* 2:387.

74 *Ant* 14:72, 105.

75 Gk *lepta dyo, ho esti kodrantēs.*

76 Andrews, *Life of Our Lord*, 443; Schürer, *Jewish People* 2.2:316ff. See Ex 20:10; Dt 5:14; 14:21; 24:14; Ac 15:20, 29; 21:25.

77 Dods, *Gospel of St. John*, on Jn 12:21.

78 Farrar, *Life of Christ* 2:207.

79 Dods, *Gospel of St. John*, on Jn 12:32.

80 Here a general term for the Old Testament. Compare Jn 10:34.

81 As compared with Jn 3:14.

82 The evangelist John reports but a few. However, compare Jn 20:30.

83 Kretzmann, *Popular Commentary* 1:482.

CHAPTER 30
TUESDAY AFTERNOON OF PASSION WEEK

1 Farrar, *Life of Christ* 2:255.

2 *Ant* 15:392.

3 *War* 5:205.

4 *Ant* 12:64–84.

5 *Ant* 15:395; *War* 5:210.

6 See ch. 3, §§ 6–14.

7 *War* 5:223.

8   Gk *kai ti to sēmeion tēs sēs parousias, kai syn-teleias tou aiōnos* (Mt 24:3). *Parousia* appears again in vv. 27, 37, and 39, but it is found nowhere else in the Gospels, though frequently in the epistles. *Synteleia tou aiōnos* appears in Mt 13:39, 49; 28:20; and Heb 9:26. The questioners took for granted that the three things went together: destruction of the temple, advent of the Son of Man, and the end of the current age. *Parousia* (literally, presence, namely, second presence) and *synteleia tou aiōnos* (end of the world) are the technical terms in the apostolic age for the close of the present order of things; and Matthew is the only one of the Gospel writers who uses these terms. See Bruce, *Synoptic Gospels*, on Mt 24:3.

9   As our chief purpose is to tell the Gospel story, the detailed interpretation of these difficult prophecies, those now fulfilled as well as those still to be fulfilled, is beyond the scope of this work.

10 Compare Mt 10:19–20; Lk 12:11–12.

11 Bruce, *Synoptic Gospels*, on Mt 24:8.

12 See Bruce, *Synoptic Gospels*, on Mk 13:19.

13 Eusebius, *NPNF2* 1:138.

14 Kretzmann, *Popular Commentary* 1:136.

15 Gk *hē parousia*.

16 Kretzmann, *Popular Commentary* 1:136.

17 Bruce, *Synoptic Gospels*, on Mt 24:30.

18 Bruce, *Synoptic Gospels*, on Mt 24:31.

19 Gk *hē genea hautē*.

20 Gk *genētai*.

21 Of *genētai*.

22 See § 2 above.

23 See ch. 25, § 5.

24 Small domestic mills, usually operated by women.

25 Gk *poiai hēmera*. Day, time of the day, indefinite period of time.

26 Gk *Kyrios hymōn*. Jesus here calls Himself Lord. In narrative, the title is given to Jesus especially by Luke (10:1; 11:39; 12:42; etc.).

27 Not strictly parallel, and the order is not stated. General concluding exhortations to watchfulness. Each evangelist brings his own epilogue before presenting the Passion history. Our arrangement is (1) Luke: Warning against dissipation and drunkenness. (2) Mark: Parable of the

doorkeeper. (3) Matthew: Parable of the master of the house and the two servants. Followed by: Parable of the ten virgins; parable of the talents; picture of the Day of Judgment.

28 Gk *grēgoreite* (cf. Mk 13:33).

29 See ch. 16, § 5.

30 Ch. 21, § 22.

31 Ch. 21, § 23.

32 For this form of punishment, see 2Sm 12:31; 1Ch 20:3; Heb 11:37 (Suetonius, *Caligula*, 27).

33 See ch. 21, § 22.

34 *ISBE* under "Marriage."

35 Bruce, *Synoptic Gospels*, on Mt 25:1.

36 Gk *lampadas*.

37 Meyer, *Commentary on the N.T.*, on Mt 25:5. On account of Gk *exerchesthe* in v. 6.

38 See Kretzmann, *Popular Commentary* 1:140.

39 Compare Lk 19:11–28, the parable of the ten minas. See ch. 25, § 26.

40 Gk *dynamis*.

41 Gk *ide*.

42 Gk *dynamis*.

43 Gk *chara*. Not feast, but joy. Salvation as the "joy of the Lord."

44 Gk *ide*.

45 Gk *trapezitais*. See Lk 19:23. Ch. 25, § 28.

46 Gk *ek dexiōn autou*.

47 Gk *ex euōnymōn*.

48 Gk *aiōnios*.

49 Gk *kolasis*.

50 Without strict regard to actual sequence at this place, the evangelist gives a summary of the Lord's activity of the final week. Otherwise it would seem that he is out of agreement with the two other Synoptists, as appears from Mk 13:1, 3 and Mt 24:1, 3, where we are told that Jesus had already left the temple, without apparently entering it again.—Curiously four cursive manuscripts have placed the section of the woman caught in adultery (Jn 7:53–8:11) after Lk 21:37–38 (Nestle, *Einführung*, 29).

51 It is probably of interest in this connection to make a comparison of the records of a few busy days in the life of our Lord.

The Day of the Sermon on the Mount

Matthew	Mark	Luke	
5:1–7:29	3:13–19	6:12–49	
111	6	37 verses	Total verses: 154

The Day of the Parables in Galilee

Matthew	Mark	Luke	
12:22–13:52	3:22–4:41	8:4–25	
8:18–27			
90	54	21 verses	Total verses: 165

Tuesday of Passion Week

Matthew	Mark	Luke	
21:19b–26:5	11:20–14:2	20:1–22:2	
214	96	87 verses	Total verses: 397

52 There were many references in the records to His death. At this time, we remind ourselves of the following predictions:

	Matthew	Mark	Luke	John
1. At the first cleansing of the temple				2:19–22
2. At Caesarea Philippi	16:21–23	8:31–33	9:22	
3. At the close of the Galilean ministry	17:22–23	9:31–32	9:43b–45	
4. On the final journey to Jerusalem	20:17–19	10:32–34	18:31–34	
5. Two days before the final Passover	26:1–2			
(6. Thursday night)	(26:31–32)	(14:27–28)		

53 Not in the temple, the regular meeting place of the Council in the Hall of Polished Stones, which would be closed by this time, but in the nearby palace of Caiaphas.

54 *The anointment of Jesus in the house of Simon the leper.* Here follows in the order of Matthew and Mark the anointing of Jesus at Bethany in the house of Simon the leper. The incident is probably related by the Synoptists at this point for the purpose of completing their narrative and for the reason that the base deed of Judas brought back to their minds one of the immediate motives of the betrayal, namely, Judas's resentment of what he pretended to believe was a waste of money, in connection with an incident in Bethany, of which, however, they had as yet not informed the reader. The account is now brought in parenthetically. While we try to satisfy ourselves with this explanation, we must admit that it does not remove all difficulties. Probably the anointing

did take place here. In that event, some explanation must be found for the transposition in John. For it is not Matthew and Mark, but *John* who pointed out the resentment of Judas. See ch. 26, § 5.

55 Not a meager sum, if you remember that one denarius was a day's wage for a laborer.

56 The term used is *paradidōmi*.

57 Gk *stratēgoi* (Ac 4:1).

58 Gk *estēsan*, from *histēmi*.

59 Gk *triakonta argyria*.

60 Joseph was sold for twenty pieces of silver (Gn 37:28). Compare Zec 11:12–13.

61 Bruce, *Synoptic Gospels*, on Mt 26:15.

CHAPTER 31
THURSDAY AFTERNOON TO THURSDAY NIGHT OF PASSION WEEK

1 See ch. 26, n. 3.

2 Later it became customary for no fewer than ten nor more than twenty to participate in one meal.

3 Edersheim, *Life and Times of Jesus* 2:487; *Temple*, 191. Other voluntary festive sacrifices were made, which, if the paschal lamb did not suffice, were added to it. These were called the first *chagigah*, festive sacrifice (Robinson, *Greek Harmony*, 213; Edersheim, *Life and Times of Jesus* 2:484; *Temple*, 186).

4 *War* 6:424–25.

5 Because according to Jewish interpretation of the history of creation the day belonged to the previous night. For rabbinic references, see Edersheim, *Life and Times of Jesus* 2:469, note. It is distinctly stated that the Passover began with the darkness on the fourteenth of Nisan.

6 One part wine, two parts water (Edersheim, *Temple*, 202ff. or *Life and Times of Jesus* 2:485). Even the poorest must have "at least four cups, though he were to receive the money for it from the poor-box."

7 Andrews, *Life of Our Lord*, 471; Edersheim, *Temple*, 186. It was this *chagigah*, says Edersheim, that the Jews were afraid they might be unable to eat if they contracted defilement in the judgment hall (Jn 18:28). But the term *Passover* was probably used by John to denote the whole festival, in this case the whole remaining festival, since the

eating of the paschal lamb was by this time presumably already past.

8 And other sacrifices were made (Lv 23:5–14). No distinct reference to this by the evangelists. "The day after the Sabbath," in Lv 23:11, is not the weekly Sabbath, but the day after the fifteenth of Nisan, the festival Sabbath, regardless on whatever day of the week it might fall. According to the rule, though it were a Sabbath, the grain was cut down on the evening before, Friday evening, the 15th, though the Sabbath had actually begun (Edersheim, *Temple*, 221ff.).

9 Edersheim, *Temple*, 225.

10 Edersheim, *Life and Times of Jesus* 2:480.

11 Bruce, *Synoptic Gospels*, on Mt 26:18; and others.

12 A traveler and his friend were walking in Nazareth towards the Virgin's Fountain several years ago, when suddenly the friend, who had been a resident in Palestine for over thirty years, exclaimed: "See that man. He is carrying a water jar. Only once have I seen that done as long as I am living in Palestine." A photograph was taken on the occasion and included in Basil Mathew's *Life of Jesus* opposite p. 416. See p. 413.

13 *Anagaion* or *anōgeon* = *ana-gaia*, *gē* = above the earth.

14 *Estrōmenon*, from *strōnnyō*, furnished; not paved. See Schirlitz, *Wörterbuch*.

15 There is a tradition, of little importance, however, and of questionable reliability, that John was a priest and wore the sacerdotal plate (Eusebius, *NPNF2* 1:242).

16 The traditional site of the Upper Room where the paschal supper was eaten—the *Coenaculum*—is on the southwestern hill of Jerusalem, generally known as Mount Zion, near the traditional house of Caiaphas. It is a room in a mosque known as Neby Daud. It was early held that the apostles were assembled in the same room at Pentecost when the Holy Spirit descended upon them (Ac 1:13; 2:1). For traditional claims, see Andrews, *Life of Our Lord*, 498.

17 Detailed descriptions are found in Edersheim, *Life and Times of Jesus* 2:496ff.; *Temple*, 204ff.; Ylvisaker, *Gospels*, 648ff.; Farrar, *Life of Christ* 2:290ff; Andrews, *Life of Our Lord*, 484.

18 Ch. 7.

19 Ch. 8.

20 Ch. 16.

21 Namely, again, after this meal, from henceforth, until—Lk 22:18, compared with Mt 26:29. Not to be taken as an absolute refusal on the part of Jesus to partake of wine. This is a gratuitous implication on the part of Meyer (*Commentary on the N.T.* on Lk 22:18). The drinking of wine was an essential part of the Jewish Passover Feast.

22 Farrar, *Life of Christ* 2:278.

23 Called *triclinia*, couches for three. But sometimes used for four or five.

24 Davis, *Dictionary of the Bible.*

25 Edersheim, *Life and Times of Jesus* 2:207.

26 Mt 26:25, compared with Jn 13:24, 29.

27 Probably more by signs than words, like Zechariah in Lk 1:22, *dianeuōn.*

28 Of course, there is no certainty in the matter. Our only interest is in helping picture the scene. For details, see Edersheim, *Life and Times of Jesus* 2:493ff., compared with p. 207ff. and other writers. Farrar, *Life of Christ* 2:278; Andrews, *Life of Our Lord*, 485–86; *ISBE* under "Meals"; likewise the article under "Meals" in Davis, *Bible Dictionary.*

29 Luke places the reference to the traitor and the disciples' dispute about rank after the institution of the Lord's Supper. But it seems that he does not insist upon strict chronological order in this place. Possibly for the purpose of completing his account, he brings in both incidents before passing on, without, however, claiming that his order must be followed against the order of Matthew and Mark as compared with John. We are reminded of the circumstance that Luke at other times completes his account of logically related subjects, even though the chronology may be disturbed; for instance, in Lk 1, vv. 65 and 66 belong after v. 79; in Lk 5, vv. 1 to 11 probably belong after 4:31, as compared with Matthew and Mark. See also the question: "Did Judas receive Holy Communion?" in this chapter, § 14, n. 38.

30 Lk 9:46, after the Transfiguration; Mt 20:25–28 and Mk 10:42–45, after the request of James and John to sit at the right and left in the kingdom of Jesus.

31 For instance, Ptolemy Euergetes of Egypt and others (Deissmann, *Licht vom Osten*, 215).

A Syrian coin has been found, issued by King Antiochus VII (138–127 BC), with the inscription: (Money of the) King Antiochus Euergetes (Williamson, *Money of the Bible*, 33).

32 The defection of Judas not taken into account (Mt 19:28).

33 *Did Christ eat the Passover?* Matthew, Mark, and Luke clearly claim Jesus' Last Supper was the Passover (Mt 26:19; Mk 14:16; Lk 22:15), while the Gospel of John only refers to it as the "supper" or "evening meal" (Jn 13:2). John only uses the word *Passover* in connection with the Jewish leaders, who on Friday morning "did not enter the governor's headquarters, so that they would not be defiled, but could eat the Passover" (Jn 18:28). Critics claim a contradiction between the Synoptic Gospels, which have the Passover meal proper on Thursday evening, and the Gospel of John, which has it Friday evening. But John's reference to the Passover is ambiguous because it could apply either to the Passover meal proper, or to the broader Passover and the Festival of Unleavened Bread, which lasted eight days. If John was referring to the broader Passover and Festival of Unleavened Bread, then the chief priests had already eaten the Passover meal Thursday night, but still wanted to be ceremonially clean to continue with the week-long festival Friday night. But if John meant the chief priests were eating the Passover meal proper Friday evening, the solution is that different groups of Jews observed different calendars at this time, so Jesus may have kept a different feast day from that kept at the temple by the priests.—For a detailed discussion of the problem, see: Robertson, *Harmony of the Gospels*, 279ff.; Robinson, *Greek Harmony*, 241ff.; Andrews, *The Life of Our Lord*, 461ff.; Ylvisaker, *Gospels*, 637ff.; Wieseler, *Chronological Synopsis*, 208ff., 363ff.

34 Gk *deipnou genomenou*, not "after supper." Compare vv. 4 and 12. "Supper having arrived," not, "Supper being ended." If we read *ginomenou*, the meaning is substantially the same; "supper arriving," at "supper time." See Dods, *Gospel of St. John*, on Jn 13:2.

35 The view of Chrysostom, as quoted by Andrews, *Life of Our Lord*, 483, and Meyer, *Commentary on the N.T.*, on Jn 13:5.

36 We have already pointed out (ch. 6, § 20, n. 59) that the double *amēn*, truly, does not occur in other parts of the New Testament; but in John we find it twenty-five times, and only as spoken by Jesus.

37 Compare Mt 10:24; Lk 6:40.

38 *Did Judas receive Holy Communion?* That depends upon when the identity of the betrayer was revealed and whether or not the order of Luke is to be adopted. According to Matthew and Mark, the traitor was revealed during the Passover meal and before the institution of Holy Communion. According to John, who does not mention the Lord's Supper, it was during the meal that we believe to have been the Passover supper. Jerome, Augustine, Chrysostom, Quenstedt, and others believe that the disclosure was made after the words of the institution were spoken and that Judas therefore took part in the first Communion service. The Formula of Concord likewise seems to support this view (FC SD VII 33, 60). But the opposite view is held by many scholars: McKnight, Meyer, Tischendorf, Robinson, Robertson, Ebrard, Wieseler, Edersheim, and others. See Stöckhardt, *Biblische Geschichte*, 265. Our arrangement is not prompted by doctrinal interests. Whether or not Judas received the Lord's Supper, the doctrine concerning this Sacrament remains the same. The argument of St. Paul stands that such as are known to be unworthy communicants should not be permitted to partake of Holy Communion (1Co 11:28–29). But suppose that Jesus, though knowing all things, nevertheless permitted an unworthy communicant to partake of the very first Communion; our argument is that He did so, (1) because He would not pass public judgment upon Judas as long as his sin was generally unknown; (2) because the betrayal, while fully decided upon by Judas, had not yet been actually committed. Ministers of the Gospel, therefore, who do not know the hearts, must content themselves with what seems to make it evident that the person whom they admit to the Sacrament is a worthy communicant. In endeavoring to bring Luke into agreement with Matthew and Mark and also with John, we are prompted by the considerations that Luke does not insist upon strict

chronological sequence of his particular arrangement and that at other places, he has permitted strict chronology to be disturbed by the connection of incidents that were logically joined, cf. § 9 above. See Stöckhardt, *Biblische Geschichte*, 265; Ylvisaker, *Gospels*, 654ff.; Andrews, *Life of Our Lord*, 493.

39 Probably Ahithophel (Ps 41:9, compared with 2Sm 15:12, 31, 34, etc.) (Farrar, *Life of Christ* 2:285).

40 Edersheim, *Life and Times of Jesus* 2:506; Bruce, *Synoptic Gospels*, on Mt 26:23.

41 In Matthew and Mark, the term refers to the dish; in John, to the contents.

42 Matthew.

43 Not to make preparation for the Passover supper, which was now past. See § 3 above. The second *chagigah*.

44 The expression is frequent in 1 John; in John's Gospel only here (Dods, *Gospel of St. John*, on Jn 13:33).

45 Paul and Luke: *meta to deipnēsai.*

46 Gk *parelabon apo tou kyriou.*

47 1Co 10:16: *potērion tēs eulogias.*

48 Compare Mt 26:30; Mk 14:26. Findlay under 1Co 10:16 in Nicoll, *Expositor's Greek Testament;* Meyer, *Commentary on the N.T.*, on Mt 26:27. The third cup was technically called "the cup of blessing" from the standpoint of the Jewish ritual, but from the Christian standpoint, probably the fourth cup would be meant.

49 Gk *kainē diathēkē.*

50 After the eating of the Passover lamb, no one was at liberty in that night to eat anything more (Meyer, *Commentary on the N.T.*, on Mt 26:26).

51 Gk *artos.*

52 Gk *eulogēsas* (Matthew and Mark); *eucharistēsas* (Luke and St. Paul). The name *Eucharist* clings to the Holy Supper due to the expression "when He had given thanks," as *Eucharist* means "giving of thanks" in Greek.

53 Kretzmann, *Popular Commentary,* or Meyer, *Commentary on the N.T.*, on Mt 26:26.

54 It is not correct to make the "breaking of bread" an essential aspect of the observance of the Lord's Supper. In fact, historically, it was the Calvinists who made a point of breaking the bread to indicate that it is *not* the body of Christ. From that

point forward, Lutherans were careful to avoid physically breaking the bread in order to make clear that we do confess the actual presence of Christ under the eucharistic bread.

55 Gk *dabete, phagete.*

56 Gk *estin.*

57 Meyer, *Commentary on the N.T.*, on Mt 26:27.

58 Gk *potērion.*

59 There should be nothing substituted for wine. It matters not if the wine is red or white or a certain vintage or alcohol content, but it must be actual wine, nothing else. We dare not interject doubt when there should be nothing but certainty about what is being received in the Lord's Supper. It should also go without saying that it is sacrilege and a great act of disobedience to substitute elements for the bread and wine of the Supper. Such actions, such as using Kool-Aid and potato chips or something equally absurd, is a sin against our Lord's institution.

60 Gk *to peri pollōn ekchynomenon eis aphesin hamartiōn.*

61 Gk *hyper hymōn.*

62 Gk *peri pollōn ekchynomenon.*

63 Every-Sunday Communion is the norm set forth in the Confessions of the Lutheran Church. Less frequent offering of the Lord's Supper was an unfortunate historical development in the Lutheran Church, but in more recent decades, there has been an increasing return to the practice of every-Sunday Communion.

64 Gk *ek tou gennēmatos tou ampelou.* Technical name for the Passover cup.

65 Here follows in the order of Luke: the traitor being revealed (Lk 22:21–23) and the contention of the disciples (Lk 22:24–30). A strict chronological order does not seem to have been intended by Luke at this place. See §§ 9–10 and 14.

Chapter 32
Thursday Night of Passion Week— Farewell Discourses

1 Probably Ps 136.

2 Variously placed by the different harmonists. The order we have followed is prompted by the desire to avoid wherever possible all transpositions. In this place, we notice that Robertson, who consistently follows the order of Mark in his *Harmony of the Gospels,* so as even to give him first place in the parallel columns, for the first time allows a transposition in the Gospel of Mark.

3 See ch. 30, § 20.

4 Dods, *Gospel of St. John,* on Jn 13:36.

5 Bruce, *Synoptic Gospels,* on Mt 26:33.

6 Plural in Gk, *exēitēsato hymas.*

7 Mark gives the more exact wording as coming probably from Peter himself. The warning may have been repeated in the conversation as reported by the other evangelists. "Before the rooster crows" (Gk *prin alektora phōnēsai*) of Matthew may also be taken as a watch of the night. Compare Mk 13:35. Roosters are not mentioned in the Old Testament. The fowl was probably introduced into Palestine after the exile, likely from Babylon. Even if the fowl was not permitted to be kept in Jerusalem on account of possible Levitical defilement, the prohibition would not have applied to the Romans occupying the nearby judgment hall of Pilate and Fort Antonia in the temple complex. See Edersheim, *Life and Times of Jesus* 2:537 n. 1; Bruce, *Synoptic Gospels,* on Mt 26:34.

8 Bruce, *Synoptic Gospels,* on Lk 22:36.

9 Edersheim, *Life and Times of Jesus* 2:536.

10 Edersheim, *Life and Times of Jesus* 2:537.

11 Bruce, *Synoptic Gospels,* on Lk 22:38.

12 Kretzmann, *Popular Commentary* 1:489.

13 See Dods, *Gospel of St. John,* on Jn 14:8.

14 Kretzmann, *Popular Commentary* 1:490.

15 Gk *paraklētos.*

16 See ch. 11, § 14.

17 Persecutions for the "name," *nomen ipsum,* in the Roman Empire. See Hardy, *Christianity and the Roman Government,* 87.

18 Gk *dia to onoma mou.*

19 "Their Law" is here, as in 10:34, used of the Old Testament Scriptures as a whole. Not a direct quotation; but similar expressions are found in Ps 69:4 and 35:19 (Dods, *Gospel of St. John,* on Jn 15:25).

20 Gk *aposynagōgos genētai* (Jn 9:22; 12:42).

21 By David Chytraeus (Ylvisaker, *Gospels,* 687).

22 See Meyer *Commentary on the N.T.*, on Jn 14:31; 15:1.

23 Dods, *Gospel of St. John*, on Jn 14:30.

24 Edersheim, *Life and Times of Jesus* 2:511.

25 Meyer, quoting Luther, *Commentary on the N.T.*, on Jn 17:25–26.

26 Meyer, *Commentary on the N.T.*, on Jn 17:25–26.

27 Kretzmann, *Popular Commentary* 1:503.

28 We notice that Jesus here solemnly in the third person speaks of Himself as Jesus Christ, the promised Messiah. See Mk 9:41.

29 Ch. 31, § 13.

30 Gk *hyios tēs apōleias*. The form "son of destruction" is in accordance with Hebrew usage. Compare 2Th 2:3; Is 57:4; Mt 23:15.

31 Gk *ek tou ponērou*. "Evil" may be neuter or masculine in the sense of "the evil one" (1Jn 2:13; or Mt 6:13).

32 Farrar, *Life of Christ* 2:304.

CHAPTER 33
THURSDAY NIGHT TO FRIDAY MORNING OF PASSION WEEK

1 Matthew and Mark narrate the Lord's announcement of Peter's denial as if it had taken place after they had left the Upper Room and were on their way to the Mount of Olives; Luke and John, as taking place before they had left the room. For our arrangement, see ch. 32, §§ 1, 12. John does not mention Jesus' agony in Gethsemane. It is, however, implied in the reference to the cup that the Father had given Him to drink (Jn 18:11), compared with the prayer to remove the cup recorded by the Synoptists in the present section.

2 At other times, the brook over which David had fled before Absalom (2Sm 15:23) was only a dry ravine, but at this time of the year, it was filled with water, *tou cheimarrou tou Kedrōn* (Jn 18:1). (The meaning of the term for brook is "winter flowing," and the expression *Kidron* is variously explained as "of the cedars," "to become black," and "a spot for enclosure of cattle.") See Dods, *Gospel of St. John*, on Jn 18:1.

3 *ISBE* under "Gethsemane."

4 Gk *agōnia* (Lk 22:44). Here only in the New Testament. From this word comes the expression "agony in the Garden" (Bruce, *Synoptic Gospels*, on Lk 22:44).

5 As Luke alone mentions the appearing of an angel, it is not certain where this should be inserted in the accounts of Matthew and Mark. Some place it between the first and second prayer, believing that the angel came at this juncture to strengthen Him for that still more terrible struggle, when He was sweating great drops of blood. Others think the death agony and the sweating of blood took place before the appearance of the angel, indeed, that he was sent by the Father after this culmination of the Lord's soul-suffering had been reached, although narrated after it. The latter would not have been contrary to the practice of Luke, as may be seen from other sections of his Gospel. See ch. 31, § 8 and Andrews, *Life of Our Lord*, 502.

6 *ISBE* under "Sweat" and Edersheim, *Life and Times of Jesus* 2:540 n. 3. Vv. 43–44 are missing in some codices. Gk *ho hidrōs autou hōsei thromboi haimatos*. *Thromboi*, clots, not drops, of blood. Here only in the New Testament. A lump, or curd, of blood. Nowhere else used in the sense of drops. But the disciples may have seen this mark of agony as clots of blood on His forehead or on the ground.

7 Ylvisaker, *Gospels*, 698.

8 As inferred from Luke, who does not mention the three.

9 Not ironically or sarcastically, hardly interrogatively. See Bruce, *Synoptic Gospels*, on Mt 26:45.

10 One of those puzzling expressions of Mark for which many explanations are given (Bruce, *Synoptic Gospels*, on Mt 26:45). *Apechei* (Gk), *sufficit*. "I have conquered in the struggle. I no longer need your sympathy," etc.

11 Gk *labōn tēn speiran* (Jn 18:3). Cohort, a tenth of a legion, about 600 men. Under the command of a *chiliarchos* (Gk), captain, or master of a thousand (Jn 18:12). See *TLSB* note on Jn 18:3.

12 The servants of the high priests, led by the officers of the temple, *stratēgous tou hierou* (Lk 22:52). They had no independent criminal jurisdiction outside the temple area. The Council, not possessing the power of the sword, had of course neither soldiers nor a regularly armed band at command (Edersheim, *Life and Times of Jesus* 2:541). However, see Schürer, *Jewish People*

2.1:187: "Possessed the right of ordering and making arrests."

13 *War* 2:176.

14 Especially regarding whether John's account fits before or after the kiss as recorded by the Synoptists.

15 Gk *asphalōs* (Mk 14:44). The ESV translates this as "under guard."

16 Farrar, *Life of Christ* 2:319 n. 1.

17 Gk *katephilēsen*.

18 Gk *hetaire, eph' hoi* or *ho parei*. The KJV translates this phrase as a question: "Wherefore are thou come?" See commentaries on Mt 26:50.

19 Farrar, *Life of Christ* 2:322.

20 Gk *eate heōs toutou*.

21 Farrar, *Life of Christ* 2:324.

22 *War* 7:253–62.

23 Bruce, *Synoptic Gospels*, on Mt 26:56.

24 Bruce, *Synoptic Gospels*, on Mk 14:52.

25 Gk *sindōn*.

26 The Jewish trial consisted of three stages: the preliminary examination by Annas, the informal trial by the Council, and the formal trial after dawn. With these are related Peter's denials of Jesus and the suicide of Judas. Each of the four Gospels records Peter's denials, but the details differ considerably, as must be the case where various reports point out certain features and pass over the rest. Of these three stages of the trial, John apparently gives the first stage, Matthew and Mark give the second stage fully and mention the third only briefly, while Luke mentions the last part of the Jewish trial.—Between vv. 14 and 19 and following v. 24, John records Peter's denial of Jesus. Likewise, the other three evangelists insert the incident into their account, Matthew and Mark as running through the second stage of the trial and Luke as preceding that of the final session. In separating the trials and throwing together the denials, we are following the lead of the Gospels in an attempt to give a combined arrangement of the progress of events. We must, however, confess our inability to arrange exactly all circumstances into a complete program. See Robertson, *Harmony of the Gospels*, notes on pp. 209 and 212.

27 Farrar, *Life of Christ* 2:328.

28 *Ant* 18:55; *War* 2:171, etc.

29 *War* 2:301, 328.

30 Stalker, *Trial and Death of Jesus*, 16.

31 On the Council and the high priests, see Schürer, *Jewish People* 2.1:163ff.

32 Annas, AD 6–15; Eleazer (son), AD 16–17; Caiaphas (son-in-law), AD 18–36; Jonathan (son), AD 36–37; Theophilos (son), AD 37; Matthias (son), AD 41; Annas (son), AD 62 (Schürer, *Jewish People* 2.1:198ff.).

33 Farrar, *Life of Christ* 2:329.

34 *Ant* 20:250.

35 *Ant* 20:199.

36 Stalker, *Life of Jesus Christ*, 18.

37 Klausner, a Jewish writer from Jerusalem (*Jesus of Nazareth*, 337).

38 Farrar, *Life of Christ* 2:335.

39 Farrar, *Life of Christ* 2:335.

40 At first, the chief priests thought they would have to wait until the crowds left Jerusalem after the feast to kill Jesus (Mk 14:2).

41 Stalker, *Life of Jesus Christ*, 19.

42 Farrar, *Life of Christ* 2:336.

43 The account interspaced with Peter's denials of Jesus.

44 The regular place of meeting was the Hall Gazith, the Hall of Hewn Stones, in the temple buildings. We must regard this meeting in the palace of Caiaphas as an exception to the rule. For meetings of the Council, see Schürer, *Jewish People* 2.1:190ff.; Edersheim, *Life and Times of Jesus* 2:553ff.; Stalker, *Trial and Death of Jesus*, 20ff.

45 Farrar, *Life of Christ* 2:340.

46 Gk *sy eipas* = *Egō eimi*, I am, in current usage.

47 See Ps 110:1; Dn 7:13.

48 Stalker, *Life of Jesus Christ*, 25.

49 As may be seen from 2Ki 18:37, the tearing of garments indicated an unusual provocation, especially upon hearing a blasphemy uttered. The Mosaic Law forbade the high priest from tearing his robes (Lv 10:6; cf. also 21:10).

50 See Lv 24:15; Dt 18:20. Death was the penalty for blasphemy and for a false prophet (Bruce, *Synoptic Gospels*, on Mt 26:66).

51 For arrangement, see § 10 n. 26.

52 Stalker, *Life of Jesus Christ*, 32.

53 The view of Nonnus, an Egyptian scholar, writing about AD 400. He wrote a paraphrase on the Gospel of John (Mathews, *Life of Jesus*, 447).

54 Farrar, *Life of Christ* 2:347.

55 Stalker, *Life of Jesus Christ*, 37.

56 Farrar, *Life of Christ* 2:348.

57 Making ש sound like ת (Meyer, *Commentary on the N.T.*, on Mt 26:73). Something on the order of saying *share* for *chair* and *ting* for *thing*.

58 Stalker, *Life of Jesus Christ*, 38.

59 Gk *kyrios* in narrative. Thus in many places in Luke.

60 Farrar, *Life of Christ* 2:349.

61 Gk *epibalōn*. Another one of those puzzling words in Mark's vocabulary. The choice is between "thinking upon it" or "covering his head and flinging himself out" (Bruce, *Synoptic Gospels*, on Mk 14:72). We prefer the latter.

62 Farrar, *Life of Christ* 2:350.

63 Lange, quoted by Farrar, *Life of Christ* 2:350.

64 The account of Matthew and Mark was interrupted by the narration of Peter's denials.

65 Schürer, *Jewish People* 2.1:194.

66 Stalker, *Life of Jesus Christ*, 30.

67 The last phrase of the *textus receptus*, "nor let Me go," is omitted in leading codices.

68 Schürer, *Jewish People* 2.1:194.

69 If he was absent from the meeting, as some think, then Mk 14:64, "They all condemned Him as deserving death," is to be interpreted as "all those present."

CHAPTER 34
FRIDAY OF PASSION WEEK—
"SUFFERED UNDER PONTIUS PILATE"

1   *Ant* 18:55; *War* 2:171.

2   Farrar, *Life of Christ* 2:364.

3   *War* 2:301, 328; Edersheim, *Life and Times of Jesus* 2:566.

4   *War* 1:401; 5:173.

5   Gk *metamelētheis*, from *metamelomai*. Used in Mt 21:29, 32; 2Co 7:8; Heb 7:21. The usual word for repent in the scriptural sense is *metanoeō* (Edersheim, *Life and Times of Jesus* 2:573).

6   Edersheim, *Life and Times of Jesus* 2:574.

7   Gk *naos*. Bruce, *Synoptic Gospels*, and Meyer, *Commentary on the N.T.*, on Mt 27:5.

8   According to tradition, to the south of Jerusalem, somewhat to the west, and above where the Kidron and Hinnom valleys merge (Edersheim,

Life and Times of Jesus 2:577; Andrews, *Life of Our Lord*, 526).

9   An extension of Dt 23:18. See Bruce, *Synoptic Gospels*, on Mt 27:6. A disturbance was caused in Jerusalem because Pilate expended "that sacred treasure which is called corban upon aqueducts" (*War* 2:175).

10 Matthew does not name Zechariah, though he quotes him three times: 21:5; 26:31; 27:9. But it was a common saying among the Jews that Zechariah had the spirit of Jeremiah (Farrar, *Life of Christ* 2:359 n. 1). "Ridderwold believes that the prophecy of Zechariah refers to a prophecy in Jeremiah 19, and that, because the prophecy in Zechariah is fully understood only by the light shed upon it in Jeremiah 1:9, therefore Matthew says that the words are from Jeremiah, although they are found in Zechariah" (Ylvisaker, *Gospels*, 720).

11 Most likely the royal palace of Herod the Great, which by this time had become state property. It occupied the highest part of the southwest hill, near the northwest angle of the ancient city, now traditionally called Zion. It is needless to point out how greatly this view of the site of the praetorium must modify the traditional claims of the Via Dolorosa, the whole course of which depends on the theory that the praetorium is identified with Castle Antonia, located on the northwestern corner of the temple complex (Edersheim, *Life and Times of Jesus* 2:566; Farrar, *Life of Christ*, ch. 60). See "Praetorium" in *ISBE*.

12 The phrase "eat the Passover" is to be understood as referring to the observation of the whole festival or to the sacrifices of this particular day, the second *chagigah*, and not to the Passover meal itself, which, as we have seen, was already eaten the evening before. See ch. 31, §§ 3, 11, and references.

13 Stalker, *Life of Jesus Christ*, 50.

14 Farrar, *Life of Christ* 2:367.

15 Cf. *War* 2:117.

16 Ch. 33, § 4.

17 Stalker, *Life of Jesus Christ*, 53.

18 Farrar, *Life of Christ* 2:370.

19 *War* 2:169–74; *Ant* 18:55–59.

20 Stalker, *Life of Jesus Christ*, 63.

21 Stalker, *Life of Jesus Christ*, 63.

22 *War* 2:344. See "Praetorium" in *ISBE*.
23 See also chs. 4 and 15.
24 Stalker, *Life of Jesus Christ*, 66.
25 Edersheim, *Life and Times of Jesus* 1:674.
26 Edersheim, *Life and Times of Jesus* 1:674.
27 Stalker, *Life of Jesus Christ*, 67.
28 Stalker, *Life of Jesus Christ*, 76.
29 Stalker, *Life of Jesus Christ*, 77.
30 Stalker, *Life of Jesus Christ*, 77.
31 Stalker, *Life of Jesus Christ*, 82.
32 Literally, son of the father. The Syriac variant with double *r* (Barrabban) would mean son of a Rabbi. Jerome, in his commentary on Matthew, says that in the Hebrew Gospel, the word was interpreted *filius magistti eotum*. Origen mentions that in some manuscripts, this man bore the name of Jesus Barabbas, which makes the contrast of character all the more striking. See commentaries under Mt 27:16.
33 Stalker, *Life of Jesus Christ*, 85.
34 The name given to her by tradition. Claudia Procula, or Procla, is said to have been a Jewish proselyte at the time of Jesus' death and afterward to have become a Christian. Her name is honored along with Pilate's in the Coptic Church, and in the calendar of saints honored by the Greek Church her name is found on the date of October 27. See *ISBE* under "Pilate."
35 Stalker, *Life of Jesus Christ*, 81.
36 That the gable of their house fell and that her husband was stabbed in her arms (Suetonius, *Iulius*, LXXXI).
37 Farrar, *Life of Christ* 2:378.
38 Stalker, *Life of Jesus Christ*, 87.

39 Our arrangement in bringing this incident at this point (following Stalker, Cadman, Kerr, Edersheim, Stevens and Burton, Robinson, Davis, and others) rather than at the usual dramatic close is prompted by the desire to follow the natural order of the combined account (without transposition) and to avoid the arrangement that would presumably have Jesus scourged twice: Jn 19:1, followed by vv. 2–15 in John, as compared with the arrangement that would make Mt 27:26 and Mk 15:15 follow Jn 19:15. Our arrangement follows this natural order:

Mt 27:24–25			
Mt 27:26	Mk 15:15	Lk 23:24–25	
Mt 27:26	Mk 15:15		Jn 19:1
Mt 27:27–31a	Mk 15:16–20a		Jn 19:2–3
			Jn 19:4–15
Mt 27:31b	Mk 15:20b	Lk 23:26a	Jn 19:16

40 Reminding us of the rite prescribed in Dt 21:6–9 of marking the freedom from guilt of the elders of a city where untracked murder had been committed. The expression is Jewish (2Sm 3:28; Ps 26:6; 73:13). Pilate may have known of the custom, although we find allusions to some such custom also among the Gentiles; but it was all the more forceful as appealing to the Jews. See Edersheim, *Life and Times of Jesus* 2:578.
41 Stalker, *Life of Jesus Christ*, 87.
42 Gk *phragellōsas*, Matthew and Mark. A Latinism from *flagello*. John: *emastigōsen*. The same term used by Josephus in *War* 5:449 (Bruce, *Synoptic Gospels*, on Mt 27:26).
43 Farrar, *Life of Christ* 2:379.
44 As to the beating, or whipping, of a culprit sanctioned by the Mosaic Law, see Dt 25:2–3; 2Co 11:24.
45 For a horribly realistic picture, see Eusebius, *NPNF*2 1:189.
46 Gk *speira*, at most a cohort of 600 men. At Passover time, a large guard would be at hand (Bruce, *Synoptic Gospels*, on Mt 27:27).
47 Stalker, *Life of Jesus Christ*, 92.
48 Farrar, *Life of Christ* 2:387.

49 Matthew, "scarlet"; Mark and John, "purple." Probably the color was actually scarlet, but the purpose of the mockery was to convey the idea of purple.

50 As regards the particular species of thorn, nothing definite is known.

51 *Qaneh* (Hbr)—*kalamos* (Gk), *canna,* cane. Probably a reed or cane walking stick (Is 36:6).

52 Stalker, *Life of Jesus Christ*, 93.

53 Farrar, *Life of Christ* 2:382.

54 Stalker, *Life of Jesus Christ*, 103.

55 Farrar, *Life of Christ* 2:383.

56 Referring probably to Lv 24:16.

57 Before Caiaphas (Mt 26:63; Mk 14:61); before Pilate (Mt 27:12; Mk 15:4–5); before Herod (Lk 23:9); and here (Jn 19:9).

58 Stalker, *Life of Jesus Christ*, 106.

59 Farrar, *Life of Christ* 2:385.

60 At the beginning of the trial, after the return of Jesus from Herod, and now.

61 "Now it was the day of Preparation of the Passover." The term *preparation* (Gk *paraskeuē*) was the usual designation of Friday, the day of preparation for the weekly Sabbath. Here the addition of "the Passover" indicates that it was the Friday of Passover Week. Compare Mt 27:62; Mk 15:42; Lk 23:54; Jn 19:31, 42. "Preparation" is still the name for Friday in modern Greek. As regards the question of the day, see ch. 31, § 11. The time is given as "about the sixth hour." It appears that John, who wrote in Asia Minor after the destruction of Jerusalem, makes the day begin at midnight, as the Greeks and Romans did. In the language of the Roman court, it was about 6 a.m., the time set for the beginning of the trial. Mark, who used Jewish reckoning (which makes the day start at dawn [about 6 a.m.]), says that it was the third hour when they crucified Him (Mk 15:25). Thus, according to Jewish time, the crucifixion took place about 9 a.m. (For a full discussion, see Steinmann, *From Abraham to Paul*, 293–96; Andrews, *Life of Our Lord*, 545ff.) We might add that the reading *tritē* for *hektē*, third for sixth hour, is found in some manuscripts. See Nestle, *Einführung*, 2.

CHAPTER 35
FRIDAY OF PASSION WEEK—"CRUCIFIED"

1 Edersheim, *Life and Times of Jesus* 2:582.

2 Andrews, *Life of Our Lord*, 543.

3 Stalker, *Life of Jesus Christ*, 131.

4 In this case, it was a man whom tradition remembers by the name of Longinus (Andrews, *Life of Our Lord*, 562). Becoming a believer, he was afterward said to have been the bishop of Cappadocia.

5 Andrews, *Life of Our Lord*, 550.

6 At any rate, it was not, and could not have been, the massive and lofty structure of considerable weight with which thousands of pictures have made us familiar (Farrar, *Life of Christ* 2:393). We also need not enter into the intrinsically improbable story of the discovery of the true cross by Helena, the mother of Constantine, in AD 325, related by the Early Church historians: Socrates 1:17; Sozomenus 2:1; Rufinus 1:7; and Theodoret 1:18. It is very significant that Eusebius, whose writings carry more weight than those of the above-named together, omits the story in his *Life of Constantine* 3:26–28 (*NPNF*2 1:527–28). It is apparently "but a version of the old Edessa legend, which tells of an identical discovery of the cross, under the very same circumstances, by the wife of the emperor Claudius, who had been converted to Christianity by the preaching of Peter" (*ISBE* under "Cross").

7 Stalker, *Life of Jesus Christ*, 132.

8 For the various arguments, see Wilson, *In Scripture Lands*, 223ff.; Andrews, *Life of Our Lord*, 575ff.; and *ISBE* under "Golgotha."

9 The story of Ahasuerus, the Wandering Jew, doomed to wander until the second coming of Christ because he taunted Jesus as He leaned against his door when passing it, bearing the cross. According to the legend, he struck Jesus and commanded Him to go on, to which the Lord replied, "I go, but thou shalt wait till I return" (Stalker, *Life of Jesus Christ*, 143).

10 See Mk 15:22: "They brought Him." Gk *pherousin auton*, carry Him.

11 Compare Ac 2:10.

12 These names are too common to enable us to identify them with those of the same name in Ac 19:33; 1Tm 1:20; Rm 16:13.

13   Stalker, *Life of Jesus Christ*, 147.

14   A close examination will reveal a few apparent discrepancies in the order of events; but there are no contradictions.

15   Mark says *pherousin* (Gk), as if Jesus were half carried to the cross.

16   The thieves in the time of Felix. The Zealots, the so-called *Sicarii*, who committed murder daily in broad daylight with their short, curved daggers, especially in the festival seasons, from the time of Nero onward to the end of the last Jewish war (*War* 2:253–57).

17   First mentioned by Origen (AD 185–254), who lived in Palestine for twenty years.

18   Edersheim, *Life and Times of Jesus* 2:590.

19   Farrar, *Life of Christ* 2:401.

20   Quoted by Stalker, *Life of Jesus Christ*, 163.

21   The passage in Mark appears in the *textus receptus* but is omitted in many manuscripts.

22   Raising what appears to be a harmonistic problem as compared with Jn 19:14, but see ch. 34, § 24, n. 61.

23   *Life*, 420–21.

24   LXX version quoted verbatim (Dods, *Gospel of St. John*, on Jn 19:24).

25   The title on the cross, based upon the text of John.

26   Not in the exact order of Matthew and Mark, but it need not disturb us in the least.

27   Edersheim, *Life and Times of Jesus* 2:594.

28   Andrews, *Life of Our Lord*, 554; Edersheim, *Life and Times of Jesus* 2:598. The names Titus and Dumachus are also found (Jones, *Apocryphal New Testament*, I, Infancy, 8:2–8).

29   *Bonus latro.*

30   The traditional text reads "in." The prayer then means: "When You come as King to earth again, may I be among those whom You shall raise from the dead to share its joys!"

31   A synonym for heaven in 2Co 12:3.

32   Weiss, *Life of Christ* 1:366 n. 1; Meyer, *Commentary on the N.T.*, on Jn 19:25.

33   Lk 6:15–16 and Ac 1:13, compared with Mt 27:56; 13:55–56. See ch. 4, n. 183 and ch. 11, § 13.

34   But not to be identified with the unknown sinner of Lk 7:37. See ch. 12, §§ 9, 11.

35   This is our view. But, of course, there are others. A change in punctuation reduces the number to three women: (1) His mother; (2) His mother's sister, Mary, the wife of Clopas (This view, besides eliminating Salome, would place two Marys into one family.); (3) and Mary Magdalene. We need not go into the whole question again here. See Andrews, *Life of Our Lord*, 111ff.; Edersheim, *Life and Times of Jesus* 2:602ff.; Dods, *Gospel of St. John*, and Meyer, *Commentary on the N.T.*, on Jn 19:24. For Joseph and Mary, Alphaeus and Mary, Zebedee and Salome, relation and family, see ch. 4, § 43. For James, Judas, and Simon, see ch. 11, § 13.

36   In Greek not a term of disrespect.

37   Gk *eis ta idia* does not necessarily mean that John had a house in Jerusalem.

38   Luke introduces the rending of the veil in the temple at this point (v. 45b), which, however, probably occurred later. The arrangement of this section seems to be as follows:

The darkness	Matthew	Mark	Luke	
"Eli, Eli"	Matthew	Mark		
"I thirst"				John
"It is finished"				John
A loud cry	Matthew	Mark	Luke	
"Father, into Your hands"			Luke	

39 "A solar eclipse is astronomically possible only at the new moon, not during a full moon as is always the case at Passover" (Ware, *When Was Jesus Really Born?*, 78). For that reason, an eclipse mentioned by Phlegon in the 202d Olympiad (AD 29–32) is out of the question (Wieseler, *Synopsis*, 353ff.).

40 Gk *skotos*.

41 Gk *tou hēliou eklipontos*, a well-attested reading in Lk 23:45 (Bruce, *Synoptic Gospels*, on Lk 23:45).

42 This is the first reference in Matthew to the time of day (Bruce, *Synoptic Gospels*, on Mt 27:45).

43 Farrar, *Life of Christ* 2:414.

44 Edersheim, *Life and Times of Jesus* 2:605.

45 Farrar, *Life of Christ* 2:417.

46 The plant has not been definitely identified (Dods, *Gospel of St. John*, on Jn 19:29).

47 "God from the machine." In ancient Greek plays, an actor playing a god was lowered onto stage using a cable device (the machine). The god miraculously entered the scene and radically changed the course of the play. This phrase refers to a drastic and unforeseen divine intervention that alters the expected outcome.

48 Still, impiously and contrary to the word of Christ, "I lay down My life. . . . I lay it down of My own accord" (Jn 10:17–18), some writers state that Jesus died of a ruptured heart. See Bruce, *Synoptic Gospels*, on Mt 27:50.

49 In the language of an early Christian hymn. Quoted by Edersheim, *Life and Times of Jesus* 2:609.

Chapter 36
Friday of Passion Week—
"Dead and Buried"

1 The rending of the veil is introduced by Luke in connection with the darkness.

2 Edersheim, *Life and Times of Jesus* 2:616.

3 Ylvisaker, *Gospels*, 752; Edersheim, *Life and Times of Jesus* 2:610.

4 Gk *meta tēn egersin autou*. The only place in the New Testament where the term *egersis* is used. Active rising of Christ. The usual word is *anastasis*. See Bruce, *Synoptic Gospels*, on Mt 27:53.

5 Meyer, *Commentary on the N.T.*, on Mt 4:5.

6 Andrews, *Life of Our Lord*, 562. Tradition has it that he later became bishop of Cappadocia (*Life of Our Lord*, 562 n. 4; Stalker, *Life of Jesus Christ*, 293).

7 Luke.

8 Matthew and Mark.

9 See ch. 11, § 13. Of this Joses, nothing further is known. His name appears among the "brothers" of Jesus (Mk 6:3 and Mt 13:55 in the KJV).

10 See ch. 31, § 3.

11 Edersheim, *Life and Times of Jesus* 2:613.

12 For the various views, see Andrews, *Life of Our Lord*, 567ff.

13 Ylvisaker, *Gospels*, 754.

14 The incident of the water and the blood is also brought into connection with the disputed passage of the three witnesses in 1Jn 5:6–8. To the witness of the Spirit there is added the witness of the water and the blood.

15 Some identify it with Ramathaim-zophim, the Ramah of Ephraim and the birth- and burial-place of Samuel (1Sm 1:1, 19; 25:1); others, with, it seems, greater likelihood, identify it with the Ramah in Benjamin, a few miles north of Jerusalem, which for a time belonged to Samaria, but later was joined to the province of Judah (1Macc 10:38; 11:28, 34). Hence "a city of the Jews."

16 The Gospel of St. Peter. Legends of a later origin claim that Joseph was sent by the apostle Philip from Gaul to Britain in AD 63 and that he built an oratory at Glastonbury, brought the Holy Grail to England, and freed Ireland from snakes (*ISBE* under "Joseph of Arimathea").

17 See ch. 7, § 5.

18 Gk has "one hundred litras." A *litra* (or Roman pound) was about 11.5 ounces (see ESV footnote on Jn 19:39).

19 Compare Is 53:9: "Made His grave . . . with a rich man in His death."

20 There probably is no significance in the *ēn*, "was," as if the place was no longer in existence when John wrote his Gospel.

21 This is stated to inform the reader that the body of Christ was not disemboweled. The Egyptians also wrapped the mummies; but when *they* embalmed the dead, the intestines were removed (Ylvisaker, *Gospels*, 756).

22 The sunset of Friday evening was the dawn of Sabbath.

23 See ch. 35, § 12 and ch. 36, § 5.

24 Gk *planos*, vagabond.

25 Or else imperative: "Have your watch!" Gk *echete koustōdian*. Notice also the Latinism, which would be quite natural in the case of Pilate (Bruce, *Synoptic Gospels*, on Mt 27:65).

26 Meyer, *Commentary on the N.T.*, on Mt 27:66.

27 Mt 28:1: "Now after the Sabbath, toward the dawn of the first day of the week" (ESV). Gk *Opse de sabbatōn*, "Now late on the Sabbath-day" (Revised Version). This phrase once gave much trouble, but the usage of the vernacular Koine Greek amply justifies the translation. The women went to inspect the tomb before the Sabbath was over (before 6 p.m. on Saturday). But the same Greek idiom was occasionally used in the sense of after. See Robertson, *Grammar*, 645. The distance from Jerusalem or Bethany to Golgotha was not more than a Sabbath-day's journey. The spices could be purchased after sundown either in Bethany or Jerusalem. It must be remembered that the Jewish first day of the week began at sundown on our Saturday (Robertson, *Harmony of the Gospels*, 239 n.).

Chapter 37
The Risen and Exalted Savior

1 Chuza probably was the court official whose son Jesus had healed by the word spoken at Cana. See chs. 12, § 11; 7, § 22.

2 Although some take these to be angels, Luke uses the words *kai idou andres duo*, "And behold, two men." He used this same construction when he introduced the appearance of Moses and Elijah at Jesus' transfiguration (Lk 9:30). It is possible these two men standing in dazzling apparel at the empty tomb were Moses and Elijah. Luke will use this same construction at Jesus' ascension (Ac 1:10).

3 Called the Eleven, although at the moment Peter and John may have been absent.

4 The plural proves the presence of other women with Mary, as related by the Synoptists. When alone, she uses the singular "I know not" (Jn

20:13), etc. See Dods, *Gospel of St. John*, on Jn 20:13.

5 Gk *othonia*.

6 Gk *soudarion*.

7 Gk *chōris entetyligmenon eis hena topon*.

8 See articles in *Lehre und Wehre*, 1914, 159ff.; 1927, 167ff.

9 This is not the place to enter into a discussion of the disputed close of Mark (16:9–20). Though missing in many manuscripts, it is found in others. It is present in Tatian's *Diatessaron*. And it is included in an important and very ancient uncial, the Washington (Freer) Manuscript, Codex W (Robertson, *Studies in the Text of the N.T.*, 100).

10 Dods, *Gospel of St. John*, on Jn 20:13.

11 Compare Mk 10:51: *Rabbouni*. The steps of honor in the title are said to be: Rab, Rabbi, Rabban, Rabboni.

12 Dods, *Gospel of St. John*, on Jn 20:13.

13 Dods, *Gospel of St. John*, on Jn 20:13.

14 Bruce, *Synoptic Gospels*, on Mt 28:12.

15 Not identical with Clopas (KJV: Cleophas) of Jn 19:25.

16 Edersheim, *Life and Times of Jesus* 2:638.

17 Which has supposedly, among other things, caused a change to be made in the original close of Mark—on account of Lk 24:34. (Rohrbach, quoted by Bruce [*Synoptic Gospels*] under Mk 16:9–20). In that case, the removal ought to have begun with Mk 16:7: "Tell His disciples and *Peter*"!

18 Since the sad decrease of their number, the apostles are now called the Eleven. But in reality, as we shall presently see, there were only ten, because Thomas was not with them (Jn 20:24).

19 A remarkable interpolation follows in Codex W (after v. 14): "And they defended themselves, saying: This world of lawlessness and unbelief is under Satan, who does not permit those unclean things that are under the dominion of spirits to comprehend the power of God. On this account reveal Your righteousness now. They said [these things] to Christ. And Christ replied to them: The term of years of the authority of Satan has been fulfilled, but other dreadful things are drawing near [even to those] for whose sake as sinners I was delivered up to death in order that they

566 / PAGES 462–81

might return to the truth and sin no more; in order that they might inherit the spiritual and incorruptible glory of righteousness which is in heaven. But go into all the world," etc. The first few lines of this insertion had been previously known in a Latin translation from Jerome (*Against Pelagians*, 2, 15), who states that he had seen the lines in some Greek manuscripts. See *Biblical World* (March, 1908): 206. Robertson brings the Greek text in *Studies in the Text of the N.T.*, 100.

20 The phrase about the honey is missing in leading manuscripts.

21 Compare Mt 16:19. See ch. 18, § 5.

22 Pieper, *Christian Dogmatics*, 459.

23 See ch. 11, § 12. It was common in those days, as seen in the example of Cephas or Peter, to have corresponding Hebrew and Greek names.

24 Type, Gk *typon*.

25 According to our chronology April 2–9, AD 33, Nisan (or Abib) 14–21. This Sunday would bring us to April 12, AD 33.

26 *Letters* 10:96. AD 112.

27 Stöckhardt, *Biblische Geschichte*, 324.

28 We are glad to see Thomas with the disciples, happily cured of all doubt.

29 Farrar, *Life of Christ* 2:441.

30 The familiar *paidia*, boys, or lads.

31 Gk *paidia, mē ti prosphagion echete. Prosphagion* really means a side dish. In that sense, fish was the ordinary side dish eaten with bread. The word was commonly used in the meaning of fish (Dods, *Gospel of St. John*, on Jn 21:5).

32 Dods, *Gospel of St. John*, on Jn 21:6.

33 ESV: "stripped for work"; KJV: "naked." One might have on the *chitōn*, the inner garment, and still be called naked (Dods, *Gospel of St. John*, on Jn 21:7).

34 Gk *hōs apo pēchōn diakosiōn*, about 200 cubits. *Pēchys*, cubit, 16–18 inches.

35 Some of the Fathers understood 100 for the Gentiles, 50 for the Jews, and 3 for the Trinity. Jerome says that there are 153 varieties of fishes. And other like inventions. See Meyer, *Commentary on the N.T.*, or Dods, *Gospel of St. John*, on Jn 21:11.

36 Gk *agapais*.

37 Gk *philō*. Jesus used the word *agapais*. Peter said *philō*. The Vulgate distinguishes by using the term *diligis* and *amo*. But probably there is no difference in the words. Different terms used for euphonic reasons. The distinction is usually made that *agapan* is based on judgment and esteem and *philein* on the affection of the heart. If the two words differed in meaning to the extent of giving each a special significance, it could not be said that Peter was grieved because Jesus had said *phileis* a third time; for Jesus had not used the same word three times. He said *agapais* twice in succession and *phileis* the third time.—The same applies to the term *feed*. The first time Jesus said *boske*, the second time *poimaine*, the third time *boske*. The function is the same (Dods, *Gospel of St. John*, Jn 21:17).

38 Eusebius, *NPNF2* 1:129, 132. Crucified head downward.

39 Gk *sy moi akolouthei*.

40 Dods, *Gospel of St. John*, on Jn 21:22.

41 Compare Mt 16:28; Mk 9:1; Lk 9:27.

42 Gk *oidamen*.

43 Eusebius, *NPNF2* 1:132, 163. According to tradition, he lived until the reign of Trajan, AD 98–117 (Eusebius, *NPNF2* 1:150). Jerome says he died in 98, a hundred years old.

44 St. Paul wrote these words about twenty-two years after Christ's resurrection.

45 Lenski, *Eisenach Gospel Selections*, 705; Walther, *Brosamen*, 121.

46 The unbaptized criminal on the cross as compared with the Baptism-despising Pharisees (Lk 23:43; 7:30).

47 Not ecstatic glossolalia, incomprehensible utterances (1Co 12:10; 14:2, etc.), but the much more wonderful speaking of previously unknown languages to the praise of God and the spiritual welfare of benighted souls, as in Ac 2:4ff. See Meyer, *Commentary on the N.T.*, on Mk 16:18.

48 Ylvisaker, *Gospels*, 783.

49 See ch. 11, § 7.

50 See ch. 11, § 13.

51 See Findlay under 1Co 15:7 in Nicoll, *Expositor's Greek Testament*.

52 Or was there another appearance? 1Co 11:23: "For I received from the Lord," etc.

53 Even from Luke it is clear that Jesus' ascension did not take place on the same day of the week as His resurrection; for the same writer explains in the Book of Acts (1:3) that Jesus showed Himself alive for forty days after His Passion.

54 Separating Lk 24:44 from the foregoing.

55 Jl 2:28–29, compared with vv. 30–31.

56 Gk *exousia*.

57 Gk *dynamis*.

58 Gk *ekathisen—kathizō*. The same term in Lk 4:20.

59 See ch. 37, § 4 note.

Appendixes

1 "The son of God." This refers to the ultimate source to which also the human ancestry of Jesus is traced.
Weiss, in his *Life of Christ*, 1:220, sees an "artistically planned" arrangement in the order of Luke:
3 × 7 from Adam to Abraham
2 × 7 from Isaac to David
3 × 7 from Nathan to Shealtiel
3 × 7 from Zerubbabel to Jesus
11 × 7 or in all 77 generations from Adam to Christ

2 Pedaiah and Shealtiel were brothers. Because Zerubbabel is called son of Shealtiel in Matthew (1:12) and Luke (3:27), a levirate marriage or adoption is commonly supposed, and Ezr 3:2 and 5:2 are followed. With Zerubbabel, the pedigree of Christ in the Old Testament becomes obscure and passes out. See Ebrard, *Gospel History*, 149–63; Robinson, *Greek Harmony*, 184ff.; Andrews, *Life of Our Lord*, 62ff.

3 See *ISBE*, under "Zerubbabel."

4 See note 3 above.

5 Africanus in Eusebius (*NPNF*2 1:91–92) seems to confuse Matthat with Melchi, 72 with 74. For tradition, see Andrews, *Life of Our Lord*, 62ff.

6 There is a remarkable reference to Mary as the daughter of Heli in the Talmud. See Weiss, *Life of Christ*, 1:221, note; *ISBE*, under "Genealogy of Christ," 1198.

7 Of whom "was born," Gk *egennēthē*. In all other cases, *egennēsen* is used, translated in the KJV as "begat." Joseph did not "beget" Jesus. This is a proof of the virgin birth.

8 Jesus, "being the son (as was supposed) of Joseph," but in reality the maternal grandson of Heli. See Eusebius, *NPNF*2 1:91–92.

9 Quoted in Farrar, *Life of Christ* 2:464; also in McClintock and Strong's *Cyclopedia of Biblical, Theological, and Ecclesiastical Literature* under "Jesus Christ" (www.biblicalcyclopedia.com). Compare also Pieper, *Christian Dogmatics* 2:82–84, and Mueller, *Christian Dogmatics*, 261.

BIBLIOGRAPHY

LIST OF AUTHORITIES CHIEFLY USED IN WRITING THIS BOOK

The references to page or chapter as given in the endnotes follow the year, edition, or publisher of each book as indicated in this list.

Andrews, Samuel J. *The Life of Our Lord upon the Earth*. New York: Charles Scribner's Sons, 1891.

Arndt, William. *Does the Bible Contradict Itself? A Discussion of Alleged Contradictions in the Bible*. St. Louis: Concordia, 1976.

Barton, George A. *Archaeology and the Bible*. Philadelphia: American Sunday-School Union, 1937.

Blunt, Alfred W. F. *Israel in World History*. London: Oxford University Press, 1927.

Brandes, Georg. *Jesus: A Myth*. Translated by Edwin Björkman. New York: Albert & Charles Boni, 1926.

Breasted, James Henry. *The Conquest of Civilization*. New York: Harper, 1938.

Broadus, John A. *A Harmony of the Gospels for Students of the Life of Christ*. New York: George H. Doran, 1922.

Brown, Raymond E. *The Birth of the Messiah: A Commentary on the Infancy Narratives in the Gospels of Matthew and Luke*. New York: Doubleday, 1993 new updated edition.

Bruce, Alexander Balmain. *The Synoptic Gospels*. Vol. 1. in *The Expositor's Greek Testament*. Edited by W. Robertson Nicoll. New York: Dodd, Mead & Co., 1897.

Burton, Ernest DeWitt and Edgar J. Goodspeed. *A Harmony of the Synoptic Gospels in Greek*. New York: Charles Scribner's Sons, 1917.

Cadman, James P. *A Critical Harmony of the Gospels, or, The Life of Our Lord in the Words of the Evangelists*. New York: Fleming H. Revell, 1885.

Catholic Encyclopedia. New York: The Robert Appleton Co., 1914.

Cremer, Hermann. *Biblico-Theological Lexicon of the N. T. Greek*. New York: Charles Scribner's Sons, 1895.

Crossway ESV Bible Atlas. Edited by John D. Currid and David P. Barrett. Wheaton, IL: Crossway, 2010.

Davis, John D. *The Westminster Dictionary of the Bible*. Philadelphia: Westminster Press, 1944.

Deissmann, Adolf. *Licht vom Osten: Das Neue Testament und die neuentdeckten Texte der hellenistisch-römischen Welt*. Tuebingen: J. C. B. Mohr, 1923.

Dods, Marcus. *The Gospel of St. John*. Vol. 1 in *The Expositor's Greek Testament*. Edited by W. Robertson Nicoll. New York: Dodd, Mead & Co., 1897.

Ebrard, J. H. A. *The Gospel History*. Edinburgh: T. & T. Clark, 1863.

Edersheim, Alfred. *The Life and Times of Jesus the Messiah*. New York: Longman, Green & Co., 1923.

———. *Sketches of Jewish Social Life in the Days of Christ*. London: The Religious Tract Society, 1876.

———. *The Temple, Its Ministry and Services*. Boston: Ira Bradley & Co., 1881.

Encyclopedia Britannica. Chicago: Encyclopedia Britannica, 2002.

Engelbrecht, Edward, ed. *The Church from Age to Age*. St. Louis: Concordia, 2011.

Farrar, F. W. *The Life of Christ*. New York: E. P. Dutton & Co., 1874.

Fritz, John H. C. *Pastoral Theology*. St. Louis: Concordia, 1932.

Fuerbringer, Ludwig. *Einleitung in das Neue Testament*. St. Louis: Concordia, 1914.

Gibbon, Edward. *Decline and Fall of the Roman Empire*. 5 vols. Philadelphia: Porter & Coates, 1845.

Gibbs, Jeffrey A. *Matthew 1:1–11:1*. Concordia Commentary. St. Louis: Concordia, 2006.

Graetz, Heinrich. *History of the Jews*. Philadelphia: The Jewish Publication Society, 1891.

Guthe, Hermann. *Bibelatlas in 21 Haupt- und 30 Nebenkarten*. Leipzig: H. Wagner & E. Debes, 1926.

Hardy, Ernest George. *Christianity and the Roman Government: A Study in Imperial Administration*. New York: The Macmillan Co., 1925.

Harris, J. Rendel. *The Twelve Apostles*. Cambridge: W. Heffer & Sons, 1927.

Hauber, Eberhard D. *Harmonie der 4. Evangelisten*. In the Greek-German *Original-Bibel*. Lemgo: Meyer, 1737.

Henry, Matthew. *Commentary on the Whole Bible: Matthew to John*. Vol. 5 of 6. New York: Fleming H. Revell Co., 1706.

Herodotus. *The History*. Translated by David Grene. Chicago: The University of Chicago Press, 1987.

Hill, J. Hamlyn. *The Earliest Life of Christ Ever Compiled from the Four Gospels, Being the Diatessaron of Tatian*. Edinburgh: T. & T. Clark, 1894.

Hummel, Horace. *Ezekiel 21–48*. Concordia Commentary. St. Louis: Concordia, 2007.

Hurlbut, Jesse Lyman. *Bible Atlas: A Manual of Biblical Geography and History*. Chicago: Rand McNally & Co., 1919.

Jones, Jeremiah, trans. *The Apocryphal New Testament*. New York: The Worthington, 1890.

Just, Arthur A., Jr. *Luke 1:1–9:50*. Concordia Commentary. St. Louis: Concordia, 1996.

Kerr, John H. *A Harmony of the Gospels in the Words of the American Standard Edition of the Revised Bible and Outline of the Life of Christ*. New York: Association Press, 1912.

Klausner, Joseph. *Jesus of Nazareth: His Life, Times, and Teaching*. New York: The Macmillan Co., 1929.

Kretzmann, Paul E. *Popular Commentary of the Bible: New Testament*. 2 vols. St. Louis: Concordia, 1921–22.

Lange, John Peter. *Lange's Commentary on the Holy Scriptures: Matthew*. New York: Charles Scribner's Sons, 1895.

Lenski, R. C. H. *The Eisenach Gospel Selections*. Columbus: Lutheran Book Concern, 1916.

Lightfoot, J. B. "The Lord's Brethren," in *St. Paul's Epistle to the Galatians*. London: Macmillan & Co., 1874.

Lodder, W. *Die Schätzung des Quirinius bei Flavius Josephus. Eine Untersuchung: Hat sich Flavius Josephus in der Datierung der Bekannten Schätzung (Lk 2:2) Geirrt?* Leipzig: Dörffling & Franke, 1930.

Ludwig, Emil. *The Son of Man: The Story of Jesus*. New York: Boni & Liveright, 1928.

MacCoun, Townsend. *The Holy Land in Geography and History*. New York: F. H. Revell, 1897.

Macknight, James. *A Harmony of the Four Gospels in Which the Natural Order of Each Is Preserved*. London: Longman, Hurst, Rees & Orme, 1809.

Madden, Frederic W. *The History of Jewish Coinage and of Money in the Old and New Testament*. London: Bernard Quaritch, 1864.

Maier, Paul L. *In the Fullness of Time: A Historian Looks at Christmas, Easter, and the Early Church*. San Francisco: HarperCollins, 1991.

Mathews, Basil. *A Life of Jesus*. New York: Richard R. Smith, Inc., 1931.

McRay, John. *Archaeology and the New Testament*. Grand Rapids, MI: Baker, 1991.

Metzger, Bruce M. *A Textual Commentary on the Greek New Testament*. New York: United Bible Societies, 1971.

Meyer, Heinrich August Wilhelm. *Commentary on the New Testament*. 11 vols. New York: Funk & Wagnalls, 1883–87.

Milman, H. H. *The History of Christianity*. New York: Harper & Bros., 1861.

———. *History of Latin Christianity*. New York: Sheldon & Co., 1860.

Mueller, John Theodore. *Christian Dogmatics: A Handbook of Doctrinal Theology for Pastors, Teachers, and Laymen*. St. Louis: Concordia, 1934.

Myers, Philip Van Ness. *General History*. 2nd revised ed. Boston: Ginn & Co., 1921.

Nestle, Eberhard. *Einführung in das Griechische Neue Testament*. 4th ed., revised by Ernst von Dobschütz. Göttingen: Vandenhoeck & Ruprecht, 1923.

New Catholic Encyclopedia. New York: McGraw-Hill Book Co., 1967.

Nicoll, W. Robertson, ed. *The Expositor's Greek Testament*. New York: George H. Doran, 1897–1910.

Oxford Bible Atlas. 4th ed. Edited by Adrian Curtis. Oxford: Oxford University Press, 2007.

Pieper, Franz. *Christian Dogmatics*. St. Louis: Concordia, 1924.

Ramsay, W. M. *The Bearing of Recent Discovery on the Trustworthiness of the New Testament*. London: Hodder & Stoughton, 1915.

———. *Was Christ Born at Bethlehem?* London: Hodder & Stoughton, 1898.

Robertson, Archibald Thomas. *A Grammar of the Greek New Testament in the Light of Historical Research*. Nashville: Broadman, 1934.

———. *A Harmony of the Gospels for Students of the Life of Christ*. New York: Harper & Bros., 1922.

———. *Luke the Historian in the Light of Recent Research*. New York: Scribner's Sons, 1920.

———. *Studies in the Text of the New Testament*. New York: George H. Doran Co., 1926.

Robinson, Edward. *A Harmony of the Gospels in Greek*. Boston: Crocker & Brewster, 1845.

Robinson, Theodore H., J. W. Hunkin, and F. C. Burkitt. *Palestine in General History*. London: Oxford University Press, 1929.

Schama, Simon. *The Story of the Jews*. London: Vintage Books, 2013.

Schirlitz, Samuel Christoph. *Griechisch-Deutsches Wörterbuch zum Neuen Testamente*. Giessen: E. Roth, 1893.

Schneemelcher, Wilhelm, ed. *New Testament Apocrypha*. Vol. 1. Philadelphia: Westminster Press, 1963.

Schürer, Emil. *A History of the Jewish People in the Time of Jesus Christ*. Edinburgh: T. & T. Clark, 1905.

Shepherd, William R. *Historical Atlas*. New York: Henry Holt & Co., 1926.

Smith, George Adam. *Atlas of the Historical Geography of the Holy Land*. London: Hodder & Stoughton, 1915.

Smith, W. W. *Students' Historical Geography of the Holy Land*. New York: George H. Doran Co., 1924.

Stalker, James. *The Life of Jesus Christ*. New York: Fleming H. Revell Co., 1909.

———. *The Trial and Death of Jesus Christ: A Devotional History of Our Lord's Passion*. Grand Rapids: Zondervan, 1961.

Stanley, Arthur P. *Lectures on the History of the Jewish Church*. New York: Charles Scribner's Sons, 1884.

Steinmann, Andrew. *From Abraham to Paul: A Biblical Chronology*. St. Louis: Concordia, 2011.

Stevens, William Arnold, and Ernest Burton. *A Harmony of the Gospels for Historical Study: An Analytical Synopsis of the Four Gospels*. New York: Scribner, 1904.

Stöckhardt, G. *Die Biblische Geschichte des Neuen Testaments*. St. Louis: Concordia, 1898.

Suetonius. *The Lives of the Caesars*. In *The Loeb Classical Library*. New York: The Macmillan Co., 1914.

Tacitus. *The Annals.* Translated by Arthur Murphy. New York: E. P. Dutton Co., 1907.

———. *History of the Jews.* In *The Works of Josephus.* Translated by William Whiston. Peabody, MA: Hendrickson Publishers, 1987.

Tatian. *The Diatessaron.* Translated by J. Hamlyn Hill. Edinburgh: T. & T. Clark, 1894.

Thackeray, H. St. J. *Selections from Josephus.* New York: The Macmillan Co., 1919.

Tholuck, August. *Philologisch-theologische Auslegung der Bergpredigt Christi nach Matthäus: zugleich ein Beitrag zur Begründung einer rein-biblischen Glaubens-und Sittenlehre.* Hamburg: Friedrich Perthes, 1833.

Voelz, James. *Mark 1:1–8:26.* Concordia Commentary. St. Louis: Concordia, 2013.

Walther, C. F. W. *Lutherische Brosamen.* St. Louis: Concordia, 1876.

Ware, Steven. *When Was Jesus Really Born? Early Christianity, the Calendar, and the Life of Jesus.* St. Louis: Concordia, 2013.

Watkins, H. W. *The Gospel According to St. John: With Commentary.* New York: Cassell, 1880.

Weiss, Bernhard. *The Life of Christ.* 3 vols. Edinburgh: T. & T. Clark, 1883.

———. *A Manual of Introduction to the New Testament.* Translated by A. J. K. Davidson. 2 vols. New York: Funk & Wagnalls, 1889.

Whiston, William, trans. *The Works of Josephus.* Peabody, MA: Hendrickson Publishers, 1987.

Wieseler, Karl. *A Chronological Synopsis of the Four Gospels.* London: George Bell & Sons, 1877.

Williamson, George Charles. *The Money of the Bible.* London: Religious Tract Society, 1894.

Wilson, Edward L. *In Scripture Lands: New Views of Sacred Places.* New York: Charles Scribner's Sons, 1890.

Ylvisaker, Johannes. *The Gospels.* Minneapolis: Augsburg Publishing House, 1932.

Zahn, Theodor. *Introduction to the New Testament.* 3 vols. Edinburgh: T. & T. Clark, 1909.

IMAGE CREDITS

SCRIPTURE INDEX

Old Testament

DANIEL

2:2 . . . . 502n54
2:40 11
2:48 . . . . 502n54
5:28–31 30
7:13 . . . . 559n47
7:13–14 . . . . 509n60, 518n41
8:16 . . . . 496n47
9:21 . . . . 496n47
9:26–27 370
9:27 371
11:31 371
12:3 336
12:9–13 370
12:11 371

HOSEA

6:2 . . . . 543n9
6:6 . . . . 155, 158
7:11 215
9:3 27
10:8 442
11:1 . . . . 76, 504n107
14:1–3 27

JOEL

2:28 469
2:28–29 . . . . 567n55
2:30–31 . . . . 567n55
2:31 447

AMOS

1:6 . . . . 537n30
7:8–11 27
7:14–15 137
9:9 17

JONAH

1:2 27
1:17 194
3:5 27

MICAH

5:2 . . . . 66, 75, 268
7:4 355

NAHUM

2:10–13 28
3:7–19 28

ZEPHANIAH

2:4–6 . . . . 491n8

HAGGAI

2:8 95
2:9 30

ZECHARIAH

1:1 . . . . 541n53
1:7 . . . . 541n53
3:1 68
3:8 . . . . 499n106
6:12 . . . . 54, 505n140
7:1–12 . . . . 519n72
8:19 . . . . 519n72
9:9 346
11:12–13 . . . . 554n60
11:13 425
12:10 452
13:7 400

MALACHI

3:1 . . . . 30, 51, 86, 187, 252
3–4 219
4:5 . . . . 96–97, 252, 446, 534n11, 535n55
4:5–6 188

The Apocrypha

THE WISDOM OF SOLOMON

9:13–19 112

TOBIT

4:15 . . . . 523n111, 540n19

ECCLESIASTICUS (SIRACH)

11:18–19 . . . . 541n61

1 MACCABEES

1:9 . . . . 492n37
1:10 . . . . 492n39
1:20–28 32
1:47 32
2:1 . . . . 65, 529n18
2:1 482
2:17 65
2:23–48 . . . . 492n43
2:42 . . . . 492n41, 492n51
2:70 65
3:13 . . . . 492n51
4:29–35 . . . . 491n16
4:42–59 33
4:46 . . . . 542n6
4:47 47
4:52–59 299
5:9–58 53
5:15 52
6:30–47 . . . . 492n46
7:47 46
8:17–20 359
8:17–29 34
9:55–56 150
10:18–21 33
10:38 . . . . 564n15
11:28 . . . . 564n15
11:34 . . . . 564n15
12:2–23 34
13:31–41 33
14:20–23 34
14:41 . . . . 33, 97, 299, 538n21
15:1–9 34
15:15–24 19
15:16–21 34

2 MACCABEES

2:1–8 247
4:30–38 33
15:35 46

New Testament

LUKE

JOHN

**Statue of
Caesar Augustus**
See ch. 1, § 6
and ch. 4, § 2.

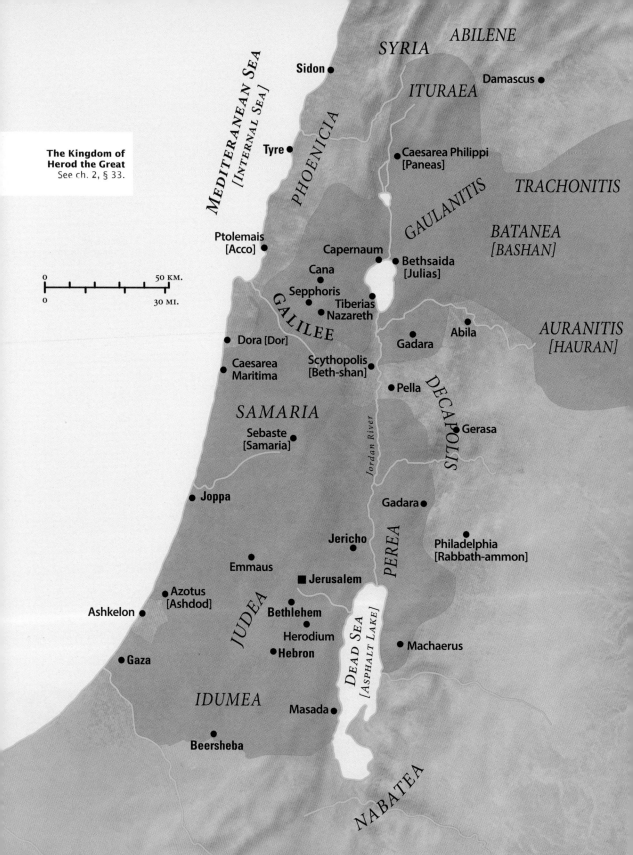

The Kingdom of
Herod the Great
See ch. 2, § 33.

MEDITERANEAN SEA
[INTERNAL SEA]

Sidon

SYRIA

ABILENE

Damascus

ITURAEA

Tyre

PHOENICIA

Caesarea Philippi
[Paneas]

TRACHONITIS

GAULANITIS

BATANEA
[BASHAN]

Ptolemais
[Acco]

Capernaum

Bethsaida
[Julias]

Cana

Sepphoris

Tiberias

GALILEE

Nazareth

Gadara

Abila

AURANITIS
[HAURAN]

Dora [Dor]

Caesarea
Maritima

Scythopolis
[Beth-shan]

Pella

DECAPOLIS

SAMARIA

Gerasa

Sebaste
[Samaria]

Jordan River

Joppa

Gadara

Jericho

PEREA

Philadelphia
[Rabbath-ammon]

Emmaus

Jerusalem

Azotus
[Ashdod]

Bethlehem

JUDEA

Ashkelon

Herodium

Hebron

DEAD SEA
[ASPHALT LAKE]

Machaerus

Gaza

IDUMEA

Masada

Beersheba

NABATEA

0   50 KM.

0   30 MI.

The Jordan River flowing into the Sea of Galilee
See ch. 6, § 1.

Judean desert beyond the oasis of Jericho
See ch. 6, § 4.

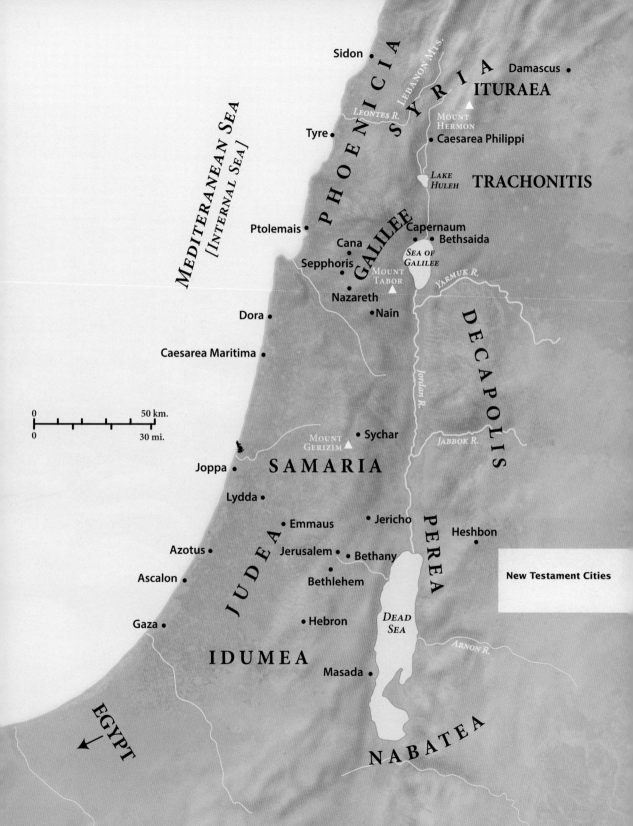

Sidon

Damascus •

PHOENICIA

SYRIA

ITURAEA

Lebanon Mts.

Leontes R.

Mount Hermon △

Tyre •

• Caesarea Philippi

Lake Huleh

TRACHONITIS

Mediteranean Sea [Internal Sea]

Ptolemais •

• Capernaum

Cana •

• Bethsaida

Sepphoris •

GALILEE

Sea of Galilee

Mount Tabor △

Yarmuk R.

Nazareth •

• Nain

Dora •

DECAPOLIS

Caesarea Maritima •

Jordan R.

0 — 50 km.

0 — 30 mi.

Mount Gerizim △

• Sychar

Jabbok R.

Joppa •

SAMARIA

Lydda •

• Emmaus

• Jericho

Azotus •

Jerusalem •

• Bethany

Heshbon •

PEREA

New Testament Cities

Ascalon •

• Bethlehem

JUDEA

Gaza •

• Hebron

Dead Sea

IDUMEA

Masada •

Arnon R.

EGYPT ←

NABATEA

**The shore of the
Sea of Galilee**
See ch. 13, § 7.

Looking from the
Jordan valley to the
central highland, where
Jesus carried out His
Galilean ministry
See ch. 16.

**Jesus proceeded
north to the borders
of Caesarea Philippi**
See ch. 18, § 3.

**Mount Hermon,
possible site of the
Transfiguration**
See ch. 18, § 8.

The road between Jerusalem and Jericho
See ch. 21, § 9.

**Ripe figs ready
for harvest**
See ch. 21, § 28.

Tomb of Lazarus
See ch. 24, § 5.

The road from Jerusalem to the Mount of Olives
See ch. 33, § 1.

**The base of the
Mount of Olives**
See ch. 33, § 1.

Ancient tree in the Garden of Gethsemane
See ch. 33, § 1.

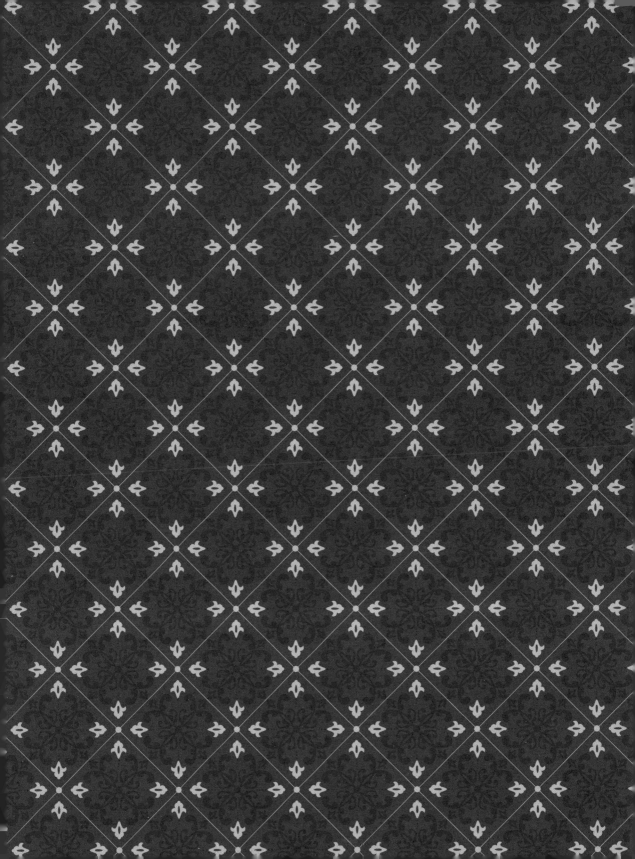